CONCISE HISTORICAL ATLAS OF CANADA

CONCISE HISTORICAL ATLAS OF CANADA

EDITED BY

*William G. Dean, Conrad E. Heidenreich,
Thomas F. McIlwraith, and John Warkentin*

CARTOGRAPHY BY

Geoffrey J. Matthews and Byron Moldofsky

UNIVERSITY OF TORONTO PRESS

Toronto Buffalo London

© University of Toronto Press Incorporated
Toronto Buffalo London
Printed in Canada

ISBN 0-8020-4203-1

Printed on acid-free paper

Canadian Cataloguing in Publication Data

Main entry under title:

Concise historical atlas of Canada

Selection of 67 plates from the Historical atlas of Canada.
Includes bibliographical references.
ISBN 0-8020-4203-1

1. Canada – Historical geography – Maps.   I. Dean, W.G. (William G.), 1921–   .
II. Matthews, Geoffrey J., 1932–   .   III. Moldofsky, Byron, 1953–   .
IV. Title: Historical atlas of Canada.

G1116.S1C66 1998   911′.71   C98-931325-5

University of Toronto Press acknowledges the
financial assistance to its publishing program
of the Canada Council for the Arts
and the Ontario Arts Council.

The research, cartography, and publication of
the three-volume *Historical Atlas of Canada*
were funded in part by the
Social Sciences and Humanities Research Council of Canada.

The *Concise Historical Atlas of Canada* is based on
the three-volume *Historical Atlas of Canada*.

Director
William G. Dean, University of Toronto

Cartographer/Designer
Geoffrey J. Matthews, University of Toronto

Co-ordinating Editors
J.-P. Wallot, National Archivist
John Warkentin, York University

Volume I: From the Beginning to 1800

Editor: R. Cole Harris
Cartographer/Designer: Geoffrey J. Matthews
ISBN: 0-8020-2495-5

Volume II: The Land Transformed, 1800–1891

Editor: R. Louis Gentilcore
Associate Editors: Don Measner and Ronald H. Walder
Cartographer/Designer: Geoffrey J. Matthews
Production Co-ordinator: Byron Moldofsky
ISBN: 0-8020-3447-0

Volume III: Addressing the Twentieth Century, 1891–1961

Editors: Donald Kerr and Deryck W. Holdsworth
Assistant Editor: Susan L. Laskin
Cartographer/Designer: Geoffrey J. Matthews
ISBN: 0-8020-3448-9

Brief Contents

This brief contents is provided to give readers an overview of the thematic groupings of plates, and to assist them in quickly locating plates that deal with like periods across these groupings. The original plate numbers from the three-volume Historical Atlas of Canada are given in square brackets following plate titles.

Contents

PART ONE:
NATIONAL PERSPECTIVES

Prehistoric and Native Canada

Exploration

Territorial Extent

Population

Transport and Urbanization

The Economy

Society

PART TWO: DEFINING EPISODES

PART THREE:
REGIONAL PATTERNS

The East

The West and the North

Publisher's Note

It is unusual for a publisher to comment on a book outside the confines of the office, and even more unusual for a publisher's note of this kind to be written. But everything about the publication of the *Historical Atlas of Canada* has been unusual, so by including this note we are simply upholding the project's tradition.

This project had a tremendous effect on the University of Toronto Press, and we believe that the story of its publication serves to demonstrate its excellence – but we recognize our bias. We have been gratified by what others have written about the scholarly significance of this magnificent publication, and about the beauty of its production.

Through the spring and summer of 1987, the staff of the University of Toronto Press worked in anticipation of a major event in Canadian publishing – the release of the first volume of the *Historical Atlas of Canada*. Our involvement in the project had begun years earlier – it sometimes seemed that it would never reach completion – but we were finally going to press, and the book was about to become a reality.

Because of the remarkable fund-raising ability of Bill Dean and others, the Press was able to reduce its financial risk, making the project publishable. Our goal was then to publish it in the most effective way possible.

Early in the year, we began to see the first proofs of the maps for the volume, and it was only then that we realized what an unusual project this was. Most of us thought of maps as tools to get us from one point to another. Some of us had seen historical atlases, and we were familiar with their use of graphs and charts to illustrate historical trends. But this atlas was something much more – it offered nothing less than the physical rendering, in two dimensions, of a wealth of historical information.

Our initial response was one of caution. Since no one had ever produced such a volume, how could anyone estimate how the public would react to it? Our first major challenge was to make as accurate an assessment as possible of the size of the first printing, because the paper required for the book had to be specially ordered. The economics of book publishing told us that it would not be feasible to reprint only a small quantity, should we underestimate slightly. We had a great deal of incentive to get things right the first time.

As part of the assessment, our sales manager travelled to Washington in the spring, and showed the early plates to the director of cartography for *National Geographic*. His reaction was so enthusiastic that we were convinced the *Atlas* would be our best seller, perhaps of all time. His response was just the first in what would become a general chorus among map-makers: How could we afford to produce such a marvel for the small Canadian market? When we talked to the marketing director for Rand McNally, he suggested that a print run of 5 000 copies would be about right for an American historical atlas – designed for a market 10 times the size of ours. It seemed we had to temper our enthusiasm.

We set the initial print run for volume I at 7 000 copies. Considering that the average sale for non-fiction books in this country – and that is not necessarily scholarly books – is about 1 500 copies, this was clearly an ambitious number. Moreover, the book would be a huge volume that would sell for $95 – more than three times the price of an average work of non-fiction in 1987.

We began the marketing program, listing the book in our fall catalogue and presenting it to buyers from bookstores across the country. It soon became obvious that a first printing of 7 000 copies would fall far short of demand. By the time all the orders were tallied, in September (a few weeks before publication), we had orders in hand for more than 23 000 copies. We printed 35 000, and today we have only about 1 500 copies of this original printing on hand. More than 25 000 copies of the *Atlas* were sold in that first glorious year, making it the best-selling book in the history of Canadian academic publishing.

And who could forget the reviews? Most commentators were simply in awe of what they had before them, and their reviews were mostly strings of superlatives. In addition to positive reviews and many major awards, the *Atlas* was largely responsible for UTP's being honoured as publisher of the year by the Canadian Booksellers' Association.

Nineteen eighty-seven was also the year in which Lester & Orpen Dennys published the *Illustrated History of Canada*. For the first time in anyone's memory, the two best-selling non-fiction books of the year were scholarly studies of Canadian history and geography.

Volumes II and III of the *Atlas* were produced in 1990 and 1993, also to great acclaim.

By the fall of 1995 both the University of Toronto Press and some of the former Atlas project staff recognized that there were people perhaps unaware of this scholarly achievement who would welcome a one-volume version of the original three-volume set. The result is the book you hold in your hands, bringing together selected plates from the full *Historical Atlas of Canada*.

Of course, it takes dedicated people to bring a project like this to fruition. Four people need to be mentioned: Bill Dean, who conceived the idea of the *Atlas* thirty years ago and whose tenacity and genius are the reasons why the project continued to completion despite severe financial setbacks; Geoff Matthews, cartographer *extraordinaire*; Peter Scaggs, who as production manager for all four volumes literally reinvented the production process; and Carl Amrhein, then head of the Department of Geography.

Publishing successfully is difficult; publishing a book like the *Historical Atlas* and having it succeed in the marketplace is particularly gratifying for a scholarly publisher. We are indeed fortunate to have published the three magnificent volumes of the *Historical Atlas of Canada*, and we are confident that the concise edition will make the information contained in the original *Atlas* accessible to an even wider audience.

George Meadows
Publisher and President

Preface

This volume comprises 67 plates selected from the *Historical Atlas of Canada*, published by the University of Toronto Press between 1987 and 1993 as a three-volume set of nearly two hundred plates. In this context, 'plates' refers to double-page spreads of maps, graphics, legends, and texts. Each plate constitutes a single subject or theme, and is accompanied by a bibliographical note at the back of the volume. The plates singled out from the original three volumes are reproduced here substantially unchanged. The selection was made by a small committee, all of whom have been deeply involved in the Atlas project throughout the thirty years since its conception. The committee members are William G. Dean (Director), Conrad E. Heidenreich, Thomas F. McIlwraith, and John Warkentin. R. Cole Harris, Jean-Claude Robert, Don Measner, and Donald Kerr provided critical advice.

Our aim has been to select plates that summarize Canadian history from prehistoric times through the European experience, starting with the Norse, a thousand years ago, to the 1960s. We hope that, collectively, they represent both crucial events and the continuity of life over this lengthy period, and that they do so in an easily readable fashion. We have directed our attention to those plates that mirror the social and economic experiences of ordinary people rather than the political and military activities associated with individual heroes. Even so, our short list included far more than the 67 plates reproduced here, and this final selection was reached only after lengthy discussions – discussions during which our own understanding of Canada, after all these years, was deepened.

We were also guided in our choice of plates by the wish to demonstrate our initial purpose, in the original three volumes, of creating innovative cartography to depict thematic topics. An atlas, of course, is essentially a narrative form of cartography, and it was our aim to enhance the form with new ideas about the kind, character, and range of information mapped. To this end, our chief cartographer, Geoffrey Matthews, was an outstanding contributor. His plate designs, augmented by input from the volume editors and the Atlas project director, resulted in novel, effective, and attractive graphics. When it became imperative, late in the project, to switch into computer-generated maps, Byron Moldofsky became our pioneer and leading electronic cartographer. The plates made on our computers are indistinguishable from their hand-made predecessors. Such graphics undoubtedly led to our winning coveted awards both in Canada and internationally. The *Historical Atlas of Canada* has added significantly to the reputation of Canadian map-making and to the world-wide development of thematic cartography.

Furthermore, our selection of plates reflects our interest in reaching as wide an audience as possible. We believe that there are many potential readers who will react favourably to this less expensive, and we hope more manageable, summary of the original three volumes. Brief essays associated with each of the three major parts in which the plates are grouped have been specially composed for this volume, and are worded with a view to making readers comfortable with the graphic expression of ideas that they may previously have encountered only as written text. We hope that this volume will be useful in both history and geography classes in schools across the country, as well as in the households of general readers interested in a visual depiction of Canada's development. For some readers this may be a book for dipping into in spare moments; for others it may serve as a guide to the full three-volume set and the pursuit of particular subjects in greater detail.

The organizational structure of the *Concise Historical Atlas of Canada* differs from that of the original three-volume set. Plates have been grouped under three headings: 'National Perspectives,' 'Defining Episodes,' and 'Regional Patterns.' The plates in the 'National Perspectives' section give overarching views of the entire land mass that came to be known as Canada. The progress of exploration, the establishment of boundaries, the spread of settlement, the development of transport facilities, and the exploitation of resources are among the nation-building subjects covered here. 'Defining Episodes' refers to important historical events – turning points of national importance such as the Seven Years' War, the War of 1812, dramatic migrations, the Depression, and the two world wars. Yet even in the plates covering these unique occurrences, our attention is drawn to the commonly shared experiences of ordinary people.

Plates in the 'Regional Patterns' section focus on smaller parts of the Canadian experience, considering events and developments in greater detail over limited periods. Regions have frequently reflected happenings on the larger national stage, and as such provide case studies of historical trends. Of course, all three categories in this volume's organization in fact represent regionalizations at varying scales. As Cole Harris asserts in the Preface to volume I, 'from the beginning of the European encounter with North America, developments in the north, which led to Canada, were different from those farther south, which led to the United States. The country's southern boundary is not a geographical absurdity.'

Any selection necessarily reflects a compromise, and we had to make hard choices in putting this volume together. If our selection underrepresents some themes, readers may have to turn to the three full volumes for more detailed information. We have sought to create an intellectually satisfying and comprehensive overview of the life of Canada's ordinary people, and to do so in a balanced way in which all parts of the land are fairly represented. We hope that both the general reader and the serious researcher may be served adequately by our choices. Furthermore, this volume is designed to be in itself a unique tribute to our history, one that will make a significant contribution to Canadians' understanding of one another and foster fuller knowledge and pride in their country.

A brief cumulative history of the Atlas project, which dates back to 1969, is to be found in the Foreword to each of the original three volumes. A summary of the intent and of the means of compilation appears in the Preface of each volume, and recorded in the Acknowledgments of each are the names of the hundreds of scholars across the country, and beyond, who have contributed to the project. Scattered throughout each of the three volumes are thematic essays binding the various sections into a coherent whole. Finally, each volume concludes with a section of notes, comprising a plate-by-plate collation of the source materials upon which the mapping is based, as well as explanations of techniques used for complex presentations. The notes that correspond to the plates chosen for this *Concise Historical Atlas of Canada* have been included here. They are a trove of information. An index to the full *Historical Atlas of Canada*, to be published separately by the University of Toronto Press, will afford access to specific information contained in the original three volumes as well as in this one.

Acknowledgments

The University of Toronto Press wishes to express its thanks first to the four scholars invited, in 1996, to develop this concise edition. William G. Dean is a member of the Originating Committee of the full Historical Atlas of Canada project, and became its director; he is also a contributor to volume II. Conrad E. Heidenreich is a member of the editorial board for volume I and a contributor; Thomas F. McIlwraith is a member of the Originating Committee and a contributor; John Warkentin is a member of the Originating Committee and a co-ordinating editor of the Atlas project. These four spent many hours discussing, selecting, and organizing the plates into suitable groups, and writing the texts that introduce each of the three sections. Professor McIlwraith acted as co-ordinator for the concise edition.

The basis for the concise edition is the three volumes of the *Historical Atlas*, and our principal debt is to those persons responsible for their publication between 1987 and 1993. We recognize particularly the editors: R. Cole Harris (volume I); R. Louis Gentilcore (deceased), Don Measner, and Ronald H. Walder (volume II); and Donald Kerr, Deryck W. Holdsworth, and Susan L. Laskin (volume III). In addition, dozens of researchers, plate authors, cartographers, and volume editorial board members were involved in the project. They were supported by the Atlas project co-ordinating group, by members of the staff of the University of Toronto Press (here we should single out the copy-editor, Joan Bulger), and financially by the Social Sciences and Humanities Research Council of Canada and a number of generous corporate and private donors. All of these people and institutions are named and their roles fully acknowledged in the three individual volumes; readers who turn there will get a small sense of the complexity of the original project. The Press and the editors of the *Concise Atlas* have remarked on how few corrections have been necessary in preparing plates and notes for republication. This fact is testament to the care with which the Atlas material was initially executed. The names of all those whose plates have been included in this concise edition appear on the individual plates.

For cartographic work, including necessary refinements to suit the concise edition, we are indebted to Byron Moldofsky and Mariange Beaudry, Cartography Laboratory, University of Toronto. We are grateful also to Darlene Zeleney, John St James, and Peter Scaggs for the editorial preparation and production of the volume. Finally, we wish to acknowledge the generous financial and other support of the Faculty of Arts and Science, University of Toronto, through its dean, Carl Amrhein.

PART ONE

NATIONAL PERSPECTIVES

Prehistoric and Native Canada

The prehistory of Canada can be viewed as a long period of human cultural adaptation to moderating post-Pleistocene environmental conditions. By the time conditions stabilized around 4000 to 2000 BCE, the land's resourceful inhabitants had developed intricate relationships with their environments, based on an intimate knowledge of the biotic setting and reinforced by spiritual bonds.

There is undisputed evidence that the first human beings crossed on a land bridge from Siberia to the unglaciated parts of Alaska sometime before 12 000 BCE. As the continental glaciers melted back, an ice-free corridor developed, about 10 000 BCE, along the eastern flanks of the Rocky Mountains (Plate 1). When the land bridge became inundated as a result of rising water levels, this corridor was used by people to migrate south into the Americas.

The earliest clearly defined group of people in the Americas is known as the Fluted Point culture. These were spear hunters who travelled in small groups, taking such game as mammoth, mastodon, camel, horse, bison, and caribou. The first four of these species became extinct about 8700 BCE, perhaps because of overhunting but more likely as a result of environmental change. As the ice sheets continued to melt back, these hunting groups became culturally more diverse and gradually spread into what are now the southern margins of Canada, where they hunted species such as bison and caribou. By 8000 BCE, the further retreat of the glaciers, ameliorating climate, and the greater diversity of biota permitted more cultural diversification and led to the rise of the Archaic period. On the East Coast a seafaring culture developed, specializing in fishing and hunting sea mammals. Throughout the woodlands the big-game hunters transformed themselves into mixed fishing and hunting groups, while on the plains and tundra big-game hunting persisted, focused on bison and caribou. West Coast groups settled along streams and coastal valleys to take advantage of the abundance of fish and marine mammals.

By about 4000 BCE the biotic environments had achieved considerable stability. The Archaic cultures moved in small clusters of interrelated families, following a seasonal cycle based on the exploitation of aquatic and forest resources. Use of the bow and arrow had spread to all groups. About 2000 BCE, with the rapid expansion of the Palaeo-Eskimo people from Siberia and Alaska, the Arctic was becoming inhabited for the first time; people reached Labrador no more than 200 years later. Between 1000 and 1400 CE these people were replaced by another wave of migrants out of Siberia, the Thule culture, who were ancestors of the modern Inuit (Plate 2). By 1000 BCE environmental conditions had become similar to those later encountered by Europeans, and the basic cultural patterns of the historic period were in place across most of the territory that is Canada.

The last major stimulus to the eastern Native cultures before European contact was the northward diffusion of maize about 500 CE, followed by tobacco four centuries later and then squash, bean, and sunflower about 1100 CE (Plate 2). Societies that developed horticulture grew rapidly, and their social and political institutions became increasingly complex. By the end of the 15th century, the Huron, Neutral, Iroquois, and others lived in villages of up to 3 000 people and were linked politically in sophisticated intertribal confederacies.

At the time of European contact Canada had been inhabited for more than 4 000 years. The Native population stood at about 300 000, with the largest concentrations in the lower Great Lakes area and on the West Coast (Plate 3). The population was culturally very diverse, and the variety of languages spoken was far greater than in Europe.

Permanent contact with Europeans, starting with itinerant fishermen and whalers, began early in the 16th century. During the 1580s fur trading became a profitable undertaking on the East Coast, and it expanded rapidly, early in the 17th century, up the St Lawrence River valley. Fur trading demanded permanent posts, and these attracted settlers and missionaries. In order to explore, to settle, and to exploit resources in safety, the French were obliged to join existing Native alliance systems that stretched from the Montagnais at Tadoussac to the Huron near Georgian Bay. These allies were pitted against the Iroquois League, which eventually forged an alliance with the Dutch and later the English.

The uneven introduction of muskets to Native allies upset the balances of power that had prevailed among them before European contact. At first this new technology was used by the Native people to settle old conflicts, but gradually the European powers armed their Native allies and used them to promote imperial ambitions. Trade, missionary efforts, increasingly devastating warfare, and the gradual depletion of fur and game animals all placed Native cultures under severe stress. But nothing had the cataclysmic impact on the Native population of the epidemic diseases spread unwittingly by the Europeans. Beginning in 1634 (or perhaps earlier), wave after wave of smallpox, measles, influenza, and other diseases swept through the Native populations. Lacking biological resistance, most perished. By the 1820s Canada's Native population had been reduced to about 175 000 (Plate 4) and in 1900 it was down to 99 000. The depletion of game accelerated with the spread of the fur trade and European settlement, resulting in Native migration and, often, starvation. Added to these disasters was the growing incidence of Native land being transferred to Europeans.

Over thousands of years Native societies everywhere had thoroughly integrated their ways of life with their natural environments. Although they had survived the intolerance of Europeans and had tried to withstand their persistent efforts to remake them into Europeans, Native societies began to disintegrate after they were confined to reserves and their relationship with the land was severed. Evidence of decline was apparent in Eastern Canada by the early 19th century, and within 100 years conditions had worsened and spread across most of the country.

Exploration

In the year 986 the Norse merchant Bjarni Herjolfsson was blown off course on his way from Iceland to Greenland. When the weather cleared, he saw a land 'not mountainous, but well wooded and with low hills.' This was the first reported sighting of Canada by a European. The land's remoteness from Greenland and Iceland, and especially a chronic inability on the part of the Norse to get along with the Natives, prevented them from settling the area.

The Norse voyages forgotten, Europe was confronted in 1492 with the electrifying news that Columbus had sailed west across the Atlantic Ocean and found islands off the coast of either India or Japan. England was the first European country to augment these discoveries, when John Cabot made a northern voyage in 1497 (Plate 5, lower map). Cabot was quickly followed by the Portuguese, who returned from Newfoundland in 1501 with a cargo of 57 Native people, who were sold into slavery in Lisbon. The prevailing opinion at the time was that these northern voyages had reached a vast easterly extension of Asia, but by about 1510 the contention that these lands might be a new continent was gaining respectability. In the 1520s expeditions were undertaken to link the northern English and Portuguese discoveries with the southern Spanish ones and to find a route through this new but inconvenient land mass. These searches led to the exploration of the St Lawrence River valley by the French and to English voyages into Davis and Hudson Straits in quest of a northern route.

Champlain solved the problem of inland exploration (Plate 6). During his first voyage in 1603, he recognized that exploration could be carried out only with Native help. He needed the geographical knowledge, the canoes, and the guidance of the Native people, as well as their expertise in living off the land. The French were drawn inland in search not only of an overland route to the Orient, but of ever more Native groups to engage in the fur trade. They were also motivated to undertake mission work among the Native population and to enlist them as allies against English encirclement. The French reached the Great Lakes in 1615, James Bay in 1671, the Mississippi River in 1673, and the Rocky Mountains in 1751.

Systematic English exploration of the Canadian interior began in 1754, when the Hudson's Bay Company (HBC) at last responded to French competition in its hinterland (Plate 7). After 1763, English- and French-Canadian traders alike pushed westward from Montréal to renew and expand the earlier French fur trade. Again the HBC was forced to react, and rapid exploration of the Canadian interior resulted. By the late 18th century Russian, Spanish, and British expeditions had defined the West Coast, and Mackenzie had crossed overland to reach the Arctic and Pacific Oceans (Plate 8).

During the early 19th century, British explorers resumed the quest for the Northwest Passage. Following the disastrous Franklin expedition of 1845, the Royal Navy and others intensified their search; they finally charted the passage during the 1850s (Plate 9). In 1944, the RCMP schooner *St Roch*, commanded by Inspector H.A. Larsen, navigated the Northwest Passage for the first time in a single season (Plate 11, upper right).

Inland, along the margins of the Canadian Shield, the first systematic scientific surveys were taking place in the mid-19th century. The intention was to determine the suitability of the Canadian interior for European settlement and resource exploitation (Plate 9, small maps).

Territorial Extent

Canada became a federal state in 1867, occupying far less area than it does today (Plates 10 and 11). It attained its present limits only in 1949, with the addition of Newfoundland and the Labrador coast. In the East, Canada evolved out of Québec and Acadia – the old core of New France, which Britain had acquired by conquest (in 1760) and by treaty (in 1763). Additional pieces date from the Treaty of Paris (in 1783), following the American Revolution. Between 1818 and 1849, as the United States expanded westward, the 49th parallel was forced on Britain, in segments, as Canada's southern boundary west of Lake of the Woods. The northwestern boundary along the 141st meridian was established by negotiations between Britain and Russia in 1825. In 1867, Alaska was purchased by the United States, and the boundary line with British Columbia became a matter of contention that was not settled until 1903 (Plate 10, middle left).

Internally, Canada's districts and provinces were shaped and reshaped as settlement proceeded westward and northward, their administrators each time demanding larger measures of local autonomy. The last territorial challenge remaining to Canada is to work out a just solution to the land claims of the Native people (Plate 11, middle left).

Population

It is estimated that in 1800 the population of what is now Eastern Canada was about 340 000; by 1825 it had grown to about 850 000, and by 1851 to 2.4 million. In 1871 the population of Canada as a whole was 3.7 million; it rose to 4.8 million by 1891, and to 18.2 million by 1961. In 1998 it was over 30 million. This section analyses Canadian population changes over the period 1800–1961, using maps and diagrams that summarize some of the country's most basic historical and geographical features. The plates depict three important elements of population: distribution patterns; demographic processes that explain the distributions; and selected characteristics of the population, such as rural-urban proportions and ethnic composition.

By 1800 a Europe-based civilization was overpowering Native lands and Native civilizations and bringing immigrants into northeastern North America. The map in Plate 12 shows a necklace of outports in eastern Newfoundland, narrow belts of settlement in the Maritimes, and a fuller band along the St Lawrence River in Lower Canada. Tiny impressions of settlement were evident in the forests of Upper Canada and in the Eastern Townships of Lower Canada, just north of the American boundary. The map reveals fundamental contrasts in language. The swirling trade patterns of Native peoples and fur traders in the vast northern country make a striking contrast with the solidly occupied area of the United States in the south, where 5.3 million people lived and sent population spurs edging northward. Close Native contact with Eurocanadians was occurring at this time not only on the Canadian Shield; in the Montréal district the Native communities of Caughnawaga and Lac-des-Deux-Montagnes were in place, as were the communities on the Grand River, north of Lake Erie, in Upper Canada.

In all the colonies the first half of the 19th century was a time of clearing forests to make farmland. Populations expanded quickly through large migrations, especially from Great Britain. Numbers almost tripled between 1825 and 1851 (Plate 13). By 1851 a net of urban centres was dispersed over Canada West, just before the first railways opened. The plate makes apparent the intriguing changes that were taking place in Canada East: the push into the Canadian Shield had begun along the Saguenay River and around Lac Saint-Jean; the Eastern Townships were filling in; and the Gaspé Peninsula finally had a population on the St Lawrence River shore to match that on the Chaleur Bay side. In the Maritimes the valleys and periphery were filling out. By mid-century every colony had its leading urban centres – cities of great importance today – and the initial lead of Montréal is clearly seen in the plate.

By 1871 a transcontinental Canada had been created, and Plate 14 follows some of the consequent population changes, to 1891. In the Maritimes the limits of rural agricultural settlement had become evident, and an urban system serving most parts had emerged, with Saint John and Halifax clear rivals. Québec's frontier lands were filling up, and in Ontario colonization roads had assisted settlers in penetrating the southern margins of the Canadian Shield. Farther west the only settlement sites evident in 1871 are those at the Red River (Winnipeg) and in southwestern British Columbia, along with tiny clusters in the BC interior that in part are relics of the gold rushes. By 1891 the impact of the Canadian Pacific Railway (CPR) is seen in the settlements on the Prairies. An urban system, led by Montréal and dependent on the railways, was in place throughout Canada. Regional centres in different sections of the country were poised to fight for supremacy nationally or regionally in the next century.

Canada is generally thought of as a country to which people came, but it has simultaneously been a place from which many departed (Plate 15). Immigration exceeded emigration in the 1850s, but outflow was greater than inflow for every decade over the rest of the century. Because of a high rate of natural increase, however, Canada's population did not actually fall. The rate of out-migration from many rural areas in Eastern Canada between 1871 and 1891 is astonishing; only a few rural counties in Québec and Ontario still received immigrants. People were moving from farms to the cities and the new industrial jobs they offered. A considerable proportion of the outflow headed to the United States, to factory jobs in New England and New York, and to farmlands farther west, before the Canadian Prairies were made easily accessible by the CPR.

From the mid-1890s to 1914 Canada experienced both enormous immigration and large internal population shifts (Plate 16). There were two great international waves of immigration, one from Europe and one from the United States, as well as a trickle from Asia. Canada had not seen such large numbers of immigrants before, nor has it since. The British Isles continued to provide the largest numbers of people, but many poured in from elsewhere in Europe, especially the central and eastern parts. Most migrated to the Prairie farmlands and towns, but many also took industrial and service jobs in other provinces, particularly Ontario. Many of the American immigrants were experienced farmers from North Dakota and Minnesota seeking larger farms in the Prairies. Emigration resulted in concentrations of Canadian-born people in New England, New York, and the Great Lakes states, as would be expected. Washington state, Oregon, and the San Francisco and Los Angeles areas were other popular destinations. Within Canada, large numbers of easterners moved to the West. Ontario and the Maritimes together contributed more than seven times as many migrants as did Québec.

After the Second World War two significant population forces were at work: renewed migration to Canada and the post-war baby boom (Plate 17). The map of demographic change between 1951 and 1961 (centre), relating natural increase and migration within small areas, reveals the complexity of the factors at work. International migrations resumed after the war, producing the largest flows since before the First World War. British immigrants led in numbers, followed by Italians, Germans, and Dutch, and then many others. Canada's ethnic composition (map, lower left) quickly changed, particularly in Ontario, Québec (mainly Montréal), and British Columbia. Though interprovincial migration numbers (upper centre) were not great in relation to the total population, they reflect the fact that there were always some internal migrants whose destinations were governed largely by where the best economic opportunities were to be found.

It is particularly difficult to map the distribution of ethnic groups in Canada, because people of either British or French origin predominate so overwhelmingly in distinct sections of the country. The maps in Plate 18 are therefore drawn to show the ethnic origin of the dominant non-British groups outside Québec and the dominant non-French groups inside Québec. These maps, for 1901, 1931, and 1961, demonstrate the penetration of French Canadians beyond Québec, the pronounced ethnic diversity of the Prairie Provinces, and the strong presence of German Canadians in many parts of Canada. In most parts of Québec, people of British origin were persistently second in numbers to French Canadians. The three-dimensional block diagrams of ethnic groups in major cities illustrate what the maps cannot: Canada's sheer ethnic diversity. The pie charts on the maps reveal that, over the course of these sixty years, French Canadians were consistently dominant in Québec, British Canadians began to relinquish dominance in Ontario, and the ethnic mix remained fairly stable in the Maritimes. British Canadians have stayed numerically strong in the West, but there has been considerable ethnic diversity in that region since 1901.

Transport and Urbanization

Canada is held together by an effective transportation system that emerged over many decades, but the 19th century was a time of critical change. In the first half of that century water and roads were the main means of transportation (Plate 19). Steamboats had been in use since 1809, and by 1850 they efficiently connected the Atlantic region to Central Canada. Roads were another matter, however, and long-distance travel on land was tiresome and slow. Yet in 1850, just before the railway age, there was scheduled passenger service by water and road in all the settled parts of eastern British North America. The Welland and St Lawrence River canals were operating, and ships could travel from the Atlantic to the Great Lakes. Transatlantic travel remained slow, but between 1837 and 1852 passage times were greatly reduced (green and brown maps, right).

The second half of the 19th century was Canada's great railway-building age, which transformed the country. Railway lines connected important centres within each settled region; the pace of life changed, and communities were better able to get to know one another. If the chief act of statesmanship creating Canada was Confederation in 1867 followed by the addition of western territories, then the building of the transcontinental railway was the great bonding and inspirational force that breathed life into the immense new country. Plate 20 shows the route of the Canadian Pacific Railway, opened in 1885 between Montréal and Vancouver, and the formidable physical barriers that were overcome. Eastward, the other vital element of a transcontinental link was the Intercolonial Railway between Montréal and Halifax, completed in 1876. Travel time within Canada was revolutionized by the new means of transportation (lower left).

Urban centres, linked by various transport systems, had an essential role, first in developing and then in organizing Canadian life. Canadians lived in widely separated domains, and each cluster of rural settlement had its system of urban centres. Canada urbanized rapidly: in 1891, 30 per cent of the population lived in places of 1 000 people or more; by 1931, more than half the population was urban; by 1951, the figure was 63 per cent. Plates 21 and 22, depicting urban networks in 1891, 1921, and 1951, use the frequency of passenger train service as an indicator of the level of interaction between places. Telephone connections, when they came, facilitated an increased flow of information, and by 1961 air travel had also become important. A comparison of the 1921 and 1951 maps reveals that the generally settled areas expanded only modestly in that period, yet town and city growth pushed the total population from 8.8 million to 14 million. Only a few small centres serving agricultural areas stagnated. A national urban system had developed by 1951, dominated by Montréal and Toronto in Central Canada; important regional centres flourished in the other major sections of the country.

In the 19th century railways changed life in Canada; in the 20th century the motor vehicle was the revolutionary force, with a dramatic impact on economic development and society (Plate 23, brown tones). Beginning in the 1920s, networks of improved highways expanded quickly in each of the major sections of Canada, but not until the 1960s was the highly engineered Trans-Canada Highway completed from coast to coast. Regional airlines began operating in the 1930s, and thirty years later transcontinental flights were commonplace, with connections throughout the North (Plate 23, green tones).

The Economy

More than half a century has passed since Harold Innis enunciated the staples hypothesis: that the export of commodities such as fish, fur, timber, wheat, and minerals played a leading role in Canadian economic development (Plate 24). The flow of exports from the port of Québec in the 18th century illustrates this concept. In this period furs and hides accounted for almost all shipments, although wheat, timber, and fish were also exported. Two basic patterns are evident from the map, governed by whether France or Great Britain was the colonial power in control. In 1736 most of the commodities went to France; in 1771 they went to Britain. In both years some goods also went to markets in the Gulf of St Lawrence, the West Indies, and southern Europe.

The geography of Canada at the end of the 19th century is summed up in Plate 25. Native people dependent on hunting, fishing, and trapping were still the only inhabitants in most of the Canadian territory, and many interior lands remained unknown to Europeans. A transcontinental economy existed in the south, with considerable regional diversification in economic activities. In Eastern Canada most of the areas suited to agriculture were settled; expansion to the northern clay belts came later. In the West, however, settlers were just on the threshold of greatly expanding the farm areas. Fishing continued to be important in the Atlantic region, and forestry was significant in all of Eastern Canada. Both of these activities were in the early stages of expansion in British Columbia, and mining was starting in the Canadian Shield. Manufacturing was concentrated in Montréal and Toronto, with lesser production in smaller centres.

In the first two decades of the 20th century the primary sector constituted about one-quarter of the Canadian economy (Plate 26), but manufacturing and service activities were gaining in importance. In 1921 agriculture was by far the most important primary activity everywhere except in British Columbia and Newfoundland (lower elements of the plate). Coal was a vital source of energy, important in Nova Scotia, Alberta, and British Columbia. From 1941 to 1961 there was a marked decrease in farm acreage in the East and expansion in western regions (Plate 27, main map); Canada was to achieve its maximum area in farmland in 1966. Plate 27 (upper middle and right) also shows that fishing continued to be an international activity on the Atlantic continental shelf, and remained an important resource until the devastation of the cod fishery in the 1990s.

Manufacturing has persistently been centred in Ontario and Québec since the late 19th century. By value of goods produced, about 50 per cent of Canada's manufacturing is usually concentrated in Ontario and 25 per cent in Québec. Plate 28 shows some factors at work in the critical formative period from 1885 to 1930, when Central Canada's vast growth was stimulated. Tariff protection assisted manufacturing, Ontario and Québec formed a large home market, and access to markets in Atlantic and Western Canada was good. The nucleus of American industry was close by, and it was convenient for firms to jump the border and establish branch plants to serve the Canadian market (upper right). After the First World War the motor-vehicle industry centred in Ontario became increasingly important (lower right), and has remained vital to the economic health of the country ever since.

Society

Both landscapes and building styles vary greatly across Canada. The artists of the Group of Seven were not the first to paint in different parts of the country; they were preceded by fully a century of artists and photographers whose landscapes from the Appalachians, Great Lakes–St Lawrence lowland, Canadian Shield, Cordillera, and Barren Grounds are reproduced in Plate 29. Places where selected artists painted are marked on the map, and the travel routes of four painters and photographers are laid out. The development of photography in Canada is analysed in the notes to Plate 29. Plate 30 shows regional differences that had emerged in domestic building design by 1891 Many factors influenced styles in Canada: folk-housing patterns carried from former homelands, influential designs from particular periods in Europe and the United States, and the mix of ideas and technologies existing in particular regions as settlement progressed from pioneer to mature stages.

Literacy and education changed life in 19th-century Canada. Literacy is one of the great human achievements, the basis of the present information age (Plate 31). In the 19th century, more and more books and journals were published, newspapers founded, and public libraries established. Provision of schooling for the general population furthermore became a great state endeavour (Plate 32). Tax-supported schools were built, teachers were trained and certified, and new technologies, such as blackboards, were introduced. School boards increasingly hired female teachers, in part because they commanded lower wages than men, as an increasing proportion of the school-age population across the country started attending school. Through these opportunities people gained access to a wider world and could more easily learn about one another.

Immigrants bring their religion with them, and migrations from Europe account for the predominance, and diversity, of Christian denominations in Canada (Plate 33, two main maps). The strong regional concentrations of Roman Catholics east of the Ottawa River valley and Protestants west from there in 1921 are distinctive. The union of several Protestant denominations to form the United Church of Canada in 1925 resolved factional stresses that had existed among Christian communities for well over a century (chart, lower left, and lower maps). It was an important event in consolidating the transcontinental nation.

ENVIRONMENTAL CHANGE AFTER 9000 BCE

Authors: J.H. McAndrews, K.-B. Liu, G.C. Manville (Palaeobotany); V.K. Prest, J.-S. Vincent (Glacial geology)

POLLEN DIAGRAM AT EDWARD LAKE, ONTARIO

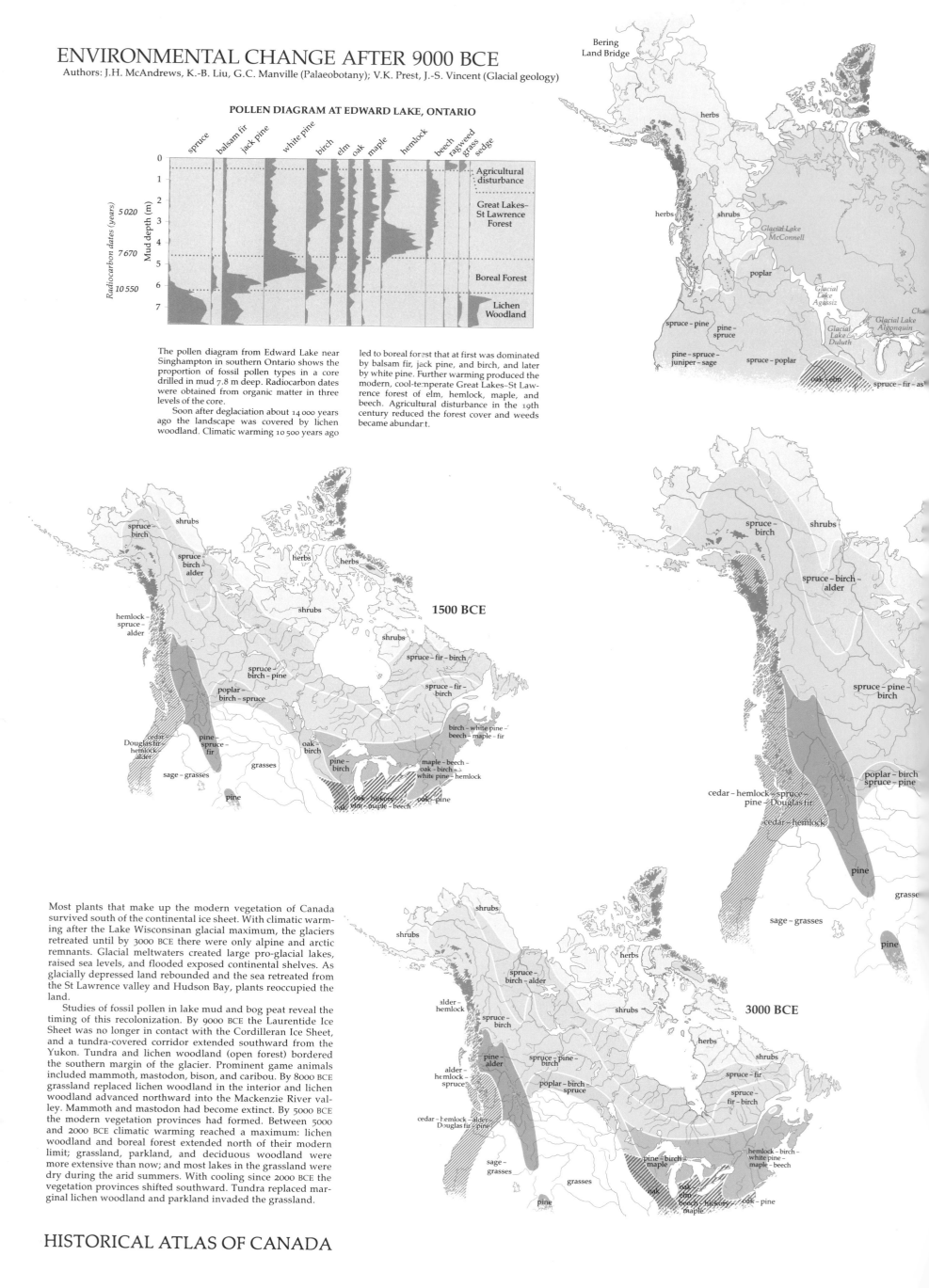

The pollen diagram from Edward Lake near Singhampton in southern Ontario shows the proportion of fossil pollen types in a core drilled in mud 7.8 m deep. Radiocarbon dates were obtained from organic matter in three levels of the core.

Soon after deglaciation about 14 000 years ago the landscape was covered by lichen woodland. Climatic warming 10 500 years ago led to boreal forest that at first was dominated by balsam fir, jack pine, and birch, and later by white pine. Further warming produced the modern, cool-temperate Great Lakes–St Lawrence forest of elm, hemlock, maple, and beech. Agricultural disturbance in the 19th century reduced the forest cover and weeds became abundant.

Most plants that make up the modern vegetation of Canada survived south of the continental ice sheet. With climatic warming after the Lake Wisconsinan glacial maximum, the glaciers retreated until by 3000 BCE there were only alpine and arctic remnants. Glacial meltwaters created large pro-glacial lakes, raised sea levels, and flooded exposed continental shelves. As glacially depressed land rebounded and the sea retreated from the St Lawrence valley and Hudson Bay, plants reoccupied the land.

Studies of fossil pollen in lake mud and bog peat reveal the timing of this recolonization. By 9000 BCE the Laurentide Ice Sheet was no longer in contact with the Cordilleran Ice Sheet, and a tundra-covered corridor extended southward from the Yukon. Tundra and lichen woodland (open forest) bordered the southern margin of the glacier. Prominent game animals included mammoth, mastodon, bison, and caribou. By 8000 BCE grassland replaced lichen woodland in the interior and lichen woodland advanced northward into the Mackenzie River valley. Mammoth and mastodon had become extinct. By 5000 BCE the modern vegetation provinces had formed. Between 5000 and 2000 BCE climatic warming reached a maximum: lichen woodland and boreal forest extended north of their modern limit; grassland, parkland, and deciduous woodland were more extensive than now; and most lakes in the grassland were dry during the arid summers. With cooling since 2000 BCE the vegetation provinces shifted southward. Tundra replaced marginal lichen woodland and parkland invaded the grassland.

HISTORICAL ATLAS OF CANADA

PLATE 1

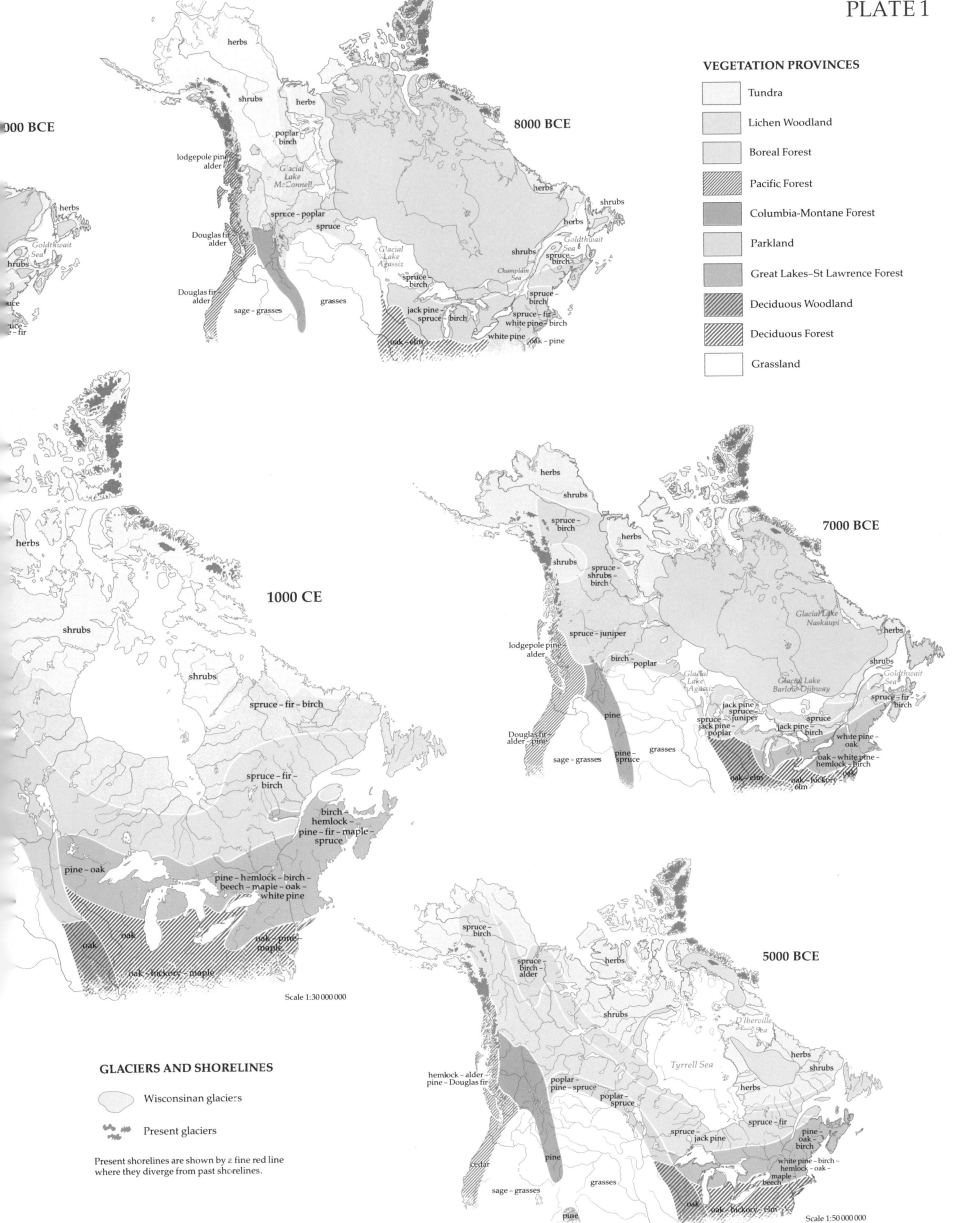

VEGETATION PROVINCES

Tundra

Lichen Woodland

Boreal Forest

Pacific Forest

Columbia-Montane Forest

Parkland

Great Lakes–St Lawrence Forest

Deciduous Woodland

Deciduous Forest

Grassland

000 BCE

8000 BCE

1000 CE

7000 BCE

5000 BCE

Scale 1:30 000 000

Scale 1:50 000 000

GLACIERS AND SHORELINES

Wisconsinan glaciers

Present glaciers

Present shorelines are shown by a fine red line where they diverge from past shorelines.

CONCISE EDITION

Author: J.V. Wright

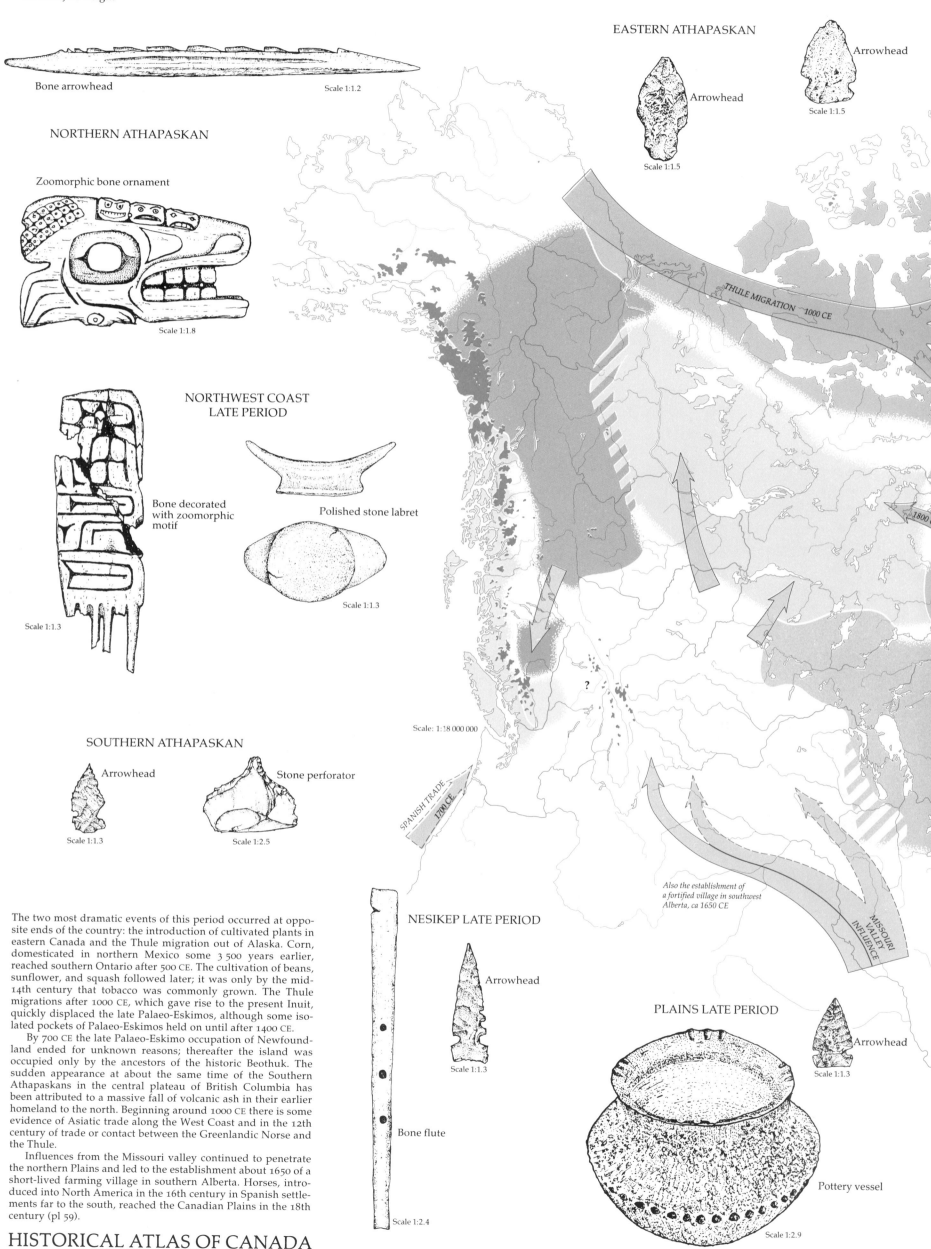

Bone arrowhead

Scale 1:1.2

EASTERN ATHAPASKAN

Arrowhead

Arrowhead

Scale 1:1.5

Scale 1:1.5

NORTHERN ATHAPASKAN

Zoomorphic bone ornament

Scale 1:1.8

NORTHWEST COAST LATE PERIOD

Bone decorated with zoomorphic motif

Polished stone labret

Scale 1:1.3

Scale 1:1.3

THULE MIGRATION 1000 CE

1800 CE

Scale: 1:18 000 000

?

SOUTHERN ATHAPASKAN

Arrowhead

Stone perforator

Scale 1:1.3

Scale 1:2.5

SPANISH TRADE 1700 CE

Also the establishment of
a fortified village in southwest
Alberta, ca 1650 CE

MISSOURI VALLEY INFLUENCE

The two most dramatic events of this period occurred at opposite ends of the country: the introduction of cultivated plants in eastern Canada and the Thule migration out of Alaska. Corn, domesticated in northern Mexico some 3 500 years earlier, reached southern Ontario after 500 CE. The cultivation of beans, sunflower, and squash followed later; it was only by the mid-14th century that tobacco was commonly grown. The Thule migrations after 1000 CE, which gave rise to the present Inuit, quickly displaced the late Palaeo-Eskimos, although some isolated pockets of Palaeo-Eskimos held on until after 1400 CE.

By 700 CE the late Palaeo-Eskimo occupation of Newfoundland ended for unknown reasons; thereafter the island was occupied only by the ancestors of the historic Beothuk. The sudden appearance at about the same time of the Southern Athapaskans in the central plateau of British Columbia has been attributed to a massive fall of volcanic ash in their earlier homeland to the north. Beginning around 1000 CE there is some evidence of Asiatic trade along the West Coast and in the 12th century of trade or contact between the Greenlandic Norse and the Thule.

Influences from the Missouri valley continued to penetrate the northern Plains and led to the establishment about 1650 of a short-lived farming village in southern Alberta. Horses, introduced into North America in the 16th century in Spanish settlements far to the south, reached the Canadian Plains in the 18th century (pl 59).

NESIKEP LATE PERIOD

Arrowhead

Scale 1:1.3

PLAINS LATE PERIOD

Arrowhead

Scale 1:1.3

Bone flute

Scale 1:2.4

Pottery vessel

Scale 1:2.9

HISTORICAL ATLAS OF CANADA

PLATE 2

ARCHAEOLOGICAL CULTURAL CONSTRUCTS

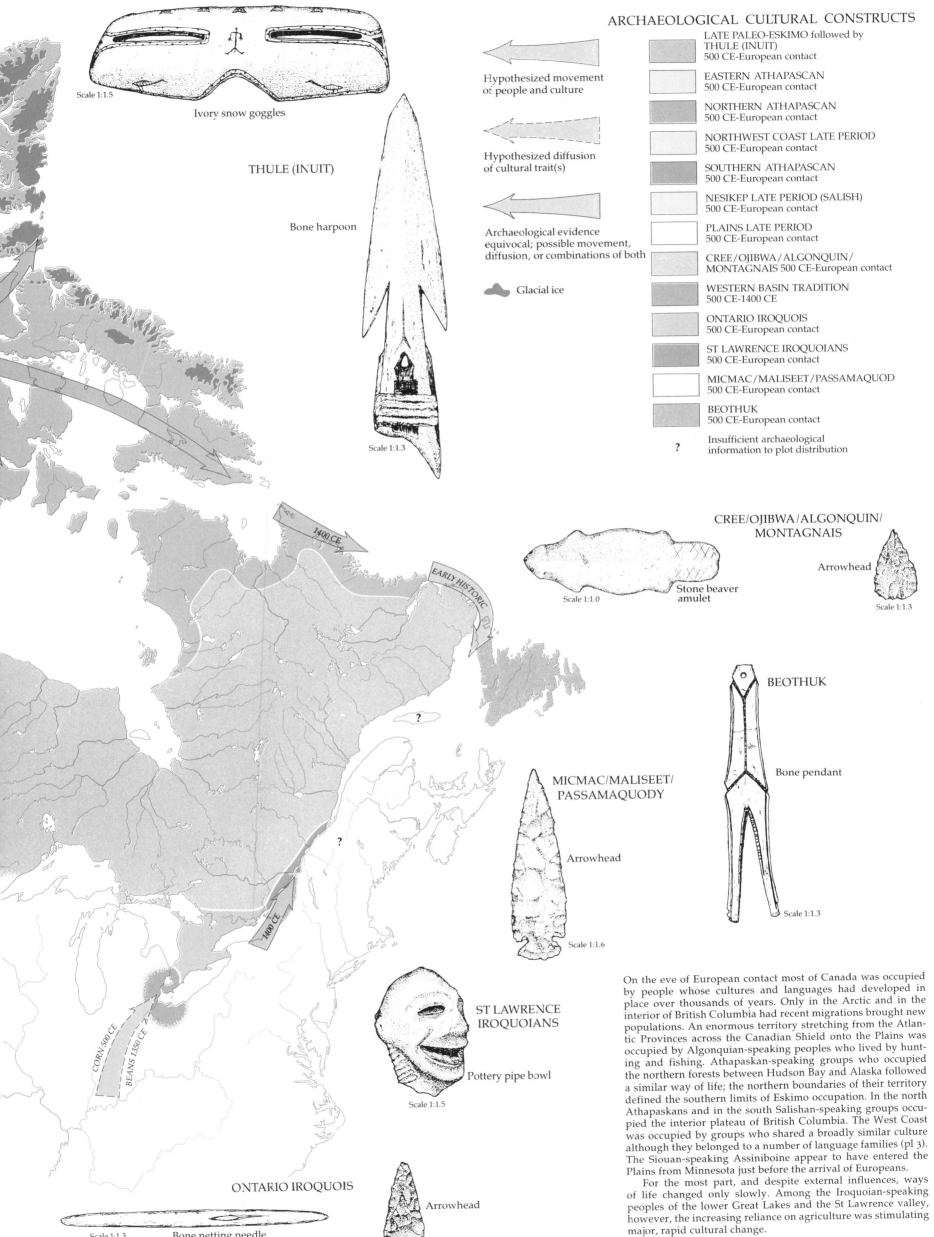

Scale 1:1.5

Ivory snow goggles

THULE (INUIT)

Bone harpoon

Scale 1:1.3

Hypothesized movement of people and culture

Hypothesized diffusion of cultural trait(s)

Archaeological evidence equivocal; possible movement, diffusion, or combinations of both

Glacial ice

LATE PALEO-ESKIMO followed by THULE (INUIT)
500 CE–European contact

EASTERN ATHAPASCAN
500 CE–European contact

NORTHERN ATHAPASCAN
500 CE–European contact

NORTHWEST COAST LATE PERIOD
500 CE–European contact

SOUTHERN ATHAPASCAN
500 CE–European contact

NESIKEP LATE PERIOD (SALISH)
500 CE–European contact

PLAINS LATE PERIOD
500 CE–European contact

CREE/OJIBWA/ALGONQUIN/
MONTAGNAIS 500 CE–European contact

WESTERN BASIN TRADITION
500 CE–1400 CE

ONTARIO IROQUOIS
500 CE–European contact

ST LAWRENCE IROQUOIANS
500 CE–European contact

MICMAC/MALISEET/PASSAMAQUOD
500 CE–European contact

BEOTHUK
500 CE–European contact

? Insufficient archaeological
information to plot distribution

CREE/OJIBWA/ALGONQUIN/
MONTAGNAIS

Arrowhead

Scale 1:1.3

Scale 1:1.0 Stone beaver amulet

1400 CE

EARLY HISTORIC

?

?

BEOTHUK

Bone pendant

Scale 1:1.3

MICMAC/MALISEET/
PASSAMAQUODY

Arrowhead

Scale 1:1.6

1400 CE

ST LAWRENCE
IROQUOIANS

Pottery pipe bowl

Scale 1:1.5

CORN 500 CE

BEANS 1350 CE

On the eve of European contact most of Canada was occupied by people whose cultures and languages had developed in place over thousands of years. Only in the Arctic and in the interior of British Columbia had recent migrations brought new populations. An enormous territory stretching from the Atlantic Provinces across the Canadian Shield onto the Plains was occupied by Algonquian-speaking peoples who lived by hunting and fishing. Athapaskan-speaking groups who occupied the northern forests between Hudson Bay and Alaska followed a similar way of life; the northern boundaries of their territory defined the southern limits of Eskimo occupation. In the north Athapaskans and in the south Salishan-speaking groups occupied the interior plateau of British Columbia. The West Coast was occupied by groups who shared a broadly similar culture although they belonged to a number of language families (pl 3). The Siouan-speaking Assiniboine appear to have entered the Plains from Minnesota just before the arrival of Europeans.

For the most part, and despite external influences, ways of life changed only slowly. Among the Iroquoian-speaking peoples of the lower Great Lakes and the St Lawrence valley, however, the increasing reliance on agriculture was stimulating major, rapid cultural change.

ONTARIO IROQUOIS

Arrowhead

Scale 1:1.3 Bone netting needle

Scale 1:1.3

CONCISE EDITION

NATIVE POPULATION AND SUBSISTENCE, 17th CENTURY

Authors: Conrad E. Heidenreich; J.V. Wright (Prehistoric subsistence)

LINGUISTIC FAMILIES AND IDENTIFIABLE GROUPS

ALGONQUIAN LINGUISTIC FAMILY

Eastern Algonquian Groups

Mc	Micmac	Mc1 Gaspegeoag
		2 Sigentigteog
		3 Epigoitnag
		4 Pigtogeoag
		5 Onamag
		6 Esgigeoag
		7 Segepenegatig
		8 Gespogoitnag
Ma	Maliseet-Passamaquoddy	Ma1 Maliseet
		2 Passamaquoddy
Ae	Eastern Abenaki	Ae1 Penobscot
		2 Kennebec
		3 Arosaguntacook
		4 Pigwaket
Aw	Western Abenaki	Aw1 Sokoki
		2 Cowasuk
		3 Winnepesaukee
		4 Penacook
		5 Amoskeag
M	Mahican	
Ar	Southern New England groups	Ar1 Pawtucket
		2 Massachusett
		3 Pokanokett
		4 Naragansett
		5 Pequot-Mohegan
De	Delaware	De1 Munsee
		2 Northern Umami
		3 Southern Umami

Northern Algonquian Groups

O	Ojibwa	O1 Outchibous
		2 Marameg
		3 Mantouek
		4 Noquet
		5 Saulteaux
		6 Mississauga
		7 Nikikouet
		8 Amikwa
		9 Achiligouan (N,Ot)
		10 Ouchougai (N,Ot)
		11 Ouasouarini
		12 Sagahanirini
Ot	Ottawa	
Me	Menominee	
Pt	Potawatomi	
N	Nipissing	
S	Sauk-Fox-Kikapoo-Mascouten	S1 Sauk
		2 Fox
		3 Kikapoo
		4 Mascouten
M	Miami-Illinois	M1 Miami
		2 Illinois
Al	Algonquin	Al1 Onontchataronon
		2 Weskarini
		3 Matouweskarini
		4 Keinouche
		5 Kichesipirini
		6 Ottagoutouemin
		7 Sagnitaouigama
		8 Outimagami (N)
Cr	Cree-Gens de Terre	Cr1 Alimbegouek
		2 Monsoni
		3 Ataouabouskatouek
		4 Nisibourounik
		5 Pitchibourounik
		6 Gesseiriniouetch
		7 Opinagauiriniouetch
		8 Grand Mistassirini
		9 Petit Mistassirini
		10 Attikiriniouetch
		11 Nitchikiriniouetch
		12 Outchichagamiouetch
		13 Escurieux
		14 Nopeming-dach-iriniouek
		15 Outoulibi
		16 Timiscimi
		17 Abitibi
		18 Piscoutagami
Mt	Montagnais-Naskapi	Mt1 Tadoussacien
		2 Kakouchaki
		3 Chicoutimi
		4 Attikamek
		5 Nekoubaniste
		6 Chomonchouaniste
		7 Oumatachirini
		8 Papinachois
		9 Oukesestigouek
		10 Chisedech
		11 Bersiamites
		12 Oueneskapi
		13 Oumamiouek
		14 Outakouamiouek
		15 Outabitibec

Western Algonquian Groups

Ch Cheyenne

BEOTHUK LINGUISTIC FAMILY

Be Beothuk

IROQUOIAN LINGUISTIC FAMILY

Ir	Iroquoian	Ir1 Huron
		2 Petun (Tionontate)
		3 Neutral
		4 Wenro
		5 Erie
		6 Seneca
		7 Cayuga
		8 Onondaga
		9 Oneida
		10 Mohawk
		11 Susquehannock

SIOUAN LINGUISTIC FAMILY

Da Dakota
W Winnebago
A Assiniboine

In the east, where the French compiled much ethnographic information before European diseases spread through the Great Lakes basin in the 1630s, the distribution of early 17th-century populations is approximately known. Most of the St Lawrence valley was uninhabited. Population densities were low wherever the economy depended on hunting, fishing, and gathering, and sharply higher where agriculture was practised. Non-agricultural peoples were highly mobile; although territories were extensive, contact between neighbouring groups was frequent.

Linguistic groups

- Algonquian
- Beothuk
- Iroquoian
- Siouan

Scale 1:12 500 000

The analysis of discarded bones and shells from an archaeological site can indicate when the site was occupied, what animals were eaten, and the relative importance of different foods. Where soils are acidic, as in the Canadian Shield, such remains are rarely preserved, however, and very little prehistoric hunting and fishing equipment survives: stone, bone, and copper tips for spears and arrows are most common, whereas objects such as sinew or rope snares, nets, and traps usually have disappeared. Some stone structures used to channel caribou and trap fish, as well as portions of wooden fishing weirs buried under water in mud, have survived. Over all, archaeological data permit only a partial picture of patterns of subsistence in late prehistoric Canada.

SUBSISTENCE
Archaeological Data

- Corn, deer, fish
- Fish, sea mammals, caribou
- Fish, shellfish, moose, sea mammals
- Deer, fish
- Caribou, fish
- Caribou, fish, moose
- Bison
- Shellfish, fish, sea mam

- ■ Wooden caribou surrour
- ■ Stone caribou drive-lane
- ✳ Bison entrapment
- ⋅ Stone fish weir
- ⋅ Wooden fish weir

Scale 1:35 000 000

HISTORICAL ATLAS OF CANADA

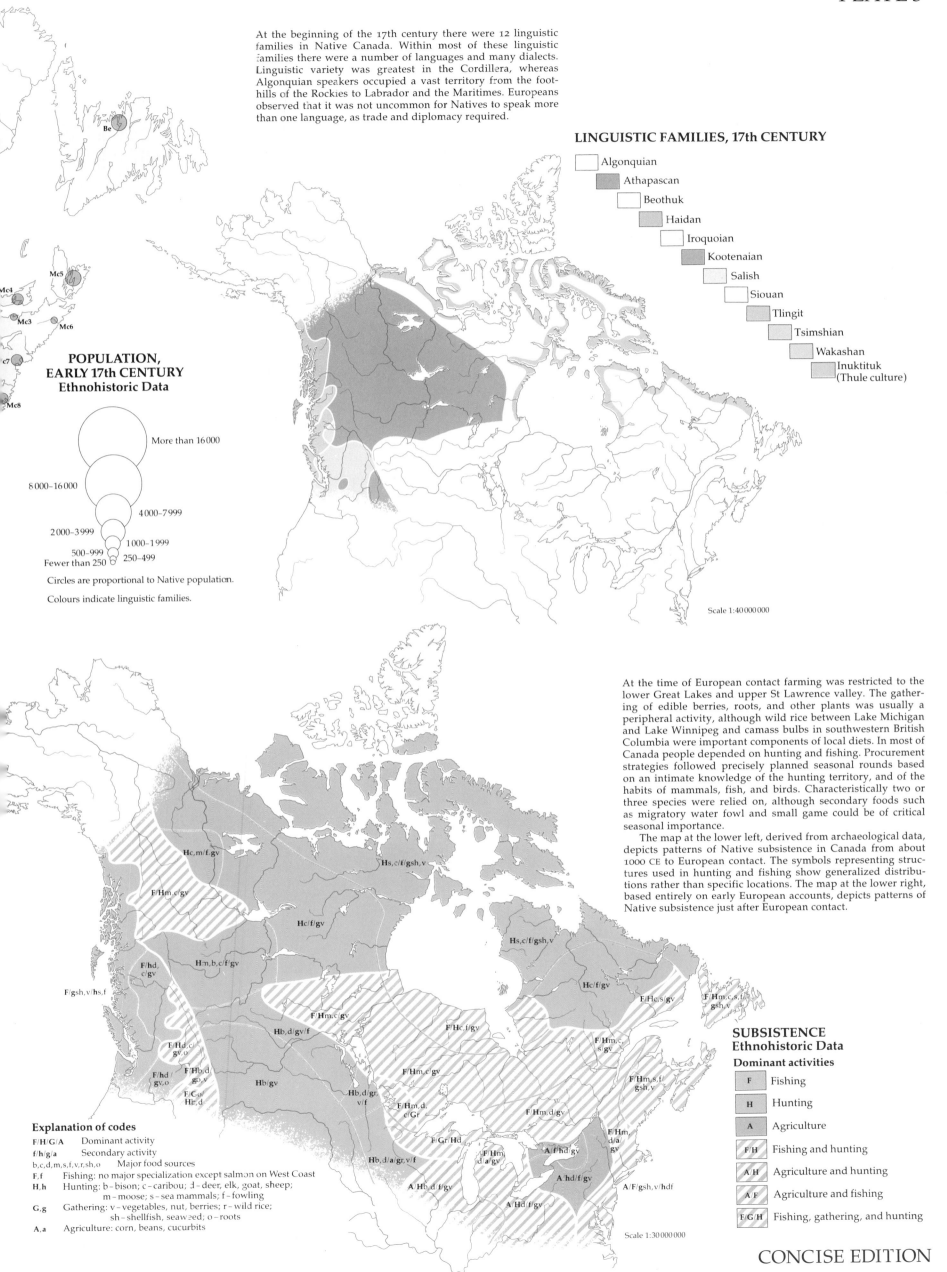

At the beginning of the 17th century there were 12 linguistic families in Native Canada. Within most of these linguistic families there were a number of languages and many dialects. Linguistic variety was greatest in the Cordillera, whereas Algonquian speakers occupied a vast territory from the foothills of the Rockies to Labrador and the Maritimes. Europeans observed that it was not uncommon for Natives to speak more than one language, as trade and diplomacy required.

LINGUISTIC FAMILIES, 17th CENTURY

Algonquian
Athapascan
Beothuk
Haidan
Iroquoian
Kootenaian
Salish
Siouan
Tlingit
Tsimshian
Wakashan
Inuktituk (Thule culture)

Scale 1:40 000 000

POPULATION, EARLY 17th CENTURY
Ethnohistoric Data

More than 16 000
8 000 – 16 000
4 000 – 7 999
2 000 – 3 999
1 000 – 1 999
500 – 999
250 – 499
Fewer than 250

Circles are proportional to Native population.

Colours indicate linguistic families.

At the time of European contact farming was restricted to the lower Great Lakes and upper St Lawrence valley. The gathering of edible berries, roots, and other plants was usually a peripheral activity, although wild rice between Lake Michigan and Lake Winnipeg and camass bulbs in southwestern British Columbia were important components of local diets. In most of Canada people depended on hunting and fishing. Procurement strategies followed precisely planned seasonal rounds based on an intimate knowledge of the hunting territory, and of the habits of mammals, fish, and birds. Characteristically two or three species were relied on, although secondary foods such as migratory water fowl and small game could be of critical seasonal importance.

The map at the lower left, derived from archaeological data, depicts patterns of Native subsistence in Canada from about 1000 CE to European contact. The symbols representing structures used in hunting and fishing show generalized distributions rather than specific locations. The map at the lower right, based entirely on early European accounts, depicts patterns of Native subsistence just after European contact.

SUBSISTENCE
Ethnohistoric Data
Dominant activities

F	Fishing
H	Hunting
A	Agriculture
F/H	Fishing and hunting
A/H	Agriculture and hunting
A/F	Agriculture and fishing
F/G/H	Fishing, gathering, and hunting

Explanation of codes

F/H/G/A   Dominant activity
f/h/g/a   Secondary activity
b,c,d,m,s,f,v,r,sh,o   Major food sources
F,f   Fishing: no major specialization except salmon on West Coast
H,h   Hunting: b – bison; c – caribou; d – deer, elk, goat, sheep; m – moose; s – sea mammals; f – fowling
G,g   Gathering: v – vegetables, nut, berries; r – wild rice; sh – shellfish, seaweed; o – roots
A,a   Agriculture: corn, beans, cucurbits

Scale 1:30 000 000

NATIVE CANADA, ca 1820

Authors: Conrad E. Heidenreich, Robert Galois (New Caledonia)

In the early 1820s the Native population of what is now Canada was about 175 000, a large drop from the 250 000 estimated for the early 17th century (pl 3). Until the late 18th century epidemic disease and, to a degree, warfare were the principal causes of population decline. In the 19th century, starvation took an increasing toll as some areas were overhunted, and as European settlement increasingly restricted the seasonal mobility of Native peoples. The search for provisions and furs led to gradual movements of population, particularly towards the grasslands and tundra (for food) and the northwest (for furs and food). In some areas where the population was expanding, bitter warfare ensued as traditional enemies came into closer contact. Seasonal movement was extensive where Native groups had access to migratory game.

On the east coast Native hunting was destroyed, seasonal movements disrupted, and the transition to agriculture made difficult as Natives were confined to small parcels of poor land. Harassed and barred from coastal resources, the Beothuk were nearing extinction. Along the upper St Lawrence and lower Great Lakes traditionally agricultural peoples, most ethnically and linguistically diverse refugees from the United States, practised a viable mixed farming. The groups of the eastern boreal forest, still masters of their land, were deeply involved in the fur trade and fishing, but faced seasonal food shortages as big game became scarce. Throughout the west and northwest, traditional economies based on hunting and fishing persisted, enmeshed with the fur and pemmican trades. The sea-otter trade had all but disappeared from the northwest coast, but other marine resources remained plentiful and supported large populations. Throughout the intermontane area and the eastern Arctic, European–Native contact was infrequent, and it had not yet taken place in the High Arctic.

BEAUFORT
SEA

RUSSIAN
AMERICA
(1825)

Great
Bear Lake

Great Slave
Lake

Lake Athabasca

PACIFIC
OCEAN

NEW
CALEDONIA

Lake
Winnipeg

COLUMBIA DISTRICT

SPANISH AMERICA

UNITED STATES OF AMERICA

HISTORICAL ATLAS OF CANADA

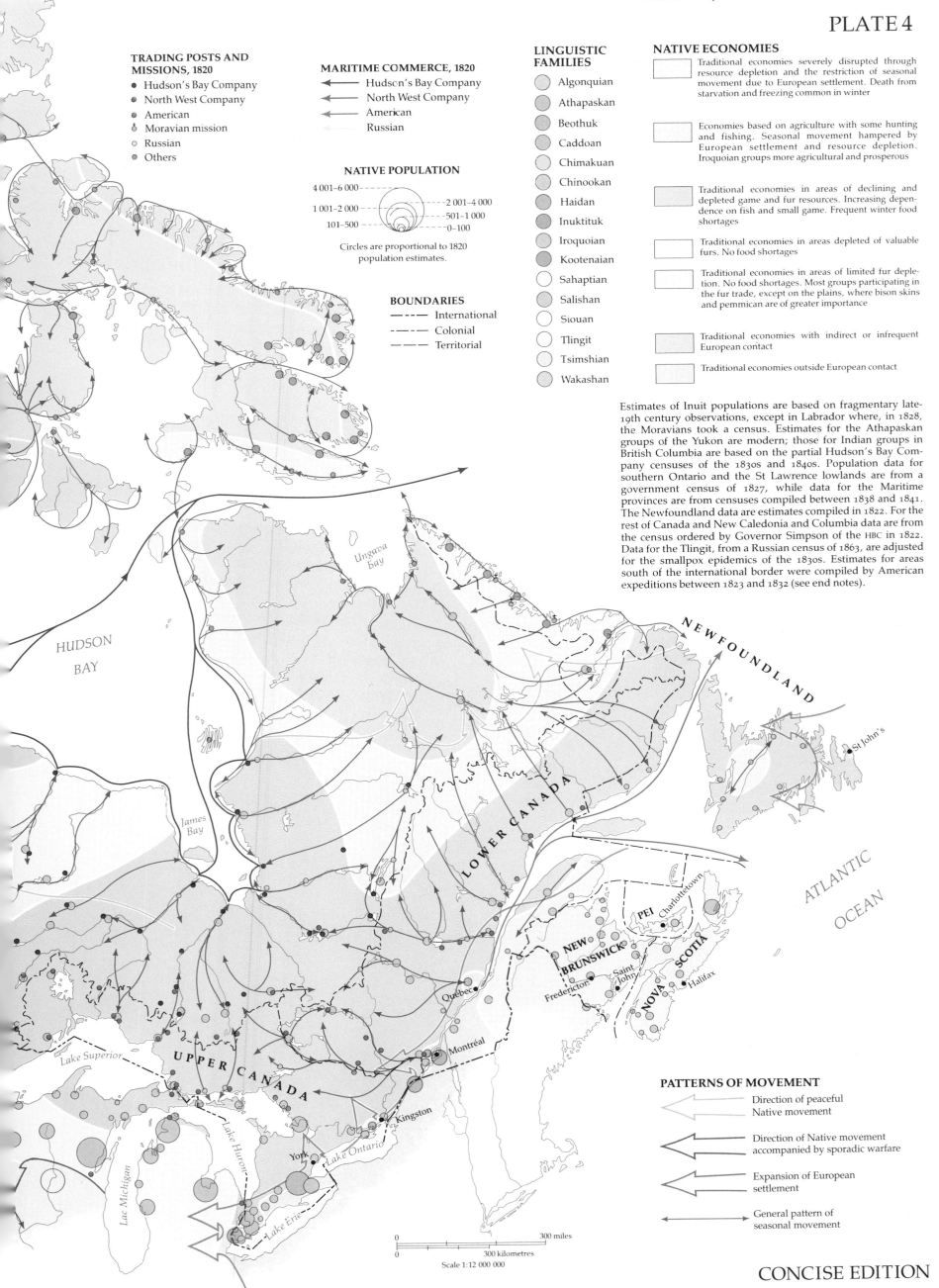

TRADING POSTS AND MISSIONS, 1820

- Hudson's Bay Company
- North West Company
- American
- Moravian mission
- Russian
- Others

MARITIME COMMERCE, 1820

- Hudson's Bay Company
- North West Company
- American
- Russian

NATIVE POPULATION

4 001–6 000
1 001–2 000
101–500
2 001–4 000
501–1 000
0–100

Circles are proportional to 1820 population estimates.

BOUNDARIES

- International
- Colonial
- Territorial

LINGUISTIC FAMILIES

- Algonquian
- Athapaskan
- Beothuk
- Caddoan
- Chimakuan
- Chinookan
- Haidan
- Inuktituk
- Iroquoian
- Kootenaian
- Sahaptian
- Salishan
- Siouan
- Tlingit
- Tsimshian
- Wakashan

NATIVE ECONOMIES

Traditional economies severely disrupted through resource depletion and the restriction of seasonal movement due to European settlement. Death from starvation and freezing common in winter

Economies based on agriculture with some hunting and fishing. Seasonal movement hampered by European settlement and resource depletion. Iroquoian groups more agricultural and prosperous

Traditional economies in areas of declining and depleted game and fur resources. Increasing dependence on fish and small game. Frequent winter food shortages

Traditional economies in areas depleted of valuable furs. No food shortages

Traditional economies in areas of limited fur depletion. No food shortages. Most groups participating in the fur trade, except on the plains, where bison skins and pemmican are of greater importance

Traditional economies with indirect or infrequent European contact

Traditional economies outside European contact

Estimates of Inuit populations are based on fragmentary late-19th century observations, except in Labrador where, in 1828, the Moravians took a census. Estimates for the Athapaskan groups of the Yukon are modern; those for Indian groups in British Columbia are based on the partial Hudson's Bay Company censuses of the 1830s and 1840s. Population data for southern Ontario and the St Lawrence lowlands are from a government census of 1827, while data for the Maritime provinces are from censuses compiled between 1838 and 1841. The Newfoundland data are estimates compiled in 1822. For the rest of Canada and New Caledonia and Columbia data are from the census ordered by Governor Simpson of the HBC in 1822. Data for the Tlingit, from a Russian census of 1863, are adjusted for the smallpox epidemics of the 1830s. Estimates for areas south of the international border were compiled by American expeditions between 1823 and 1832 (see end notes).

HUDSON BAY

NEWFOUNDLAND

Ungava Bay

James Bay

LOWER CANADA

St John's

ATLANTIC OCEAN

PEI
Charlottetown

NEW BRUNSWICK

NOVA SCOTIA

Fredericton
Saint John
Halifax

Quebec

Lake Superior

UPPER CANADA

Montréal

Kingston

York

Lac Michigan

Lake Huron

Lake Ontario

Lake Erie

PATTERNS OF MOVEMENT

Direction of peaceful Native movement

Direction of Native movement accompanied by sporadic warfare

Expansion of European settlement

General pattern of seasonal movement

0   300 miles

0   300 kilometres

Scale 1:12 000 000

CONCISE EDITION

EXPLORING THE ATLANTIC COAST, 16th AND 17th CENTURIES

Author: Richard I. Ruggles

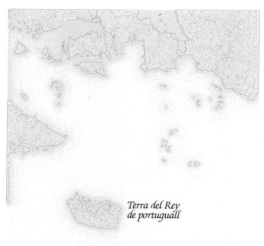

CANTINO MAP, 1502 (detail)

An anonymous Portuguese map of the world, obtained by Alberto Cantino, agent for the Duke of Ferrara, depicts the land discovered by John Cabot and the brothers Miguel and Gaspar Corte-Real as an island far south and west of Greenland. Most of the Caribbean islands were fairly well known.

RIBEIRO MAP, 1529 (detail)

Diogo Ribeiro, a Portuguese cartographer, recorded new discoveries on the official Spanish map of the world. By 1529 Esteban Gómez and Giovanni da Verrazano had established that there was a continuous coastline between Florida and the Gulf of St Lawrence. Between C. del breton and C. rasso (Cape Race) Ribeiro located a broad bay, an indication, perhaps, that the existence of the Gulf of St Lawrence was known. To the north Ribeiro named Labrador and Greenland.

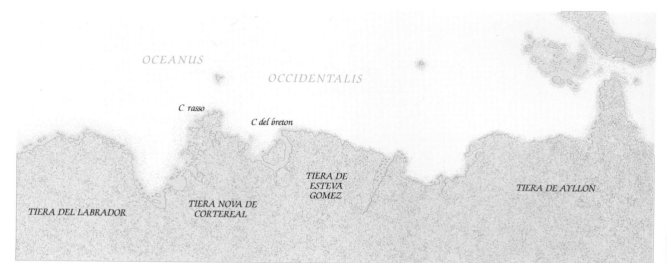

JAMES MAP, 1632 (detail)

By 1616 William Baffin had established the general outline of Baffin Bay; by 1632 Luke Foxe and Thomas James had explored the western shores of Hudson Bay and James Bay. A northwest passage had not been found, although there were still reports, not to be followed up until much later, of openings to the west.

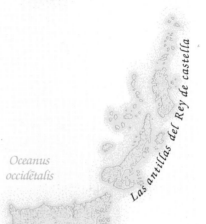

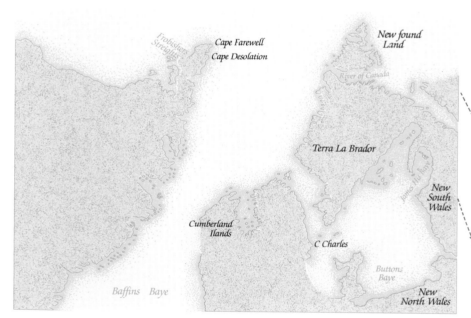

Shoreline known to explorers

PRINCIPAL EXPLORATIONS

English

Cabot (after Morison), 1497 . . . . . _____

Frobisher, 1576, 1577, 1578 . . . . . __ __ __

Davis, 1585, 1586, 1587 . . . . - - - - -

Hudson, 1610–11 . . . . · · · · ·

Button, 1612–13 . . . . · — · —

Baffin and Bylot, 1615, 1616 . . . . . — · · —

Foxe, 1631 . . . . — · —

James, 1631–2 . . . . — — —

Portuguese

Corte-Real (after Morison), 1500, 1501 . . . . _____

Fagundes, 1520?, 1521–5? . . . . . . __ __ __

French

Verrazano, 1524 . . . . _____

Cartier, 1534, 1535–6 . . . . __ __ __

Bellenger, 1583 . . . . _____

Spanish

Gómez, 1524–5 . . . . _____

Danish

Munk, 1619–20 . . . . _____

MER OCCEANE:

MER DESPAIGNE:

MER DE FRAN CE:

TIQVE:

Terre des bretons

Canada

Ochelaga

CANADA

Canada

Sagne

Terre du Laberador

ATLANTIC

OCEAN

Cabot Strait

Gulf of
St Lawrence

U N K N O W N

James Bay

By permission of The British Library

DESCELIERS MAP, 1550 (portion)

The voyages of Jacques Cartier and Jean-François La Rocque de Roberval greatly enlarged European knowledge of northeastern North America, and enabled cartographers to represent the complex shoreline of the Gulf of St Lawrence with some accuracy. This map by Pierre Desceliers, a cartographer-artist working near Dieppe, illustrates the great expansion of geographical understanding since pre-Cartier days. The delightful illustrations are largely fanciful.

As far as we know, English and Portuguese navigators were the first modern Europeans to reach the eastern coast of North America. They and their successors found a disconcertingly continuous landmass which they soon realized was not Asia, and which blocked the sea route to it. By 1530 French and Spanish explorers had skirted the coast from the south without entering any of the prospective passages: Chesapeake Bay, the Hudson River, the Bay of Fundy, the Gulf of St Lawrence, or Hudson Strait. Jacques Cartier, the first known explorer of the Gulf of St Lawrence, found a large river rather than a sea channel. Later the English delineated the massive embayments of Baffin Bay and Hudson Bay. In each case early expectations that a northwest passage to the western ocean had been found

were not fulfilled as further exploration revealed western shores to these enormous chambers rather than open ocean.

The maps of 1502, 1529, 1550, and 1632 show four stages of the European understanding of northeastern North America: the first (Cantino, 1502) after the landfalls of Cabot and the Corte-Reals but before the continent of North America was recognized; the second (Ribeiro, 1529) after an approximately continuous coastline had been identified between Labrador and the Caribbean; the third (Desceliers, 1550) after Cartier had explored the Gulf of St Lawrence and the lower St Lawrence River; and the fourth (James, 1632) more than fifty years after the English began the search for a northwest passage.

CONCISE EDITION

EXPLORATION, 17th, 18th CENTURIES

Authors: Richard I. Ruggles, Conrad E. Heidenreich

Early in the 17th century the French began to explore the rivers draining into the St Lawrence valley. Usually they gathered geographical information from Natives, set objectives for exploration based on these accounts, and, when opportunity arose, travelled with Native guides. Verbal accounts, maps, and journals transmitted the French discoveries. By the early 1680s officials in Québec were responsible for compiling and sending maps to the Ministère de la Marine in Paris, where authorized personnel had access to them.

The search for a route across the continent was a continuing motive for exploration throughout the French regime, but usually was set within more limited objectives. Fur traders sought Indian suppliers; missionaries sought Indian converts. Territorial claims and the search for minerals were sometimes important motives for exploration. Occasionally military expeditions yielded new geographical knowledge.

The direction and speed of exploration varied with motives and opportunities. By helping Natives in their wars Champlain was able to explore much of the eastern Great Lakes basin; by expanding their missions Recollet, Jesuit, and Sulpician priests obtained new geographical information. After 1681, when the interior trade was legalized, French traders explored well beyond the Great Lakes. In the 18th century westward exploration accelerated under the pressure of British competition from Hudson Bay and the Ohio valley.

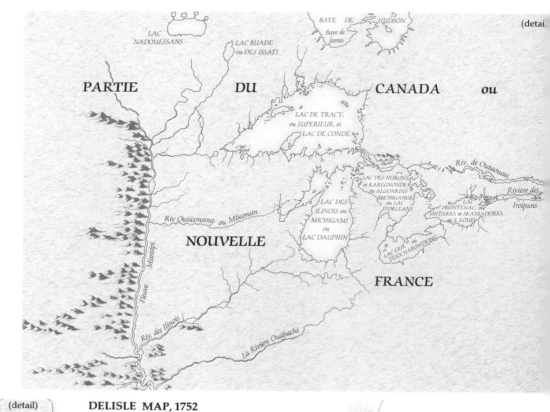

DELISLE MAP, 1752

Joseph-Nicholas Delisle and his nephew by marriage, Philippe Buache, were obsessed by the idea of a vast sea, connected to the Pacific in northwestern North America. Beginning in 1752, Delisle and Buache published a series of maps and memoirs describing this mythical 'Mer de l'ouest'; some of their maps appeared as late as 1779 in Diderot's *Encyclopédie*. The 'Mer de l'ouest' had been a strong motive for exploration but as early as the 1740s few others dared place it on a map.

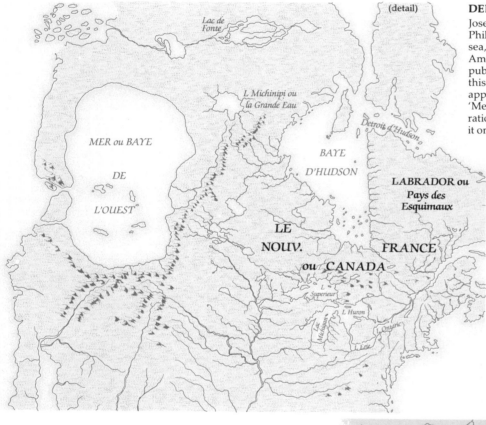

BELLIN MAP, 1755

When he made this map, Jacques-Nicolas Bellin was chief engineer of the cartographic section of the *Ministère de la Marine*, the depository for journals and maps from New France. Bellin used this material to good advantage and, beginning in 1743, produced a series of maps of New France that incorporated the latest available information about the North American interior. His map of 1755, the last original map in this set, includes data from La Vérendrye (1750), Bonnécamps (1749), Chaussegros de Léry and La Ronde (1735), and Father Laure (1731–3).

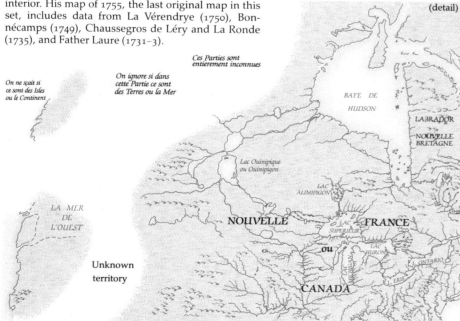

FRENCH EXPLORATION

0   300 miles
0   300 kilometres

Scale 1:12 500 000

CORONELLI MAP, 1688

Vincenzo Coronelli, an Italian friar in the Minorite Order of Franciscans, was commissioned to construct a huge globe for Louis XIV. His sojourn in Paris 1681–3 brought him into contact with cartographic material from New France, in particular the manuscripts of J.-B. Franquelin, then chief hydrographer at Québec, and La Salle. Coronelli's map of the Great Lakes, probably compiled in 1684–5 and published in 1688, was the first printed map of Canada to incorporate information from the explorations of Allouez, La Salle, Hennepin, and Jolliet.

SANSON MAP, 1656

Nicolas Sanson, founder of the great French school of cartography, was appointed Géographe ordinaire du Roi in 1630 and had access to the latest geographical information from New France. His maps of 1650 and 1656 are the first to show portions of all the Great Lakes more or less in their true positions. Sanson relied on the Jesuits, whose understanding of the Great Lakes basin derived from their own observations, Native accounts, and informants such as Étienne Brûlé and Jean Nicollet.

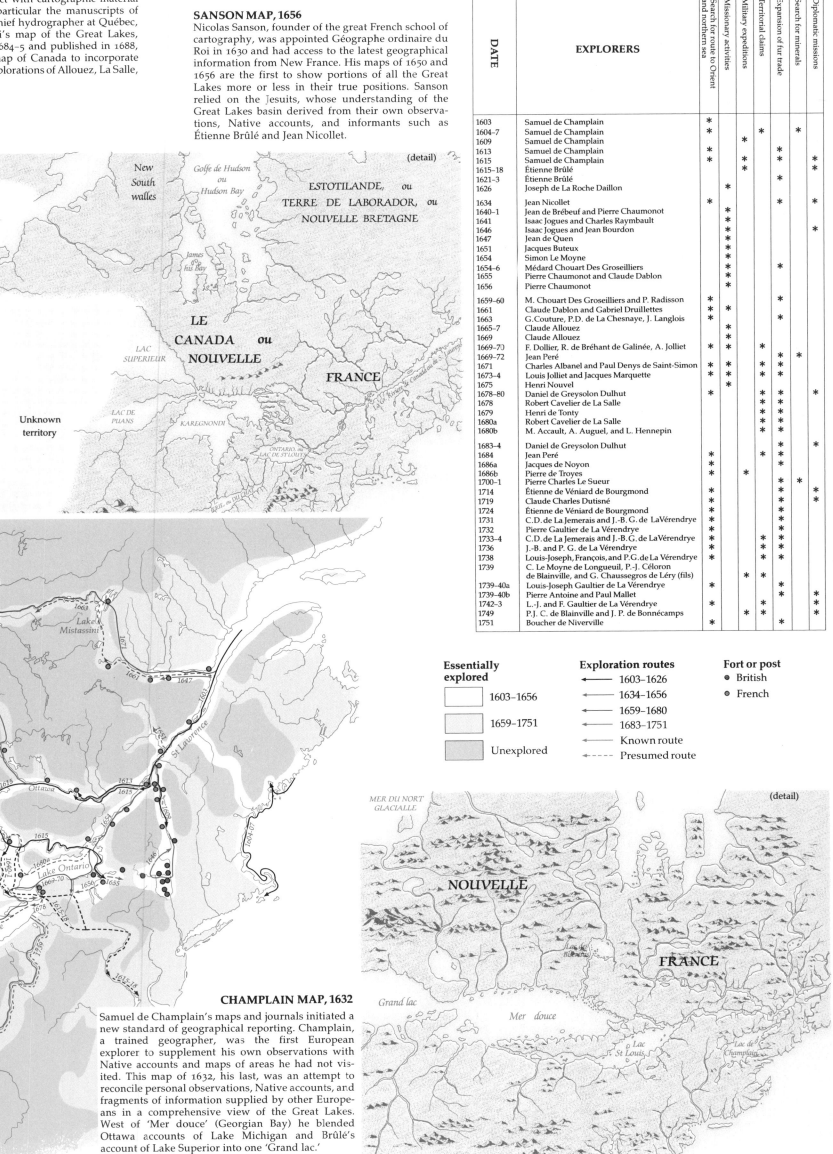

DATE	EXPLORERS	Search for route to Orient and northern sea	Missionary activities	Military expeditions	Territorial claims	Expansion of fur trade	Search for minerals	Diplomatic missions
1603	Samuel de Champlain	*						
1604-7	Samuel de Champlain	*			*		*	
1609	Samuel de Champlain			*				
1613	Samuel de Champlain							
1615	Samuel de Champlain	*		*	*	*		*
1615-18	Étienne Brûlé			*				
1621-3	Étienne Brûlé					*		
1626	Joseph de La Roche Daillon		*					
1634	Jean Nicollet	*				*		
1640-1	Jean de Brébeuf and Pierre Chaumonot		*					
1641	Isaac Jogues and Charles Raymbault		*					
1646	Isaac Jogues and Jean Bourdon		*					*
1647	Jean de Quen		*					
1651	Jacques Buteux		*					
1654	Simon Le Moyne		*					
1654-6	Médard Chouart Des Groseilliers		*			*		
1655	Pierre Chaumonot and Claude Dablon		*					
1656	Pierre Chaumonot		*					
1659-60	M. Chouart Des Groseilliers and P. Radisson	*	*			*		
1661	Claude Dablon and Gabriel Druillettes	*	*					
1663	G.Couture, P.D. de La Chesnaye, J. Langlois	*	*					
1665-7	Claude Allouez		*					
1669	Claude Allouez		*					
1669-70	F. Dollier, R. de Bréhant de Galinée, A. Jolliet	*			*	*		
1669-72	Jean Peré					*	*	
1671	Charles Albanel and Paul Denys de Saint-Simon	*	*		*	*		
1673-4	Louis Jolliet and Jacques Marquette	*	*		*	*		
1675	Henri Nouvel		*					
1678-80	Daniel de Greysolon Dulhut	*			*	*		*
1678	Robert Cavelier de La Salle				*	*		
1679	Henri de Tonty				*	*		
1680a	Robert Cavelier de La Salle				*	*		
1680b	M. Accault, A. Auguel, and L. Hennepin				*	*		
1683-4	Daniel de Greysolon Dulhut				*	*		*
1684	Jean Peré	*				*		
1686a	Jacques de Noyon	*						
1686b	Pierre de Troyes	*		*				
1700-1	Pierre Charles Le Sueur	*					*	
1714	Étienne de Véniard de Bourgmond	*						*
1719	Claude Charles Dutisné	*						
1724	Étienne de Véniard de Bourgmond	*				*		*
1731	C.D.de La Jemerais and J.-B. G. de LaVérendrye	*				*		
1732	Pierre Gaultier de La Vérendrye	*				*		
1733-4	C.D.de La Jemerais and J.-B.G. de LaVérendrye	*			*	*		
1736	J.-B. and P. G. de La Vérendrye	*				*		
1738	Louis-Joseph, François, and P.G.de La Vérendrye	*			*	*		
1739	C. Le Moyne de Longueuil, P.-J. Céloron de Blainville, and G. Chaussegros de Léry (fils)			*	*			
1739-40a	Louis-Joseph Gaultier de La Vérendrye	*				*		*
1739-40b	Pierre Antoine and Paul Mallet					*		*
1742-3	L.-J. and F. Gaultier de La Vérendrye	*			*			*
1749	P.J. C. de Blainville and J. P. de Bonnécamps			*	*	*		
1751	Boucher de Niverville	*						

MOTIVATION

Essentially explored
- ☐ 1603–1656
- ◩ 1659–1751
- ▨ Unexplored

Exploration routes
- ← 1603–1626
- ← 1634–1656
- ← 1659–1680
- ← 1683–1751
- ← Known route
- ←--- Presumed route

Fort or post
- ● British
- ● French

CHAMPLAIN MAP, 1632

Samuel de Champlain's maps and journals initiated a new standard of geographical reporting. Champlain, a trained geographer, was the first European explorer to supplement his own observations with Native accounts and maps of areas he had not visited. This map of 1632, his last, was an attempt to reconcile personal observations, Native accounts, and fragments of information supplied by other Europeans in a comprehensive view of the Great Lakes. West of 'Mer douce' (Georgian Bay) he blended Ottawa accounts of Lake Michigan and Brûlé's account of Lake Superior into one 'Grand lac.'

CONCISE EDITION

EXPLORATION FROM HUDSON BAY, 18th CENTURY
Author: Richard I. Ruggles

Exploration of the interior was an intended by-product of the fur trades conducted out of Montréal and Hudson Bay. Traders from Montréal frequented Lake Winnipeg by the 1730s (pl 6), and established posts on the Saskatchewan River by the 1750s (pl 44). Although the Hudson's Bay Company (HBC) did not open an interior trading post until 1774, as early as 1691 one of its young traders, Henry Kelsey, crossed the boreal forest and the parkland belt to reach the edge of the grasslands, and then wintered with Indian bands on their trapping grounds. After 1754 HBC traders visited the parkland and grasslands annually; one of them, Anthony Henday, may have been the first European to see the Rocky Mountains from the Canadian plains.

In 1772 another HBC employee, Samuel Hearne, finally succeeded in crossing the barren ground to reach the Arctic Ocean at the mouth of the Coppermine River. He found Native reports of rich deposits of copper to be greatly exaggerated, and demonstrated that there was not a water passage to the Pacific from Hudson Bay. Navigators had long probed the inlets of the northwestern bay, looking for such a passage (pl 5).

NORTON MAP, 1760
Moses Norton, a HBC trader at Fort Churchill, questioned Indians about their homelands when they came to trade. On the basis of their accounts and sketch maps he drafted a remarkably comprehensive map of northern Canada. The map shown here, a re-oriented and amended version of the original, suggests the identity of many geographical features.

GRAHAM MAP, 1772–1774
Andrew Graham, a HBC trader at Fort York, collected geographical information from Indians and from company traders who wintered inland. This map, a composite of two of Graham's, draws particularly on William Tomison, who journeyed up the Severn River and across Lakes Winnipeg (Frenchman's Lake or Little Sea) to reach the grasslands in the Assiniboine valley; and on Matthew Cocking, who explored upstream from the forks of the Saskatchewan River and south through Eagle Hills.

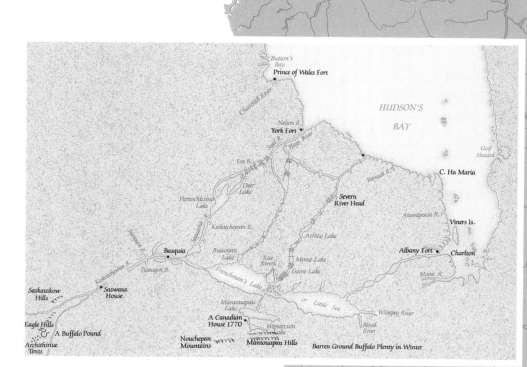

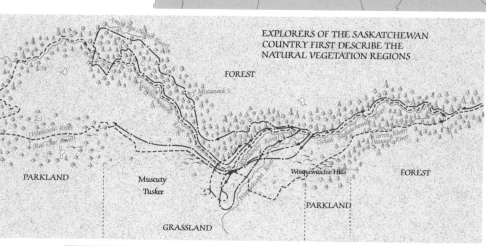

Interpreted from Hudson's Bay Company explorers' journals

EXPLORERS OF THE SASKATCHEWAN COUNTRY FIRST DESCRIBE THE NATURAL VEGETATION REGIONS

This map shows how HBC traders understood the Saskatchewan country in the early 1770s, by which time many of them had penetrated the region by canoe or on foot. Some (notably Kelsey, Henday, Pink, and Cocking) kept daily journals and made regular environmental notations. Henday, who in 1754–5 was perhaps the first European trader to traverse the regions between northern Manitoba and the foothills of the Rocky Mountains, lived with Indians and relied on Indian guides; he left the most comprehensive survey.

Scale 1:12 500 000

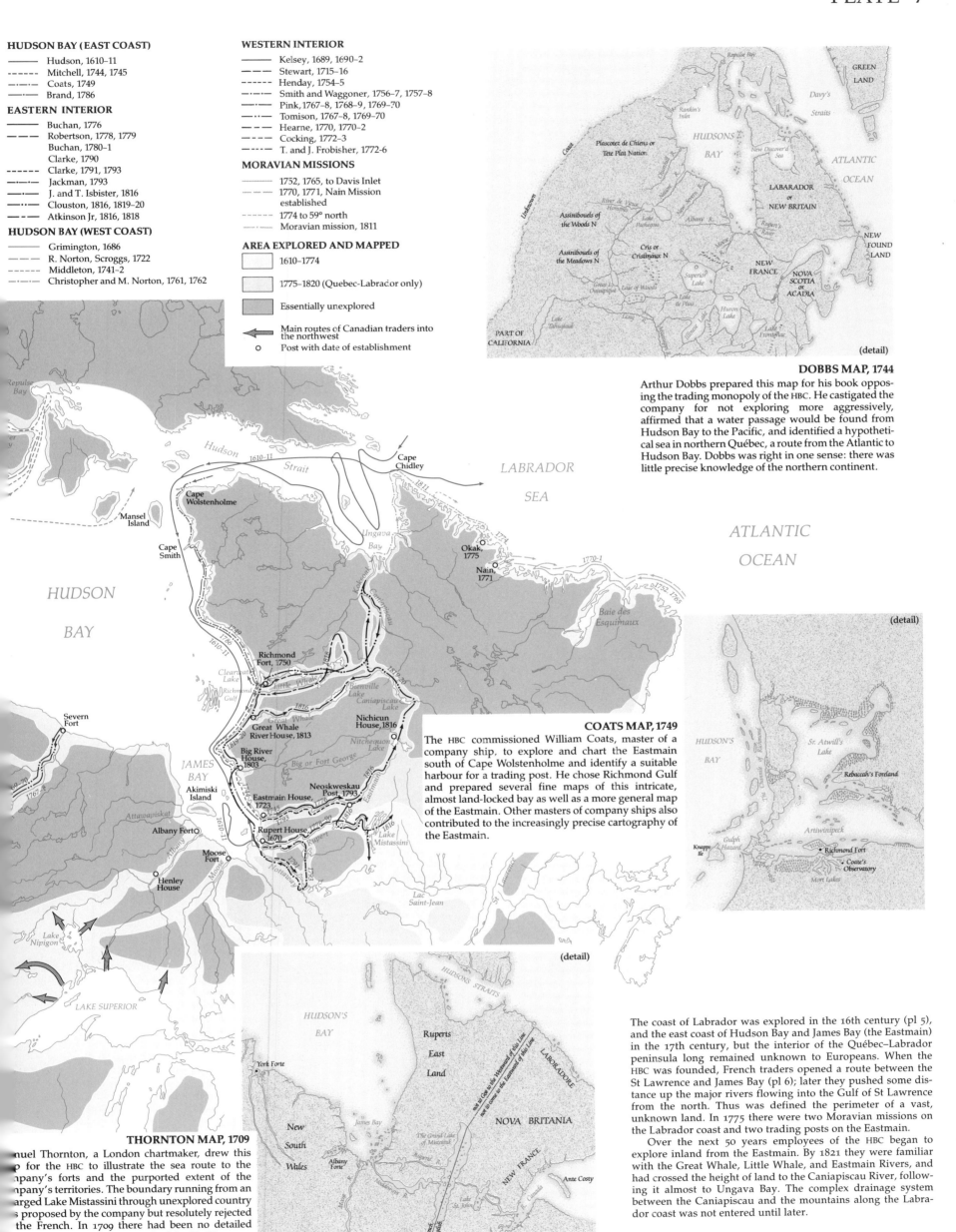

HUDSON BAY (EAST COAST)
- Hudson, 1610–11
- Mitchell, 1744, 1745
- Coats, 1749
- Brand, 1786

EASTERN INTERIOR
- Buchan, 1776
- Robertson, 1778, 1779
- Buchan, 1780–1
- Clarke, 1790
- Clarke, 1791, 1793
- Jackman, 1793
- J. and T. Isbister, 1816
- Clouston, 1819–20
- Atkinson Jr, 1816, 1818

HUDSON BAY (WEST COAST)
- Grimington, 1686
- R. Norton, Scroggs, 1722
- Middleton, 1741–2
- Christopher and M. Norton, 1761, 1762

WESTERN INTERIOR
- Kelsey, 1689, 1690–2
- Stewart, 1715–16
- Henday, 1754–5
- Smith and Waggoner, 1756–7, 1757–8
- Pink, 1767–8, 1768–9, 1769–70
- Tomison, 1767–8, 1769–70
- Hearne, 1770, 1770–2
- Cocking, 1772–3
- T. and J. Frobisher, 1772–6

MORAVIAN MISSIONS
- 1752, 1765, to Davis Inlet
- 1770, 1771, Nain Mission established
- 1774 to 59° north
- Moravian mission, 1811

AREA EXPLORED AND MAPPED
- 1610–1774
- 1775–1820 (Quebec–Labrador only)
- Essentially unexplored
- Main routes of Canadian traders into the northwest
- ○ Post with date of establishment

DOBBS MAP, 1744

Arthur Dobbs prepared this map for his book opposing the trading monopoly of the HBC. He castigated the company for not exploring more aggressively, affirmed that a water passage would be found from Hudson Bay to the Pacific, and identified a hypothetical sea in northern Québec, a route from the Atlantic to Hudson Bay. Dobbs was right in one sense: there was little precise knowledge of the northern continent.

COATS MAP, 1749

The HBC commissioned William Coats, master of a company ship, to explore and chart the Eastmain south of Cape Wolstenholme and identify a suitable harbour for a trading post. He chose Richmond Gulf and prepared several fine maps of this intricate, almost land-locked bay as well as a more general map of the Eastmain. Other masters of company ships also contributed to the increasingly precise cartography of the Eastmain.

THORNTON MAP, 1709

...muel Thornton, a London chartmaker, drew this ...p for the HBC to illustrate the sea route to the ...pany's forts and the purported extent of the ...pany's territories. The boundary running from an ...arged Lake Mistassini through unexplored country ...proposed by the company but resolutely rejected ...the French. In 1709 there had been no detailed ...loration of the Eastmain north of the Big River.

The coast of Labrador was explored in the 16th century (pl 5), and the east coast of Hudson Bay and James Bay (the Eastmain) in the 17th century, but the interior of the Québec–Labrador peninsula long remained unknown to Europeans. When the HBC was founded, French traders opened a route between the St Lawrence and James Bay (pl 6); later they pushed some distance up the major rivers flowing into the Gulf of St Lawrence from the north. Thus was defined the perimeter of a vast, unknown land. In 1775 there were two Moravian missions on the Labrador coast and two trading posts on the Eastmain.

Over the next 50 years employees of the HBC began to explore inland from the Eastmain. By 1821 they were familiar with the Great Whale, Little Whale, and Eastmain Rivers, and had crossed the height of land to the Caniapiscau River, following it almost to Ungava Bay. The complex drainage system between the Caniapiscau and the mountains along the Labrador coast was not entered until later.

EXPLORATION IN THE FAR NORTHWEST, 18th AND 19th CENTURIES
Author: Richard I. Ruggles

Except for the few Russian traders who obtained sea-otter pelts in western Alaska and sold them in Mongolia, the northwestern corner of North America remained outside the range of European knowledge until the last quarter of the 18th century. In 1770 trade in land furs had not reached the Mackenzie drainage basin and barely touched the Rocky Mountains (pll 7, 60), while the Spanish (who claimed the entire West Coast of the New World) had just begun to establish outposts in southern California. On world maps of the day northwestern North America was blank.

This was soon changed. In the mid-1770s the Spaniards Pérez and Quadra sailed north along the West Coast in search of Russian interlopers. Finding none, they quickly left. In 1778 a British expedition under James Cook spent a month at Nootka on Vancouver Island, then sailed northward to search for the passage that the admiralty thought might lie about 60°N. After Cook the broad outline of the Northwest Coast was known. In the early 1790s British and Spanish surveys, the most extensive by George Vancouver, filled in many details.

PACIFIC COASTAL EXPLORATION

Russian
- Bering, 1741
- Chirikov, 1741
- Shelikov, 1783–6
- Izmailov and Bocharev, 1788
- Billings and Sharychev, 1789–90

Spanish
- Pérez, 1774; Quadra, 1775
- Eliza, 1790
- Fidalgo, 1790–3
- Valdés and Galiano, 1792
- Caamaño, 1792

British
- Cook, 1778–9
- Vancouver, 1792–4

WESTERN INTERIOR
- Pond, 1778–80, 1787–8
- Mackenzie, 1789, 1793
- Turnor, Fidler, Ross, 1790–2
- Fidler, 1793
- Thompson, 1795–6
- Jarvis, 1775, 1776
- Kipling, 1777
- G. Sutherland, 1777–8
- J. Hudson, 1778
- J. Sutherland, 1784
- Fidler, 1799–1800, 1800–1, 1807
- Fraser, 1806, 1808
- Thompson, 1797–1812
- Lewis and Clark, 1804–6

ARCTIC
- Ross, 1818
- Parry, 1819–20, 1821–2
- Franklin, Richardson, Back, 1819–22

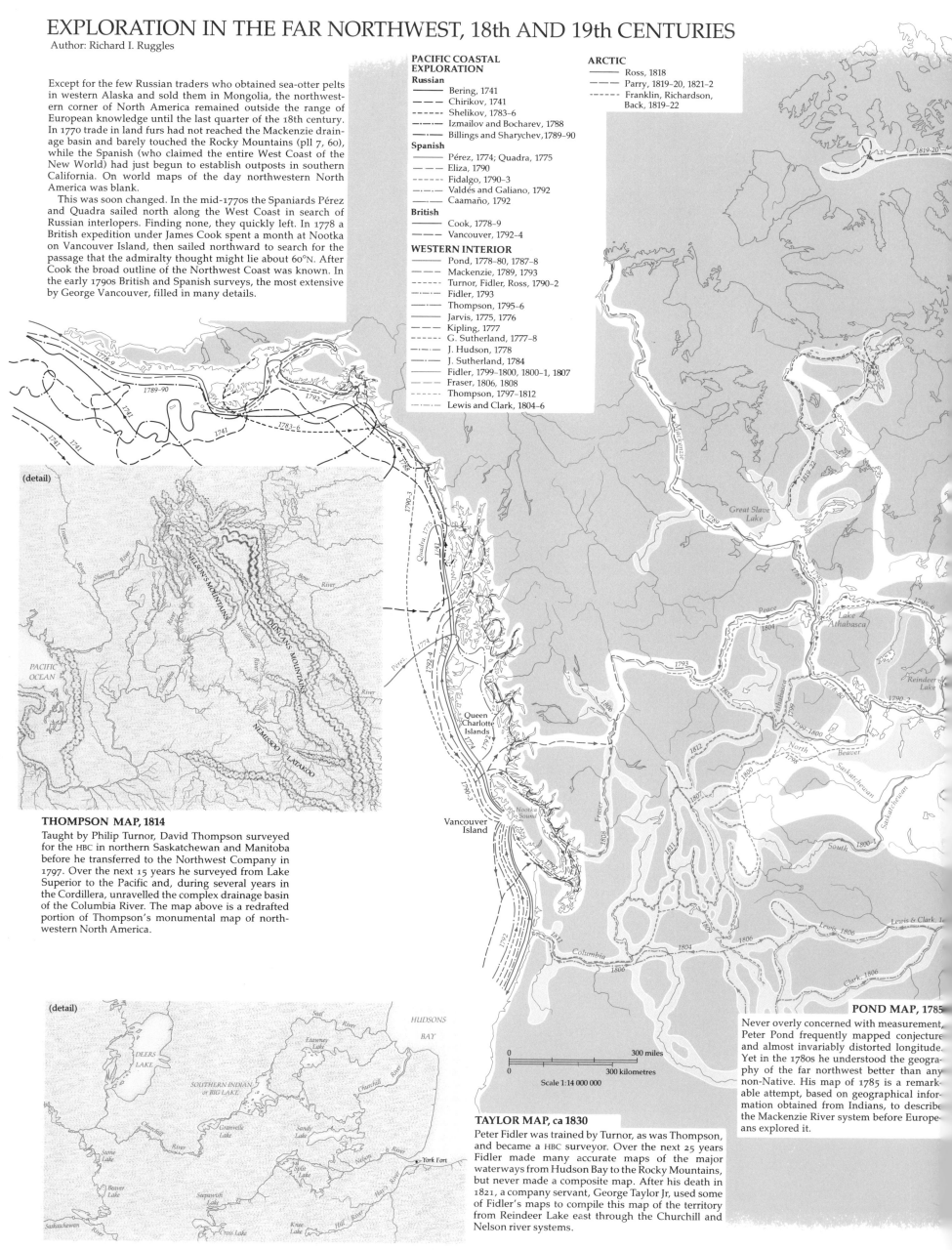

THOMPSON MAP, 1814
Taught by Philip Turnor, David Thompson surveyed for the HBC in northern Saskatchewan and Manitoba before he transferred to the Northwest Company in 1797. Over the next 15 years he surveyed from Lake Superior to the Pacific and, during several years in the Cordillera, unravelled the complex drainage basin of the Columbia River. The map above is a redrafted portion of Thompson's monumental map of northwestern North America.

TAYLOR MAP, ca 1830
Peter Fidler was trained by Turnor, as was Thompson, and became a HBC surveyor. Over the next 25 years Fidler made many accurate maps of the major waterways from Hudson Bay to the Rocky Mountains, but never made a composite map. After his death in 1821, a company servant, George Taylor Jr, used some of Fidler's maps to compile this map of the territory from Reindeer Lake east through the Churchill and Nelson river systems.

POND MAP, 1785
Never overly concerned with measurement, Peter Pond frequently mapped conjecture and almost invariably distorted longitude. Yet in the 1780s he understood the geography of the far northwest better than any non-Native. His map of 1785 is a remarkable attempt, based on geographical information obtained from Indians, to describe the Mackenzie River system before Europeans explored it.

Scale 1:14 000 000

0   300 miles

0   300 kilometres

HISTORICAL ATLAS OF CANADA

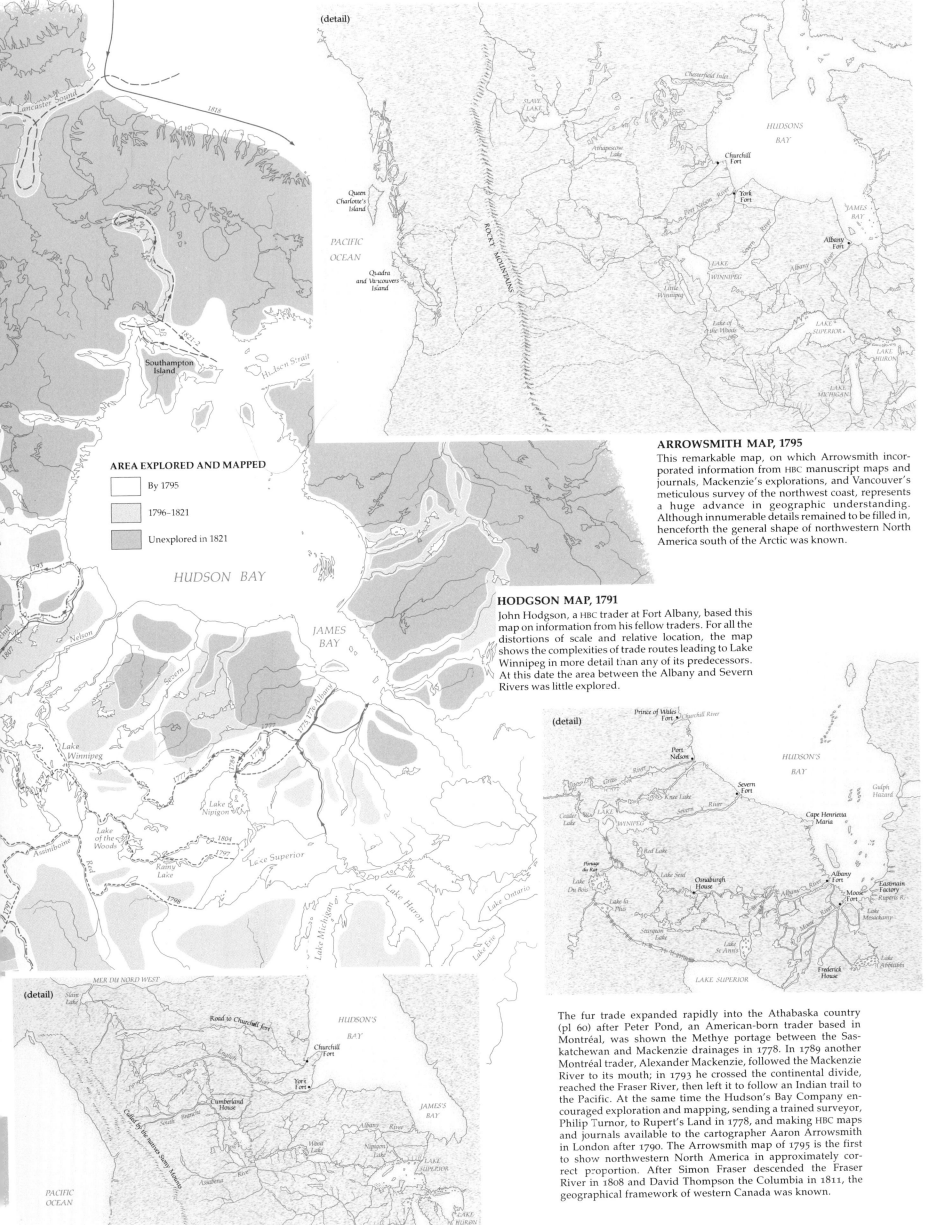

(detail)

AREA EXPLORED AND MAPPED

By 1795

1796–1821

Unexplored in 1821

ARROWSMITH MAP, 1795

This remarkable map, on which Arrowsmith incorporated information from HBC manuscript maps and journals, Mackenzie's explorations, and Vancouver's meticulous survey of the northwest coast, represents a huge advance in geographic understanding. Although innumerable details remained to be filled in, henceforth the general shape of northwestern North America south of the Arctic was known.

HODGSON MAP, 1791

John Hodgson, a HBC trader at Fort Albany, based this map on information from his fellow traders. For all the distortions of scale and relative location, the map shows the complexities of trade routes leading to Lake Winnipeg in more detail than any of its predecessors. At this date the area between the Albany and Severn Rivers was little explored.

(detail)

The fur trade expanded rapidly into the Athabaska country (pl 60) after Peter Pond, an American-born trader based in Montréal, was shown the Methye portage between the Saskatchewan and Mackenzie drainages in 1778. In 1789 another Montréal trader, Alexander Mackenzie, followed the Mackenzie River to its mouth; in 1793 he crossed the continental divide, reached the Fraser River, then left it to follow an Indian trail to the Pacific. At the same time the Hudson's Bay Company encouraged exploration and mapping, sending a trained surveyor, Philip Turnor, to Rupert's Land in 1778, and making HBC maps and journals available to the cartographer Aaron Arrowsmith in London after 1790. The Arrowsmith map of 1795 is the first to show northwestern North America in approximately correct proportion. After Simon Fraser descended the Fraser River in 1808 and David Thompson the Columbia in 1811, the geographical framework of western Canada was known.

(detail)

EXPLORATION AND ASSESSMENT TO 1891

Author: Richard I. Ruggles

After the disappearance of Sir John Franklin and his crew in 1845, the search for survivors of the expedition continued to motivate Canadian Arctic exploration in the latter part of the 19th century. The British Navy, Lady Franklin's private search groups, various American parties sponsored by scientific societies, public subscriptions, whaling enterprises, and overland journeys by employees of the HBC sought out the shores, straits, and inlets of much of the southern Arctic and of many of the Queen Elizabeth Islands. During the search significant additions were made to the store of scientific and geographical knowledge of the northern part of North America.

British maritime activity was concentrated on both sides of the major passage from Lancaster Sound west through M'Clure Strait. To the south, naval and private expeditions completed the coastal mapping of Victoria, Prince of Wales, and Somerset islands and Boothia Peninsula. Francis L. McClintock and Allen W. Young circled King William Island, where the Franklin party had perished. Venturing farthest north was the British Navy's George S. Nares, who dispatched sledge parties over the ice towards the Pole and along the north coasts of Ellesmere Island and Greenland. This series of straits and basins was also the setting for most American activity. But it was the most experienced player in the North, the HBC, which gathered the first definite information on the fate of the Franklin expedition when John Rae reached Pelly Bay from Repulse Bay in 1854. The HBC followed with a voyage down the Back River to the Arctic coast by James Anderson and James G. Stewart. Other HBC treks, such as those by Roderick MacFarlane, Warburton Pike, and James Mackinlay, were made to further the fur trade.

The first geological map of a large part of Canada was prepared by Sir John Richardson in 1851 to accompany his book on his search for the Franklin expedition. The map, based on observations made during his earlier expeditions in the western interior and the North, commencing in 1819, includes two geological units, 'Metamorphic or Primitive Rocks' and 'Fossiliferous Rocks from the Silurian strata upwards,' depicting for the first time the boundaries of the Canadian Shield.

GENERAL EXPLORATION

British
— W. Kennedy and J. Bellot, 1851–2
— — R. Collinson and C. Jago, 1852–4
– – – E. Inglefield, 1852
- - - - E. Belcher, S. Osborn, and G. Richards, 1852–4
·········· H. Kellett and F. McClintock, 1852–4
— F. McClintock and A. Young, 1859
–··–··– W. Adams, 1872
–·–·– G. Nares, 1875–6

Hudson's Bay Company
–···–···– J. Rae, 1853–4
–··–··– J. Anderson and J. Stewart, 1855
— — R. MacFarlane, 1857
— W. Pike and J. Mackinlay, 1890

American
— E. Kane, 1853–4
– – – I. Hayes, 1861
·········· C. Hall, 1868–9, 1871
— E. Fisher, 1868–9
— F. Schwatka, 1878–80
–··–··– J. Spicer, 1879–80
–·–·– A. Greely, 1881–4

AREA EXPLORED AND MAPPED
☐ By 1891
▨ Essentially unexplored

SCIENTIFIC EXPEDITIONS

British
— J. Palliser, J. Hector, et al., 1857, 1858

Canadian
— H. Hind et al., 1857, 1858
– – – H. Hind and W. Hind, 1861
–·–·– A. Gordon and R. Bell, 1884–5, 1885–6, 1886

American
— R. Kennicott, 1859–62
·········· C. Drexler, 1860
–··–··– F. Schwatka, 1883

German
–··–··– F. Boas, 1883–4

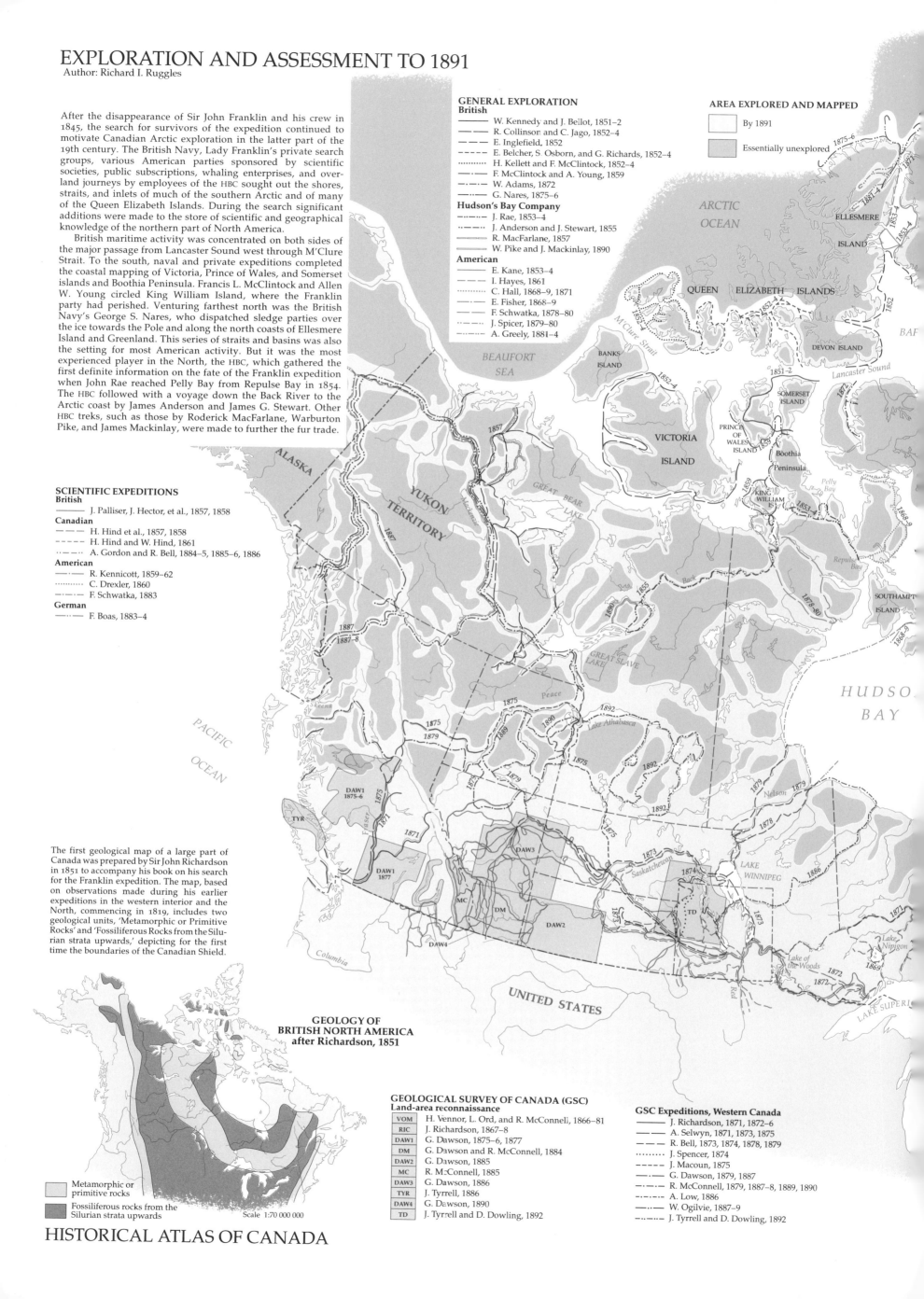

GEOLOGY OF BRITISH NORTH AMERICA
after Richardson, 1851

☐ Metamorphic or primitive rocks
■ Fossiliferous rocks from the Silurian strata upwards

Scale 1:70 000 000

HISTORICAL ATLAS OF CANADA

GEOLOGICAL SURVEY OF CANADA (GSC)
Land-area reconnaissance

VOM	H. Vennor, L. Ord, and R. McConnell, 1866–81
RIC	J. Richardson, 1867–8
DAW1	G. Dawson, 1875–6, 1877
DM	G. Dawson and R. McConnell, 1884
DAW2	G. Dawson, 1885
MC	R. McConnell, 1885
DAW3	G. Dawson, 1886
TYR	J. Tyrrell, 1886
DAW4	G. Dawson, 1890
TD	J. Tyrrell and D. Dowling, 1892

GSC Expeditions, Western Canada
— J. Richardson, 1871, 1872–6
— A. Selwyn, 1871, 1873, 1875
– – – R. Bell, 1873, 1874, 1878, 1879
·········· J. Spencer, 1874
– – – – J. Macoun, 1875
—·— G. Dawson, 1879, 1887
–··–··– R. McConnell, 1879, 1887–8, 1889, 1890
—··— A. Low, 1886
–··–··– W. Ogilvie, 1887–9
–···–···– J. Tyrrell and D. Dowling, 1892

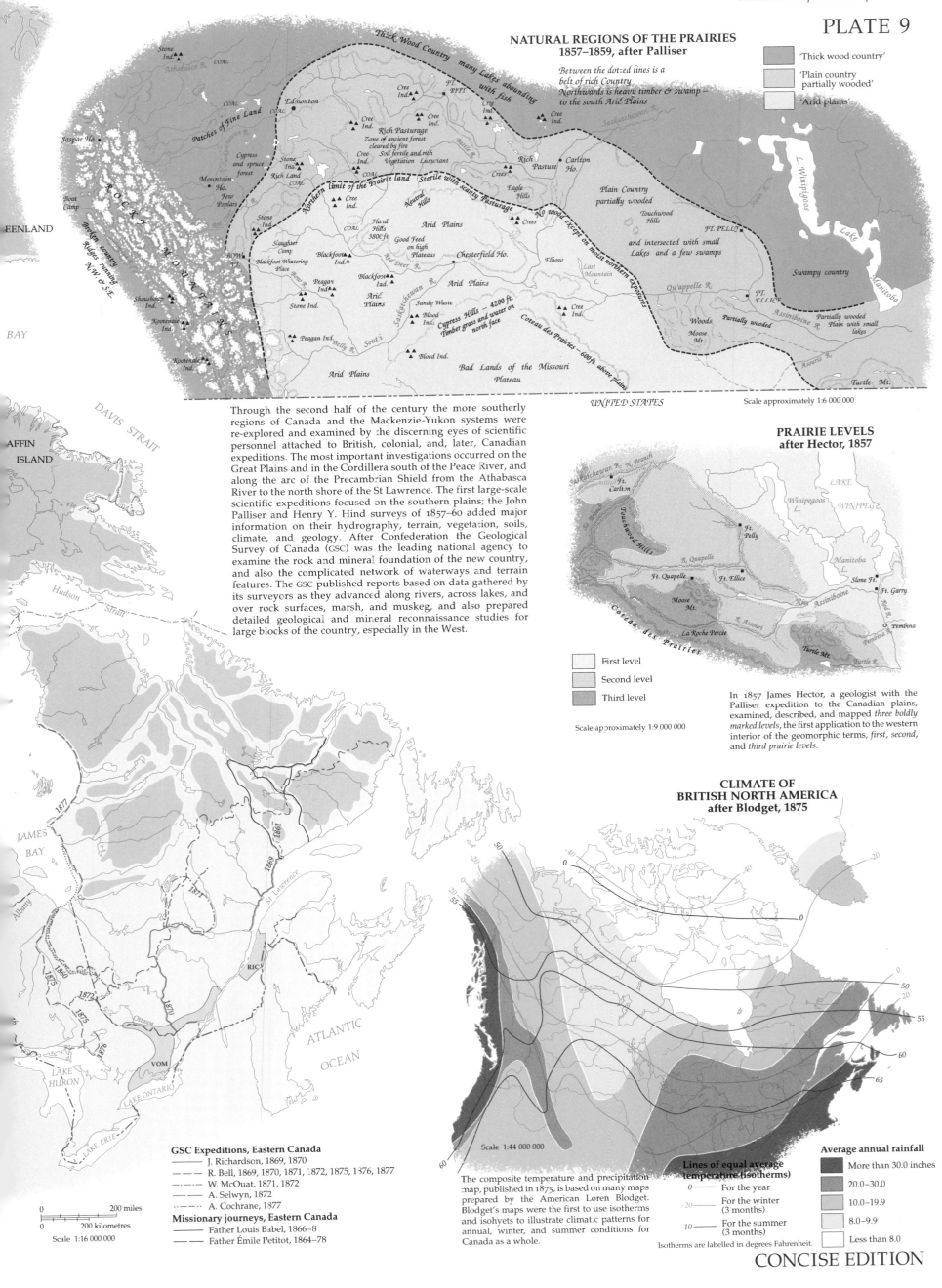

PLATE 9

NATURAL REGIONS OF THE PRAIRIES
1857–1859, after Palliser

Between the dotted lines is a belt of rich Country. Northwards is heavy timber & swamp — to the south Arid Plains

'Thick wood country'

'Plain country partially wooded'

'Arid plains'

Scale approximately 1:6 000 000

Map labels (Natural Regions):
Thick Wood Country many Lakes abounding with fish
Patches of Fine Land
Stone Ind.
COAL
Athabasca R.
Jaspar Ho.
Edmonton
Cree Ind.
PT. PITT
Saskatchewan R.
Battle R.
Cypress and spruce forest
Rich Land
COAL
Mountain Ho.
Few Poplars
ROCKY MOUNTAINS
Broken country
Ridges running N.W. & S.E.
Shouskoup Ind.
Kootenaie Ind.
BOW Rr.
Slaughter Camp
Blackfoot Wintering Place
Blackfoot Ind.
Peagan Ind.
Stone Ind.
Arid Plains
Cree Ind.
Neutral Hills
Hard Hills 3800 ft.
Good Feed on high Plateaux
Red Deer R.
Saskatchewan R.
Bow R.
Belly R.
Sandy Waste
Blood Ind.
Cypress Hills – 4200 ft. Timber grass and water on north face
Peagan Ind.
Blood Ind.
Arid Plains
Bad Lands of the Missouri Plateau
Coteau des Prairies – 600 ft. above plains
Chesterfield Ho.
Elbow
Last Mountain
Qu'appelle R.
Zone of ancient forest cleared by fire. Soil fertile and rich. Vegetation Luxuriant
Rich Pasturage
Sterile with scanty Pasturage
Northern limit of the Prairie land
Crees
Rich Pasture
Carlton Ho.
Eagle Hills
Plain Country partially wooded and intersected with small Lakes and a few swamps
No wood except on moist northern exposures
Touchwood Hills
PT. PELLY
L. Winnipegoos
Lake Manitoba
Swampy country
Woods
Moose Mt.
Partially wooded
PT. ELLICE
Assiniboine R.
Partially wooded Plain with small lakes
Souris R.
Turtle Mt.
UNITED STATES
EENLAND
BAY

Through the second half of the century the more southerly regions of Canada and the Mackenzie-Yukon systems were re-explored and examined by the discerning eyes of scientific personnel attached to British, colonial, and, later, Canadian expeditions. The most important investigations occurred on the Great Plains and in the Cordillera south of the Peace River, and along the arc of the Precambrian Shield from the Athabasca River to the north shore of the St Lawrence. The first large-scale scientific expeditions focused on the southern plains; the John Palliser and Henry Y. Hind surveys of 1857–60 added major information on their hydrography, terrain, vegetation, soils, climate, and geology. After Confederation the Geological Survey of Canada (GSC) was the leading national agency to examine the rock and mineral foundation of the new country, and also the complicated network of waterways and terrain features. The GSC published reports based on data gathered by its surveyors as they advanced along rivers, across lakes, and over rock surfaces, marsh, and muskeg, and also prepared detailed geological and mineral reconnaissance studies for large blocks of the country, especially in the West.

PRAIRIE LEVELS
after Hector, 1857

Map labels (Prairie Levels):
Saskatchewan R. N. Branch
Ft. Carlton
Touchwood Hills
S. Saskatchewan R.
R. Quapelle
Ft. Pelly
Ft. Quapelle
Ft. Ellice
Moose Mt.
La Roche Percée
Coteau des Prairies
R. Assiniboine
Rivière Assiniboine
R. Assouri
Turtle Mt.
Turtle L.
Winipegoos L.
LAKE WINNIPEG
Manitoba L.
Stone Ft.
Ft. Garry
Red R.
Pembina R.
Pembina

First level

Second level

Third level

Scale approximately 1:9 000 000

In 1857 James Hector, a geologist with the Palliser expedition to the Canadian plains, examined, described, and mapped *three boldly marked levels*, the first application to the western interior of the geomorphic terms, *first, second,* and *third prairie levels.*

CLIMATE OF BRITISH NORTH AMERICA
after Blodget, 1875

Scale 1:44 000 000

The composite temperature and precipitation map, published in 1875, is based on many maps prepared by the American Loren Blodget. Blodget's maps were the first to use isotherms and isohyets to illustrate climatic patterns for annual, winter, and summer conditions for Canada as a whole.

Lines of equal average temperature (isotherms)

0 — For the year

−20 — For the winter (3 months)

10 — For the summer (3 months)

Isotherms are labelled in degrees Fahrenheit.

Average annual rainfall

More than 30.0 inches

20.0–30.0

10.0–19.9

8.0–9.9

Less than 8.0

Map labels (eastern Canada):
DAVIS STRAIT
AFFIN ISLAND
BAFFIN ISLAND
Hudson Strait
JAMES BAY
Albany
St Lawrence
Ottawa
ATLANTIC OCEAN
LAKE HURON
LAKE ONTARIO
LAKE ERIE
1877
1861
1869
1871
1870
1860
1872
1875
1876
RIC
VOM
1871

GSC Expeditions, Eastern Canada
——— J. Richardson, 1869, 1870
– – – R. Bell, 1869, 1870, 1871, 1872, 1875, 1876, 1877
–··–··– W. McOuat, 1871, 1872
········· A. Selwyn, 1872
–·–·–· A. Cochrane, 1877

Missionary journeys, Eastern Canada
——— Father Louis Babel, 1866–8
——— Father Émile Petitot, 1864–78

0 ———— 200 miles
0 ———— 200 kilometres
Scale 1:16 000 000

CONCISE EDITION

FROM SEA TO SEA: TERRITORIAL GROWTH TO 1900

Authors: Norman L. Nicholson, Charles F.J. Whebell

Canada and the United States both originated in European-controlled settler colonies clinging to the shores of the Atlantic and along the St Lawrence valley. Most of these colonies engaged in long-term attempts to expand inland. In 1783 the southern thirteen colonies gained sovereign autonomy as the new United States. The northern colonies, however, remained fully dependent on Britain until after the mid-19th century, and even after the Confederation of 1867 Britain retained control of external relations.

The parallel expansion westwards of the United States and British North America brought about considerable territorial competition. Canada's external boundaries mainly derive from this competition: the St Lawrence watershed, partitioned through the Great Lakes basin; the arbitrary line of 49°N from the Great Lakes to the Rockies, extended later to the Pacific shore; and the Alaska Panhandle, another watershed-like boundary. Competition occurred, too, between individual colonies or provinces for valuable resource land; though analogous to those on the continental scale, such cases did not enter the international arena. At the end of the century only two external boundaries remained under dispute: the Alaska Panhandle, aggravated by the Klondike gold rush; and the Labrador coast, between Canada and Newfoundland, then still a separate self-governing colony.

1884 British Order in Council: Settled boundary between Ontario and Manitoba
1889 Ontario Boundary Act: Ontario enlarged west to Lake of the Woods and north to Albany River
1895 Ungava, Mackenzie, Yukon, and Franklin established as districts in the North-West Territories. Districts of Athabaska and Keewatin enlarged
1897 Boundaries of Ungava, Keewatin, Mackenzie, Yukon, and Franklin slightly changed
1898 Yukon established as a separate territory. Quebec boundary extended north to Eastmain River

ALASKA PANHANDLE BOUNDARY DISPUTE 1873–1903

1713 Treaty of Utrecht: France ceded Nova Scotia, excluding Île Royale (Cape Breton Island) but including present-day New Brunswick, to Great Britain; relinquished interest in Newfoundland, except fishing rights; and recognized British rights to Rupert's Land
1763 Treaty of Paris: France ceded Louisiana to Spain and all her other territories in North America to Britain, except Saint-Pierre and Miquelon Islands. Royal Proclamation: Described the boundaries of Québec; assigned to Newfoundland the Labrador coast together with the Anticosti and Madeleine Islands. St John's Island and Cape Breton Island annexed to Nova Scotia. Established new government for Québec (formerly part of New France)
1769 St John's Island established as a separate colony after absentee landlords petitioned for separation from mainland Nova Scotia
1774 Québec Act: Enlarged Québec to include Labrador, Anticosti and Madeleine Islands, the Indian country both north and west to Rupert's Land and to the southwest to the junction of the Ohio and Mississippi rivers
1783 Treaty of Paris: Independence of the United States recognized and boundaries between it and British North America described (imperfectly) from the Atlantic Ocean to Lake of the Woods
1784 Colonial government established in New Brunswick and Cape Breton
1790 Nootka Convention: Opened northwest coast to occupation by any country
1791 Constitutional Act, followed by Order in Council, divided Québec into Lower Canada and Upper Canada

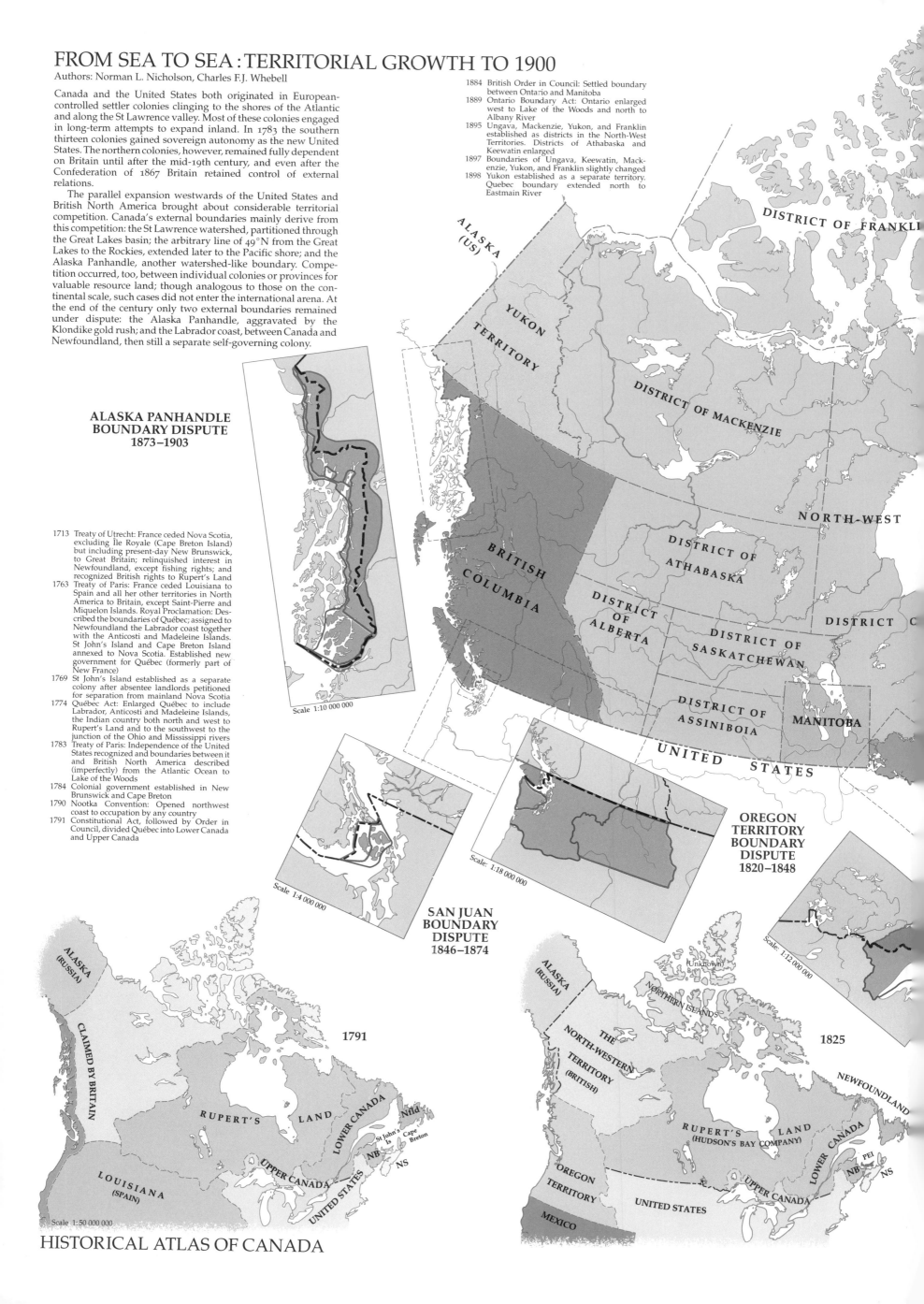

Scale 1:10 000 000

Scale 1:4 000 000

SAN JUAN BOUNDARY DISPUTE 1846–1874

Scale: 1:18 000 000

OREGON TERRITORY BOUNDARY DISPUTE 1820–1848

Scale: 1:12 000 000

1791

Scale 1:50 000 000

1825

HISTORICAL ATLAS OF CANADA

1874 New provisional northern and western boundaries of Ontario described
1876 District of Keewatin created from part of North-West Territories
1878 Award of Arbitration: Western and northern boundaries of Ontario defined
1880 Imperial Order in Council: Transferred to Canada all British islands in North America not already in Canada, except for Newfoundland and its dependencies. The Arctic Islands were annexed to Canada as part of the North-West Territories
1881 Act of Dominion: Boundaries of Manitoba extended. Extension to east contested by Ontario
1882 Provisional Districts of Assiniboia, Saskatchewan, Alberta, and Athabaska established from parts of the North-West Territories and District of Keewatin

1873

Scale 1:50 000 000

CANADA IN 1900

— · — · — International boundary
— · · — · · — Provincial boundary
— — — District boundary

1851 Agreement between British-appointed arbitrators on adjustments to Canada–New Brunswick boundary promulgated by an Act of Parliament
1858 A Bill to provide for the government of New Caledonia established new boundaries and the area was renamed British Columbia
1859 Indian Territories Act: Established British jurisdiction over land not in Rupert's Land or British Columbia which was called The North-Western Territory
1862 British Order in Council created Stickeen Territory immediately north of British Columbia and south of the 62nd parallel
1863 Western possessions amalgamated into British Columbia with present boundaries excluding Vancouver Island. Rest of Stickeen Territory above 60th parallel amalgamated back into The North-Western Territory
1866 British Columbia and Vancouver Island united into one colony
1867 British North America Act: United provinces of New Brunswick, Nova Scotia, and Canada into a federal state, the Dominion of Canada. Canada East and West renamed Québec and Ontario
1868 Rupert's Land Act: Authorized acquisition of Rupert's Land and The North-Western Territory from the Hudson's Bay Company
1870 British Order in Council: Transferred Rupert's Land and The North-Western Territory to Canada and renamed The North-West Territories
1870 Act of Dominion: Established Manitoba as fifth province
1871 Treaty of Washington: Anglo-American agreement submitted San Juan boundary dispute to arbitration by Emperor of Germany. Act of Dominion: British Columbia entered Dominion of Canada as sixth province
1872 Award of Arbitration: San Juan water boundary settled
1873 Act of Dominion: Prince Edward Island became seventh province

TERRITORIAL DISPUTES

United States territory not in dispute
British territory not in dispute
Territory awarded to the United States
Territory awarded to Britain

— — — Previously established
——— British extreme claim
——— United States extreme claim
——— Interim proposals
— — — Final-compromise boundary

QUÉBEC–NEW BRUNSWICK BOUNDARY DISPUTE 1798–1851

Saint-Pierre Miquelon (France)

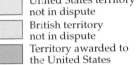

Scale 1:10 000 000

Territory awarded to Québec
Territory awarded to New Brunswick
— — — Previously established
——— Québec extreme claim
——— New Brunswick extreme claim
——— Interim proposal
——— Final-compromise boundary

0 ___ 250 miles
0 ___ 250 kilometres
Scale 1:18 000 000

1842
1798
1842
1798

1

2

MAINE BOUNDARY DISPUTE, 1798–1842

1 Granted to USA 1831 and then to Britain 1842
2 Granted to Britain 1831 and then to USA 1842

LAKE SUPERIOR BOUNDARY DISPUTE 1826–1842

1794 Treaty of London (Jay's Treaty): Established Saint-Croix River (NB) as boundary described in Treaty of Paris, 1783, and started process of rectifying errors in boundary descriptions of the 1783 treaty
1798 St John's Island renamed Prince Edward Island
1809 Labrador Act: Re-annexed the Labrador Coast and Anticosti Island to Newfoundland
1814 Treaty of Ghent: Provided for adjustments of all boundary disputes arising out of Treaty of Paris, 1783
1817 Commissioners affixed international boundary among islands between Passamaquoddy Bay and Bay of Fundy
1818 Convention: International boundary extended along 49th parallel from Lake of the Woods to the Rocky Mountains. Oregon Territory to west to be administered jointly by US and Britain for 10 years
1820 Cape Breton Island re-annexed to Nova Scotia
1825 Labrador Act: Labrador Coast between Saint-Jean River and Anse Sablon and Anticosti Island re-annexed to Lower Canada. Anglo-Russian Treaty: Defined lines of demarcation between Alaska and British North America

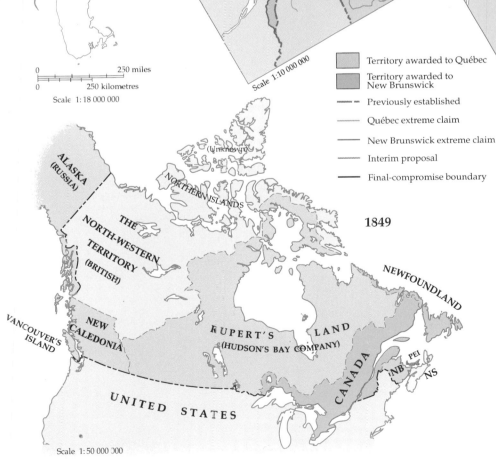

1849

Scale 1:50 000 000

1827 Gallatin-Addington negotiation extended joint British-American occupation of the Oregon Territory indefinitely. Negotiations under Treaty of Ghent referred settlement of boundary between New Brunswick and Maine to arbitration by the King of the Netherlands
1831 Award of arbitrator not accepted by either Britain or the United States
1840 Act of Union: United Upper and Lower Canada into Province of Canada. Provinces renamed Canada East and Canada West
1842 Ashburton-Webster Treaty: Settled boundaries still undefined by Treaty of 1783: between Canada East and New Hampshire, New Brunswick and Maine; and between Canada West and Minnesota
1846 Oregon Boundary Treaty: extended 49th parallel to Pacific excluding Vancouver's Island. Northern area called New Caledonia. A British-appointed commission failed to settle the dispute over the boundary between Canada and New Brunswick
1849 Vancouver's Island established as a Crown Colony

CONCISE EDITION

TERRITORIAL EVOLUTION, 1891–1961

Authors: Norman L. Nicholson, Robert Galois (BC), Michael Staveley (Nfld)

With the transfer of the Arctic Islands to Canada in the 1880s Britain completed its withdrawal from the new country. The integration of the vast Northwest Territories (NWT) into a dominion that stretched from the Atlantic to the Pacific proceeded in piecemeal fashion. The Yukon segment of the NWT became a separate territory in 1898 in order to cope better with the Klondike gold rush, but it was the formation of the provinces of Alberta and Saskatchewan in 1905 that brought a significant level of administrative autonomy to the region. In 1912 Ontario, Québec, and Manitoba were also extended northward; thereafter the NWT became an area synonymous with Canada 'north of 60.' On the Labrador coast the historical claims of Newfoundland conflicted with those of an expanded Québec, especially as new timber and mineral resources became accessible. Newfoundland joined the Canadian Confederation in 1949 after an acrimonious internal debate. Across the country, throughout the 20th century, the territorial laws and management systems of Native peoples were largely ignored by the demands of resource capital and homesteaders. Amerindians had little success in resolving land claims or in determining their own way of life.

REGIONAL SHARE OF TERRITORY

1891

Maritimes, Québec, Ontario, Manitoba, British Columbia, Keewatin, Assiniboia, Saskatchewan, Athabaska, Alberta, Rest of Northwest Territories

Total land area
3 315 647 sq mi
8 587 194 sq km

1949

Mackenzie, Keewatin, Franklin, Northwest Territories, Yukon Territory, British Columbia, Alberta, Saskatchewan, Manitoba, Ontario, Québec, Maritimes, Newfoundland

Total land area
3 560 238 sq mi
9 220 660 sq km

TWO VIEWS OF LAND IN BRITISH COLUMBIA

Compiled under the authority of the hereditary Gitksan and Wet'suwet'en chiefs

GITKSAN AND WET'SUWET'EN TERRITORIES

TAHLTAN
GITKSAN
MISGA'A
SEKANI
TSIMSHIAN
WET'SUWET'EN
HAISLA
CARRIER

Takla Lake
Babine Lake
Nass
Skeena

See detail below.

PACIFIC OCEAN

Clan Group

- Wolf
- Fireweed and Beaver
- Frog
- Eagle

Scale 1:4 000 000

In most of British Columbia the absence of treaties between government (imperial, colonial, or federal) and indigenous peoples contributed to conflict as settlement advanced. Assertions of ownership by the province and its alienation of land and resources were challenged by Indian claims of an extant aboriginal title to the land. As illustrated in the upper Skeena, the provincial system of land tenure, with Indians confined to reserves, was superimposed on a continuing aboriginal system of territorial ownership and resource allocation. A federal/provincial royal commission (1913–16) endeavoured to resolve this conflict but the ensuing 'settlement' of 1927 between the federal government and British Columbia was never accepted by the Indians.

PRE-EMPTOR'S MAP

BRITISH COLUMBIA

Kispiox
Hazelton
New Hazelton
Kitwanga
Cedarvale
Skeena Crossing
Smithers
Pacific

BC Department of Lands Bulkley Sheet, 1922 (detail)

- Indian Reserve
- Pre-empted
- Open for pre-emption
- Timber licence
- Government reserve
- BC Land Settlement Board
- Unsurveyed land

- ○ Post office
- ╌╌ Telegraph
- —— Road
- ┼┼ Grand Trunk Pacific Railway

Scale 1:735 000

NORTH POLE

ARCTIC OCEAN
BEAUFORT SEA
PACIFIC OCEAN

CANADA 1925

QUEEN ELIZABETH ISLANDS
SVERDRUP ISLANDS
ELLESMERE ISLAND
DISTRICT OF FRANKLIN 1895
PRINCE PATRICK ISLAND
MELVILLE ISLAND
BANKS ISLAND
BATHURST ISLAND
CORNWALLIS
PRINCE OF WALES ISLAND
VICTORIA ISLAND
KING WILLIAM
DISTRICT OF KEEWATIN

ALASKA (USA)

YUKON TERRITORY 1898
Whitehorse
DISTRICT OF YUKON 1895

DISTRICT OF MACKENZIE
Great Bear Lake
Great Slave Lake
Yellowknife
ARCTIC CIRCLE

NORTHWEST DISTRICT OF MACKENZIE

DISTRICT OF KEEWATIN

QUEEN CHARLOTTE ISLANDS

BRITISH COLUMBIA

Dixon Entrance
Queen Charlotte Sound

VANCOUVER ISLAND
Victoria

Peace
Athabasca
Lake Athabasca
Reindeer Lake

ALBERTA 1905
Edmonton

SASKATCHEWAN 1905

DISTRICT OF ATHABASKA 1882 1895
DISTRICT OF ALBERTA 1882 1895
DISTRICT OF SASKATCHEWAN 1882
DISTRICT OF ASSINIBOIA 1882

Regina
Qu'Appelle
Lake Winnipeg
Winnipeg

MANITOBA 1912

UNITED STATES OF AMERICA

It is tempting to conjecture what would have been the outcome of later federal/provincial relations had the Prairies been one province, or had any of the other five options that were seriously considered in 1905 been chosen.

PROPOSALS FOR THE PRAIRIE PROVINCES, 1905

1. 32nd Correction Line, Approx 60° N, 3rd Meridian 106° W, A, To Manitoba
2. 57° N, A
3. 32nd Correction Line, A, 9th Correction Line Approx 52° N, B
4. 32nd Correction Line, West of 10th Range, West of 4th Mer, A, B, 9th Correction Line, C
5. West of 10th Range, West of 4th Mer, 55° N, A, B, C, 9th Correction Line, D
6. 58°40' N, West of 21st Range, West of 2nd Mer, 54°30' N, 111° W, A, B, C, D

HISTORICAL ATLAS OF CANADA

PLATE 11

The exploration and discovery of the Arctic Islands, long associated with the search for a northwest passage, extended further north in the late 19th and early 20th centuries. Many of the important voyages were by Scandinavians and Americans. The Arctic explorer Vilhjalmur Stefansson, working for the Canadian government, made the last substantial discovery of new islands in the 1910s. It was not until 1940–4 that an RCMP patrol boat, the *St Roch*, succeeded in traversing the Northwest Passage both ways. While this voyage was a symbolic expression of Canadian sovereignty in the area, NORAD early-warning stations (pl 67) testify to the changing geopolitical position of the Canadian Arctic.

ARCTIC EXPLORATION

NORTH POLE
claimed by Peary
6 Apr 1909

87°06′ Lat
21 Apr 1906

84°17′ Lat
21 Apr 1902

GREENLAND
(DENMARK)

Norwegian Capt O. Sverdrup
1898–1902 (*Fram*)

American Lieut R.E. Peary, USN
1898–1902 (*Windward*)
1905–1906 (*Roosevelt*)
1908–1909 (*Roosevelt*)

Canadian A.P. Low
1904 (*Neptune*)

Canadian Capt J.E. Bernier
1906–1907 (*Arctic*)
1908–1909 (*Arctic*)
1910–1911 (*Arctic*)

Canadian V. Stefansson
1913–1918 (dog sled)

Canadian Staff-Sgt H.A. Larsen RCMP
1940–1942 (*St Roch*)
1944 (*St Roch*)

1916 WC Winter camp and anchorage of vessel
◄ Movement of exploration

(*St Roch*)
Depart Vancouver,
23 June 1940
Arrive Vancouver,
16 Oct 1944,
86 days from east to west

Low departed Halifax,
Aug 1903; spent a year
in Hudson Bay area.

(*St Roch*)
Arrive Halifax,
11 Oct 1942
Depart Halifax,
22 July 1944

Scale 1:20 000 000

From
Kristtiansund, Nor
To
Stavanger, Nor
From New York
From Sydney,
NS
To Sydney,
NS
To
New York
From Québec

The interior of Labrador was first divided in 1825: south of the 52nd parallel and west of a line that lay 'due north and south of a line from … Ance Sablon' was Québec territory; north and east was Newfoundland territory. Canada/Québec claimed areas north of that boundary in 1867 and 1898 but these claims were refuted by Newfoundland. When both Québec and Newfoundland sought to control the licensing of mineral and lumber resources, the British Privy Council in 1927 ruled in favour of Newfoundland. Québec did not recognize that Canada confirmed the boundary in 1949.

FIRST POLL OF THE REFERENDUM
3 June 1948

Labrador

St John's East
16 322

St John's West
19 880

Grand Falls
12 580

Humber
11 588

Harbour Main-
Bell Island
8 103

St-Georges-
Port-au-Port
6 465

Scale 1:8 200 000

NEWFOUNDLAND JOINS CONFEDERATION

Bankrupted during the Depression, the Colony of Newfoundland was administered by a British-appointed commission between 1934 and 1949. In 1948 Newfoundlanders debated three options: union with Canada, which promised social and economic revitalization; a continuation of government by commission; or a return to responsible government. For some, responsible government would safeguard traditional links: St John's merchants feared being swamped by Canadian firms and the Catholic hierarchy feared the loss of separate schooling. Others aspired to a customs union with the United States. The debate was bitter and the vote extremely close.

SECOND POLL OF THE REFERENDUM
22 June 1948

Labrador

St John's East
15 679

St John's West
18 706

Grand Falls
11 030

Humber
10 378

Harbour Main-
Bell Island
8 215

St-Georges-
Port-au-Port
6 728

Number of voters
4 000–4 999 · 5 000–5 999
2 000–3 999

* Uninhabited district

Scale 1:8 200 000

CANADA, 1891–1961

Boundary, 1961 **Historical**

––––– International –––––

––––– Provincial or territorial –––––

––––– District –––––

THE FINAL RESULTS OF THE REFERENDUM

Poll 1

Responsible
Government
44.6%

Confederation
with Canada
41.3%

Commission
of Government
14.3%

Total
155 777 votes

Poll 2

Responsible
Government
47.7%

Confederation
with Canada
52.3%

Total
149 657 votes

0 ––––– 300 miles
0 ––––– 300 kilometres
Scale 1:18 000 000

CONCISE EDITION

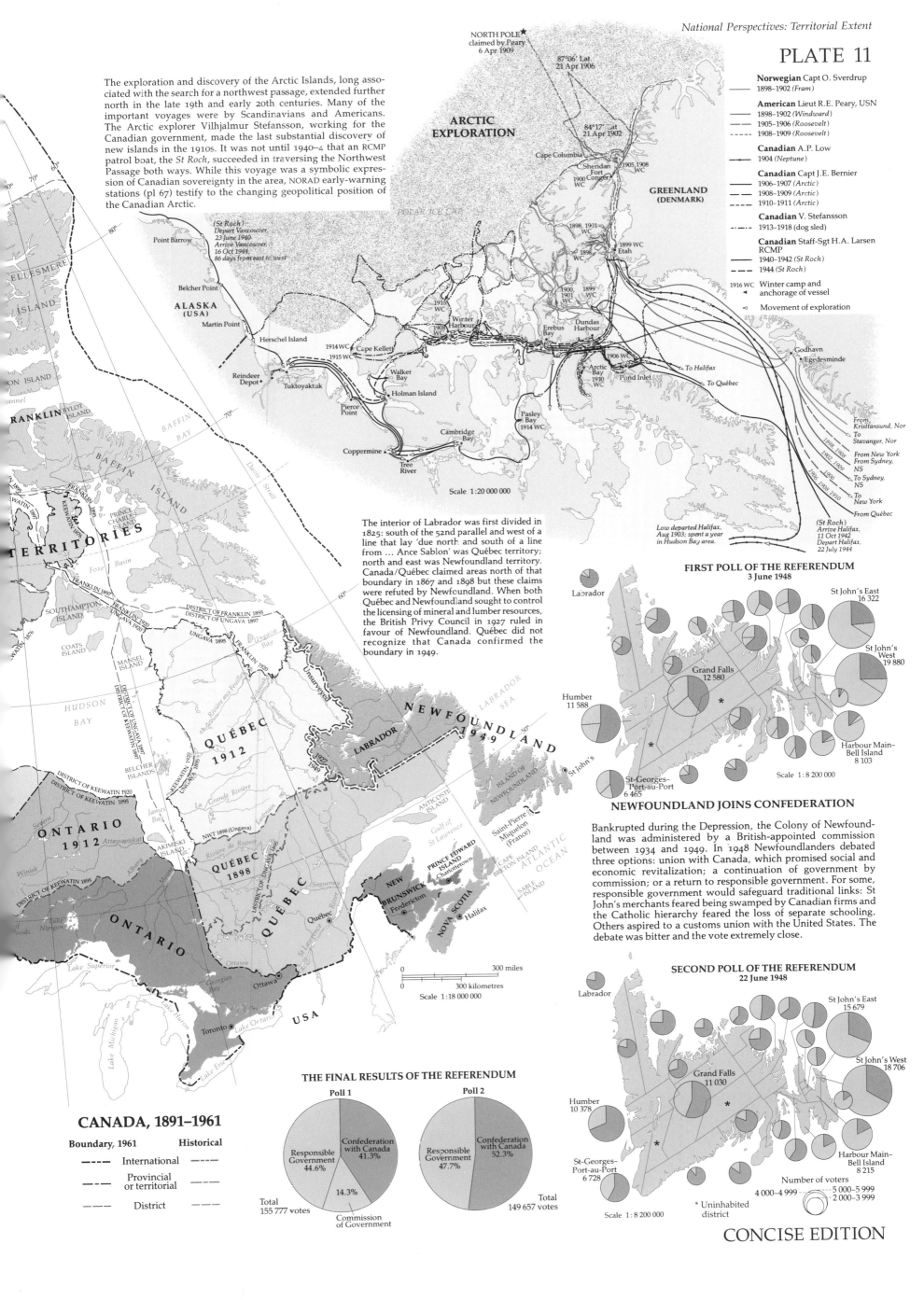

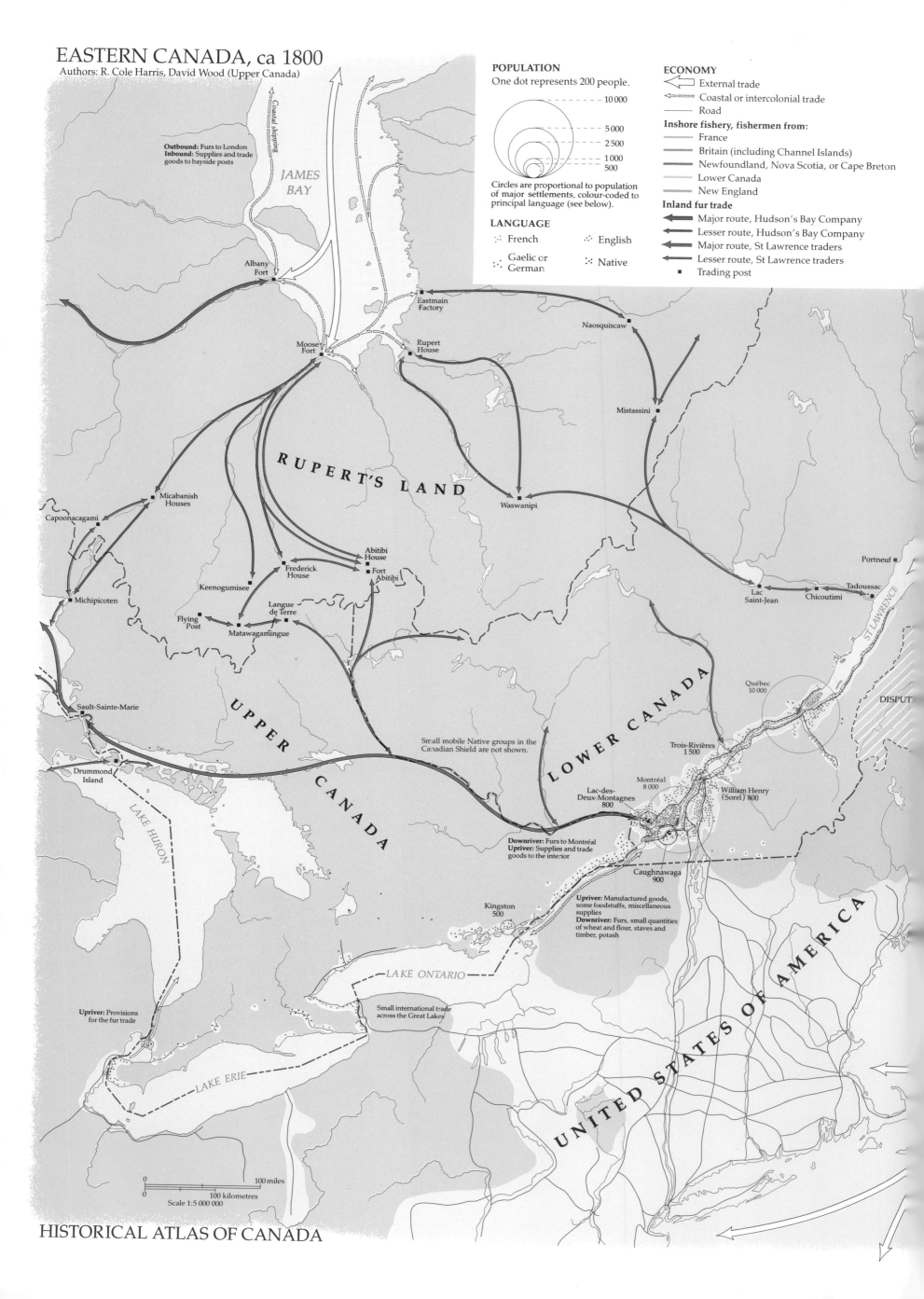

EASTERN CANADA, ca 1800
Authors: R. Cole Harris, David Wood (Upper Canada)

POPULATION
One dot represents 200 people.

— 10 000
— 5 000
— 2 500
— 1 000
— 500

Circles are proportional to population of major settlements, colour-coded to principal language (see below).

LANGUAGE
French
English
Gaelic or German
Native

ECONOMY
External trade
Coastal or intercolonial trade
Road

Inshore fishery, fishermen from:
France
Britain (including Channel Islands)
Newfoundland, Nova Scotia, or Cape Breton
Lower Canada
New England

Inland fur trade
Major route, Hudson's Bay Company
Lesser route, Hudson's Bay Company
Major route, St Lawrence traders
Lesser route, St Lawrence traders
Trading post

JAMES BAY

Outbound: Furs to London
Inbound: Supplies and trade goods to bayside posts

Coastal shipping

Albany Fort

Eastmain Factory

Moose Fort

Rupert House

Naosquiscaw

RUPERT'S LAND

Mistassini

Waswanipi

Micabanish Houses

Capoonacagami

Abitibi House

Frederick House

Fort Abitibi

Keenogumisee

Michipicoten

Langue de Terre

Flying Post

Matawagamingue

Lac Saint-Jean

Chicoutimi

Tadoussac

Portneuf

ST LAWRENCE

Québec 10 000

DISPUT

Sault-Sainte-Marie

UPPER CANADA

LOWER CANADA

Small mobile Native groups in the Canadian Shield are not shown.

Trois-Rivières 1 500

Drummond Island

LAKE HURON

Montréal 8 000

William Henry (Sorel) 800

Lac-des-Deux-Montagnes 800

Downriver: Furs to Montréal
Upriver: Supplies and trade goods to the interior

Caughnawaga 900

Upriver: Manufactured goods, some foodstuffs, miscellaneous supplies
Downriver: Furs, small quantities of wheat and flour, staves and timber, potash

Kingston 500

LAKE ONTARIO

Small international trade across the Great Lakes

Upriver: Provisions for the fur trade

LAKE ERIE

UNITED STATES OF AMERICA

0   100 miles
0   100 kilometres
Scale 1:5 000 000

HISTORICAL ATLAS OF CANADA

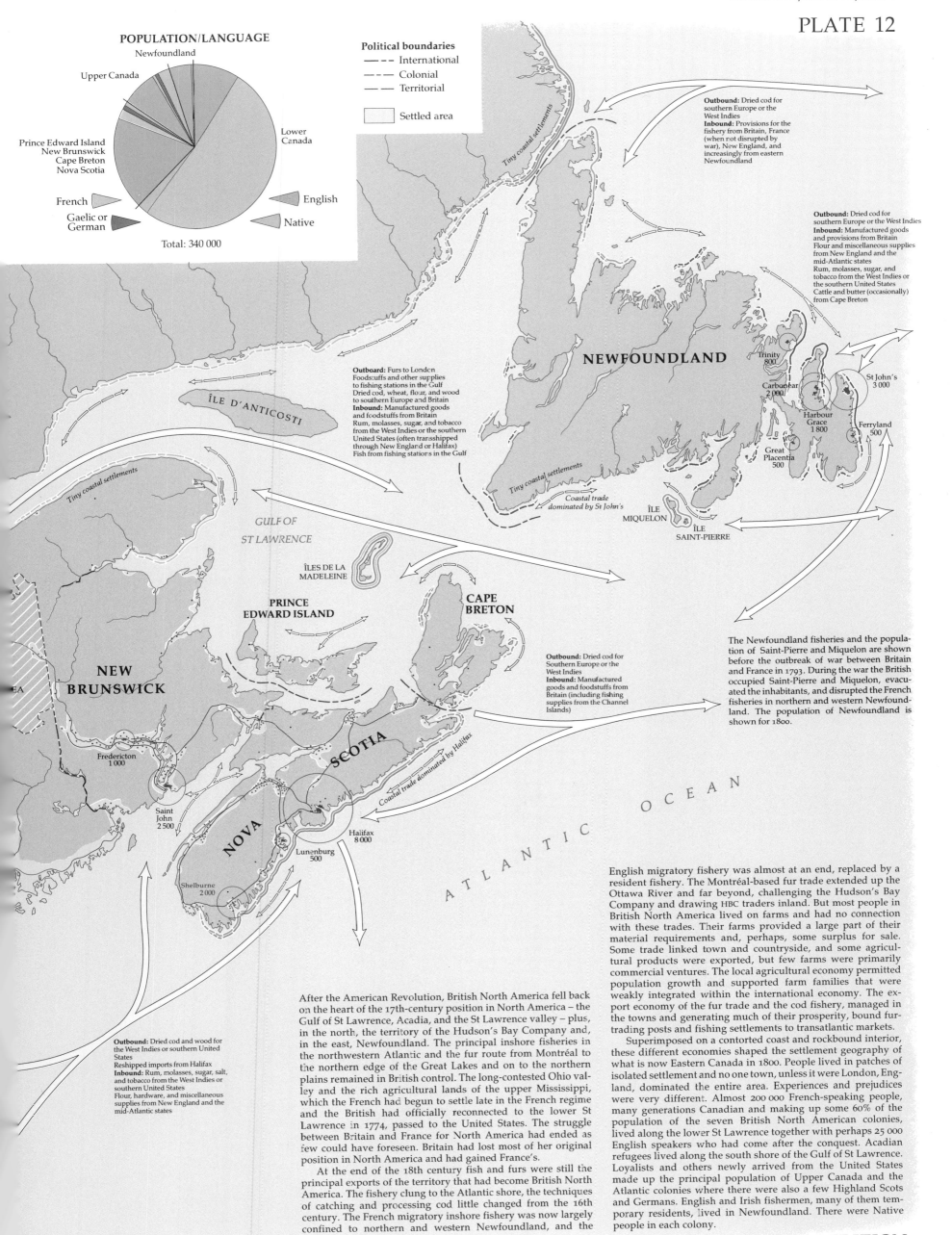

POPULATION/LANGUAGE

Newfoundland
Upper Canada

Prince Edward Island
New Brunswick
Cape Breton
Nova Scotia

Lower Canada

French
Gaelic or German
English
Native

Total: 340 000

Political boundaries
– – – International
– – – Colonial
– – – Territorial

Settled area

Outbound: Dried cod for southern Europe or the West Indies
Inbound: Provisions for the fishery from Britain, France (when not disrupted by war), New England, and increasingly from eastern Newfoundland

Outbound: Dried cod for southern Europe or the West Indies
Inbound: Manufactured goods and provisions from Britain
Flour and miscellaneous supplies from New England and the mid-Atlantic states
Rum, molasses, sugar, and tobacco from the West Indies or the southern United States
Cattle and butter (occasionally) from Cape Breton

Outbound: Furs to London
Foodstuffs and other supplies to fishing stations in the Gulf
Dried cod, wheat, flour, and wood to southern Europe and Britain
Inbound: Manufactured goods and foodstuffs from Britain
Rum, molasses, sugar, and tobacco from the West Indies or the southern United States (often transshipped through New England or Halifax)
Fish from fishing stations in the Gulf

NEWFOUNDLAND

Trinity 800
Carbonear 2 000
Harbour Grace 1 800
St John's 3 000
Ferryland 500
Great Placentia 500

ÎLE D'ANTICOSTI

Tiny coastal settlements

GULF OF ST LAWRENCE

ÎLES DE LA MADELEINE

PRINCE EDWARD ISLAND

CAPE BRETON

ÎLE MIQUELON
ÎLE SAINT-PIERRE

Coastal trade dominated by St John's

Tiny coastal settlements

NEW BRUNSWICK

Fredericton 1 000

Saint John 2 500

NOVA SCOTIA

Lunenburg 500

Halifax 8 000

Shelburne 2 000

Outbound: Dried cod for Southern Europe or the West Indies
Inbound: Manufactured goods and foodstuffs from Britain (including fishing supplies from the Channel Islands)

Coastal trade dominated by Halifax

ATLANTIC OCEAN

The Newfoundland fisheries and the population of Saint-Pierre and Miquelon are shown before the outbreak of war between Britain and France in 1793. During the war the British occupied Saint-Pierre and Miquelon, evacuated the inhabitants, and disrupted the French fisheries in northern and western Newfoundland. The population of Newfoundland is shown for 1800.

Outbound: Dried cod and wood for the West Indies or southern United States
Reshipped imports from Halifax
Inbound: Rum, molasses, sugar, salt, and tobacco from the West Indies or southern United States
Flour, hardware, and miscellaneous supplies from New England and the mid-Atlantic states

After the American Revolution, British North America fell back on the heart of the 17th-century position in North America – the Gulf of St Lawrence, Acadia, and the St Lawrence valley – plus, in the north, the territory of the Hudson's Bay Company and, in the east, Newfoundland. The principal inshore fisheries in the northwestern Atlantic and the fur route from Montréal to the northern edge of the Great Lakes and on to the northern plains remained in British control. The long-contested Ohio valley and the rich agricultural lands of the upper Mississippi, which the French had begun to settle late in the French regime and the British had officially reconnected to the lower St Lawrence in 1774, passed to the United States. The struggle between Britain and France for North America had ended as few could have foreseen. Britain had lost most of her original position in North America and had gained France's.

At the end of the 18th century fish and furs were still the principal exports of the territory that had become British North America. The fishery clung to the Atlantic shore, the techniques of catching and processing cod little changed from the 16th century. The French migratory inshore fishery was now largely confined to northern and western Newfoundland, and the English migratory fishery was almost at an end, replaced by a resident fishery. The Montréal-based fur trade extended up the Ottawa River and far beyond, challenging the Hudson's Bay Company and drawing HBC traders inland. But most people in British North America lived on farms and had no connection with these trades. Their farms provided a large part of their material requirements and, perhaps, some surplus for sale. Some trade linked town and countryside, and some agricultural products were exported, but few farms were primarily commercial ventures. The local agricultural economy permitted population growth and supported farm families that were weakly integrated within the international economy. The export economy of the fur trade and the cod fishery, managed in the towns and generating much of their prosperity, bound fur-trading posts and fishing settlements to transatlantic markets.

Superimposed on a contorted coast and rockbound interior, these different economies shaped the settlement geography of what is now Eastern Canada in 1800. People lived in patches of isolated settlement and no one town, unless it were London, England, dominated the entire area. Experiences and prejudices were very different. Almost 200 000 French-speaking people, many generations Canadian and making up some 60% of the population of the seven British North American colonies, lived along the lower St Lawrence together with perhaps 25 000 English speakers who had come after the conquest. Acadian refugees lived along the south shore of the Gulf of St Lawrence. Loyalists and others newly arrived from the United States made up the principal population of Upper Canada and the Atlantic colonies where there were also a few Highland Scots and Germans. English and Irish fishermen, many of them temporary residents, lived in Newfoundland. There were Native people in each colony.

POPULATION IN THE CANADAS AND THE ATLANTIC REGION TO 1857

Authors: Brian S. Osborne, Jean-Claude Robert, David A. Sutherland

During the first half of the 19th century the Canadas (Québec and Ontario) experienced considerable population growth in response to immigration and high birth rates. The population of Québec almost doubled from some 480 000 in 1825 to 890 000 in 1851, while that of Ontario multiplied sixfold from 158 000 in 1825 to 952 000 in 1851. The period also witnessed an expansion of the settled area. Whereas Québec's 1825 population had been concentrated in the Québec City–Montréal heartland, by 1851 settlement had spread into the Eastern Townships and along the Chaudière valley, and was stretching out along the north and south shores of the St Lawrence and the Gaspé coast. During the same period the concentration of Ontario's population along the Great Lakes–St Lawrence corridor extended some 50 km inland but had not yet expanded into the area between the Ottawa River and Lake Huron. By 1851 the Toronto-Hamilton-London region was emerging as the economic core of the province.

Both provinces continued to be predominantly rural with less than 20% of their population living in the eight largest urban centres. By 1851 the urban system was dominated by Montréal (58 000) and Québec City (42 000), although Toronto had exploded from under 2 000 in 1825 to over 30 000. Kingston (11 700) had fallen behind Hamilton (14 100) and was being challenged by Ottawa (7 800) and London (7 000).

The red bars on the population pyramids show male/female ratios for each age group, that is the number of males per 100 females or the number of females per 100 males.

* The 'average percentage' axis at the bottom of each population pyramid represents the average percentage of the total population, by sex, in each year for each age group represented by the orange and green bars.

As an example, for Rural Canada West in 1851 (shown above), there were 96 000 males in the 0–4 age group representing 10.6% of the total population (907 500). Within this 0–4 'male' age group, each year had an average of 2.1% of the total population for each of the five years. This percentage is shown visually on the pyramid.

This method has been used to take into account the varying ranges of age groups in the census data for different areas and dates.

HISTORICAL ATLAS OF CANADA

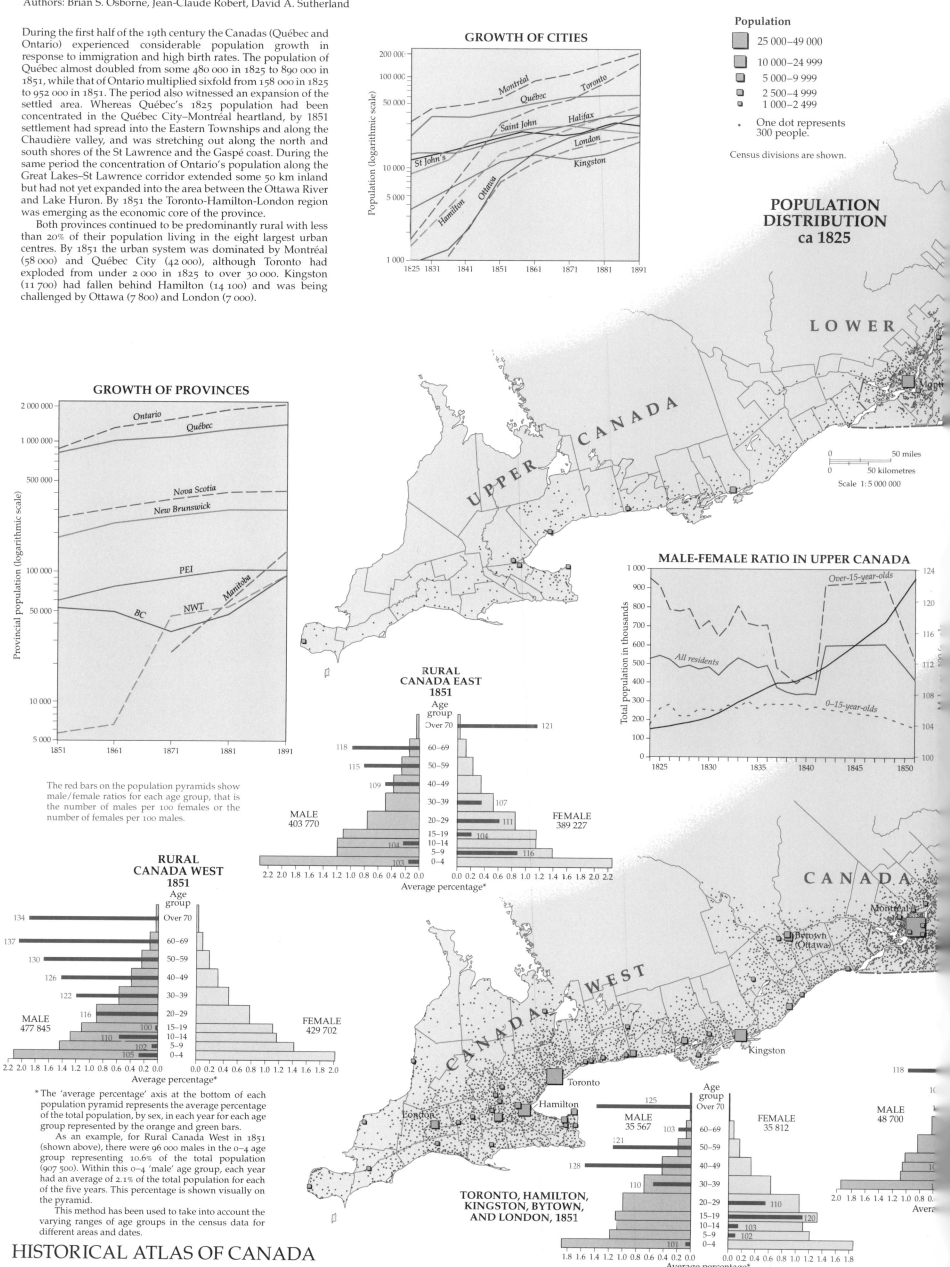

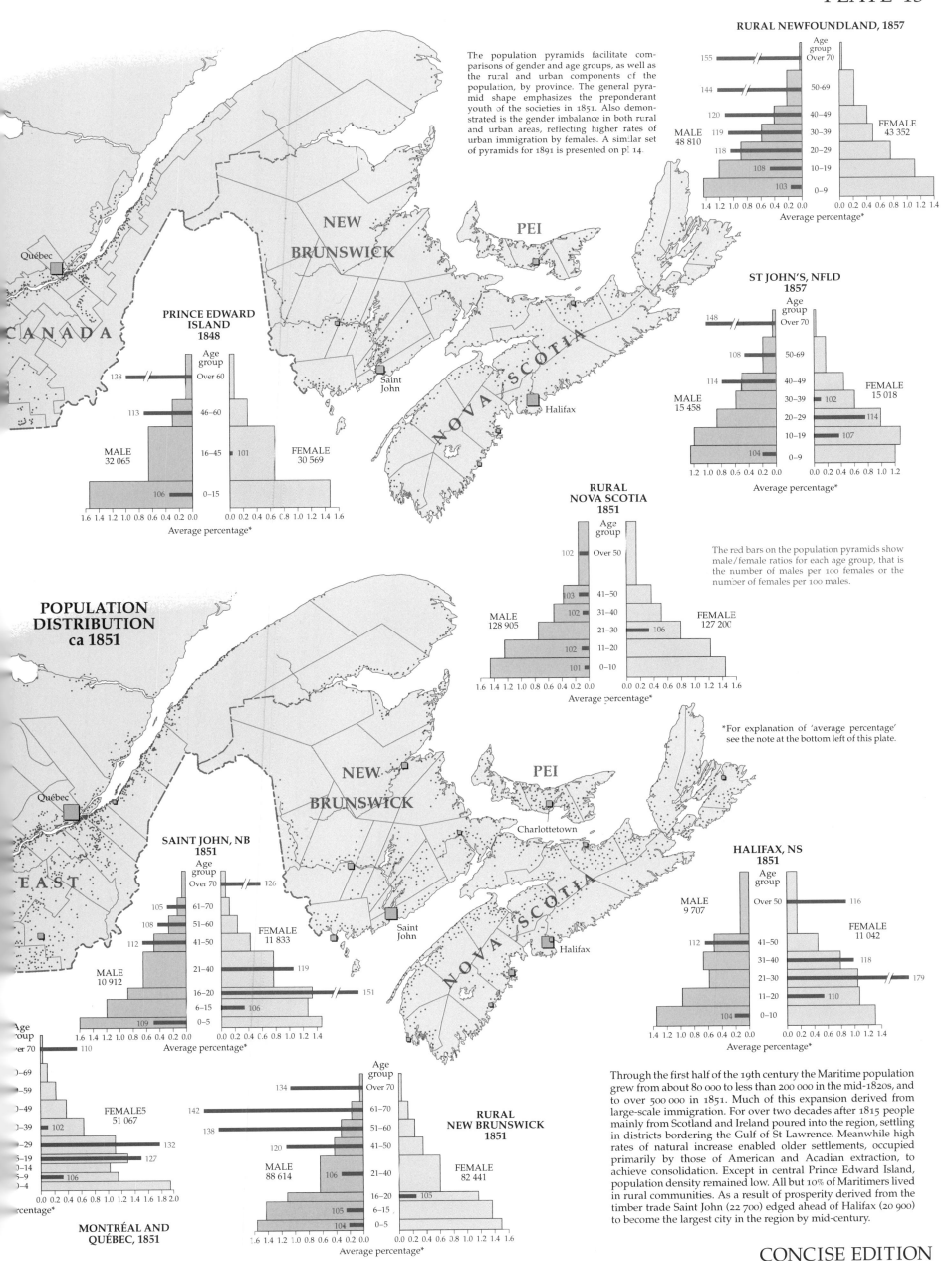

RURAL NEWFOUNDLAND, 1857

MALE 48 810 — FEMALE 43 352

Age group: Over 70, 50–69, 40–49, 30–39, 20–29, 10–19, 0–9

155, 144, 120, 119, 118, 108, 103

Average percentage*

The population pyramids facilitate comparisons of gender and age groups, as well as the rural and urban components of the population, by province. The general pyramid shape emphasizes the preponderant youth of the societies in 1851. Also demonstrated is the gender imbalance in both rural and urban areas, reflecting higher rates of urban immigration by females. A similar set of pyramids for 1891 is presented on pl 14.

ST JOHN'S, NFLD 1857

MALE 15 458 — FEMALE 15 018

Age group: Over 70, 50–69, 40–49, 30–39, 20–29, 10–19, 0–9

148, 108, 114, 102, 114, 107, 104

Average percentage*

PRINCE EDWARD ISLAND 1848

MALE 32 065 — FEMALE 30 569

Age group: Over 60, 46–60, 16–45, 0–15

138, 113, 101, 106

Average percentage*

RURAL NOVA SCOTIA 1851

MALE 128 905 — FEMALE 127 200

Age group: Over 50, 41–50, 31–40, 21–30, 11–20, 0–10

102, 103, 102, 106, 102, 101

Average percentage*

The red bars on the population pyramids show male/female ratios for each age group, that is the number of males per 100 females or the number of females per 100 males.

POPULATION DISTRIBUTION ca 1851

*For explanation of 'average percentage' see the note at the bottom left of this plate.

SAINT JOHN, NB 1851

MALE 10 912 — FEMALE 11 833

Age group: Over 70, 61–70, 51–60, 41–50, 21–40, 16–20, 6–15, 0–5

126, 105, 108, 112, 119, 151, 106, 109

Average percentage*

HALIFAX, NS 1851

MALE 9 707 — FEMALE 11 042

Age group: Over 50, 41–50, 31–40, 21–30, 11–20, 0–10

116, 112, 118, 179, 110, 104

Average percentage*

MONTRÉAL AND QUÉBEC, 1851

FEMALE 51 067

Age group: Over 70, 60–69, 50–59, 40–49, 30–39, 20–29, 15–19, 10–14, 5–9, 0–4

110, 102, 132, 127, 106

Average percentage*

RURAL NEW BRUNSWICK 1851

MALE 88 614 — FEMALE 82 441

Age group: Over 70, 61–70, 51–60, 41–50, 21–40, 16–20, 6–15, 0–5

134, 142, 138, 120, 106, 105, 105, 104

Average percentage*

Through the first half of the 19th century the Maritime population grew from about 80 000 to less than 200 000 in the mid-1820s, and to over 500 000 in 1851. Much of this expansion derived from large-scale immigration. For over two decades after 1815 people mainly from Scotland and Ireland poured into the region, settling in districts bordering the Gulf of St Lawrence. Meanwhile high rates of natural increase enabled older settlements, occupied primarily by those of American and Acadian extraction, to achieve consolidation. Except in central Prince Edward Island, population density remained low. All but 10% of Maritimers lived in rural communities. As a result of prosperity derived from the timber trade Saint John (22 700) edged ahead of Halifax (20 900) to become the largest city in the region by mid-century.

CONCISE EDITION

THE CANADIAN POPULATION, 1871, 1891

Authors: Don Measner, Christine Hampson

Canada in 1891 had attained a population of approximately 4.8 million, a doubling of its numbers since 1851. The rate of increase varied both by decade and by region. In the central and eastern provinces a substantial growth of over 50% from 1851 to 1871 fell off to an increase of only 21% from 1871 to 1891. By contrast, in the new farmlands of the West dramatic increases occurred in the latter period, setting the stage for major growth to follow.

By 1871 the main areas of population concentration were well in place. Three-quarters of the country's inhabitants lived in the southern parts of Québec and Ontario, almost all of them (over 90%) in areas occupied in 1851. In the Maritimes as well increases reinforced the existing pattern, a coastal distribution inherited from earlier in the century. In the West population had begun to spread westward, beyond Manitoba, following the newly built railway lines.

The population was predominantly rural. At the same time the rate of urban growth had surpassed that in rural areas. In urban centres with at least 1 000 inhabitants population increased from 23% of the total population in 1871 to 33% in 1891, with much of the growth in larger centres. In 1891 over 38% of urban residents lived in centres with populations over 25 000.

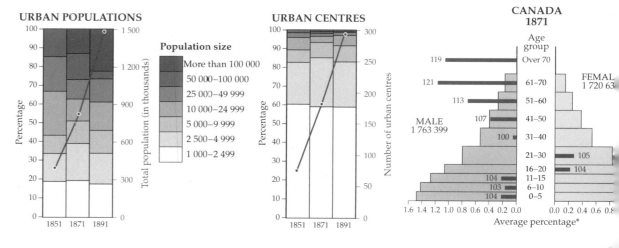

Natives were under-enumerated in both the 1871 and 1891 censuses, especially in the West.

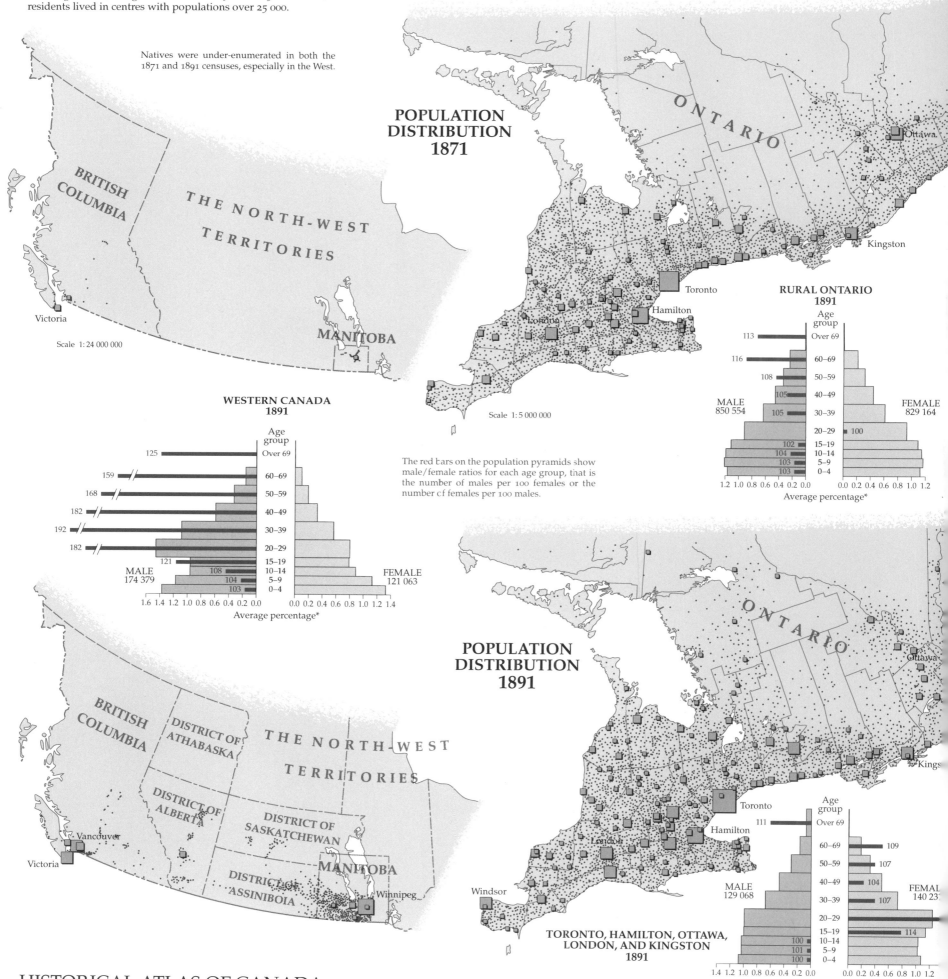

The red bars on the population pyramids show male/female ratios for each age group, that is the number of males per 100 females or the number of females per 100 males.

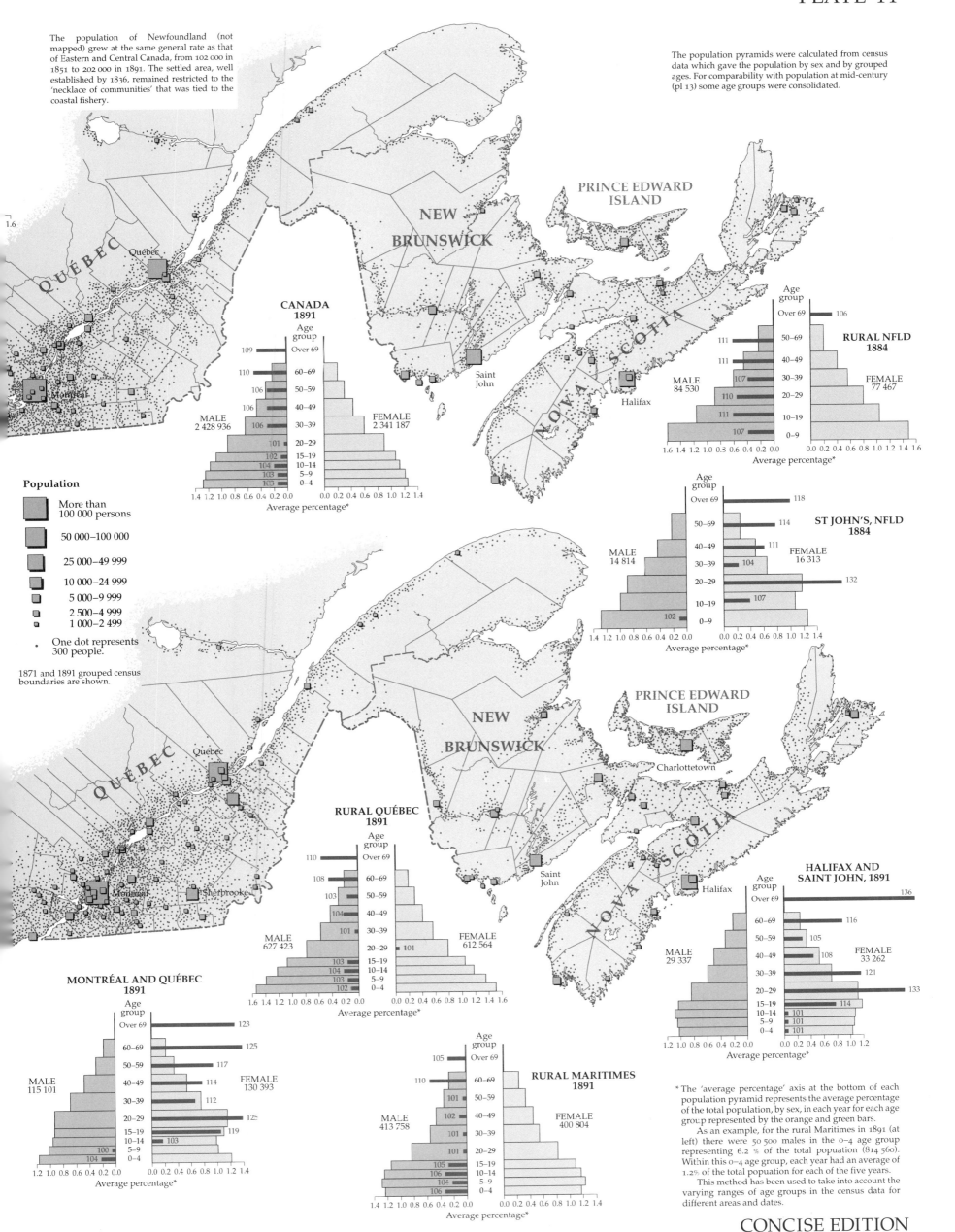

The population of Newfoundland (not mapped) grew at the same general rate as that of Eastern and Central Canada, from 102 000 in 1851 to 202 000 in 1891. The settled area, well established by 1836, remained restricted to the 'necklace of communities' that was tied to the coastal fishery.

The population pyramids were calculated from census data which gave the population by sex and by grouped ages. For comparability with population at mid-century (pl 13) some age groups were consolidated.

PRINCE EDWARD ISLAND

NEW BRUNSWICK

QUÉBEC

Québec

Montréal

NOVA SCOTIA

Saint John

Halifax

CANADA 1891

Age group

Over 69	109
60–69	110
50–59	106
40–49	106
30–39	106
20–29	101
15–19	102
10–14	104
5–9	103
0–4	103

MALE 2 428 936

FEMALE 2 341 187

Average percentage*

RURAL NFLD 1884

Age group

Over 69	106
50–69	111
40–49	111
30–39	107
20–29	110
10–19	111
0–9	107

MALE 84 530

FEMALE 77 467

Average percentage*

Population

	More than 100 000 persons
	50 000–100 000
	25 000–49 999
	10 000–24 999
	5 000–9 999
	2 500–4 999
	1 000–2 499
•	One dot represents 300 people.

1871 and 1891 grouped census boundaries are shown.

ST JOHN'S, NFLD 1884

Age group

Over 69	118
50–69	114
40–49	111
30–39	104
20–29	132
10–19	107
0–9	102

MALE 14 814

FEMALE 16 313

Average percentage*

PRINCE EDWARD ISLAND

NEW BRUNSWICK

QUÉBEC

Québec

Montréal

Sherbrooke

NOVA SCOTIA

Saint John

Halifax

Charlottetown

RURAL QUÉBEC 1891

Age group

Over 69	110
60–69	108
50–59	103
40–49	104
30–39	101
20–29	101
15–19	103
10–14	104
5–9	103
0–4	102

MALE 627 423

FEMALE 612 564

Average percentage*

HALIFAX AND SAINT JOHN, 1891

Age group

Over 69	136
60–69	116
50–59	105
40–49	108
30–39	121
20–29	133
15–19	114
10–14	101
5–9	101
0–4	101

MALE 29 337

FEMALE 33 262

Average percentage*

MONTRÉAL AND QUÉBEC 1891

Age group

Over 69	123
60–69	125
50–59	117
40–49	114
30–39	112
20–29	125
15–19	119
10–14	103
5–9	100
0–4	104

MALE 115 101

FEMALE 130 393

Average percentage*

RURAL MARITIMES 1891

Age group

Over 69	105
60–69	110
50–59	101
40–49	102
30–39	101
20–29	101
15–19	105
10–14	106
5–9	104
0–4	106

MALE 413 758

FEMALE 400 804

Average percentage*

* The 'average percentage' axis at the bottom of each population pyramid represents the average percentage of the total population, by sex, in each year for each age group represented by the orange and green bars.

As an example, for the rural Maritimes in 1891 (at left) there were 50 500 males in the 0–4 age group representing 6.2 % of the total popuation (814 560). Within this 0–4 age group, each year had an average of 1.2% of the total popuation for each of the five years.

This method has been used to take into account the varying ranges of age groups in the census data for different areas and dates.

THE EXODUS: MIGRATIONS, 1860–1900

Authors: Patricia A. Thornton, Ronald H. Walder, Elizabeth Buchanan (kinship linkages)

The flow of population to and from Canada changed dramatically in the second half of the 19th century. British immigration fell off rapidly; at the same time emigration from Canada, overwhelmingly to the United States, rose sharply. The 1880s were to become known as the time of 'the exodus.'

The immigrant stream, although diminished, still flowed. For a large number of European immigrants, however, Canada was merely a way-station on the road to the American frontier; all provinces lost population to the United States. From the Maritimes young single males and females from farm or traditional-craft families in coastal areas strongly tied to a declining commercial economy emigrated to the major ports of New England. A high rate of natural increase in rural Québec, coupled with limited agricultural opportunities, forced many French Canadians south to the mill towns of New England. With most of its agricultural land occupied, rural Ontario lost young men to Detroit and Chicago, or to the agricultural and lumbering frontiers in the western United States.

Coinciding with entry and exodus, large numbers of people were also moving from one part of the country to another, as colonization of rural areas came to an end and industrialization and urbanization gathered momentum. In the 1870s some interior parts of Canada were still experiencing frontierward in-migration, although in smaller numbers than in the preceding decades. Much of this originated from more densely settled rural areas, which were also losing young people to the emerging cities and industrial towns. By the 1880s frontierward migration had almost ceased and out-migration was occurring on a massive scale towards the highly centralized industrial heartland and its resource hinterlands.

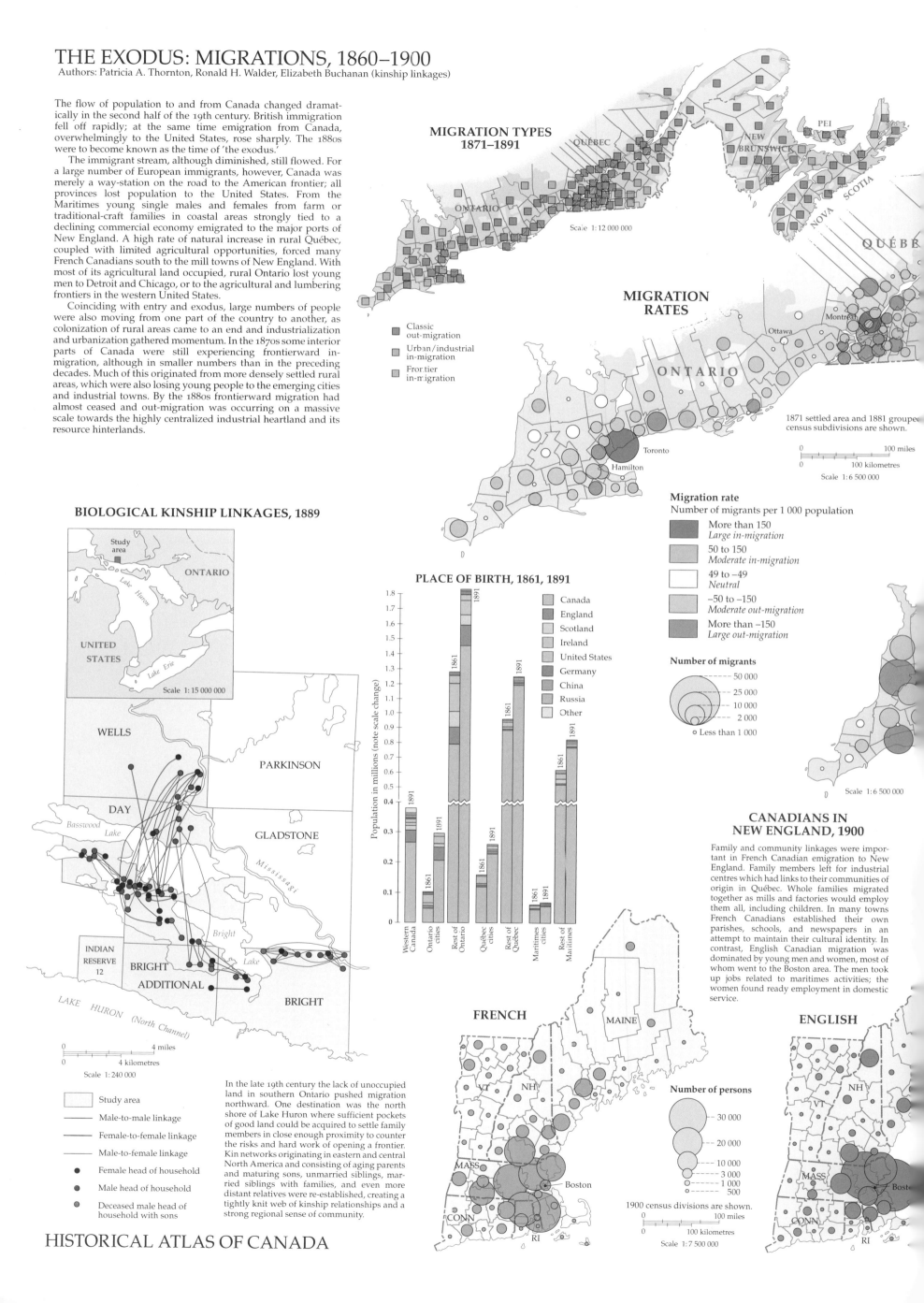

MIGRATION TYPES 1871–1891

Scale 1:12 000 000

- Classic out-migration
- Urban/industrial in-migration
- Frontier in-migration

MIGRATION RATES

1871 settled area and 1881 grouped census subdivisions are shown.

0 — 100 miles
0 — 100 kilometres
Scale 1:6 500 000

Migration rate
Number of migrants per 1 000 population

- More than 150 — *Large in-migration*
- 50 to 150 — *Moderate in-migration*
- 49 to –49 — *Neutral*
- –50 to –150 — *Moderate out-migration*
- More than –150 — *Large out-migration*

Number of migrants
- 50 000
- 25 000
- 10 000
- 2 000
- Less than 1 000

Scale 1:6 500 000

BIOLOGICAL KINSHIP LINKAGES, 1889

Study area — ONTARIO
UNITED STATES
Lake Huron
Lake Erie
Scale 1:15 000 000

WELLS — PARKINSON
DAY — GLADSTONE
Basswood Lake
Mississagi
Bright
INDIAN RESERVE 12 — BRIGHT — ADDITIONAL — Lake — BRIGHT
LAKE HURON (North Channel)

0 — 4 miles
0 — 4 kilometres
Scale 1:240 000

- Study area
- Male-to-male linkage
- Female-to-female linkage
- Male-to-female linkage
- ● Female head of household
- ● Male head of household
- ● Deceased male head of household with sons

In the late 19th century the lack of unoccupied land in southern Ontario pushed migration northward. One destination was the north shore of Lake Huron where sufficient pockets of good land could be acquired to settle family members in close enough proximity to counter the risks and hard work of opening a frontier. Kin networks originating in eastern and central North America and consisting of aging parents and maturing sons, unmarried siblings, married siblings with families, and even more distant relatives were re-established, creating a tightly knit web of kinship relationships and a strong regional sense of community.

HISTORICAL ATLAS OF CANADA

PLACE OF BIRTH, 1861, 1891

Population in millions (note scale change)

- Canada
- England
- Scotland
- Ireland
- United States
- Germany
- China
- Russia
- Other

(bars labelled: Western Canada 1891; Ontario cities 1861/1891; Rest of Ontario 1861/1891; Québec cities 1861/1891; Rest of Québec 1861/1891; Maritimes cities 1861/1891; Rest of Maritimes 1861/1891)

CANADIANS IN NEW ENGLAND, 1900

Family and community linkages were important in French Canadian emigration to New England. Family members left for industrial centres which had links to their communities of origin in Québec. Whole families migrated together as mills and factories would employ them all, including children. In many towns French Canadians established their own parishes, schools, and newspapers in an attempt to maintain their cultural identity. In contrast, English Canadian migration was dominated by young men and women, most of whom went to the Boston area. The men took up jobs related to maritimes activities; the women found ready employment in domestic service.

FRENCH
MAINE
VT — NH
MASS — Boston
CONN — RI

Number of persons
- 30 000
- 20 000
- 10 000
- 3 000
- 1 000
- 500

1900 census divisions are shown.

0 — 100 miles
0 — 100 kilometres
Scale 1:7 500 000

ENGLISH
NH
VT
MASS — Boston
CONN — RI

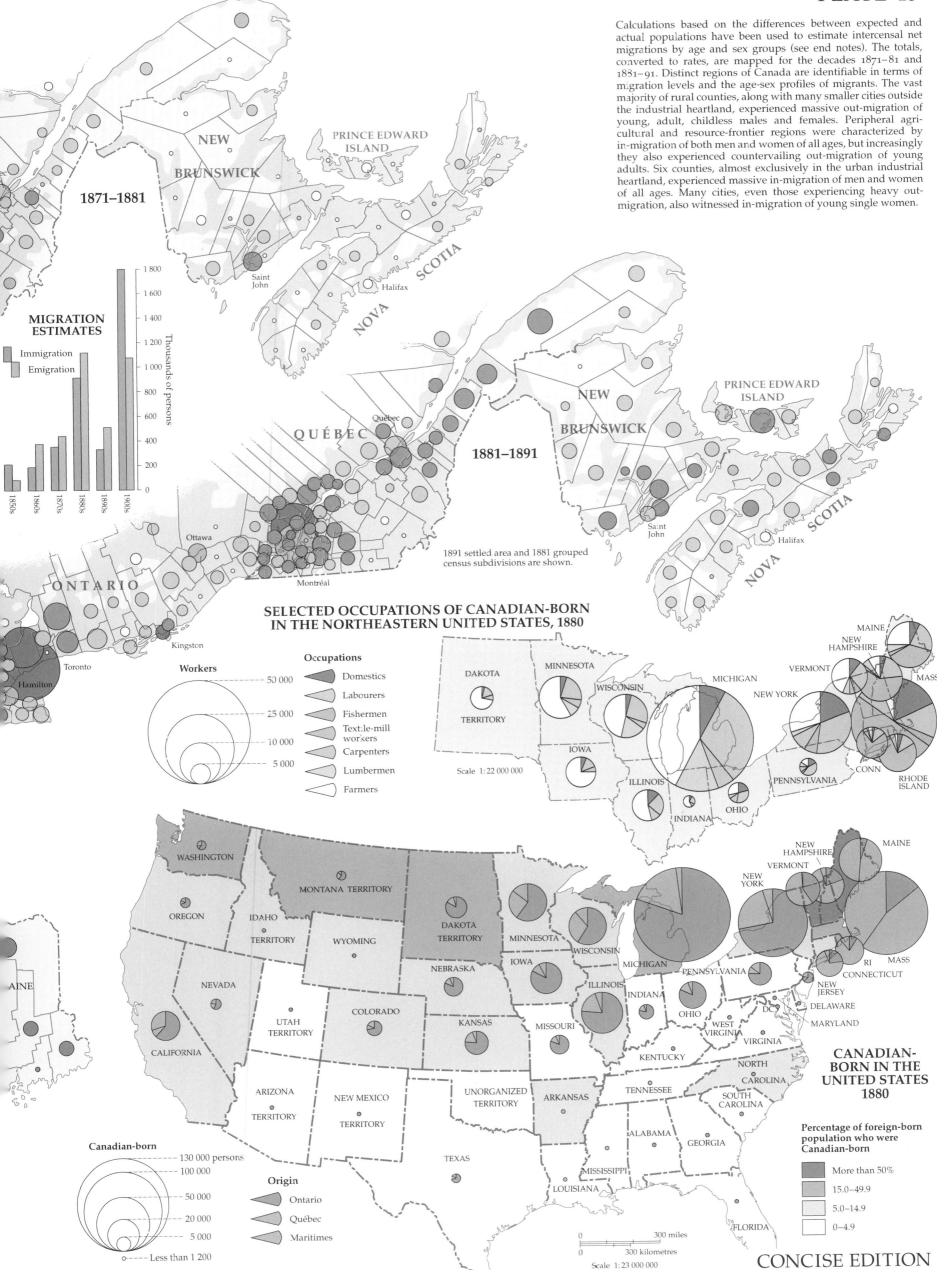

Calculations based on the differences between expected and actual populations have been used to estimate intercensal net migrations by age and sex groups (see end notes). The totals, converted to rates, are mapped for the decades 1871–81 and 1881–91. Distinct regions of Canada are identifiable in terms of migration levels and the age-sex profiles of migrants. The vast majority of rural counties, along with many smaller cities outside the industrial heartland, experienced massive out-migration of young, adult, childless males and females. Peripheral agricultural and resource-frontier regions were characterized by in-migration of both men and women of all ages, but increasingly they also experienced countervailing out-migration of young adults. Six counties, almost exclusively in the urban industrial heartland, experienced massive in-migration of men and women of all ages. Many cities, even those experiencing heavy out-migration, also witnessed in-migration of young single women.

1871–1881

MIGRATION ESTIMATES

Immigration

Emigration

1881–1891

1891 settled area and 1881 grouped census subdivisions are shown.

SELECTED OCCUPATIONS OF CANADIAN-BORN IN THE NORTHEASTERN UNITED STATES, 1880

Workers
- 50 000
- 25 000
- 10 000
- 5 000

Occupations
- Domestics
- Labourers
- Fishermen
- Textile-mill workers
- Carpenters
- Lumbermen
- Farmers

Scale 1:22 000 000

CANADIAN-BORN IN THE UNITED STATES 1880

Canadian-born
- 130 000 persons
- 100 000
- 50 000
- 20 000
- 5 000
- Less than 1 200

Origin
- Ontario
- Québec
- Maritimes

Percentage of foreign-born population who were Canadian-born
- More than 50%
- 15.0–49.9
- 5.0–14.9
- 0–4.9

0   300 miles

0   300 kilometres

Scale 1:23 000 000

CONCISE EDITION

MIGRATION, 1891–1930

Author: Marvin McInnis

As the 19th century drew to a close the influx of immigrants to Canada accelerated greatly, reaching a peak in the years 1909–13. There were many immigrants from eastern Europe, especially Poland, Austria, and Russia. Scandinavians also came in large numbers, often having first emigrated to the United States. A significant number of Americans came, mostly to the areas of agricultural settlement in the West. Britain, the traditional source of immigrants to Canada, continued to provide the greatest number. Canada was not, however, equally open to all immigrants: Asians were required to pay restrictive head taxes.

The outstanding attraction of Canada was farming on the plains, where 160-acre farms were offered free under homestead policy. Almost as many immigrants came to non-agricultural jobs, however, especially in railway construction, mining, and logging in the West and manufacturing and other jobs in the cities of Central Canada. Canadians continued to emigrate to the United States in large numbers, particularly to industrial cities near the border such as Detroit and Buffalo.

THE MOVE TO THE WEST, 1891–1914

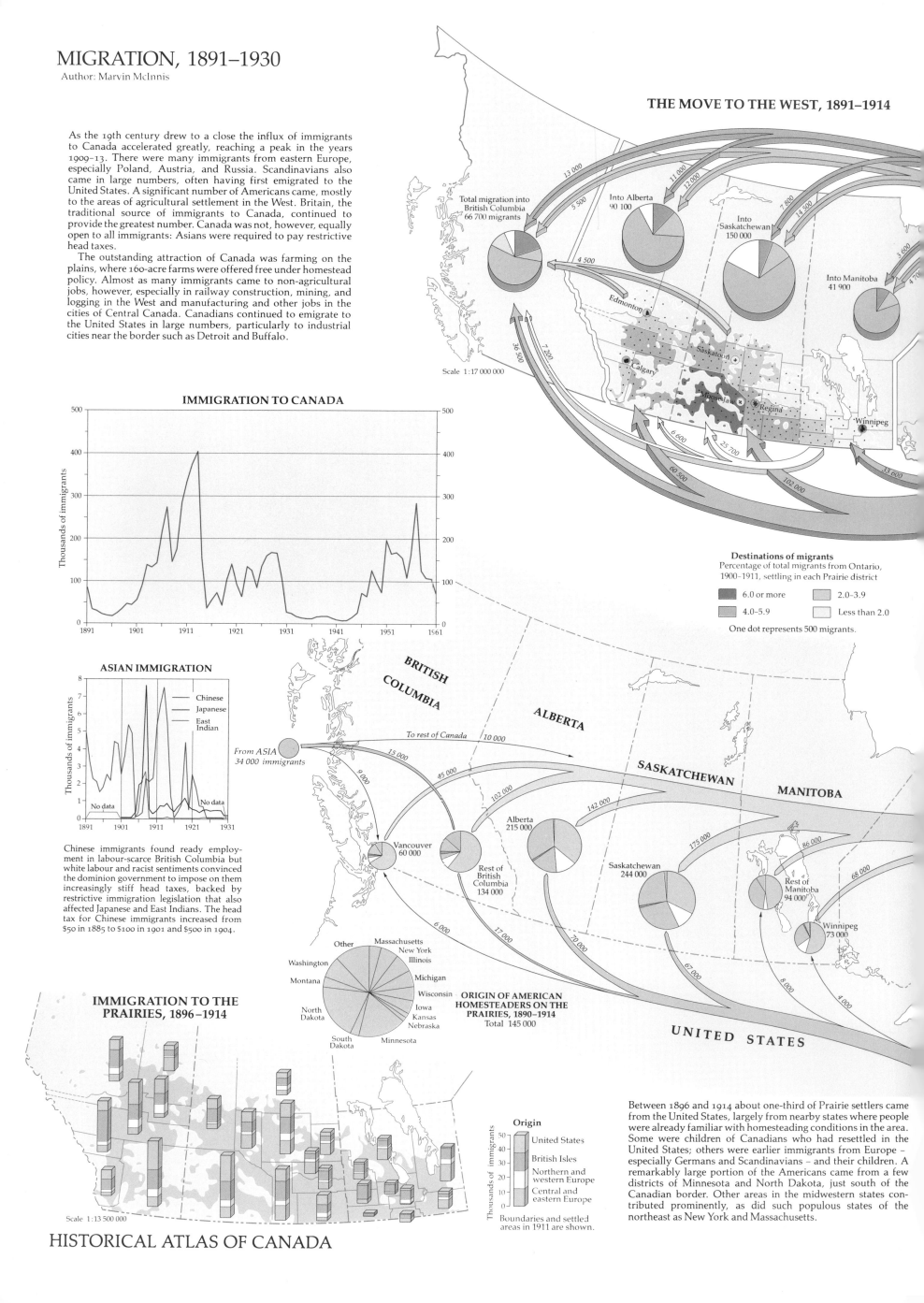

Total migration into British Columbia 66 700 migrants

Into Alberta 90 100

Into Saskatchewan 150 000

Into Manitoba 41 900

Edmonton

Calgary · Saskatoon · Regina · Moose Jaw · Winnipeg

Scale 1:17 000 000

Destinations of migrants
Percentage of total migrants from Ontario, 1900–1911, settling in each Prairie district

- 6.0 or more
- 4.0–5.9
- 2.0–3.9
- Less than 2.0

One dot represents 500 migrants.

IMMIGRATION TO CANADA

Thousands of immigrants

1891 1901 1911 1921 1931 1941 1951 1961

ASIAN IMMIGRATION

Thousands of immigrants

— Chinese
— Japanese
— East Indian

No data   No data

1891 1901 1911 1921 1931

Chinese immigrants found ready employment in labour-scarce British Columbia but white labour and racist sentiments convinced the dominion government to impose on them increasingly stiff head taxes, backed by restrictive immigration legislation that also affected Japanese and East Indians. The head tax for Chinese immigrants increased from $50 in 1885 to $100 in 1901 and $500 in 1904.

BRITISH COLUMBIA

ALBERTA

SASKATCHEWAN

MANITOBA

From ASIA 34 000 immigrants

To rest of Canada 10 000

15 000
9 000
45 000
102 000
142 000
175 000
86 000
68 000

Vancouver 60 000

Rest of British Columbia 134 000

Alberta 215 000

Saskatchewan 244 000

Rest of Manitoba 94 000

Winnipeg 73 000

6 000
17 000
70 000
67 000
8 000
4 000

ORIGIN OF AMERICAN HOMESTEADERS ON THE PRAIRIES, 1890–1914
Total 145 000

Other
Massachusetts
New York
Illinois
Michigan
Wisconsin
Iowa
Kansas
Nebraska
Minnesota
South Dakota
North Dakota
Montana
Washington

UNITED STATES

IMMIGRATION TO THE PRAIRIES, 1896–1914

Thousands of immigrants

Origin
- United States
- British Isles
- Northern and western Europe
- Central and eastern Europe

Boundaries and settled areas in 1911 are shown.

Scale 1:13 500 000

Between 1896 and 1914 about one-third of Prairie settlers came from the United States, largely from nearby states where people were already familiar with homesteading conditions in the area. Some were children of Canadians who had resettled in the United States; others were earlier immigrants from Europe – especially Germans and Scandinavians – and their children. A remarkably large portion of the Americans came from a few districts of Minnesota and North Dakota, just south of the Canadian border. Other areas in the midwestern states contributed prominently, as did such populous states of the northeast as New York and Massachusetts.

HISTORICAL ATLAS OF CANADA

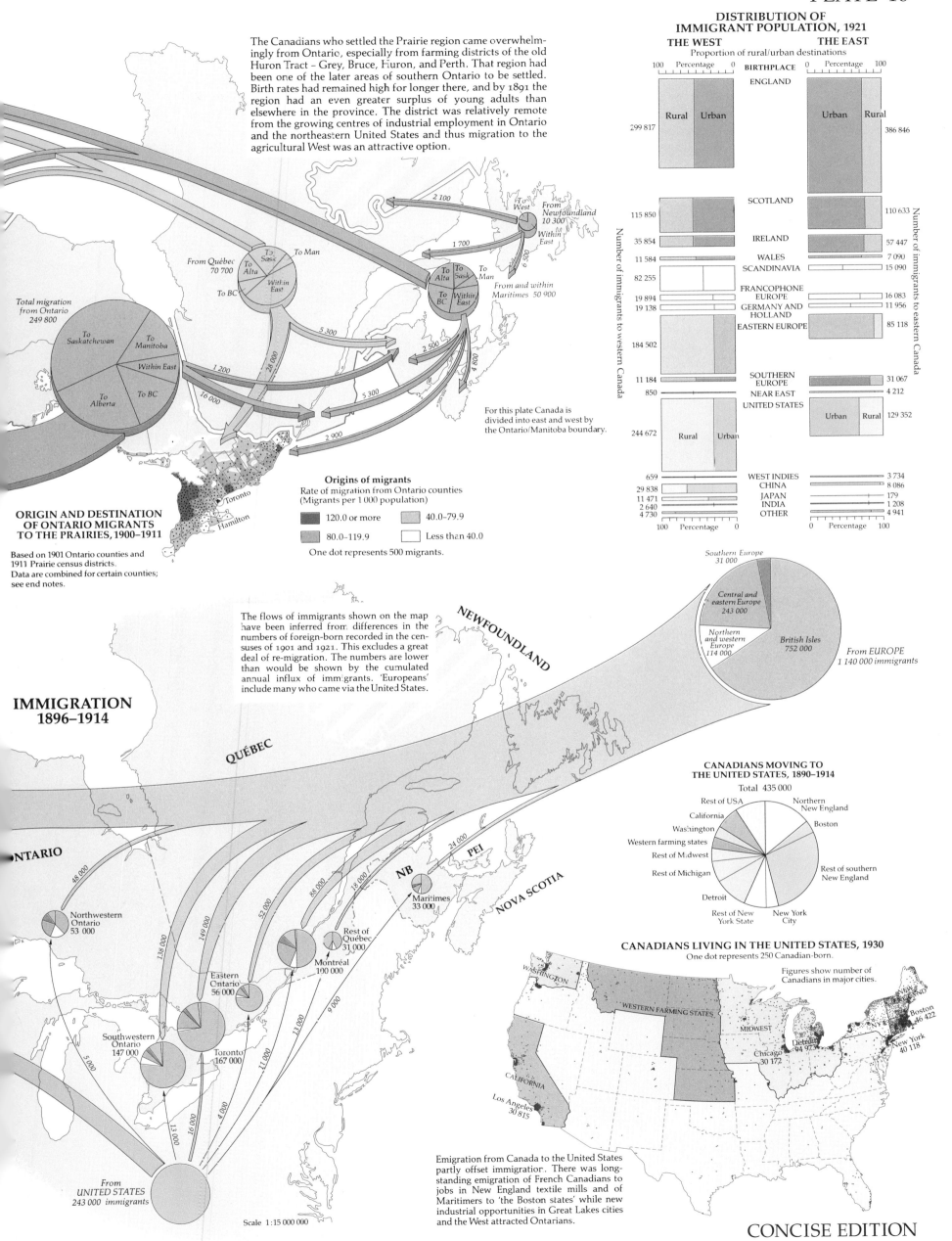

The Canadians who settled the Prairie region came overwhelmingly from Ontario, especially from farming districts of the old Huron Tract – Grey, Bruce, Huron, and Perth. That region had been one of the later areas of southern Ontario to be settled. Birth rates had remained high for longer there, and by 1891 the region had an even greater surplus of young adults than elsewhere in the province. The district was relatively remote from the growing centres of industrial employment in Ontario and the northeastern United States and thus migration to the agricultural West was an attractive option.

DISTRIBUTION OF IMMIGRANT POPULATION, 1921

THE WEST   THE EAST
Proportion of rural/urban destinations

For this plate Canada is divided into east and west by the Ontario/Manitoba boundary.

BIRTHPLACE	West	East
ENGLAND	299 817	386 846
SCOTLAND	115 850	110 633
IRELAND	35 854	57 447
WALES	11 584	7 090
SCANDINAVIA	82 255	15 090
FRANCOPHONE EUROPE	19 894	16 083
GERMANY AND HOLLAND	19 138	11 956
EASTERN EUROPE	184 502	85 118
SOUTHERN EUROPE	11 184	31 067
NEAR EAST	850	4 212
UNITED STATES	244 672	129 352
WEST INDIES	659	3 734
CHINA	29 838	8 086
JAPAN	11 471	179
INDIA	2 640	1 208
OTHER	4 730	4 941

Number of immigrants to western Canada
Number of immigrants to eastern Canada

ORIGIN AND DESTINATION OF ONTARIO MIGRANTS TO THE PRAIRIES, 1900–1911

Based on 1901 Ontario counties and 1911 Prairie census districts.
Data are combined for certain counties; see end notes.

Total migration from Ontario 249 800

To Saskatchewan
To Manitoba
Within East
To Alberta
To BC

From Québec 70 700
To Sask
To Alta
Within East
To Man
To BC

To West
From Newfoundland 10 300
Within East

From and within Maritimes 50 900
To Alta
To Sask
To Man
To BC
Within East

2 100
1 700
6 500
28 000
5 300
1 200
16 000
2 500
4 800
5 300
2 900

Toronto
Hamilton

Origins of migrants
Rate of migration from Ontario counties
(Migrants per 1 000 population)

- 120.0 or more
- 80.0–119.9
- 40.0–79.9
- Less than 40.0

One dot represents 500 migrants.

IMMIGRATION 1896–1914

The flows of immigrants shown on the map have been inferred from differences in the numbers of foreign-born recorded in the censuses of 1901 and 1921. This excludes a great deal of re-migration. The numbers are lower than would be shown by the cumulated annual influx of immigrants. 'Europeans' include many who came via the United States.

NEWFOUNDLAND

QUÉBEC

ONTARIO

NB   PEI
NOVA SCOTIA

Southern Europe 31 000
Central and eastern Europe 243 000
Northern and western Europe 114 000
British Isles 752 000

From EUROPE 1 140 000 immigrants

Northwestern Ontario 53 000
138 000
48 000
149 000
52 000
88 000
18 000
24 000
Maritimes 33 000
Rest of Québec 31 000
Montréal 100 000
Eastern Ontario 56 000
Southwestern Ontario 147 000
Toronto 167 000
11 000
9 000
13 000
4 000
5 000
13 000
16 000
4 000

From UNITED STATES 243 000 immigrants

Scale 1:15 000 000

CANADIANS MOVING TO THE UNITED STATES, 1890–1914
Total 435 000

Rest of USA
California
Washington
Western farming states
Rest of Midwest
Rest of Michigan
Detroit
Rest of New York State
New York City
Rest of southern New England
Boston
Northern New England

CANADIANS LIVING IN THE UNITED STATES, 1930
One dot represents 250 Canadian-born.

Figures show number of Canadians in major cities.

WASHINGTON
WESTERN FARMING STATES
MIDWEST
CALIFORNIA
Los Angeles 30 815
Chicago 30 172
Detroit 94 973
Boston 46 422
New York 40 118

Emigration from Canada to the United States partly offset immigration. There was long-standing emigration of French Canadians to jobs in New England textile mills and of Maritimers to 'the Boston states' while new industrial opportunities in Great Lakes cities and the West attracted Ontarians.

CONCISE EDITION

POPULATION CHANGES, 1941–1961

Authors: Marvin McInnis, Warren Kalbach, Donald Kerr

From 1946 to 1961 Canada's population grew remarkably, from
12 million to 18 million. The union of Newfoundland with
Canada added 360 000 people, but the main reason for rapid
growth was a great increase in immigration combined with
a dramatic rise in the birth rate. The 'baby boom' was unex-
pected and involved a significant and sustained increase in
average family size. It was an experience shared with the
United States and a few other countries, though the rise in fertility was greatest in Canada. By the end of the 1950s the birth
rate had reached its peak. Immigration surged after the Second
World War as Canada accepted many people displaced from
Europe by the war and its aftermath. The prosperity of the
Canadian economy also attracted large numbers from a Europe
still struggling to recover from the war. The immigrants came
at a time when the natural growth of Canada's labour force,
reflecting the low birth rate of the 1930s, was unusually small.
Rapidly growing urban Ontario was the favoured destination
of immigrants. By 1961 the great wave of immigration had
passed and the inflow had dropped to a modest level.

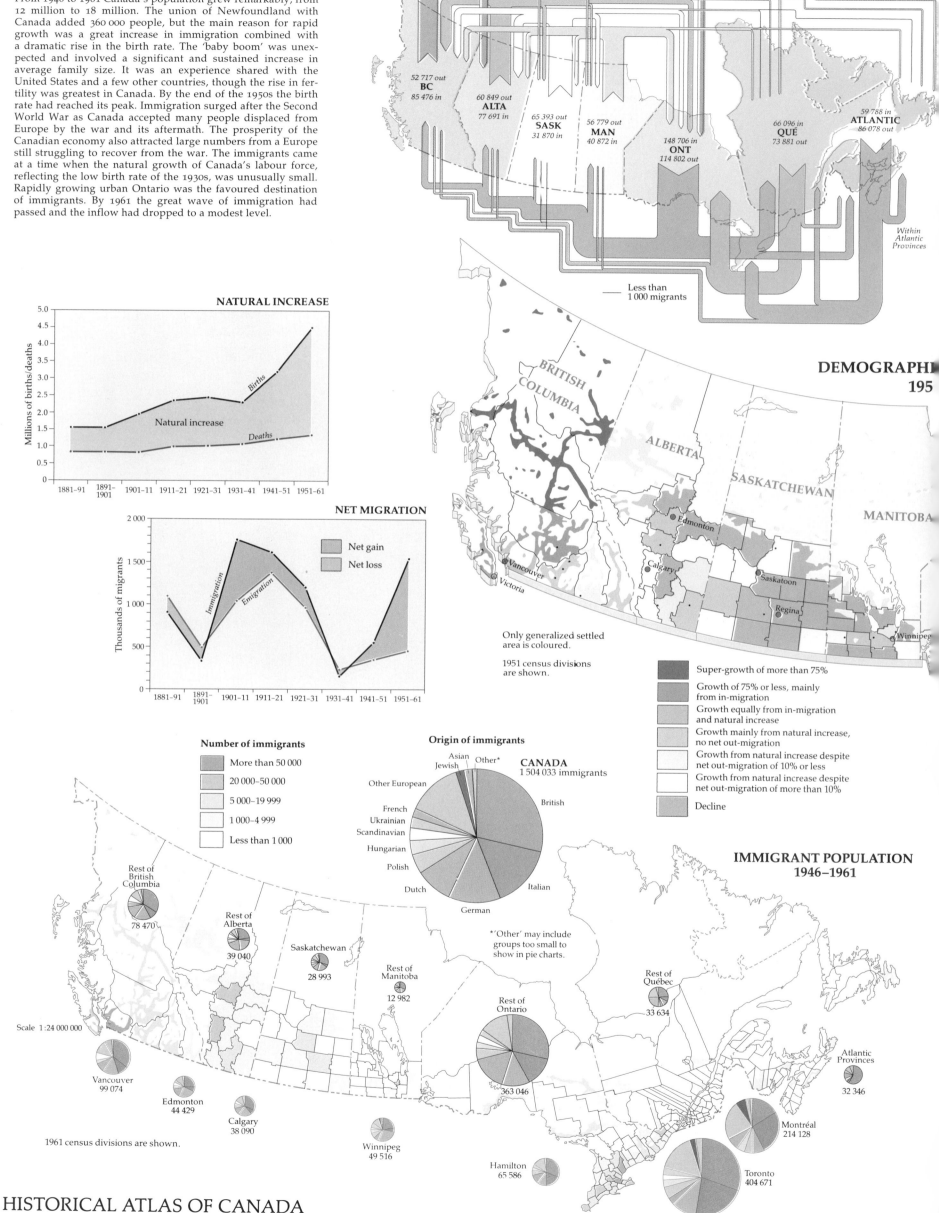

INTERPROVINCIAL MIGRATION 1956–1961

52 717 out
85 476 in
BC

60 849 out
77 691 in
ALTA

65 393 out
31 870 in
SASK

56 779 out
40 872 in
MAN

148 706 in
114 802 out
ONT

66 096 in
73 881 out
QUÉ

59 788 in
86 078 out
ATLANTIC

Within Atlantic Provinces

— Less than 1 000 migrants

NATURAL INCREASE

Births
Natural increase
Deaths

Millions of births/deaths

1881–91 · 1891–1901 · 1901–11 · 1911–21 · 1921–31 · 1931–41 · 1941–51 · 1951–61

NET MIGRATION

Net gain
Net loss

Immigration
Emigration

Thousands of migrants

1881–91 · 1891–1901 · 1901–11 · 1911–21 · 1921–31 · 1931–41 · 1941–51 · 1951–61

DEMOGRAPH... 195...

Only generalized settled
area is coloured.

1951 census divisions
are shown.

- Super-growth of more than 75%
- Growth of 75% or less, mainly from in-migration
- Growth equally from in-migration and natural increase
- Growth mainly from natural increase, no net out-migration
- Growth from natural increase despite net out-migration of 10% or less
- Growth from natural increase despite net out-migration of more than 10%
- Decline

BRITISH COLUMBIA · ALBERTA · SASKATCHEWAN · MANITOBA
Vancouver · Victoria · Edmonton · Calgary · Saskatoon · Regina · Winnipeg

Number of immigrants

- More than 50 000
- 20 000–50 000
- 5 000–19 999
- 1 000–4 999
- Less than 1 000

Origin of immigrants

Asian · Jewish · Other*
Other European
French
Ukrainian
Scandinavian
Hungarian
Polish
Dutch
German
Italian
British

CANADA
1 504 033 immigrants

*'Other' may include
groups too small to
show in pie charts.

IMMIGRANT POPULATION 1946–1961

Rest of British Columbia
78 470

Rest of Alberta
39 040

Saskatchewan
28 993

Rest of Manitoba
12 982

Rest of Ontario
363 046

Rest of Québec
33 634

Atlantic Provinces
32 346

Montréal
214 128

Vancouver
99 074

Edmonton
44 429

Calgary
38 090

Winnipeg
49 516

Hamilton
65 586

Toronto
404 671

Scale 1:24 000 000

1961 census divisions are shown.

HISTORICAL ATLAS OF CANADA

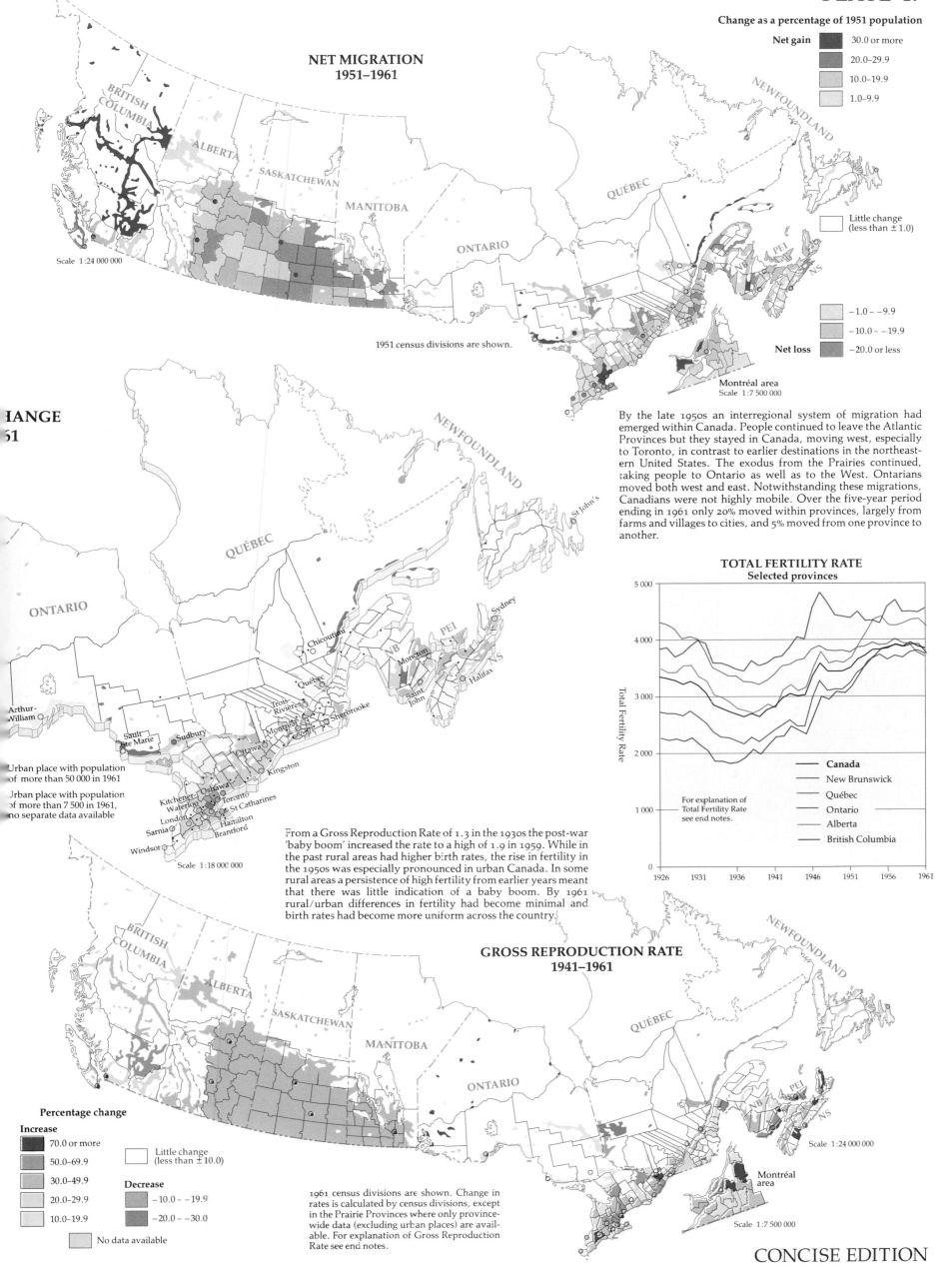

Change as a percentage of 1951 population

Net gain
- 30.0 or more
- 20.0–29.9
- 10.0–19.9
- 1.0–9.9

Little change (less than ±1.0)

- −1.0 – −9.9
- −10.0 – −19.9

Net loss
- −20.0 or less

NET MIGRATION 1951–1961

Scale 1:24 000 000

1951 census divisions are shown.

Montréal area
Scale 1:7 500 000

By the late 1950s an interregional system of migration had emerged within Canada. People continued to leave the Atlantic Provinces but they stayed in Canada, moving west, especially to Toronto, in contrast to earlier destinations in the northeastern United States. The exodus from the Prairies continued, taking people to Ontario as well as to the West. Ontarians moved both west and east. Notwithstanding these migrations, Canadians were not highly mobile. Over the five-year period ending in 1961 only 20% moved within provinces, largely from farms and villages to cities, and 5% moved from one province to another.

TOTAL FERTILITY RATE
Selected provinces

Total Fertility Rate

For explanation of Total Fertility Rate see end notes.

- **Canada**
- New Brunswick
- Québec
- Ontario
- Alberta
- British Columbia

1926 1931 1936 1941 1946 1951 1956 1961

Urban place with population of more than 50 000 in 1961

Urban place with population of more than 7 500 in 1961, no separate data available

Scale 1:18 000 000

From a Gross Reproduction Rate of 1.3 in the 1930s the post-war 'baby boom' increased the rate to a high of 1.9 in 1959. While in the past rural areas had higher birth rates, the rise in fertility in the 1950s was especially pronounced in urban Canada. In some rural areas a persistence of high fertility from earlier years meant that there was little indication of a baby boom. By 1961 rural/urban differences in fertility had become minimal and birth rates had become more uniform across the country.

GROSS REPRODUCTION RATE 1941–1961

Percentage change

Increase
- 70.0 or more
- 50.0–69.9
- 30.0–49.9
- 20.0–29.9
- 10.0–19.9

Little change (less than ±10.0)

Decrease
- −10.0 – −19.9
- −20.0 – −30.0

No data available

1961 census divisions are shown. Change in rates is calculated by census divisions, except in the Prairie Provinces where only province-wide data (excluding urban places) are available. For explanation of Gross Reproduction Rate see end notes.

Scale 1:24 000 000

Montréal area

Scale 1:7 500 000

CONCISE EDITION

POPULATION COMPOSITION, 1891–1961

Authors: Donald Cartwright, Murdo MacPherson

ETHNIC ORIGIN, 1901

The three maps show the ethnic origin of the dominant non-British group outside Québec and the dominant non-French group inside Québec. Circles are proportional to provincial population. Figures indicate population for provinces and cities.

Age
85 +
80–84
75–79
70–74
65–69
60–64
55–59
50–54
45–49
40–44
35–39
30–34
25–29
20–24
15–19
10–14
5–9
0–4

Male   Female

400 200   0   0 200 400
Thousands of persons

Québec
68 841

British Columbia
178 657

The Territories
211 649

Manitoba
255 211

Newfoundland

No data available

Québec
1 648 898

Ontario
2 182 947

Prince Edward Island
103 259

Nova Scotia
459 574

New Brunswick
331 120

Edmonton

Vancouver

Scale 1 : 26 000 000

Regina

Winnipeg

Vancouver
27 010

Edmonton
2 626

Regina
2 645

Winnipeg
42 340

Toronto
156 098

Ottawa
57 640

Montréal
203 078

Halifax
74 662

Québec

Montréal

Ottawa

Toronto

Halifax

From 1891 to 1961 the population of Canada almost quadrupled, from 4.8 million to 18.2 million. Before the Great War much of the growth was rural, especially in the rapid occupation of the western Prairies (pl 62). From the 1920s, and especially after the Second World War, urban population growth outstripped rural and by 1961 at least 70% of the population lived in urban centres, two-thirds of that number in metropolitan centres of over 100 000. Throughout the period the historical character of the population, largely British or French in origin, was significantly modified in much of Canada as a result of two great waves of European migration (1896–1913, 1946–61) (pll 16, 17). Ukrainian, German, and other European groups established rural settlements in the Prairies (pl 62), and in the 1950s a combination of large-scale immigration and migration from rural to urban areas increased the ethnic diversity of most Canadian cities dramatically.

ETHNIC ORIGIN, 1961

POPULATION PROFILE

Male

1200 1000 800 600 400 200
Thousands of persons

1 629 082

BRITISH COLUMBIA

1 331 944

ALBERTA

925 181

SASKATCHEWAN

921 686

MANITOBA

Edmonton

Vancouver

Regina

Winnipeg

Vancouver
384 522

Edmonton
281 027

Regina
112 141

Winnipeg
265 429

0   300 miles
0   300 kilometres
Scale 1 : 16 000 000

URBAN AND RURAL POPULATION

1901

NFLD

QUÉ

PEI

NB

NS

MAN

ONT

BC

Montréal

Toronto

1931

NFLD

QUÉ

PEI

NB

NS

SASK

MAN

ALTA

ONT

BC

Montréal

Québec

Winnipeg

Vancouver

Windsor

Ottawa

Toronto

Hamilton

1961

NFLD

QUÉ

PEI

NB

NS

Chicoutimi

Québec

Sydney

Halifax

SASK

MAN

ALTA

ONT

BC

Winnipeg

Sudbury

Regina

Edmonton

Calgary

Victoria

Vancouver

Montréal

Ottawa

Kitchener

Windsor

Hamilton

London

Toronto

Size of population
1 000 000 persons
500 000
100 000

Type of population
Rural
Urban
Metropolitan
Less than 1 000 or dispersed
1 000–100 000
More than 100 000

POPULATION GROWTH

Millions of persons

20

15

10

5

0

Total population

Urban

Rural

1891 1901 1911 1921 1931 1941 1951 1961

ETHNIC ORIGIN

British
French
German
Ukrainian
Italian
Dutch
No dominant non-British or non-French group

Scandinavian
Polish
Indian, Inuit
Jewish
Asian
Other

* Indicates majority status (see note)

1 Austro-Hungarian (includes Ukrainian, Bukovynian, Galician, and Ruthenian in 1901)
2 Austrian (1931, 1961)
3 Hungarian (1931, 1961)
4 Russian (largely Doukhobor)

'Other' may include some ethnic groups which are less than 1% of provincial or city populations; see end notes.

HISTORICAL ATLAS OF CANADA

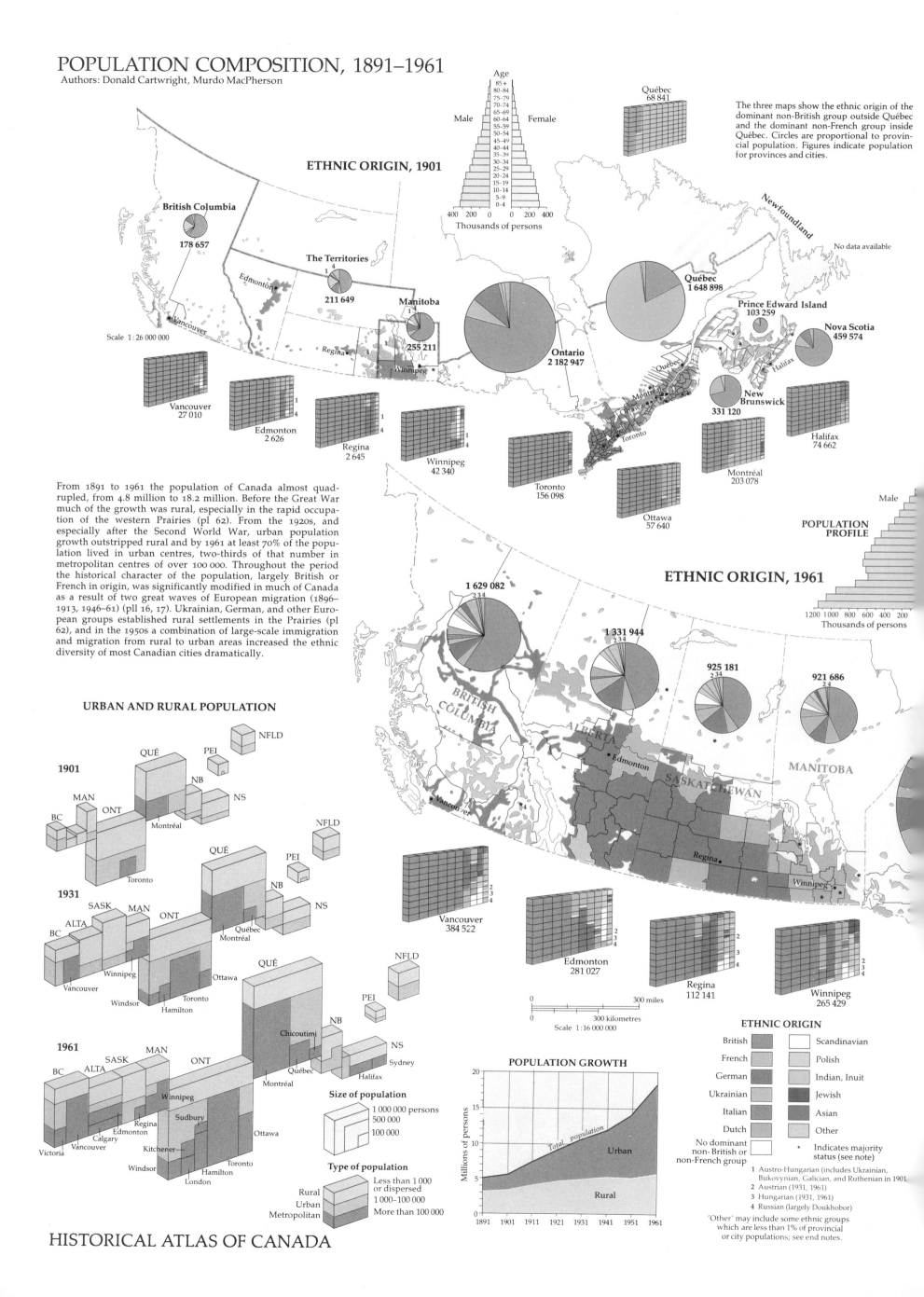

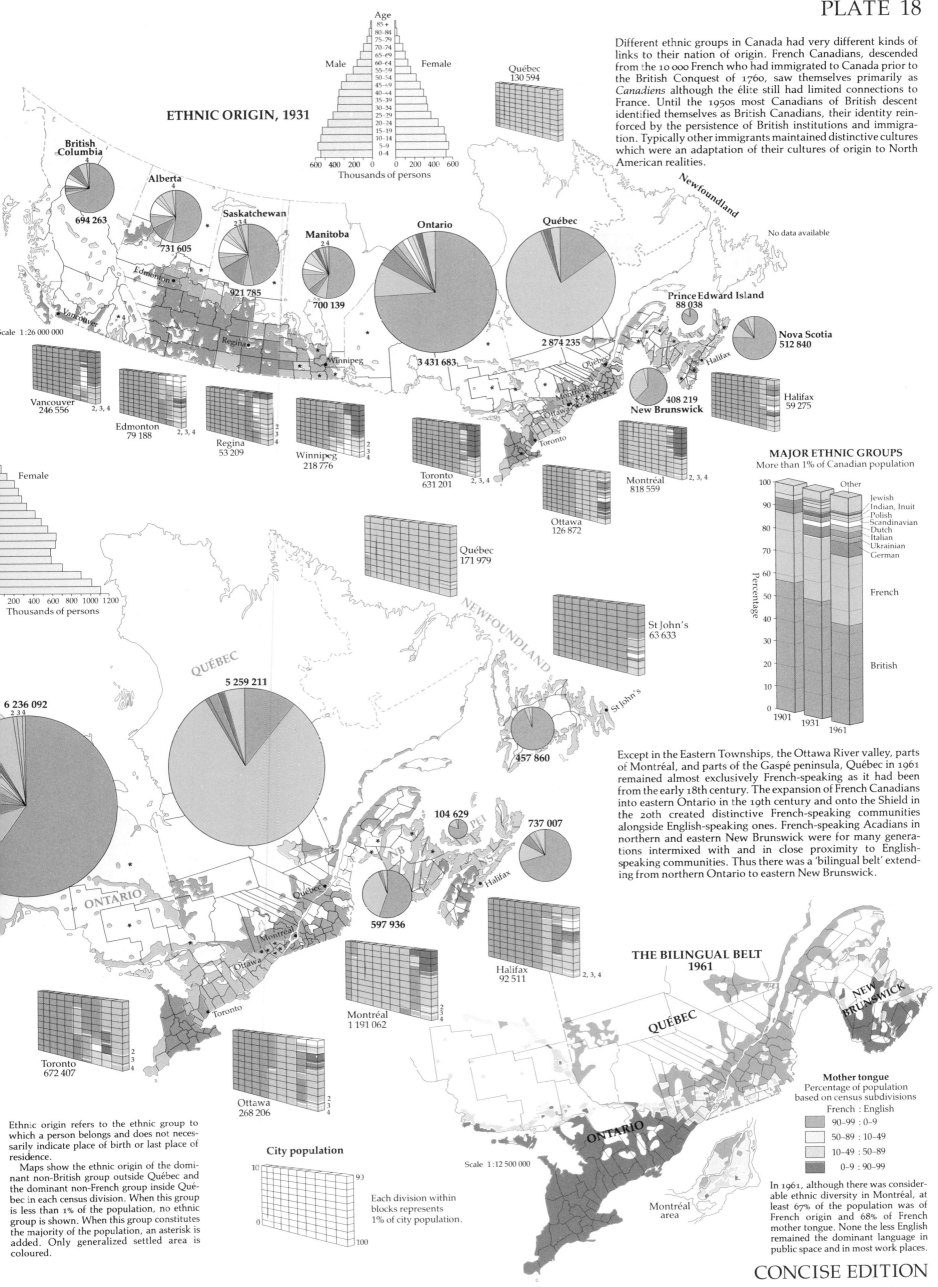

Different ethnic groups in Canada had very different kinds of links to their nation of origin. French Canadians, descended from the 10 000 French who had immigrated to Canada prior to the British Conquest of 1760, saw themselves primarily as *Canadiens* although the élite still had limited connections to France. Until the 1950s most Canadians of British descent identified themselves as British Canadians, their identity reinforced by the persistence of British institutions and immigration. Typically other immigrants maintained distinctive cultures which were an adaptation of their cultures of origin to North American realities.

ETHNIC ORIGIN, 1931

Age
85 +
80–84
75–79
70–74
65–69
60–64
55–59
50–54
45–49
40–44
35–39
30–34
25–29
20–24
15–19
10–14
5–9
0–4

Male · Female

600 400 200 0 0 200 400 600
Thousands of persons

British Columbia
694 263

Alberta
731 605

Saskatchewan
921 785

Manitoba
700 139

Ontario
3 431 683

Québec
2 874 235

Newfoundland
No data available

Prince Edward Island
88 038

Nova Scotia
512 840

New Brunswick
408 219

Québec
130 594

Scale 1:26 000 000

Vancouver
246 556 — 2, 3, 4

Edmonton
79 188 — 2, 3, 4

Regina
53 209

Winnipeg
218 776

Toronto
631 201 — 2, 3, 4

Montréal
818 559 — 2, 3, 4

Ottawa
126 872

Halifax
59 275

Female

200 400 600 800 1000 1200
Thousands of persons

MAJOR ETHNIC GROUPS
More than 1% of Canadian population

100
90
80
70
60
50
40
30
20
10
0

Percentage

1901 1931 1961

Other
Jewish
Indian, Inuit
Polish
Scandinavian
Dutch
Italian
Ukrainian
German
French
British

Québec
171 979

St John's
63 633

Ottawa
268 206

6 236 092 — 2 3 4

QUÉBEC
5 259 211

NEWFOUNDLAND

St John's
457 860

104 629

PEI

737 007

ONTARIO

597 936

104 629

Québec

Montréal

Ottawa

Toronto

Halifax
92 511 — 2, 3, 4

Toronto
672 407 — 2 3 4

Montréal
1 191 062 — 2 3 4

Ottawa
268 206 — 2 3 4

Except in the Eastern Townships, the Ottawa River valley, parts of Montréal, and parts of the Gaspé peninsula, Québec in 1961 remained almost exclusively French-speaking as it had been from the early 18th century. The expansion of French Canadians into eastern Ontario in the 19th century and onto the Shield in the 20th created distinctive French-speaking communities alongside English-speaking ones. French-speaking Acadians in northern and eastern New Brunswick were for many generations intermixed with and in close proximity to English-speaking communities. Thus there was a 'bilingual belt' extending from northern Ontario to eastern New Brunswick.

THE BILINGUAL BELT 1961

NEW BRUNSWICK

QUÉBEC

ONTARIO

Montréal area

Scale 1:12 500 000

Ethnic origin refers to the ethnic group to which a person belongs and does not necessarily indicate place of birth or last place of residence.

Maps show the ethnic origin of the dominant non-British group outside Québec and the dominant non-French group inside Québec in each census division. When this group is less than 1% of the population, no ethnic group is shown. When this group constitutes the majority of the population, an asterisk is added. Only generalized settled area is coloured.

City population

10 90

0 100

Each division within blocks represents 1% of city population.

Mother tongue
Percentage of population based on census subdivisions
French : English

90–99 : 0–9
50–89 : 10–49
10–49 : 50–89
0–9 : 90–99

In 1961, although there was considerable ethnic diversity in Montréal, at least 67% of the population was of French origin and 68% of French mother tongue. None the less English remained the dominant language in public space and in most work places.

CONCISE EDITION

THE EMERGENCE OF A TRANSPORTATION SYSTEM, 1837–1852

Author: Andrew F. Burghardt

An adequate system of transportation developed very slowly in British North America. Most of the population lived next to shorelines and rivers, and people and freight moved by water. In 1812 the only stage runs were around the St Lawrence rapids and Niagara Falls, from Montréal to Québec, and from Québec to Boston. By 1837 steamboats ran daily, from April to November, between Montréal and Québec, between Prescott and Kingston, and from Kingston to Toronto, Niagara, and Oswego. Elsewhere boats ran at best three times a week. Macadamization of roads began in 1837, making scheduled stage runs possible. Daily coach service (except Sundays) existed only between Montréal and Prescott and north of Toronto. Travellers from Britain could reach Montréal (via Boston) more quickly than they could get to Québec. A trip from Toronto to London, Ontario, cost a labourer one month's wages. Except for migration, travel was beyond the means of most people.

The pre-rail transport network, dominated by the steamboat, reached its climax in 1852. The linear Québec-Windsor corridor was in place. The deepening of the St Lawrence canals by 1848 completed the water transport network. The cut at Burlington Bay had opened up Hamilton Harbour; the Chambly Canal opened the Richelieu to Lake Champlain; St Anne's Canal tied in the Ottawa River; and the Welland Canal linked Lakes Ontario, Erie, and Huron. In addition to the expected centres – Montréal, Québec, Toronto, Halifax, and Saint John – the major nodes included Hamilton, the principal land-water interchange, and Kingston, the boat centre *par excellence*. Pictou and Arichat, NS, Shediac, NB, and Cobourg, Port Hope, and Chatham in Canada West (Ontario) were enjoying their zenith as transportation centres. The only true feeder network of stage lines developed west of Hamilton. One integrated system had been organized: William Weller's Royal Mail from Niagara to Montréal.

TRANSPORTATION SERVICE SUMMER 1837

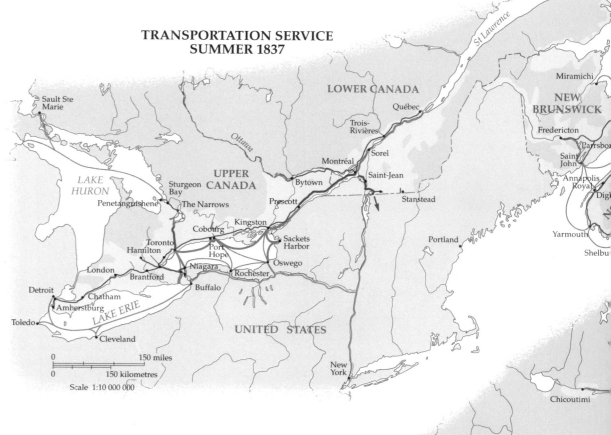

CARGO ORIGINS AND DESTINATIONS, 1851–1852

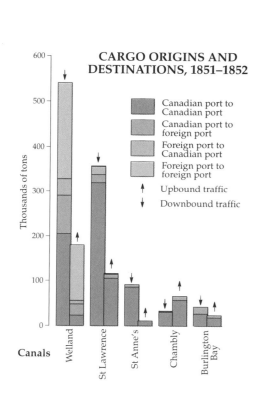

- Canadian port to Canadian port
- Canadian port to foreign port
- Foreign port to Canadian port
- Foreign port to foreign port
- ↑ Upbound traffic
- ↓ Downbound traffic

Thousands of tons

Canals: Welland, St Lawrence, St Anne's, Chambly, Burlington Bay

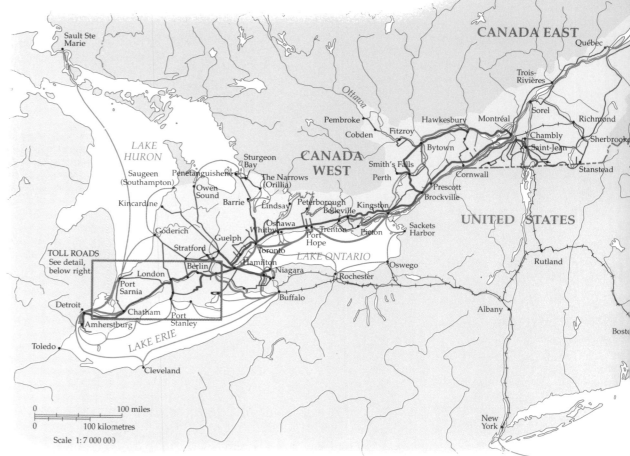

WELLAND CANAL SYSTEM, 1851

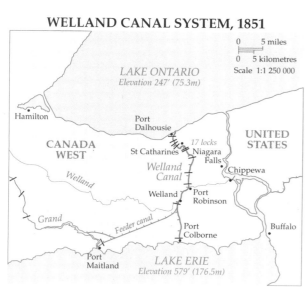

LAKE ONTARIO
Elevation 247' (75.3m)

LAKE ERIE
Elevation 579' (176.5m)

0 — 5 miles
0 — 5 kilometres
Scale 1:1 250 000

WELLAND CANAL CARGO

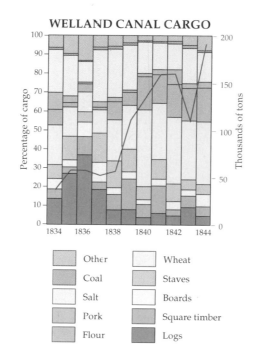

Percentage of cargo / Thousands of tons

1834 1836 1838 1840 1842 1844

- Other
- Coal
- Salt
- Pork
- Flour
- Wheat
- Staves
- Boards
- Square timber
- Logs

The Royal Mail, drawing by C.W. Jefferys

Courtesy of National Archives of Canada, Ottawa, C 69849, and Robert Stacey

HISTORICAL ATLAS OF CANADA

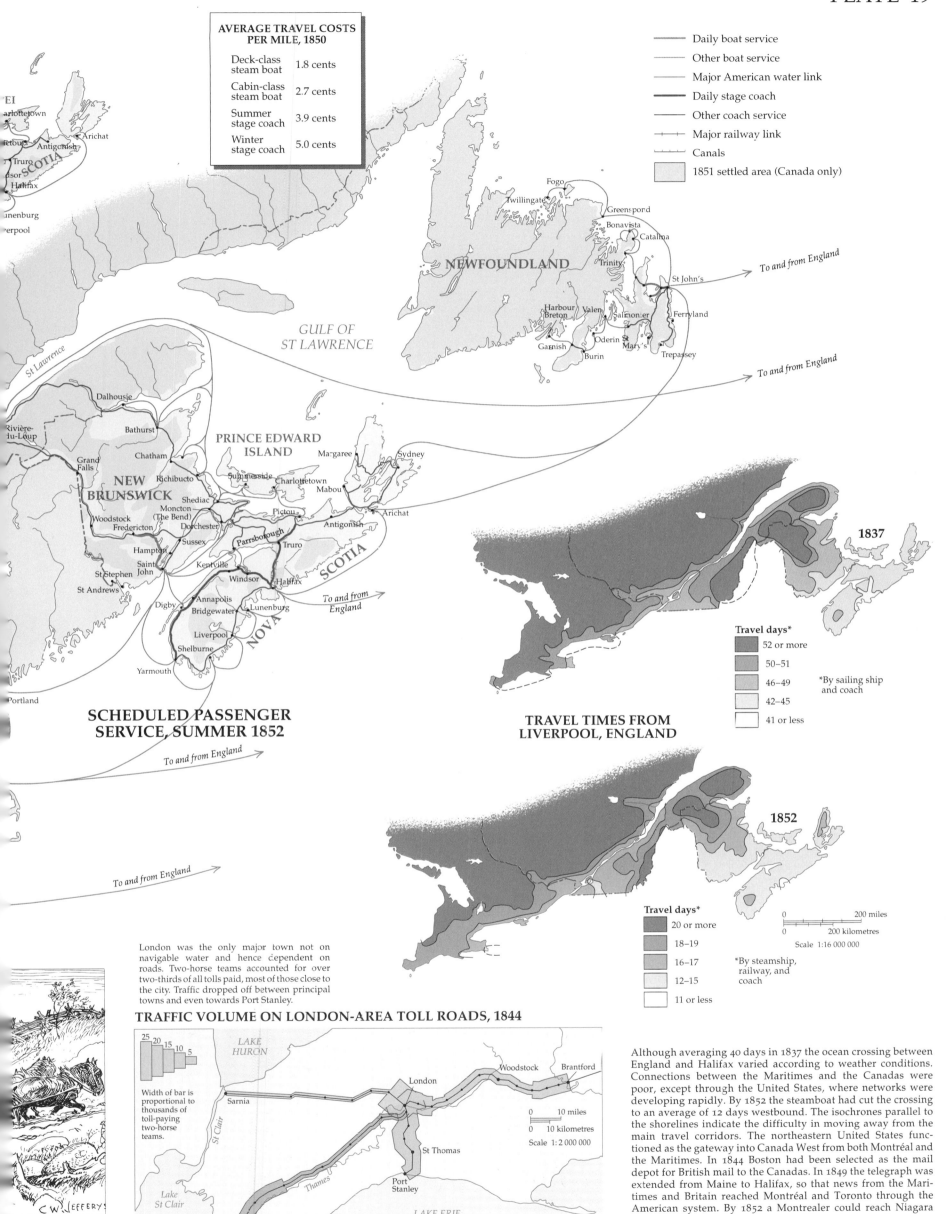

AVERAGE TRAVEL COSTS PER MILE, 1850

Deck-class steam boat	1.8 cents
Cabin-class steam boat	2.7 cents
Summer stage coach	3.9 cents
Winter stage coach	5.0 cents

Daily boat service
Other boat service
Major American water link
Daily stage coach
Other coach service
Major railway link
Canals
1851 settled area (Canada only)

NEWFOUNDLAND

GULF OF ST LAWRENCE

To and from England

PRINCE EDWARD ISLAND

NEW BRUNSWICK

NOVA SCOTIA

To and from England

SCHEDULED PASSENGER SERVICE, SUMMER 1852

TRAVEL TIMES FROM LIVERPOOL, ENGLAND

1837

Travel days*
52 or more
50–51
46–49
42–45
41 or less

*By sailing ship and coach

1852

Travel days*
20 or more
18–19
16–17
12–15
11 or less

*By steamship, railway, and coach

0   200 miles
0   200 kilometres
Scale 1:16 000 000

London was the only major town not on navigable water and hence dependent on roads. Two-horse teams accounted for over two-thirds of all tolls paid, most of those close to the city. Traffic dropped off between principal towns and even towards Port Stanley.

TRAFFIC VOLUME ON LONDON-AREA TOLL ROADS, 1844

25 20 15 10 5

Width of bar is proportional to thousands of toll-paying two-horse teams.

LAKE HURON

Sarnia
London
Woodstock
Brantford

St Thomas
Port Stanley
Chatham

St Clair
Thames
Lake St Clair
LAKE ERIE

0   10 miles
0   10 kilometres
Scale 1:2 000 000

C W JEFFERYS

Although averaging 40 days in 1837 the ocean crossing between England and Halifax varied according to weather conditions. Connections between the Maritimes and the Canadas were poor, except through the United States, where networks were developing rapidly. By 1852 the steamboat had cut the crossing to an average of 12 days westbound. The isochrones parallel to the shorelines indicate the difficulty in moving away from the main travel corridors. The northeastern United States functioned as the gateway into Canada West from both Montréal and the Maritimes. In 1844 Boston had been selected as the mail depot for British mail to the Canadas. In 1849 the telegraph was extended from Maine to Halifax, so that news from the Maritimes and Britain reached Montréal and Toronto through the American system. By 1852 a Montrealer could reach Niagara more quickly and cheaply through Albany, by train, than along Lake Ontario. The St Lawrence estuary was a transportational backwater.

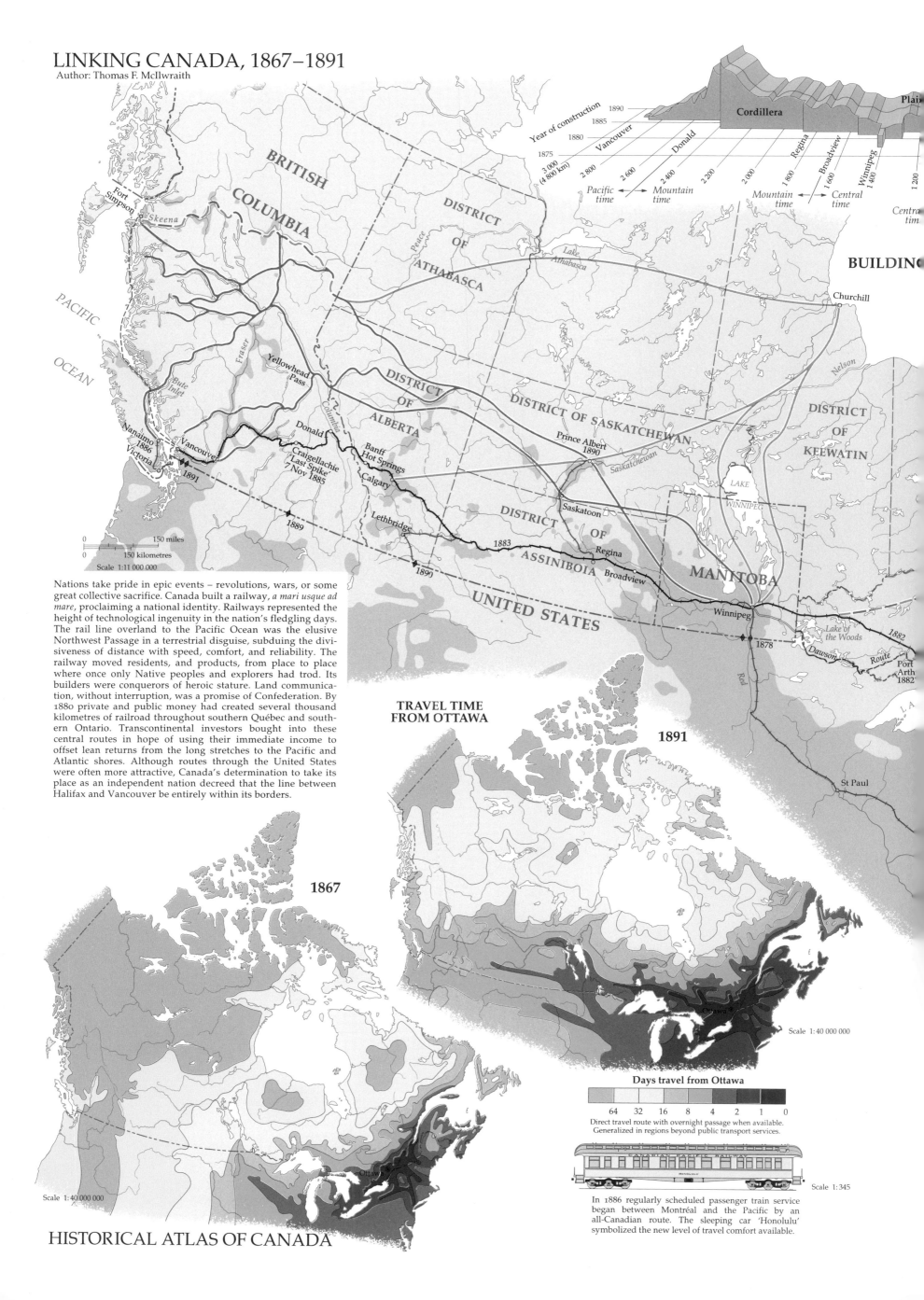

LINKING CANADA, 1867–1891
Author: Thomas F. McIlwraith

BUILDING

Nations take pride in epic events – revolutions, wars, or some great collective sacrifice. Canada built a railway, *a mari usque ad mare*, proclaiming a national identity. Railways represented the height of technological ingenuity in the nation's fledgling days. The rail line overland to the Pacific Ocean was the elusive Northwest Passage in a terrestrial disguise, subduing the divisiveness of distance with speed, comfort, and reliability. The railway moved residents, and products, from place to place where once only Native peoples and explorers had trod. Its builders were conquerors of heroic stature. Land communication, without interruption, was a promise of Confederation. By 1880 private and public money had created several thousand kilometres of railroad throughout southern Québec and southern Ontario. Transcontinental investors bought into these central routes in hope of using their immediate income to offset lean returns from the long stretches to the Pacific and Atlantic shores. Although routes through the United States were often more attractive, Canada's determination to take its place as an independent nation decreed that the line between Halifax and Vancouver be entirely within its borders.

TRAVEL TIME FROM OTTAWA

1891

1867

Scale 1:40 000 000

Scale 1:40 000 000

Days travel from Ottawa

| 64 | 32 | 16 | 8 | 4 | 2 | 1 | 0 |

Direct travel route with overnight passage when available. Generalized in regions beyond public transport services.

Scale 1:345

In 1886 regularly scheduled passenger train service began between Montréal and the Pacific by an all-Canadian route. The sleeping car 'Honolulu' symbolized the new level of travel comfort available.

HISTORICAL ATLAS OF CANADA

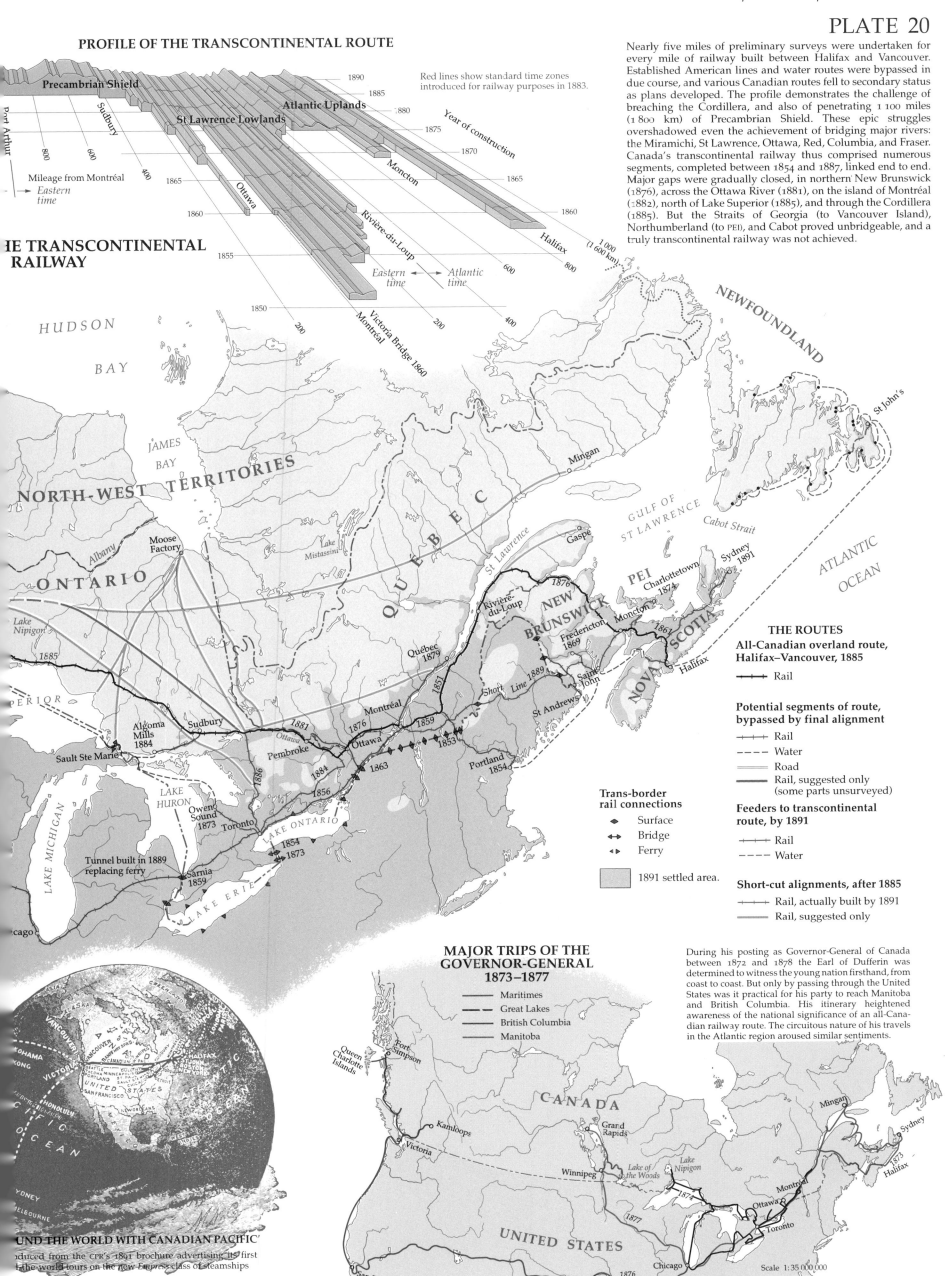

PROFILE OF THE TRANSCONTINENTAL ROUTE

Precambrian Shield

Port Arthur

Sudbury

St Lawrence Lowlands

Atlantic Uplands

Red lines show standard time zones introduced for railway purposes in 1883.

Year of construction

Mileage from Montréal

Eastern time

800

600

400

200

Moncton

Rivière-du-Loup

Ottawa

Victoria Bridge 1860

Montréal

Eastern time ←→ *Atlantic time*

Halifax

1 000 (1 600 km)

800

600

400

200

1890
1885
1880
1875
1870
1865
1860
1855
1850

THE TRANSCONTINENTAL RAILWAY

Nearly five miles of preliminary surveys were undertaken for every mile of railway built between Halifax and Vancouver. Established American lines and water routes were bypassed in due course, and various Canadian routes fell to secondary status as plans developed. The profile demonstrates the challenge of breaching the Cordillera, and also of penetrating 1 100 miles (1 800 km) of Precambrian Shield. These epic struggles overshadowed even the achievement of bridging major rivers: the Miramichi, St Lawrence, Ottawa, Red, Columbia, and Fraser. Canada's transcontinental railway thus comprised numerous segments, completed between 1854 and 1887, linked end to end. Major gaps were gradually closed, in northern New Brunswick (1876), across the Ottawa River (1881), on the island of Montréal (±882), north of Lake Superior (1885), and through the Cordillera (1885). But the Straits of Georgia (to Vancouver Island), Northumberland (to PEI), and Cabot proved unbridgeable, and a truly transcontinental railway was not achieved.

HUDSON BAY

JAMES BAY

NORTH-WEST TERRITORIES

ONTARIO

QUEBEC

NEWFOUNDLAND

St John's

Mingan

GULF OF ST LAWRENCE

Cabot Strait

ATLANTIC OCEAN

Gaspé

St Lawrence

PEI

Charlottetown 1874

Sydney 1891

Moose Factory

Albany

Lake Mistassini

Lake Nipigon

Québec 1879

Rivière-du-Loup

NEW BRUNSWICK

Fredericton 1869

Moncton

NOVA SCOTIA

1861

Halifax

1885

SUPERIOR

Sudbury

1881

Montréal

1876

Ottawa

1859

Saint John

Short Line 1889

St Andrews

Algoma Mills 1884

Pembroke

Ottawa

1884

1863

1853

Portland 1854

Sault Ste Marie

1886

1856

LAKE HURON

Owen Sound 1873

Toronto

1854

1873

LAKE ONTARIO

LAKE MICHIGAN

Tunnel built in 1889 replacing ferry

Sarnia 1859

LAKE ERIE

Chicago

THE ROUTES

All-Canadian overland route, Halifax–Vancouver, 1885

─┼─┼─ Rail

Potential segments of route, bypassed by final alignment

─┼─┼─ Rail

– – – Water

═══ Road

━━━ Rail, suggested only (some parts unsurveyed)

Feeders to transcontinental route, by 1891

─┼─┼─ Rail

– – – Water

Trans-border rail connections

◆ Surface

◆▶ Bridge

◀▶ Ferry

▨ 1891 settled area.

Short-cut alignments, after 1885

─┼─┼─ Rail, actually built by 1891

──── Rail, suggested only

MAJOR TRIPS OF THE GOVERNOR-GENERAL 1873–1877

──── Maritimes

━ ━ ━ Great Lakes

──── British Columbia

──── Manitoba

During his posting as Governor-General of Canada between 1872 and 1878 the Earl of Dufferin was determined to witness the young nation firsthand, from coast to coast. But only by passing through the United States was it practical for his party to reach Manitoba and British Columbia. His itinerary heightened awareness of the national significance of an all-Canadian railway route. The circuitous nature of his travels in the Atlantic region aroused similar sentiments.

Queen Charlotte Islands

Fort Simpson

CANADA

Kamloops

Victoria

Grand Rapids

Lake of the Woods

Lake Nipigon

Winnipeg

1874

1877

Mingan

Montréal

Ottawa

Toronto

1873

Halifax

Sydney

UNITED STATES

Chicago

San Francisco

1876

Scale 1:35 000 000

'OUND THE WORLD WITH CANADIAN PACIFIC'

duced from the CPR's 1891 brochure advertising its first the world tours on the new *Empress* class of steamships

VANCOUVER

VICTORIA

HONOLULU

YOKOHAMA

HONG KONG

SAN FRANCISCO

UNITED STATES

HALIFAX

ATLANTIC OCEAN

PACIFIC OCEAN

SYDNEY

MELBOURNE

CONCISE EDITION

THE EMERGENCE OF THE URBAN SYSTEM, 1888–1932

Authors: James W. Simmons, Michael Conzen (railways), Donald Kerr (telephones)

In 1891 30% of the population lived in 297 places of 1 000 people or more, and these urban centres were concentrated in the Maritimes, southern Québec, and southern Ontario. One example of the level of interaction between places is the frequency of passenger-train service. Here it indicates that, although the regions were linked, contacts were generally infrequent and many peripheral locations were still not connected to the rest of the system. Only in southern Ontario were there sufficient branch lines to integrate the region effectively.

THE URBAN NETWORK, 1891

Scale 1:30 000 000

Scale 1:12 500 000

THE URBAN NETWORK, 1921

Scale 1:15 000 000

The long-distance telephone network indicates the possibility of connections among places but not the frequency of calls. With the gradual introduction of copper open-wire transmission lines in the late 1880s, the range of calls increased from about 80 km to several hundred kilometres. Capacity remained limited; the single circuit between Montréal and Toronto, for example, was able to carry only five three-minute calls per hour in 1905. The introduction of loading coils and electronic repeaters just before the First World War and more rapidly in the 1920s increased the range, frequency, and quality of calls significantly.

THE LONG-DISTANCE TELEPHONE NETWORK, 1888–1932

Data incomplete for Nova Scotia

Although Canada was served by transcontinental railways early in the 20th century, the evolution of a long-distance telephone network came more slowly. The divided jurisdictions of eight provincial and regional companies and the technical and economic problems of transmitting signals across great and often sparsely populated distances worked against effective interregional communication. Long-distance calls between regions in Canada often travelled through the United States, being switched at centres such as Chicago and Boston along the lines of the American Telephone and Telegraph Company. Improvements in technology and, above all, the strong resolve of Canadian companies to establish a transcontinental system eventually made possible the completion of an all-Canadian trunk-line (Trans-Canada Telephone System) in 1932.

Scale 1:33 000 000

- - - Trans-Canada Telephone System and repeater stations, 1932

HISTORICAL ATLAS OF CANADA

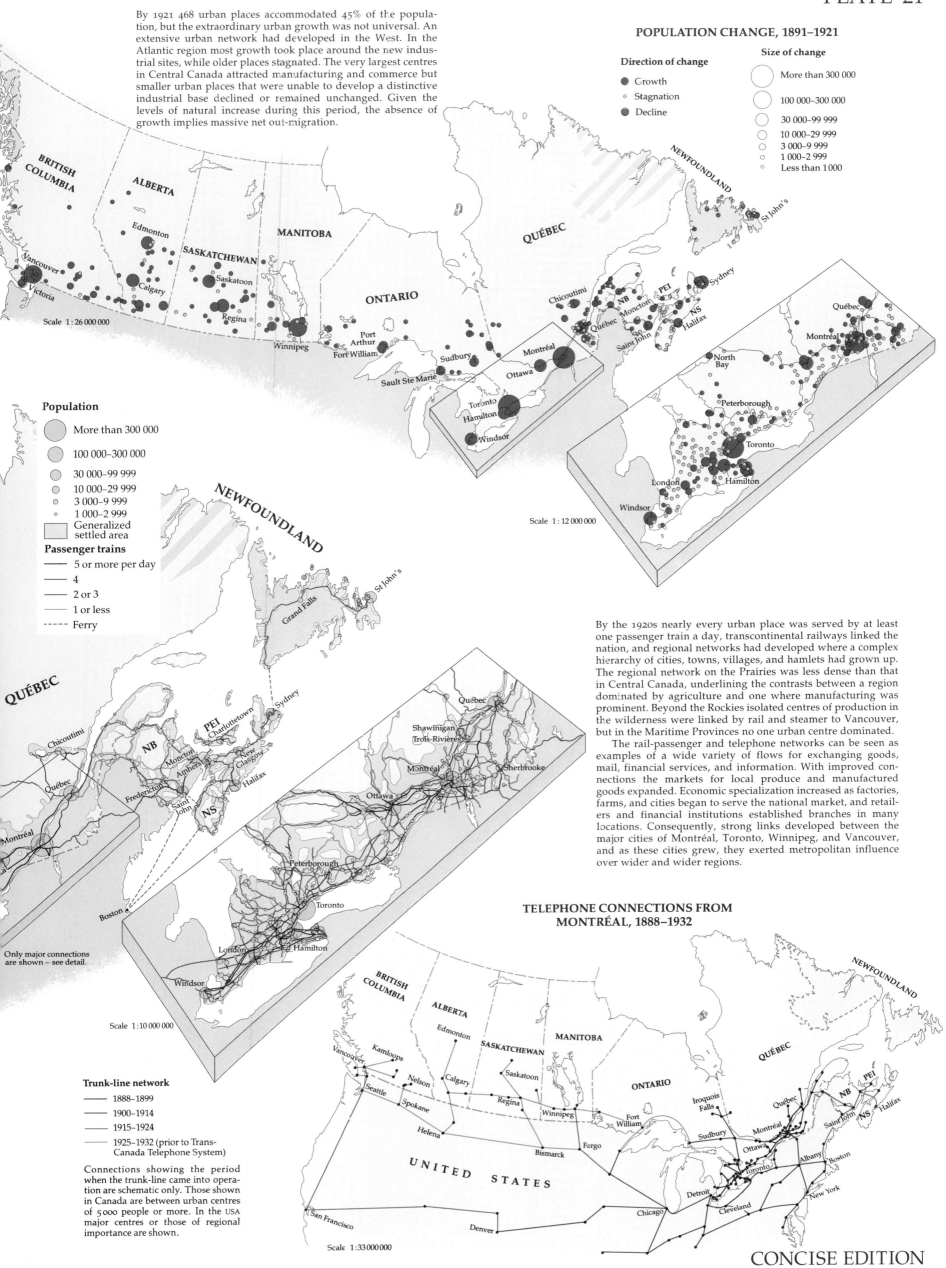

By 1921 468 urban places accommodated 45% of the population, but the extraordinary urban growth was not universal. An extensive urban network had developed in the West. In the Atlantic region most growth took place around the new industrial sites, while older places stagnated. The very largest centres in Central Canada attracted manufacturing and commerce but smaller urban places that were unable to develop a distinctive industrial base declined or remained unchanged. Given the levels of natural increase during this period, the absence of growth implies massive net out-migration.

POPULATION CHANGE, 1891–1921

Direction of change
- Growth
- Stagnation
- Decline

Size of change
- More than 300 000
- 100 000–300 000
- 30 000–99 999
- 10 000–29 999
- 3 000–9 999
- 1 000–2 999
- Less than 1 000

Scale 1 : 12 000 000

Population
- More than 300 000
- 100 000–300 000
- 30 000–99 999
- 10 000–29 999
- 3 000–9 999
- 1 000–2 999
- Generalized settled area

Passenger trains
- 5 or more per day
- 4
- 2 or 3
- 1 or less
- Ferry

Scale 1 : 26 000 000

Only major connections are shown – see detail.

Scale 1:10 000 000

Trunk-line network
- 1888–1899
- 1900–1914
- 1915–1924
- 1925–1932 (prior to Trans-Canada Telephone System)

Connections showing the period when the trunk-line came into operation are schematic only. Those shown in Canada are between urban centres of 5 000 people or more. In the USA major centres or those of regional importance are shown.

By the 1920s nearly every urban place was served by at least one passenger train a day, transcontinental railways linked the nation, and regional networks had developed where a complex hierarchy of cities, towns, villages, and hamlets had grown up. The regional network on the Prairies was less dense than that in Central Canada, underlining the contrasts between a region dominated by agriculture and one where manufacturing was prominent. Beyond the Rockies isolated centres of production in the wilderness were linked by rail and steamer to Vancouver, but in the Maritime Provinces no one urban centre dominated.

The rail-passenger and telephone networks can be seen as examples of a wide variety of flows for exchanging goods, mail, financial services, and information. With improved connections the markets for local produce and manufactured goods expanded. Economic specialization increased as factories, farms, and cities began to serve the national market, and retailers and financial institutions established branches in many locations. Consequently, strong links developed between the major cities of Montréal, Toronto, Winnipeg, and Vancouver, and as these cities grew, they exerted metropolitan influence over wider and wider regions.

TELEPHONE CONNECTIONS FROM MONTRÉAL, 1888–1932

Scale 1:33 000 000

CONCISE EDITION

THE INTEGRATION OF THE URBAN SYSTEM, 1921–1961

Authors: James W. Simmons, Michael Conzen (railways)

ECONOMIC SPECIALIZATION, 1961

ECONOMIC BASE OF URBAN-CENTRED REGIONS[1]

Primary sector[2]
- Fishing
- Forestry
- Mining
- Agriculture
- Two or more primary industries

Secondary sector
- Manufacturing
- Manufacturing and primary industries
- Manufacturing and tertiary industries

Tertiary sector
- Transportation
- Public administration
- Tertiary and primary industries

1 Based on census divisions
2 Includes processing of primary commodities

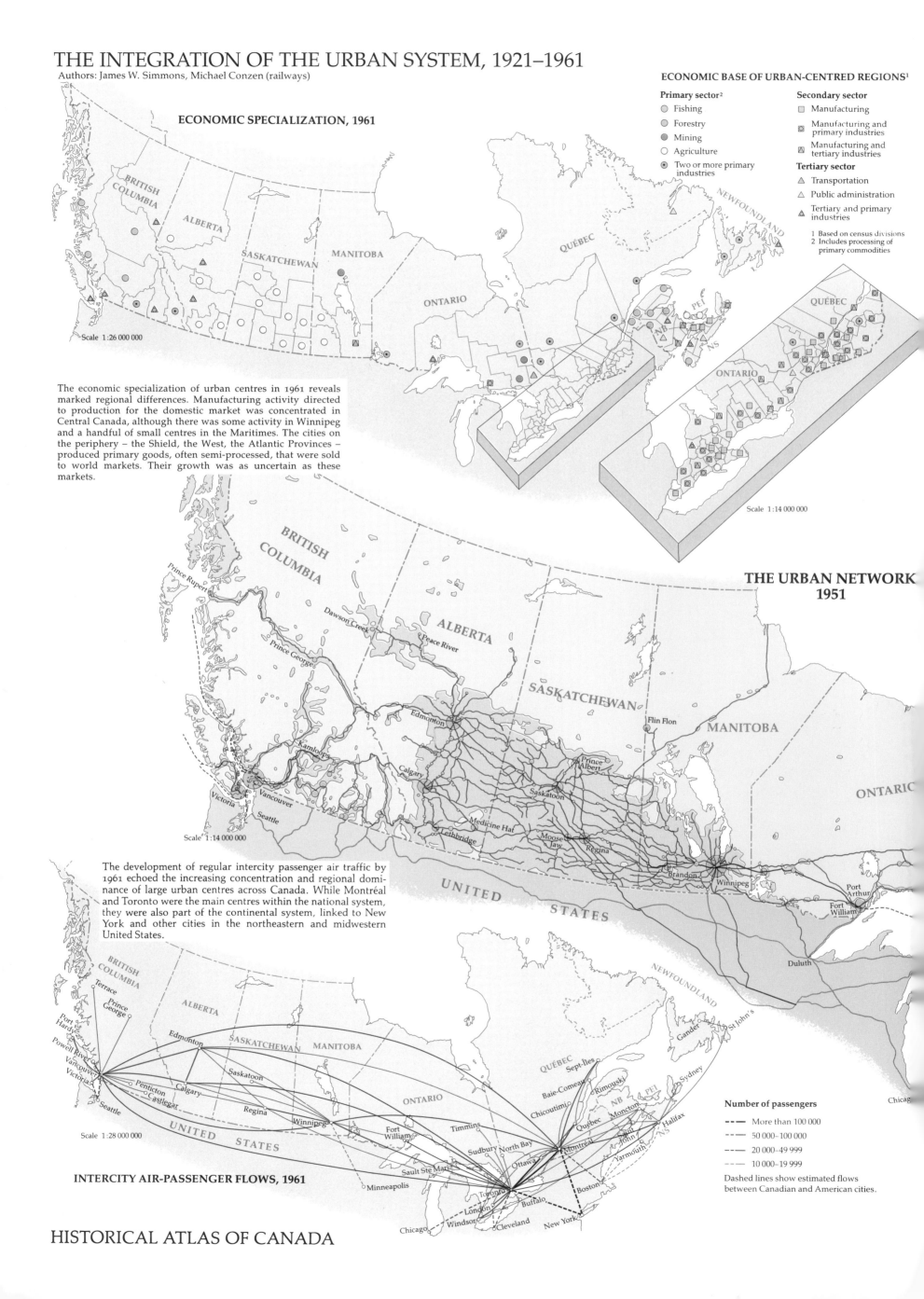

Scale 1:26 000 000

Scale 1:14 000 000

The economic specialization of urban centres in 1961 reveals marked regional differences. Manufacturing activity directed to production for the domestic market was concentrated in Central Canada, although there was some activity in Winnipeg and a handful of small centres in the Maritimes. The cities on the periphery – the Shield, the West, the Atlantic Provinces – produced primary goods, often semi-processed, that were sold to world markets. Their growth was as uncertain as these markets.

THE URBAN NETWORK 1951

Scale 1:14 000 000

The development of regular intercity passenger air traffic by 1961 echoed the increasing concentration and regional domi-nance of large urban centres across Canada. While Montréal and Toronto were the main centres within the national system, they were also part of the continental system, linked to New York and other cities in the northeastern and midwestern United States.

INTERCITY AIR-PASSENGER FLOWS, 1961

Scale 1:28 000 000

Number of passengers
- More than 100 000
- 50 000–100 000
- 20 000–49 999
- 10 000–19 999

Dashed lines show estimated flows between Canadian and American cities.

HISTORICAL ATLAS OF CANADA

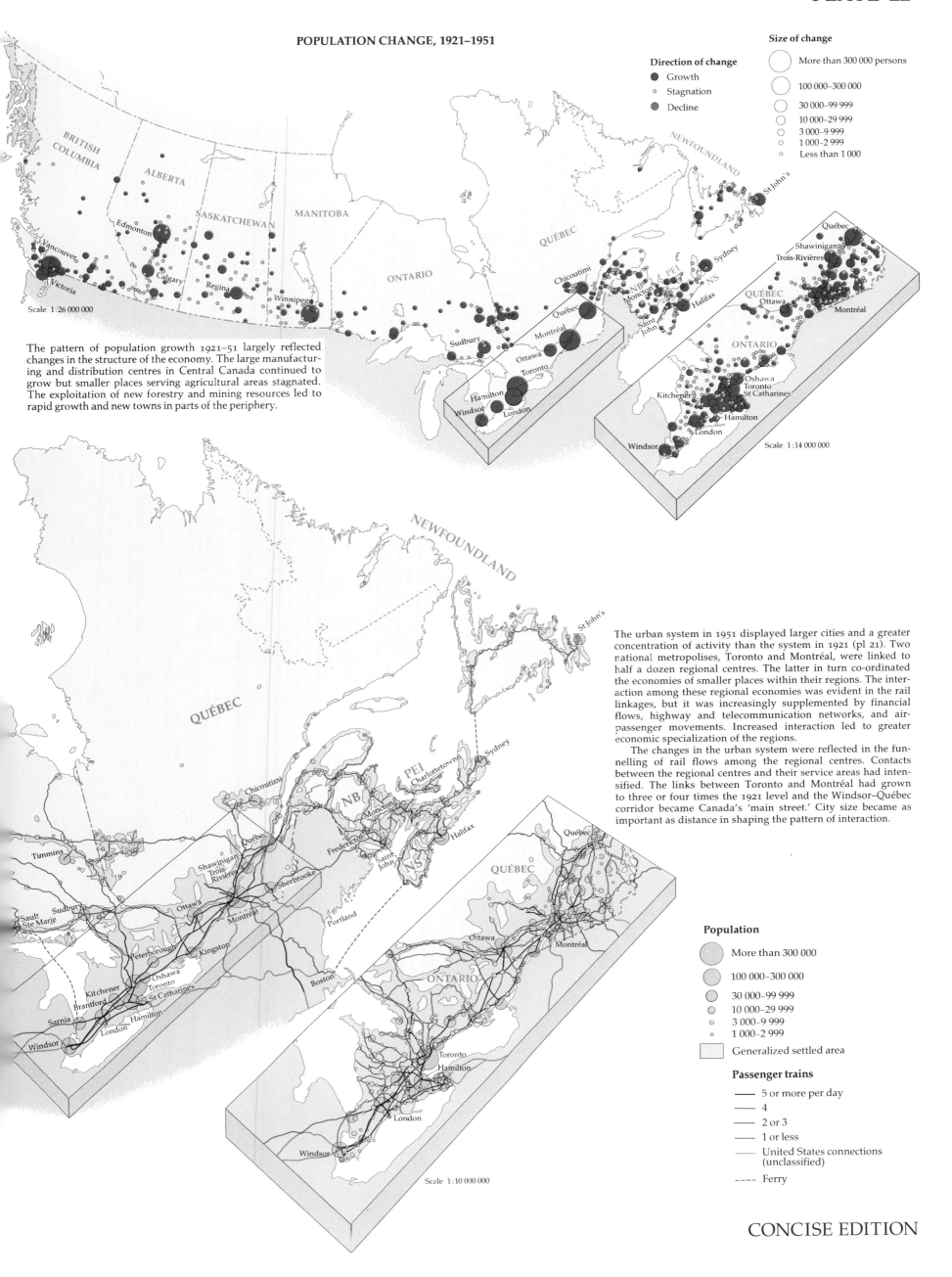

POPULATION CHANGE, 1921–1951

Direction of change
● Growth
○ Stagnation
● Decline

Size of change
More than 300 000 persons
100 000–300 000
30 000–99 999
10 000–29 999
3 000–9 999
1 000–2 999
Less than 1 000

Scale 1:26 000 000

The pattern of population growth 1921–51 largely reflected changes in the structure of the economy. The large manufacturing and distribution centres in Central Canada continued to grow but smaller places serving agricultural areas stagnated. The exploitation of new forestry and mining resources led to rapid growth and new towns in parts of the periphery.

Scale 1:14 000 000

The urban system in 1951 displayed larger cities and a greater concentration of activity than the system in 1921 (pl 21). Two national metropolises, Toronto and Montréal, were linked to half a dozen regional centres. The latter in turn co-ordinated the economies of smaller places within their regions. The interaction among these regional economies was evident in the rail linkages, but it was increasingly supplemented by financial flows, highway and telecommunication networks, and air-passenger movements. Increased interaction led to greater economic specialization of the regions.

The changes in the urban system were reflected in the funnelling of rail flows among the regional centres. Contacts between the regional centres and their service areas had intensified. The links between Toronto and Montréal had grown to three or four times the 1921 level and the Windsor–Québec corridor became Canada's 'main street.' City size became as important as distance in shaping the pattern of interaction.

Population
More than 300 000
100 000–300 000
30 000–99 999
10 000–29 999
3 000–9 999
1 000–2 999
▢ Generalized settled area

Passenger trains
—— 5 or more per day
—— 4
—— 2 or 3
—— 1 or less
—— United States connections (unclassified)
---- Ferry

Scale 1:10 000 000

CONCISE EDITION

THE GROWTH OF ROAD AND AIR TRANSPORT, 20th CENTURY

Authors: Gerald Bloomfield, Murdo MacPherson, David Neufeld (airlines)

MOVEMENT OF PASSENGERS

CANADIAN AIRLINES, 1937

CARGO VOLUME BY REGION

AIR FREIGHT
Total
11 024 600 kg

AIR MAIL
Total
599 400 kg

Scheduled routes

— Freight, mail, and passenger

- - - Freight and passenger only

∘∘∘ Proposed Trans-Canada Airli[nes]

Scale 1:38 000 000

Paved roads

— By 1937
— By 1950
— By 1961

Other important roads
Gravel
— By 1937*
— By 1950
— By 1961

Improved earth
- - - By 1950
- - - By 1961

*For Newfoundland all 'highroads' in 1941 are shown (surface type undifferentiated).

Trans-Canada Highway

∘∘∘ Route, 1961

Total expenditure, 1951–1963

Provincial   Federal

Total in dollars

British Columbia
$248 346 000

Alberta
$35 689 000

National parks in BC and Alta
$75 523 000

Saskatchewan
$28 265 000

Manitoba
$40 190 000

Ontario
$202 653 000

While railway development had passed its zenith before the Depression, road and air transportation expanded through the 1930s and grew dramatically in the post-war period. In 1930 Canada's road network was regionally focused, and east-west connections often required the use of the more developed highway system in the United States and its north-south feeders into Canada. Only with the completion of links along the North Bay–Cochrane–Hearst–Port Arthur–Fort William route in 1946 was it possible to cross Canada by car. The quality of route surface varied considerably, however, with few paved roads in the Prairies and difficult connections through the Rockies.

In the post-war period the extension of paving was rapid, spurred by increasing automobile ownership and 'good roads' lobbies; by 1961 virtually all the major intercity routes were completely paved. Other significant roads had at least a gravel surface. Although Toronto and Buffalo and the cities of the Golden Horseshoe were linked by a 'super-highway' as early as 1939, construction of a good-quality, coast-to-coast route did not begin until 1950. The Trans-Canada Highway Act of 1949 provided for cost sharing between the federal and provincial governments. Difficulties in construction in Newfoundland, through the Shield in northern Ontario, and across the Rockies delayed the opening of the highway until July 1962; even then some 3 000 km were still unpaved.

Scale 1:13 500 000

0 _____ 200 miles

0 _____ 200 kilometres

MAIN HIGHWAYS, 1930

No comparable data available for Newfoundland

— Primary road
— Secondary road
— US highway used as connecting route by Canadia[ns]

Scale 1:25 000 000

UNITED STATES

HISTORICAL ATLAS OF CANADA

PLATE 23

CANADIAN AIRLINES, 1963

National	Trans-Canada
	Canadian Pacific
Regional	Pacific Western
	Transair
	Quebecair
	Eastern Provincial

ORIGINS OF THE MAJOR AIRLINES

Regional origin of constituent airlines

.... Maritime Provinces
- - - - Québec and N Ontario
— — — NW Ontario and N Manitoba
—·—·— Prairie Provinces
—+—+— N Alberta, Yukon, NWT
———— British Columbia
━━━━ Multiple regions
↑ Subsidiary relationship

EASTERN PROVINCIAL AIRWAYS

NORDAIR

QUEBECAIR

TRANSAIR

PACIFIC WESTERN AIRLINES

CANADIAN PACIFIC AIRLINES

TRANS-CANADA AIRLINES

1921   1931   1941   1951   1961 1964

Lines represent airline connections and may not show actual routes.

Scale 1:35 000 000

Prior to the Depression there was little development of airline services. However, with the expansion of gold mining through the 1930s and the exploitation of metallic minerals after the mid-1930s, a north-south pattern in scheduled airline services into remote areas developed. Air freight, especially to north-western Ontario gold fields, drew much traffic but air mail was also an important cargo to isolated settlements and northern resource communities. The late 1930s saw the heyday of Canadian bush flying.

The development of east-west interurban links for passenger service transformed the organization of the airline industry. In the face of increasingly important regional private carriers the federal government created Trans-Canada Airlines (TCA) in April 1937 as the national carrier and through strict regulation after the Second Word War thwarted Canadian Pacific's national airline aspirations. Fiercely independent operators were gradually absorbed into larger regional companies, but TCA did not have a rival until 1960 when Canadian Pacific services into Winnipeg, Toronto, and Montréal were licensed. By then the feeder pattern of regional airlines had been rationalized considerably.

PASSENGER MILES AND COMMERCIAL PILOTS

—— Commercial pilots
—— Passenger miles

MOTOR-VEHICLE REGISTRATIONS, 1938, 1951, 1961

Vehicles per thousand persons

More than 300
200–300
100–199.9
Less than 100

1961
1951
1938

PEI   NFLD   NB   NS   MAN   SASK   ALTA   BC   QUE   ONT

EVOLUTION OF THE ROAD NETWORK

Québec
$102 832 000

Newfoundland
$61 796 000

PEI
$10 414 000

Nova Scotia
$27 049 000

New Brunswick
$66 352 000

While Ontario had an extensive network of paved roads by the 1930s, it was not until the post-war period that Québec and the Maritimes expanded their systems. The Prairies and British Columbia lagged behind; in the former the need for paved roads on prairie land was not pressing whereas in the latter problems of construction over mountainous terrain were acute.

PAVED ROADS

BC
Prairie Provinces
Total length
Ontario
Québec
Maritimes
No data

The considerable interprovincial variation in the registration of automobiles was the result of many interrelated factors, including levels of urbanization, rural population density, economic prosperity, the quality and extent of road networks, and recreational use.

SURFACED ROADS

Total length
Gravel, crushed stone
Paved
No data

MOTOR-VEHICLE REGISTRATIONS

—— Total vehicles
—— Passenger cars
- - - Commercial vehicles

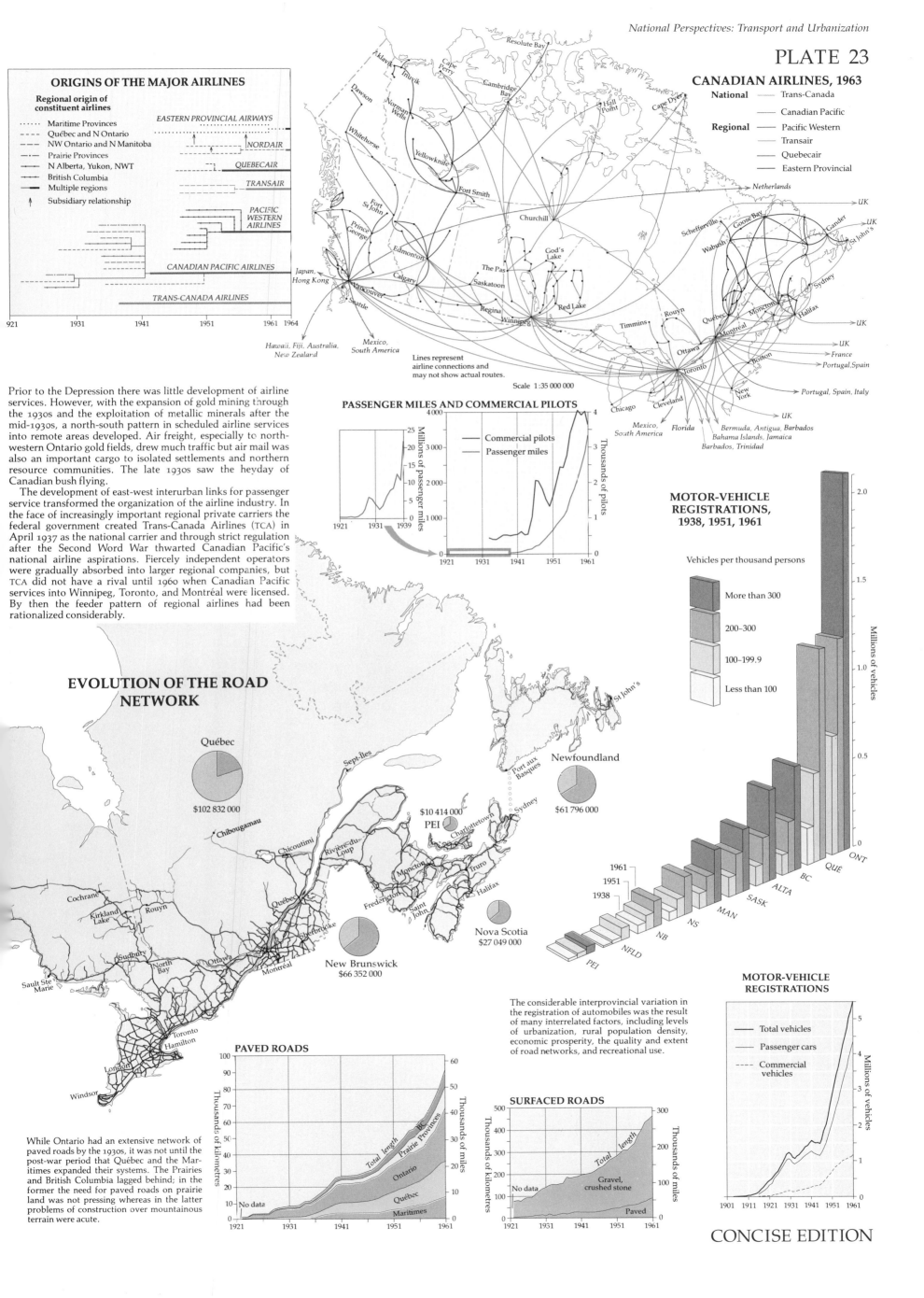

CANADIAN NORTH ATLANTIC TRADE, 17th AND 18th CENTURIES

Authors: Thomas Wien, James Pritchard

Two export trades, united by a common demand for European goods, dominated Canadian commerce in the later 17th and 18th centuries. Although it required few ships, the fur trade was the colony's *grand commerce*, accounting for almost all exports in the 17th century and for some 60% towards the end of the 18th century. A very different trade, involving more and usually smaller ships, dealt in products of the St Lawrence valley: chiefly wheat, timber, and fish. At various times there were markets for these goods at fishing stations in the Gulf of St Lawrence, at Louisbourg, on the slave plantations in the French and British West Indies, in neighbouring British colonies, and in southern Europe. But Québec, icebound for part of the year and remote, was not an ideal Atlantic port. Its exports apart from furs were usually available at more advantageous locations. Canada's commerce remained relatively small, accounting for less than 10% of the value of French colonial trade in the 1730s and for less than 5% of British trade with North America in the 1770s.

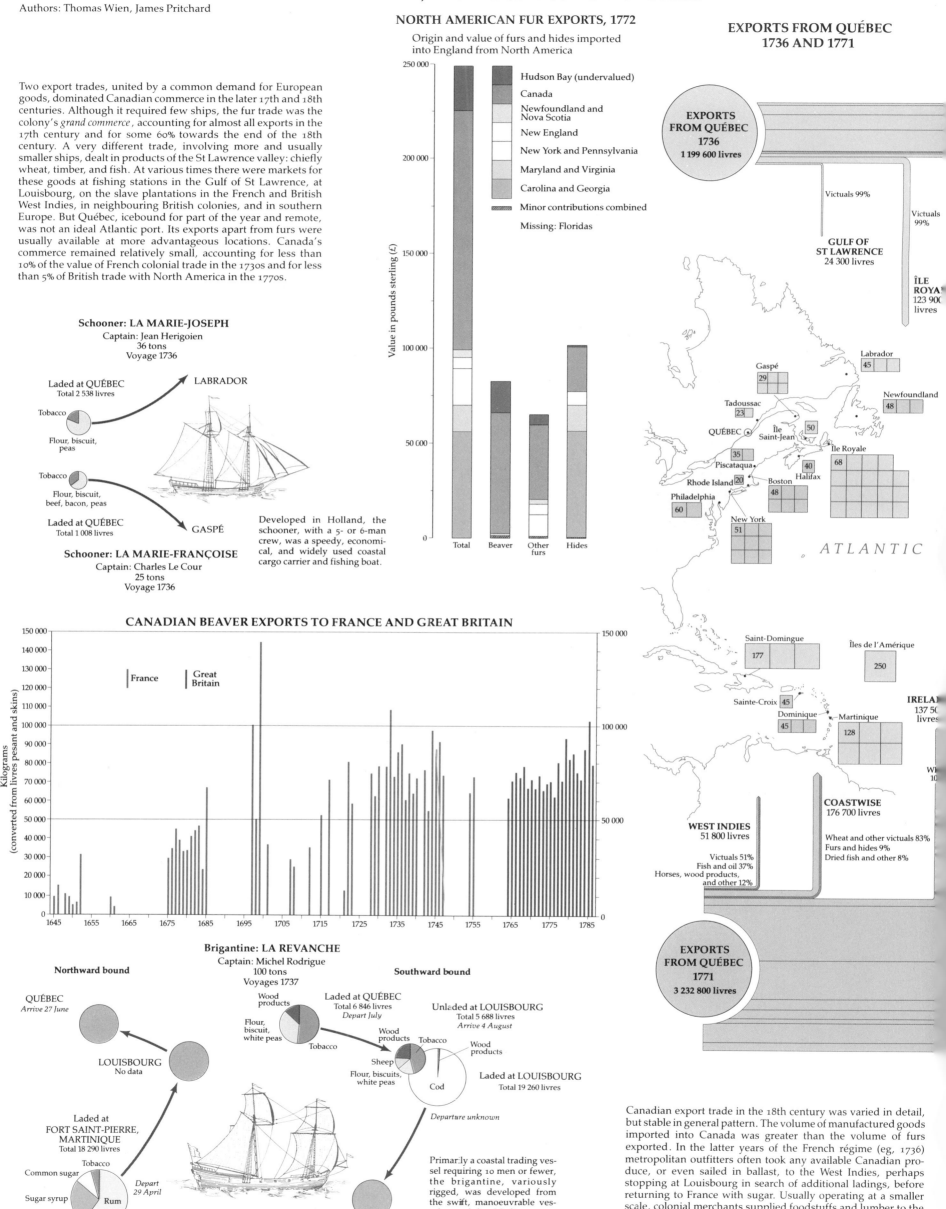

NORTH AMERICAN FUR EXPORTS, 1772

Origin and value of furs and hides imported into England from North America

- Hudson Bay (undervalued)
- Canada
- Newfoundland and Nova Scotia
- New England
- New York and Pennsylvania
- Maryland and Virginia
- Carolina and Georgia
- Minor contributions combined
- Missing: Floridas

Value in pounds sterling (£)

Total · Beaver · Other furs · Hides

Schooner: LA MARIE-JOSEPH
Captain: Jean Herigoien
36 tons
Voyage 1736

Laded at QUÉBEC
Total 2 538 livres
LABRADOR
Tobacco
Flour, biscuit, peas

Laded at QUÉBEC
Total 1 008 livres
GASPÉ
Tobacco
Flour, biscuit, beef, bacon, peas

Schooner: LA MARIE-FRANÇOISE
Captain: Charles Le Cour
25 tons
Voyage 1736

Developed in Holland, the schooner, with a 5- or 6-man crew, was a speedy, economical, and widely used coastal cargo carrier and fishing boat.

CANADIAN BEAVER EXPORTS TO FRANCE AND GREAT BRITAIN

Kilograms (converted from livres pesant and skins)

France   Great Britain

1645 1655 1665 1675 1685 1695 1705 1715 1725 1735 1745 1755 1765 1775 1785

Brigantine: LA REVANCHE
Captain: Michel Rodrigue
100 tons
Voyages 1737

Northward bound

QUÉBEC
Arrive 27 June

LOUISBOURG
No data

Laded at FORT SAINT-PIERRE, MARTINIQUE
Total 18 290 livres
Tobacco
Common sugar
Sugar syrup
Rum
Depart 29 April

Southward bound

Laded at QUÉBEC
Total 6 846 livres
Depart July
Wood products
Flour, biscuit, white peas
Tobacco

Unladed at LOUISBOURG
Total 5 688 livres
Arrive 4 August
Wood products
Tobacco
Sheep
Flour, biscuits, white peas
Cod
Wood products

Laded at LOUISBOURG
Total 19 260 livres
Departure unknown

WEST INDIES
No data

Primarily a coastal trading vessel requiring 10 men or fewer, the brigantine, variously rigged, was developed from the swift, manoeuvrable vessels used by Mediterranean pirates.

EXPORTS FROM QUÉBEC 1736 AND 1771

EXPORTS FROM QUÉBEC 1736
1 199 600 livres

Victuals 99%

GULF OF ST LAWRENCE
24 300 livres

Victuals 99%

ÎLE ROYALE
123 900 livres

Gaspé 29
Labrador 45
Tadoussac 23
Newfoundland 48
QUÉBEC
Île Saint-Jean 50
Île Royale 68
Piscataqua 35
Boston 40 / Halifax
Rhode Island 20
Philadelphia 60
Boston 48
New York 51

ATLANTIC

Saint-Domingue 177
Îles de l'Amérique 250
Sainte-Croix 45
Dominique 45
Martinique 128
IRELAND 137 500 livres

COASTWISE
176 700 livres

Wheat and other victuals 83%
Furs and hides 9%
Dried fish and other 8%

WEST INDIES
51 800 livres

Victuals 51%
Fish and oil 37%
Horses, wood products, and other 12%

EXPORTS FROM QUÉBEC 1771
3 232 800 livres

Canadian export trade in the 18th century was varied in detail, but stable in general pattern. The volume of manufactured goods imported into Canada was greater than the volume of furs exported. In the latter years of the French régime (eg, 1736) metropolitan outfitters often took any available Canadian produce, or even sailed in ballast, to the West Indies, perhaps stopping at Louisbourg in search of additional ladings, before returning to France with sugar. Usually operating at a smaller scale, colonial merchants supplied foodstuffs and lumber to the Gulf, Louisbourg, and the slave colonies. Later (eg, 1771) Canadian grain and flour were increasingly marketed in southern Europe, but many vessels returned lightly loaded to Britain.

HISTORICAL ATLAS OF CANADA

The width of the flow arrows is proportional to the value of trade goods at an approximate scale of one mm to 50 000 livres. The values represented here include only trade goods and not bills of exchange. Beaver were undervalued in 1736 as were other furs and hides in 1771.

Fish and other 6%
Hides 19%
Furs 32%
Beaver 43%

FRANCE
954 000 livres

Victuals 71%
Fish 19%
Timber 10%

WEST INDIES
97 400 livres

Great Britain
112

Ireland
101

Cork
101

Bristol
112

London
112

Le Havre
90

La Rochelle
300

Southern Europe
103

Oporto
103

Lisbon
103

Barcelona
103

Livorno
103

Gibraltar
103

Madeira
103

OCEAN

SOUTHERN EUROPE AND MADEIRA
542 200 livres

Wheat and cereals 72%
Fish 28%

Wood products, wheat, and other 4%

GREAT BRITAIN
2 324 600 livres

Beaver 46%
Other furs 33%
Hides 9%
Oil 8%

The number of ships sailing to Québec increased in the mid-1660s when the Crown assumed direct control of Canada, and again in the 1680s and 1690s when the colony was at war with the English colonies and the Iroquois. The growth of shipping after 1740, and particularly after 1755, also reflected French military support. British shipping to Québec in the 1760s fell well below the French wartime level, then grew in the 1770s in response to expanding trade and the American Revolution. The perennial Canadian problem of establishing an export other than furs is reflected in the decline of trade in the 1780s.

In response to changes in European demand, merchants altered the composition of their fur shipments over the long term. In general, beaver dominated 17th-century exports, while other furs and hides accounted for much of the growth of 18th-century exports. The relative importance of particular furs and hides and of different regional trades in these commodities is shown for 1772.

The graphs of exports and imports of furs and hides should be used cautiously. Data are lacking on the volume of shipments to Albany during the first half of the 18th century, and to Le Havre in the 1730s. The proportion of La Rochelle's fur imports that came from Louisiana is unclear. While the La Rochelle records underestimate the value of imports, the London records probably err in the opposite direction.

Average annual number of vessels sailing from
Other French ports
Bordeaux — Southern Europe and Madeira
La Rochelle — Britain and Ireland
Average annual tonnage ———

EUROPEAN SHIPPING TO QUÉBEC, 1640–1789

Ship: LE FIER
Captain: Pierre Chiron
140 tons
Voyage 1725

Laded at QUÉBEC
For owners and as freight, 40 tons
Total 38 901 livres

Cod
Cash and bills of exchange
Wood products
Hides
Furs
Arrive 22 August
Depart 29 October

Laded at LA ROCHELLE
For owners, 70 tons, valued at 9 782 livres
60 tons freight, value unknown

Foodstuffs
Miscellaneous earthenware, glass, etc
Wine and brandy
Depart 25 May
Arrive 18 December

A great variety of ship-rigged craft of 100 to 200 tons and 20- to 30-man crews carried the bulk of the world's trade goods.

The block graphs above show the number and average tonnage of vessels departing Québec in 1736 and 1771. Each square represents one vessel.

25 50 100 200 300

Average tonnage per vessel

In 1736 some vessels of the Île Royale block continued to the West Indies; vessels arriving in La Rochelle averaged nearer 200 tons in other years. London often received fewer vessels than in 1771.

FUR AND HIDE IMPORTS, LA ROCHELLE AND LONDON, 1718–1778

La Rochelle   London
Hides
Other furs
Beaver

Additional shipments to Le Havre, 1730–43

Livres tournois

Pounds sterling (£)

LA ROCHELLE (undervalued)
Does not include beaver smuggled to New York

LONDON (approximate market value)

CONCISE EDITION

CANADA IN 1891

Authors: Marvin McInnis, Peter J. Usher (native land use)

In 1891, five years after British Columbia was linked to eastern Canada by rail, the country was still rather fragmented. Vast stretches of territory separated pockets of settled areas where agricultural activity supported most of the people. Southern Ontario and southern Québec, which were better integrated than the rest of the country, had three-quarters of the Canadian population, and their principal cities were founded on a prosperous agricultural economy. A commercially viable farming community had begun in Manitoba. In the Maritime Provinces and in eastern Québec, where the population was much more thinly scattered and the agricultural economy less successful, fishing and forestry still played an important role. The vast Precambrian Shield was only beginning to yield timber and mineral wealth and the abundant resources west of the Rockies were still largely untapped.

Beyond the settled South and its contiguous resource frontier traditional fur trading and fisheries shaped the contact between indigenous and non-indigenous peoples. From a southern Canadian perspective the North was a vast and unknown country. Missions, whaling stations, and fur-trading posts were the only white colonial outposts. From the perspective of the Native peoples life still revolved around seasonal limits of resources, although they adapted their traditional way of life to include fur trading.

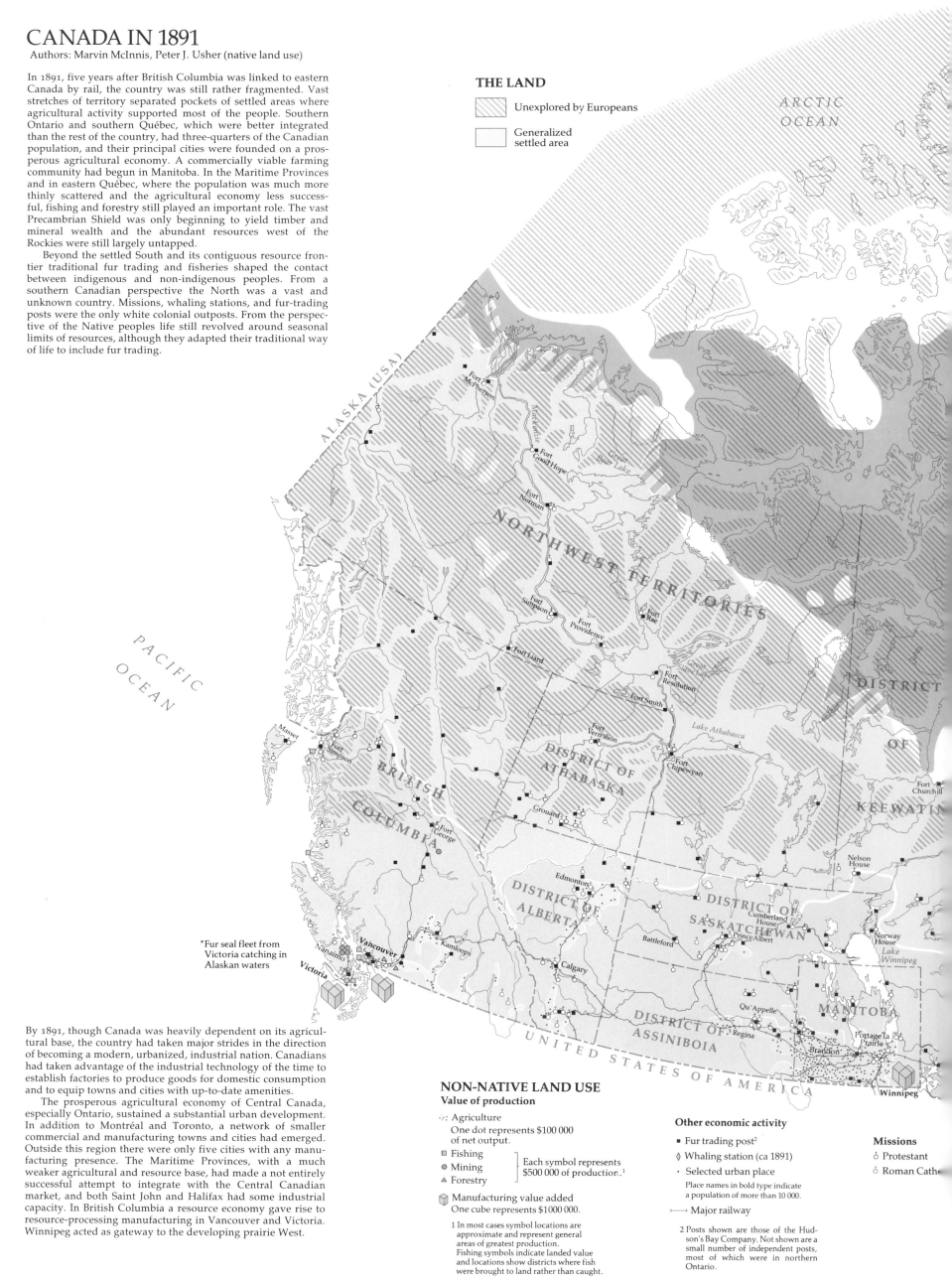

THE LAND

Unexplored by Europeans

Generalized settled area

*Fur seal fleet from Victoria catching in Alaskan waters

By 1891, though Canada was heavily dependent on its agricultural base, the country had taken major strides in the direction of becoming a modern, urbanized, industrial nation. Canadians had taken advantage of the industrial technology of the time to establish factories to produce goods for domestic consumption and to equip towns and cities with up-to-date amenities.

The prosperous agricultural economy of Central Canada, especially Ontario, sustained a substantial urban development. In addition to Montréal and Toronto, a network of smaller commercial and manufacturing towns and cities had emerged. Outside this region there were only five cities with any manufacturing presence. The Maritime Provinces, with a much weaker agricultural and resource base, had made a not entirely successful attempt to integrate with the Central Canadian market, and both Saint John and Halifax had some industrial capacity. In British Columbia a resource economy gave rise to resource-processing manufacturing in Vancouver and Victoria. Winnipeg acted as gateway to the developing prairie West.

NON-NATIVE LAND USE
Value of production

∴ Agriculture
One dot represents $100 000 of net output.

▣ Fishing
◉ Mining   Each symbol represents $500 000 of production.[1]
▲ Forestry

⬚ Manufacturing value added
One cube represents $1000 000.

1 In most cases symbol locations are approximate and represent general areas of greatest production. Fishing symbols indicate landed value and locations show districts where fish were brought to land rather than caught.

Other economic activity

■ Fur trading post[2]
◊ Whaling station (ca 1891)
· Selected urban place

Place names in bold type indicate a population of more than 10 000.

⟼ Major railway

2 Posts shown are those of the Hudson's Bay Company. Not shown are a small number of independent posts, most of which were in northern Ontario.

Missions

ŏ Protestant
ŏ Roman Catho

Canada in 1891 was still a thinly populated land. More than one-quarter of the population of almost five million were urban dwellers (places with over 1 000 people), yet only Montréal (219 000) and Toronto (181 000) had populations greater than 70 000. Most of the non-indigenous population lived in cities, towns, and farms within a southern band of agricultural settlement that had almost reached its limits in eastern Canada but which was still expanding rapidly on the central and western Prairies. At the margins of the agricultural frontier in the eastern provinces, and just beginning to expand in British Columbia, were areas of forest exploitation. Much of the population along the Atlantic coast was oriented to the fishing economy. The disparate regions of European settlement in Canada were bound together by a transcontinental railway and a growing number of branch lines, supplemented sometimes by inland-waterway steamship lines, to outlying agricultural and resource communities.

Spread unevenly across Canada were some 100 000 indigenous people. The northward and westward advance of the resource frontier was accompanied by the formal surrender of Indian lands to the Crown, usually through the signing of treaties. Where this had already occurred, Indians were confined to small reserves of land and their activities off the reserves were severely constrained, especially where land was taken up for agriculture by the non-indigenous population. To the north, however, Indians and Inuit continued to live as mobile hunting and fishing bands, using large tracts of land and water with few effective restrictions, although non-Native activity – fur-trade posts in the sub-Arctic, whaling stations in the Arctic, and missions – reoriented Native land use and trade and provided focal points for settlement of the indigenous people.

NATIVE LAND USE

Inuit

Virtually self-sufficient hunting and fishing economy; fur trapping for trade exceptional. Some trade in fur and meat established with British and American whaling ships

Indians in non-surrendered areas

Hunting and fishing for subsistence; trapping for trade, mostly with Hudson's Bay Company. As with Inuit, continued extensive use of traditional lands

Indians in surrendered areas

Some hunting and fishing for subsistence, and trapping for trade, in forested areas and along northwestern British Columbia coast; however, use of traditional lands eliminated where taken up for settlement in agricultural areas. Some involvement in wage labour and agriculture

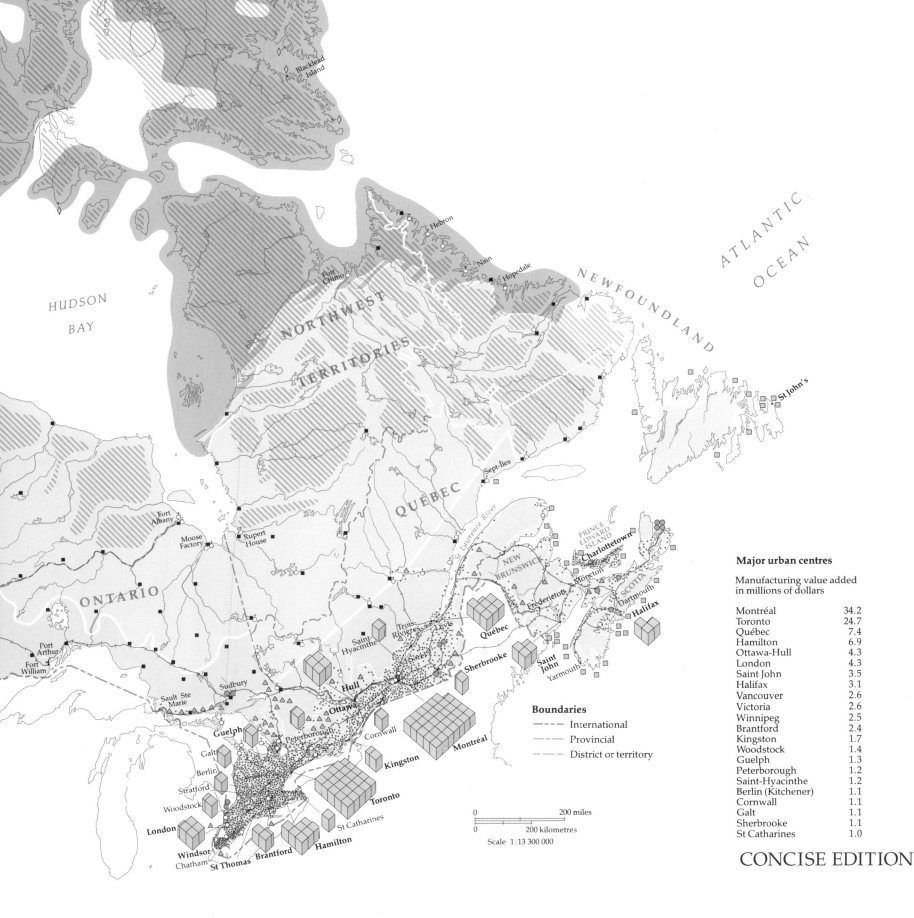

Major urban centres

Manufacturing value added in millions of dollars

Montréal	34.2
Toronto	24.7
Québec	7.4
Hamilton	6.9
Ottawa-Hull	4.3
London	4.3
Saint John	3.5
Halifax	3.1
Vancouver	2.6
Victoria	2.6
Winnipeg	2.5
Brantford	2.4
Kingston	1.7
Woodstock	1.4
Guelph	1.3
Peterborough	1.2
Saint-Hyacinthe	1.2
Berlin (Kitchener)	1.1
Cornwall	1.1
Galt	1.1
Sherbrooke	1.1
St Catharines	1.0

Boundaries

- - - - - International
— - — - Provincial
— — — District or territory

0   200 miles
0   200 kilometres
Scale 1:13 300 000

CONCISE EDITION

PRIMARY PRODUCTION, 1891–1926

Author: Marvin McInnis

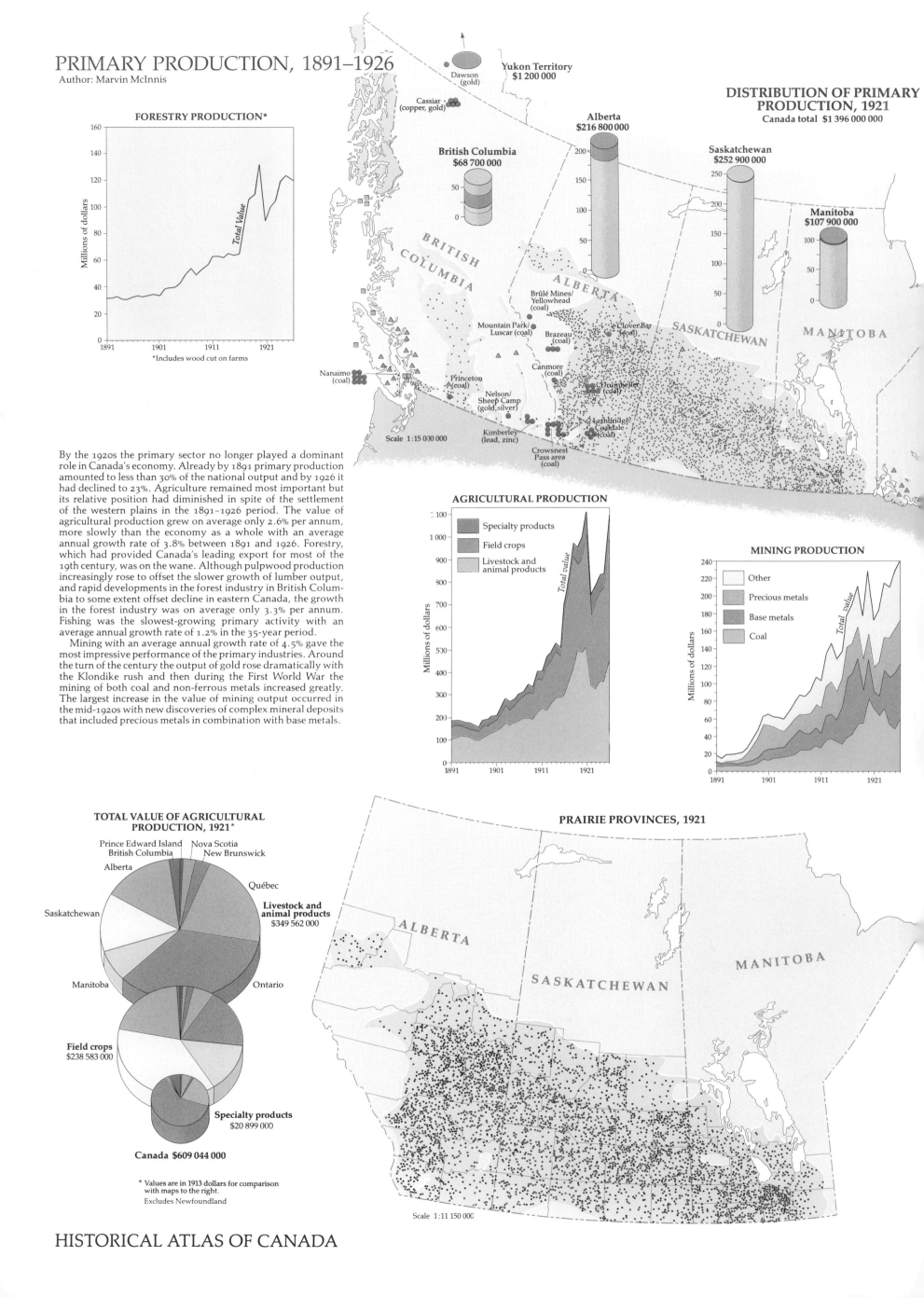

FORESTRY PRODUCTION*

*Includes wood cut on farms

Yukon Territory
$1 200 000

Dawson (gold)

Cassiar (copper, gold)

Alberta $216 800 000

Saskatchewan $252 900 000

Manitoba $107 900 000

British Columbia $68 700 000

BRITISH COLUMBIA

ALBERTA

SASKATCHEWAN

MANITOBA

Brûlé Mines/ Yellowhead (coal)

Mountain Park/ Luscar (coal)

Brazeau (coal)

Clover Bar (coal)

Nanaimo (coal)

Princeton (coal)

Nelson/ Sheep Camp (gold, silver)

Canmore (coal)

Drumheller (coal)

Kimberley (lead, zinc)

Lethbridge/ Coaldale (coal)

Crowsnest Pass area (coal)

Scale 1:15 000 000

By the 1920s the primary sector no longer played a dominant role in Canada's economy. Already by 1891 primary production amounted to less than 30% of the national output and by 1926 it had declined to 23%. Agriculture remained most important but its relative position had diminished in spite of the settlement of the western plains in the 1891–1926 period. The value of agricultural production grew on average only 2.6% per annum, more slowly than the economy as a whole with an average annual growth rate of 3.8% between 1891 and 1926. Forestry, which had provided Canada's leading export for most of the 19th century, was on the wane. Although pulpwood production increasingly rose to offset the slower growth of lumber output, and rapid developments in the forest industry in British Columbia to some extent offset decline in eastern Canada, the growth in the forest industry was on average only 3.3% per annum. Fishing was the slowest-growing primary activity with an average annual growth rate of 1.2% in the 35-year period.

Mining with an average annual growth rate of 4.5% gave the most impressive performance of the primary industries. Around the turn of the century the output of gold rose dramatically with the Klondike rush and then during the First World War the mining of both coal and non-ferrous metals increased greatly. The largest increase in the value of mining output occurred in the mid-1920s with new discoveries of complex mineral deposits that included precious metals in combination with base metals.

AGRICULTURAL PRODUCTION

- Specialty products
- Field crops
- Livestock and animal products

Total value

MINING PRODUCTION

- Other
- Precious metals
- Base metals
- Coal

Total value

TOTAL VALUE OF AGRICULTURAL PRODUCTION, 1921*

Prince Edward Island
British Columbia
Nova Scotia
Alberta
New Brunswick
Québec
Saskatchewan
Livestock and animal products $349 562 000
Manitoba
Ontario

Field crops $238 583 000

Specialty products $20 899 000

Canada $609 044 000

* Values are in 1913 dollars for comparison with maps to the right.
Excludes Newfoundland

PRAIRIE PROVINCES, 1921

ALBERTA

SASKATCHEWAN

MANITOBA

Scale 1:11 150 000

HISTORICAL ATLAS OF CANADA

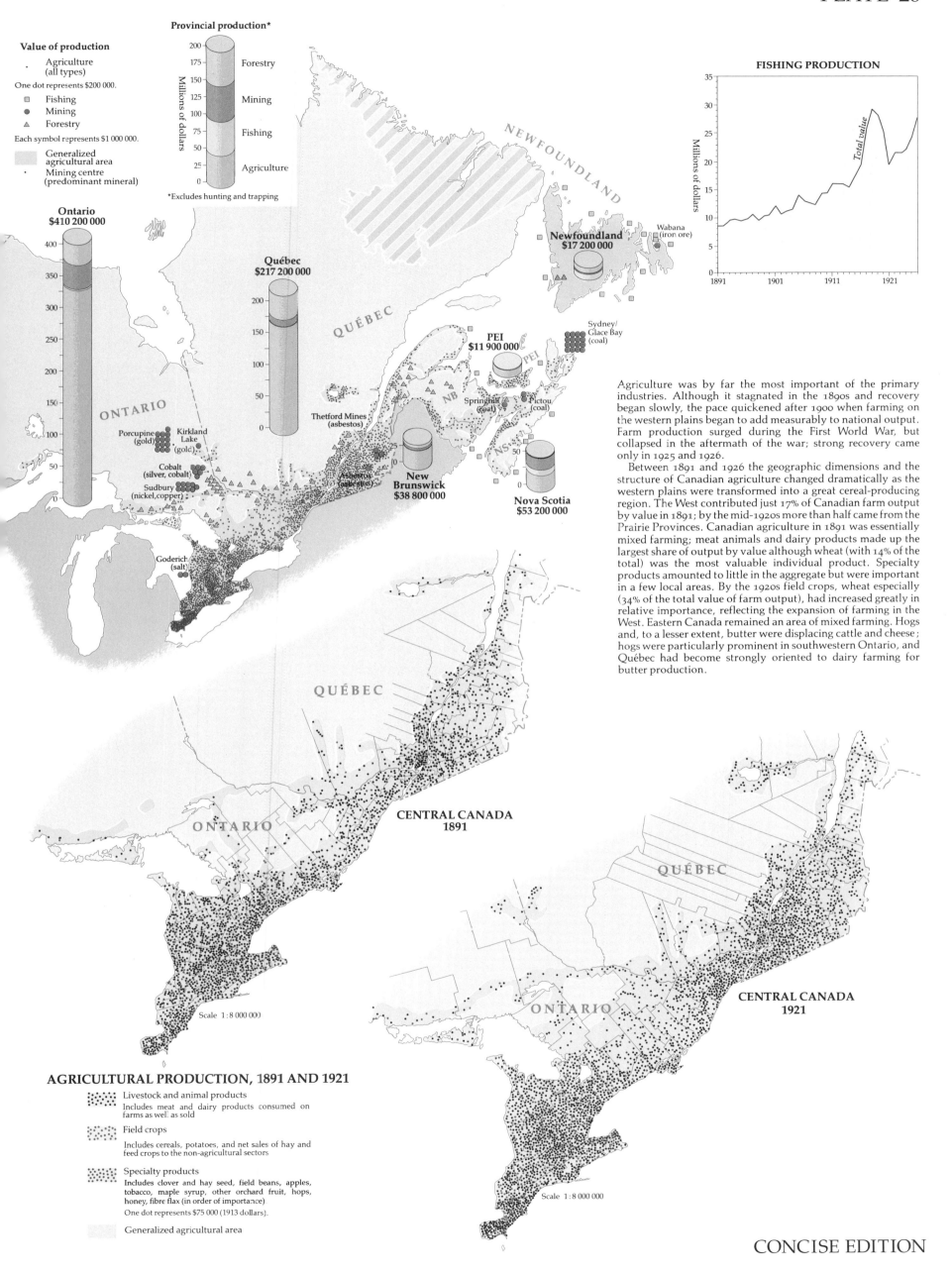

Value of production

. Agriculture
(all types)
One dot represents $200 000.

▢ Fishing
● Mining
▲ Forestry
Each symbol represents $1 000 000.

Generalized
agricultural area
• Mining centre
(predominant mineral)

Provincial production*

Millions of dollars

Forestry
Mining
Fishing
Agriculture

*Excludes hunting and trapping

FISHING PRODUCTION

Millions of dollars

Total value

1891   1901   1911   1921

Ontario
$410 200 000

Québec
$217 200 000

QUÉBEC

ONTARIO

Porcupine
(gold)   Kirkland
Lake
(gold)

Cobalt
(silver, cobalt)

Sudbury
(nickel, copper)

Goderich
(salt)

Thetford Mines
(asbestos)

Asbestos
(asbestos)

**New
Brunswick**
$38 800 000

NB

PEI
$11 900 000

PEI

NS

Springhill
(coal)

Pictou
(coal)

Nova Scotia
$53 200 000

Sydney/
Glace Bay
(coal)

Newfoundland
$17 200 000

NEWFOUNDLAND

Wabana
(iron ore)

Agriculture was by far the most important of the primary
industries. Although it stagnated in the 1890s and recovery
began slowly, the pace quickened after 1900 when farming on
the western plains began to add measurably to national output.
Farm production surged during the First World War, but
collapsed in the aftermath of the war; strong recovery came
only in 1925 and 1926.

Between 1891 and 1926 the geographic dimensions and the
structure of Canadian agriculture changed dramatically as the
western plains were transformed into a great cereal-producing
region. The West contributed just 17% of Canadian farm output
by value in 1891; by the mid-1920s more than half came from the
Prairie Provinces. Canadian agriculture in 1891 was essentially
mixed farming; meat animals and dairy products made up the
largest share of output by value although wheat (with 14% of the
total) was the most valuable individual product. Specialty
products amounted to little in the aggregate but were important
in a few local areas. By the 1920s field crops, wheat especially
(34% of the total value of farm output), had increased greatly in
relative importance, reflecting the expansion of farming in the
West. Eastern Canada remained an area of mixed farming. Hogs
and, to a lesser extent, butter were displacing cattle and cheese;
hogs were particularly prominent in southwestern Ontario, and
Québec had become strongly oriented to dairy farming for
butter production.

QUÉBEC

ONTARIO

**CENTRAL CANADA
1891**

Scale 1 : 8 000 000

QUÉBEC

ONTARIO

**CENTRAL CANADA
1921**

Scale 1 : 8 000 000

AGRICULTURAL PRODUCTION, 1891 AND 1921

Livestock and animal products
Includes meat and dairy products consumed on
farms as well as sold

Field crops
Includes cereals, potatoes, and net sales of hay and
feed crops to the non-agricultural sectors

Specialty products
Includes clover and hay seed, field beans, apples,
tobacco, maple syrup, other orchard fruit, hops,
honey, fibre flax (in order of importance).
One dot represents $75 000 (1913 dollars).

Generalized agricultural area

CONCISE EDITION

FARMING AND FISHING, 1941–1961

Authors: Gerald Bloomfield, Philip D. Keddie, Eric W. Sager

Canadian farmland underwent a period of adjustment in the post-war years. In the East there was a net decline of about 6.3 million acres (2.5 million hectares) of improved farmland, some abandoned, notably on the Shield margins and in the Maritimes, and some lost to urbanization. However, there were important additions in the Québec clay belt and in counties of southwestern Ontario where the introduction of hybrid corn helped encourage the conversion of permanent pasture and sandy scrubland into cropland. In the four western provinces there was a net gain of 15.2 million acres (about 6 million hectares), mostly along the 'pioneer fringe,' in part facilitated by government assistance for clearing the land and post-war settlement schemes. Improved agricultural practices prompted the expansion of arable farming on more marginal lands while in southeastern Saskatchewan and southwestern Manitoba 'pothole' filling and drainage schemes also contributed to the increase. Notwithstanding the east/west patterns of change in improved farmland area, the value of farm output generally increased in both regions, and Ontario especially remained an important agricultural producer.

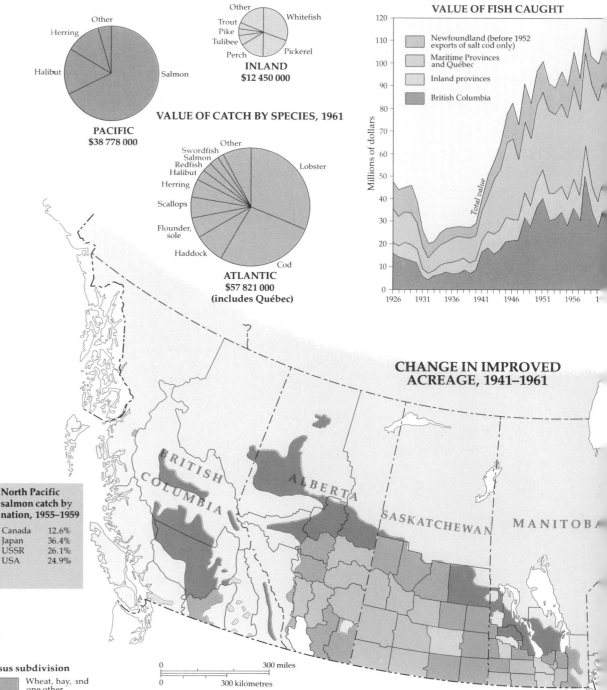

VALUE OF CATCH BY SPECIES, 1961

PACIFIC
$38 778 000

INLAND
$12 450 000

ATLANTIC
$57 821 000
(includes Québec)

VALUE OF FISH CAUGHT

- Newfoundland (before 1952 exports of salt cod only)
- Maritime Provinces and Québec
- Inland provinces
- British Columbia

Millions of dollars

Total value

1926 1931 1936 1941 1946 1951 1956

CHANGE IN IMPROVED ACREAGE, 1941–1961

BRITISH COLUMBIA   ALBERTA   SASKATCHEWAN   MANITOBA

0   300 miles
0   300 kilometres
Scale 1:17 000 000

NET FARMING INCOME

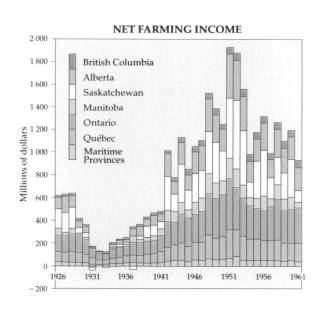

- British Columbia
- Alberta
- Saskatchewan
- Manitoba
- Ontario
- Québec
- Maritime Provinces

Millions of dollars

1926 1931 1936 1941 1946 1951 1956 1961

North Pacific salmon catch by nation, 1955–1959	
Canada	12.6%
Japan	36.4%
USSR	26.1%
USA	24.9%

CROP COMBINATIONS IN THE PRAIRIES

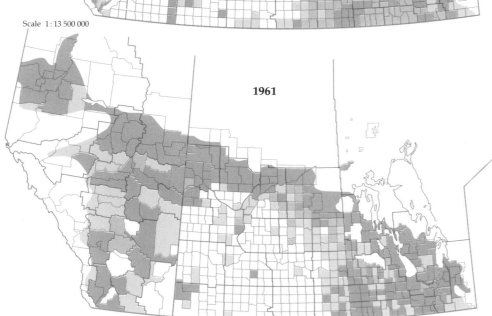

1941

Crop combinations by census subdivision

- Wheat
- Wheat and one other
- Wheat, oats, and barley
- Wheat, hay, and one other
- One to three crops (excluding wheat)
- Four or more crops (including wheat)

Only generalized agricultural area is coloured.

Scale 1:13 500 000

1961

Farming devoted exclusively to wheat continued to dominate the cropland areas in the Prairie Provinces, shifting east and north through the period as new rust-resistant varieties were introduced. Elsewhere cropping systems tended to become more diversified: there was a decline in oats, a growth in hay and flax, and the appearance of rapeseed (canola) as a locally important crop. Large areas of rangeland in southwest Saskatchewan and southeast Alberta sustained cow-calf enterprises, with wheat dominating the limited cropland in those areas.

Percentage change

Increase | Decrease
- 40.0 or more
- 20.0–39.9
- 10.0–19.9
- Less than 10.0

The census division is used as the unit of analysis. Only generalized agricultural area is coloured.

VARIETIES OF PRAIRIE BREAD WHEAT

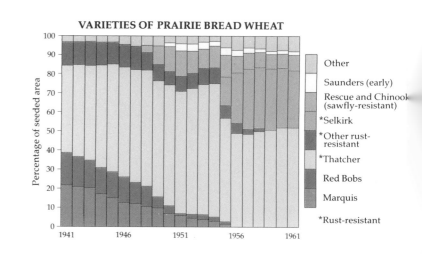

Percentage of seeded area

- Other
- Saunders (early)
- Rescue and Chinook (sawfly-resistant)
- *Selkirk
- *Other rust-resistant
- *Thatcher
- Red Bobs
- Marquis

*Rust-resistant

1941 1946 1951 1956 1961

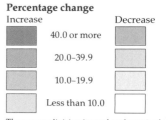

HISTORICAL ATLAS OF CANADA

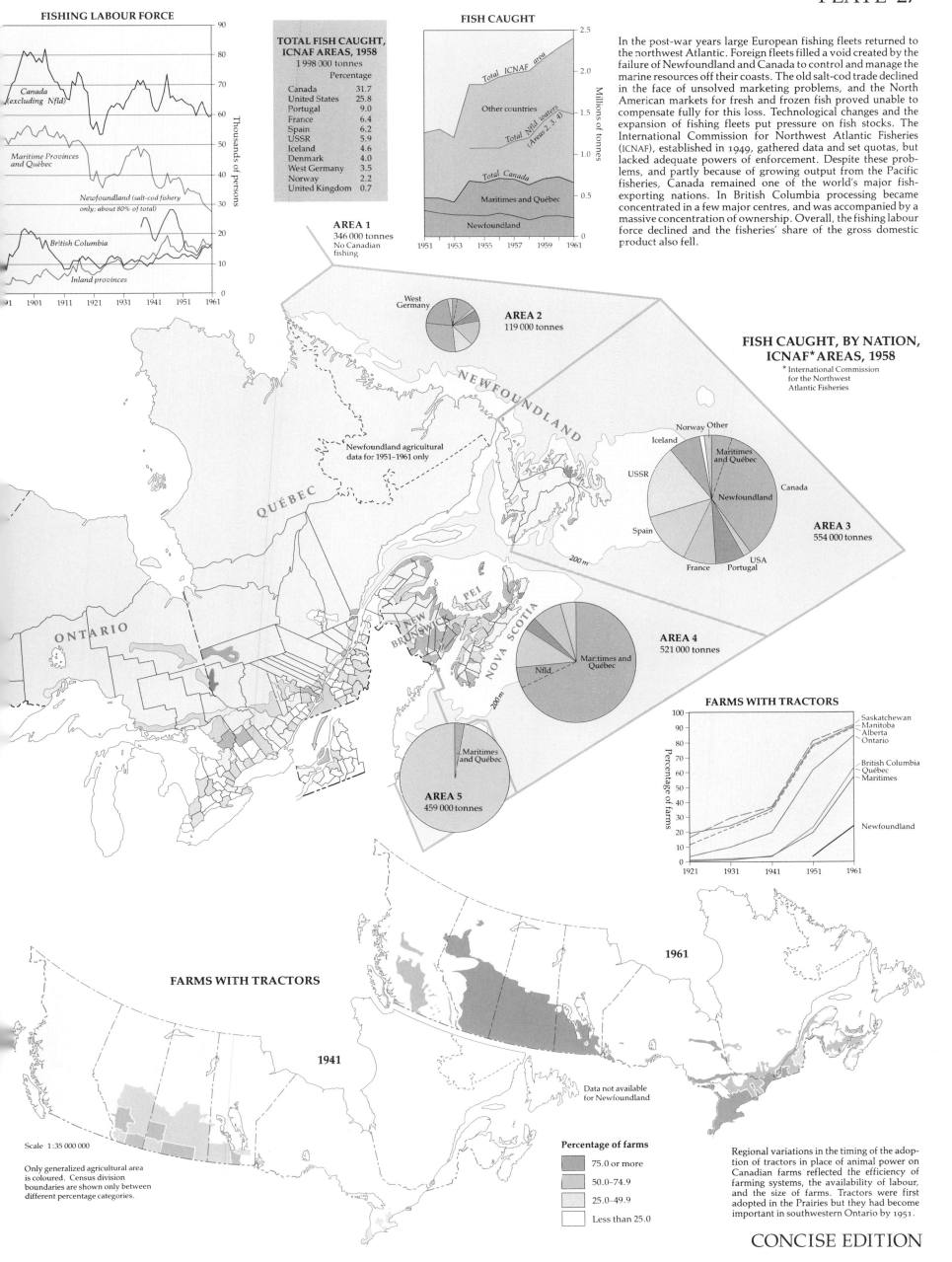

FISHING LABOUR FORCE

Canada (excluding Nfld)

Maritime Provinces and Québec

Newfoundland (salt-cod fishery only; about 80% of total)

British Columbia

Inland provinces

Thousands of persons

1901 1911 1921 1931 1941 1951 1961

TOTAL FISH CAUGHT, ICNAF AREAS, 1958
1 998 000 tonnes

	Percentage
Canada	31.7
United States	25.8
Portugal	9.0
France	6.4
Spain	6.2
USSR	5.9
Iceland	4.6
Denmark	4.0
West Germany	3.5
Norway	2.2
United Kingdom	0.7

FISH CAUGHT

Total ICNAF area

Other countries

Total Nfld waters (Areas 2, 3, 4)

Total Canada

Maritimes and Québec

Newfoundland

Millions of tonnes

1951 1953 1955 1957 1959 1961

In the post-war years large European fishing fleets returned to the northwest Atlantic. Foreign fleets filled a void created by the failure of Newfoundland and Canada to control and manage the marine resources off their coasts. The old salt-cod trade declined in the face of unsolved marketing problems, and the North American markets for fresh and frozen fish proved unable to compensate fully for this loss. Technological changes and the expansion of fishing fleets put pressure on fish stocks. The International Commission for Northwest Atlantic Fisheries (ICNAF), established in 1949, gathered data and set quotas, but lacked adequate powers of enforcement. Despite these problems, and partly because of growing output from the Pacific fisheries, Canada remained one of the world's major fish-exporting nations. In British Columbia processing became concentrated in a few major centres, and was accompanied by a massive concentration of ownership. Overall, the fishing labour force declined and the fisheries' share of the gross domestic product also fell.

AREA 1
346 000 tonnes
No Canadian fishing

West Germany

AREA 2
119 000 tonnes

NEWFOUNDLAND

FISH CAUGHT, BY NATION, ICNAF* AREAS, 1958
* International Commission for the Northwest Atlantic Fisheries

Newfoundland agricultural data for 1951–1961 only

QUÉBEC

Norway Other
Iceland
USSR
Maritimes and Québec
Newfoundland
Canada
Spain
France Portugal
USA

AREA 3
554 000 tonnes

ONTARIO

PEI
NEW BRUNSWICK
NOVA SCOTIA

200 m

Nfld
Maritimes and Québec

AREA 4
521 000 tonnes

FARMS WITH TRACTORS

Saskatchewan
Manitoba
Alberta
Ontario

British Columbia
Québec
Maritimes

Newfoundland

Percentage of farms

1921 1931 1941 1951 1961

Maritimes and Québec

AREA 5
459 000 tonnes

1961

FARMS WITH TRACTORS

1941

Data not available for Newfoundland

Scale 1:35 000 000

Only generalized agricultural area is coloured. Census division boundaries are shown only between different percentage categories.

Percentage of farms

▨	75.0 or more
▨	50.0–74.9
▨	25.0–49.9
☐	Less than 25.0

Regional variations in the timing of the adoption of tractors in place of animal power on Canadian farms reflected the efficiency of farming systems, the availability of labour, and the size of farms. Tractors were first adopted in the Prairies but they had become important in southwestern Ontario by 1951.

CONCISE EDITION

THE CHANGING STRUCTURE OF MANUFACTURING, 1879–1930

Authors: Gerald Bloomfield, Michael Hinton (cotton), Ted Regehr (newsprint), Glen Williams (investment)

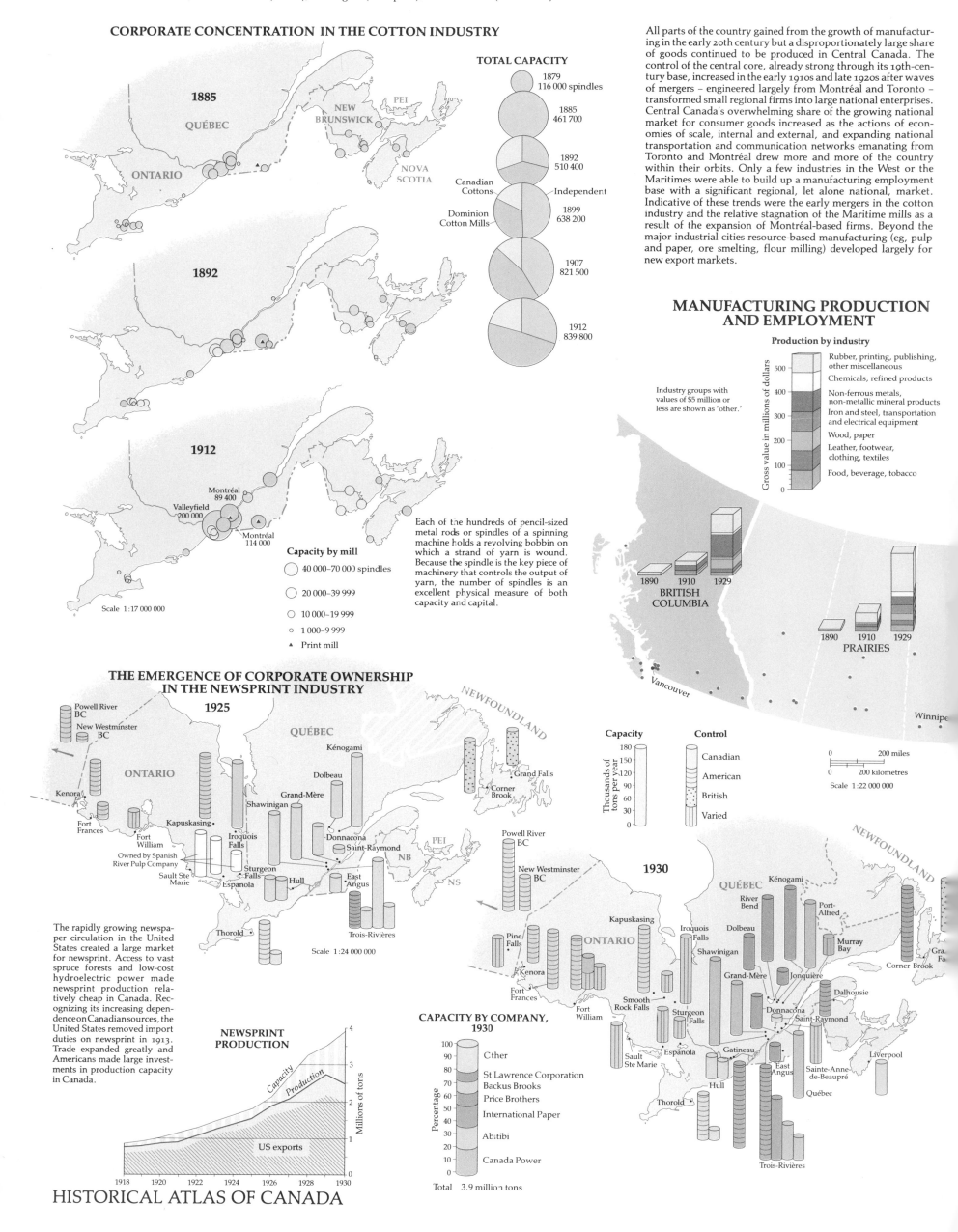

CORPORATE CONCENTRATION IN THE COTTON INDUSTRY

TOTAL CAPACITY

1879
116 000 spindles

1885
461 700

1892
510 400

Canadian Cottons — Independent

Dominion Cotton Mills

1899
638 200

1907
821 500

1912
839 800

1885
QUÉBEC
NEW BRUNSWICK
PEI
ONTARIO
NOVA SCOTIA

1892

1912
Montréal 89 400
Valleyfield 200 000
Montréal 114 000

Scale 1:17 000 000

Capacity by mill
- 40 000–70 000 spindles
- 20 000–39 999
- 10 000–19 999
- 1 000–9 999
- ▲ Print mill

Each of the hundreds of pencil-sized metal rods or spindles of a spinning machine holds a revolving bobbin on which a strand of yarn is wound. Because the spindle is the key piece of machinery that controls the output of yarn, the number of spindles is an excellent physical measure of both capacity and capital.

All parts of the country gained from the growth of manufacturing in the early 20th century but a disproportionately large share of goods continued to be produced in Central Canada. The control of the central core, already strong through its 19th-century base, increased in the early 1910s and late 1920s after waves of mergers – engineered largely from Montréal and Toronto – transformed small regional firms into large national enterprises. Central Canada's overwhelming share of the growing national market for consumer goods increased as the actions of economies of scale, internal and external, and expanding national transportation and communication networks emanating from Toronto and Montréal drew more and more of the country within their orbits. Only a few industries in the West or the Maritimes were able to build up a manufacturing employment base with a significant regional, let alone national, market. Indicative of these trends were the early mergers in the cotton industry and the relative stagnation of the Maritime mills as a result of the expansion of Montréal-based firms. Beyond the major industrial cities resource-based manufacturing (eg, pulp and paper, ore smelting, flour milling) developed largely for new export markets.

MANUFACTURING PRODUCTION AND EMPLOYMENT

Production by industry

Industry groups with values of $5 million or less are shown as 'other.'

Gross value in millions of dollars

- Rubber, printing, publishing, other miscellaneous
- Chemicals, refined products
- Non-ferrous metals, non-metallic mineral products
- Iron and steel, transportation and electrical equipment
- Wood, paper
- Leather, footwear, clothing, textiles
- Food, beverage, tobacco

1890 1910 1929
BRITISH COLUMBIA

1890 1910 1929
PRAIRIES

Vancouver

Winnipe

Capacity
Thousands of tons per year
180 150 120 90 60 30 0

Control
- Canadian
- American
- British
- Varied

0 — 200 miles
0 — 200 kilometres
Scale 1:22 000 000

THE EMERGENCE OF CORPORATE OWNERSHIP IN THE NEWSPRINT INDUSTRY

1925
Powell River BC
New Westminster BC
NEWFOUNDLAND
QUÉBEC
Kénogami
ONTARIO
Grand Falls
Kenora
Corner Brook
Fort Frances
Kapuskasing
Shawinigan
Grand-Mère
Dolbeau
Fort William
Iroquois Falls
Donnacona
Saint-Raymond
Owned by Spanish River Pulp Company
Sault Ste Marie
Sturgeon Falls
Espanola
Hull
East Angus
PEI
NB
NS
Thorold
Trois-Rivières

Scale 1:24 000 000

The rapidly growing newspaper circulation in the United States created a large market for newsprint. Access to vast spruce forests and low-cost hydroelectric power made newsprint production relatively cheap in Canada. Recognizing its increasing dependence on Canadian sources, the United States removed import duties on newsprint in 1913. Trade expanded greatly and Americans made large investments in production capacity in Canada.

NEWSPRINT PRODUCTION

Millions of tons
4 3 2 1 0
Capacity
Production
US exports
1918 1920 1922 1924 1926 1928 1930

CAPACITY BY COMPANY, 1930

Percentage
100 90 80 70 60 50 40 30 20 10 0
- Other
- St Lawrence Corporation
- Backus Brooks
- Price Brothers
- International Paper
- Abitibi
- Canada Power

Total 3.9 million tons

1930
Powell River BC
New Westminster BC
NEWFOUNDLAND
QUÉBEC
Kénogami
River Bend
Port-Alfred
Kapuskasing
Iroquois Falls
Dolbeau
Murray Bay
ONTARIO
Pine Falls
Shawinigan
Grand-Mère
Jonquière
Corner Brook
Kenora
Smooth Rock Falls
Sturgeon Falls
Donnacona
Saint-Raymond
Dalhousie
Fort Frances
Fort William
Espanola
Gatineau
Sault Ste Marie
East Angus
Sainte-Anne-de-Beaupré
Liverpool
Hull
Québec
Thorold
Trois-Rivières

HISTORICAL ATLAS OF CANADA

AMERICAN BRANCH PLANTS, 1913

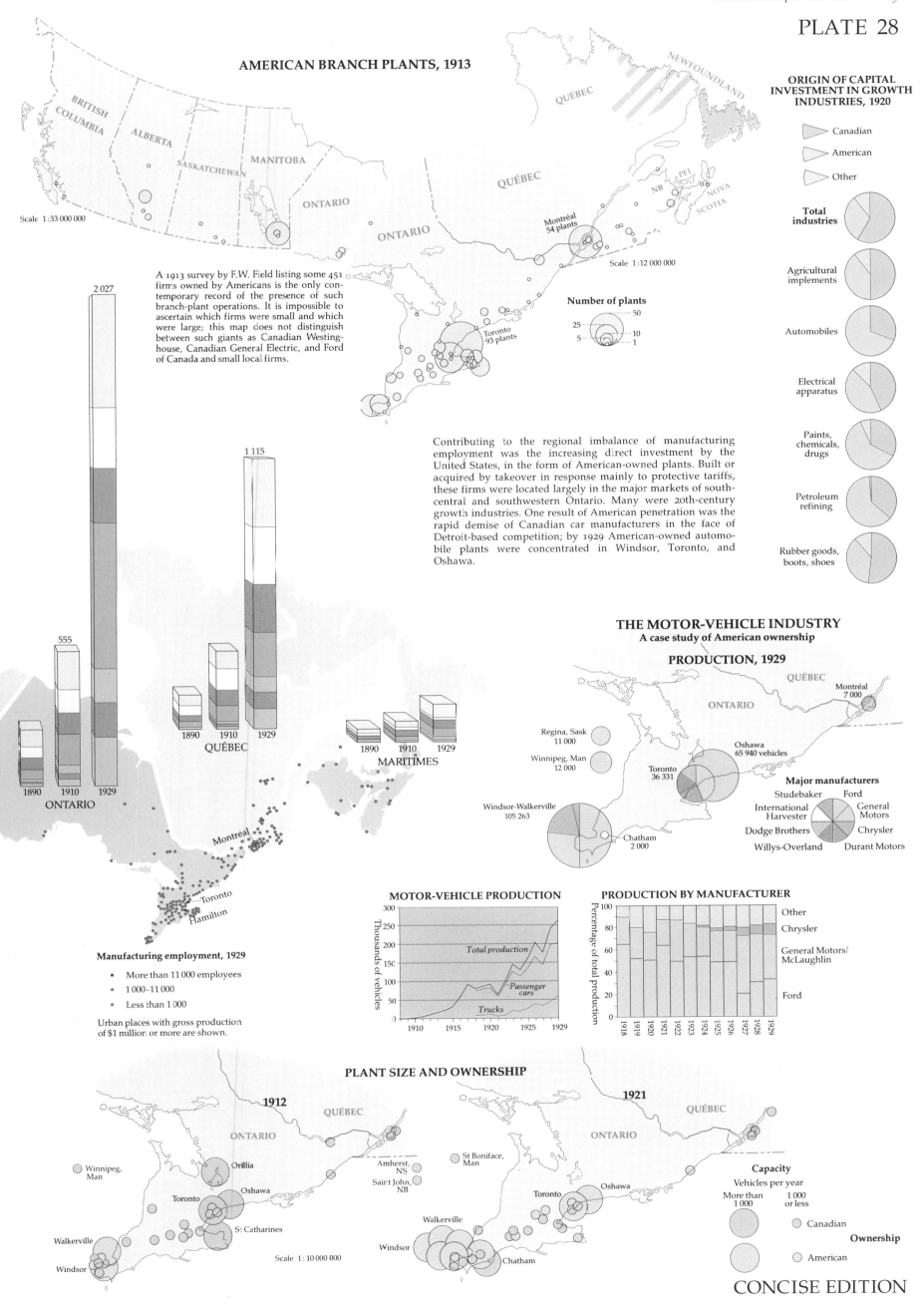

Scale 1:33 000 000

Scale 1:12 000 000

Montréal
54 plants

Toronto
93 plants

Number of plants

25
50
10
5
1

**ORIGIN OF CAPITAL
INVESTMENT IN GROWTH
INDUSTRIES, 1920**

Canadian

American

Other

Total industries

Agricultural implements

Automobiles

Electrical apparatus

Paints, chemicals, drugs

Petroleum refining

Rubber goods, boots, shoes

A 1913 survey by F.W. Field listing some 451 firms owned by Americans is the only contemporary record of the presence of such branch-plant operations. It is impossible to ascertain which firms were small and which were large; this map does not distinguish between such giants as Canadian Westinghouse, Canadian General Electric, and Ford of Canada and small local firms.

Contributing to the regional imbalance of manufacturing employment was the increasing direct investment by the United States, in the form of American-owned plants. Built or acquired by takeover in response mainly to protective tariffs, these firms were located largely in the major markets of south-central and southwestern Ontario. Many were 20th-century growth industries. One result of American penetration was the rapid demise of Canadian car manufacturers in the face of Detroit-based competition; by 1929 American-owned automobile plants were concentrated in Windsor, Toronto, and Oshawa.

2 027

1 115

555

1890 1910 1929
ONTARIO

1890 1910 1929
QUÉBEC

1890 1910 1929
MARITIMES

THE MOTOR-VEHICLE INDUSTRY
A case study of American ownership

PRODUCTION, 1929

Montréal
7 000

Regina, Sask
11 000

Winnipeg, Man
12 000

Oshawa
65 940 vehicles

Toronto
36 331

Windsor-Walkerville
105 263

Chatham
2 000

Major manufacturers

Studebaker   Ford
International   General
Harvester   Motors
Dodge Brothers   Chrysler
Willys-Overland Durant Motors

Montreal

Toronto
Hamilton

Manufacturing employment, 1929

• More than 11 000 employees
• 1 000–11 000
• Less than 1 000

Urban places with gross production of $1 million or more are shown.

MOTOR-VEHICLE PRODUCTION

Total production

Passenger cars

Trucks

1910 1915 1920 1925 1929

PRODUCTION BY MANUFACTURER

Other
Chrysler
General Motors/McLaughlin
Ford

1918 1919 1920 1921 1922 1923 1924 1925 1926 1927 1928 1929

PLANT SIZE AND OWNERSHIP

1912

QUÉBEC

ONTARIO

Winnipeg, Man

Orillia

Oshawa

Toronto

St Catharines

Walkerville

Windsor

Amherst, NS

Saint John, NB

St Boniface, Man

Scale 1:10 000 000

1921

QUÉBEC

ONTARIO

Toronto

Oshawa

Walkerville

Windsor

Chatham

Capacity
Vehicles per year
More than 1 000

1 000 or less

Canadian

Ownership

American

CONCISE EDITION

19th-CENTURY IMAGES OF CANADA

Authors: John H. Wadland, Margaret Hobbs

During the 19th century many artists travelled within Canada, recording their sense of its diverse landscapes. A young Swiss immigrant, Peter Rindisbacher, recorded his arrival aboard the ship *Wellington* at Fort Churchill in 1821, following this with a series of detailed images tracing his overland travels to the Red River colony. Paul Kane and W.G.R. Hind crossed the country before the arrival of the railway and the land survey, representing the land in works which were both sensitive to the Native inhabitants and also reflective of the changes attending the arrival of another culture.

Born in Ontario and essentially self-taught, Lucius R. O'Brien became the first president of the Royal Canadian Academy (RCA) in 1880. J.A. Fraser, also a charter member of the RCA, emigrated from England in 1858 after receiving instruction at the South Kensington School. O'Brien was trained as a civil engineer while Fraser began by tinting photographs in the Montréal studio of William Notman. Their emergence as professional landscape painters paralleled the evolution of the technologies which launched their careers. The locations of the O'Brien works shown on this plate suggest a relationship between his fascination for the railway and the views he captured. Both O'Brien and Fraser lived in the East, where topography, light, and colour differed dramatically from the West, to which they travelled on the Canadian Pacific Railway (CPR). On the way they created regional images of the country which strongly affected the perception of Canadians for the next two generations, before the Group of Seven.

1 Dally, Ox team at Clinton, BC, photograph, 1868

Courtesy of Glenbow Archives, Calgary, NA674-38

2 Hind, *Strait of San Juan, BC*, watercolour, ca 1862

Courtesy of McCord Museum of Canadian History, Montréal, M473

4 Tyrrell, Eskimo camp on the barren land, photograph, 1894

Courtesy of National Archives of Canada, PA-050939

3 O'Brien, *Through the Rocky Mountains, a Pass on the Canadian Highway*, watercolour, 1887

Private collection, Toronto / Photograph courtesy of Art Gallery of Ontario.

5 Horetzky, Peace River at Fort Dunvegan, photograph, 1872

Courtesy of National Archives of Canada, PA-92

6 Kane, *Camping on the Prairie*, oil, 1845

Courtesy of Stark Museum of Art, Orange, Texas

- Railways
- 1891 settled area

1889 boundaries are shown.

7 Royal Engineers, Ox train at Dead Horse Creek, photo, ca 1873

Courtesy of National Archives of Canada, PA-74645

8 Rindisbacher,

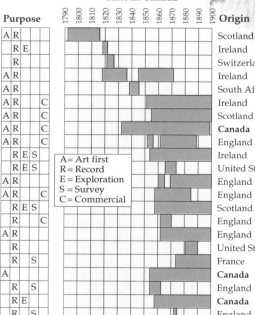

SELECTED PAINTERS AND PHOTOGRAPHERS

Name	Dates	Purpose	Time in Canada 1790 1800 1810 1820 1830 1840 1850 1860 1870 1880 1890 1900	Origin
Heriot, George	ca1759–1839	A R		Scotland
Hood, Robert	ca1796–1821	R E		Ireland
Rindisbacher, Peter	1806–1834	R		Switzerland
Kane, Paul	1810–1871	A R		Ireland
Warre, H.J.	1819–1898	A R		South Africa
Armstrong, William	1822–1914	A R C		Ireland
*Henderson, Alexander	1831–1913	A R C		Scotland
O'Brien, Lucius R.	1832–1899	A R C		**Canada**
Hind, W.G.R.	1833–1889	A R C		England
*Hime, Humphrey L.	1833–1903	R E S		Ireland
*Baltzly, Benjamin	1835–1883	R E S		United States
Matthews, Marmaduke	1837–1913	A R		England
Fraser, J.A.	1838–1898	A R C		England
*Horetzky, Charles	1838–1900	R E S		Scotland
*Dally, Frederick	1838–1914	R C		England
Martin, T. Mower	1838–1934	A R		England
*Dossetter, Edward	1842–1927	R		United States
*Deville, Édouard	1849–1924	R S		France
Watson, Homer	1855–1936	A		**Canada**
*Royal Engineers, BC		R S		England
*Tyrrell, Joseph B.	1858–1957	R E		**Canada**
*Royal Engineers, Prairies		R S		England

A = Art first
R = Record
E = Exploration
S = Survey
C = Commercial

*Photographers

HISTORICAL ATLAS OF CANADA

10 Rindisbacher, *Occupation of the Unfortunate Colonists*, watercolour, 1821

Courtesy of National Archives of Canada, C-1505

13 O'Brien, *Sunrise on the Saguenay*, oil, ca 1882

Courtesy of National Gallery of Canada, Ottawa, 113

Lowe, *View of Cobourg*, wood engraving, 1853, after oil by O'Brien

Courtesy Metropolitan Toronto Reference Library, J Ross Robertson Collection, T 18073

12 O'Brien, *Among the Islands of Georgian Bay*, watercolour, 1886

Courtesy Art Gallery of Ontario, T 260 1

14 Fraser, *September Afternoon, Eastern Townships*, oil, 1873

Courtesy of National Gallery of Canada, Ottawa, 18159

15 Henderson, Intercolonial Railway, Matapedia River, photo, ca 1872

Courtesy of National Archives of Canada, PA-022071

16 Hind, *Harvesting Hay*, Sussex, New Brunswick, oil, ca 1880

Courtesy of National Archives of Canada, C-103003

GREENLAND
(Denmark)

NEWFOUNDLAND

For more information
about the images on this
plate, see end notes.

UDSON
BAY

ERRITORIES

JAMES
BAY

Moose
Factory

ONTARIO

QUEBEC

PEI

NEW
BRUNSWICK

NOVA SCOTIA

Montreal

Ottawa

LAKE SUPERIOR

LAKE
HURON

LAKE MICHIGAN

Toronto

LAKE
ONTARIO

LAKE ERIE

To St Louis

Images of Canada

■ 2 Approximate locations
of selected illustrations

▲ Known locations of
O'Brien landscapes

● Known locations in BC
of Dally photographs

Four itineraries

—— Peter Rindisbacher
—— Paul Kane
—— W.G.R. Hind
—— Charles Horetzky

Scale 1:17 000 000

nter Fishing on the Ice, watercolour, 1821

Courtesy of National Archives of Canada, C-001932

9 Kane, *French River Rapids*, oil 1845

Courtesy of Stark Museum of Art, Orange, Texas

Fraser and O'Brien are known to have copied the work of photographers like Alexander Henderson and Frederick Dally. Henderson chronicled the construction of the Intercolonial Railway and took views of the West after 1885, before establishing the photography department of the CPR. Dally took up photography in 1866 and by 1870 had created an extraordinary portfolio documenting coastal and interior British Columbia. Charles Horetzky, an immigrant of Polish and British extraction, learned photography from a group of amateurs in Moose Factory. As an exploratory engineer on the CPR Survey from 1871 to 1881 he pioneered the use of collodion dry-plate technology. Employing the more cumbersome wet-plate process, the Royal Engineers photographed the length of the 49th parallel in two separate expeditions between 1858 and 1874. Images in the far North include those captured by the box camera of J.B. Tyrrell during his tenure (1881–98) with the Geological Survey.

CONCISE EDITION

THE LOOK OF DOMESTIC BUILDING, 1891

Authors: Peter Ennals, Deryck W. Holdsworth

In 1891 the built landscape of Canada's settler society encompassed a wide variety of structures old and new. As cultural mixing occurred throughout the century, various house-building approaches gave way to a few regional prototypes. Their histories followed a typical sequence in which various immigrant housing forms, many of them based on old world folk-culture types, were tested and refined in response to regional and local experiences.

Whereas old dwellings had been simple in plan, typically consisting of one to three multi-purpose rooms, vernacular housing (as this new dwelling type came to be called) provided a more complex floor plan emphasizing a lifestyle lived in functionally specific rooms, eg, kitchen, bedroom, and parlour. During the 19th century the nature and form of the vernacular dwelling became more standardized and international, as pattern-books gained currency and mass-produced design components, such as doors and trim, revolutionized the technology of construction. Thus, the vernacular designer was able to mimic the style of the élite who employed architects to reproduce aesthetically correct high-style designs. In this way ordinary people sought to use housing to display taste and social achievement. Distinctions also increased between houses in rural and urban areas, reflecting differences in class, the exposure to new ideas, and the requirements of municipal fire and other regulations. Despite these many differences, regional types evolved both in towns and in rural areas. By the end of the century the built landscapes of Newfoundland, the Maritimes, Québec, Ontario, and the West could be distinguished from one another.

FOLK AND FORMAL IDIOMS

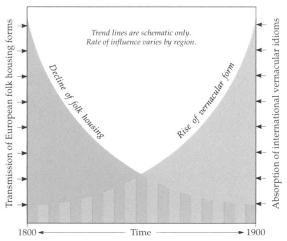

Trend lines are schematic only.
Rate of influence varies by region.

Transmission of European folk housing forms

Decline of folk housing

Rise of vernacular form

Absorption of international vernacular idioms

1800 ← Time → 1900

OKOTOKS, DISTRICT OF ALBERTA

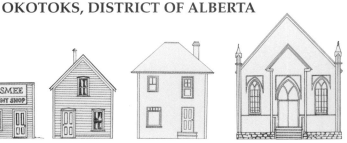

MAIN STREETS

The juxtaposition of buildings in smaller urban places frequently produced a characteristic townscape, a visual profile or signature that was regionally distinct. Arrayed along a typical 'main street' were manufacturing establishments, commercial and institutional buildings, residences, and other components of the municipal apparatus. Even when expressed as a composite of a larger reality, the streetscapes, as shown here, with their accumulations of structures spanning several years, attest to a dynamic process of growth. There was still no cohesiveness or planning control in the design of Canada's urban places. Instead, towns developed organically by integrating a complex matrix of individual economic, political, and aesthetic decisions.

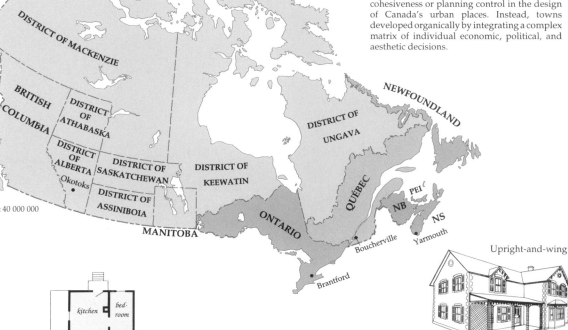

Scale 1: 40 000 000

Upright-and-wing

Farmers' Gothic

ONTARIO

Initially pioneers reproduced folk housing based on Scots and Irish hall-and-parlour variants, though rendered in one or other of the log-construction techniques carried to Ontario by Loyalists and other settlers from the New York and Pennsylvania frontier. Early in the century the style of vernacular housing became one of the many ways by which people expressed their material and social success. In the second half of the century, following heavy immigration from the British Isles, an explosion of building introduced the Gothic revival and other features, replacing, in the process, most of the earlier folk housing. The use of more expensive building materials such as brick and stone and manufactured stylistic elements differentiated social classes in both rural and urban areas.

Settler's lean-to

Western vernacular

stove / cabin

West Coast bungalow

kitchen / bedroom / parlour / bedroom / porch

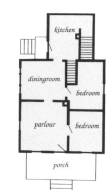

kitchen / diningroom / bedroom / parlour / bedroom / porch

Log hall-and-parlour

bedroom / kitchen / stove

NORTH AND WEST

A regional design idiom had yet to emerge in this area of new settlement. Diversity and flux marked its house-building history in the 19th century. The landscape was a disconnected patchwork of log dwellings, sod dugouts or stamped-earth huts, and vernacular farm cottages built by migrants from Ontario and adjacent American states. In British Columbia only Victoria could claim an established Anglo-American settlement landscape; hastily built false-fronted shacktowns and log houses marked the resource frontier that predominated elsewhere.

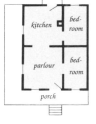

Pattern-book vernacular

dining-room / kitchen / porch / parlour

Log hall-and-parlour

bedroom / kitchen / living-room

service shed / kitchen / bedroom / dining-room / parlour

BRANTFORD, ONTARIO

HOTEL

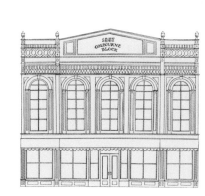

GOLBOURNE BLOCK

POST

HISTORICAL ATLAS OF CANADA

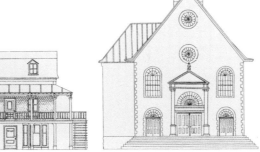

BOUCHERVILLE, QUÉBEC

QUÉBEC

By the beginning of the 19th century Québec's domestic buildings displayed a visually distinct folk idiom. During the century many old houses were expanded and adapted to reflect changes in heating technology and to incorporate the changing fashions that marked a general vernacular shift. Late in the century American vernacular architectural influences were being carried even to rural areas through family visits of Québec labourers who had migrated to New England's mill towns. These ideas fused with existing idioms to produce distinctive houses.

Québec vernacular

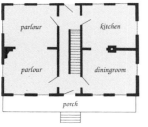

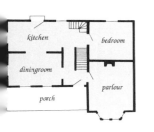

Québec hall-and-parlour
with kitchen wing

Newfoundland vernacular

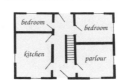

NEWFOUNDLAND

Newfoundland society was isolated from the impulses affecting architectural change in Canada. Strong folk-culture transplants from southern Ireland and West Country England reduced the range of house forms. The houses, invariably constructed of timber, preserved a characteristic hall-and-parlour form with the addition of a rear lean-to or 'linhay.' Vernacular housing filtered into the colony primarily through resident merchants in centres like St John's. By the end of the century frame houses with a centre-hall plan and a shallow pitched gable or mansard roof had become a distinctive feature of the Newfoundland landscape.

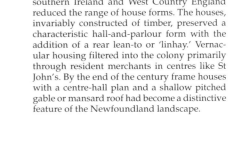

Centre-hall with linhay

Hall-and-parlour with linhay

YARMOUTH, NOVA SCOTIA

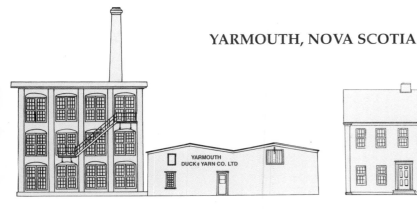

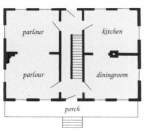

Settler's shanty

All buildings are depicted at a similar scale.

Multi-storey buildings show plan for ground floor only.

Hall-and-parlour

MARITIMES

By the early 19th century Acadian, Scots, Irish, and American folk-housing ideas had become part of the Maritime landscape (pl 48). Two- and three-room hall-and-parlour timber houses were common. Beside them appeared larger vernacular houses inspired by 18th-century Georgian and other classical idioms derived from New England. By the 1840s builders of these folk houses used New England exterior finishes although interior spaces maintained older patterns. By the end of the century a distinctive wooden Maritime vernacular house had emerged.

Colonial and Georgian

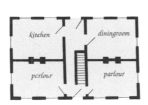

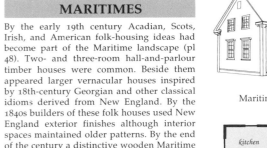

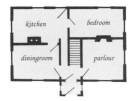

Maritime vernacular

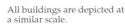

CONCISE EDITION

THE PRINTED WORD, 18th AND 19th CENTURIES

Authors: John H. Wadland, Margaret Hobbs

In 19th-century British North America the tasks of daily survival were all-consuming, leaving little time for cultural pursuits. The vastness of the land and the inhospitable terrain were formidable impediments to the movements of people, goods, and ideas, and travel was slow. Before 1850 a newspaper sent by steamship from London (England) might reach London (Ontario) in six weeks. But what could it tell its readers about Canada? In the 1750s Halifax brought the country into the information age with the establishment of the first press, the first indigenous newspaper, the first published advertisement, the first post office, and the first bookstore. While ships, canoes, and stagecoaches could move newspapers and books between the colonies, rapid duplication of the Halifax experience throughout British North America showed there was no substitute for a local press, a local bookstore, and a reading room or library.

Early colonial newspapers benefited financially but suffered intellectually from their dependence on government or religious patronage. Invariably the most independent newspapers were those based in major urban centres, where there was a large market. As the century advanced, published political and economic opinion became more sophisticated as the relationships between advertising and circulation strengthened. But the partisan preoccupations of mid-century continued. Printer, publisher, editor, and owner were often united in one person, serving Canadians the printed fare they most loved, the tangle of contentious debate.

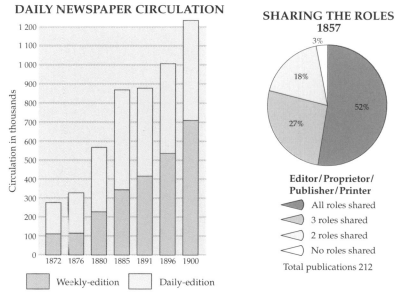

DAILY NEWSPAPER CIRCULATION

Circulation in thousands

1872, 1876, 1880, 1885, 1891, 1896, 1900

Weekly-edition   Daily-edition

SHARING THE ROLES 1857

3%
18%
27%
52%

Editor/Proprietor/
Publisher/Printer

All roles shared
3 roles shared
2 roles shared
No roles shared

Total publications 212

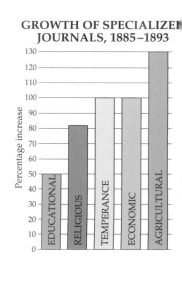

GROWTH OF SPECIALIZED JOURNALS, 1885–1893

Percentage increase

EDUCATIONAL, RELIGIOUS, TEMPERANCE, ECONOMIC, AGRICULTURAL

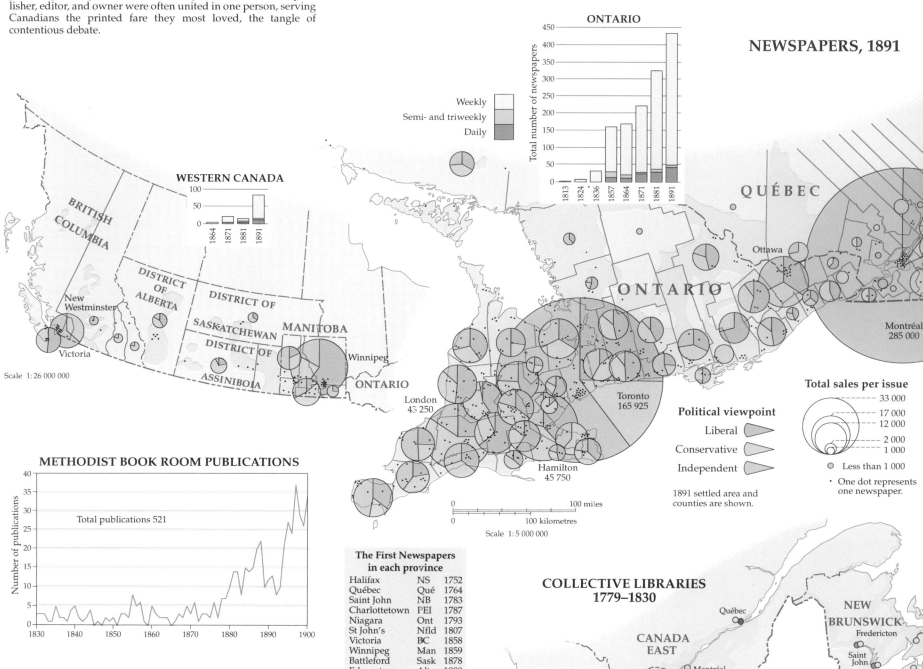

ONTARIO

Total number of newspapers

1813, 1824, 1836, 1857, 1864, 1871, 1881, 1891

Weekly
Semi- and triweekly
Daily

NEWSPAPERS, 1891

QUÉBEC

ONTARIO

Ottawa

Montréal
285 000

WESTERN CANADA

1864, 1871, 1881, 1891

BRITISH COLUMBIA

DISTRICT OF ALBERTA

DISTRICT OF SASKATCHEWAN

DISTRICT OF ASSINIBOIA

MANITOBA

New Westminster

Victoria

Winnipeg

ONTARIO

Scale 1:26 000 000

London
43 250

Toronto
165 925

Hamilton
45 750

Political viewpoint

Liberal
Conservative
Independent

1891 settled area and counties are shown.

Total sales per issue

33 000
17 000
12 000
2 000
1 000

○ Less than 1 000

• One dot represents one newspaper.

0   100 miles
0   100 kilometres
Scale 1:5 000 000

METHODIST BOOK ROOM PUBLICATIONS

Number of publications

Total publications 521

1830, 1840, 1850, 1860, 1870, 1880, 1890, 1900

The First Newspapers in each province

Halifax	NS	1752
Québec	Qué	1764
Saint John	NB	1783
Charlottetown	PEI	1787
Niagara	Ont	1793
St John's	Nfld	1807
Victoria	BC	1858
Winnipeg	Man	1859
Battleford	Sask	1878
Edmonton	Alta	1880

COLLECTIVE LIBRARIES 1779–1830

Québec

CANADA EAST

CANADA WEST

Bytown

Montréal

York
Niagara

Kingston

Founded

● 1779–1799
● 1800–1819
○ 1820–1830

Scale 1:12 000 000

NEW BRUNSWICK

Fredericton

Saint John

Halifax

REGIONAL SPREAD OF NEWSPAPERS

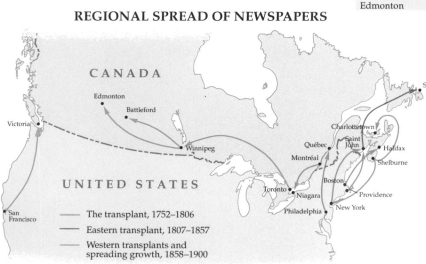

CANADA

Edmonton
Battleford
Victoria
Winnipeg

UNITED STATES

San Francisco

St John's
Charlottetown
Saint John
Québec
Halifax
Montréal
Shelburne
Toronto
Niagara
Boston
Providence
Philadelphia
New York

— The transplant, 1752–1806
— Eastern transplant, 1807–1857
— Western transplants and spreading growth, 1858–1900

Scale 1:50 000 000

The largest and most powerful publishing operation in Canada in the 19th century was the Methodist Book Room in Toronto, originally established in 1829 to produce a church newspaper, the influential *Christian Guardian*. Separated from the newspaper in 1843, the Book Room broadened its publishing list to include a more eclectic mix of text and trade books. After 1879 its new director, William Briggs, nurtured a stable of well-respected Canadian authors and began an agency to serve several prominent British and American publishers. Among those apprenticed in the Book Room were Thomas Allen, John McClelland, and George Stewart, who would leave to create their own publishing companies.

MECHANICS' INSTITUTES 1828–1852

CANADA WEST

Bytown

Toronto

London
Hamilton
Niagara
Kingston

Scale 1:12 000 000

HISTORICAL ATLAS OF CANADA

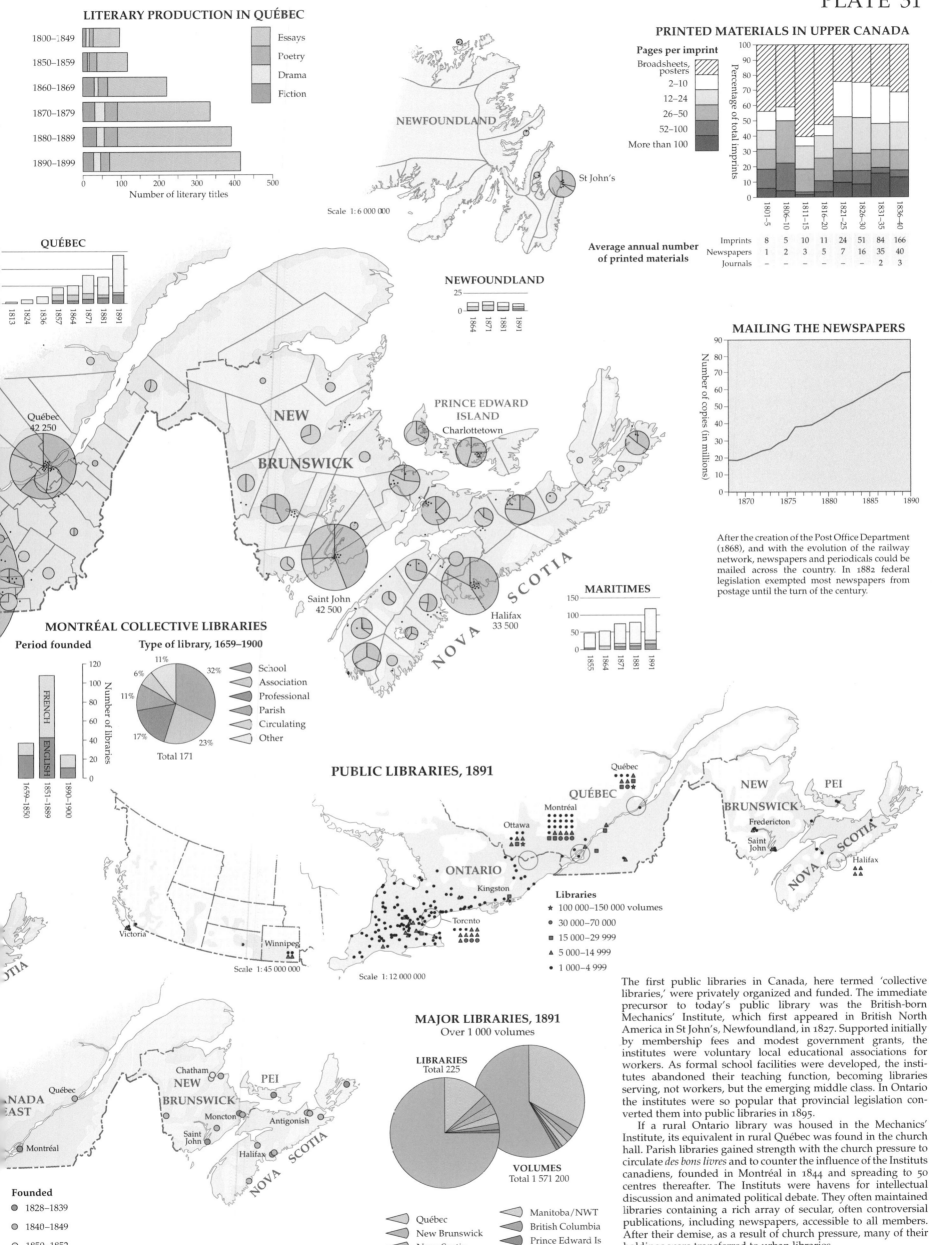

LITERARY PRODUCTION IN QUÉBEC

1800–1849
1850–1859
1860–1869
1870–1879
1880–1889
1890–1899

Essays
Poetry
Drama
Fiction

Number of literary titles

PRINTED MATERIALS IN UPPER CANADA

Pages per imprint

Broadsheets, posters
2–10
12–24
26–50
52–100
More than 100

Percentage of total imprints

	1801–5	1806–10	1811–15	1816–20	1821–25	1826–30	1831–35	1836–40
Imprints	8	5	10	11	24	51	84	166
Newspapers	1	2	3	5	7	16	35	40
Journals	–	–	–	–	–	–	2	3

Average annual number of printed materials

NEWFOUNDLAND

St John's

Scale 1:6 000 000

QUÉBEC

1813 1824 1836 1857 1864 1871 1881 1891

NEWFOUNDLAND

25

1864 1871 1881 1891

MAILING THE NEWSPAPERS

Number of copies (in millions)

1870 1875 1880 1885 1890

After the creation of the Post Office Department (1868), and with the evolution of the railway network, newspapers and periodicals could be mailed across the country. In 1882 federal legislation exempted most newspapers from postage until the turn of the century.

Québec 42 250

NEW BRUNSWICK

PRINCE EDWARD ISLAND
Charlottetown

Saint John 42 500

Halifax 33 500

NOVA SCOTIA

MARITIMES

150

1855 1864 1871 1881 1891

MONTRÉAL COLLECTIVE LIBRARIES

Period founded

Type of library, 1659–1900

Number of libraries

FRENCH
ENGLISH

1659–1850 1851–1889 1890–1900

11%
6%
11%
17%
32%
23%

School
Association
Professional
Parish
Circulating
Other

Total 171

PUBLIC LIBRARIES, 1891

Québec
QUÉBEC
Montréal
Ottawa

NEW BRUNSWICK
Fredericton
Saint John

PEI

NOVA SCOTIA
Halifax

ONTARIO
Kingston
Toronto

Libraries
★ 100 000–150 000 volumes
● 30 000–70 000
■ 15 000–29 999
▲ 5 000–14 999
• 1 000–4 999

Victoria

Winnipeg

Scale 1:45 000 000

Scale 1:12 000 000

MAJOR LIBRARIES, 1891
Over 1 000 volumes

LIBRARIES
Total 225

VOLUMES
Total 1 571 200

Québec
New Brunswick
Nova Scotia

Manitoba/NWT
British Columbia
Prince Edward Is
Ontario

Chatham
NEW BRUNSWICK
Moncton
Saint John
Halifax

Québec
Montréal

CANADA EAST

PEI
Antigonish

NOVA SCOTIA

Founded
● 1828–1839
● 1840–1849
○ 1850–1852

The first public libraries in Canada, here termed 'collective libraries,' were privately organized and funded. The immediate precursor to today's public library was the British-born Mechanics' Institute, which first appeared in British North America in St John's, Newfoundland, in 1827. Supported initially by membership fees and modest government grants, the institutes were voluntary local educational associations for workers. As formal school facilities were developed, the institutes abandoned their teaching function, becoming libraries serving, not workers, but the emerging middle class. In Ontario the institutes were so popular that provincial legislation converted them into public libraries in 1895.

If a rural Ontario library was housed in the Mechanics' Institute, its equivalent in rural Québec was found in the church hall. Parish libraries gained strength with the church pressure to circulate *des bons livres* and to counter the influence of the Instituts canadiens, founded in Montréal in 1844 and spreading to 50 centres thereafter. The Instituts were havens for intellectual discussion and animated political debate. They often maintained libraries containing a rich array of secular, often controversial publications, including newspapers, accessible to all members. After their demise, as a result of church pressure, many of their holdings were transferred to urban libraries.

THE QUEST FOR UNIVERSAL SCHOOLING, 1851–1891

Authors: Alison Prentice, Susan L. Laskin

Separation in schooling both masked and was a reaction against a powerful thrust towards uniformity. Dissatisfied with the uneven, family-oriented, and highly idiosyncratic formal education experienced by most children and also worried by what they believed was a related rise in juvenile idleness, political agitation, and crime, educational reformers turned increasingly to the state. Sectarian, political, ethnic, and class rivalries, they argued, would disappear in tax-supported schools as these came under the control of provincial and local governments. Reduced work opportunities for the young complemented a rising tide of propaganda favouring more and better government schooling. Family or local poverty and new industrial employment for children meant uneven patterns of change but, overall, increasing enrolment and attendance suggest growing acceptance of the school as the normal week-day environment for the young. Also increasingly accepted was the employment of women teachers in community schools. Here too change was uneven, with frontier regions poor in resources and rapidly expanding cities appearing to lead the way. The Catholic School Commission of Montréal made that city an exception to the general rule for urban centres; it favoured schools for boys and male teachers. The general trend almost everywhere else, however, was towards co-educational public schooling and a predominantly female teaching force in elementary schools.

EDUCATIONAL PATTERNS IN ONTARIO

--- Urban   ——— Rural

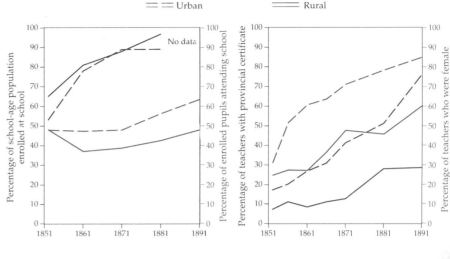

SCHOOL REGISTRATIONS

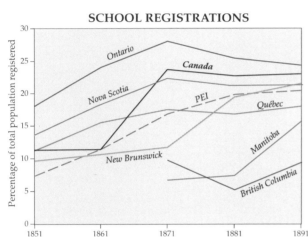

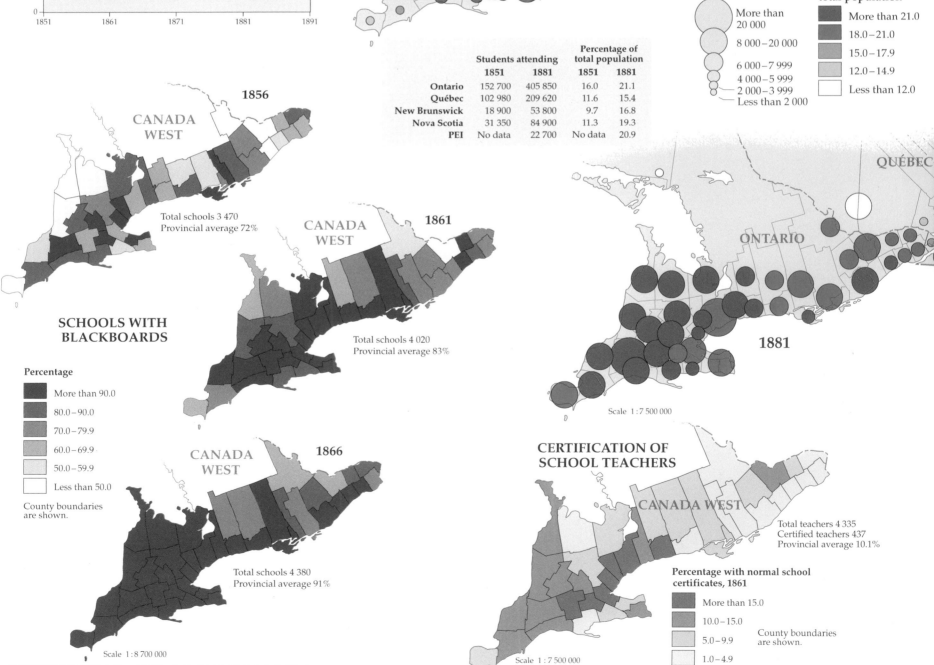

1851 grouped census districts are shown.

1851

STUDENTS IN SCHOOL

Students attending

- More than 20 000
- 8 000–20 000
- 6 000–7 999
- 4 000–5 999
- 2 000–3 999
- Less than 2 000

Percentage of total population

- More than 21.0
- 18.0–21.0
- 15.0–17.9
- 12.0–14.9
- Less than 12.0

	Students attending		Percentage of total population	
	1851	1881	1851	1881
Ontario	152 700	405 850	16.0	21.1
Québec	102 980	209 620	11.6	15.4
New Brunswick	18 900	53 800	9.7	16.8
Nova Scotia	31 350	84 900	11.3	19.3
PEI	No data	22 700	No data	20.9

1856

CANADA WEST

Total schools 3 470
Provincial average 72%

1861

CANADA WEST

Total schools 4 020
Provincial average 83%

ONTARIO

1881

Scale 1 : 7 500 000

SCHOOLS WITH BLACKBOARDS

Percentage

- More than 90.0
- 80.0–90.0
- 70.0–79.9
- 60.0–69.9
- 50.0–59.9
- Less than 50.0

County boundaries are shown.

1866

CANADA WEST

Total schools 4 380
Provincial average 91%

Scale 1 : 8 700 000

HISTORICAL ATLAS OF CANADA

CERTIFICATION OF SCHOOL TEACHERS

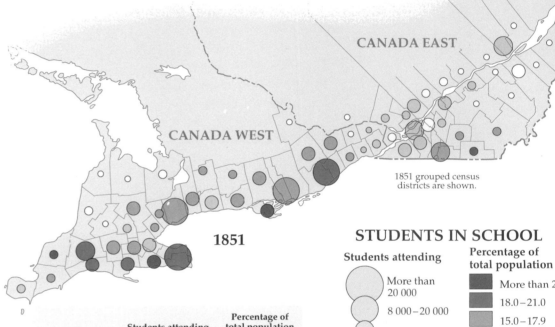

CANADA WEST

Total teachers 4 335
Certified teachers 437
Provincial average 10.1%

Percentage with normal school certificates, 1861

- More than 15.0
- 10.0–15.0
- 5.0–9.9
- 1.0–4.9

County boundaries are shown.

Scale 1 : 7 500 000

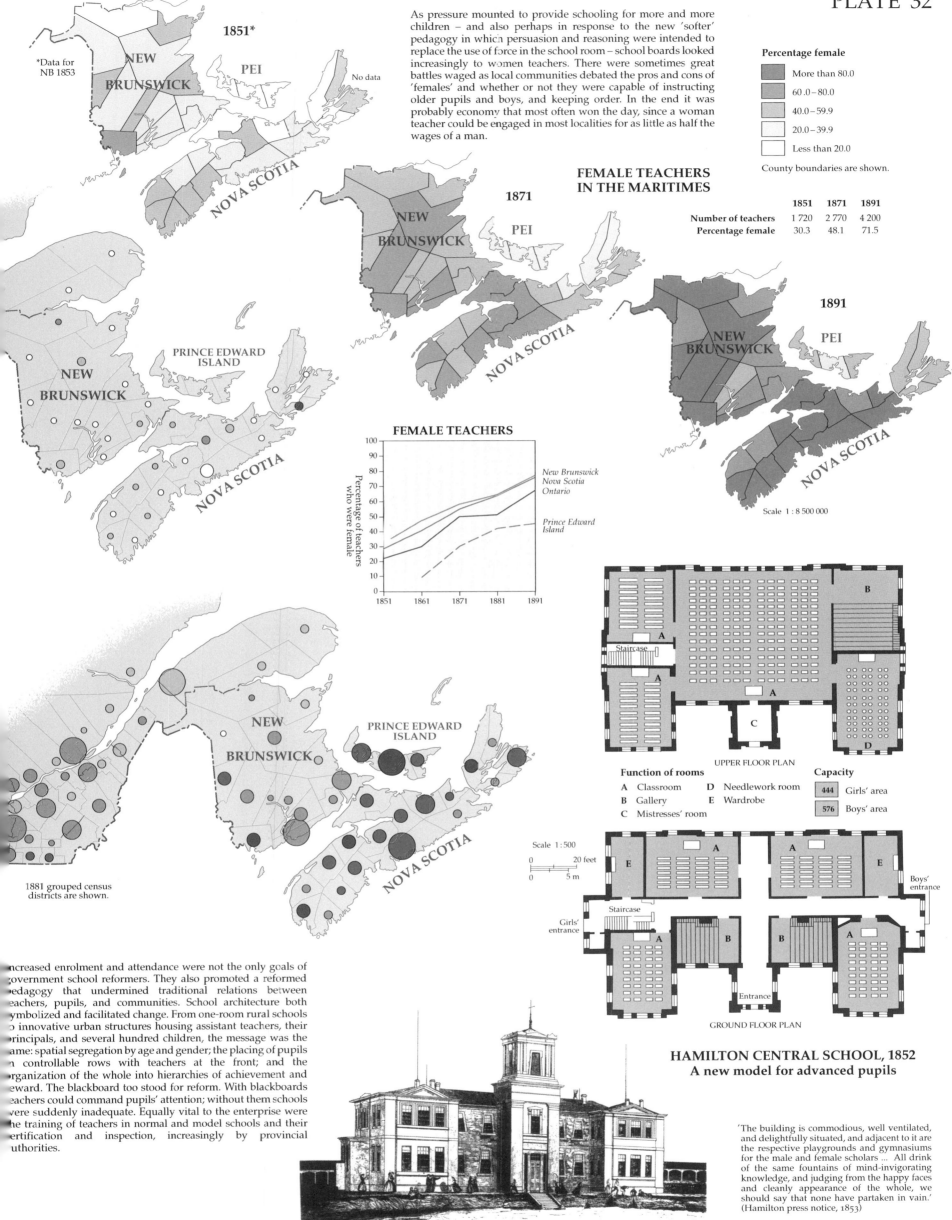

As pressure mounted to provide schooling for more and more children – and also perhaps in response to the new 'softer' pedagogy in which persuasion and reasoning were intended to replace the use of force in the school room – school boards looked increasingly to women teachers. There were sometimes great battles waged as local communities debated the pros and cons of 'females' and whether or not they were capable of instructing older pupils and boys, and keeping order. In the end it was probably economy that most often won the day, since a woman teacher could be engaged in most localities for as little as half the wages of a man.

1851*

*Data for NB 1853

NEW BRUNSWICK

PEI

No data

NOVA SCOTIA

Percentage female

More than 80.0

60.0–80.0

40.0–59.9

20.0–39.9

Less than 20.0

County boundaries are shown.

FEMALE TEACHERS IN THE MARITIMES

1871

NEW BRUNSWICK

PEI

NOVA SCOTIA

	1851	1871	1891
Number of teachers	1 720	2 770	4 200
Percentage female	30.3	48.1	71.5

1891

NEW BRUNSWICK

PEI

NOVA SCOTIA

Scale 1 : 8 500 000

PRINCE EDWARD ISLAND

NEW BRUNSWICK

NOVA SCOTIA

FEMALE TEACHERS

Percentage of teachers who were female

New Brunswick
Nova Scotia
Ontario

Prince Edward Island

1851 1861 1871 1881 1891

NEW BRUNSWICK

PRINCE EDWARD ISLAND

NOVA SCOTIA

1881 grouped census districts are shown.

Increased enrolment and attendance were not the only goals of government school reformers. They also promoted a reformed pedagogy that undermined traditional relations between teachers, pupils, and communities. School architecture both symbolized and facilitated change. From one-room rural schools to innovative urban structures housing assistant teachers, their principals, and several hundred children, the message was the same: spatial segregation by age and gender; the placing of pupils in controllable rows with teachers at the front; and the organization of the whole into hierarchies of achievement and reward. The blackboard too stood for reform. With blackboards teachers could command pupils' attention; without them schools were suddenly inadequate. Equally vital to the enterprise were the training of teachers in normal and model schools and their certification and inspection, increasingly by provincial authorities.

B

A

Staircase

A

A

C

D

UPPER FLOOR PLAN

Function of rooms

A Classroom   D Needlework room
B Gallery   E Wardrobe
C Mistresses' room

Capacity

444 Girls' area

576 Boys' area

Scale 1 : 500

0   20 feet
0   5 m

E

A

A

E

Boys' entrance

Staircase

Girls' entrance

A

B

B

A

Entrance

GROUND FLOOR PLAN

HAMILTON CENTRAL SCHOOL, 1852
A new model for advanced pupils

'The building is commodious, well ventilated, and delightfully situated, and adjacent to it are the respective playgrounds and gymnasiums for the male and female scholars ... All drink of the same fountains of mind-invigorating knowledge, and judging from the happy faces and cleanly appearance of the whole, we should say that none have partaken in vain.' (Hamilton press notice, 1853)

The Hamilton Central School, 1852

RELIGIOUS ADHERENCE, 20th CENTURY

Authors: Murdo MacPherson, Douglas Campbell (Votes of congregations, NS)

Except for the formation of the United Church of Canada in 1925, the modern patterns of religious adherence across Canada had largely emerged by 1921. In eastern Canada these patterns reflected traditions brought by migrants from Europe and the United States over three centuries. The varied origins of late 19th- and early 20th-century immigrants were apparent in the patchwork pattern of adherence on the Prairies. The diversity was even more dramatic at the local level. In Saskatchewan, for example, the band of Presbyterians and Methodists mirrored the earliest line of settlement by migrants from Ontario, the United States, and Britain, while the scattering of Lutherans on either side corresponded with settlement by Germans and Scandinavians. The presence of adherents of Greek churches* indicated Ukrainian group settlement on the prairie fringes. In British Columbia the predominance of Anglicans was a consequence of the largely British background of the population; however, the Confucian and Buddhist elements of Vancouver's population showed the significant presence of Chinese and Japanese migrants. Similarly, it is clear that Winnipeg, Toronto, and Montréal were the preferred destinations of most Jewish immigrants.

Percentage of population

	Roman Catholic	Anglican	Baptist
	50.0 or more	50.0 or more	50.0 or more
	25.0–49.9	25.0–49.9	25.0–49.9
	10.0–24.9	10.0–24.9	10.0–24.9
	Presbyterian	Methodist	Lutheran
	50.0 or more	50.0 or more	25.0–49.9
	25.0–49.9	25.0–49.9	10.0–24.9
	10.0–24.9	10.0–24.9	

First statistical rank refers to the single religious group with the greatest number of adherents per census unit and second statistical rank is the group with the next highest percentage of adherents. Religious populations are most diverse in census units where under 25% of adherents belong to the first rank.

RELIGIOUS ADHERENCE, 1921
First statistical rank

RELIGIOUS DIVERSITY IN SASKATCHEWAN, 1921

Census subdivisions

Colour shows major group only, not percentage of adherence. See central legend.

FIRST RANK

Saskatoon

Regina

Mormons 17.6%

SECOND RANK

Saskatoon

Regina

Scale 1:11 300 000

Congregationalists 11.6%

VANCOUVER

WINNIPEG

RELIGIOUS ADHERENCE, 1921
Second statistical rank

BRITISH COLUMBIA

ALBERTA

SASKATCHEWAN

MANITOBA

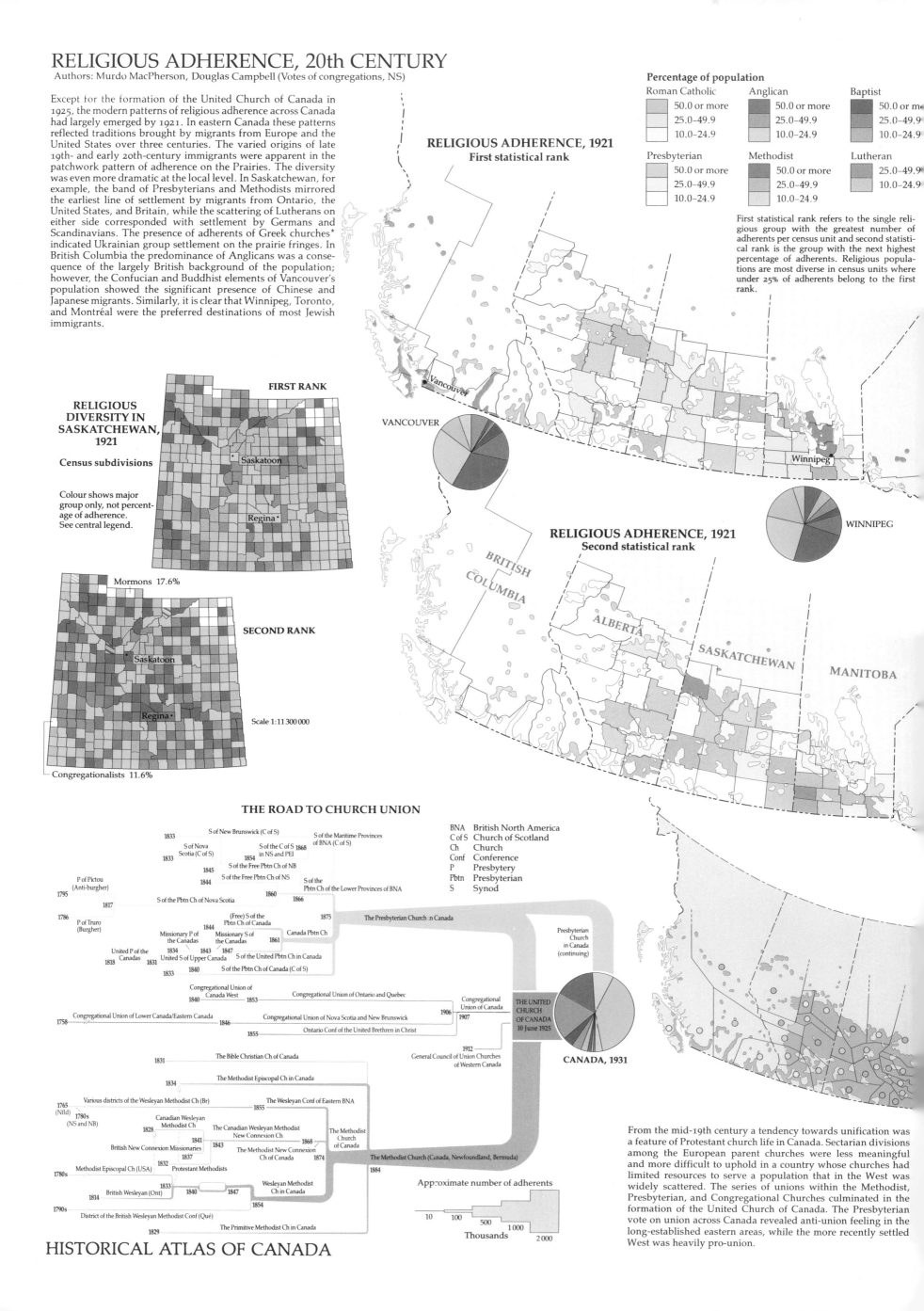

THE ROAD TO CHURCH UNION

BNA	British North America
C of S	Church of Scotland
Ch	Church
Conf	Conference
P	Presbytery
Pbtn	Presbyterian
S	Synod

S of New Brunswick (C of S) 1833

S of Nova Scotia (C of S) 1833

S of the C of S in NS and PEI 1854 1868

S of the Maritime Provinces of BNA (C of S)

S of the Free Pbtn Ch of NB 1845

S of the Free Pbtn Ch of NS 1844

S of the Pbtn Ch of the Lower Provinces of BNA 1860

P of Pictou (Anti-burgher) 1795 — 1817

S of the Pbtn Ch of Nova Scotia 1866

P of Truro (Burgher) 1786

(Free) S of the Pbtn Ch of Canada 1844 1875

The Presbyterian Church in Canada

Missionary P of the Canadas 1834

Missionary S of the Canadas 1843 1861

Canada Pbtn Ch 1847

United P of the Canadas 1818 1831

S of the United Pbtn Ch in Canada

United S of Upper Canada 1840

S of the Pbtn Ch of Canada (C of S) 1833

Presbyterian Church in Canada (continuing)

Congregational Union of Canada West 1840 1853

Congregational Union of Ontario and Quebec

Congregational Union of Canada 1906 1907

Congregational Union of Lower Canada/Eastern Canada 1758

Congregational Union of Nova Scotia and New Brunswick 1846

Ontario Conf of the United Brethren in Christ 1855

THE UNITED CHURCH OF CANADA 10 June 1925

General Council of Union Churches of Western Canada 1912

CANADA, 1931

The Bible Christian Ch of Canada 1831

The Methodist Episcopal Ch in Canada 1834

Various districts of the Wesleyan Methodist Ch (Br) 1765 (Nfld) 1780s (NS and NB)

The Wesleyan Conf of Eastern BNA 1855

Canadian Wesleyan Methodist Ch 1828

The Canadian Wesleyan Methodist New Connexion Ch 1841 1868

The Methodist Church of Canada

British New Connexion Missionaries 1837 1843

The Methodist New Connexion Ch of Canada 1874

Methodist Episcopal Ch (USA) 1780s

Protestant Methodists 1832

The Methodist Church (Canada, Newfoundland, Bermuda) 1884

British Wesleyan (Ont) 1814 1833 1840

Wesleyan Methodist Ch in Canada 1847 1854

District of the British Wesleyan Methodist Conf (Qué) 1790s

The Primitive Methodist Ch in Canada 1829

Approximate number of adherents

10   100   500   1000   2000

Thousands

HISTORICAL ATLAS OF CANADA

From the mid-19th century a tendency towards unification was a feature of Protestant church life in Canada. Sectarian divisions among the European parent churches were less meaningful and more difficult to uphold in a country whose churches had limited resources to serve a population that in the West was widely scattered. The series of unions within the Methodist, Presbyterian, and Congregational Churches culminated in the formation of the United Church of Canada. The Presbyterian vote on union across Canada revealed anti-union feeling in the long-established eastern areas, while the more recently settled West was heavily pro-union.

PLATE 33

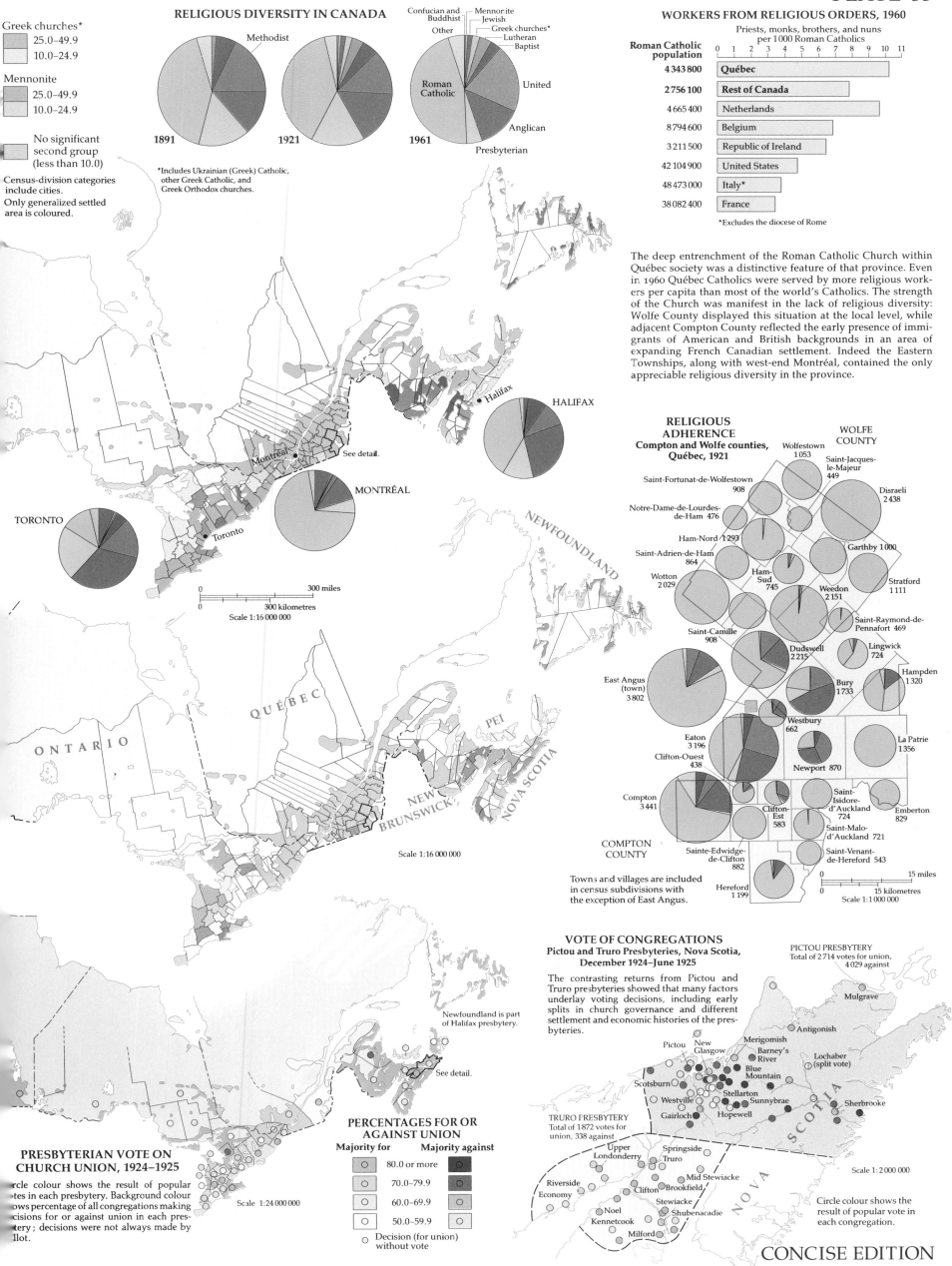

RELIGIOUS DIVERSITY IN CANADA

Greek churches*
25.0–49.9
10.0–24.9

Mennonite
25.0–49.9
10.0–24.9

No significant
second group
(less than 10.0)

Census-division categories
include cities.
Only generalized settled
area is coloured.

Methodist

Confucian and Buddhist
Other
Mennonite
Jewish
Greek churches*
Lutheran
Baptist

Roman
Catholic

United

Anglican

Presbyterian

1891   **1921**   **1961**

*Includes Ukrainian (Greek) Catholic,
other Greek Catholic, and
Greek Orthodox churches.

WORKERS FROM RELIGIOUS ORDERS, 1960

Priests, monks, brothers, and nuns
per 1000 Roman Catholics

Roman Catholic
population

0 1 2 3 4 5 6 7 8 9 10 11

4 343 800   Québec
2 756 100   **Rest of Canada**
4 665 400   Netherlands
8 794 600   Belgium
3 211 500   Republic of Ireland
42 104 900   United States
48 473 000   Italy*
38 082 400   France

*Excludes the diocese of Rome

The deep entrenchment of the Roman Catholic Church within
Québec society was a distinctive feature of that province. Even
in 1960 Québec Catholics were served by more religious workers per capita than most of the world's Catholics. The strength
of the Church was manifest in the lack of religious diversity:
Wolfe County displayed this situation at the local level, while
adjacent Compton County reflected the early presence of immigrants of American and British backgrounds in an area of
expanding French Canadian settlement. Indeed the Eastern
Townships, along with west-end Montréal, contained the only
appreciable religious diversity in the province.

HALIFAX

MONTRÉAL

TORONTO

Montréal

Toronto

Halifax

See detail.

NEWFOUNDLAND

QUÉBEC

ONTARIO

NEW
BRUNSWICK

PEI

NOVA
SCOTIA

0   300 miles
0   300 kilometres
Scale 1:16 000 000

Scale 1:16 000 000

RELIGIOUS
ADHERENCE
Compton and Wolfe counties,
Québec, 1921

WOLFE
COUNTY

Wolfestown 1053
Saint-Jacques-le-Majeur 449
Saint-Fortunat-de-Wolfestown 908
Disraeli 2438
Notre-Dame-de-Lourdes-de-Ham 476
Ham-Nord 1293
Garthby 1000
Saint-Adrien-de-Ham 864
Ham-Sud 745
Stratford 1111
Wotton 2029
Weedon 2151
Saint-Raymond-de-Pennafort 469
Saint-Camille 908
Dudswell 2215
Lingwick 724
Hampden 1320
East Angus (town) 3802
Bury 1733
Westbury 662
La Patrie 1356
Eaton 3196
Clifton-Ouest 438
Newport 870
Compton 3441
Clifton-Est 583
Saint-Isidore-d'Auckland 724
Emberton 829
Saint-Malo-d'Auckland 721
Sainte-Edwidge-de-Clifton 882
Saint-Venant-de-Hereford 543
Hereford 1199

COMPTON
COUNTY

Towns and villages are included
in census subdivisions with
the exception of East Angus.

0   15 miles
0   15 kilometres
Scale 1:1 000 000

PRESBYTERIAN VOTE ON
CHURCH UNION, 1924–1925

Circle colour shows the result of popular
votes in each presbytery. Background colour
shows percentage of all congregations making
decisions for or against union in each presbytery; decisions were not always made by
ballot.

Newfoundland is part
of Halifax presbytery.

See detail.

Scale 1:24 000 000

PERCENTAGES FOR OR
AGAINST UNION

Majority for   **Majority against**

80.0 or more
70.0–79.9
60.0–69.9
50.0–59.9

Decision (for union)
without vote

VOTE OF CONGREGATIONS
Pictou and Truro Presbyteries, Nova Scotia,
December 1924–June 1925

The contrasting returns from Pictou and
Truro presbyteries showed that many factors
underlay voting decisions, including early
splits in church governance and different
settlement and economic histories of the presbyteries.

PICTOU PRESBYTERY
Total of 2714 votes for union,
4029 against

Mulgrave
Antigonish
Pictou   New Glasgow   Merigomish
Barney's River
Lochaber (split vote)
Scotsburn   Blue Mountain
Westville   Stellarton
Sunnybrae   Sherbrooke
Gairloch   Hopewell

TRURO PRESBYTERY
Total of 1872 votes for union, 338 against

Upper Londonderry   Springside
Truro
Riverside   Mid Stewiacke
Economy   Clifton   Brookfield
Noel   Stewiacke
Kennetcook   Shubenacadie
Milford

NOVA SCOTIA

Scale 1:2 000 000

Circle colour shows the
result of popular vote in
each congregation.

CONCISE EDITION

PART TWO

DEFINING EPISODES

Throughout Canada's history there have been episodes that, in the reflective light of subsequent generations, we recognize now as landmarks along the path to modern nationhood. Some have involved the relocation of people or boundaries, others concern our stature in the world. All stand out as moments when the course of Canada's development took a new direction.

Migration from France to Canada began as the 17th century opened. It proceeded by fits and starts, in response to varying circumstances in the homeland, and stopped suddenly and permanently almost exactly 150 years later (Plate 34). This was one of history's most distinctly circumscribed population movements. Virtually all persons of French heritage in Canada trace their roots to that period, and everyone who moved into the St Lawrence valley at that time had emigrated from France. Despite their rural style in New France, the graph shows that immigrants were as likely as not to have come from cities or towns in old France. The spatter of tiny dots on the main map shows that many left for the St Lawrence in ones and twos, and as the decades passed they came from further inland (three purple maps). But the marine regions of the north and west – most isolated and outward-looking – were the predominant places of origin, and homogeneity in New France was high. Exceptional numbers emigrated in the 1660s and 1750s (table), periods when New France was threatened by the English. In the earlier instance, the threat subsided and a properly founded colony took shape; in the latter case, the threat was a harbinger of war, and of eventual British authority. A century and a half of sporadic settling activity was enough to plant a French society in America, and then the pipeline was shut off.

By the middle of the 18th century New France had grown into a crescent-shaped territory, arcing from Louisbourg, on Cape Breton Island, through the St Lawrence River valley, the Great Lakes, and the Mississippi River valley to New Orleans on the Gulf of Mexico. France's was an inland claim, and a provocative confinement of the British colonies on the East Coast, from Massachusetts southward. In this unstable situation, war inevitably erupted between these traditional enemy nations (Plate 35). The first action took place deep in the continent, in western New York and wilderness Pennsylvania, where the French troops successfully used guerrilla tactics and outmanoeuvred the British at every opportunity (main map, blue stars). The survival and prosperity of New France depended on free passage overseas, however, and here British seapower was clearly supreme (red stars). The extent of French settlement (blue shading) was feeble in comparison with the rapid colonization of the British (pink shading), and the French claim to America could not long withstand British pressure. With the extinction of French power following the British conquest of the town of Québec in 1759, British authority extended from Florida to the Arctic Islands and well inland. For tens of thousands of French people, life carried on as in a foreign country.

In Acadia – that part of New France that we speak of today as the Maritimes – the transfer from French to British authority proceeded very differently (Plate 36). In 1750, several thousand people of French descent (map, upper left, purple circles) were living in what had become British land a generation before, and had been resolutely defying British authority. The stress mounted steadily through mid-century, and in 1755 Great Britain precipitated a refugee problem that would persist for half a century. British forces undertook the deportation – the scattering, more accurately – of French people from the Baie Française (Bay of Fundy) to other English colonies as a means of breaking their resistance. Flowlines on the three buff-coloured maps depict a chaotic mixture of expulsion, escape, and relocation that continued for years throughout the Atlantic world. Many Acadians, or their descendants, eventually made their way back to the region, although seldom to precisely the same places (map, lower right). Henry W. Longfellow's epic poem 'Evangeline' recounts one couple's lifelong search for each other and the Acadian homeland they had lost.

Some three decades later yet another refugee crisis occurred, this time involving British loyalists (Plate 37). In 1776, British colonies from Massachusetts to Georgia declared independence from the rule of Great Britain, leaving about half a million people (one-quarter of the entire anglophone population in America) foreigners in their own land. Most stayed in place during the Revolutionary War (1776–83), but thereafter a few thousand departed northward to the Québec colony (central map). Some of these people had borne arms for Britain, and had to leave, while other 'United Empire Loyalists' left voluntarily in order to remain British subjects. Among those who emigrated from the United States were nearly 2 000 members of First Nations societies (yellow map, left). Hundreds more who sought a haven in southwestern New Brunswick found limited opportunity there and subsequently re-migrated – principally to Upper Canada (Ontario), but sometimes back to the United States (maps, upper right; also Plate 48, upper left). Displaced Loyalists and deeply rooted *habitants* made a potent combination, and from this unstable situation emerged Canada's two solitudes – French Québec in the St Lawrence River valley and English Ontario along the Great Lakes. A large proportion of this group were children (Plate 37, main map), lifeblood for a new society. The farmlot survey (plan, lower left) for permanent rural land-holdings, made before occupants were received, shows Britain's encouragement of, and support for, a substantial influx. Strung out from Nova Scotia to Lake Huron, and nowhere far from the new United States, a new component of the British Empire of the 19th century was taking hold and would gradually flourish.

Canada consolidated its English-speaking, British character during the second quarter of the 19th century, but only after a close call. The United States nearly won the War of 1812 (Plate 38), but the thin scattering of settlers in British America and the small, professional British garrison – about one person for every twenty Americans – proved a worthy opponent. Peace was declared in 1815, and open warfare never again erupted along the border. But a wariness of American expansionist tendencies was established at this time, and has been a central part of Canadian life ever since.

Heavy, steady immigration swelled Canada's numbers to some 1 000 000 inhabitants by about 1830 and to more than twice that number twenty years later (Plate 39). Growth was most intense in Upper Canada (Ontario), where, following a generation in which civil institutions were established and the land survey started, tens of thousands of settlers from Ireland, Scotland, and England arrived to start new, better lives. The flow lines on the main maps on Plate 39 largely bypass Lower Canada (Québec), but a substantial number of people continued on to the United States. The earlier comers tended to be independent, skilled, and not a burden on society; those who came later, and especially those seeking a haven after the Irish famine of 1846–7, were in the opposite position. Once uprooted, people are prone to relocate more than once before settling back into a new permanence. Whereas this pattern was obvious in the case of the Acadians and the United Empire Loyalists, it was more subtly manifested in this later instance, as evident in the case study of immigrants in Wellington County, Ontario, depicted in the lower left corner of the plate.

With the start of the First World War, a full century of peace and its opportunities for civilian migration came to a close. The story of population movements took a new, darker turn. From coast to coast, thousands of ordinary Canadians and Newfoundlanders found themselves involved in a distinctive counter-migration, voluntarily returning overseas to fight an Old World war (Plate 40). Enlistments were particularly strong in Manitoba, and not a street – indeed, hardly a house – in St John's failed to send its sons and daughters into service (main map). The city was literally at war. Canada's industrial heartland of southern Ontario and southern Québec produced munitions and spearheaded unprecedented fund-raising activities (map and graphs, lower left). Of the various battlefields on which Canadian forces distinguished themselves (map, centre right), none has been as significant as Vimy Ridge, taken in 1917 amid enormous sacrifice and the failure of other nations' forces. Canada is said to have come of age as a nation here, and received recognition for having effectively turned the war around.

The Great Depression of the 1930s put thousands of Canadians involuntarily on the move within their own country, in search of work and of answers to their loss of relevance in such a resource-rich country (Plate 41). The idea that this was to be 'Canada's Century' was an illusion, as Canadians attempted to support their fellow citizens in this domestic battle for survival. There surely was no depression in the record-keeping offices, as is evident from the variety of statistical material given graphic display on this plate.

The eruption of the Second World War once again directs our focus to the Atlantic Ocean and overseas (Plate 42). The Canadian army, in Italy and the Low Countries, fought as well as anybody and, considering that they were badly equipped, better than the polished German machine. The landing at Dieppe (1944) once again placed Canadians in the vanguard of turning the war around. Canadian flyers formed the backbone of the Royal Air Force after heavy losses in the Battle of Britain; thousands of European and other pilots trained all across Canada (map, upper left). The Navy, also badly equipped, escorted convoys and, along with the Merchant Marine, heroically faced German U-boats in the North Atlantic, a theatre of military activity wider than any since the Napoleonic era 130 years earlier.

THE FRENCH ORIGINS OF THE CANADIAN POPULATION, 1608–1759

Authors: Hubert Charbonneau, Normand Robert

Of some 9 000 Europeans who settled in the St Lawrence valley before 1760, only about 350 were not French. Marriage certificates usually indicate the parish of origin of couples married in Canada. Other sources–marriage contracts, confirmation lists, indenture contracts, and death certificates–provide additional information, so that in the great majority of cases the origin of an immigrant, whether married in Canada or not, can be established.

Four times as many men as women and nearly as many urban as rural people emigrated to Canada, about half of them in the 17th century. Two periods of heavy immigration, almost a hundred years apart, can be identified. The first, under Jean Talon's administration, coincided with the arrival in Canada of the 'Filles du roi' and the Carignan regiment, the second with the arrival of troops during the Seven Years' War. These two waves of immigration contributed 40% of male immigrants and the majority of female immigrants. In the 17th century women accounted for a third of all immigrants. However, after 1673 their number dropped to an average of three per year, a level maintained until the end of the French regime. Nearly all immigrants were single: one man in twenty and one woman in five were married or widowed. Couples married in France accounted for only 250 families.

Over all, the rate of emigration from the towns was nearly five times as high as from the countryside. One woman in three came from Rouen, La Rochelle, or Paris. Paris alone contributed 10% of all immigrants, and one woman in five. Indeed, two-thirds of the female immigrants were of urban origin.

IMMIGRANTS BY SEX AND DECADE, 1608–1759

Period	Men	Women	Total
Before 1630	15	6	21
1630-1639	88	51	139
1640-1649	141	86	227
1650-1659	403	239	642
1660-1669	1075	623	1698
1670-1679	429	369	798
1680-1689	486	56	542
1690-1699	490	32	522
1700-1709	283	24	307
1710-1719	293	18	311
1720-1729	420	14	434
1730-1739	483	16	499
1740-1749	576	16	592
1750-1759	1699	52	1751
Unknown	27	17	44
TOTAL	**6 908**	**1 619**	**8 527**

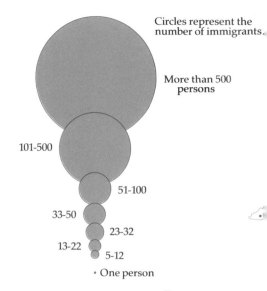

Circles represent the number of immigrants.

More than 500 persons
101-500
51-100
33-50
23-32
13-22
5-12
• One person

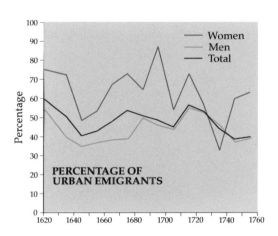

PERCENTAGE OF URBAN EMIGRANTS

Women
Men
Total

Percentage

Brest
Quimper
BRETAGNE

Before 1670

Total immigration: 2 727
Province unknown: 194

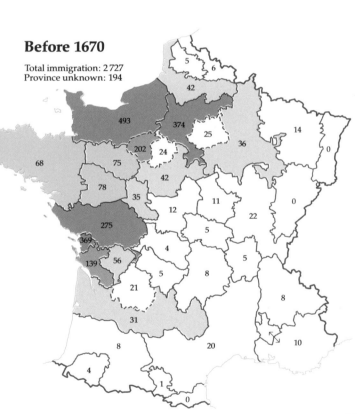

1670–1699

Total immigration: 1 862
Province unknown: 162

1700–1759

Total immigration: 3 894
Province unknown: 227

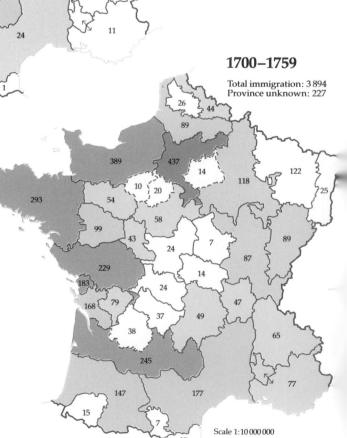

IMMIGRATION BY PROVINCE OF ORIGIN

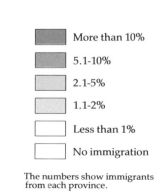

■	More than 10%
■	5.1-10%
■	2.1-5%
■	1.1-2%
□	Less than 1%
□	No immigration

The numbers show immigrants from each province.

Settlers came from all the provinces of France, but about three-quarters were from west of a line between Bordeaux and Soissons. Besides Paris, the main regions of emigration lay in the hinterlands of the major ports of embarkation: La Rochelle, Bordeaux, Rouen, Dieppe, Saint-Malo, Granville. The foremost provinces were Normandy and Île-de-France, followed by Poitou, Aunis, Brittany, and Saintonge. Prior to 1670 Normandy ranked first, but it was later superseded by the Île-de-France. Along with Poitou-Charentes, these three areas contributed two-thirds of all the 17th century immigrants. After 1700 the Midi also contributed immigrants; soldiers from the southwest and east tended to succeed the indentured servants of the central west and northwest.

Scale 1:10 000 000

HISTORICAL ATLAS OF CANADA

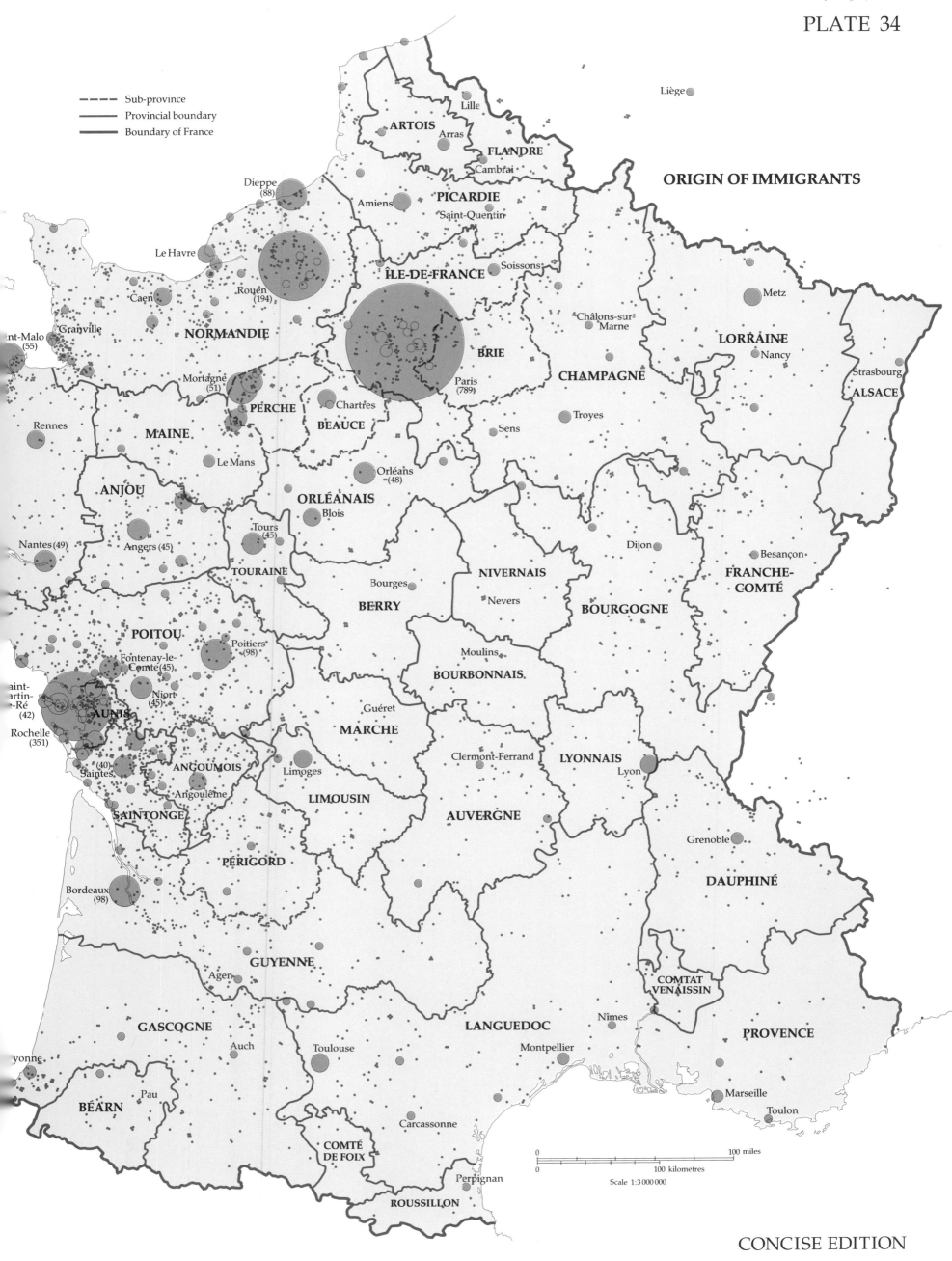

ORIGIN OF IMMIGRANTS

- - - Sub-province
——— Provincial boundary
━━━ Boundary of France

Liège

ARTOIS
Lille
Arras
FLANDRE
Cambrai
PICARDIE
Amiens
Saint-Quentin
Dieppe (88)
Le Havre
Soissons
ÎLE-DE-FRANCE
Rouen (194)
Caen
Granville
NORMANDIE
BRIE
Metz
LORRAINE
Nancy
Strasbourg
ALSACE
Châlons-sur-Marne
CHAMPAGNE
Saint-Malo (55)
Mortagne (51)
PERCHE
Chartres
BEAUCE
Paris (789)
Troyes
Sens
Rennes
MAINE
Le Mans
ANJOU
Orléans (48)
ORLÉANAIS
Blois
Dijon
Besançon
FRANCHE-COMTÉ
Nantes (49)
Angers (45)
Tours (45)
TOURAINE
Bourges
NIVERNAIS
Nevers
BOURGOGNE
POITOU
Poitiers (98)
BERRY
Fontenay-le-Comté (45)
Niort (45)
Moulins
Saint-Martin-de-Ré (42)
AUNIS
BOURBONNAIS
Guéret
MARCHE
Clermont-Ferrand
LYONNAIS
Lyon
Rochelle (351)
(40)
Saintes
ANGOUMOIS
Limoges
Angoulême
SAINTONGE
LIMOUSIN
AUVERGNE
Grenoble
DAUPHINÉ
PÉRIGORD
Bordeaux (98)
GUYENNE
Agen
COMTAT VENAISSIN
GASCOGNE
Auch
Toulouse
LANGUEDOC
Nîmes
PROVENCE
Bayonne
Pau
Montpellier
Marseille
BÉARN
Toulon
Carcassonne
COMTÉ DE FOIX
Perpignan
ROUSSILLON

0   100 miles
0   100 kilometres
Scale 1:3 000 000

CONCISE EDITION

THE SEVEN YEARS' WAR

Authors: W.J. Eccles, Susan L. Laskin

THE LAKE CHAMPLAIN CORRIDOR

CANADA

Ottawa

Montréal

Fort Chambly
ABANDONED by French
1 Sep 1760

Fort Saint-Jean
ABANDONED by French
29 Aug 1760

ST LAWRENCE RIVER

Fort de l'Île-aux-Noix
ABANDONED by French
28 Aug 1760

NEW YORK

LAKE CHAMPLAIN

NAVAL SKIRMISH
17 Oct 1759

BRITISH ADVANCE ON MONTRÉAL
11 Aug 1760
3 400 British (1 750 British regulars,
1 500 American provincials, 150 Indians)

Fort Saint-Frédéric/
Crown Point

ABANDONED by French 31 July 1759
British build Crown Point

ATTACK ON CARILLON 8 July 1758
Defenders: 3 510 French (3 100 Troupes de
Terre, 250 Canadian militia, 150 Troupes
de la Marine, 10 Indians)
Attackers: 15 390 British (9 020 American
provincials, 6 370 British regulars)
Outcome: British repulsed: 550 British killed,
1 360 wounded; 110 French killed, 270 wounded

Carillon/
Ticonderoga

ADVANCE ON CARILLON 27 July 1759
Defenders: 2 300 French
Attackers: 6 300 British
Outcome: French withdraw and Carillon
renamed Ticonderoga

Fort William Henry/
Fort George

SIEGE OF FORT WILLIAM HENRY 9 Aug 1757
Defenders: 2 450 British (1 400 American militia,
850 British regulars, 100 Royal Artillery, 100 Rangers)
Attackers: 8 030 French (2 950 Canadian militia and
volunteers, 2 570 Troupes de Terre, 1 800 Indians,
520 Troupes de la Marine, 190 gunners)
Outcome: Captured by French: 40 British killed,
70 wounded; 20 French killed, 40 wounded
REBUILT by British 9 Aug 1759
and renamed Fort George

Fort Edward

Fort Miller

BATTLE 8 Sep 1755
1 700 British (1 500 American
militia, 200 Indians)
1 500 French (700 Indians,
600 Canadian militia,
200 Troupes de Terre)
Outcome: Stalemate: 190 British
killed, 100 wounded; 100–120 French
killed, 130 wounded

Fort
Saratoga

Fort
Stillwater

Fort Half
Moon

Albany

Hudson

0   30 miles
0   30 kilometres
Scale 1:2 500 000

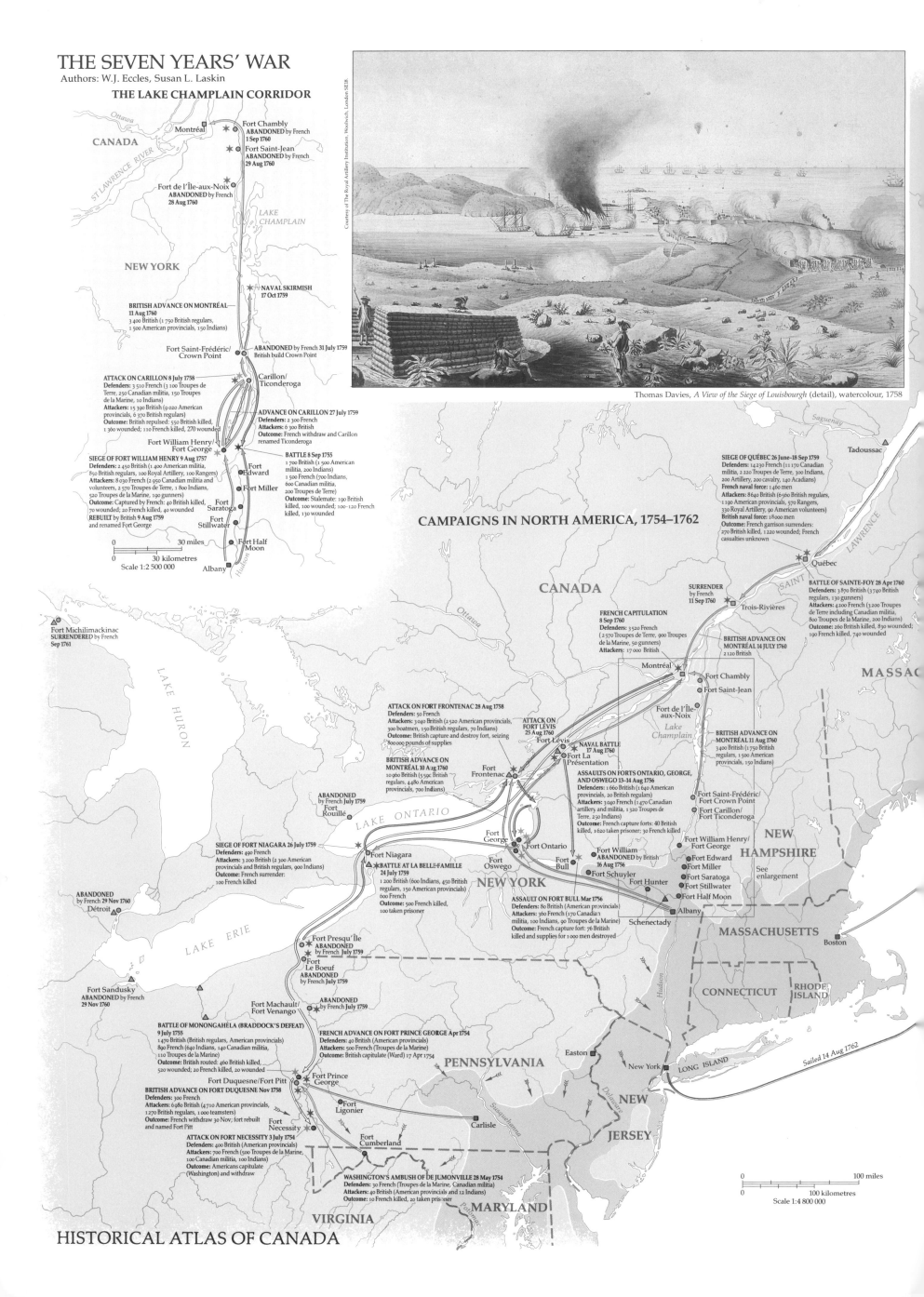

Thomas Davies, *A View of the Siege of Louisbourgh* (detail), watercolour, 1758

CAMPAIGNS IN NORTH AMERICA, 1754–1762

Saguenay

Tadoussac

SAINT LAWRENCE

SIEGE OF QUÉBEC 26 June–18 Sep 1759
Defenders: 14 230 French (11 170 Canadian
militia, 2 220 Troupes de Terre, 300 Indians,
200 Artillery, 200 cavalry, 140 Acadians)
French naval force: 1 460 men
Attackers: 8 640 British (6 560 British regulars,
1 190 American provincials, 570 Rangers,
330 Royal Artillery, 90 American volunteers)
British naval force: 18 000 men
Outcome: French garrison surrenders:
270 British killed, 1 220 wounded; French
casualties unknown

Québec

CANADA

SURRENDER
by French
11 Sep 1760

Trois-Rivières

FRENCH CAPITULATION
8 Sep 1760
Defenders: 3 520 French
(2 570 Troupes de Terre, 900 Troupes
de la Marine, 50 gunners)
Attackers: 17 000 British

BATTLE OF SAINTE-FOY 28 Apr 1760
Defenders: 3 870 British (3 740 British
regulars, 130 gunners)
Attackers: 4 200 French (3 200 Troupes de
Terre including Canadian militia,
800 Troupes de la Marine, 200 Indians)
Outcome: 260 British killed, 830 wounded;
190 French killed, 740 wounded

Ottawa

Montréal

**BRITISH ADVANCE ON
MONTRÉAL 14 JULY 1760**
2 120 British

Fort Chambly

Fort Saint-Jean

Fort de l'Île-
aux-Noix

*Lake
Champlain*

**BRITISH ADVANCE ON
MONTRÉAL 11 Aug 1760**
3 400 British (1 750 British
regulars, 1 500 American
provincials, 150 Indians)

MASSAC[HUSETTS]

LAKE HURON

Fort Michilimackinac
SURRENDERED by French
Sep 1761

ATTACK ON FORT FRONTENAC 28 Aug 1758
Defenders: 50 French
Attackers: 3 040 British (2 520 American provincials,
300 boatmen, 150 British regulars, 70 Indians)
Outcome: British capture and destroy fort, seizing
800 000 pounds of supplies

**ATTACK ON
FORT LÉVIS
25 Aug 1760**
Fort Lévis

**NAVAL BATTLE
17 Aug 1760**
Fort La
Présentation

**BRITISH ADVANCE ON
MONTRÉAL 10 Aug 1760**
10 960 British (5 590 British
regulars, 4 480 American
provincials, 700 Indians)

Fort
Frontenac

**ASSAULTS ON FORTS ONTARIO, GEORGE,
AND OSWEGO 13–14 Aug 1756**
Defenders: 1 660 British (1 640 American
provincials, 20 British regulars)
Attackers: 3 040 French (1 470 Canadian
artillery and militia, 1 320 Troupes de
Terre, 250 Indians)
Outcome: French capture forts: 40 British
killed, 1 620 taken prisoner; 30 French killed

Fort Saint-Frédéric/
Fort Crown Point

Fort Carillon/
Fort Ticonderoga

ABANDONED
by French July 1759
Fort
Rouillé

LAKE ONTARIO

Fort
George

Fort Ontario

Fort
Bull

Fort William
ABANDONED by British
16 Aug 1756

Fort Schuyler

**NEW
HAMPSHIRE**

Fort William Henry/
Fort George

Fort Edward

Fort Miller

Fort Saratoga

See
enlargement

SIEGE OF FORT NIAGARA 26 July 1759
Defenders: 490 French
Attackers: 3 200 British (2 300 American
provincials and British regulars, 900 Indians)
Outcome: French surrender:
100 French killed

Fort Niagara

△ **BATTLE AT LA BELLE-FAMILLE
24 July 1759**
1 200 French (600 Indians, 450 British
regulars, 150 American provincials)
600 French
Outcome: 500 French killed,
100 taken prisoner

Fort
Oswego

NEW YORK

Fort Hunter

Fort Stillwater

Fort Half
Moon

ASSAULT ON FORT BULL Mar 1756
Defenders: 80 British (American provincials)
Attackers: 360 French (170 Canadian
militia, 100 Indians, 90 Troupes de la Marine)
Outcome: French capture fort: 76 British
killed and supplies for 1 000 men destroyed

Schenectady

Albany

Hudson

MASSACHUSETTS

Boston

ABANDONED
by French 29 Nov 1760
Détroit

LAKE ERIE

Fort Sandusky
ABANDONED by French
29 Nov 1760

Fort Presqu'Île
ABANDONED
by French July 1759

Fort
Le Boeuf
ABANDONED
by French July 1759

Fort Machault/
Fort Venango

ABANDONED
by French July 1759

BATTLE OF MONONGAHÉLA (BRADDOCK'S DEFEAT)
9 July 1755
1 470 British (British regulars, American provincials)
890 French (640 Indians, 140 Canadian militia,
110 Troupes de la Marine)
Outcome: British routed: 460 British killed,
520 wounded; 20 French killed, 20 wounded

FRENCH ADVANCE ON FORT PRINCE GEORGE Apr 1754
Defenders: 40 British (American provincials)
Attackers: 500 French (Troupes de la Marine)
Outcome: British capitulate (Ward) 17 Apr 1754

Fort Duquesne/Fort Pitt

Fort Prince
George

Fort

BRITISH ADVANCE ON FORT DUQUESNE Nov 1758
Defenders: 300 French
Attackers: 6 980 British (4 710 American provincials,
1 270 British regulars, 1 000 teamsters)
Outcome: French withdraw 30 Nov; fort rebuilt
and named Fort Pitt

Fort
Ligonier

Fort
Necessity

ATTACK ON FORT NECESSITY 3 July 1754
Defenders: 400 British (American provincials)
Attackers: 700 French (500 Troupes de la Marine,
100 Canadian militia, 100 Indians)
Outcome: Americans capitulate
(Washington) and withdraw

Fort Cumberland

Carlisle

Easton

PENNSYLVANIA

New York

LONG ISLAND

Sailed 14 Aug 1762

Delaware

**NEW
JERSEY**

Susquehanna

CONNECTICUT

**RHODE
ISLAND**

WASHINGTON'S AMBUSH OF DE JUMONVILLE 28 May 1754
Defenders: 30 French (Troupes de la Marine, Canadian militia)
Attackers: 40 British (American provincials and 12 Indians)
Outcome: 10 French killed, 20 taken prisoner

Potomac

MARYLAND

VIRGINIA

0   100 miles
0   100 kilometres
Scale 1:4 800 000

HISTORICAL ATLAS OF CANADA

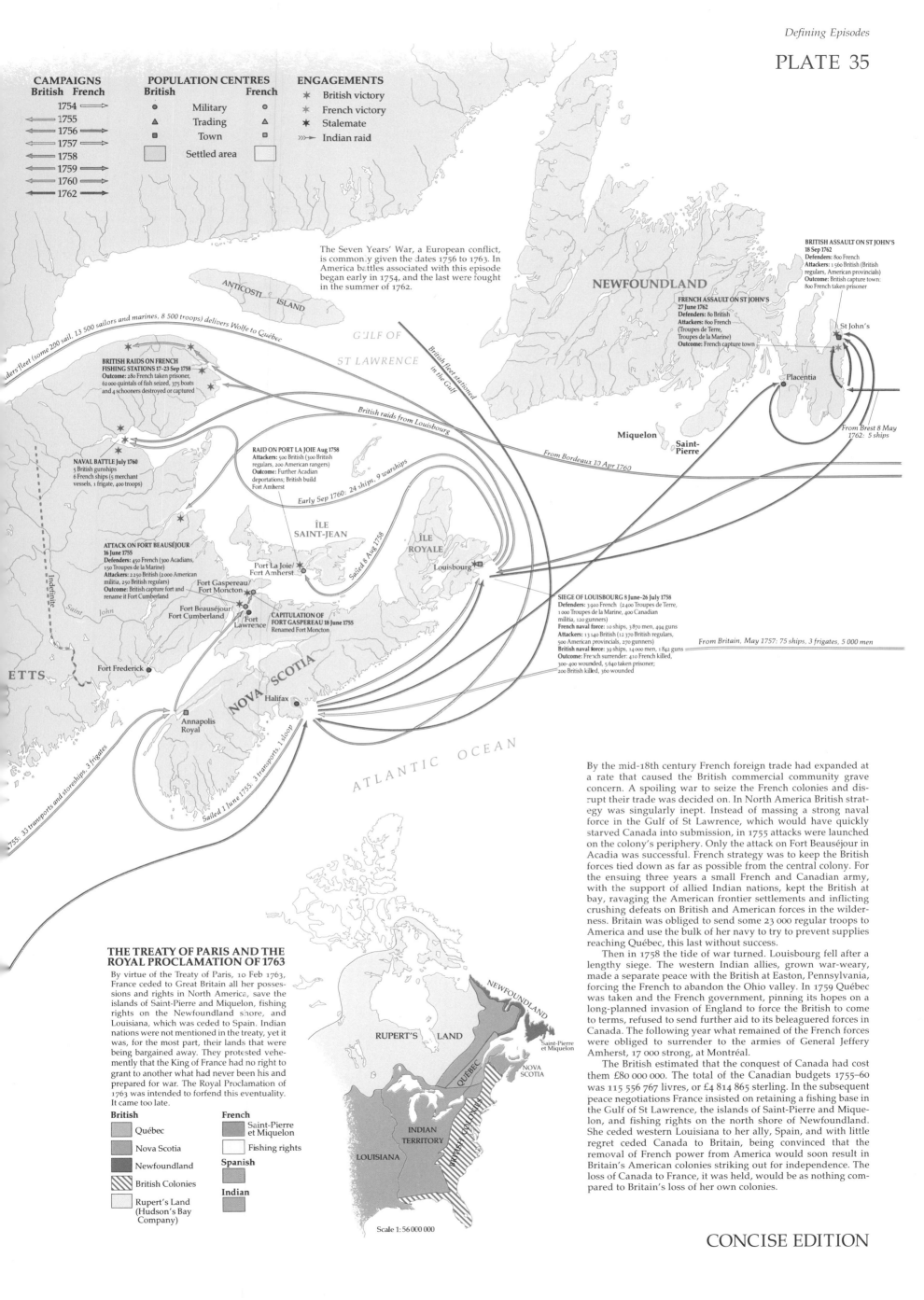

CAMPAIGNS

British	French
1754	
1755	
1756	
1757	
1758	
1759	
1760	
1762	

POPULATION CENTRES

British		French
●	Military	●
▲	Trading	▲
■	Town	■
▢	Settled area	▢

ENGAGEMENTS

✳ British victory
✳ French victory
✳ Stalemate
⋙ Indian raid

The Seven Years' War, a European conflict, is commonly given the dates 1756 to 1763. In America battles associated with this episode began early in 1754, and the last were fought in the summer of 1762.

ANTICOSTI ISLAND

NEWFOUNDLAND

GULF OF ST LAWRENCE

British fleet stationed in the Gulf

BRITISH ASSAULT ON ST JOHN'S
18 Sep 1762
Defenders: 800 French
Attackers: 1 560 British (British regulars, American provincials)
Outcome: British capture town; 800 French taken prisoner

FRENCH ASSAULT ON ST JOHN'S
27 June 1762
Defenders: 80 British
Attackers: 800 French (Troupes de Terre, Troupes de la Marine)
Outcome: French capture town

St John's

Placentia

Miquelon

Saint-Pierre

From Brest 8 May 1762: 5 ships

anders' fleet (some 200 sail, 13 500 sailors and marines, 8 500 troops) delivers Wolfe to Québec

British raids from Louisbourg

From Bordeaux 19 Apr 1760

BRITISH RAIDS ON FRENCH FISHING STATIONS 17–23 Sep 1758
Outcome: 280 French taken prisoner, 62 000 quintals of fish seized, 375 boats and 4 schooners destroyed or captured

NAVAL BATTLE July 1760
5 British gunships
6 French ships (5 merchant vessels, 1 frigate, 400 troops)

ATTACK ON FORT BEAUSÉJOUR
16 June 1755
Defenders: 450 French (300 Acadians, 150 Troupes de la Marine)
Attackers: 2 250 British (2 000 American militia, 250 British regulars)
Outcome: British capture fort and rename it Fort Cumberland

RAID ON PORT LA JOIE Aug 1758
Attackers: 500 British (300 British regulars, 200 American rangers)
Outcome: Further Acadian deportations; British build Fort Amherst

Early Sep 1760: 24 ships, 9 warships

ÎLE SAINT-JEAN

ÎLE ROYALE

Port La Joie/ Fort Amherst

Sailed 8 Aug 1758

Louisbourg

SIEGE OF LOUISBOURG 8 June–26 July 1758
Defenders: 3 920 French (2 400 Troupes de Terre, 1 000 Troupes de la Marine, 400 Canadian militia, 120 gunners)
French naval force: 10 ships, 3 870 men, 494 guns
Attackers: 13 140 British (12 370 British regulars, 500 American provincials, 270 gunners)
British naval force: 39 ships, 14 000 men, 1 842 guns
Outcome: French surrender: 410 French killed, 300–400 wounded, 5 640 taken prisoner; 200 British killed, 360 wounded

From Britain, May 1757: 75 ships, 3 frigates, 5 000 men

Fort Gaspereau/ Fort Moncton

Fort Beauséjour/ Fort Cumberland

Fort Lawrence

CAPITULATION OF FORT GASPEREAU 18 June 1755
Renamed Fort Moncton

St John

Indefinite

Fort Frederick

ETTS

NOVA SCOTIA

Halifax

Annapolis Royal

1755: 33 transports and storeships, 3 frigates

Sailed 1 June 1755: 3 transports, 1 sloop

ATLANTIC OCEAN

By the mid-18th century French foreign trade had expanded at a rate that caused the British commercial community grave concern. A spoiling war to seize the French colonies and disrupt their trade was decided on. In North America British strategy was singularly inept. Instead of massing a strong naval force in the Gulf of St Lawrence, which would have quickly starved Canada into submission, in 1755 attacks were launched on the colony's periphery. Only the attack on Fort Beauséjour in Acadia was successful. French strategy was to keep the British forces tied down as far as possible from the central colony. For the ensuing three years a small French and Canadian army, with the support of allied Indian nations, kept the British at bay, ravaging the American frontier settlements and inflicting crushing defeats on British and American forces in the wilderness. Britain was obliged to send some 23 000 regular troops to America and use the bulk of her navy to try to prevent supplies reaching Québec, this last without success.

Then in 1758 the tide of war turned. Louisbourg fell after a lengthy siege. The western Indian allies, grown war-weary, made a separate peace with the British at Easton, Pennsylvania, forcing the French to abandon the Ohio valley. In 1759 Québec was taken and the French government, pinning its hopes on a long-planned invasion of England to force the British to come to terms, refused to send further aid to its beleaguered forces in Canada. The following year what remained of the French forces were obliged to surrender to the armies of General Jeffery Amherst, 17 000 strong, at Montréal.

The British estimated that the conquest of Canada had cost them £80 000 000. The total of the Canadian budgets 1755–60 was 115 556 767 livres, or £4 814 865 sterling. In the subsequent peace negotiations France insisted on retaining a fishing base in the Gulf of St Lawrence, the islands of Saint-Pierre and Miquelon, and fishing rights on the north shore of Newfoundland. She ceded western Louisiana to her ally, Spain, and with little regret ceded Canada to Britain, being convinced that the removal of French power from America would soon result in Britain's American colonies striking out for independence. The loss of Canada to France, it was held, would be as nothing compared to Britain's loss of her own colonies.

THE TREATY OF PARIS AND THE ROYAL PROCLAMATION OF 1763

By virtue of the Treaty of Paris, 10 Feb 1763, France ceded to Great Britain all her possessions and rights in North America, save the islands of Saint-Pierre and Miquelon, fishing rights on the Newfoundland shore, and Louisiana, which was ceded to Spain. Indian nations were not mentioned in the treaty, yet it was, for the most part, their lands that were being bargained away. They protested vehemently that the King of France had no right to grant to another what had never been his and prepared for war. The Royal Proclamation of 1763 was intended to forfend this eventuality. It came too late.

British	French
▢ Québec	▢ Saint-Pierre et Miquelon
▢ Nova Scotia	▢ Fishing rights
▢ Newfoundland	**Spanish**
▨ British Colonies	▢
▢ Rupert's Land (Hudson's Bay Company)	**Indian**
	▢

RUPERT'S LAND

NEWFOUNDLAND

QUÉBEC

Saint-Pierre et Miquelon

NOVA SCOTIA

BRITISH COLONIES

INDIAN TERRITORY

LOUISIANA

Scale 1:56 000 000

ACADIAN DEPORTATION AND RETURN, 1750–1803

Authors: Jean Daigle, Robert LeBlanc

POPULATION DISTRIBUTION 1750

French control	British control
■ French fort	■ British fort

4 000
2 000
1 000
500

- Acadians
- Other French
- British

Circles are proportional to
population of major settlements.

· One dot represents 25 people.

The British captured Port-Royal in 1710. In 1713, when the Treaty of Utrecht confirmed British control of peninsular Nova Scotia, most Acadians found themselves in British territory.

For more than thirty years they were left alone; their settlements filled the Fundy marshes. Then, during most of the 1740s, Britain and France were again at war. Louisbourg fell to New England militiamen in 1745, and when the British returned it after the Treaty of Aix-la-Chapelle in 1748, they embarked on a rival fortification at Halifax. The French strengthened Louisbourg. In 1755, at the start of the Seven Years' War (pl 35), nervous British officials in Nova Scotia, suspecting Acadian claims of neutrality, decided to deport the Acadians, who by then numbered almost 13 000 people.

BAIE DES CHALEURS

Nepisiguit

Miramichy

ÎLE SAINT-JEAN

Niganiche

Malpèque
Tracadie
Pointe-de-l'Est
Bedèque
Rivière-du-Nord
Saint-Pierre
Rivière-du-Nord-Est
Anse-de-la-Fortune

ÎLE ROYALE

Baie-des-Espagnols

Baie de Miré

Fort Gédaïque
Memramkook
Fort Beauséjour
Port-Lajoie
Pointe-à-Prime
Baie Verte
Fort Gaspareau
Louisbourg (3 990)

Fort Nashouat
Petitcoudiac
Fort Lawrence
Tatmagouche
Port-Toulouse
Petite-Framboise
Nérichac

Fort Jemseg
Chepoudy
Baie de Chignectou

ACADIA

Fort Nerepis
Fort Latour
Fort Ménagouèche
Bassin des Mines
Cobeguit
Canso

BAIE FRANÇAISE
Rivière-aux-Canards (750)
Grand-Pré (1 350)
NOVA SCOTIA
Pigiguit (600)
Fort Edward
(300)
Port-Royal (500)
Fort Anne
Chezzetkouk
Halifax (1 675)
La Hève
Mirliguèche

Scale 1:2 900 000

Tebouque

Pobomcoup

Ministigueshe

1758–1762

Scale 1:19 000 000

NOUVELLE-FRANCE / CANADA

NEWFOUNDLAND

SAINT-PIERRE ET MIQUELON

1758 (3 500)
To France
1758–60 (500)
1759 (200)
1759 (?)
1760 (300)
To France

MAINE
N.H.
NEW YORK
MASS.
1762 (1 500)
CONN.
R.I.
1762 (1 500)
1758–62
PENNSYLVANIA
N.J.
MD.
DELAWARE
VIRGINIA
1758–62
NORTH CAROLINA
GEORGIA
SOUTH CAROLINA
1758–9 (200)
1758–9 (?)
1758–9 (?)
To New Orleans

⬅ 1 000
⬅ 500
⬅ 250 or less
⬅ Number unknown

Arrows are proportional to Acadian population movements.

1755–1757

NOUVELLE-FRANCE / CANADA

NEWFOUNDLAND

SAINT-PIERRE ET MIQUELON

1755 (500)
(?)
1755–8 (1 500)
(2 000)

MAINE
N.H.
(2 000)
(700)
NEW YORK
MASS.
R.I.
CONN.
(250)
PENNSYLVANIA
N.J.
(500)
MD.
(1)
DELAWARE
(1 000)
VIRGINIA
(1 100)
(1 100)
To England
1756
(500)
NORTH CAROLINA
SOUTH CAROLINA
(500)
GEORGIA
(400)

⬅ Acadian deportation
⬅ Acadian flight
⬅ Acadian migration
■ Origin of deported Acadians

Deportation began without consultation with the British government or notification of officials in the colonies to which the Acadians were being sent. Before the end of 1755 more than half of the Acadians had been sent to British colonies south of Acadia. Authorities in Virginia, fearing that the Acadians would be a public expense, rerouted them to England. Refugees from the deportation of 1755 escaped to the south shore of the Gulf of St Lawrence, Île Saint-Jean (Prince Edward Island), or the French settlements along the St Lawrence River. In 1758, when Louisbourg was captured for the second time and the French could no longer protect the Gulf, the British rounded up another 2 500 Acadians, sending them to England or France. Others fled to the Miramichi River or to the islands of Saint-Pierre and Miquelon where, before 1763, most were caught and deported. Finally, during the American Revolution the remaining Acadian refugees on Saint-Pierre and Miquelon were sent to France.

1763–1785

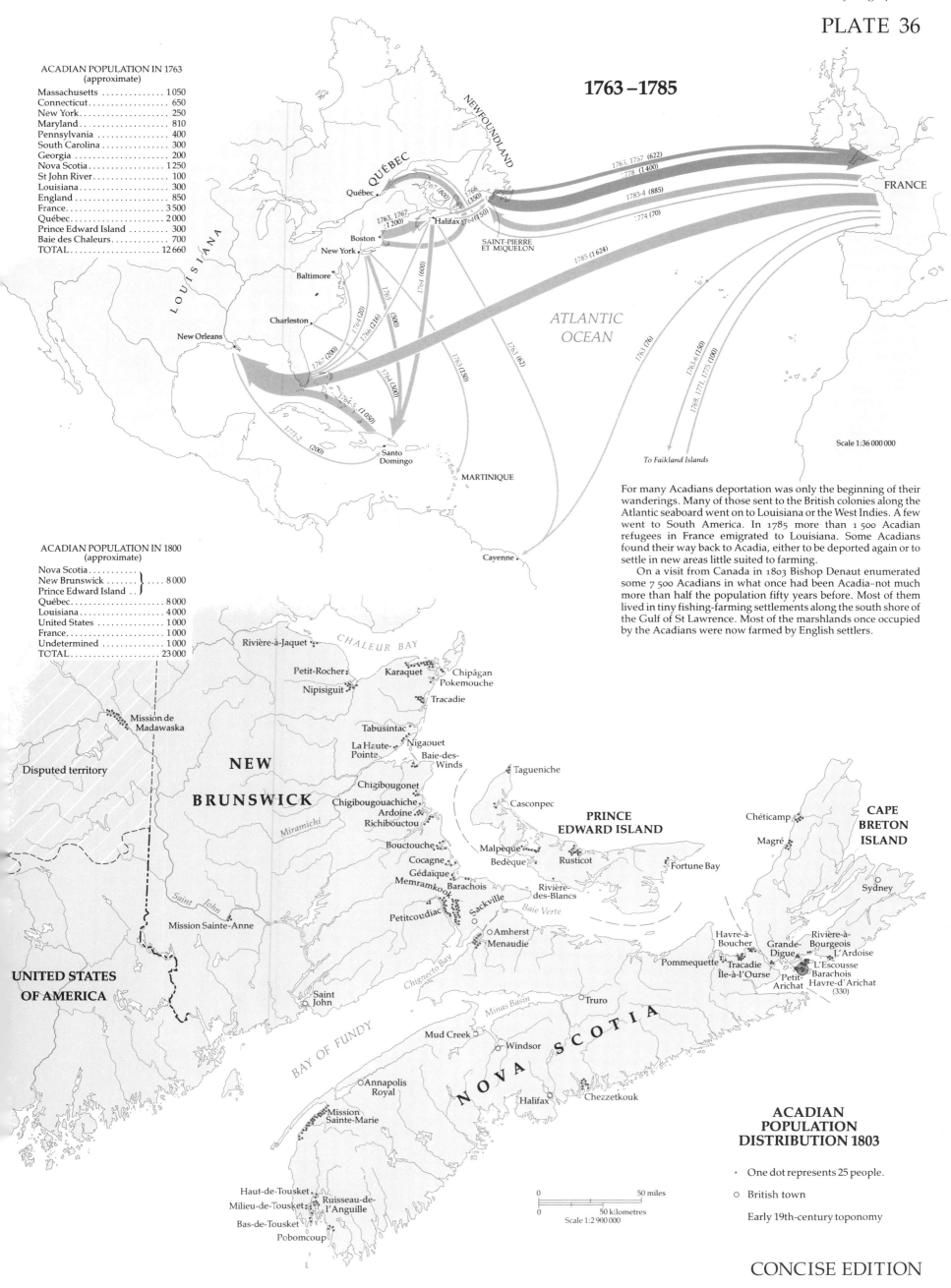

ACADIAN POPULATION IN 1763
(approximate)

Massachusetts	1 050
Connecticut	650
New York	250
Maryland	810
Pennsylvania	400
South Carolina	300
Georgia	200
Nova Scotia	1 250
St John River	100
Louisiana	300
England	850
France	3 500
Québec	2 000
Prince Edward Island	300
Baie des Chaleurs	700
TOTAL	12 660

ACADIAN POPULATION IN 1800
(approximate)

Nova Scotia	
New Brunswick	8 000
Prince Edward Island	
Québec	8 000
Louisiana	4 000
United States	1 000
France	1 000
Undetermined	1 000
TOTAL	23 000

For many Acadians deportation was only the beginning of their wanderings. Many of those sent to the British colonies along the Atlantic seaboard went on to Louisiana or the West Indies. A few went to South America. In 1785 more than 1 500 Acadian refugees in France emigrated to Louisiana. Some Acadians found their way back to Acadia, either to be deported again or to settle in new areas little suited to farming.

On a visit from Canada in 1803 Bishop Denaut enumerated some 7 500 Acadians in what once had been Acadia–not much more than half the population fifty years before. Most of them lived in tiny fishing-farming settlements along the south shore of the Gulf of St Lawrence. Most of the marshlands once occupied by the Acadians were now farmed by English settlers.

ACADIAN POPULATION DISTRIBUTION 1803

· One dot represents 25 people.

○ British town

Early 19th-century toponomy

CONCISE EDITION

THE COMING OF THE LOYALISTS, LATE 18th CENTURY

Authors: R. Louis Gentilcore, Don Measner, David Doherty

For much of British North America (BNA) European settlement began in the wake of the American Revolution, with the arrival of Loyalist refugees from the newly independent United States. Some 50 000 exiles turned to what remained of the British colonies in North America, ensuring a British presence on the continent. By 1784 the Loyalist settlements spanned half a continent, from the Atlantic provinces to the lower Great Lakes. They created the new colonies of New Brunswick (1784) and Upper Canada (1791).

The Loyalists arrived in two major migrations, to the Maritimes (shown in pl 48) and to the colony of Québec, where migration was much smaller but took place over a longer period of time. Beginning in 1774 and continuing throughout the Revolutionary War, groups of Loyalists passed into Québec from the frontier areas of nearby colonies, especially New York. With the new arrivals in 1783 the numbers awaiting settlement in Québec swelled to several thousand. Their future lay not in the well-populated parts of the province but in the relatively empty western interior above Montréal. Lands were made available to some 5 000 settlers in newly surveyed townships along the upper St Lawrence River, eastern Lake Ontario, and the Niagara River. Smaller numbers remained in Québec or went to the coastlands of the Bay of Chaleur and the Gaspé Peninsula. A separate group, over 6 000 Six Nations Indian allies, dispossessed from their lands in western New York, were offered land along the Grand River. Approximately one-third this number were enumerated here in the 1780s.

LOYALIST POPULATIONS*

Area	Year	Population	Status
Niagara Indians	Dec 1778	6 515	RL
Montréal	Sep 1779	1 025	RL
Montréal	Oct 1780	1 395	RL
Montréal	Jan 1782	1 700	RL
Niagara	Jul 1782	85	RL
Montréal	Mar 1783	1 720	RL
Montréal	Jan 1784	1 105	RL
Niagara	Jul 1784	620	RL
NS and NB	Nov 1785	26 315	RL
Chaleur Bay	Aug 1784	435	SR
St Lawrence	Jul 1784	3 775	SR
Cape Breton	1784	140	SR
Six Nations	1785	1 845	SR
Prince Edward Is	1785	380	SR
New Brunswick	Nov 1785	10 825	SR
Nova Scotia	1785	16 425	SR
NS, NB, and PEI	1785	35 000	TS
Québec	1785	15 000	TS
United Kingdom	1785	2 000	TS
Africa	ca 1790	2 000	TS
Upper and Lower Canada	1791	25 000	TS

*See end notes.

RL = Ration lists
SR = Settled refugees
TS = Total settled

LAND GRANT PROPOSALS, 1783

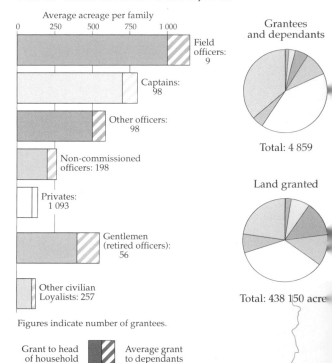

Average acreage per family

Field officers: 9
Captains: 98
Other officers: 98
Non-commissioned officers: 198
Privates: 1 093
Gentlemen (retired officers): 56
Other civilian Loyalists: 257

Figures indicate number of grantees.

Grant to head of household
Average grant to dependants

Grantees and dependants
Total: 4 859

Land granted
Total: 438 150 acre

The unprecedented Loyalist migration called for massive assistance. The distribution of food, equipment, and supplies taxed the limited administrative facilities of the colony. Most important was the fair allocation of land. The scale of land grants shown here was set out in the Royal Instruction of 1783, with special authorizations made to regiments recruited under specific promises.

SIX NATIONS LAND GRANTS

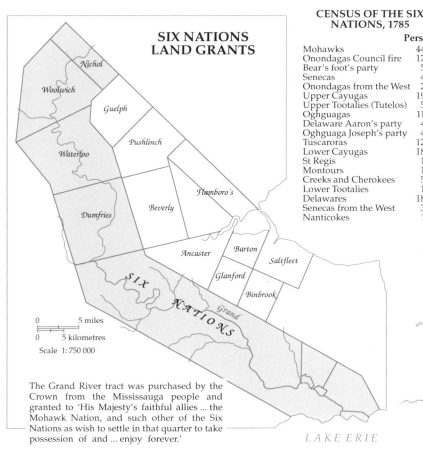

CENSUS OF THE SIX NATIONS, 1785

	Persons
Mohawks	448
Onondagas Council fire	174
Bear's foot's party	51
Senecas	47
Onondagas from the West	20
Upper Cayugas	198
Upper Tootalies (Tutelos)	55
Oghguagas	113
Delaware Aaron's party	48
Oghguaga Joseph's party	49
Tuscaroras	129
Lower Cayugas	183
St Regis	16
Montours	15
Creeks and Cherokees	53
Lower Tootalies	19
Delawares	183
Senecas from the West	31
Nanticokes	11

The Grand River tract was purchased by the Crown from the Mississauga people and granted to 'His Majesty's faithful allies ... the Mohawk Nation, and such other of the Six Nations as wish to settle in that quarter to take possession of and ... enjoy forever.'

LOYALISTS IN QUÉBEC 1784

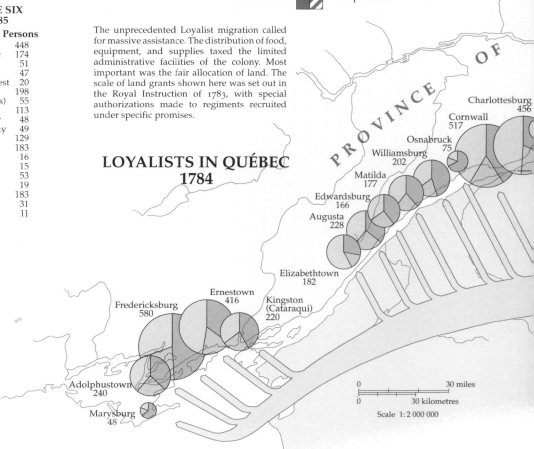

Charlottesburg 456
Cornwall 517
Osnabruck 75
Williamsburg 202
Matilda 177
Edwardsburg 166
Augusta 228
Elizabethtown 182
Ernestown 416
Kingston (Cataraqui) 220
Fredericksburg 580
Adolphustown 240
Marysburg 48

FIRST SURVEY FOR SETTLEMENT
Township 1, Cataraqui, Province of Québec

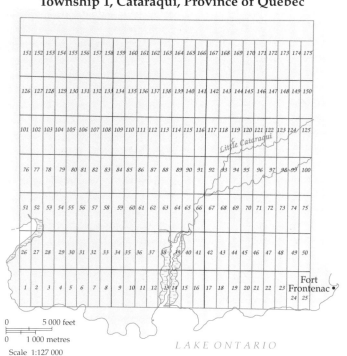

DISBANDED BUTLER'S RANGERS

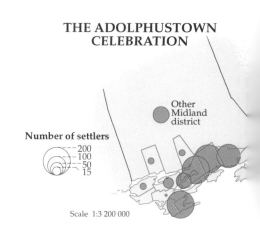

Number of Rangers

Settled
Granted land

Colonel John Butler's Rangers were made up of New York and Pennsylvania Loyalists. With headquarters at Niagara, they campaigned vigorously on the British side during the Revolutionary War. By 1780 many of them had taken up land along the Niagara River in what would become the first permanent British settlement in western Québec.

THE ADOLPHUSTOWN CELEBRATION

Other Midland district

Number of settlers
200
100
50
15

Scale 1:3 200 000

In western Québec (later Upper Canada) allotments of land were identified and transferred as parts of townships. The first township survey, Number 1 at Cataraqui (Kingston), initiated a system which would spread throughout the province as a basis for the granting and occupancy of land. The survey and plan of this township, completed 27 Oct 1783, began with a row of 25 lots, each 120 acres, along the base line. Behind them other rows of lots (concessions) would follow. Under the system every holding in the province could be given a specific address, made up of the name of the township and its lot and concession numbers.

HISTORICAL ATLAS OF CANADA

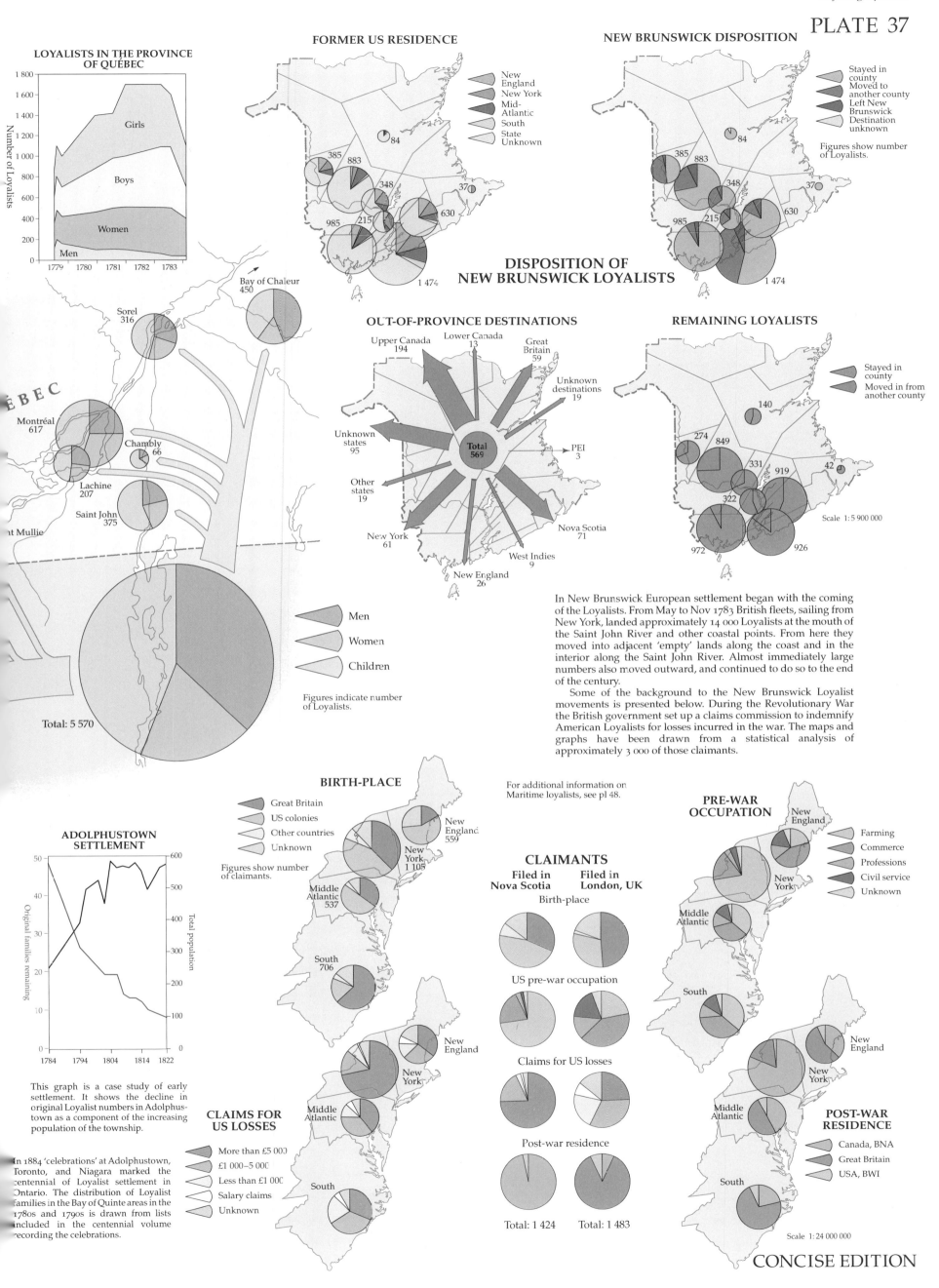

LOYALISTS IN THE PROVINCE OF QUÉBEC

Number of Loyalists

Girls
Boys
Women
Men

1779 1780 1781 1782 1783

FORMER US RESIDENCE

New England
New York
Mid-Atlantic
South
State Unknown

84
385 883
348
37
630
985 215
1 474

NEW BRUNSWICK DISPOSITION

Stayed in county
Moved to another county
Left New Brunswick
Destination unknown

Figures show number of Loyalists.

84
385 883
348
37
630
985 215
1 474

DISPOSITION OF NEW BRUNSWICK LOYALISTS

OUT-OF-PROVINCE DESTINATIONS

Upper Canada 194
Lower Canada 13
Great Britain 59
Unknown destinations 19
Total 569
PEI 3
Unknown states 95
Other states 19
Nova Scotia 71
New York 61
West Indies 9
New England 26

REMAINING LOYALISTS

Stayed in county
Moved in from another county

140
274 849
331 919
42
322
972 926

Scale 1:5 900 000

In New Brunswick European settlement began with the coming of the Loyalists. From May to Nov 1783 British fleets, sailing from New York, landed approximately 14 000 Loyalists at the mouth of the Saint John River and other coastal points. From here they moved into adjacent 'empty' lands along the coast and in the interior along the Saint John River. Almost immediately large numbers also moved outward, and continued to do so to the end of the century.

Some of the background to the New Brunswick Loyalist movements is presented below. During the Revolutionary War the British government set up a claims commission to indemnify American Loyalists for losses incurred in the war. The maps and graphs have been drawn from a statistical analysis of approximately 3 000 of those claimants.

Bay of Chaleur 450
Sorel 316
QUÉBEC
Montréal 617
Chambly 66
Lachine 207
Saint John 375
Mullie

Men
Women
Children

Total: 5 570

Figures indicate number of Loyalists.

ADOLPHUSTOWN SETTLEMENT

Original families remaining

Total population

1784 1794 1804 1814 1822

This graph is a case study of early settlement. It shows the decline in original Loyalist numbers in Adolphustown as a component of the increasing population of the township.

In 1884 'celebrations' at Adolphustown, Toronto, and Niagara marked the centennial of Loyalist settlement in Ontario. The distribution of Loyalist families in the Bay of Quinte areas in the 1780s and 1790s is drawn from lists included in the centennial volume recording the celebrations.

BIRTH-PLACE

Great Britain
US colonies
Other countries
Unknown

Figures show number of claimants.

New England 559
New York 1 105
Middle Atlantic 537
South 706

For additional information on Maritime loyalists, see pl 48.

CLAIMANTS

	Filed in Nova Scotia	Filed in London, UK
Birth-place		
US pre-war occupation		
Claims for US losses		
Post-war residence		
Total:	1 424	1 483

CLAIMS FOR US LOSSES

More than £5 000
£1 000–5 000
Less than £1 000
Salary claims
Unknown

New England
New York
Middle Atlantic
South

PRE-WAR OCCUPATION

New England
New York
Middle Atlantic
South

Farming
Commerce
Professions
Civil service
Unknown

POST-WAR RESIDENCE

New England
New York
Middle Atlantic
South

Canada, BNA
Great Britain
USA, BWI

Scale 1:24 000 000

CONCISE EDITION

THE WAR OF 1812, 1812–1814

Author: William G. Dean

In June 1812 the United States declared war on Great Britain and promptly invaded Upper Canada. The root of this war lay as much in the American-Indian conflict along the northwestern frontier as in American-British maritime rivalry in the previous decade. After three years of fighting British, Canadian, and Indian forces, the United States had lost territory along its east coast, in the West, and on the Pacific coast. Even the few American military and naval successes could not begin to outweigh the economic stranglehold of the British blockade. The weight of British sea power determined the outcome of the war, with the United States unable to achieve its war aims. Negotiations begun by President James Madison in 1812 ultimately concluded in 1814 with the restoration of the pre-war situation. In surviving the military might of the United States, Canadians discovered the essentials of nationhood.

Lacking a navy, American strategy was based on a quick land war to be concluded before British reinforcements could cross the Atlantic. The Americans also expected that Canadians would not fight. The British, exhausted by their wars with Napoleon, relied entirely on defensive measures and a naval blockade. In order of priority the American objectives were Québec, Montréal, Kingston, and Niagara. Québec had never been taken without naval support, but Montréal was vulnerable through the well-trodden Champlain corridor. The Americans, lacking effective military leadership and hampered by reluctant New Englanders, failed to take Montréal, and simply wasted their strength in unco-ordinated thrusts on the Canadian perimeter.

MILITARY TRANSPORT

Generalized times based upon a number of averages under ideal conditions

	Miles per day	Kilometres per day
Steamboat	120	193
Schooner – upstream St Lawrence	27	43
Schooner – downstream St Lawrence	76	122
Schooner on the lakes	60	96
Bateau – upstream St Lawrence	15	24
Bateau – downstream St Lawrence	42	67
Bateau on the lakes	22	35
Durham boat	34	55
Voyageur canoe	75	120
Horseback (express)	57	92
Horseback	36	58
Packhorse (mud road)	12	19
Packhorse (winter)	4	6
Sleigh coach	48	71
Stage coach – good roads	50	80
Stage coach – poor roads	35	56
Freight wagon	18	29
Ox wagon	5	8
Marching (trained troops)	20	32
Forced march	40	64

Trans-Atlantic shipping

Liverpool to Québec (winter)	50 days
Liverpool to Québec (summer)	20 days

NAVAL WAR ON THE GREA[T]

	1812		1813	
	American	British	American	Brit[ish]
Vessels	12	6	34	1
Tonnage	1 672	920	5 139	3 89
Crew	708	720	1 960	1 38
Guns	84	78	221	14
Broadside weight in pounds	1 050	1 191	2 875	2 09
	Losses		Losses	
Vessels	2	2	4	1
Tonnage	160	160	444	2 56
Guns	6	6	41	

ECONOMIC IMPACT, LOWER CANADA

Revenue and expenses in the province of Lower Canada

Registered tonnage of ships clearing Québec customs

The Battle of Lundy's Lane, watercolour by C.W. Jefferys

Courtesy of the City of Toronto Archives, A75–61

1812

British strategy was defensive, but Major-General Isaac Brock's two offensive thrusts – the capture of Forts Michilimackinac and Detroit – profoundly influenced subsequent events, especially in keeping the Indians on the British side. The Americans, because their best armies were in the West fighting Indians, opened their offensive at Detroit and, later, Niagara. An assault on Montréal fizzled out at the border.

Scale 1:3 000 000

1813

Three major American strategic thrusts failed. First, a combined naval/military assault on the Niagara peninsula was eventually thrown back at Stoney Creek. Second, a two-pronged assault on Montréal down the St Lawrence and down the Champlain valley was halted at Crysler's Farm and Châteauguay, respectively. Full strategic advantage of the American naval control of Lake Erie was not taken, despite the victory at Moraviantown.

HISTORICAL ATLAS OF CANADA

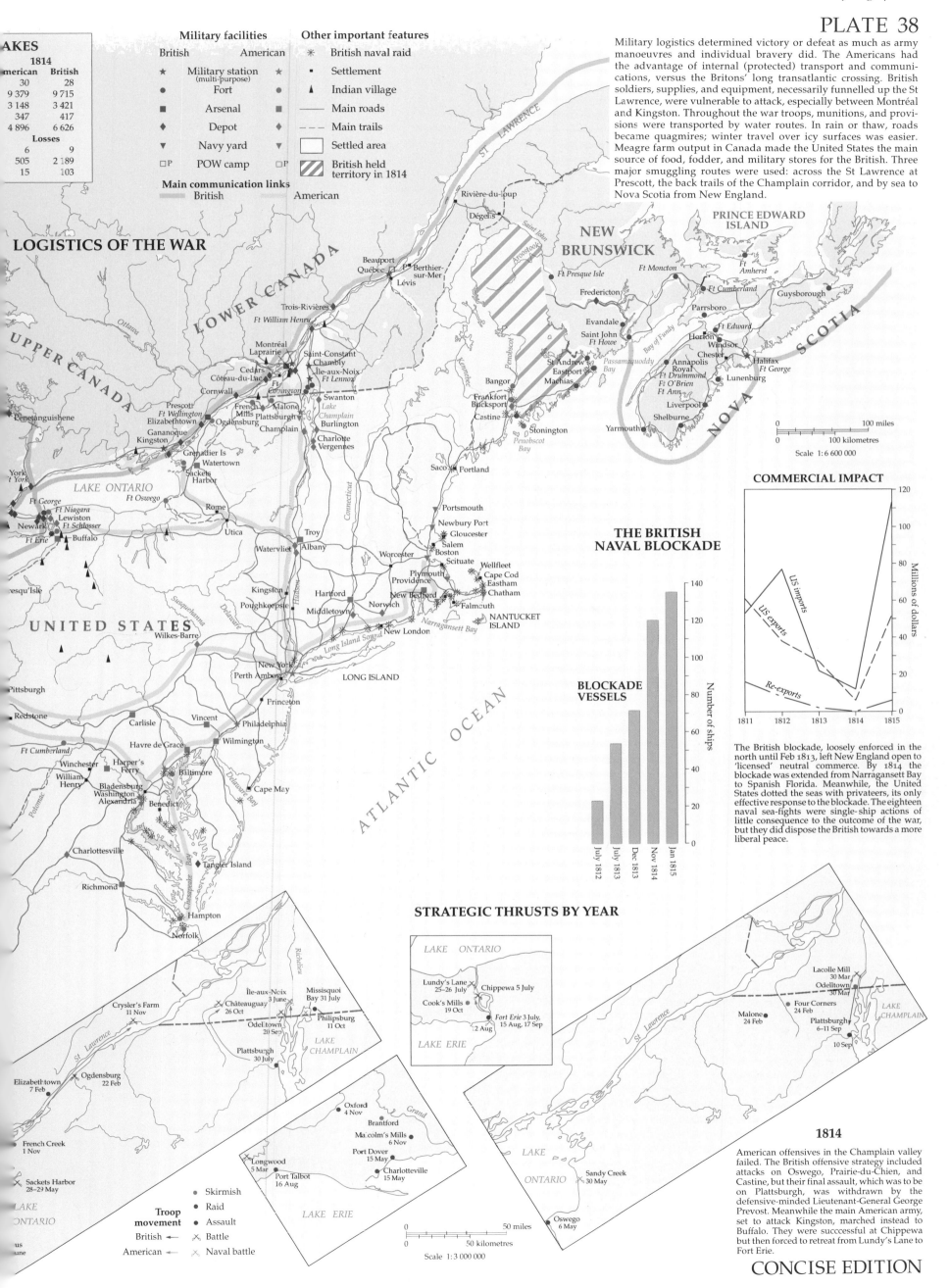

PLATE 38

Military logistics determined victory or defeat as much as army manoeuvres and individual bravery did. The Americans had the advantage of internal (protected) transport and communications, versus the Britons' long transatlantic crossing. British soldiers, supplies, and equipment, necessarily funnelled up the St Lawrence, were vulnerable to attack, especially between Montréal and Kingston. Throughout the war troops, munitions, and provisions were transported by water routes. In rain or thaw, roads became quagmires; winter travel over icy surfaces was easier. Meagre farm output in Canada made the United States the main source of food, fodder, and military stores for the British. Three major smuggling routes were used: across the St Lawrence at Prescott, the back trails of the Champlain corridor, and by sea to Nova Scotia from New England.

LOGISTICS OF THE WAR

Legend

Military facilities

	British	American
Military station (multi-purpose)	★	★
Fort	●	●
Arsenal	■	■
Depot	◆	◆
Navy yard	▼	▼
POW camp	□P	□P

Main communication links
British — American

Other important features
- ✳ British naval raid
- ■ Settlement
- ▲ Indian village
- —— Main roads
- – – Main trails
- ☐ Settled area
- ▨ British held territory in 1814

COMMERCIAL IMPACT

US imports
US exports
Re-exports

1811 1812 1813 1814 1815

Millions of dollars

THE BRITISH NAVAL BLOCKADE

BLOCKADE VESSELS

Number of ships

July 1812 | July 1813 | Dec 1813 | Nov 1814 | Jan 1815

The British blockade, loosely enforced in the north until Feb 1813, left New England open to 'licensed' neutral commerce. By 1814 the blockade was extended from Narragansett Bay to Spanish Florida. Meanwhile, the United States dotted the seas with privateers, its only effective response to the blockade. The eighteen naval sea-fights were single-ship actions of little consequence to the outcome of the war, but they did dispose the British towards a more liberal peace.

STRATEGIC THRUSTS BY YEAR

Troop movement
- British ⟵
- American ⟵
- ✕ Battle
- ✕ Naval battle
- ● Skirmish
- ● Raid
- ● Assault

Scale 1:3 000 000

0 — 50 miles
0 — 50 kilometres

1814

American offensives in the Champlain valley failed. The British offensive strategy included attacks on Oswego, Prairie-du-Chien, and Castine, but their final assault, which was to be on Plattsburgh, was withdrawn by the defensive-minded Lieutenant-General George Prevost. Meanwhile the main American army, set to attack Kingston, marched instead to Buffalo. They were successful at Chippewa but then forced to retreat from Lundy's Lane to Fort Erie.

CONCISE EDITION

Scale 1:6 600 000

0 — 100 miles
0 — 100 kilometres

TRANSATLANTIC MIGRATIONS, 1815–1865

Authors: John C. Weaver, James De Jonge, Darrell Norris

Before the 19th century, emigration from northern Europe to North America was well established, although it was interrupted at the end of the 18th century by the Napoleonic wars. The end of hostilities in 1815 opened the well-travelled Atlantic highway to renewed flows of goods and people, setting the course of settlement in British North America for the rest of the century. From 1815 to 1865 well over a million emigrants from the British Isles entered British North America. From this half-century two short periods have been selected as particularly worthy of illustration. Between 1846 and 1851 over 265 000 immigrants landed at the port of Québec; almost as many, approximately 193 000, had come between 1831 and 1836. Many immigrants were individuals in reduced circumstances, but above the poverty line. The Irish frequently came from areas which had suffered a weakened domestic textile industry caused by the depression after the Napoleonic wars and by mechanization. They chose migration as an opportunity for improvement. Thus, during the late 1830s, when a depression and the rebellions of 1837 tarnished the reputation of the Canadas, there was a decline in immigration. Canadian public-works projects in the early 1840s reinvigorated the economy, and the pace of immigration then increased. The substantial increase in the late 1840s was the product of the Irish famine of 1846–9.

EMIGRATION FROM THE BRITISH ISLES

Thousands of emigrants

To Australia, New Zealand (905 000), and all other places (126 000)

To North American colonies (1 273 000)

To United States (3 958 000)

Totals are given in parentheses.

TRAVELS OF IMMIGRANT J. THOMSON 1844–1864

IMMIGRATION TO BRITISH NORTH AMERICA 1831–1836

Number of immigrants

— 2 501–5 000

--- 1 501–2 500

····· 0–1 500

Period of immigration

1831–1836

1846–1851

Figures indicate number of immigrants flowing to the area labelled.

FINAL RESIDENCES
A sample of immigrant farmers in Wellington County

1831–1836

1846–1851

Origin

England

Scotland

Ireland

Germany

Original North American residence	Number of residences in North America			
	One	Two	Three	Four or more
Same				
Elsewhere in Wellington County				
Other Ontario				
Québec				
United States				

Newcomers commonly worked for a period as casual labourers or as seasonal workers on farms or in forests. For many there were years of residential and occupational movement. The Canada Company promoted settlement within Wellington County by advertising and recruiting in England, which may account for the fact that during the period 1831–6 most settlers went directly to the area and settled there permanently. A greater scarcity of land in 1846–51 may explain the larger proportion of multiple moves before final settlement in the later period.

Scale 1: 1 000 000

Scale 1:11 000 000

HISTORICAL ATLAS OF CANADA

GROSSE ÎLE MONUMENT

A short distance from the port of Québec, the tiny island of Grosse Île was the country's main quarantine station from 1832 to 1937. The island's most prominent structure, a 14 m granite cross, honours immigrants who died and doctors who tried to save them. The Irish Gaelic inscription at the base reads: 'Children of the Gael died in their thousands on this island having fled from the laws of the foreign tyrants and an artificial famine in the years 1847–8. God's loyal blessing upon them.'

Data on embarkation must be read with caution. Not all emigrants sailing from an English or Scottish port were English or Scottish. The Irish also sailed from Liverpool and Greenock with their superior commercial connections to British North America, and also, in the case of Liverpool, because many Irish had located in English cities. In contrast, few English or Scots embarked from Irish ports. Consequently, the number of Irish migrants was much greater than total numbers leaving Irish ports would indicate. The shift towards greater use of the ports of southern Ireland in 1846–51 indicates a change precipitated by the famine. Emigration was lowest from Ulster where the famine had least impact. However, heavier use of southern ports did not mean a drastic shift in the social composition of the immigrant stream. Puzzles and gaps remain, but it appears that generally the emigration rate in commercial farming areas was much higher than that of the southern counties with their high proportion of landless labourers. Furthermore, Protestants continued to outnumber Catholics just as they had done during the pre-famine era. There were exceptions, but large numbers of immigrants were neither paupers nor Catholics.

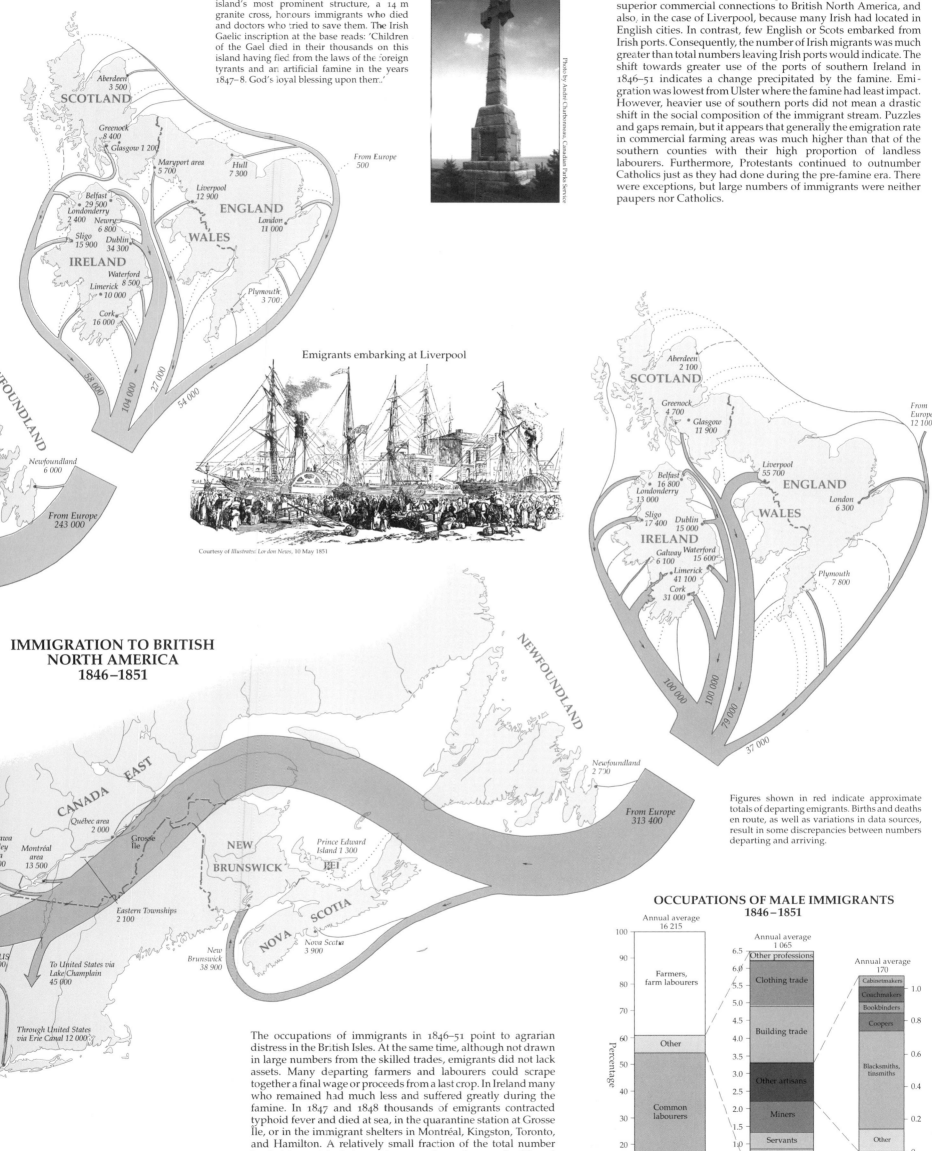

Photo by André Charbonneau, Canadian Parks Service

Emigrants embarking at Liverpool

Courtesy of *Illustrated London News*, 10 May 1851

IMMIGRATION TO BRITISH NORTH AMERICA 1846–1851

Figures shown in red indicate approximate totals of departing emigrants. Births and deaths en route, as well as variations in data sources, result in some discrepancies between numbers departing and arriving.

The occupations of immigrants in 1846–51 point to agrarian distress in the British Isles. At the same time, although not drawn in large numbers from the skilled trades, emigrants did not lack assets. Many departing farmers and labourers could scrape together a final wage or proceeds from a last crop. In Ireland many who remained had much less and suffered greatly during the famine. In 1847 and 1848 thousands of emigrants contracted typhoid fever and died at sea, in the quarantine station at Grosse Île, or in the immigrant shelters in Montréal, Kingston, Toronto, and Hamilton. A relatively small fraction of the total number landed in wretched circumstances and posed severe health and relief challenges for local government and charitable associations. The crisis that faced them has tended to obscure the fact that many arrived weakened and poorer but neither destitute nor broken.

OCCUPATIONS OF MALE IMMIGRANTS 1846–1851

CONCISE EDITION

THE GREAT WAR, 1914–1918

Author: Christopher A. Sharpe

ENLISTMENT AND MILITARY INSTALLATIONS

Yukon Territory and

British Columbia 158 272

Alberta 122 915

Saskatchewan 158 907

Manitoba 122 762

Scale 1:40 000 000

Newfoundland 33 708

Québec 390 897

Ontario 582 246

Nova Scotia and PEI 115 361

New Brunswick 68 710

Scale 1:20 000 000

- ● Canadian Expeditionary Force training camp
- ● Royal Flying Corps aerodrome
- ● Royal Canadian Navy signal station
- ▲ 'Alien' internment camp

Canadian Expeditionary Force (CEF) (excluding Newfoundland)

CEF Canada 189 588

CEF Overseas 417 486

Untapped manpower 1 112 996

Total eligible male population (18–45 years) 1 720 070

Percentage of men

Battalion	0 20 40 60 80 100	Total number of men
Royal Newfoundland Regiment		6 241
2nd (Eastern Ontario)		5 326
24th (Victoria Rifles)		4 827
46th (South Saskatchewan)		5 374
49th (Loyal Edmonton)		4 050
72nd (Seaforth Highlanders)		3 791
77th (Ottawa)		1 368

■ Killed ■ Wounded □ Not injured

VICTORY LOAN CAMPAIGNS, 1917, 1918

BC, Alta, Sask, Man, Ont, Qué, NB, NS, PEI

(1918 only)

0 40 80 120 160 200

Per capita contributions in dollars

The strain of financing the war effort led to war taxes on business profits, personal income, and luxuries. There were also three Victory Loan campaigns aimed at the patriotism of small-scale savers. In 1917 the campaign raised $546 million, far in excess of the $150 million target. A further $678 million and $587 million were realized in the next two years.

CANADIAN PATRIOTIC FUND, 1914–1919

BC, Alta, Sask, Man, Ont, Qué, NB, NS, PEI, **Canada**, Nfld

Contributions — Deficit spending — Surplus

Canada total $ 46 348 931

0 2 4 6 8 10 12 16 24 38 46

Millions of dollars

The Canadian Patriotic Fund was a voluntary organization which co-ordinated fund-raising and provided monthly grants to wives and dependents of soldiers. Widows and dependents received pensions from the fund until the federal government assumed that responsibility in 1916. While most contributions were voluntary, Alberta and New Brunswick used taxes to levy funds.

IMPERIAL MUNITIONS BOARD CONTRACTS, 1915–1919

The British government established the Imperial Munitions Board in Canada to bring order to the country's fledgling munitions industry. In addition to co-ordinating contracts for ships, aircraft, chemicals, explosives, weapons, and ammunition at existing factories, the board also established seven new 'national factories' to produce war *matériel*.

BRITISH COLUMBIA, ALBERTA, SASKATCHEWAN, MANITOBA, ONTARIO, QUÉBEC, NEWFOUNDLAND

Scale 1:40 000 000

UK, BC, Alta, Sask, Man, NB, USA, NS, Qué, Ont

Value of contracts
Millions of dollars
- ● More than 100.0
- ● 15.1–100.0
- ● 1.0–15.0
- · Less than 1.0

Total contracts $1 104 155 604

Scale 1:20 000 000

PROVINCIAL SHARE OF MANUFACTURING AND WAR TRADE, 1915

Percentage of trade

War trade — Manufacturing trade

BC, Alta, Sask, Man, Ont, Qué, NB, NS

ST JOHN'S

0 1 500 feet
0 400 metres
Scale 1:18 000

MILITARY SERVICE ACT, 1917

Thousands of men

150 140 130 120 110 100 90 80 70 60 50 40 30 20 10 0

□ Conscripted or volunteered
■ Defaulted

BC, Alta, Sask, Man, Ont, Qué, NB, NS and PEI, **Canada**

British Columbia 18 169

Alberta 28 076

Saskatchewan 45 536

Manitoba 24 512

Québec 115 602

Newfoundland 3 629 called up 1 573 medically acceptable

Ontario 122 968

New Brunswick 16 902

Nova Scotia and Prince Edward Island 30 117

Canada

Class 1 registration 401 882

Taken on strength 124 588

Occupational exemptions

Medical exemptions

Agricultural exemptions

Dis-charged

On strength as of Armistice Day

Exemption refused

Signed reports for service

HISTORICAL ATLAS OF CANADA

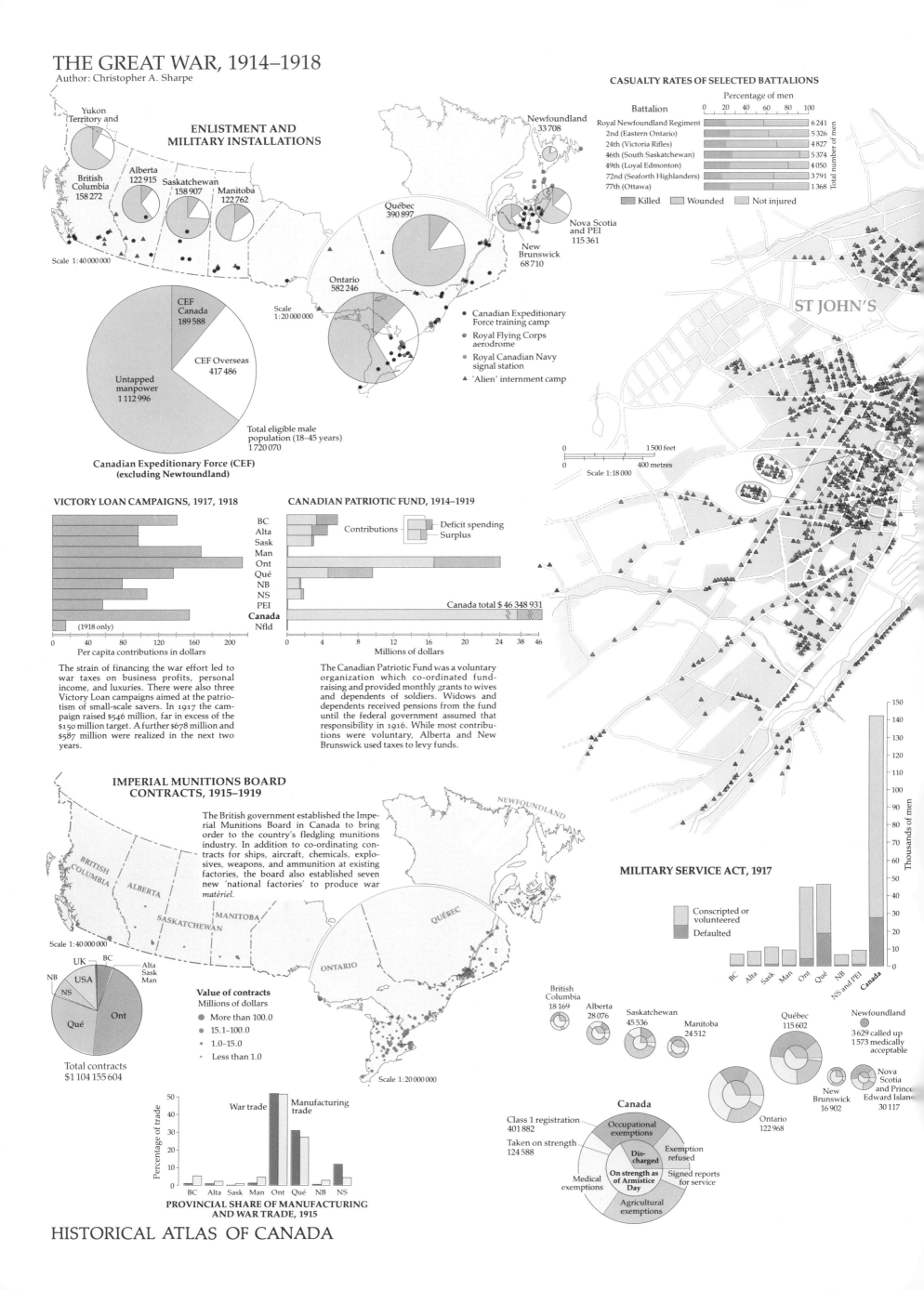

THE ROYAL NEWFOUNDLAND REGIMENT
Final tally, St John's enlistment

▲ Enlisted and returned without medical discharge 1460

▲ Killed in action or died of wounds 365

△ Discharged as medically unfit 352

Not shown are 33 men who were called up but did not serve overseas.

▢ Generalized residential areas

In most areas of Canada more than one regiment recruited men, but in St John's in Newfoundland only the Royal Newfoundland Regiment (RNR) was active. As in other places the impact of service was devastating on the local community. Of the 24% of the RNR that came from St John's almost half sustained casualties, many at Beaumont Hamel on 1 July 1916, the first day of the Battle of the Somme. The war killed or injured 15% of the city's men between 18 and 32 years of age.

REVENUE AND PUBLIC DEBT

Millions of dollars — axis 200 to 3 200, years 1900–1939

Net public debt

Total war-tax revenue

TAXES

Millions of dollars — axis 0 to 300, years 1915–1939

Business-profits war tax (to 1920); war tax on financial institutions

Total revenue

Income war tax

Custom and excise taxes

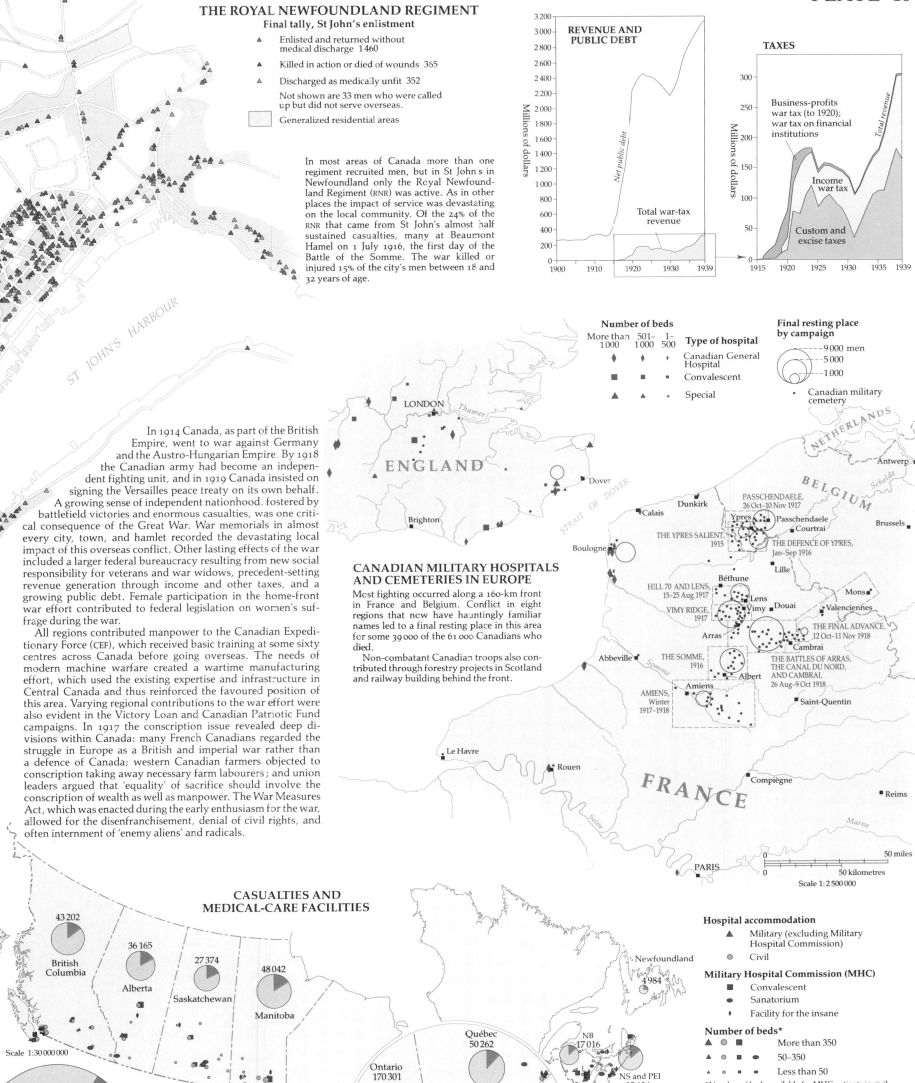

Number of beds — More than 1000 / 501–1000 / 1–500

Type of hospital
◆ Canadian General Hospital
■ Convalescent
▲ Special

Final resting place by campaign
9 000 men
5 000
1 000
· Canadian military cemetery

CANADIAN MILITARY HOSPITALS AND CEMETERIES IN EUROPE

Most fighting occurred along a 160-km front in France and Belgium. Conflict in eight regions that now have hauntingly familiar names led to a final resting place in this area for some 39 000 of the 61 000 Canadians who died.

Non-combatant Canadian troops also contributed through forestry projects in Scotland and railway building behind the front.

PASSCHENDAELE, 26 Oct–10 Nov 1917

THE YPRES SALIENT, 1915

THE DEFENCE OF YPRES, Jan–Sep 1916

HILL 70 AND LENS, 15–25 Aug 1917

VIMY RIDGE, 1917

THE FINAL ADVANCE, 12 Oct–11 Nov 1918

THE SOMME, 1916

THE BATTLES OF ARRAS, THE CANAL DU NORD, AND CAMBRAI, 26 Aug–9 Oct 1918

AMIENS, Winter 1917–1918

Scale 1:2 500 000 — 0 50 miles / 0 50 kilometres

In 1914 Canada, as part of the British Empire, went to war against Germany and the Austro-Hungarian Empire. By 1918 the Canadian army had become an independent fighting unit, and in 1919 Canada insisted on signing the Versailles peace treaty on its own behalf. A growing sense of independent nationhood, fostered by battlefield victories and enormous casualties, was one critical consequence of the Great War. War memorials in almost every city, town, and hamlet recorded the devastating local impact of this overseas conflict. Other lasting effects of the war included a larger federal bureaucracy resulting from new social responsibility for veterans and war widows, precedent-setting revenue generation through income and other taxes, and a growing public debt. Female participation in the home-front war effort contributed to federal legislation on women's suffrage during the war.

All regions contributed manpower to the Canadian Expeditionary Force (CEF), which received basic training at some sixty centres across Canada before going overseas. The needs of modern machine warfare created a wartime manufacturing effort, which used the existing expertise and infrastructure in Central Canada and thus reinforced the favoured position of this area. Varying regional contributions to the war effort were also evident in the Victory Loan and Canadian Patriotic Fund campaigns. In 1917 the conscription issue revealed deep divisions within Canada: many French Canadians regarded the struggle in Europe as a British and imperial war rather than a defence of Canada; western Canadian farmers objected to conscription taking away necessary farm labourers; and union leaders argued that 'equality' of sacrifice should involve the conscription of wealth as well as manpower. The War Measures Act, which was enacted during the early enthusiasm for the war, allowed for the disenfranchisement, denial of civil rights, and often internment of 'enemy aliens' and radicals.

CASUALTIES AND MEDICAL-CARE FACILITIES

43 202 — British Columbia

36 165 — Alberta

27 374 — Saskatchewan

48 042 — Manitoba

170 301 — Ontario

50 262 — Québec

17 016 — NB

25 124 — NS and PEI

4 984 — Newfoundland

Scale 1:30 000 000

Scale 1:20 000 000

Hospital accommodation
▲ Military (excluding Military Hospital Commission)
● Civil

Military Hospital Commission (MHC)
■ Convalescent
⬭ Sanatorium
◆ Facility for the insane

Number of beds*
▲ ● ■ — More than 350
▲ ● ■ — 50–350
▲ ● ■ — Less than 50

*Number of beds available for MHC patients in civil hospitals (except facilities for the insane)

The Military Hospital Commission was established in 1916 to provide convalescent homes for soldiers returning as invalids from overseas and to arrange for their discharge. Where facilities were not available for leasing, the commission erected new hospitals. Because of the rigours of the transatlantic voyage, active treatment (except that required by amputees) was carried out in hospitals in England and France staffed by Canadian Army Medical Corps. In Canada it was administered at municipal or private hospitals that had on-call bed-space or at military-base hospitals. Military hospitals generally served non-battle casualties.

Killed 7.2%

Died overseas 1.1%

Died in Canada 0.3%

Wounded 19.6%

Suffered from illness 66.8%

Injured 5.0%

465

CASUALTIES OF CEF CANADA AND CEF OVERSEAS (repetitions included)

Fatalities 14.2%

Survivors 85.8%

417 485

FATALITIES OF CEF OVERSEAS

CONCISE EDITION

THE IMPACT OF THE GREAT DEPRESSION, 1930s

Authors: Murdo MacPherson, Deryck W. Holdsworth (trekking)

THE UNEMPLOYED AND RELIEF

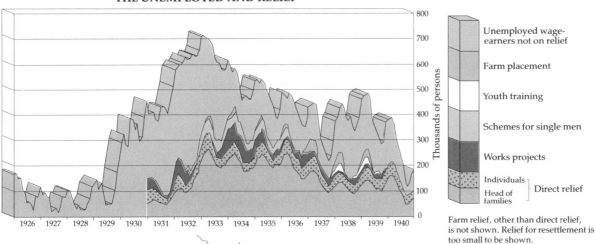

Unemployed wage-earners not on relief

Farm placement

Youth training

Schemes for single men

Works projects

Individuals / Head of families } Direct relief

Farm relief, other than direct relief, is not shown. Relief for resettlement is too small to be shown.

By the winter of 1933 some 32% of the Canadian workforce was jobless and by April over 1.5 million Canadians, 15% of the population, depended on direct relief for survival. Even by 1939 a million people were still on relief. Direct relief, formerly a public charity granted to the chronically poor, was extended in the Depression to those whose destitution was caused solely by unemployment or by loss of the means of livelihood, as in the case of drought-stricken farmers. The distribution of relief reflected the pattern of hardship across the country. Saskatchewan, with its devastated farming economy (pl 63), had the highest proportion of relief recipients in its population. In contrast, Maritimers were less likely to go on relief because of their traditional access to basic sustenance.

The relief rolls of urban areas were disproportionately large, reflecting not only the main concentrations of unemployment but also the in-migration of those seeking help. Many municipalities experienced great difficulties coping with this influx. Soup kitchens, queues for job openings, and 'hobo jungles' became the habitual world of many unemployed. Some travelled from place to place – usually 'riding the rails' on freight cars – seeking 'work and wages' instead of 'the pogey' or work in a relief camp. This could bring a stint of work on a farm, in a logging camp, or in a gold mine, sometimes interspersed with an excursion to the milder BC coast in winter.

Phyllis and Ali Knight

P Phyllis   A Ali
Began trek in Toronto, Ontario
1 P Confectionery factory worker and domestic
   A Painter
   Spring 1929 to spring 1930 (after emigrating from Germany)
2 P Odd jobs
   A Cook on tug
   Spring 1930 to fall 1930
3 P Domestic, unemployed, caretaker
   A Unemployed, trips to interior searching for gold, labouring (3a)
   Winter 1930 to spring 1934
4 P & A Washed gold
   Summer 1934 to spring 1935
   P Operated hot dog stand, unemployed
   A Odd jobs, road crew
   Summer 1935 to winter 1935
5 P Gave birth
   A Unemployed, away cooking on road crew (5a)
   Winter 1935–1936
6 P & A Cook on road crew, child rearing, operated bakeshop
   Spring 1936 to spring 1937
7 P Child rearing
   A Baking at Pilot and Bralorne mines after bakeshop went out of business
   Spring to summer 1937
8 P Returned to Germany for visit
   A Baking at various mines in Bridge River area, unemployed
   Summer 1937 to winter 1937–1938
9 P Child rearing
   A Unemployed, odd jobs
   Winter 1938–1939
10 P Kitchen help, logging camp
   A Cook
   Spring 1939 to fall 1939

Nelson Thibault

Began trek in Bankend, Saskatchewan
1 Left family farm. Fall 1934
2 Looked for work. Fall 1934
3 Stooking and threshing. Fall 1934
4 Unemployed. Fall 1934
5 'Jaunt,' unemployed. Fall 1934
6 Helped family. Winter 1934–1935
7 Unemployed. Summer 1935
8 With family. Summer 1935
9 Brief stay, unemployed. Summer 1935
10, 11 Stayed at Finnish guest house. Fall 1935
12 Toured bush camps, no work. Fall 1935
13 No work at iron works. Fall 1935
14 No work, police harassment. Winter 1935
15 Unemployed. Winter 1935
16 Various trips to California fruit belt. Winter 1935
17 Unemployed. Winter 1935
18 With family. Winter 1935–1936
19 Waiting for 'trek.' Summer 1936
20 With family. Summer 1936
21 Casual work. Fall 1936
22 Firefighting, cook. Summer and fall 1937
23 Lumbering, gambling. Fall 1937
24 Unemployed. Winter 1937
25 Contemplated farming. Early summer 1938
26 Unemployed. Summer 1938
27 Unemployed for most part, looked for farm work. Summer 1938
28 Brief look for work. Summer 1938
29 Unemployed. Winter 1938
30 Farm work. Winter and spring 1939
31 Through USA – Montana, Denver, midwest – looking for 'experience.' Summer 1939
32, 33, 34 Looking for work, unemployed. Summer 1939
35 Mining and union organizing. Fall 1939

Bill Johnstone

Began trek in Holden, Alberta
1 Family farm (after emigrating from England). Fall 1928
2 Coal mining. Winter 1928–1929
3 New family farm and farm work on neighbouring farms. Summer 1929 to winter 1931
4 Coal mining. Winter 1931
5 On family farm recovering from injury, farm work in neighbourhood. Fall 1931 to winter 1933
6 Coal mining. Winter 1933–1934
7 Coal mining. Spring 1934 to fall 1937
8 Coal mining. Fall 1937 until retirement

MONTHLY RELIEF BUDGETS
Family of five, 1936

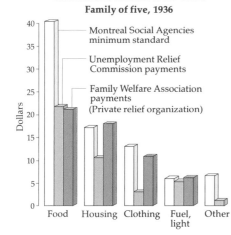

Montreal Social Agencies minimum standard

Unemployment Relief Commission payments

Family Welfare Association payments (Private relief organization)

RELIEF BUDGET
One week, for a family of five, Montréal, 1932

Food	Amount	Approximate Cost		Subtotal
Milk	13 quarts	$1.30	Dairy	1.45
Cheese	1 pound	.15		
Brown bread	10 loaves, 240 oz	.60	Grains, cereals	1.00
Rolled oats	3 pounds	.15		
Flour	2 pounds	.10		
Rice, barley	2 pounds	.15		
Tomatoes	3 tins, 6 pounds	.18		
Potatoes	25 pounds	.25		
Carrots, turnips	4 pounds	.16	Vegetables, fruits	.94
Cabbage	2 pounds	.05		
Onions	2 pounds	.08		
Dried beans	1 pound	.04		
Dried peas	1 pound	.06		
Prunes, figs	1 pound	.12		
Chuck roast	3½ pounds	.46	Meat	.54
Beef or pork liver	½ pound	.08		
Butter	1 pound	.26		
Peanut butter	½ pound	.08	Other	.65
Shortening	½ pound	.08		
Molasses	1 pound	.13		
Sugar	2 pounds	.10		
			One-week total	$4.58

MONTHLY FOOD ALLOWANCES
Family of five, 1936

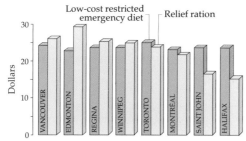

Low-cost restricted emergency diet   Relief ration

VANCOUVER EDMONTON REGINA WINNIPEG TORONTO MONTRÉAL SAINT JOHN HALIFAX

Relief allowances were small, less than could be earned even in the worst-paid jobs, and thus it was difficult for families to live entirely on relief. Eligibility rules and the funds that were available varied from municipality to municipality across the country. Rarely were the necessities of life – food, housing, fuel, and clothing – adequately covered by relief. Only in western cities did the relief ration permit the maintenance of a 'restricted emergency diet' (a minimum standard, regarded by health agencies as nutritionally inadequate for prolonged periods). Most Canadians on relief suffered from poor health and cases of scurvy and rickets attested to malnutrition.

In an attempt to deal with the enormity of the relief burden a 'Canadians first' policy surfaced and over 17 000 foreign 'public charges' were deported between 1929 and 1935. The policy was stopped after the 1935 election.

DEPORTATIONS

Other deportees, including those deported for criminal and medical reasons

Public charges

HISTORICAL ATLAS OF CANADA

RELIEF RECIPIENTS BY PROVINCE

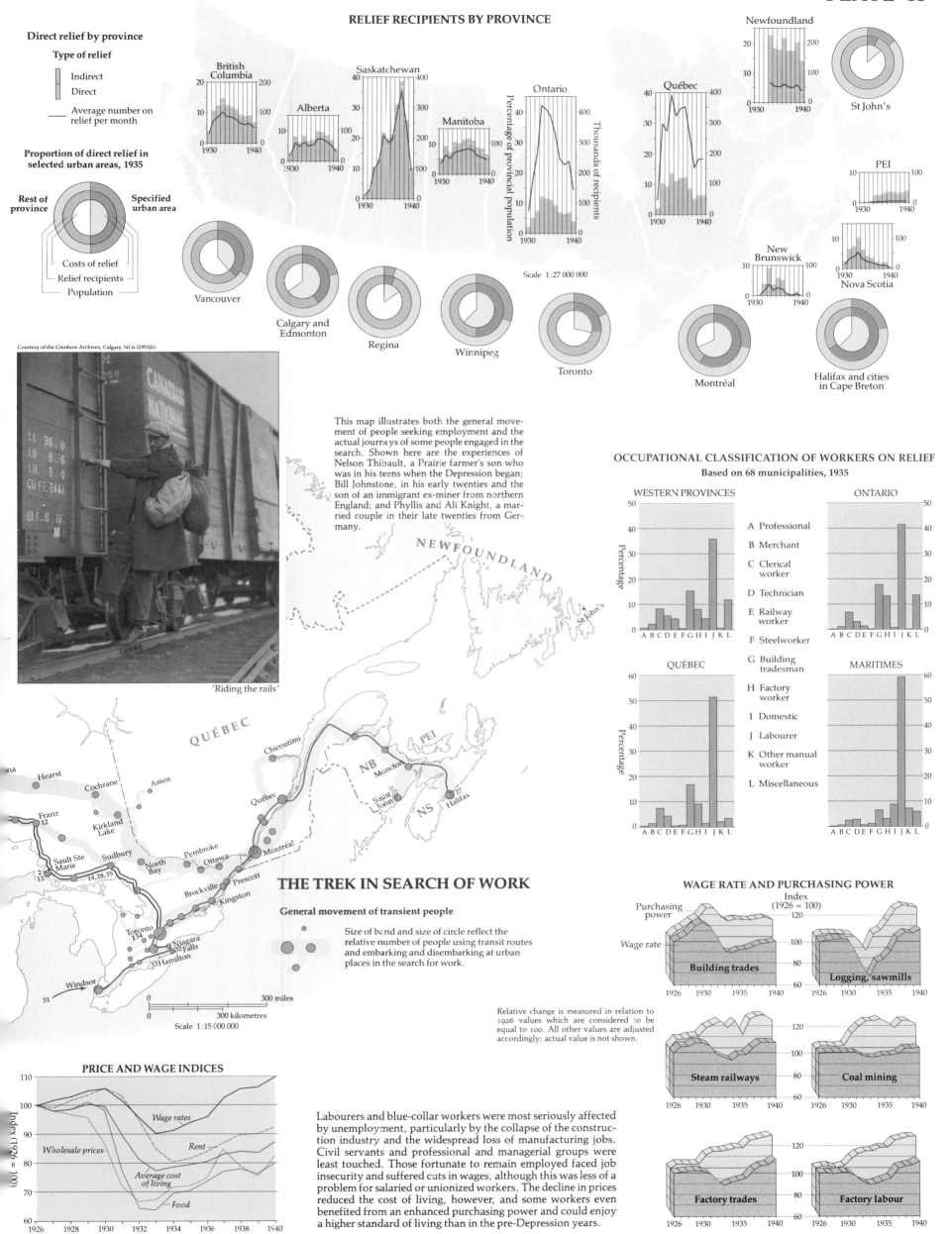

Direct relief by province

Type of relief

- Indirect
- Direct

— Average number on relief per month

Proportion of direct relief in selected urban areas, 1935

Rest of province — Specified urban area

Costs of relief
Relief recipients
Population

British Columbia
Alberta
Saskatchewan
Manitoba
Ontario
Québec
Newfoundland
St John's
PEI
Nova Scotia
New Brunswick

Percentage of provincial population
Thousands of recipients

Vancouver
Calgary and Edmonton
Regina
Winnipeg
Toronto
Montréal
Halifax and cities in Cape Breton

Scale 1:27 000 000

Courtesy of the Glenbow Archives, Calgary, NC6-12955(b)

'Riding the rails'

This map illustrates both the general movement of people seeking employment and the actual journeys of some people engaged in the search. Shown here are the experiences of Nelson Thibault, a Prairie farmer's son who was in his teens when the Depression began; Bill Johnstone, in his early twenties and the son of an immigrant ex-miner from northern England; and Phyllis and Ali Knight, a married couple in their late twenties from Germany.

OCCUPATIONAL CLASSIFICATION OF WORKERS ON RELIEF
Based on 68 municipalities, 1935

WESTERN PROVINCES
ONTARIO
QUÉBEC
MARITIMES

Percentage

A B C D E F G H I J K L

A Professional
B Merchant
C Clerical worker
D Technician
E Railway worker
F Steelworker
G Building tradesman
H Factory worker
I Domestic
J Labourer
K Other manual worker
L Miscellaneous

THE TREK IN SEARCH OF WORK

General movement of transient people

Size of band and size of circle reflect the relative number of people using transit routes and embarking and disembarking at urban places in the search for work.

Hearst
Cochrane
Amos
Chicoutimi
Franz
12
Kirkland Lake
Sault Ste Marie
13
Sudbury
North Bay
Pembroke
Ottawa
Québec
Montréal
Moncton
Saint John
Halifax
27
Brockville
Prescott
Kingston
Toronto
134
Niagara Falls
32
Hamilton
33
Windsor
31

QUÉBEC
NEWFOUNDLAND
NB
PEI
NS
St John's

0   300 miles
0   300 kilometres
Scale 1:15 000 000

Relative change is measured in relation to 1926 values which are considered to be equal to 100. All other values are adjusted accordingly; actual value is not shown.

WAGE RATE AND PURCHASING POWER

Index (1926 = 100)

Purchasing power
Wage rate

Building trades
Logging, sawmills
Steam railways
Coal mining
Factory trades
Factory labour

1926 1930 1935 1940

PRICE AND WAGE INDICES

Index (1926 = 100)

Wage rates
Wholesale prices
Rent
Average cost of living
Food

1926 1928 1930 1932 1934 1936 1938 1940

Labourers and blue-collar workers were most seriously affected by unemployment, particularly by the collapse of the construction industry and the widespread loss of manufacturing jobs. Civil servants and professional and managerial groups were least touched. Those fortunate to remain employed faced job insecurity and suffered cuts in wages, although this was less of a problem for salaried or unionized workers. The decline in prices reduced the cost of living, however, and some workers even benefited from an enhanced purchasing power and could enjoy a higher standard of living than in the pre-Depression years.

CONCISE EDITION

THE SECOND WORLD WAR, 1939–1945

Author: Christopher A. Sharpe

MILITARY MOBILIZATION

Type of centre

- ● Canadian Army (Active) 1 July 1943
- ▲ British Commonwealth Air Training Plan
- ■ Royal Canadian Navy

Figures indicate total number of eligible males (18–45 years) in each province in 1941.

British Columbia 181 000
Alberta 178 000
Saskatchewan 191 000
Manitoba 159 000

Scale 1:35 000 000

Royal Navy — Royal Artillery
Royal Air Force — Nfld Forestry Service
Untapped manpower
Nfld 55 000
NB 94 000
Québec 699 000
NS, PEI 142 000

Scale 1:15 000 000

Ontario 830 000

540 957
1 465 660
212 571
99 399
96 979
58 434

- Canadian Army (Active) (CA(A))
- Royal Canadian Air Force (RCAF)
- Royal Canadian Navy (RCN)
- Recruits home defence
- National Resources Mobilization transfers to general service
- Untapped manpower

2 474 000 eligible males (18–45 years) in Canada in 1941

ENLISTMENT OF WOMEN

Thousands of volunteers (y-axis: 0 to 18)

RCN*
RCAF*
CA*

BC, Alta, Sask, Man, Ont, Qué, NB, NS, PEI

*Women's divisions

Ill-Fated Trio by Alfred Leete (Douglas Champio... (North Atlantic Convoys ONS18 and ON202 combir...

The *St Croix* and two British vessels were lost to acoustic torpedo attack by U-boats in a fierce battle to protect the big combined convoy. This loss of three valuable and seasoned anti-submarine ships and their crews (only 3 survivors) came as a blow to the command in the North Atlantic.

Memories of the slaughter of Canadian soldiers during the First World War and the conscription crisis made the Canadian government reluctant to commit manpower to the Second World War until after the fall of France in 1940. None the less, in 1939 the British Commonwealth Air Training Plan established facilities in Canada to train much-needed aircrew for the Royal Air Force (RAF). The plan was a significant contribution to the Allied war effort, 45% of all Commonwealth aircrews receiving some or all of their training in Canada. This tie with Britain, however, retarded the development of a national air force. In 1944 63% of the more than 27 000 members of the Overseas War Establishment of the Royal Canadian Air Force (RCAF) served in RAF squadrons.

On the naval front Canada provided corvette protection to vital convoys of war matériel and foodstuffs crossing the North Atlantic Ocean. Initially, the skeletal Royal Canadian Navy (RCN) lacked expertise and equipment but by October 1943 it had grown to include 85 000 men serving in 365 warships. By 1944 virtually all transatlantic convoys were sailing under RCN protection.

Military ship losses

(RCN) warship sunk

Ottawa — Name of warship
14/9/42 — Day/month/year

U-boat sunk by RCN

U210 — Number of U-boat
Assiniboine — Name of RCN ship
6/8/42 — Day/month/year

U-boat sunk by RCAF

U520 — Number of U-boat
10/Gander — Squadron number and location
30/10/42 — Day/month/year

Merchant ship losses

Allied merchant ships sunk in the North Atlantic (except during the Battle of the St Lawrence; see below)

- · Sept 1939 to March 1941
- · April 1941 to May 1943
- · June 1943 to May 1945
- → General route of convoys

Allied air coverage

- April 1941 to May 1943
- June 1943 to May 1945

PACIFIC COAST

Almost 2 000 Canadian soldiers were involved in the ill-fated defence of Hong Kong in 1941. After Pearl Harbour threats of Japanese invasion led to the establishment of operational bases in British Columbia, although none saw action. A Canadian infantry brigade and two RCAF squadrons served under American command in the Aleutian campaign (1942-3).

Operational bases

- ■ Royal Canadian Navy

Canadian Army (Active)
- ● Headquarters and infantry
- ○ Coastal defence

- ▲ Royal Canadian Air Force
- ○ US Army
- △ US Army Air Force

A German automatic weather station, established by U537, operated in Martin Bay, Oct 1943 to Jan 1944.

Battle of the St Lawrence
May to Oct 1942

- Canadian warship sunk
- · Merchant ship sunk

Between June and December 1942 six German U-boats sank eighteen merchant and two RCN vessels in the St Lawrence and its approaches, and two U-boats sank four ore-carriers off Bell Island, Newfoundland. These losses led to the closing of the St Lawrence to non-local convoys. The threat of further German attacks persisted until mid-1943 when U-boat losses in the Atlantic soared.

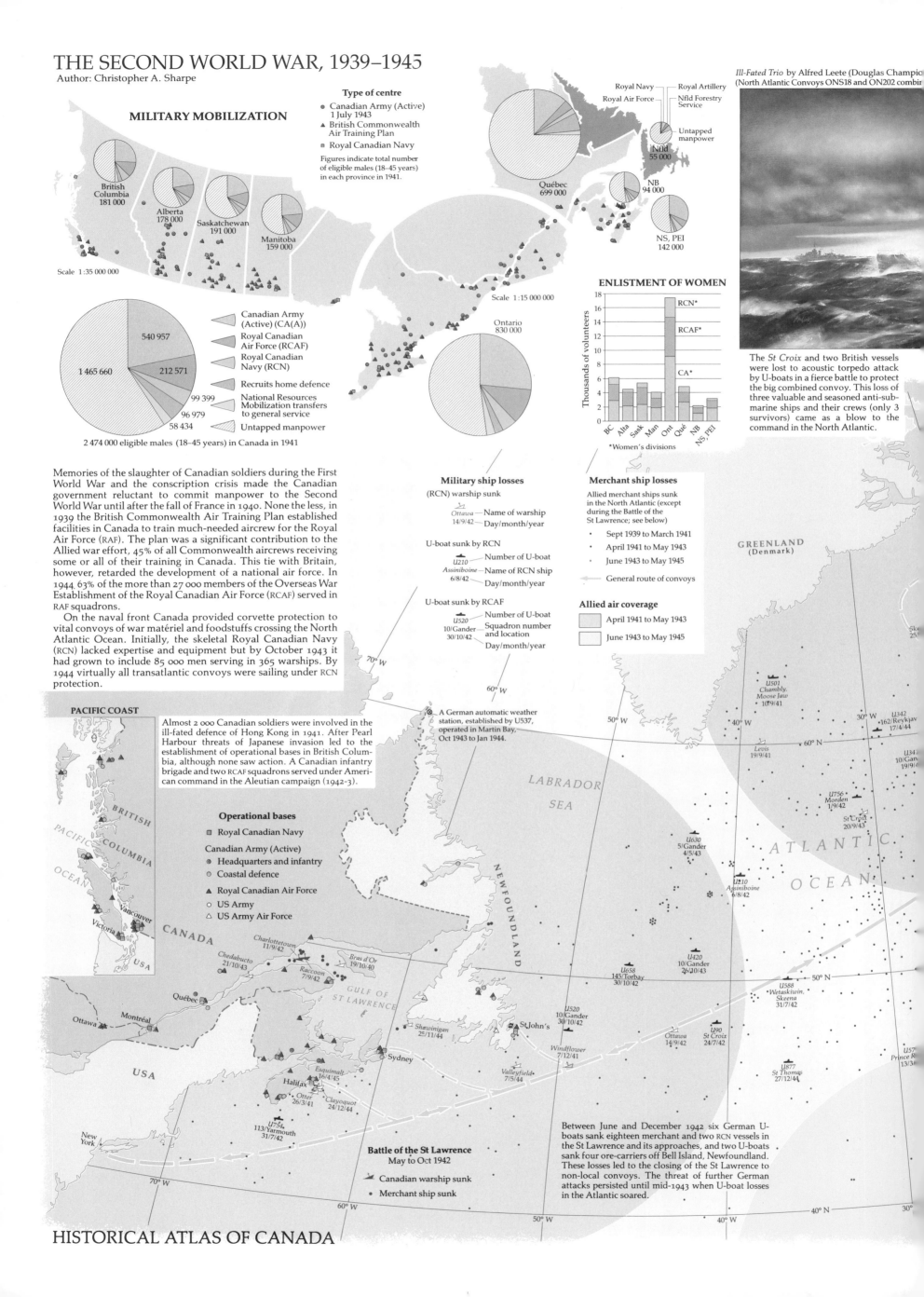

GREENLAND (Denmark)

U501 Chambly, Moose Jaw 10/9/41
U342 162/Reykjavik 17/4/44
Levis 19/9/41
U34... 10/Gan... 19/9/...
U756 Morden 1/9/42
St Croix 20/9/43
U630 5/Gander 4/5/43
U210 Assiniboine 6/8/42
U420 10/Gander 26/10/43
U658 145/Torbay 30/10/42
U588 Wetaskiwin, Skeena 31/7/42
U520 10/Gander 30/10/42
U90 St Croix 24/7/42
Ottawa 14/9/42
U57... Prince R...
U877 St Thomas 27/12/44

LABRADOR SEA
ATLANTIC OCEAN
NEWFOUNDLAND

BRITISH COLUMBIA
PACIFIC OCEAN
CANADA
USA
Vancouver
Victoria

Charlottetown 11/9/42
Chedabucto 21/10/43
Bras d'Or 19/10/40
Raccoon 7/9/42
Québec
Ottawa
Montréal
GULF OF ST LAWRENCE
Shawinigan 25/11/44
St John's
U520 10/Gander 30/10/42
Windflower 7/12/41
Valleyfield 7/5/44
Sydney
Esquimalt 16/4/45
Halifax
Otter 26/3/41
Clayoquot 24/12/44
U754 113/Yarmouth 31/7/42
New York
USA

HISTORICAL ATLAS OF CANADA

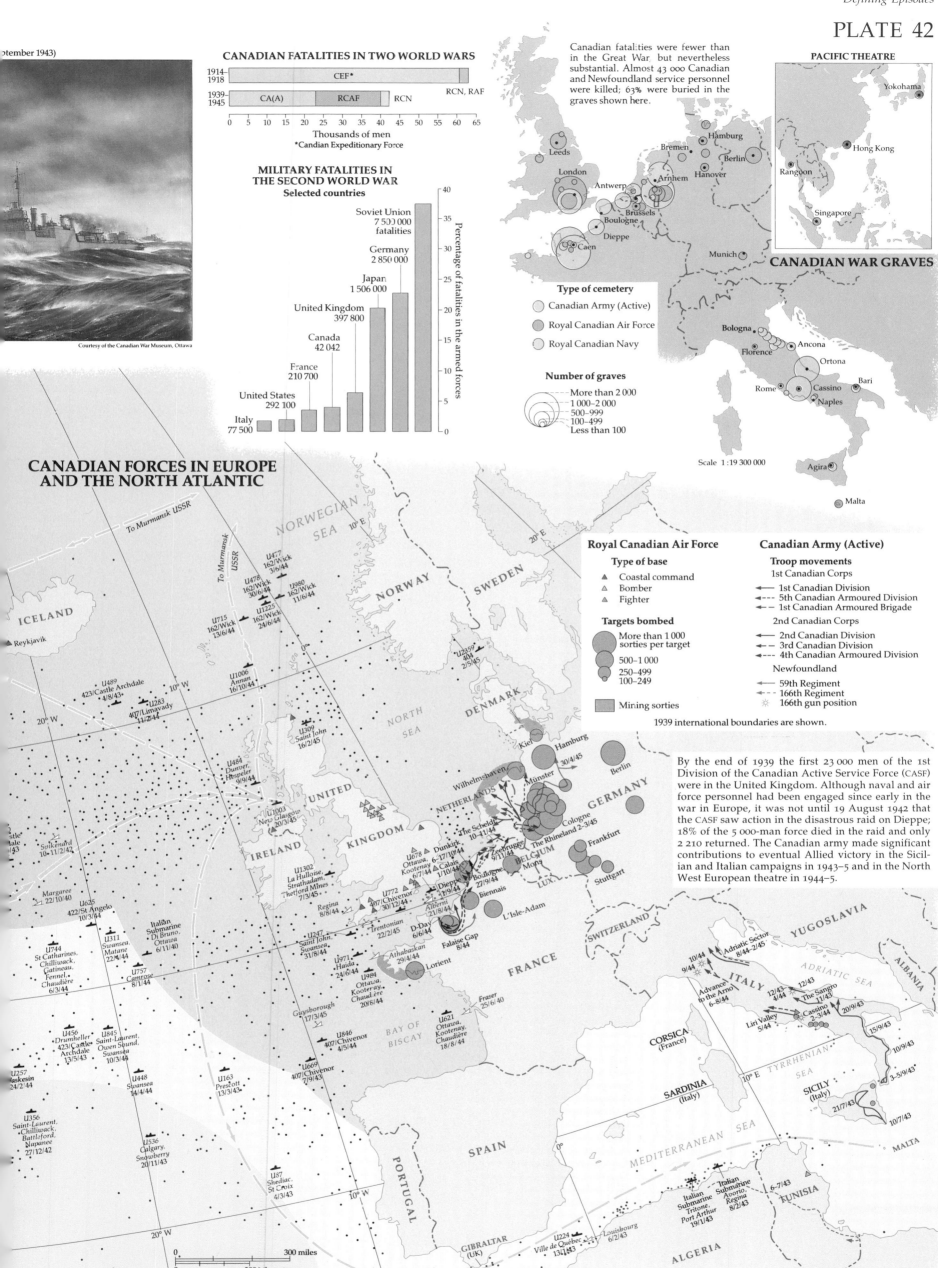

CANADIAN FATALITIES IN TWO WORLD WARS

1914–1918 — CEF*
1939–1945 — CA(A) | RCAF | RCN | RCN, RAF

Thousands of men
*Canadian Expeditionary Force

MILITARY FATALITIES IN THE SECOND WORLD WAR
Selected countries

Soviet Union 7 500 000 fatalities
Germany 2 850 000
Japan 1 506 000
United Kingdom 397 800
Canada 42 042
France 210 700
United States 292 100
Italy 77 500

Percentage of fatalities in the armed forces

Courtesy of the Canadian War Museum, Ottawa

(September 1943)

Canadian fatalities were fewer than in the Great War, but nevertheless substantial. Almost 43 000 Canadian and Newfoundland service personnel were killed; 63% were buried in the graves shown here.

PACIFIC THEATRE

Yokohama
Hong Kong
Rangoon
Singapore

CANADIAN WAR GRAVES

Leeds, London, Antwerp, Hamburg, Bremen, Berlin, Hanover, Arnhem, Brussels, Boulogne, Dieppe, Caen, Munich

Type of cemetery
- Canadian Army (Active)
- Royal Canadian Air Force
- Royal Canadian Navy

Number of graves
- More than 2 000
- 1 000–2 000
- 500–999
- 100–499
- Less than 100

Bologna, Florence, Ancona, Ortona, Rome, Cassino, Bari, Naples, Agira

Scale 1:19 300 000

Malta

CANADIAN FORCES IN EUROPE AND THE NORTH ATLANTIC

Royal Canadian Air Force

Type of base
- ▲ Coastal command
- △ Bomber
- ◮ Fighter

Targets bombed
- More than 1 000 sorties per target
- 500–1 000
- 250–499
- 100–249
- Mining sorties

Canadian Army (Active)

Troop movements

1st Canadian Corps
- ← 1st Canadian Division
- ◅-- 5th Canadian Armoured Division
- ◄- 1st Canadian Armoured Brigade

2nd Canadian Corps
- ◄- 2nd Canadian Division
- ◄- 3rd Canadian Division
- ◅-- 4th Canadian Armoured Division

Newfoundland
- ← 59th Regiment
- ◅-- 166th Regiment
- ✳ 166th gun position

1939 international boundaries are shown.

By the end of 1939 the first 23 000 men of the 1st Division of the Canadian Active Service Force (CASF) were in the United Kingdom. Although naval and air force personnel had been engaged since early in the war in Europe, it was not until 19 August 1942 that the CASF saw action in the disastrous raid on Dieppe; 18% of the 5 000-man force died in the raid and only 2 210 returned. The Canadian army made significant contributions to eventual Allied victory in the Sicilian and Italian campaigns in 1943–5 and in the North West European theatre in 1944–5.

Scale at 50° N approximately 1:15 760 000

CONCISE EDITION

PART THREE

REGIONAL PATTERNS

Canada's vast extent dictated that regionalism would become one of the country's most deep-seated and most persistent features. In a place of such immensity, the formation of smaller groupings with which people can identify is inevitable. In Canada, regions have come into focus over successive generations, only to fade into new arrangements in response to changes in population, economics, and technology. One century's core region dissolves into the periphery of somewhere else in the next century. The most stable regions – the Prairie grasslands or the St Lawrence River valley, for example – are defined by physiography. As we enter the 21st century, each region has contributed its share to Canada's personality and to building our collective view of ourselves over time. The plates in this section represent regions from all parts of the country in selected periods. Readers who turn to the three-volume *Historical Atlas of Canada* will find plates covering similar subjects in different eras, and different subjects in like eras.

The East

The North American fur trade of the 17th and 18th centuries defined a region – in effect, a huge, coherent commercial zone, though most of us have probably never thought of it this way – stretching from Chesapeake Bay and the upper Mississippi River valley northward to James Bay (Plates 43 and 44). The areas of general and seasonal occupancy shown in Plate 43 are quite opposite to the situation that exists today: southern Ontario, so central in our time, was once peripheral. Over the course of the century spanned by these two plates (together with two intermediate plates, Plates 38 and 39 in volume I), the French established control of the Great Lakes–St Lawrence watershed, as illustrated by the blue circles and flow lines in Plate 44 (lower map). Critical nodes within this region lay south of Lake Ontario – home of the Iroquois confederacy – and at the narrows west of Lake Huron, through which more and more traffic would pass. By comparison, the English fur trade through Hudson Bay seems hardly worth mentioning (Plate 44, lower map, red circles and flow lines). One's image of the great Hudson's Bay Company, founded in 1670 to trade throughout the drainage basin of the bay, is diminished by this evidence. Seasonally occupied regions (striped areas, upper maps) were all but eliminated as displaced Native communities were shunted together by the westward advance of European settlement.

Plates 45–8 depict aspects of life in the Atlantic region in the 18th century. The exquisite illustrations taken from contemporary French accounts and portfolios and reproduced in Plate 45 give us an idea of the intensive use of labour in the Newfoundland fishery of the period. Labour and capital were scarce in North America, but the fishery was exceptional in this regard, resembling European industry in its heavy reliance on both. This was certainly true of the British cod fishery, first conducted from mother ships on the Continental Shelf ('the banks') and then increasingly from shore bases. Plate 46 tells us much about the Newfoundland coastlines – the concentration of French in the northern peninsula (left map, purple and blue circles), the existence of a single Basque enclave at Port-au-Choix (green circle), and the mixing of Irish and English in the Avalon peninsula (lower right map, green and pink circles). When we compare this pattern with the geography of origin of the ships and men supplying the migratory and resident fisheries – a cluster in Normandy, a few ports in southwest England, and Waterford and Cork in Ireland (green map, upper right) – we begin to appreciate one of the great stresses of occupying new lands: living among strangers. As the 18th century progressed, Newfoundland increasingly became a place where people settled and raised families (brown circles, main map and lower left). The large proportion of children in (aptly named) Conception Bay in 1784–5 is a revealing statistic. Newfoundland territoriality was coastal, and the politics of this rocky edge are revealed in the colours used (in the central map) to delineate it; exploitation of the interior forests and minerals would await another era.

Among the earliest farming communities anywhere in Canada were those on the Bay of Fundy (Baie Française), on land recovered from the sea (Plate 47, orange areas). Here, early in the 18th century, French settlers were building dykes and aboiteaux (sluices) in order to create permanent cropland and pasture. What a contrast with the more familiar Canadian pioneering experience of clearing forests to make farmland! The Acadians borrowed the technology for controlling tide waters from the Low Countries of northern Europe and applied it to fine effect in a region with one of the world's strongest tidal flows. In the early 18th century, some 500 hectares were dyked and under cultivation. The plan and the series of enlargements of the Port-Royal area map in Plate 47 are among the most detailed landscapes that scholars have been able to trace from this early era of land occupancy in Canada (see also Plate 50).

By the end of the 18th century it was evident that the Fundy marshlands were among the best of a very few pockets of decent farmland in the Maritimes (Plate 48, main map, green shading). Indeed, trading rather than farming proved to be the better means to a living, as indicated by the commodities shown flowing in and out of dozens of little ports around the shores. With the establishment of the United States in 1783, the Maritime colonies were transformed from marginal places in the Atlantic world into Britain's central foothold in continental North America. Fears that Nova Scotia might join the United States after 1783 were allayed by the surge of British Loyalists who migrated to the area in order that they might continue to live under the British flag (map, upper left; see also Plate 37). In the late 18th century North America was on the verge of redirecting its focus from the Atlantic Ocean inland, and within a century the Maritimes would be left behind in the westward continental movement. Of all the primary products in trade, coal alone would tie the region to the industrialization of the 19th century, and even that link would weaken by the middle of the 20th century. The prospects for Maritime well-being would follow the same course.

To most French Canadians through the course of history, home has meant the St Lawrence River valley, only the thinnest strip of land in the vast area occupied by the modern province of Québec. In 1739, some 40 000 *habitants* lived scattered along the river banks, while vast tracts of reasonably good farmland farther back lay untouched, within their grasp but outside their need (Plate 49, green areas). Not for another hundred years would all this farmland be occupied and rural Québec considered full to overflowing. The importance of access – to the river front, as on the Île d'Orléans, or to central market points back from the riverfront, as at Charlesbourg – is clearly visible in the land survey (Plate 50, main map). The orderliness of the property boundary lines over long distances indicates strong central control, remarkable in such a remote place with only a rudimentary administrative structure. The productive use of tidal marshes is reminiscent of the Bay of Fundy region (see Plate 47). Québec and Montréal were monumental towns, each neatly circumscribed by walls, and each holding commanding sites over their hinterlands (Plate 51). The irregularity of streets and the prevalence of open public spaces are both very French, and perhaps their re-creation in this new land reflects the sense of exile the French colonists might have felt.

Plate 52 focuses on the forest industry in 19th-century Canada. The circumstances of forest exploitation in this country again demonstrate Harold Innis's staples theory: the vast exploitation of the forest could be accomplished with a bare minimum of infrastructure – for the simple reason that pine floats. No wonder, then, that Canadian forest exploitation followed the waterways, or that delays in introducing railways (owing to lack of capital) did not retard the growth of the forest industry (Plate 52). As the pie charts show, timber dominated the export picture, but a wide range of other wood products were also valued in the age before steam and steel. The forest industry brought large numbers of people inland, thereby encouraging construction of the major railway lines that would tie the North American interior together in the latter half of the 19th century.

Taking up land in 19th-century Ontario aroused mixed emotions among settlers (Plate 53). The thrill of owning one's own land was tempered by having to prove oneself with the axe, the adze, the shovel, the ox, and the hoe. Many newcomers had little or no farming experience and, because of the land-distribution policies that tended to disperse people widely, often found themselves living far from neighbours whose advice or support could be helpful. Dense settlement and prosperity – evidenced by the numerous substantial farmhouses from that period that are still standing today – developed first in a broad arc between Cobourg and the Niagara peninsula, gradually diminishing towards the less accessible inland areas to the north and west. As a centre of trade, Ontario had a long way to go before it could rival Montréal and Québec, the main focal points for imports and exports in Canada at mid-century (Plate 54). But Ontario's mercantile activity compared favourably with that of the Maritime Provinces – the former was growing, the latter stagnating. Notice, in the main map of Plate 54, how American railways are poised to draw southern Ontario into the continental picture. This would happen in the 1850s, and with it would come an increasingly integrated and balanced trade as industrialization took hold.

In the pre-industrial manufacturing economy, sawmilling was predominant in the areas from Saint-Maurice eastward, and economic growth would falter, in the absence of replacement activities, as the trees ran out (Plate 55). West of Saint-Maurice, industrial diversity and a higher proportion of skilled tradesmen give evidence of a society that could adapt and grow as the industrial might of inland North America developed. Central Canada's industrial strength took hold in the larger river valleys, such as the Grand River (Plate 56, lower left) and various streams in the Ottawa River region. The other focal points were the cities, notably Montréal and Toronto. A strong element of inertia assured that many small family firms would keep Ontario's small towns vibrant into the 1920s, relying on their old water mills to generate either mechanical or electrical power. Small firms prevailed in the cities as well. The relative decline of the Maritime Provinces, despite some notable growth spots, became increasingly evident as the century drew to a close.

In a city the size of Montréal the differentiation of space along social and income lines began to show well before 1900 (Plate 57). Mount Royal played an important role, for all aspired to live on its slopes, where they could take in the purer air and a finer view. Over some 60 years of transformation, merchants and professionals became established on the mountain, while labourers found themselves in residual spots along the riverfront. Such was the case in every city; from the Citadel in Halifax to the Upper Town in Québec, to Forest Hill in Toronto, to Shaughnessy Heights in Vancouver, the names tell the same story. A glimpse at downtown Toronto early in the 20th century (Plate 58) shows the intense industrial development that was driving residents to the new suburbs. Trading and commercial establishments, building upon political authority, contributed to Toronto's burgeoning industrial might. By the beginning of the 20th century the infrastructure was in place, and corporate managers, directors, and investors regarded Toronto – and particularly the corner of King and Bay Streets – as the place to be. The interconnections among these people and their firms were complex and tightly knit.

The West and the North

During the 17th and 18th centuries Hudson Bay, the Great Lakes, and the Mississippi River offered the primary means of access to the interior of America, an area long presumed by Europeans to be a great inland sea. The subregions shown on many of the maps on Plate 59 help us to understand why Canada would become an east–west nation. Transition zones – notably the water divide between Hudson Bay and the Great Lakes and the Mississippi River system – were significant in this period before surveyed political borders were in place. Economic regions (upper right), the pattern of the diffusion of horses (lower left), and seasonal modes of Indian life (upper centre) defined zones that look not at all like the political divisions on our modern maps. One of the great arteries of commerce at that time connected Great Slave Lake, Lake Athabasca, Cumberland House, Norway House, and York Factory (Plate 60). Although few Canadians today have been to any of these places, two centuries ago they were central points in a land of wandering traders and hunters. Half of all people living in what has become modern Canada were in the area featured in Plate 60 in 1800; only a tiny percentage of Canadians live there today. The attempt of the St Lawrence traders to outflank the Hudson Bay groups made the area from Lake Superior to Great Slave Lake a turbulent zone.

The Canadian Prairies were occupied in the 19th century by way of routes through the Great Plains of the United States. Settlers, supplies, railway-building materials, and labour all passed through St Paul and the Red River valley en route to this new destination (Plate 61; see also Plate 20). The CPR, building east from Winnipeg in 1881, dove into the forest after barely 50 km, and emerged from it only 600 km later, at Lake Superior. After 1885, grain exports followed that route, and gradually the railway to Montréal became Canada's commercial spine – much more than a mere symbol of the nation's coast-to-coast existence. By the time of the First World War, three transcontinental railways were complete, and had conveyed thousands of immigrants west, into the Prairies (Plate 62). In a single generation the northwesterly flow of settlement reached the edges of the territory best suited to agricultural activity, defined in the north and west by shorter growing seasons and higher altitude, and near the American line by the dryness of the Alberta–Saskatchewan borderland (main map). Nowhere in Canada were early communities so compartmentalized by ethnic group – and even by regional affiliation within the group – as they were on the Prairies (upper right). No region in Canada had a less diversified economic base than did the Prairies early in the 20th century; the region was consequently devastated by the double blow of the collapsed wheat market and the long drought of the 1930s (Plate 63). Settlement focused briefly on the northerly fringes of the Prairie region (lower centre maps, red dots), where the growing season was shorter but there were at least steady supplies of water. Around this time Canadian rural pioneering was coming to an end along the parkland belt, from Lake Manitoba to Peace River. Across the country the process of rural depopulation and retrenchment from marginal areas was well under way, as younger family members sought more rewarding lives in the cities.

British Columbia in large measure defied European occupancy. Native societies were scarcely displaced by farmer-settlers, for there was virtually no pioneering to undertake, and Native people were able to maintain their traditional territorial balance (Plate 64). The predominantly British population was concentrated in a tiny portion of the territory around the Strait of Georgia (upper right). Canada – or 'the rest of Canada,' after British Columbia joined Confederation in 1871 – seemed more remote than Great Britain, and was certainly more remote than San Francisco. The gold rush of 1858 to 1866 introduced entrepreneurs to British Columbia's resource potential (Plate 64, graphs, left centre), and there followed a massive exploitation of such resources as salmon, coal, base metals, and timber (Plate 65). Company towns sprang up, and roads and branch railways spread out through the valleys to move these bulky products in trade. Labour was scarce, and members of ethnic communities were employed in large numbers in particular areas of development – Chinese labourers in railway construction and gold digging, and Norwegians in salmon canneries, for example. British Columbia's tendency towards distinctive politics was likely influenced by the absence of the steady, conservative agricultural base that characterized other parts of the country.

The Precambrian Shield is Canada's own special physiographic region, a vast, ancient, rocky mass that consolidates Canada's east–west orientation (Plate 66). Its treasures have included gold – and yet there was no gold rush – and a wide range of industrial minerals, fibres, and sources of electrical power to serve urban development in the 20th century. No city has benefited more from exploitation of the Shield than Toronto, whose ascendancy as the business capital of Canada was closely linked to the wealth of the region.

The social and economic life of the indigenous people of the Canadian North – the Dene, the Métis, and the Inuit – has been influenced by non-Native elements since the time of the fur trade, yet as late as 1958, a large percentage of the population maintained traditional lifestyles (Plate 67). Since the 1950s the marketing of Inuit soapstone and whalebone carvings and stoneblock prints has given new vitality to Arctic communities and has raised awareness of the region among 'southern' Canadians. Today, this vast area is poised on the brink of major political change, with the establishment, in 1999, of the new territory of Nunavut in the central and eastern Arctic.

TRADE IN INTERIOR AMERICA, 1654–1666

Author: Conrad E. Heidenreich

TRADE RESUMES, 1654–1660

Between 1634 and 1651, epidemics and warfare depopulated most of the eastern Great Lakes region. After 1649 the St Lawrence valley was cut off from the west until 1654, when a group of Ottawa and Wyandot (Huron–Petun), now relocated west of Lake Michigan, came to Montréal to re-establish trade. Coureurs de bois and missionaries who followed them back to Green Bay and Lake Superior noted that these groups, as well as the Saulteaux and Potawatomi, had begun a carrying trade between their Native neighbours and the French. Meanwhile, Montagnais bands along the Saint-Maurice and Saguenay Rivers continued as middlemen between the French and more northerly bands.

From 1654 to 1658 peace between the French and all the Iroquois except the Mohawk gave the Seneca, Cayuga, and Onondaga the opportunity to disperse the Erie and the refugee Petun and Neutral and to carry the war south to the Shawnee. In the upper Mississippi a group of westward-migrating Ottawa and Wyandot initiated a protracted conflict when they tried to take hunting territory from the Dakota.

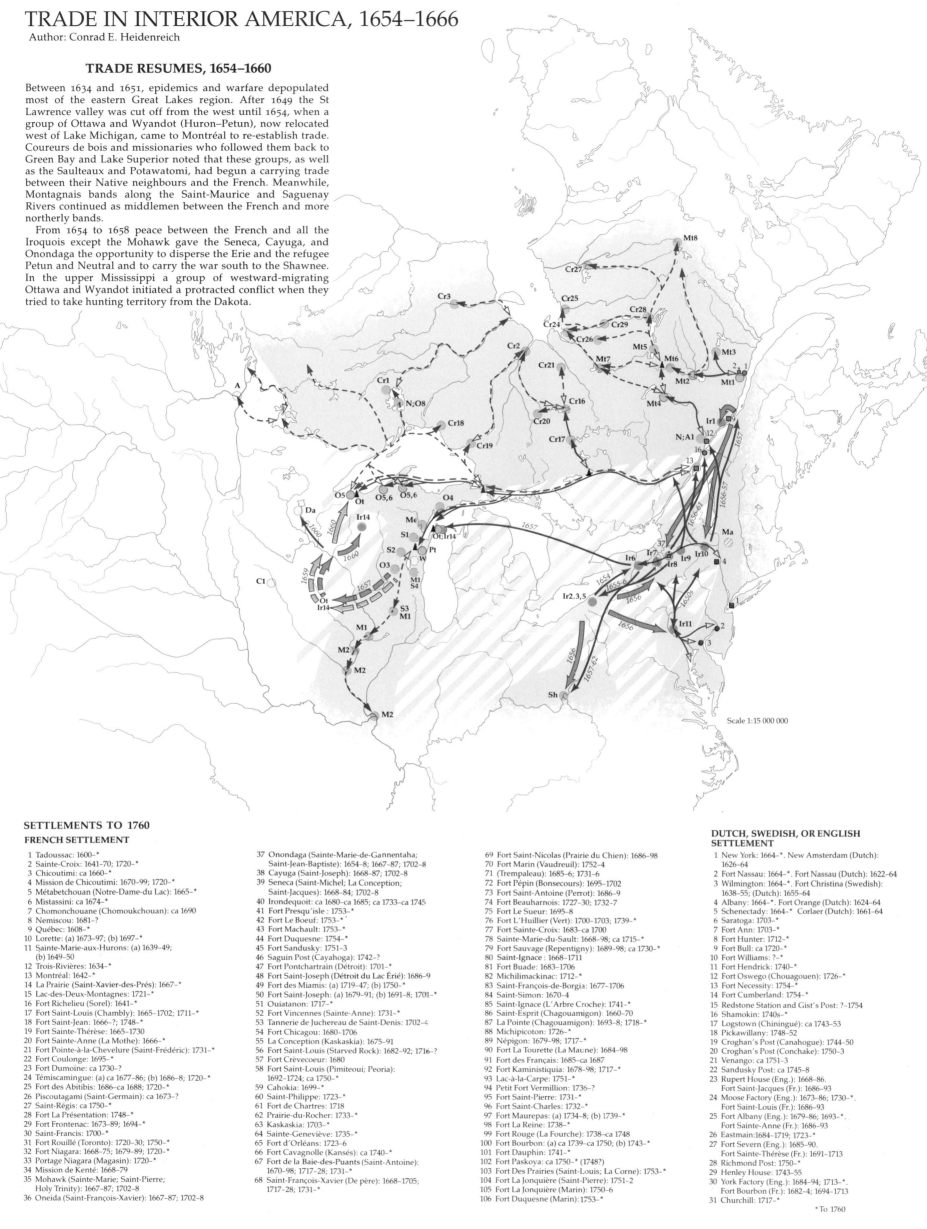

Scale 1:15 000 000

SETTLEMENTS TO 1760

FRENCH SETTLEMENT

1 Tadoussac: 1600–*
2 Sainte-Croix: 1641–70; 1720–*
3 Chicoutimi: ca 1660–*
4 Mission de Chicoutimi: 1670–99; 1720–*
5 Métabetchouan (Notre-Dame-du-Lac): 1665–*
6 Mistassini: ca 1674–*
7 Chomonchouane (Chomoukchouan): ca 1690
8 Nemiscou: 1681–?
9 Québec: 1608–*
10 Lorette: (a) 1673–97; (b) 1697–*
11 Sainte-Marie-aux-Hurons: (a) 1639–49; (b) 1649–50
12 Trois-Rivières: 1634–*
13 Montréal: 1642–*
14 La Prairie (Saint-Xavier-des-Prés): 1667–*
15 Lac-des-Deux-Montagnes: 1721–*
16 Fort Richelieu (Sorel): 1641–*
17 Fort Saint-Louis (Chambly): 1665–1702; 1711–*
18 Fort Saint-Jean: 1666–?; 1748–*
19 Fort Sainte-Thérèse: 1665–1730
20 Fort Sainte-Anne (La Mothe): 1666–*
21 Fort Pointe-à-la-Chevelure (Saint-Frédéric): 1731–*
22 Fort Coulonge: 1695–*
23 Fort Dumoine: ca 1730–?
24 Témiscamingue: (a) ca 1677–86; (b) 1686–8; 1720–*
25 Fort des Abitibis: 1686–ca 1688; 1720–*
26 Piscoutagami (Saint-Germain): ca 1673–?
27 Saint-Régis: ca 1750–*
28 Fort La Présentation: 1748–*
29 Fort Frontenac: 1673–89; 1694–*
30 Fort-Francis: 1700–*
31 Fort Rouillé (Toronto): 1720–30; 1750–*
32 Fort Niagara: 1668–75; 1679–89; 1720–*
33 Portage Niagara (Magasin): 1720–*
34 Mission de Kenté: 1668–79
35 Mohawk (Sainte-Marie; Saint-Pierre; Holy Trinity): 1667–87; 1702–8
36 Oneida (Saint-François-Xavier): 1667–87; 1702–8

37 Onondaga (Sainte-Marie-de-Gannentaha; Saint-Jean-Baptiste): 1654–8; 1667–87; 1702–8
38 Cayuga (Saint-Joseph): 1668–87; 1702–8
39 Seneca (Saint-Michel; La Conception; Saint-Jacques): 1668–84; 1702–8
40 Irondequoit: ca 1680–ca 1685; ca 1733–ca 1745
41 Fort Presqu'isle: 1753–*
42 Fort Le Boeuf: 1753–*
43 Fort Machault: 1753–*
44 Fort Duquesne: 1754–*
45 Fort Sandusky: 1751–3
46 Saguin Post (Cayahoga): 1742–?
47 Fort Pontchartrain (Détroit): 1701–*
48 Fort Saint-Joseph (Détroit du Lac Érié): 1686–9
49 Fort des Miamis: (a) 1719–47; (b) 1750–*
50 Fort Saint-Joseph: (a) 1679–91; (b) 1691–8; 1701–*
51 Ouiatanon: 1717–*
52 Fort Vincennes (Sainte-Anne): 1731–*
53 Tannerie de Juchereau de Saint-Denis: 1702–?
54 Fort Chicagou: 1680–1706
55 La Conception (Kaskaskia): 1675–91
56 Fort Saint-Louis (Starved Rock): 1682–92; 1716–?
57 Fort Crèvecoeur: 1680
58 Fort Saint-Louis (Pimiteoui; Peoria): 1692–1724; ca 1750–*
59 Cahokia: 1699–*
60 Saint-Philippe: 1723–*
61 Fort de Chartres: 1718
62 Prairie-du-Rocher: 1733–*
63 Kaskaskia: 1703–*
64 Sainte-Geneviève: 1735–*
65 Fort d'Orléans: 1723–6
66 Fort Cavagnolle (Kansés): ca 1740–*
67 Fort de la Baie-des-Puants (Saint-Antoine): 1670–98; 1717–28; 1731–*
68 Saint-François-Xavier (De père): 1668–1705; 1717–28; 1731–*

69 Fort Saint-Nicolas (Prairie du Chien): 1686–98
70 Fort Marin (Vaudreuil): 1752–4
71 (Trempaleau): 1685–6; 1731–6
72 Fort Pépin (Bonsecours): 1695–1702
73 Fort Saint-Antoine (Perrot): 1686–9
74 Fort Beauharnois: 1727–30; 1732–7
75 Fort Le Sueur: 1695–8
76 Fort L'Huillier (Vert): 1700–1703; 1739–*
77 Fort Sainte-Croix: 1683–ca 1700
78 Sainte-Marie-du-Sault: 1668–98; ca 1715–*
79 Fort Sauvage (Repentigny): 1689–98; ca 1730–*
80 Saint-Ignace: 1668–1711
81 Fort Buade: 1683–1706
82 Michilimackinac: 1712–*
83 Saint-François-de-Borgia: 1677–1706
84 Saint-Simon: 1670–4
85 Saint-Ignace (L'Arbre Croche): 1741–*
86 Saint-Esprit (Chagouamigon): 1660–70
87 La Pointe (Chagouamigon): 1693–8; 1718–*
88 Michipicoton: 1726–*
89 Népigon: 1679–98; 1717–*
90 Fort La Tourette (La Maune): 1684–98
91 Fort des Français: 1685–ca 1687
92 Fort Kaministiquia: 1678–98; 1717–*
93 Lac-à-la-Carpe: 1751–*
94 Petit Fort Vermillion: 1736–?
95 Fort Saint-Pierre: 1731–*
96 Fort Saint-Charles: 1732–*
97 Fort Maurepas: (a) 1734–8; (b) 1739–*
98 Fort La Reine: 1738–*
99 Fort Rouge (La Fourche): 1738–ca 1748
100 Fort Bourbon: (a) ca 1739–ca 1750; (b) 1743–*
101 Fort Dauphin: 1741–*
102 Fort Paskoya: ca 1750–* (1748?)
103 Fort Des Prairies (Saint-Louis; La Corne): 1753–*
104 Fort La Jonquière (Saint-Pierre): 1751–2
105 Fort La Jonquière (Marin): 1750–6
106 Fort Duquesne (Marin): 1753–*

DUTCH, SWEDISH, OR ENGLISH SETTLEMENT

1 New York: 1664–*. New Amsterdam (Dutch): 1626–64
2 Fort Nassau: 1664–*. Fort Nassau (Dutch): 1622–64
3 Wilmington: 1664–*. Fort Christina (Swedish): 1638–55; (Dutch): 1655–64
4 Albany: 1664–*. Fort Orange (Dutch): 1624–64
5 Schenectady: 1664–* Corlaer (Dutch): 1661–64
6 Saratoga: 1703–*
7 Fort Ann: 1703–*
8 Fort Hunter: 1712–*
9 Fort Bull: ca 1720–*
10 Fort Williams: ?–*
11 Fort Hendrick: 1740–*
12 Fort Oswego (Chouagouen): 1726–*
13 Fort Necessity: 1754–*
14 Fort Cumberland: 1754–*
15 Redstone Station and Gist's Post: ?–1754
16 Shamokin: 1740s–*
17 Logstown (Chiningué): ca 1743–53
18 Pickawillany: 1748–52
19 Croghan's Post (Canahogue): 1744–50
20 Croghan's Post (Conchake): 1750–3
21 Venango: ca 1751–3
22 Sandusky Post: ca 1745–8
23 Rupert House (Eng.): 1668–86. Fort Saint-Jacques (Fr.): 1686–93
24 Moose Factory (Eng.): 1673–86; 1730–*. Fort Saint-Louis (Fr.): 1686–93
25 Fort Albany (Eng.): 1679–86; 1693–*. Fort Sainte-Anne (Fr.): 1686–93
26 Eastmain: 1684–1719; 1723–*
27 Fort Severn (Eng.): 1685–90. Fort Sainte-Thérèse (Fr.): 1691–1713
28 Richmond Post: 1750–*
29 Henley House: 1743–55
30 York Factory (Eng.): 1684–94; 1713–*. Fort Bourbon (Fr.): 1682–4; 1694–1713
31 Churchill: 1717–*

* To 1760

The maps in pll 43 and 44 treat the inland development of New France for selected dates near the start and end of the process, spanning a century. The maps present an integrated view of French, English, and Indian trade, warfare, and settlement in the central interior of North America.

NATIVE GROUPS

IROQUOIAN LINGUISTIC FAMILY

Ir	Iroquoian	Ir1	Huron
		2	Petun (Tionontâte)
		3	Neutral
		4	Wenro
		5	Erie
		6	Seneca
		7	Cayuga
		8	Onondaga
		9	Oneida
		10	Mohawk
		11	Susquehannock
		12	Tuscarora
		13	Mingo (Seneca.Cayuga)
		14	Wyandot (Huron/Petun)

SIOUAN LINGUISTIC FAMILY

Da	Dakota	Da1	Santee
		2	Yankton
		3	Teton
W	Winnebago		
A	Assiniboine		
M	Mandan		
H	Hidatsa-Crow		
De	Dhegiha	De1	Omaha
		2	Ponca
		3	Osage
		4	Kansa
C	Chiwere	C1	Iowa
		2	Oto
		3	Missouri

CADDOAN LINGUISTIC FAMILY

A	Arikara
P	Pawnee

ALGONQUIAN LINGUISTIC FAMILY

Western Language Group

A	Arapaho	A1	Arapaho
		2	Atsina
B	Blackfoot	B1	Siksika
		2	Blood
		3	Piegan
C	Cheyenne		

Central Language Group

O	Ojibwa	O1	Outchibous
		2	Marameg
		3	Mantouek
		4	Noquet
		5	Saulteaux
		6	Mississauga
		7	Nikikouet
		8	Amikwa
		9	Achiligouan (N) (Ot)
		10	Ouchougai (N) (Ot)
		11	Ouasouarini
		12	Sagahanirini
		13	Graisse Ours
		14	Not specified
Ot	Ottawa		
Me	Menominee		
Pt	Potawatomi		
N	Nipissing		
S	Sauk-Fox-Kikapoo-Mascouten	S1	Sauk
		2	Fox
		3	Kikapoo
		4	Mascouten
M	Miami-Illinois	M1	Miami
		2	Illinois
Al	Algonquin		
Sh	Shawnee		
Mt	Montagnais-Naskapi	Mt1	Tadoussacien
		2	Kakouchaki
		3	Chicoutimi
		4	Attikamek
		5	Nekoubaniste
		6	Chomonchouaniste
		7	Oumatachirini (Cr)
		8	Nitchikiriniouetch (Cr)

Central Language Group

Cr	Cree–Gens de Terre		West Main Cree
		Cr1	Alimbegouek
		2	Monsoni
		3	Ataouabouskatouek
		4	Washahoe
		5	Weenusk
		6	Penneswagewan
		7	Maskegon
		8	Michinipi
		9	Nameoulini
		10	Christinaux du bois fort
		11	Christinaux du Puant
		12	Christinaux l'eau troublé
		13	Kinougeoulini
		14	Qeunebigonhelini
		15	Non-specified
			Gens de Terre
		Cr16	Abitibi
		17	Timiscimi (A1)
		18	Outoulibi
		19	Nopeming
		20	Piscoutagami
		21	Outchichagamiouetch
		22	Non-specified
			East Main Cree
		Cr24	Nisibourounik
		25	Pitchibourounik
		26	Gesseriniouetch
		27	Opinagauiriniouetch
		28	Grands Mistassirini (Mt)
		29	Escurieux

Eastern Language Group

Ma	Mahican
De	Delaware
Aw	Western Abenaki
Ae	Eastern Abenaki

Goods and traders

- ◄─── European goods
- ◁─── Native goods
- ─── Natives trading with Europeans
- --- Natives trading with Natives
- ─── Annual French traders
- - - Occasional French traders

Settlements and trading places
(see numbered list below)

- ▣ French village or town
- ⚑ French mission
- ◉ French fort or post
- ▪ Dutch village, English after 1664
- ● Dutch fort or post, English after 1664
- ▲ Known Native trading place

Warfare

- ◄─── Native warfare
- ◄═══ French warfare
- ◁══ Forced Native migration
- ◁═▢ Peaceful Native migration

Native population

- ◯ Language and Native group, eg Ir6 Iroquoian (Seneca) (see comprehensive list at right)
- ◯ Principal Native traders
- ▢ Area generally occupied
- ▢ Area seasonally occupied

Native languages

- ● Central Algonquian
- ◐ Eastern Algonquian
- ● Iroquoian
- ◯ Siouan

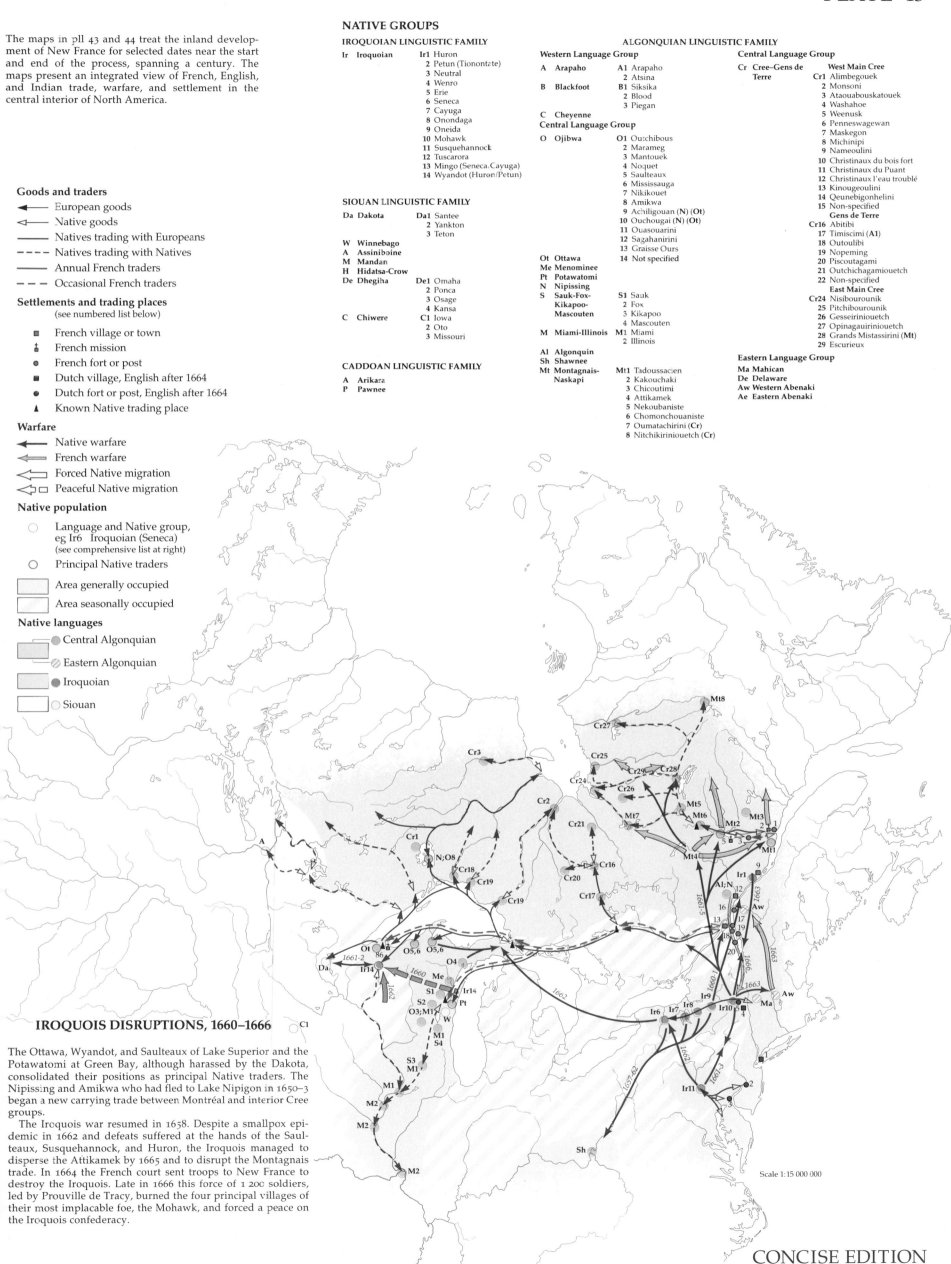

IROQUOIS DISRUPTIONS, 1660–1666

The Ottawa, Wyandot, and Saulteaux of Lake Superior and the Potawatomi at Green Bay, although harassed by the Dakota, consolidated their positions as principal Native traders. The Nipissing and Amikwa who had fled to Lake Nipigon in 1650–3 began a new carrying trade between Montréal and interior Cree groups.

The Iroquois war resumed in 1658. Despite a smallpox epidemic in 1662 and defeats suffered at the hands of the Saulteaux, Susquehannock, and Huron, the Iroquois managed to disperse the Attikamek by 1665 and to disrupt the Montagnais trade. In 1664 the French court sent troops to New France to destroy the Iroquois. Late in 1666 this force of 1 200 soldiers, led by Prouville de Tracy, burned the four principal villages of their most implacable foe, the Mohawk, and forced a peace on the Iroquois confederacy.

Scale 1:15 000 000

CONCISE EDITION

FRANCE SECURES THE INTERIOR, 1740–1755

Authors: Conrad E. Heidenreich, Françoise Noël

FRENCH STRATEGIC PROBLEMS, 1740–1751

In 1744 war between France and Britain (War of the Austrian Succession) cut short supplies to New France. After Louisbourg fell in 1745, the British blockaded the St Lawrence. Making the best of this opportunity, British traders moved into the Ohio country where they offered goods at one-third to one-quarter the French price. Attempts by the French post commanders to forbid their Native allies to trade with the British led to sullen resentment, then to open conflict. In 1744 the Miami sacked Fort Miami. The Huron burned the mission at Détroit and began attacks on French traders. The entire Wabash–Lake Erie area became unsafe for travel.

When the war ended in 1748, the French cut the price of trade goods by half and in 1749 ordered troops under Céloron de Blainville to tour the Ohio and eject British traders. The effect of this tour was slight. In 1751 the Miami destroyed Fort Vincennes and declared open support for the British.

In the northwest French trade also suffered. Although La Vérendrye and his sons had pushed trade and exploration to the Saskatchewan River, wartime scarcity and high prices induced many Native groups to trade with the Hudson's Bay Company.

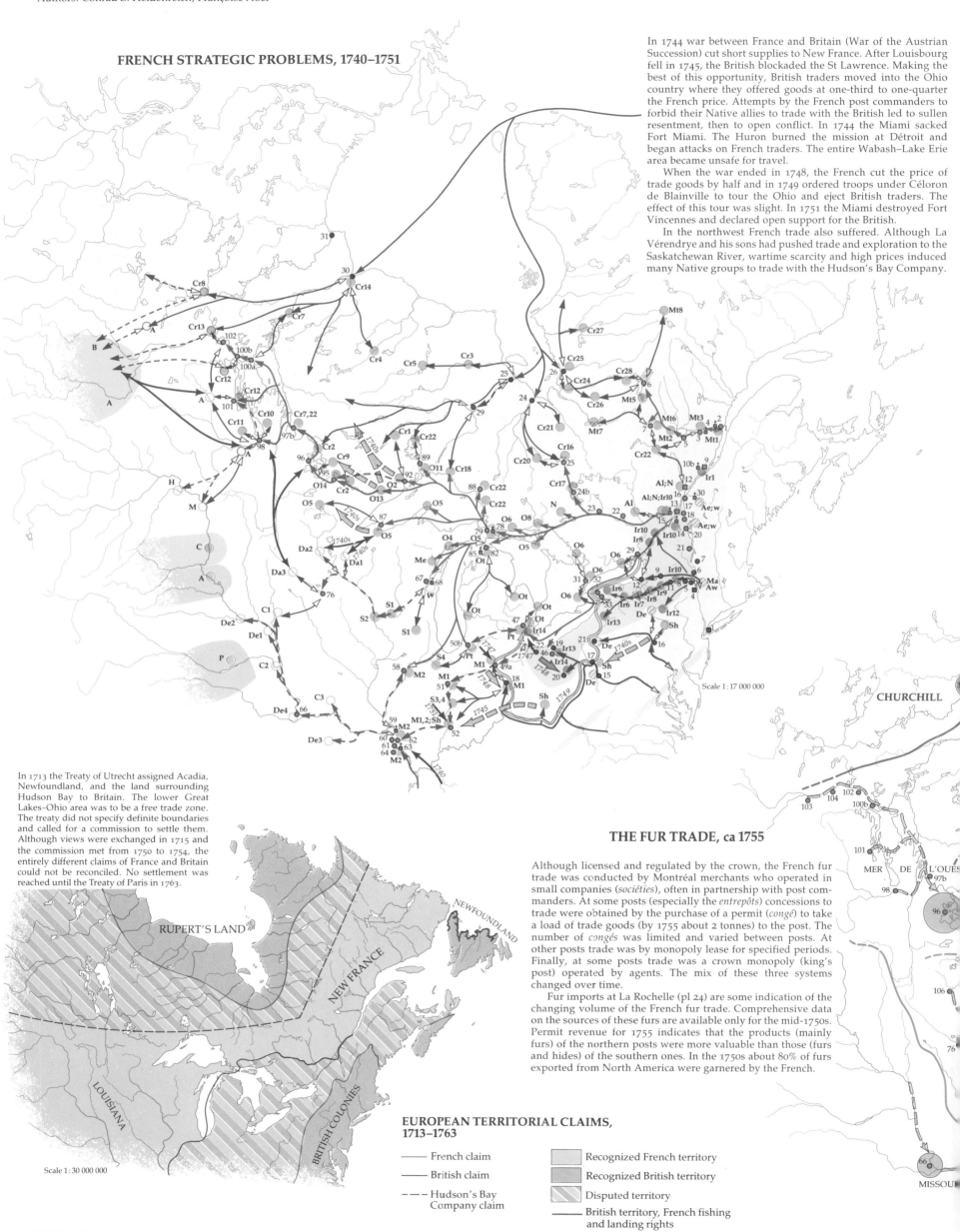

Scale 1 : 17 000 000

CHURCHILL

In 1713 the Treaty of Utrecht assigned Acadia, Newfoundland, and the land surrounding Hudson Bay to Britain. The lower Great Lakes–Ohio area was to be a free trade zone. The treaty did not specify definite boundaries and called for a commission to settle them. Although views were exchanged in 1715 and the commission met from 1750 to 1754, the entirely different claims of France and Britain could not be reconciled. No settlement was reached until the Treaty of Paris in 1763.

RUPERT'S LAND

NEWFOUNDLAND

NEW FRANCE

LOUISIANA

BRITISH COLONIES

Scale 1 : 30 000 000

THE FUR TRADE, ca 1755

Although licensed and regulated by the crown, the French fur trade was conducted by Montréal merchants who operated in small companies (sociétés), often in partnership with post commanders. At some posts (especially the entrepôts) concessions to trade were obtained by the purchase of a permit (congé) to take a load of trade goods (by 1755 about 2 tonnes) to the post. The number of congés was limited and varied between posts. At other posts trade was by monopoly lease for specified periods. Finally, at some posts trade was a crown monopoly (king's post) operated by agents. The mix of these three systems changed over time.

Fur imports at La Rochelle (pl 24) are some indication of the changing volume of the French fur trade. Comprehensive data on the sources of these furs are available only for the mid-1750s. Permit revenue for 1755 indicates that the products (mainly furs) of the northern posts were more valuable than those (furs and hides) of the southern ones. In the 1750s about 80% of furs exported from North America were garnered by the French.

MER DE L'OUES

MISSOU

EUROPEAN TERRITORIAL CLAIMS, 1713–1763

—— French claim

—— British claim

--- Hudson's Bay Company claim

 Recognized French territory

 Recognized British territory

 Disputed territory

—— British territory, French fishing and landing rights

HISTORICAL ATLAS OF CANADA

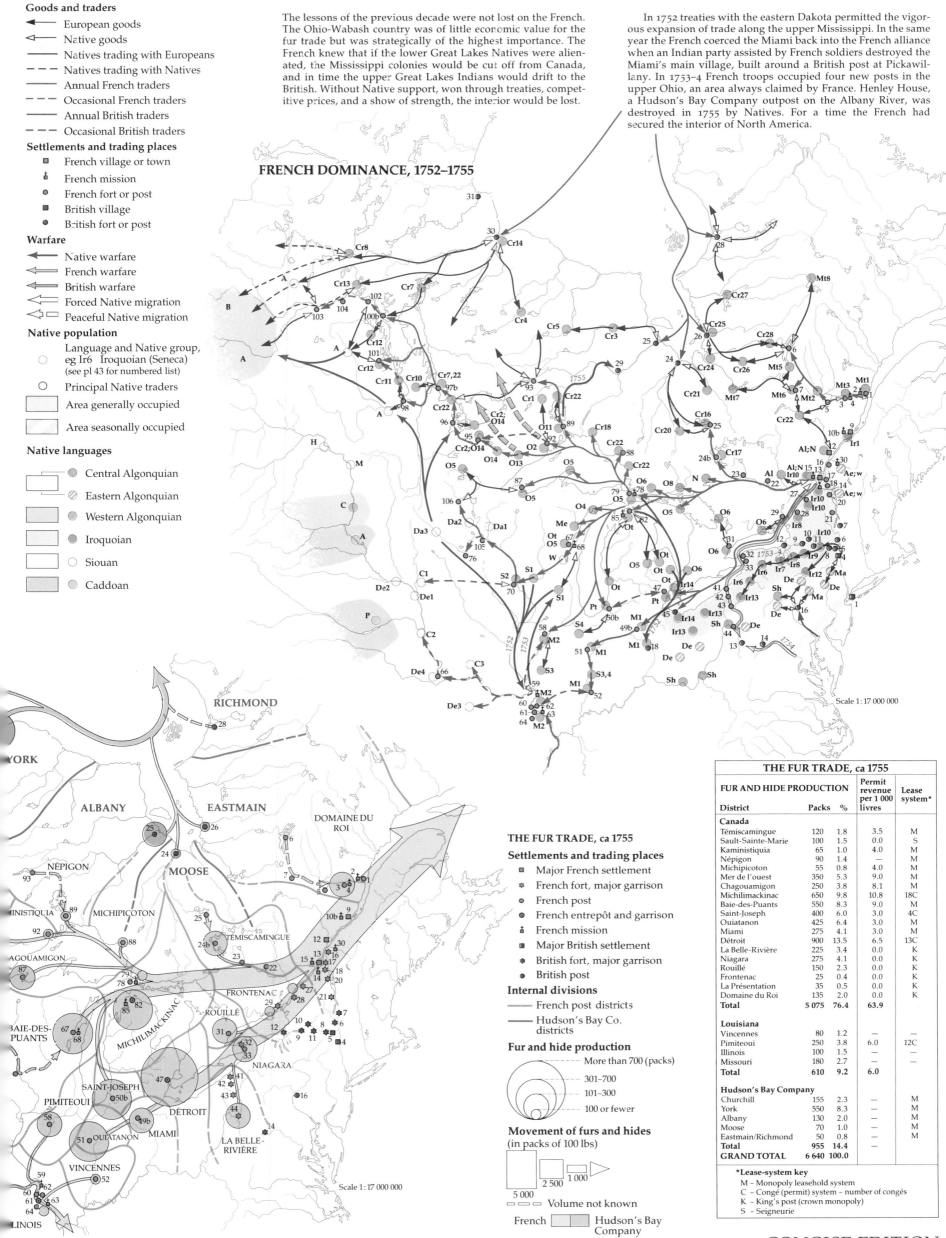

Goods and traders

- ◄—— European goods
- ◁—— Native goods
- —— Natives trading with Europeans
- - - - Natives trading with Natives
- —— Annual French traders
- - - - Occasional French traders
- —— Annual British traders
- - - - Occasional British traders

Settlements and trading places

- ■ French village or town
- ⚑ French mission
- ● French fort or post
- ■ British village
- ● British fort or post

Warfare

- ◄ Native warfare
- ◄ French warfare
- ◁ British warfare
- ◁ Forced Native migration
- ◁□ Peaceful Native migration

Native population

- ○ Language and Native group, eg Ir6 Iroquoian (Seneca) (see pl 43 for numbered list)
- ○ Principal Native traders
- ▨ Area generally occupied
- ▨ Area seasonally occupied

Native languages

- ● Central Algonquian
- ◍ Eastern Algonquian
- ● Western Algonquian
- ● Iroquoian
- ○ Siouan
- ● Caddoan

The lessons of the previous decade were not lost on the French. The Ohio-Wabash country was of little economic value for the fur trade but was strategically of the highest importance. The French knew that if the lower Great Lakes Natives were alienated, the Mississippi colonies would be cut off from Canada, and in time the upper Great Lakes Indians would drift to the British. Without Native support, won through treaties, competitive prices, and a show of strength, the interior would be lost.

In 1752 treaties with the eastern Dakota permitted the vigorous expansion of trade along the upper Mississippi. In the same year the French coerced the Miami back into the French alliance when an Indian party assisted by French soldiers destroyed the Miami's main village, built around a British post at Pickawillany. In 1753–4 French troops occupied four new posts in the upper Ohio, an area always claimed by France. Henley House, a Hudson's Bay Company outpost on the Albany River, was destroyed in 1755 by Natives. For a time the French had secured the interior of North America.

FRENCH DOMINANCE, 1752–1755

Scale 1 : 17 000 000

THE FUR TRADE, ca 1755

Settlements and trading places

- ■ Major French settlement
- ⚑ French fort, major garrison
- ● French post
- ◉ French entrepôt and garrison
- ⚑ French mission
- ■ Major British settlement
- ⚑ British fort, major garrison
- ● British post

Internal divisions

- —— French post districts
- —— Hudson's Bay Co. districts

Fur and hide production

- More than 700 (packs)
- 301–700
- 101–300
- 100 or fewer

Movement of furs and hides (in packs of 100 lbs)

- 5 000 / 2 500 / 1 000
- Volume not known
- ▨ French   ▨ Hudson's Bay Company

Scale 1 : 17 000 000

THE FUR TRADE, ca 1755

FUR AND HIDE PRODUCTION			Permit revenue per 1 000 livres	Lease system*
District	Packs	%		
Canada				
Témiscamingue	120	1.8	3.5	M
Sault-Sainte-Marie	100	1.5	0.0	S
Kaministiquia	65	1.0	4.0	M
Népigon	90	1.4	—	M
Michipicoton	55	0.8	4.0	M
Mer de l'ouest	350	5.3	9.0	M
Chagouamigon	250	3.8	8.1	M
Michilimackinac	650	9.8	10.8	18C
Baie-des-Puants	550	8.3	9.0	M
Saint-Joseph	400	6.0	3.0	4C
Ouiatanon	425	6.4	3.0	M
Miami	275	4.1	3.0	M
Détroit	900	13.5	6.5	13C
La Belle-Rivière	225	3.4	0.0	K
Niagara	275	4.1	0.0	K
Rouillé	150	2.3	0.0	K
Frontenac	25	0.4	0.0	K
La Présentation	35	0.5	0.0	K
Domaine du Roi	135	2.0	0.0	K
Total	**5 075**	**76.4**	**63.9**	
Louisiana				
Vincennes	80	1.2	—	—
Pimiteoui	250	3.8	6.0	12C
Illinois	100	1.5	—	—
Missouri	180	2.7	—	—
Total	**610**	**9.2**	**6.0**	
Hudson's Bay Company				
Churchill	155	2.3	—	M
York	550	8.3	—	M
Albany	130	2.0	—	M
Moose	70	1.0	—	M
Eastmain/Richmond	50	0.8	—	M
Total	**955**	**14.4**	—	
GRAND TOTAL	**6 640**	**100.0**		

*Lease-system key
M – Monopoly leasehold system
C – Congé (permit) system – number of congés
K – King's post (crown monopoly)
S – Seigneurie

CONCISE EDITION

THE MIGRATORY FISHERIES, 18th CENTURY
Authors: John Mannion, C. Grant Head

The roofs are colour-coded by building function.

A	Stage (A)
M	Fishermen's or shore-workers' cabin (M)
N	Officers' cabin (N)
F	Oil vat (F)
H	Flakes (H)
I	Rances (I)
K	Bed of cobbles with piles of cod (K)
O	Garden (O)
-----	Probable boundary between properties or 'rooms'

MIGRATORY INSHORE DRY FISHERY

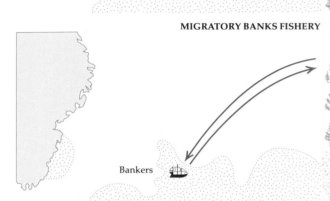

Fishing ships (usually laid up in harbour during season)

Boats, usually shallops

Banks

MIGRATORY BANKS FISHERY

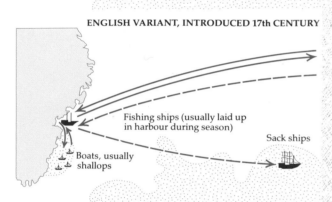

Bankers

ENGLISH VARIANT, INTRODUCED 17th CENTURY

Fishing ships (usually laid up in harbour during season)

Sack ships

Boats, usually shallops

RESIDENT BANKS FISHERY, 18th CENTURY

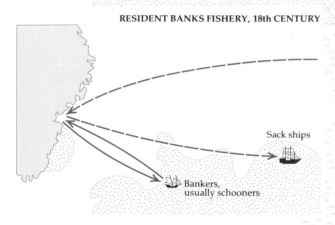

Sack ships

Bankers, usually schooners

The first European fishing ships in the northwestern Atlantic brought a migratory fishery to coastal harbours in the New World. Men fished *inshore* in small boats, usually shallops, and preserved the catch ashore by light salting, washing, and drying *(dry fishery)*. At the end of the season the fishermen returned to Europe, usually marketing the cod in southern ports. After the mid-16th century some ships (bankers) sailed directly to the *offshore* banks. The cod were heavily salted in the hold *(wet or green fishery)* and the bankers returned to Europe with the catch. In the early 17th century sack (supply) ships, usually English, transported fish from the inshore fishery to markets in southern Europe while the fishing ships returned directly to their home ports. By the early 18th century bankers based in the New World supplemented the inshore fishery. The cod, wet-salted temporarily, were later washed and dried ashore.

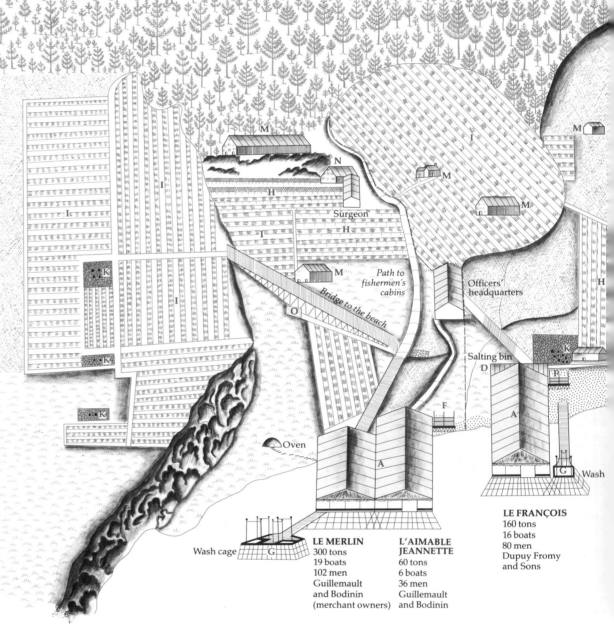

M

N

H

Surgeon

I

Path to fishermen's cabins

M

O

Bridge to the beach

Officers' headquarters

Salting bin

D

F

F

A

Oven

A

G   Wash

K

K

K

Wash cage   G

LE MERLIN
300 tons
19 boats
102 men
Guillemault and Bodinin (merchant owners)

L'AIMABLE JEANNETTE
60 tons
6 boats
36 men
Guillemault and Bodinin

LE FRANÇOIS
160 tons
16 boats
80 men
Dupuy Fromy and Sons

The map depicts a seasonally occupied harbour in the Bay of Islands in western Newfoundland in 1785. That spring seven ships averaging 157 tons arrived from Saint-Malo with 470 men. Using 84 shallops they caught and cured over 12 000 quintals (1 quintal = 112 English pounds or about 50 kilograms) of dried cod and processed 180 barrels of oil – a small, probably unprofitable production for the number of men involved.

Ships of 30–150 tons participated in the banks fishery. They came from many ports and brought many different techniques and customs to the banks, but all bankers preserved their catch by the wet process, which produced a more perishable product than the dry fishery but with much less labour.

Fishermen on the bankers stood in barrels (1) and were further protected by heavy leather aprons and by shields (2) rigged in front of them. Their hempen lines, carrying 5-lb (2.3-kg) weights and one or two baited hooks, were variously deployed. The fishermen hauled the cod on deck and cut out their tongues (as a measure of the number caught). Boys carried the cod to the header (3), who stood in a barrel beside the table on which he beheaded and gutted the cod. On the other side of the table the splitter (4) removed backbones and dropped the split cod into the hold, where the salters (5) packed them between layers of salt. A boy (6) put the livers in a barrel on deck.

HISTORICAL ATLAS OF CANADA

BANKER
Side elevation of a 100-ton banker from Sables-d'Olonne, 18th century

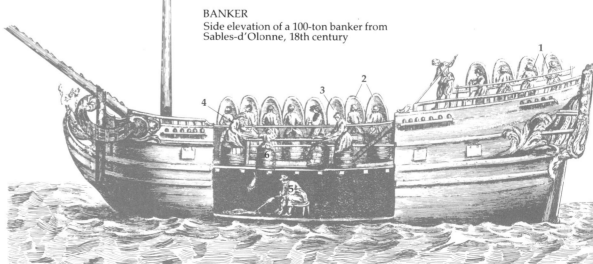

Duhamel du Monceau, 1772

PROCESSING COD AT THE STAGE

The dry fishery was capital- and labour-intensive. It required many ships, boats, and men, and created large, seasonal workplaces.

The cod, usually caught from shallops with three-man crews, were landed at the end of a stage (A), where boys passed them indoors to headers (B) and splitters (C). The split cod were carried to salters (D), who piled them between layers of salt; livers were collected in baskets and taken by boys (E) to the oil vat (F). After some days the salted cod were carried to the wash cage (G), washed, and piled again to drain. Then they were spread out to dry: on flakes (long, narrow platforms around 50 cm high and made of poles and spruce boughs) (H); on labour-saving rances, (rows of boughs placed on the beach) (I); or directly on the beach cobbles (J). The cod, turned at mid-day and piled (K) at night, were sufficiently dry after 10 days of good drying.

The shoremen usually slept in lofts (L) on the stages (A) or in cabins (M) nearby. Fishermen slept in similar cabins and officers had slightly more ample quarters (N). There might be a brewery for spruce beer, an outdoor oven, and tiny gardens (O).

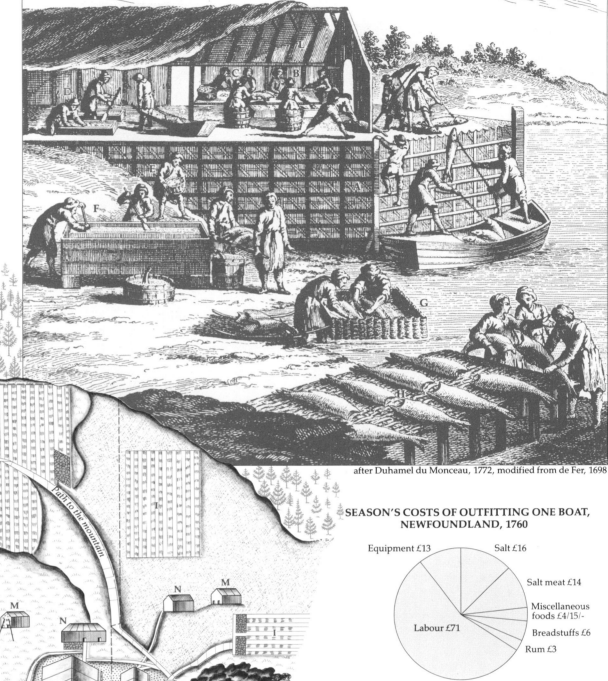

after Duhamel du Monceau, 1772, modified from de Fer, 1698

SEASON'S COSTS OF OUTFITTING ONE BOAT, NEWFOUNDLAND, 1760

Equipment £13 · Salt £16 · Salt meat £14 · Miscellaneous foods £4/15/- · Breadstuffs £6 · Rum £3 · Labour £71

Brewery

H · M · M · I · O · O · Path to the mountain · Cross · Path to the mountain · I · N · M · M · N · M · N · I

N · F · F · N · A · A · A · A · Bridge · G · Wash cage · G · Wash cage

M. Pelé's stage · **M. Morvan's stage**

AIMABLE JULIE
0 tons
boats
7 men
uguen Quenet
d Company

L'ANPHYTRIE
150 tons
11 boats
63 men
Duguen Quenet
and Company

All statistics are from French records of cod fishery from Saint-Malo at Trois-Isles, Bay of Islands (western Newfoundland), spring, summer, and fall 1785.

DRYING COD ASHORE

FISHERMAN, HEADER, AND SPLITTER
AT WORK ON A BANKER

Duhamel du Monceau, 1772

after Duhamel du Monceau, 1772

THE NEWFOUNDLAND FISHERY, 18th CENTURY

Authors: John Mannion, Gordon Handcock, Alan Macpherson

The treaty of Utrecht (1713) established British title to New-
foundland. During the following century the British fishery
expanded well beyond the old English shore in southeastern
Newfoundland; it quickly occupied the south coast when the
French fishermen moved to Île Royale, reached the west coast
by the 1760s, and established resident fisheries on the Petit-
Nord (the northern peninsula of Newfoundland) and the
Labrador coast before 1800. The small French residential fishery was confined to the islands of Saint-Pierre and Miquelon.
About a quarter of the French migratory fishery went directly
to the banks. Most of the rest crowded into the harbours of the
Petit-Nord, where France retained fishing rights and practised
an inshore fishery (pl 45).

The British fishery was even more varied. Planters (resident
fishing proprietors) hired shallop crews for the inshore fishery.
The migratory fishery, operating out of English ports, sent
ships to the inshore fishery and bankers to the Grand Bank
where cod were salted aboard and dry-cured ashore (as in the
schooner fishery, pl 45). Some migrants – masters and men
known collectively as by-boatmen – came out as passengers on
English fishing vessels and operated independently in the
inshore fishery. As late as 1790 planters and migratory men
divided production almost equally between them, but the
Napoleonic Wars eliminated the by-boatmen and drastically
reduced the migratory ship-fishery. By 1805 planters accounted
for over 90% of the catch.

BRITISH COD PRODUCTION
Total and percentage by sector

Inhabitants

Total British quintals

Fishing ships
and bankers

By-boat
keepers

FRENCH FISHERMEN,
1765–1772

**Average number of men per
year, 1765–6, 1768–9, 1771–2**

501–1 000 men
251–500
101–250
51–100
10–50

Home port of fishermen

Atlantic   Granville

Basque   Saint-Malo

For the north shore and
Saint-Pierre and Miquelon,
see the central map.

Scale 1:2 000 000

LABRADOR

STRAIT OF BELLE ISLE

Belle Isle

Dégrat-de-la-
Grande-Bay

La Bayeau-Maures

Vieux-
Férolle

Port-au-Choix

Orange

Machigonais
au vache

Fleur-de-Lys

Bay-
Verte
Les Pins et l'Île au Bois
Paquet
Coup-de-Hache
La Scie
Cape St John

WHITE BAY

NOTRE DAME BAY

Fairou
Quirpon
Criquet-
Saint-
Lunaire
Grands-Brehats
Les Grandes-Oies   Saint-Antoine
Les Petites-Oies   La Crémaillère
Hare Bay
Ficnot
Le Four
Les Islettes
Grand-Saint-Julien
Croque
Cap-Rouge
Conche
Rince
Boutitou
Les
Equillettes
Les Canaries
Sans Fonds
Fourche
Bell
Island

PETIT-NORD

Enlargement for French Fishermen, 1765–1772

LABRADOR

Chateau
Red Bay
Labrador
St Modest
Forteau

Grand Saint-Julien

Hilliard's Arm   Bell
Les Equillettes   Isla
Wild Cove   Wild Cove
Hilliard's Arm   Les Canari
Les Equillettes   French
Les Canaries   shore

Port-au-Choix

Fleur-de-Ly
St J

Sop's
Arm   Hauling Point

Sop's Arm
Hauling Point
Riverhead
Fleur-de-Lys   Riverhead

White Bay

PETIT-NORD

See enlargement for French Fishermen, 1765–1772.

Central map

NEWFOUND

St George's
Bay

Codroy
Grand Bay
Port-aux-Basques
Le Cou
Burgeo Island

Port-aux-
Basques
Grand Bay   Le Cou   Great Garia
Port-aux-Basques   Burgeo Island   Ramea Island
Le Cou
Great Garia
Burgeo Island

Hermitage
Connaigre
Pass Island
Harbour Breton   Bo

Fortune
Bay   Fo
Gran
Ban
Fort

Miquelon

Saint-Pierre

Perma
French
resider
(600)

1765s
1780s
1760s
1760s

0   40 miles
0   40 kilometres
Scale 1:2 750 000

Saint-Pierre and Miquelon, originally French, were ceded
to Britain in 1713, but were
returned to France in 1763.

BRITISH POPULATION, NEWFOUNDLAND

Summer (migrant)

Winter (resident)

Women

Thousands of people

1720   1730   1740   1750   1760   1770   1780   1790   1797

WINTER POPULATION,
1737–1738

1 001–2 000 people
601–1 000
351–600
201–350
101–200
0–100

Men   Women
Children

Bonavista Bay

Bonavista

Trinity
Bonaventure
Old
Perlican
Bay de
Verde
Conception
Bay
Carbonear
Musquito
Harbour
Grace
Torbay
Quidi
Vidi
St John's
Petty
Harbour

AVALON
PENINSULA

Placentia
Bay   Little
Placentia
Great
Placentia

Bay Bulls

Ferryland
Fermeuse
Renews

Trepassey

St Mary's Bay

Scale 1:2 500 000

WINTER POPULATION,
1784–1785

Bonavista Bay

Bonavista

Trinity Ba

Trinity
Bonaventure
Conceptio
(35
Old Perlican
Bay de
Verde
Carbonear
Musquito
Harbour
Grace
Torbay
Quidi
Vidi
St John's
Petty
Harbour

AVALON
PENINSULA

Placentia
Bay   Little
Placentia
Great
Placentia

Bay Bulls

Cape Broyle
Ferryland
Fermeuse
Renews

Placentia
Bay

St Mary's

Trepassey

St Mary's Bay

Scale 1:2 500 000

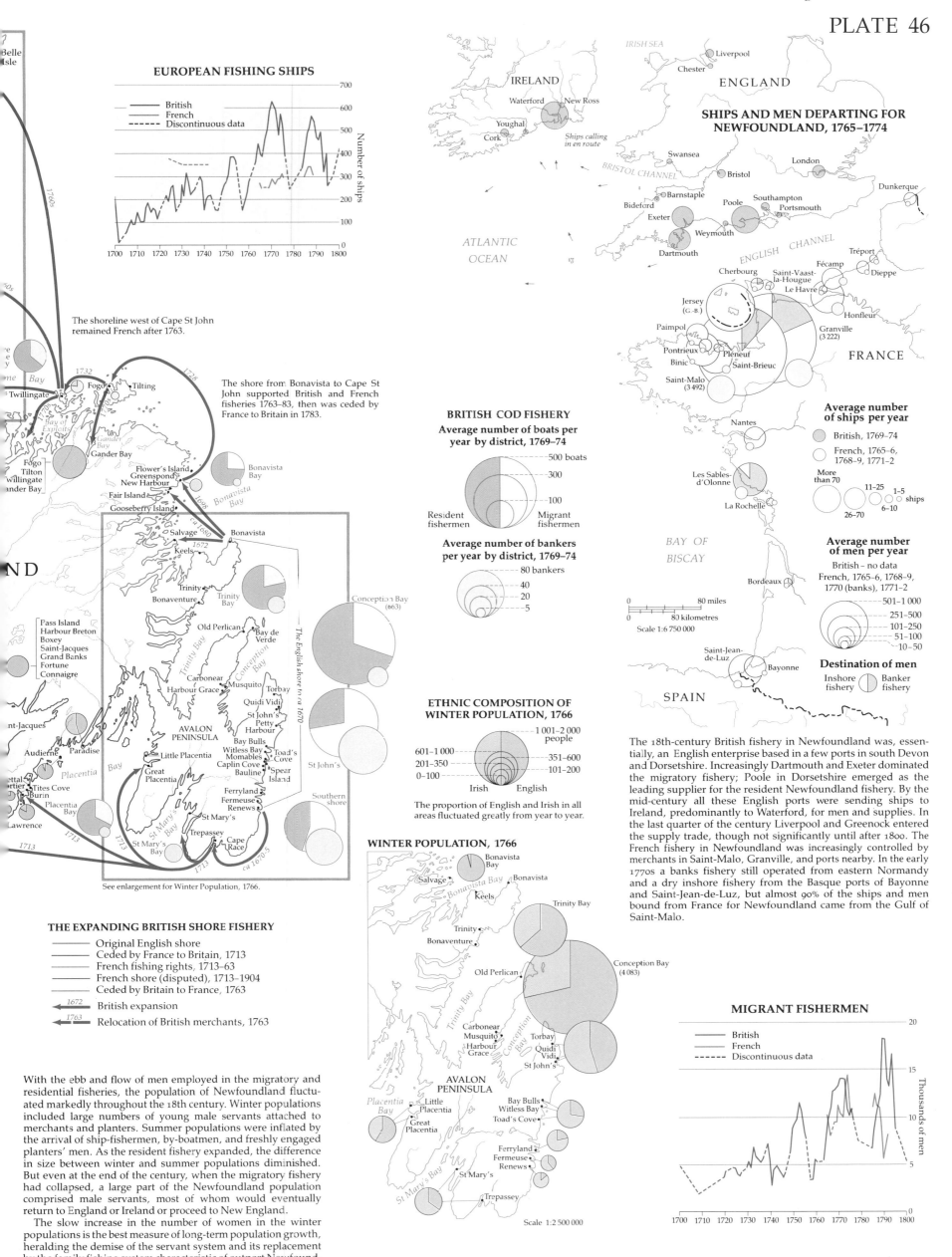

EUROPEAN FISHING SHIPS

- British
- French
- Discontinuous data

The shoreline west of Cape St John remained French after 1763.

The shore from Bonavista to Cape St John supported British and French fisheries 1763–83, then was ceded by France to Britain in 1783.

SHIPS AND MEN DEPARTING FOR NEWFOUNDLAND, 1765–1774

Ships calling in en route

Average number of ships per year

- British, 1769–74
- French, 1765–6, 1768–9, 1771–2

More than 70 · 26–70 · 11–25 · 6–10 · 1–5 ships

Average number of men per year

British – no data
French, 1765–6, 1768–9, 1770 (banks), 1771–2

- 501–1 000
- 251–500
- 101–250
- 51–100
- 10–50

Destination of men

- Inshore fishery
- Banker fishery

BRITISH COD FISHERY

Average number of boats per year by district, 1769–74

- 500 boats
- 300
- 100

Resident fishermen · Migrant fishermen

Average number of bankers per year by district, 1769–74

- 80 bankers
- 40
- 20
- 5

ETHNIC COMPOSITION OF WINTER POPULATION, 1766

- 1 001–2 000 people
- 601–1 000
- 351–600
- 201–350
- 101–200
- 0–100

Irish · English

The proportion of English and Irish in all areas fluctuated greatly from year to year.

WINTER POPULATION, 1766

Scale 1:2 500 000

See enlargement for Winter Population, 1766.

THE EXPANDING BRITISH SHORE FISHERY

- Original English shore
- Ceded by France to Britain, 1713
- French fishing rights, 1713–63
- French shore (disputed), 1713–1904
- Ceded by Britain to France, 1763
- *1672* British expansion
- *1763* Relocation of British merchants, 1763

The 18th-century British fishery in Newfoundland was, essentially, an English enterprise based in a few ports in south Devon and Dorsetshire. Increasingly Dartmouth and Exeter dominated the migratory fishery; Poole in Dorsetshire emerged as the leading supplier for the resident Newfoundland fishery. By the mid-century all these English ports were sending ships to Ireland, predominantly to Waterford, for men and supplies. In the last quarter of the century Liverpool and Greenock entered the supply trade, though not significantly until after 1800. The French fishery in Newfoundland was increasingly controlled by merchants in Saint-Malo, Granville, and ports nearby. In the early 1770s a banks fishery still operated from eastern Normandy and a dry inshore fishery from the Basque ports of Bayonne and Saint-Jean-de-Luz, but almost 90% of the ships and men bound from France for Newfoundland came from the Gulf of Saint-Malo.

Scale 1:6 750 000

With the ebb and flow of men employed in the migratory and residential fisheries, the population of Newfoundland fluctuated markedly throughout the 18th century. Winter populations included large numbers of young male servants attached to merchants and planters. Summer populations were inflated by the arrival of ship-fishermen, by-boatmen, and freshly engaged planters' men. As the resident fishery expanded, the difference in size between winter and summer populations diminished. But even at the end of the century, when the migratory fishery had collapsed, a large part of the Newfoundland population comprised male servants, most of whom would eventually return to England or Ireland or proceed to New England.

The slow increase in the number of women in the winter populations is the best measure of long-term population growth, heralding the demise of the servant system and its replacement by the family fishing system characteristic of outport Newfoundland in the 19th century.

MIGRANT FISHERMEN

- British
- French
- Discontinuous data

Thousands of men

ACADIAN MARSHLAND SETTLEMENT, 1671–1714

Author: Jean Daigle

POPULATION DISTRIBUTION, 1707

The Acadian population grew from a few immigrant families established at Port-Royal after 1640. A high birth rate and low infant mortality led to rapid population growth. In 1671 there were approximately 500 Acadians: 350 in 70 farm families near Port-Royal, the rest fishermen over-wintering along the Atlantic coast. Settlement occupied all the marshes along the Rivière au Dauphin above Port-Royal, then expanded in the 1680s to the larger marshes near the head of the Baie Française (Bay of Fundy). In 1707 there were about 1 400 Acadians; almost all of them, raised beside the marshes in settlements of closely related kin and out of range of the principal fisheries, were farmers.

Acadian dykes were made from sods of marsh grasses and often reinforced by logs and branches. Frequently there was a road along the top. Aboiteaux (sluices) were variously framed; clapets (clapper valves) kept out salt water. Dykes were as much as 2 m high and some 4 m wide.

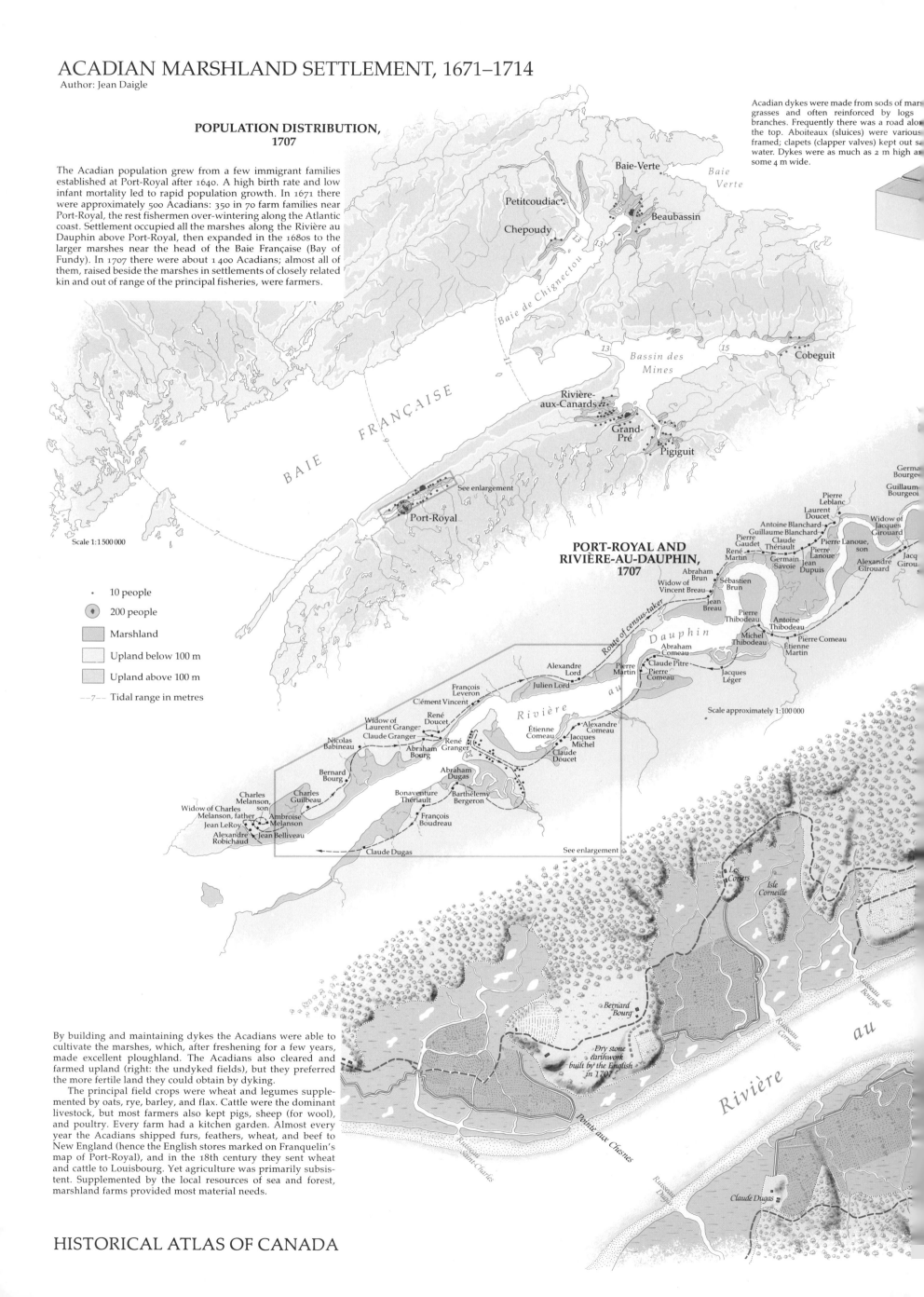

Scale 1:1 500 000

- 10 people
200 people
Marshland
Upland below 100 m
Upland above 100 m
—7— Tidal range in metres

PORT-ROYAL AND RIVIÈRE-AU-DAUPHIN, 1707

Scale approximately 1:100 000

By building and maintaining dykes the Acadians were able to cultivate the marshes, which, after freshening for a few years, made excellent ploughland. The Acadians also cleared and farmed upland (right: the undyked fields), but they preferred the more fertile land they could obtain by dyking.

The principal field crops were wheat and legumes supplemented by oats, rye, barley, and flax. Cattle were the dominant livestock, but most farmers also kept pigs, sheep (for wool), and poultry. Every farm had a kitchen garden. Almost every year the Acadians shipped furs, feathers, wheat, and beef to New England (hence the English stores marked on Franquelin's map of Port-Royal), and in the 18th century they sent wheat and cattle to Louisbourg. Yet agriculture was primarily subsistent. Supplemented by the local resources of sea and forest, marshland farms provided most material needs.

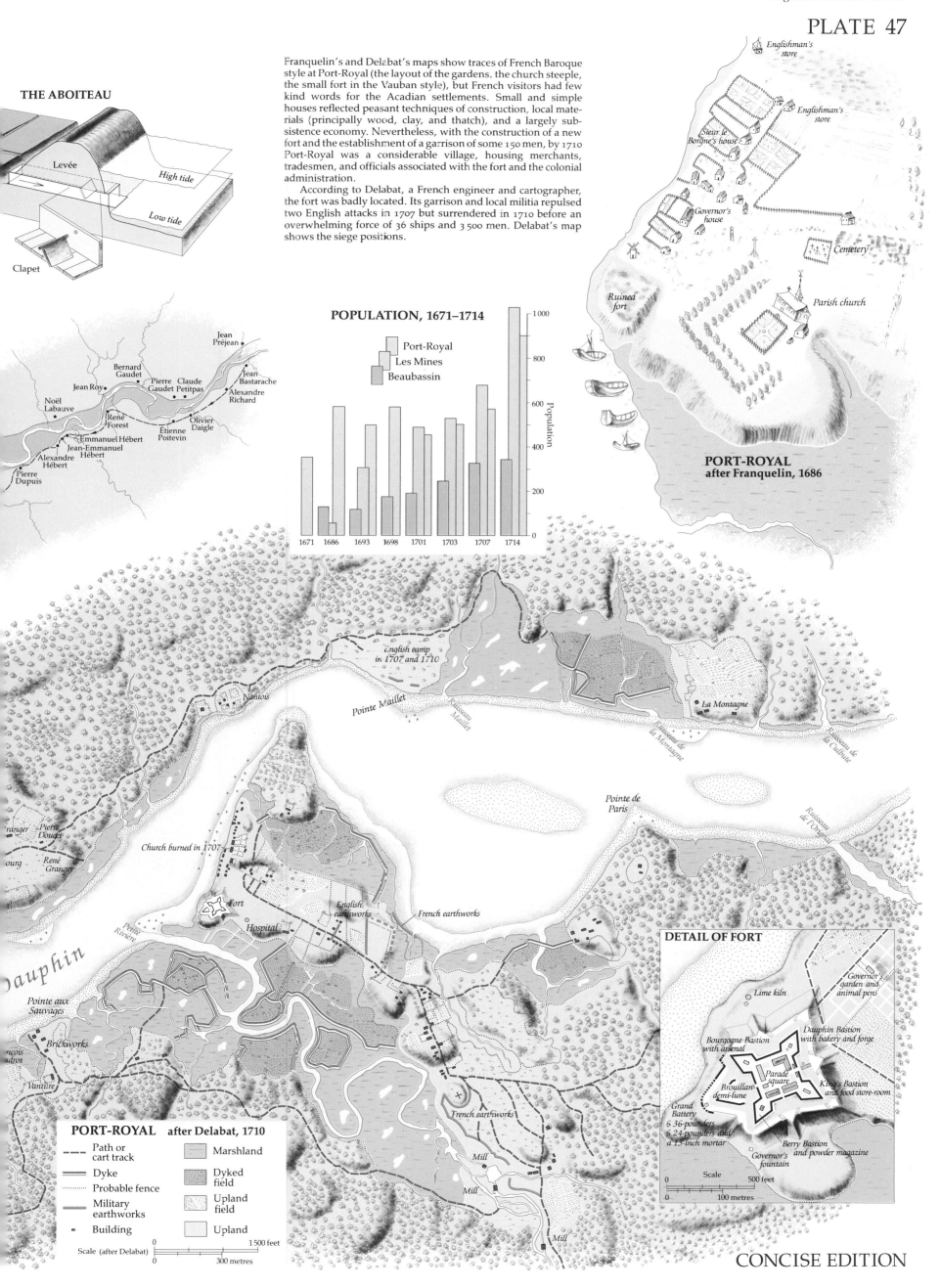

THE ABOITEAU

Levée

High tide

Low tide

Clapet

Franquelin's and Delabat's maps show traces of French Baroque style at Port-Royal (the layout of the gardens. the church steeple, the small fort in the Vauban style), but French visitors had few kind words for the Acadian settlements. Small and simple houses reflected peasant techniques of construction, local materials (principally wood, clay, and thatch), and a largely subsistence economy. Nevertheless, with the construction of a new fort and the establishment of a garrison of some 150 men, by 1710 Port-Royal was a considerable village, housing merchants, tradesmen, and officials associated with the fort and the colonial administration.

According to Delabat, a French engineer and cartographer, the fort was badly located. Its garrison and local militia repulsed two English attacks in 1707 but surrendered in 1710 before an overwhelming force of 36 ships and 3 500 men. Delabat's map shows the siege positions.

Jean Préjean

Bernard Gaudet
Jean Roy
Pierre Claude
Gaudet Petitpas
Jean Bastarache
Alexandre Richard
Noël Labauve
René Forest
Olivier Daigle
Emmanuel Hébert
Étienne Poitevin
Jean-Emmanuel Hébert
Alexandre Hébert
Pierre Dupuis

POPULATION, 1671–1714

Port-Royal
Les Mines
Beaubassin

Population

1 000
800
600
400
200
0

1671 1686 1693 1698 1701 1703 1707 1714

Englishman's store

Englishman's store

Sieur le Borgne's house

Governor's house

Ruined fort

Cemetery

Parish church

PORT-ROYAL
after Franquelin, 1686

English camp in 1707 and 1710

Le Nantois

Pointe Maillet

Ruisseau Maillet

La Montagne

Ruisseau de la Montagne

Ruisseau de la Culbute

Pointe de Paris

Ruisseau de l'Original

Pierre Doucet

René Granger

Church burned in 1707

Fort

Hospital

English earthworks

French earthworks

Dauphin

Pointe aux Sauvages

Brickworks

Vanture

French earthworks

Mill

Mill

Mill

DETAIL OF FORT

Lime kiln

Governor's garden and animal pens

Bourgogne Bastion with arsenal

Dauphin Bastion with bakery and forge

Brouillac demi-lune

Parade square

King's Bastion and food store-room

Grand Battery
6 36-pounders
5 24-pounders and a 13-inch mortar

Governor's fountain

Berry Bastion and powder magazine

Scale
0 ____ 500 feet
0 ____ 100 metres

PORT-ROYAL **after Delabat, 1710**

- – – – Path or cart track
- ──── Dyke
- ········ Probable fence
- ──── Military earthworks
- ▪▪ Building

Marshland
Dyked field
Upland field
Upland

Scale (after Delabat)
0 ____ 1 500 feet
0 ____ 300 metres

CONCISE EDITION

MARITIME CANADA, LATE 18th CENTURY

Authors: Graeme Wynn; L.D. McCann (Halifax)

ORIGINS OF NEW BRUNSWICK LOYALISTS*

Other
Carolinas
Massachusetts
Pennsylvania
Connecticut
New York
New Jersey

DISTRIBUTION OF LOYALISTS, ca 1785

(3000) ⬤ Major centre and population

∴ One dot represents 50 people.

– – – Colonial boundary

– – – County boundary

POPULATION AND LOYALISTS' GRANTS IN NOVA SCOTIA, 1780s

Escheats for non-improvement
Permanent grants
Departed Loyalists
Black Loyalists
Military Loyalists
Civilian Loyalists

Grants/population

556 414 1716 6605

ANNAPOLIS CUMBERLAND HALIFAX HANTS KINGS LUNENBURG QUEENS SYDNEY SHELBURNE

NEW BRUNSWICK

YORK NORTHUMBERLAND

SUNBURY

QUEENS

KINGS

CHARLOTTE

SAINT JOHN

U.S.

Saint John (2 000)

ISLAND OF ST JOHN

PRINCE

QUEENS KINGS

CAPE BRETON ISLAND

Sydney

WESTMORLAND

CUMBERLAND

KINGS

KINGS

HANTS

NOVA SCOTIA

SYDNEY

Halifax

HALIFAX

KINGS

ANNAPOLIS

LUNENBURG

QUEENS

SHELBURNE

Shelburne (5000)

Scale 1:3 500 000

ORIGINS OF SHELBURNE LOYALISTS**

Other
Virginia
Carolinas
Massachusetts
New Jersey
Pennsylvania
New York

*Based on 1870 family heads and single adult males
**Approximately 700 Loyalists

Almost 40 000 Loyalists came to the British colony of Nova Scotia in the early 1780s. Of these, perhaps a fifth left almost immediately, 13 500 settled in what is now New Brunswick, and some 19 000 settled in peninsular Nova Scotia. These settlers, most of whom came from the Middle Colonies, were largely American-born (90%), civilian (60%), and from the middle or lower ranks of the societies they left. With their coming instant towns sprang up on rocky shores. Shelburne soon declined, but Parrtown grew into Saint John, the largest city in the new colony of New Brunswick. Records of land grants allow the number of Loyalists per county and the distribution of Loyalists in 1785 to be established approximately. Clearly this sudden influx of new settlers was an enormous boost to local development; vacant lands were occupied, domestic markets created, and enterprise encouraged.

HALIFAX SHIPPING

Number of vessels
110 100 90 80 70 60 50 40 30 20 10 0

Tonnage of vessels (000)
12 11 10 9 8 7 6 5 4 3 2 1 0

Entering 1779 Clearing
Entering 1790 Clearing
Entering 1790 Clearing

United Kingdom
Canada
Newfoundland
New England
Mid-Atlantic States
South Atlantic States
West Indies
Other

HALIFAX, 1784

Wharf
Mauger's distillery
Dockyard
Mast pond
Store-keeper's wharf
Barriet's wharf
Proctor's wharf
Brown's wharf
Hardwell's wharf
Mauger's wharf
Gerrishe's wharf
Five-Gun battery
Nine-Gun battery
King's slip
Frederick's wharf
Governor's battery
Nood Yard wharf
Phillis' wharf
Tretton's wharf
Wilkinson's wharf
Portuguese wharf
Fourteen-Gun battery
Fairbank's wharf
Fitzpatrick wharf
Crowley's wharf
Collier's wharf
South battery
The King's lime kiln
Yard wharfs

After Charles Blaskowitz, 'Plan of the Town of Halifax 1784,' and others

0 ___ 2 000 feet
0 ___ 500 metres
Scale 1:40 000

Densely developed

Major public buildings
1 Naval hospital
2 Dutch Church (Anglican)
3 Grenadier barracks
4 Red barracks
5 Court-house
6 Public stores
7 Parade grounds
8 Market house
9 St Paul's Anglican Church
10 Governor's house
11 Powder magazine
12 Assembly house
13 St Mather's Dissenters Church
14 Provost
15 General hospital
16 Prison
17 Cemetery
18 Engineer's yard

SYDNEY, 1795

Blackbourne's wharf (decayed)
O'Brien's wharf (ruined)
Ingenville's wharf

After James Miller, 'Map of the Town of Sydney, 1795'

0 ___ 1000 feet
0 ___ 200 metres
Scale 1:14 000

Major public buildings
1 Military cemetery
2 Four-gun sod battery
3 Prison
4 Store
5 Infirmary
6 Barracks
7 Governor's house
8 Court-house
9 Church
10 Cemetery
11 Court-house
12 Ruined King's store

In 1783 Halifax was a provincial capital, garrison outpost, and mercantile town of some 5 000 people. Substantial wharves and warehouses lined the waterfront, but manufacturing was limited. In the densely built-up core people of different social, economic, and ethnic backgrounds lived close together. There was more segregation on the periphery, with labourers and German Protestants concentrated in the northern suburbs and government officials and some merchants in the south. Sydney, founded with some pretension in 1783, was a garrisoned village in 1800.

HISTORICAL ATLAS OF CANADA

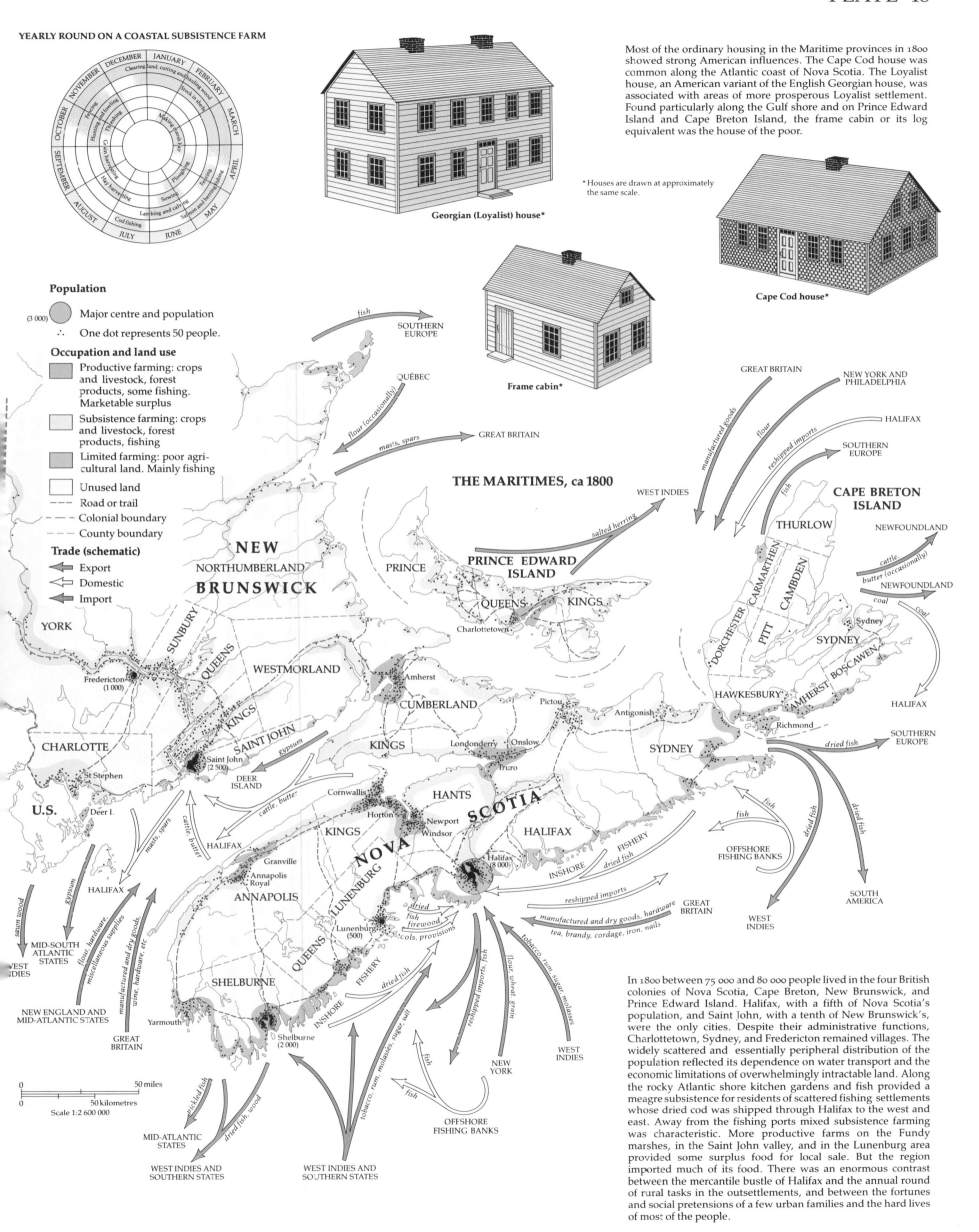

YEARLY ROUND ON A COASTAL SUBSISTENCE FARM

Most of the ordinary housing in the Maritime provinces in 1800 showed strong American influences. The Cape Cod house was common along the Atlantic coast of Nova Scotia. The Loyalist house, an American variant of the English Georgian house, was associated with areas of more prosperous Loyalist settlement. Found particularly along the Gulf shore and on Prince Edward Island and Cape Breton Island, the frame cabin or its log equivalent was the house of the poor.

* Houses are drawn at approximately the same scale.

Georgian (Loyalist) house*

Frame cabin*

Cape Cod house*

Population

(3 000)   Major centre and population

∴   One dot represents 50 people.

Occupation and land use

Productive farming: crops and livestock, forest products, some fishing. Marketable surplus

Subsistence farming: crops and livestock, forest products, fishing

Limited farming: poor agricultural land. Mainly fishing

Unused land

– – – Road or trail

– – – Colonial boundary

– – – County boundary

Trade (schematic)

⟵ Export

⟵ Domestic

⟵ Import

THE MARITIMES, ca 1800

In 1800 between 75 000 and 80 000 people lived in the four British colonies of Nova Scotia, Cape Breton, New Brunswick, and Prince Edward Island. Halifax, with a fifth of Nova Scotia's population, and Saint John, with a tenth of New Brunswick's, were the only cities. Despite their administrative functions, Charlottetown, Sydney, and Fredericton remained villages. The widely scattered and essentially peripheral distribution of the population reflected its dependence on water transport and the economic limitations of overwhelmingly intractable land. Along the rocky Atlantic shore kitchen gardens and fish provided a meagre subsistence for residents of scattered fishing settlements whose dried cod was shipped through Halifax to the west and east. Away from the fishing ports mixed subsistence farming was characteristic. More productive farms on the Fundy marshes, in the Saint John valley, and in the Lunenburg area provided some surplus food for local sale. But the region imported much of its food. There was an enormous contrast between the mercantile bustle of Halifax and the annual round of rural tasks in the outsettlements, and between the fortunes and social pretensions of a few urban families and the hard lives of most of the people.

Scale 1:2 600 000

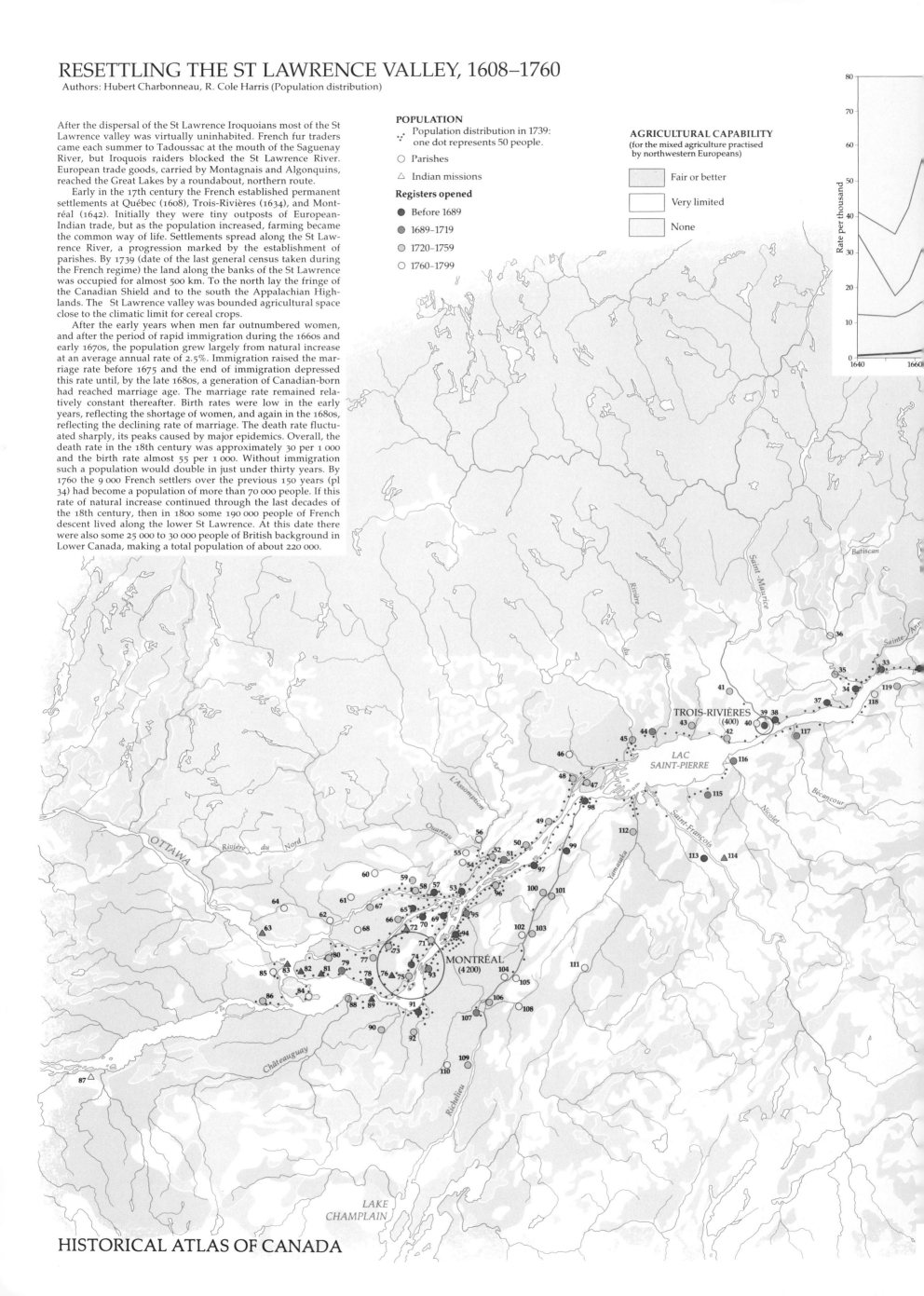

RESETTLING THE ST LAWRENCE VALLEY, 1608–1760

Authors: Hubert Charbonneau, R. Cole Harris (Population distribution)

After the dispersal of the St Lawrence Iroquoians most of the St Lawrence valley was virtually uninhabited. French fur traders came each summer to Tadoussac at the mouth of the Saguenay River, but Iroquois raiders blocked the St Lawrence River. European trade goods, carried by Montagnais and Algonquins, reached the Great Lakes by a roundabout, northern route.

Early in the 17th century the French established permanent settlements at Québec (1608), Trois-Rivières (1634), and Montréal (1642). Initially they were tiny outposts of European-Indian trade, but as the population increased, farming became the common way of life. Settlements spread along the St Lawrence River, a progression marked by the establishment of parishes. By 1739 (date of the last general census taken during the French regime) the land along the banks of the St Lawrence was occupied for almost 500 km. To the north lay the fringe of the Canadian Shield and to the south the Appalachian Highlands. The St Lawrence valley was bounded agricultural space close to the climatic limit for cereal crops.

After the early years when men far outnumbered women, and after the period of rapid immigration during the 1660s and early 1670s, the population grew largely from natural increase at an average annual rate of 2.5%. Immigration raised the marriage rate before 1675 and the end of immigration depressed this rate until, by the late 1680s, a generation of Canadian-born had reached marriage age. The marriage rate remained relatively constant thereafter. Birth rates were low in the early years, reflecting the shortage of women, and again in the 1680s, reflecting the declining rate of marriage. The death rate fluctuated sharply, its peaks caused by major epidemics. Overall, the death rate in the 18th century was approximately 30 per 1 000 and the birth rate almost 55 per 1 000. Without immigration such a population would double in just under thirty years. By 1760 the 9 000 French settlers over the previous 150 years (pl 34) had become a population of more than 70 000 people. If this rate of natural increase continued through the last decades of the 18th century, then in 1800 some 190 000 people of French descent lived along the lower St Lawrence. At this date there were also some 25 000 to 30 000 people of British background in Lower Canada, making a total population of about 220 000.

POPULATION

Population distribution in 1739: one dot represents 50 people.

○ Parishes

△ Indian missions

Registers opened

● Before 1689

● 1689–1719

● 1720–1759

○ 1760–1799

AGRICULTURAL CAPABILITY
(for the mixed agriculture practised by northwestern Europeans)

Fair or better

Very limited

None

HISTORICAL ATLAS OF CANADA

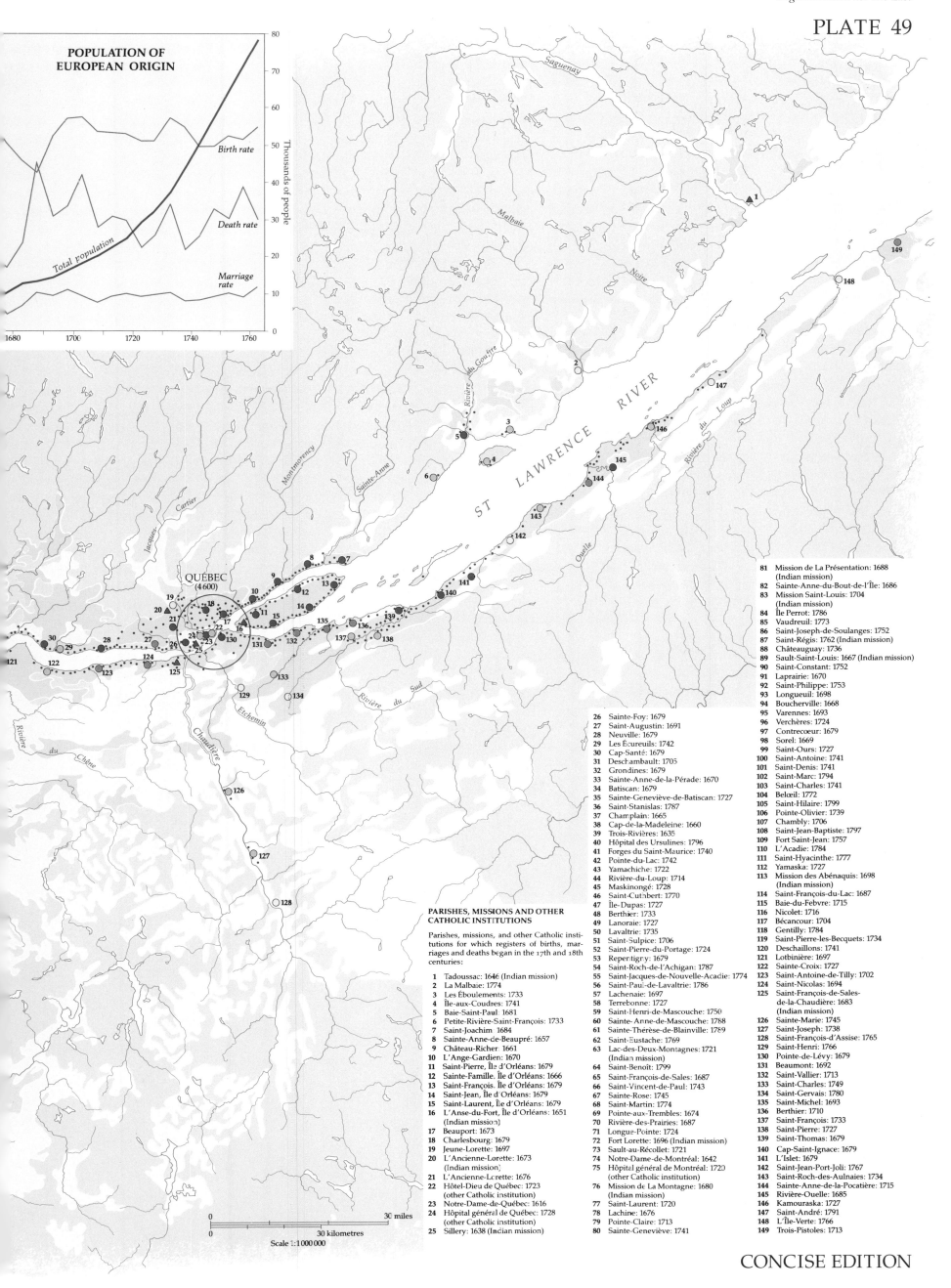

POPULATION OF EUROPEAN ORIGIN

Thousands of people

Birth rate

Death rate

Marriage rate

Total population

1680   1700   1720   1740   1760

QUÉBEC
(4 600)

ST LAWRENCE RIVER

Saguenay

Malbaie

Noire

Rivière du Loup

Ouelle

Rivière du Sud

Etchemin

Chaudière

Rivière du Chêne

Montmorency

Sainte-Anne

Jacques-Cartier

81 Mission de La Présentation: 1688 (Indian mission)
82 Sainte-Anne-du-Bout-de-l'Île: 1686
83 Mission Saint-Louis: 1704 (Indian mission)
84 Île Perrot: 1786
85 Vaudreuil: 1773
86 Saint-Joseph-de-Soulanges: 1752
87 Saint-Régis: 1762 (Indian mission)
88 Châteauguay: 1736
89 Sault-Saint-Louis: 1667 (Indian mission)
90 Saint-Constant: 1752
91 Laprairie: 1670
92 Saint-Philippe: 1753
93 Longueuil: 1698
94 Boucherville: 1668
95 Varennes: 1693
96 Verchères: 1724
97 Contrecoeur: 1679
98 Sorel: 1669
99 Saint-Ours: 1727
100 Saint-Antoine: 1741
101 Saint-Denis: 1741
102 Saint-Marc: 1794
103 Saint-Charles: 1741
104 Beloeil: 1772
105 Saint-Hilaire: 1799
106 Pointe-Olivier: 1739
107 Chambly: 1706
108 Saint-Jean-Baptiste: 1797
109 Fort Saint-Jean: 1757
110 L'Acadie: 1784
111 Saint-Hyacinthe: 1777
112 Yamaska: 1727
113 Mission des Abénaquis: 1698 (Indian mission)
114 Saint-François-du-Lac: 1687
115 Baie-du-Febvre: 1715
116 Nicolet: 1716
117 Bécancour: 1704
118 Gentilly: 1784
119 Saint-Pierre-les-Becquets: 1734
120 Deschaillons: 1741
121 Lotbinière: 1697
122 Sainte-Croix: 1727
123 Saint-Antoine-de-Tilly: 1702
124 Saint-Nicolas: 1694
125 Saint-François-de-Sales-de-la-Chaudière: 1683 (Indian mission)
126 Sainte-Marie: 1745
127 Saint-Joseph: 1738
128 Saint-François-d'Assise: 1765
129 Saint-Henri: 1766
130 Pointe-de-Lévy: 1679
131 Beaumont: 1692
132 Saint-Vallier: 1713
133 Saint-Charles: 1749
134 Saint-Gervais: 1780
135 Saint-Michel: 1693
136 Berthier: 1710
137 Saint-François: 1733
138 Saint-Pierre: 1727
139 Saint-Thomas: 1679
140 Cap-Saint-Ignace: 1679
141 L'Islet: 1679
142 Saint-Jean-Port-Joli: 1767
143 Saint-Roch-des-Aulnaies: 1734
144 Sainte-Anne-de-la-Pocatière: 1715
145 Rivière-Ouelle: 1685
146 Kamouraska: 1727
147 Saint-André: 1791
148 L'Île-Verte: 1766
149 Trois-Pistoles: 1713

26 Sainte-Foy: 1679
27 Saint-Augustin: 1691
28 Neuville: 1679
29 Les Écureuils: 1742
30 Cap-Santé: 1679
31 Deschambault: 1705
32 Grondines: 1679
33 Sainte-Anne-de-la-Pérade: 1670
34 Batiscan: 1679
35 Sainte-Geneviève-de-Batiscan: 1727
36 Saint-Stanislas: 1787
37 Champlain: 1665
38 Cap-de-la-Madeleine: 1660
39 Trois-Rivières: 1635
40 Hôpital des Ursulines: 1796
41 Forges du Saint-Maurice: 1740
42 Pointe-du-Lac: 1742
43 Yamachiche: 1722
44 Rivière-du-Loup: 1714
45 Maskinongé: 1728
46 Saint-Cuthbert: 1770
47 Île-Dupas: 1727
48 Berthier: 1733
49 Lanoraie: 1727
50 Lavaltrie: 1735
51 Saint-Sulpice: 1706
52 Saint-Pierre-du-Portage: 1724
53 Repentigny: 1679
54 Saint-Roch-de-l'Achigan: 1787
55 Saint-Jacques-de-Nouvelle-Acadie: 1774
56 Saint-Paul-de-Lavaltrie: 1786
57 Lachenaie: 1697
58 Terrebonne: 1727
59 Saint-Henri-de-Mascouche: 1750
60 Sainte-Anne-de-Mascouche: 1788
61 Sainte-Thérèse-de-Blainville: 1789
62 Saint-Eustache: 1769
63 Lac-des-Deux-Montagnes: 1721 (Indian mission)
64 Saint-Benoît: 1799
65 Saint-François-de-Sales: 1687
66 Saint-Vincent-de-Paul: 1743
67 Sainte-Rose: 1745
68 Saint-Martin: 1774
69 Pointe-aux-Trembles: 1674
70 Rivière-des-Prairies: 1687
71 Longue-Pointe: 1724
72 Fort Lorette: 1696 (Indian mission)
73 Sault-au-Récollet: 1721
74 Notre-Dame-de-Montréal: 1642
75 Hôpital général de Montréal: 1720 (other Catholic institution)
76 Mission de La Montagne: 1680 (Indian mission)
77 Saint-Laurent: 1720
78 Lachine: 1676
79 Pointe-Claire: 1713
80 Sainte-Geneviève: 1741

PARISHES, MISSIONS AND OTHER CATHOLIC INSTITUTIONS

Parishes, missions, and other Catholic institutions for which registers of births, marriages and deaths began in the 17th and 18th centuries:

1 Tadoussac: 1646 (Indian mission)
2 La Malbaie: 1774
3 Les Éboulements: 1733
4 Île-aux-Coudres: 1741
5 Baie-Saint-Paul: 1681
6 Petite-Rivière-Saint-François: 1733
7 Saint-Joachim: 1684
8 Sainte-Anne-de-Beaupré: 1657
9 Château-Richer: 1661
10 L'Ange-Gardien: 1670
11 Saint-Pierre, Île d'Orléans: 1679
12 Sainte-Famille. Île d'Orléans: 1666
13 Saint-François. Île d'Orléans: 1679
14 Saint-Jean, Île d'Orléans: 1679
15 Saint-Laurent, Île d'Orléans: 1679
16 L'Anse-du-Fort, Île d'Orléans: 1651 (Indian mission)
17 Beauport: 1673
18 Charlesbourg: 1679
19 Jeune-Lorette: 1697
20 L'Ancienne-Lorette: 1673 (Indian mission)
21 L'Ancienne-Lorette: 1676
22 Hôtel-Dieu de Québec: 1723 (other Catholic institution)
23 Notre-Dame-de-Québec: 1616
24 Hôpital général de Québec: 1728 (other Catholic institution)
25 Sillery: 1638 (Indian mission)

0   30 miles
0   30 kilometres
Scale 1:1 000 000

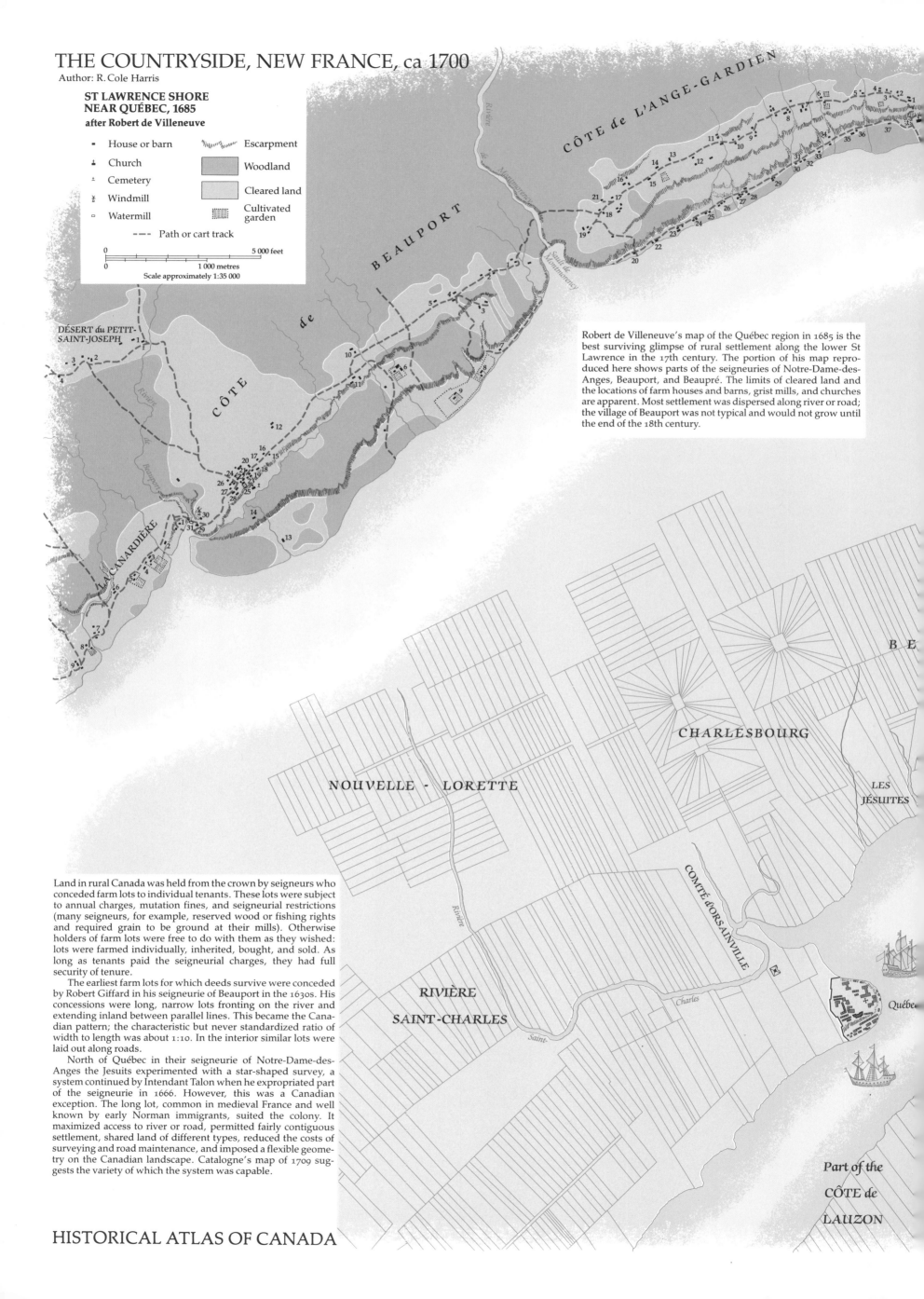

THE COUNTRYSIDE, NEW FRANCE, ca 1700

Author: R. Cole Harris

ST LAWRENCE SHORE NEAR QUÉBEC, 1685
after Robert de Villeneuve

- ▪ House or barn
- ⚑ Church
- ☖ Cemetery
- ⚙ Windmill
- ▫ Watermill

ᴴᴵᴸᴵᴵ Escarpment

▨ Woodland

▨ Cleared land

▨ Cultivated garden

- - - Path or cart track

```
0                    5 000 feet
0        1 000 metres
Scale approximately 1:35 000
```

DÉSERT du PETIT-SAINT-JOSEPH

CÔTE de BEAUPORT

CÔTE de L'ANGE-GARDIEN

CÔTE de BEAUPORT

LACANARDIÈRE

Robert de Villeneuve's map of the Québec region in 1685 is the best surviving glimpse of rural settlement along the lower St Lawrence in the 17th century. The portion of his map reproduced here shows parts of the seigneuries of Notre-Dame-des-Anges, Beauport, and Beaupré. The limits of cleared land and the locations of farm houses and barns, grist mills, and churches are apparent. Most settlement was dispersed along river or road; the village of Beauport was not typical and would not grow until the end of the 18th century.

CHARLESBOURG

NOUVELLE - LORETTE

LES JÉSUITES

COMTÉ d'ORSAINVILLE

RIVIÈRE SAINT-CHARLES

Québec

BE

Part of the CÔTE de LAUZON

Land in rural Canada was held from the crown by seigneurs who conceded farm lots to individual tenants. These lots were subject to annual charges, mutation fines, and seigneurial restrictions (many seigneurs, for example, reserved wood or fishing rights and required grain to be ground at their mills). Otherwise holders of farm lots were free to do with them as they wished: lots were farmed individually, inherited, bought, and sold. As long as tenants paid the seigneurial charges, they had full security of tenure.

The earliest farm lots for which deeds survive were conceded by Robert Giffard in his seigneurie of Beauport in the 1630s. His concessions were long, narrow lots fronting on the river and extending inland between parallel lines. This became the Canadian pattern; the characteristic but never standardized ratio of width to length was about 1:10. In the interior similar lots were laid out along roads.

North of Québec in their seigneurie of Notre-Dame-des-Anges the Jesuits experimented with a star-shaped survey, a system continued by Intendant Talon when he expropriated part of the seigneurie in 1666. However, this was a Canadian exception. The long lot, common in medieval France and well known by early Norman immigrants, suited the colony. It maximized access to river or road, permitted fairly contiguous settlement, shared land of different types, reduced the costs of surveying and road maintenance, and imposed a flexible geometry on the Canadian landscape. Catalogne's map of 1709 suggests the variety of which the system was capable.

HISTORICAL ATLAS OF CANADA

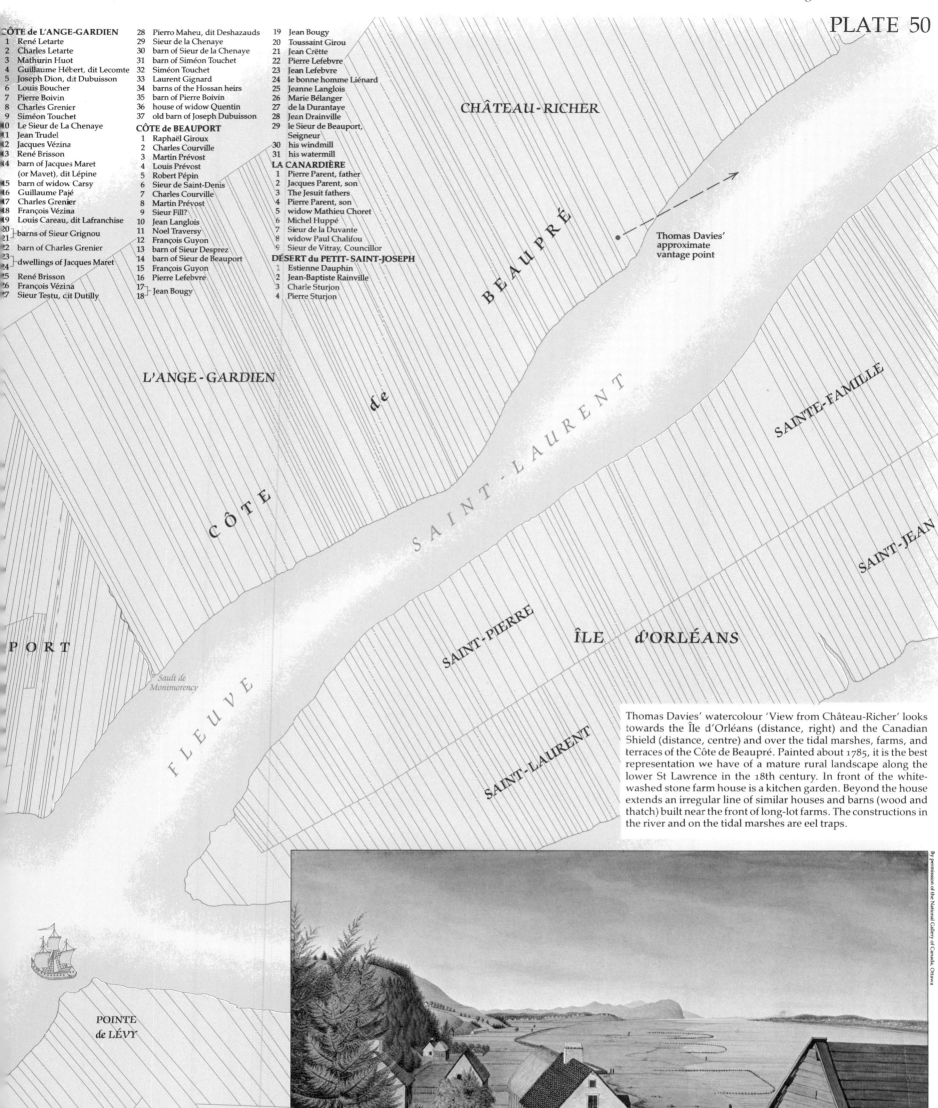

CÔTE de L'ANGE-GARDIEN
1 René Letarte
2 Charles Letarte
3 Mathurin Huot
4 Guillaume Hébert, dit Lecomte
5 Joseph Dion, dit Dubuisson
6 Louis Boucher
7 Pierre Boivin
8 Charles Grenier
9 Siméon Touchet
10 Le Sieur de La Chenaye
11 Jean Trudel
12 Jacques Vézina
13 René Brisson
14 barn of Jacques Maret (or Mavet), dit Lépine
15 barn of widow Carsy
16 Guillaume Pajé
17 Charles Grenier
18 François Vézina
19 Louis Careau, dit Lafranchise
20 ⎱ barns of Sieur Grignou
21 ⎰
22 barn of Charles Grenier
23 ⎱ dwellings of Jacques Maret
24 ⎰
25 René Brisson
26 François Vézina
27 Sieur Testu, dit Dutilly

28 Pierro Maheu, dit Deshazauds
29 Sieur de la Chenaye
30 barn of Sieur de la Chenaye
31 barn of Siméon Touchet
32 Siméon Touchet
33 Laurent Gignard
34 barns of the Hossan heirs
35 barn of Pierre Boivin
36 house of widow Quentin
37 old barn of Joseph Dubuisson

CÔTE de BEAUPORT
1 Raphaël Giroux
2 Charles Courville
3 Martin Prévost
4 Louis Prévost
5 Robert Pépin
6 Sieur de Saint-Denis
7 Charles Courville
8 Martin Prévost
9 Sieur Fill?
10 Jean Langlois
11 Noel Traversy
12 François Guyon
13 barn of Sieur Desprez
14 barn of Sieur de Beauport
15 François Guyon
16 Pierre Lefebvre
17 ⎱ Jean Bougy
18 ⎰

19 Jean Bougy
20 Toussaint Girou
21 Jean Crètte
22 Pierre Lefebvre
23 Jean Lefebvre
24 le bonne homme Liénard
25 Jeanne Langlois
26 Marie Bélanger
27 de la Durantaye
28 Jean Drainville
29 le Sieur de Beauport, Seigneur
30 his windmill
31 his watermill

LA CANARDIÈRE
1 Pierre Parent, father
2 Jacques Parent, son
3 The Jesuit fathers
4 Pierre Parent, son
5 widow Mathieu Choret
6 Michel Huppé
7 Sieur de la Duvante
8 widow Paul Chalifou
9 Sieur de Vitray, Councillor

DÉSERT du PETIT-SAINT-JOSEPH
1 Estienne Dauphin
2 Jean-Baptiste Rainville
3 Charle Sturjon
4 Pierre Sturjon

CHÂTEAU-RICHER

CÔTE de BEAUPRÉ

Thomas Davies'
approximate
vantage point

L'ANGE-GARDIEN

CÔTE de

SAINT-LAURENT

Sault de Montmorency

FLEUVE

PORT

POINTE de LÉVY

SAINT-PIERRE   ÎLE d'ORLÉANS

SAINTE-FAMILLE

SAINT-JEAN

SAINT-LAURENT

Thomas Davies' watercolour 'View from Château-Richer' looks towards the Île d'Orléans (distance, right) and the Canadian Shield (distance, centre) and over the tidal marshes, farms, and terraces of the Côte de Beaupré. Painted about 1785, it is the best representation we have of a mature rural landscape along the lower St Lawrence in the 18th century. In front of the white-washed stone farm house is a kitchen garden. Beyond the house extends an irregular line of similar houses and barns (wood and thatch) built near the front of long-lot farms. The constructions in the river and on the tidal marshes are eel traps.

LAND SURVEY NEAR QUÉBEC

after Sieur de Catalogne, 1709

0   10 000 feet

0   2 000 metres

Scale approximately 1:70 000

Thomas Davies, *View from Château-Richer*, watercolour, ca 1785

CONCISE EDITION

THE TOWNS, NEW FRANCE, 1685–1759

Authors: Marc Lafrance, André Charbonneau

Québec (1608) and Trois-Rivières (1634) began as trading posts, and Montréal (1642) as a religious mission. For years they were tiny European outposts on the banks of the St Lawrence River; eventually local authorities drew up town plans, organized the distribution of lots, and oversaw the development of small towns.

These earliest Canadian towns were commercial, military, and administrative centres. The European dichotomy between upper and lower town emerged very early, with the ecclesiastical *cité* and fortifications on higher ground and the commercial centre along the river. Gardens and orchards gave the upper towns a somewhat rural appearance, whereas the lower towns were densely built up urban areas. As the towns grew, official interest in ordered, symmetrical development was challenged by the spontaneous creation of suburbs.

Merchants and their families, colonial officials, men and women of the church, soldiers, artisans and tradespeople, domestic servants and day labourers all lived in the towns and, especially in Québec, there was also a considerable migratory population associated with the port. In 1757 Montcalm considered Québec the equal of any French town, excluding the first ten.

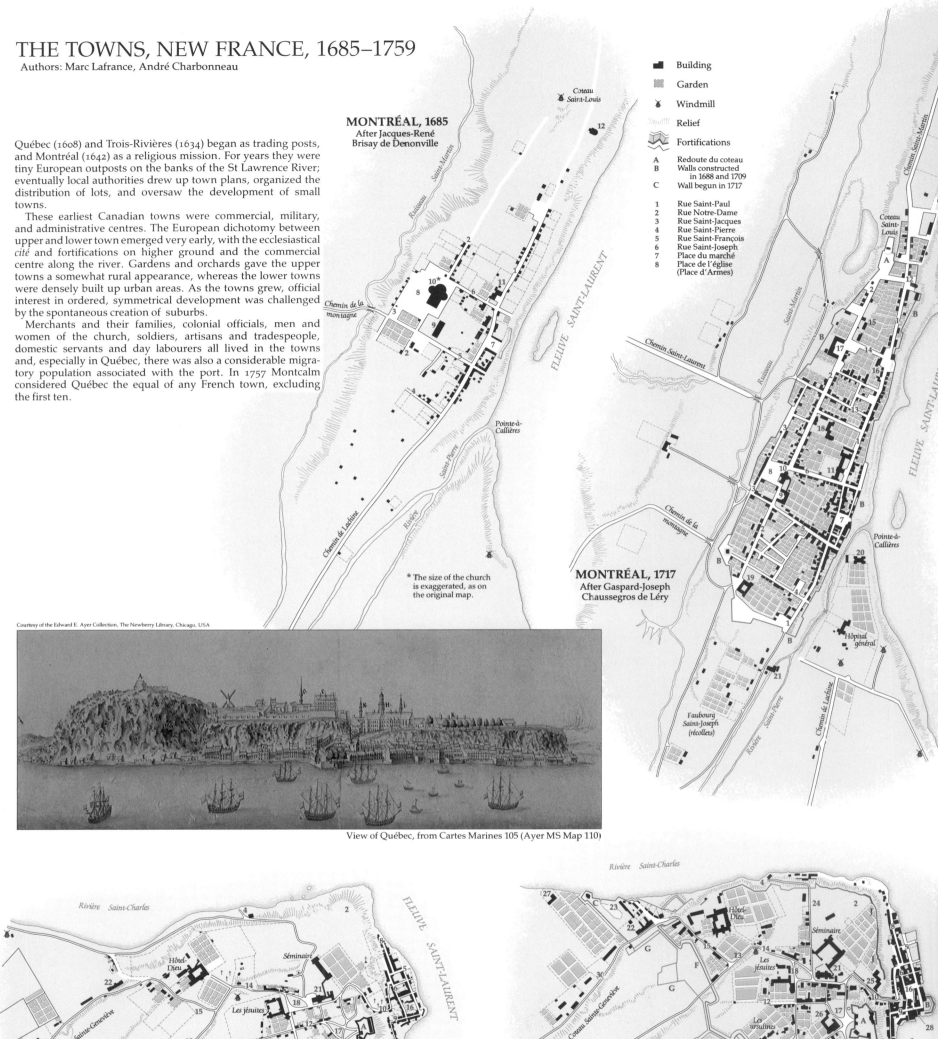

MONTRÉAL, 1685
After Jacques-René
Brisay de Denonville

* The size of the church
is exaggerated, as on
the original map.

MONTRÉAL, 1717
After Gaspard-Joseph
Chaussegros de Léry

Building
Garden
Windmill
Relief
Fortifications

A Redoute du coteau
B Walls constructed
    in 1688 and 1709
C Wall begun in 1717

1 Rue Saint-Paul
2 Rue Notre-Dame
3 Rue Saint-Jacques
4 Rue Saint-Pierre
5 Rue Saint-François
6 Rue Saint-Joseph
7 Place du marché
8 Place de l'église
    (Place d'Armes)

Courtesy of the Edward E. Ayer Collection, The Newberry Library, Chicago, USA

View of Québec, from Cartes Marines 105 (Ayer MS Map 110)

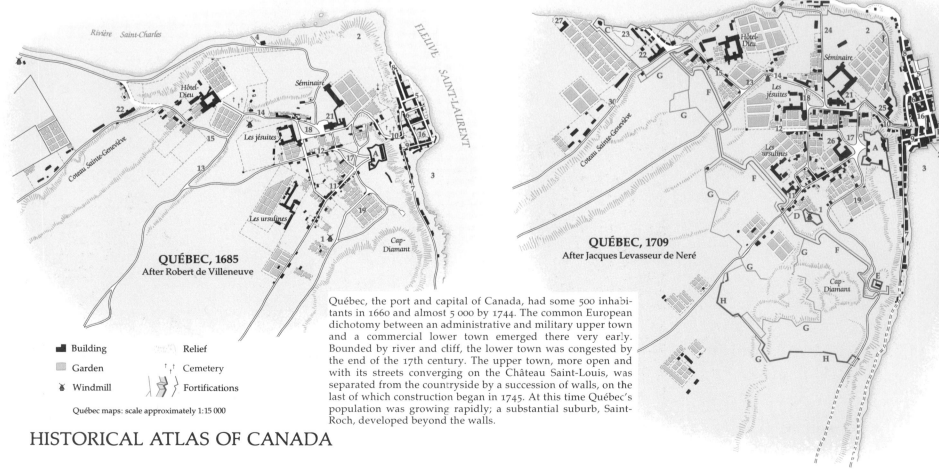

QUÉBEC, 1685
After Robert de Villeneuve

QUÉBEC, 1709
After Jacques Levasseur de Neré

Building   Relief
Garden   Cemetery
Windmill   Fortifications

Québec maps: scale approximately 1:15 000

Québec, the port and capital of Canada, had some 500 inhabitants in 1660 and almost 5 000 by 1744. The common European dichotomy between an administrative and military upper town and a commercial lower town emerged there very early. Bounded by river and cliff, the lower town was congested by the end of the 17th century. The upper town, more open and with its streets converging on the Château Saint-Louis, was separated from the countryside by a succession of walls, on the last of which construction began in 1745. At this time Québec's population was growing rapidly; a substantial suburb, Saint-Roch, developed beyond the walls.

HISTORICAL ATLAS OF CANADA

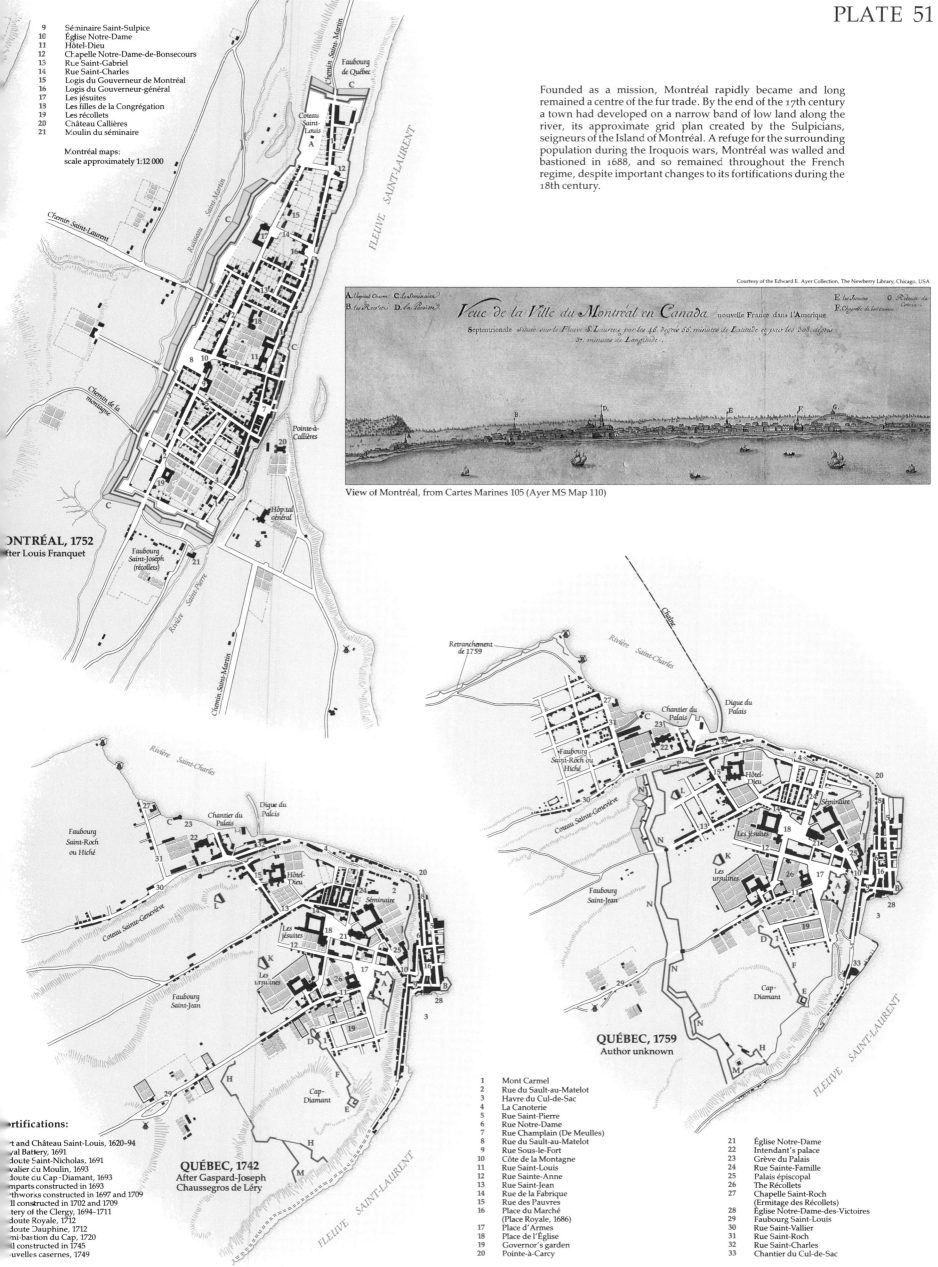

9   Séminaire Saint-Sulpice
10 Église Notre-Dame
11 Hôtel-Dieu
12 Chapelle Notre-Dame-de-Bonsecours
13 Rue Saint-Gabriel
14 Rue Saint-Charles
15 Logis du Gouverneur de Montréal
16 Logis du Gouverneur-général
17 Les jésuites
18 Les filles de la Congrégation
19 Les récollets
20 Château Callières
21 Moulin du séminaire

Montréal maps:
scale approximately 1:12 000

Founded as a mission, Montréal rapidly became and long remained a centre of the fur trade. By the end of the 17th century a town had developed on a narrow band of low land along the river, its approximate grid plan created by the Sulpicians, seigneurs of the Island of Montréal. A refuge for the surrounding population during the Iroquois wars, Montréal was walled and bastioned in 1688, and so remained throughout the French regime, despite important changes to its fortifications during the 18th century.

Courtesy of the Edward E. Ayer Collection, The Newberry Library, Chicago, USA

Veue de la Ville du Montréal en Canada nouvelle France dans l'Amerique

View of Montréal, from Cartes Marines 105 (Ayer MS Map 110)

MONTRÉAL, 1752
After Louis Franquet

QUÉBEC, 1742
After Gaspard-Joseph
Chaussegros de Léry

QUÉBEC, 1759
Author unknown

Fortifications:
Fort and Château Saint-Louis, 1620–94
Royal Battery, 1691
Redoute Saint-Nicholas, 1691
Chevalier du Moulin, 1693
Redoute du Cap-Diamant, 1693
Ramparts constructed in 1693
Earthworks constructed in 1697 and 1709
Wall constructed in 1702 and 1709
Battery of the Clergy, 1694–1711
Redoute Royale, 1712
Redoute Dauphine, 1712
Demi-bastion du Cap, 1720
Wall constructed in 1745
Nouvelles casernes, 1749

1   Mont Carmel
2   Rue du Sault-au-Matelot
3   Havre du Cul-de-Sac
4   La Canoterie
5   Rue Saint-Pierre
6   Rue Notre-Dame
7   Rue Champlain (De Meulles)
8   Rue du Sault-au-Matelot
9   Rue Sous-le-Fort
10 Côte de la Montagne
11 Rue Saint-Louis
12 Rue Sainte-Anne
13 Rue Saint-Jean
14 Rue de la Fabrique
15 Rue des Pauvres
16 Place du Marché
     (Place Royale, 1686)
17 Place d'Armes
18 Place de l'Église
19 Governor's garden
20 Pointe-à-Carcy
21 Église Notre-Dame
22 Intendant's palace
23 Grève du Palais
24 Rue Sainte-Famille
25 Palais épiscopal
26 The Récollets
27 Chapelle Saint-Roch
     (Ermitage des Récollets)
28 Église Notre-Dame-des-Victoires
29 Faubourg Saint-Louis
30 Rue Saint-Vallier
31 Rue Saint-Roch
32 Rue Saint-Charles
33 Chantier du Cul-de-Sac

CONCISE EDITION

TIMBER PRODUCTION AND TRADE TO 1850

Author: Graeme Wynn

Wood was the great staple of early-19th-century British North America. From the hemlock–white pine–northern hardwood forest that covered much of the land east of Lake Superior a bewildering variety of products – masts, spars, square (or ton) timber, deals, planks, boards, shingles, clapboards, laths, barrel staves, pot and pearl ashes, and firewood – went to markets as distant as Britain and the West Indies, and as different as shipyards, sugar plantations, steamboats, and speculative builders. Farmers who worked for a time in the woods; 'shantyboys' who spent months in remote forest camps cutting trees through the winter; raftsmen, longshoremen, and sailors who carried forest products to market; and merchants who organized the trade – all played parts in the industry. By mid-century the main characteristics of the trade are clear. Most exports came down the St Lawrence: white pine dominated square-timber shipments, but red pine was especially important in the Ottawa valley, and oak was the most significant product of the area upstream from the Welland Canal. In the Maritimes, where ton-timber output peaked in 1825, the bulk of exports came from the Saint John valley (especially from its upper reaches in the state of Maine and the still-disputed territory between New Brunswick and Québec); large, modern sawmills contributed an increasing proportion to shipments from the Saint John and Miramichi valleys; small quantities of wood left Pictou and a handful of ports with limited hinterlands in Prince Edward Island and on the Atlantic coast of Nova Scotia. Estimates of the numbers engaged in the trade are notoriously unreliable, but in 1845–6 no more than 8 000 full-time lumbermen/raftsmen would have been required to cut and bring the entire production of the Ottawa valley to Québec.

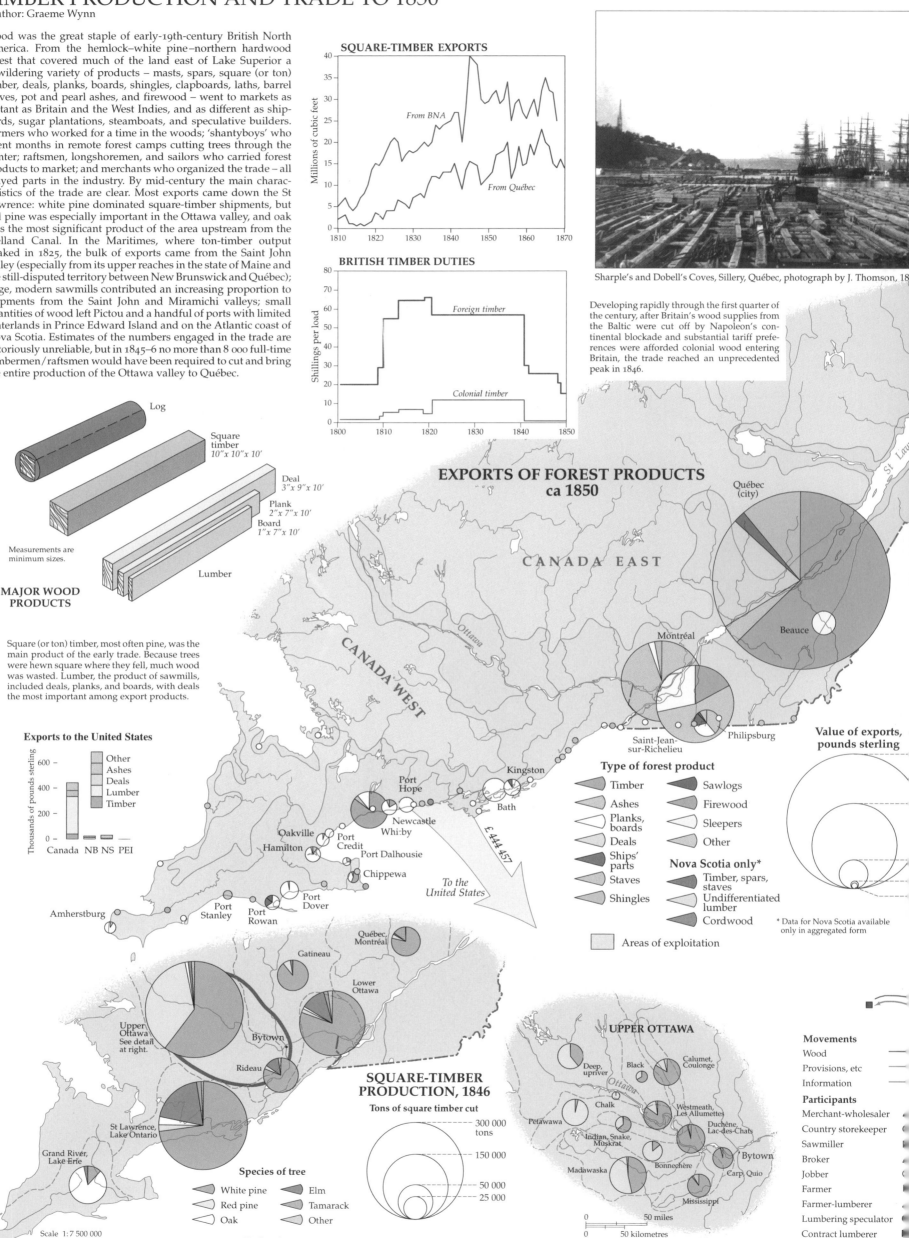

SQUARE-TIMBER EXPORTS

From BNA

From Québec

(Millions of cubic feet: 0–40; years 1810–1870)

BRITISH TIMBER DUTIES

Foreign timber

Colonial timber

(Shillings per load: 0–80; years 1800–1850)

Sharple's and Dobell's Coves, Sillery, Québec, photograph by J. Thomson, 18—

Developing rapidly through the first quarter of the century, after Britain's wood supplies from the Baltic were cut off by Napoleon's continental blockade and substantial tariff preferences were afforded colonial wood entering Britain, the trade reached an unprecedented peak in 1846.

MAJOR WOOD PRODUCTS

Log

Square timber 10" x 10" x 10'

Deal 3" x 9" x 10'

Plank 2" x 7" x 10'

Board 1" x 7" x 10'

Lumber

Measurements are minimum sizes.

Square (or ton) timber, most often pine, was the main product of the early trade. Because trees were hewn square where they fell, much wood was wasted. Lumber, the product of sawmills, included deals, planks, and boards, with deals the most important among export products.

Exports to the United States

(Thousands of pounds sterling: 0–600+)

- Other
- Ashes
- Deals
- Lumber
- Timber

Canada NB NS PEI

EXPORTS OF FOREST PRODUCTS ca 1850

CANADA EAST

CANADA WEST

Québec (city)

Montréal

Beauce

Saint-Jean-sur-Richelieu

Philipsburg

Kingston

Bath

Port Hope

Newcastle

Whitby

Oakville

Port Credit

Hamilton

Port Dalhousie

Chippewa

Port Dover

Port Rowan

Port Stanley

Amherstburg

£ 444 457

To the United States

St Lawrence

Ottawa

Type of forest product

Timber	Sawlogs
Ashes	Firewood
Planks, boards	Sleepers
Deals	Other
Ships' parts	
Staves	
Shingles	

Nova Scotia only*

- Timber, spars, staves
- Undifferentiated lumber
- Cordwood

* Data for Nova Scotia available only in aggregated form

Areas of exploitation

Value of exports, pounds sterling

SQUARE-TIMBER PRODUCTION, 1846

Québec, Montréal

Gatineau

Lower Ottawa

Upper Ottawa See detail at right.

Bytown

Rideau

St Lawrence, Lake Ontario

Grand River, Lake Erie

Tons of square timber cut

- 300 000 tons
- 150 000
- 50 000
- 25 000

Species of tree

White pine	Elm
Red pine	Tamarack
Oak	Other

--- Timber districts

Scale 1:7 500 000

UPPER OTTAWA

Deep, upriver

Black

Calumet, Coulonge

Chalk

Westmeath, Les Allumettes

Petawawa

Duchêne, Lac-des-Chats

Indian, Snake, Muskrat

Bonnechère

Bytown

Madawaska

Carp, Quio

Mississippi

Ottawa

0   50 miles
0   50 kilometres

Scale 1:5 000 000

Movements

Wood

Provisions, etc

Information

Participants

Merchant-wholesaler

Country storekeeper

Sawmiller

Broker

Jobber

Farmer

Farmer-lumberer

Lumbering speculator

Contract lumberer

HISTORICAL ATLAS OF CANADA

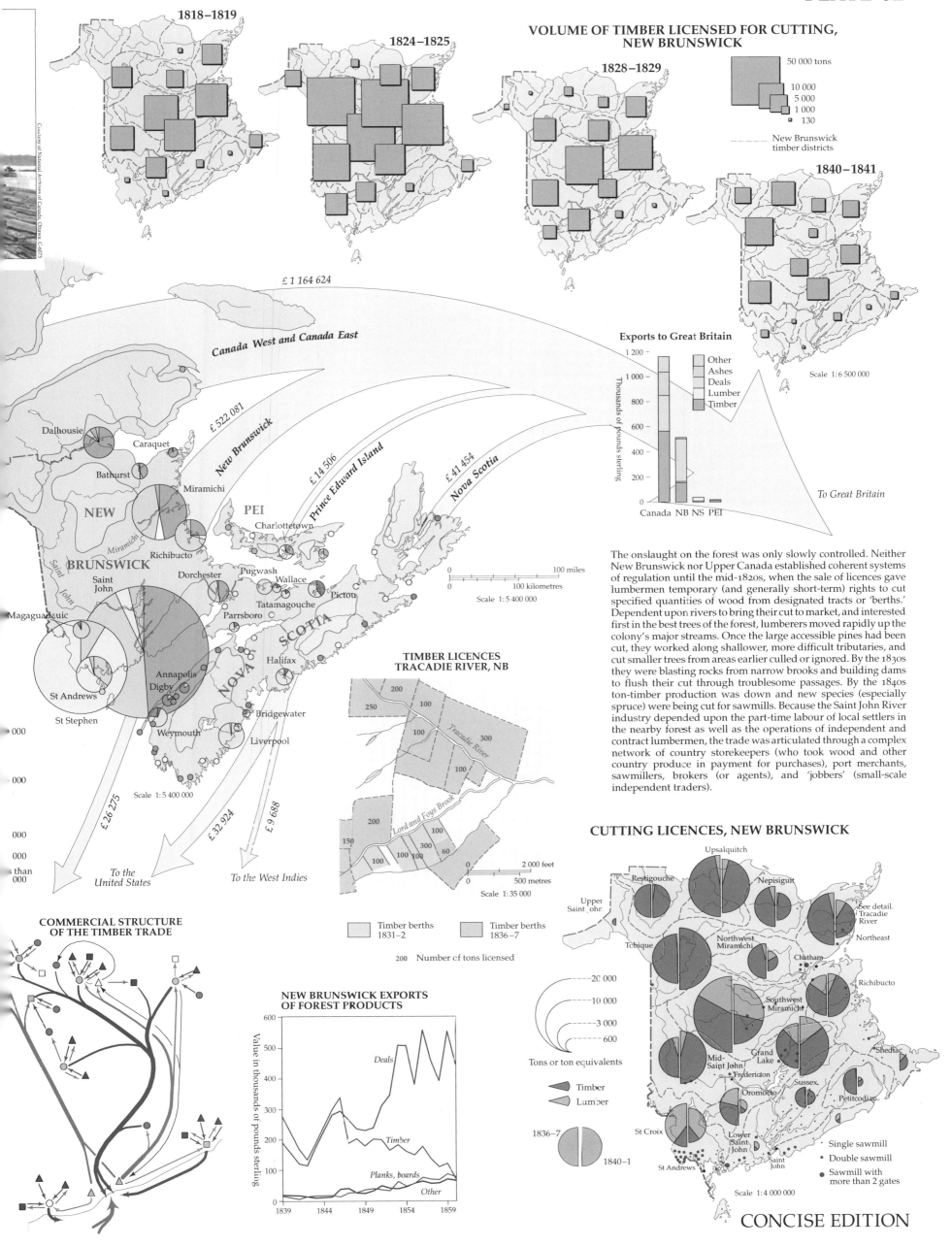

1818–1819

1824–1825

VOLUME OF TIMBER LICENSED FOR CUTTING, NEW BRUNSWICK

1828–1829

50 000 tons
10 000
5 000
1 000
130

New Brunswick timber districts

1840–1841

Scale 1:6 500 000

£ 1 164 624

Canada West and Canada East

Exports to Great Britain

Other
Ashes
Deals
Lumber
Timber

£ 522 081

New Brunswick

£ 14 506

Prince Edward Island

£ 41 454

Nova Scotia

Dalhousie
Caraquet
Bathurst
Miramichi
NEW
Richibucto
BRUNSWICK
Saint John
Magaguadauic
Dorchester
Pugwash
Wallace
PEI
Charlottetown
Tatamagouche
Pictou
Parrsboro
St Andrews
St Stephen
Annapolis
Digby
NOVA SCOTIA
Weymouth
Halifax
Bridgewater
Liverpool

Thousands of pounds sterling

Canada NB NS PEI

To Great Britain

The onslaught on the forest was only slowly controlled. Neither New Brunswick nor Upper Canada established coherent systems of regulation until the mid-1820s, when the sale of licences gave lumbermen temporary (and generally short-term) rights to cut specified quantities of wood from designated tracts or 'berths.' Dependent upon rivers to bring their cut to market, and interested first in the best trees of the forest, lumberers moved rapidly up the colony's major streams. Once the large accessible pines had been cut, they worked along shallower, more difficult tributaries, and cut smaller trees from areas earlier culled or ignored. By the 1830s they were blasting rocks from narrow brooks and building dams to flush their cut through troublesome passages. By the 1840s ton-timber production was down and new species (especially spruce) were being cut for sawmills. Because the Saint John River industry depended upon the part-time labour of local settlers in the nearby forest as well as the operations of independent and contract lumberers, the trade was articulated through a complex network of country storekeepers (who took wood and other country produce in payment for purchases), port merchants, sawmillers, brokers (or agents), and 'jobbers' (small-scale independent traders).

100 miles
100 kilometres
Scale 1:5 400 000

TIMBER LICENCES TRACADIE RIVER, NB

200
250
100
100
Tracadie River
300
100
200
Lord and Foys Brook
150
100
300
100 100 60

2 000 feet
500 metres
Scale 1:35 000

£ 26 275
£ 32 924
£ 9 688

To the United States
To the West Indies

Scale 1:5 400 000

Timber berths 1831–2
Timber berths 1836–7

200 Number of tons licensed

CUTTING LICENCES, NEW BRUNSWICK

Upsalquitch
Restigouche
Nepisiguit
Upper Saint John
Tobique
Northwest Miramichi
Chatham
Northeast
See detail, Tracadie River
Richibucto
Southwest Miramichi
Mid-Saint John
Grand Lake
Shediac
Fredericton
Sussex
Oromocto
Petitcodiac
St Croix
Lower Saint John
Saint John
St Andrews

20 000
10 000
3 000
600

Tons or ton equivalents

Timber
Lumber

1836–7
1840–1

Single sawmill
Double sawmill
Sawmill with more than 2 gates

Scale 1:4 000 000

COMMERCIAL STRUCTURE OF THE TIMBER TRADE

NEW BRUNSWICK EXPORTS OF FOREST PRODUCTS

Value in thousands of pounds sterling

600
500
400
300
200
100
0

Deals
Timber
Planks, boards
Other

1839 1844 1849 1854 1859

CONCISE EDITION

A NEW AGRICULTURE: UPPER CANADA TO 1856

Authors: J. David Wood, Peter Ennals (Hamilton Township), Thomas F. McIlwraith (cleared land, 1842)

In contrast to the well-established agricultural settlement in Lower Canada, at the beginning of the 19th century Upper Canada had just begun its agricultural development. The availability of a large expanse of good land, the opportunity to reach and serve a buoyant international market for wheat, and the influx of large numbers of land-hungry immigrants, many with capital, hastened development. Land clearing was rapid, a cash wheat economy was pervasive, and a service network of mills, merchants, and artisans, centred in small towns, was set in place. Because a vibrant agricultural economy emerged early, the pioneer stage was brief. By 1851 the last corners of the province, towards Georgian Bay and up the Ottawa valley, were being surveyed for settlement. Some of the first settlers were squatters, but in general the survey preceded settlers. In a classic frontier sequence colonization moved from a patchy clearing of the primarily hardwood forest, through the expansion of crop-land, to a scene busy with farming activities. The increasing complexity of these activities is captured in the annual farm work of Benjamin Smith of Ancaster in 1805 and 1838. By the 1830s most of the early-settled lakeshore tier of townships, of which Hamilton is an example, had a quarter to a third of their land cleared; by 1850 many had over half cleared and were close to their maximum farm population. In one generation, from 1821 to 1851, the province's population increased from 210 000 to 952 000.

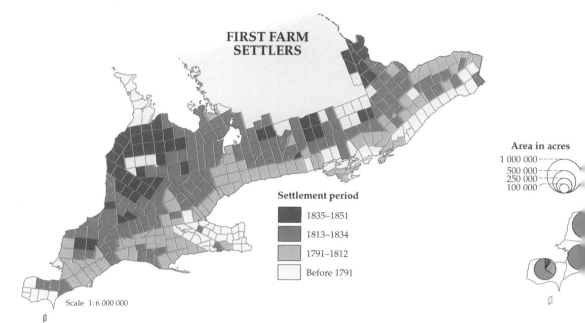

FIRST FARM SETTLERS

Area in acres
1 000 000
500 000
250 000
100 000

Settlement period
- 1835–1851
- 1813–1834
- 1791–1812
- Before 1791

Scale 1: 6 000 000

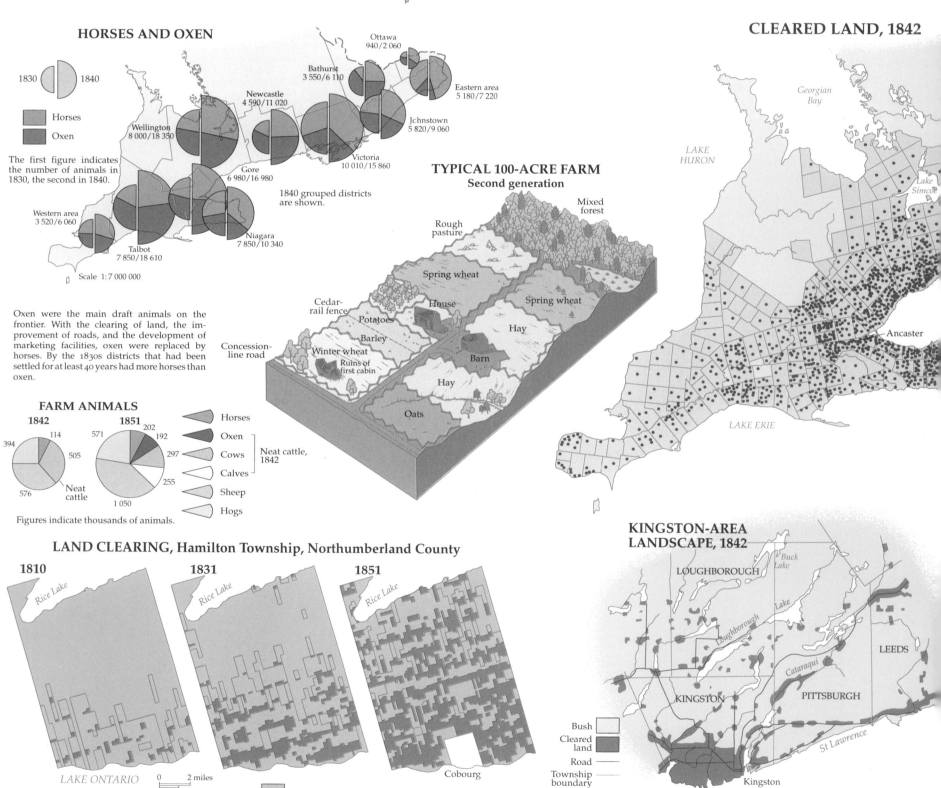

HORSES AND OXEN

1830   1840

- Horses
- Oxen

The first figure indicates the number of animals in 1830, the second in 1840.

Ottawa 940/2 060
Bathurst 3 550/6 110
Newcastle 4 590/11 020
Eastern area 5 180/7 220
Johnstown 5 820/9 060
Wellington 8 000/18 350
Victoria 10 010/15 860
Gore 6 980/16 980
1840 grouped districts are shown.
Western area 3 520/6 060
Talbot 7 850/18 610
Niagara 7 850/10 340

Scale 1: 7 000 000

Oxen were the main draft animals on the frontier. With the clearing of land, the improvement of roads, and the development of marketing facilities, oxen were replaced by horses. By the 1830s districts that had been settled for at least 40 years had more horses than oxen.

FARM ANIMALS

1842
394
114
505
576
Neat cattle

1851
571
202
192
297
255
1 050

- Horses
- Oxen
- Cows } Neat cattle, 1842
- Calves
- Sheep
- Hogs

Figures indicate thousands of animals.

TYPICAL 100-ACRE FARM
Second generation

Mixed forest
Rough pasture
Spring wheat
Spring wheat
House
Hay
Cedar-rail fence
Potatoes
Barley
Barn
Winter wheat
Ruins of first cabin
Concession-line road
Hay
Oats

CLEARED LAND, 1842

Georgian Bay
LAKE HURON
Lake Simcoe
Ancaster
LAKE ERIE

LAND CLEARING, Hamilton Township, Northumberland County

1810
Rice Lake

1831
Rice Lake

1851
Rice Lake
Cobourg

LAKE ONTARIO
0   2 miles
0   2 kilometres
Scale 1: 395 000

- Uncleared occupied land
- Cleared occupied land
- Crown land

KINGSTON-AREA LANDSCAPE, 1842

LOUGHBOROUGH
Buck Lake
Lake
Loughborough
Cataraqui
LEEDS
KINGSTON
PITTSBURGH
St Lawrence
Kingston

- Bush
- Cleared land
- Road
- Township boundary

1851 townships are shown.

0   5 miles
0   5 kilometres
Scale 1: 500 000

Small grains
- Includes barley, oats, rye, and wheat

Other field crops
- Includes beans, buckwheat, c (maize), flax, peas, potatoes, turnips

Outside contact
- Includes going to mill or mar and helping neighbours

FARM OF BENJAMIN SMITH, near Ancaster, 1805.
Farm team: one full-time worker with some seasonal helpers

| JANUARY | FEBRUARY | MARCH | APRIL | MAY | JUNE | JULY | AUGUST | SEPTEMBER | OCTOBER | NOVEMBER | DECEMBER |

HISTORICAL ATLAS OF CANADA

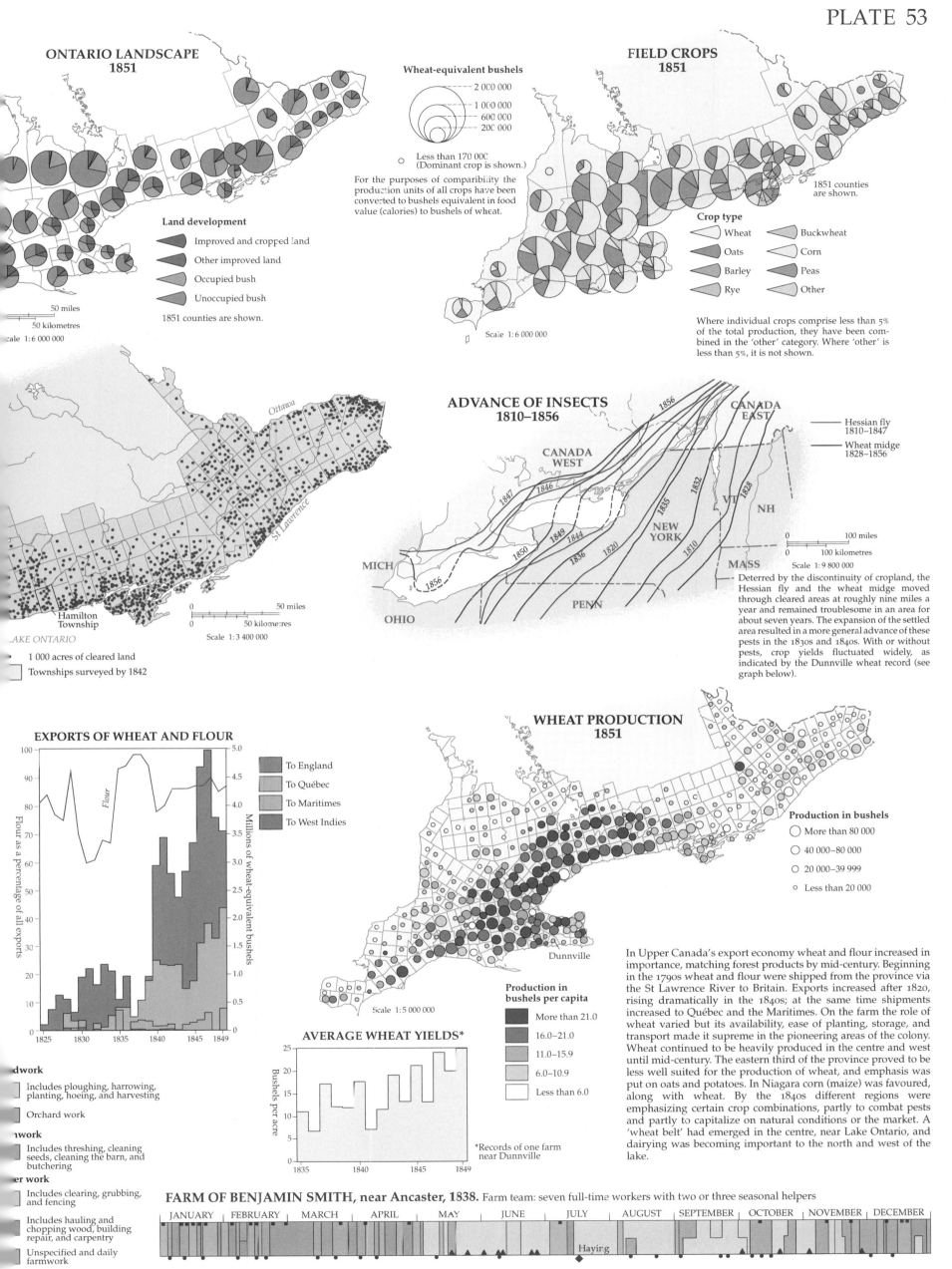

ONTARIO LANDSCAPE 1851

Wheat-equivalent bushels

2 000 000
1 000 000
600 000
200 000

○ Less than 170 000
(Dominant crop is shown.)

For the purposes of comparibility the production units of all crops have been converted to bushels equivalent in food value (calories) to bushels of wheat.

Land development

Improved and cropped land
Other improved land
Occupied bush
Unoccupied bush

50 miles
50 kilometres
Scale 1:6 000 000

1851 counties are shown.

FIELD CROPS 1851

1851 counties are shown.

Crop type

Wheat | Buckwheat
Oats | Corn
Barley | Peas
Rye | Other

Scale 1:6 000 000

Where individual crops comprise less than 5% of the total production, they have been combined in the 'other' category. Where 'other' is less than 5%, it is not shown.

Ottawa
St Lawrence

Hamilton Township

LAKE ONTARIO

• 1 000 acres of cleared land

Townships surveyed by 1842

50 miles
0   50 kilometres
Scale 1:3 400 000

ADVANCE OF INSECTS 1810–1856

—— Hessian fly 1810–1847
—— Wheat midge 1828–1856

CANADA EAST
CANADA WEST
MICH
MASS
OHIO
PENN
NEW YORK
VT
NH

Scale 1:9 800 000

0   100 miles
0   100 kilometres

Deterred by the discontinuity of cropland, the Hessian fly and the wheat midge moved through cleared areas at roughly nine miles a year and remained troublesome in an area for about seven years. The expansion of the settled area resulted in a more general advance of these pests in the 1830s and 1840s. With or without pests, crop yields fluctuated widely, as indicated by the Dunnville wheat record (see graph below).

EXPORTS OF WHEAT AND FLOUR

To England
To Québec
To Maritimes
To West Indies

Flour

Flour as a percentage of all exports
Millions of wheat-equivalent bushels

1825 1830 1835 1840 1845 1849

dwork

Includes ploughing, harrowing, planting, hoeing, and harvesting

Orchard work

work

Includes threshing, cleaning seeds, cleaning the barn, and butchering

er work

Includes clearing, grubbing, and fencing

Includes hauling and chopping wood, building repair, and carpentry

Unspecified and daily farmwork

WHEAT PRODUCTION 1851

Production in bushels

○ More than 80 000
○ 40 000–80 000
○ 20 000–39 999
○ Less than 20 000

Dunnville

Scale 1:5 000 000

Production in bushels per capita

More than 21.0
16.0–21.0
11.0–15.9
6.0–10.9
Less than 6.0

AVERAGE WHEAT YIELDS*

Bushels per acre

1835 1840 1845 1849

*Records of one farm near Dunnville

In Upper Canada's export economy wheat and flour increased in importance, matching forest products by mid-century. Beginning in the 1790s wheat and flour were shipped from the province via the St Lawrence River to Britain. Exports increased after 1820, rising dramatically in the 1840s; at the same time shipments increased to Québec and the Maritimes. On the farm the role of wheat varied but its availability, ease of planting, storage, and transport made it supreme in the pioneering areas of the colony. Wheat continued to be heavily produced in the centre and west until mid-century. The eastern third of the province proved to be less well suited for the production of wheat, and emphasis was put on oats and potatoes. In Niagara corn (maize) was favoured, along with wheat. By the 1840s different regions were emphasizing certain crop combinations, partly to combat pests and partly to capitalize on natural conditions or the market. A 'wheat belt' had emerged in the centre, near Lake Ontario, and dairying was becoming important to the north and west of the lake.

FARM OF BENJAMIN SMITH, near Ancaster, 1838. Farm team: seven full-time workers with two or three seasonal helpers

JANUARY	FEBRUARY	MARCH	APRIL	MAY	JUNE	JULY	AUGUST	SEPTEMBER	OCTOBER	NOVEMBER	DECEMBER

Haying

CONCISE EDITION

TRADE TO THE MIDDLE OF THE 19th CENTURY

Author: David A. Sutherland

Trade was crucial for British North America (BNA) in the pre-Confederation period. Far from being self-sufficient, the colonists relied on imports and exports for survival and development. The St Lawrence valley and Great Lakes basin accounted for approximately 60% of all colonial trade. Montréal and Québec, along with six other major ports, handled the bulk of the goods flowing in and out of British North America. The colonies differed in terms of the goods they produced for export: Canada West traded largely in flour and lumber; Canada East and New Brunswick were timber country; Prince Edward Island specialized in oats and potatoes; while fish was the main export of Nova Scotia and Newfoundland. What contemporaries were beginning to dream of by 1850 was a shift of capital and labour away from staples towards factories, so that British North America could become less dependent on imports as a source for manufactured goods. Railways had also begun to be discussed but at mid-century most long-haul trade involved use of rivers, lakes, and the ocean. Wooden-hulled and sail-powered craft, ranging from small canal barges to 300-ton deep-sea ships, carried most of the goods involved in colonial trade.

TRADE BY COMMODITY, 1850

Legend:
- Agricultural products
- Fish and sea products
- Textile products
- Forest products
- Metals and minerals
- Miscellaneous

Prince Edward Island — Imports / Exports
New Brunswick — Imports / Exports
Newfoundland — Imports / Exports
Nova Scotia — Imports / Exports
Canada East and West — Imports / Exports

Value in millions of dollars

IMPORTS

Millions of dollars

- Québec and Montréal
- Nova Scotia and Cape Breton
- Newfoundland
- New Brunswick
- Prince Edward Island

IMPORTS FROM GREAT BRITAIN

Millions of dollars

- New Brunswick and PEI
- Nova Scotia and Cape Breton
- Newfoundland

IMPORTS 1850

Figures indicate value in thousands of dollars, rounded off.

Great Britain **14 200**
Within BNA **2 460**
Other Europe **1 560**
British West Indies **100**
United States **9 830**

Scale 1:24 000 000

IMPORTS AND EXPORTS 1850–1852

Within BNA **1 790**
United States **6 010**

Scale 1:24 000 000

Value of export or import

Imports / Exports

- $8 000 000
- $6 000 000
- $2 000 000
- $400 000
- $40 000

Less than $10 000

- American entry points
- Canal (1851)
- Railway (1851)
- Settled area (1851)

Circles are proportional to average annual values by port, 1850–1852. Values converted from pounds; see end notes.

0   100 miles
0   100 kilometres
Scale 1:4 900 000

HISTORICAL ATLAS OF CANADA

VESSEL DESTINATIONS

Port of Québec   **Port of Halifax**

27 093 tons   **1804–1806**   23 628 tons

98 652   **1808–1810**   49 582

219 044   **1828–1830**   158 889

- Great Britain
- British North America
- British West Indies
- United States
- Other Europe

NEWFOUNDLAND LIGHTHOUSE DUTIES, 1850

Newfoundland trade was shared among St John's and a host of small outports scattered along the island's northeast and southwest coasts. The red arrows indicate the extent of the three coastal areas. Port ranking for 1850 is an estimate, based on lighthouse fees collected at mid-century. Lighthouse duties were fees charged, probably on a tonnage basis, on incoming vessels in support of lighthouses.

Northeast coast
$2 280

NEWFOUNDLAND

St John's
$5 796

Southwest coast
$1 080

SAINT-PIERRE
AND MIQUELON
(France)

GULF OF
ST LAWRENCE

Gaspé

New Carlisle

Dalhousie

Bathurst

Miramichi

NEW BRUNSWICK

Richibucto

Buctouche

Shediac

Hillsborough

Magaguadavic

St Stephen

St Andrews

Saint John

Digby

PRINCE EDWARD ISLAND

Charlottetown

Pictou

NOVA SCOTIA

Sydney

Arichat

Halifax

Liverpool

Yarmouth

QUÉBEC EXPORTS TO GREAT BRITAIN

1835   1850

Figures indicate thousands of tons.

Bars define approximate destination of Québec exports.

West coast of Scotland 20.6

14.0   26.9   East coast of Scotland

SCOTLAND

Ulster-Belfast 11.5   17.5

IRELAND

Ireland 12.3   30.2

Midlands-Liverpool 52.2

Northeast 15.7   46.5

132.5

ENGLAND

Bristol and Wales 68.5   32.1   London 42.3

WALES

West country 20.5   35.7   The South

Scale 1:10 800 000

EXPORTS

Millions of dollars

25
20
15
10
5

1820   1825   1830   1835   1840   1845   1850

- Québec and Montréal
- Nova Scotia and Cape Breton
- Newfoundland
- New Brunswick
- Prince Edward Island

EXPORTS 1850

Figures indicate value in thousands of dollars, rounded off.

Great Britain
9 750

Other Europe
2 050

British West Indies **510**

BNA 280
BNA 40
170
1 430
2 040
100
70
810
BNA 90
BNA
700
280
70
360
200
220
1 630
250
50

Overall trade grew significantly through the first half of the 19th century, giving employment to thousands of sailors, dockers, and construction workers and also building the careers of the scores of merchants who presided over the colonial business community. The British Isles persisted as the colonists' chief source of supply and their leading market, but commercial links with the United States became more significant through the 1830s and 1840s. Intercolonial trade, especially between the Canadas and the Atlantic colonies, was of only marginal importance in this era. Although internally fragmented, British North America was indirectly tied together through the operation of the larger North Atlantic economy, which shaped demand for colonial staples and governed access to capital and credit. This had the effect of exposing the colonists to common experiences in terms of cyclical episodes of commercial expansion and contraction. For example, almost all settlers prospered during the War of 1812 but then felt the pinch of acute hard times during the protracted adaptation to peace. Similarly, distress was widespread through the late 1840s, so much so that many colonists began looking for new options involving expansion of trade with one another and also with the United States.

CONCISE EDITION

BY HAND AND BY WATER: MANUFACTURING TO 1854

Authors: Ronald H. Walder, David A. Sutherland (Maritime shipbuilding)

Before the 1850s the colonies of British North America supplied staples to Great Britain under the imperial economic policy of mercantilism. Under these conditions manufacturing lagged. In what might be termed a pioneer, pre-industrial manufacturing economy, most activity took place in water-powered mills or in small 'manufactories' where artisans plied a specialized trade. Sawmills and grist mills located at suitable water-power sites were the dominant features of the industrial landscape. The most successful might be joined by other enterprises such as wool-carding and fulling mills, tanneries, metal foundries, potasheries, breweries, and distilleries. In growing urban centres artisans and skilled tradesmen operated relatively small enterprises, supplying local markets with consumer goods too expensive to import from Great Britain and the United States.

The emphasis on staples had a substantial impact on the structure and distribution of manufacturing. In the Atlantic colonies preferential access to the imperial trade system, accessible forest resources, and the demands of the fishery led to the development of a flourishing shipbuilding industry. In New Brunswick and Lower Canada, and later in Upper Canada, the timber industry developed a major sawmilling component which supplied deals to Great Britain and later sawn lumber to the United States. By mid-century sawmilling was the single most important manufacturing activity in British North America. By processing their grain in Upper Canada Americans could gain access to the protected British market. With farmers producing a wheat surplus, merchant millers in the province used advanced technologies to build large-capacity mills at sites along the Lake Ontario shore.

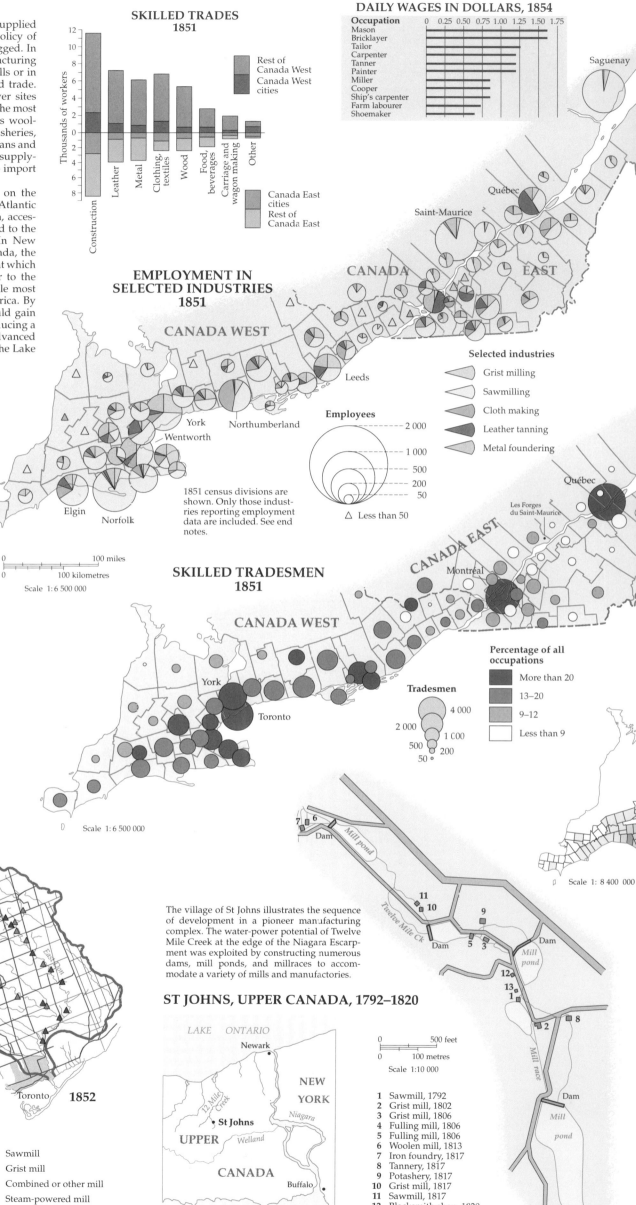

SKILLED TRADES 1851

Thousands of workers

Construction, Leather, Metal, Clothing, textiles, Wood, Food, beverages, Carriage and wagon making, Other

Rest of Canada West
Canada West cities
Canada East cities
Rest of Canada East

DAILY WAGES IN DOLLARS, 1854

Occupation	0 0.25 0.50 0.75 1.00 1.25 1.50 1.75
Mason	
Bricklayer	
Tailor	
Carpenter	
Tanner	
Painter	
Miller	
Cooper	
Ship's carpenter	
Farm labourer	
Shoemaker	

EMPLOYMENT IN SELECTED INDUSTRIES 1851

Saguenay

Québec

Saint-Maurice

CANADA EAST

CANADA WEST

Leeds

York
Wentworth
Northumberland

Elgin
Norfolk

Selected industries
Grist milling
Sawmilling
Cloth making
Leather tanning
Metal foundering

Employees
2 000
1 000
500
200
50
△ Less than 50

1851 census divisions are shown. Only those industries reporting employment data are included. See end notes.

Scale 1:6 500 000

UPPER CANADA GRIST-MILL CAPACITY

Average number of operating millstones per mill

1825 1830 1835 1840 1845 1850

MILLS IN UPPER CANADA

Number of mills / Population in thousands

Sawmills
Population
Grist mills

1825 1830 1835 1840 1845 1850

SKILLED TRADESMEN 1851

Québec
Les Forges du Saint-Maurice

CANADA EAST

Montréal

CANADA WEST

York
Toronto

Percentage of all occupations
More than 20
13–20
9–12
Less than 9

Tradesmen
4 000
2 000
1 000
500
200
50

Scale 1:6 500 000

Scale 1:8 400 000

MILL DEVELOPMENT IN THE DON VALLEY

Toronto

1852

1825

York

△ Sawmill
△ Grist mill
▲ Combined or other mill
△ Steam-powered mill

0 4 miles
0 4 kilometres
Scale 1:400 000

The village of St Johns illustrates the sequence of development in a pioneer manufacturing complex. The water-power potential of Twelve Mile Creek at the edge of the Niagara Escarpment was exploited by constructing numerous dams, mill ponds, and millraces to accommodate a variety of mills and manufactories.

ST JOHNS, UPPER CANADA, 1792–1820

LAKE ONTARIO
Newark

NEW YORK
Niagara

UPPER CANADA
Welland

Buffalo
LAKE ERIE

St Johns

Scale 1:100 000

0 500 feet
0 100 metres
Scale 1:10 000

1 Sawmill, 1792
2 Grist mill, 1802
3 Grist mill, 1806
4 Fulling mill, 1806
5 Fulling mill, 1806
6 Woolen mill, 1813
7 Iron foundry, 1817
8 Tannery, 1817
9 Potashery, 1817
10 Grist mill, 1817
11 Sawmill, 1817
12 Blacksmith shop, 1820
13 Wagon shop, 1820

Mill pond
Dam
Twelve Mile Ck
Mill race

HISTORICAL ATLAS OF CANADA

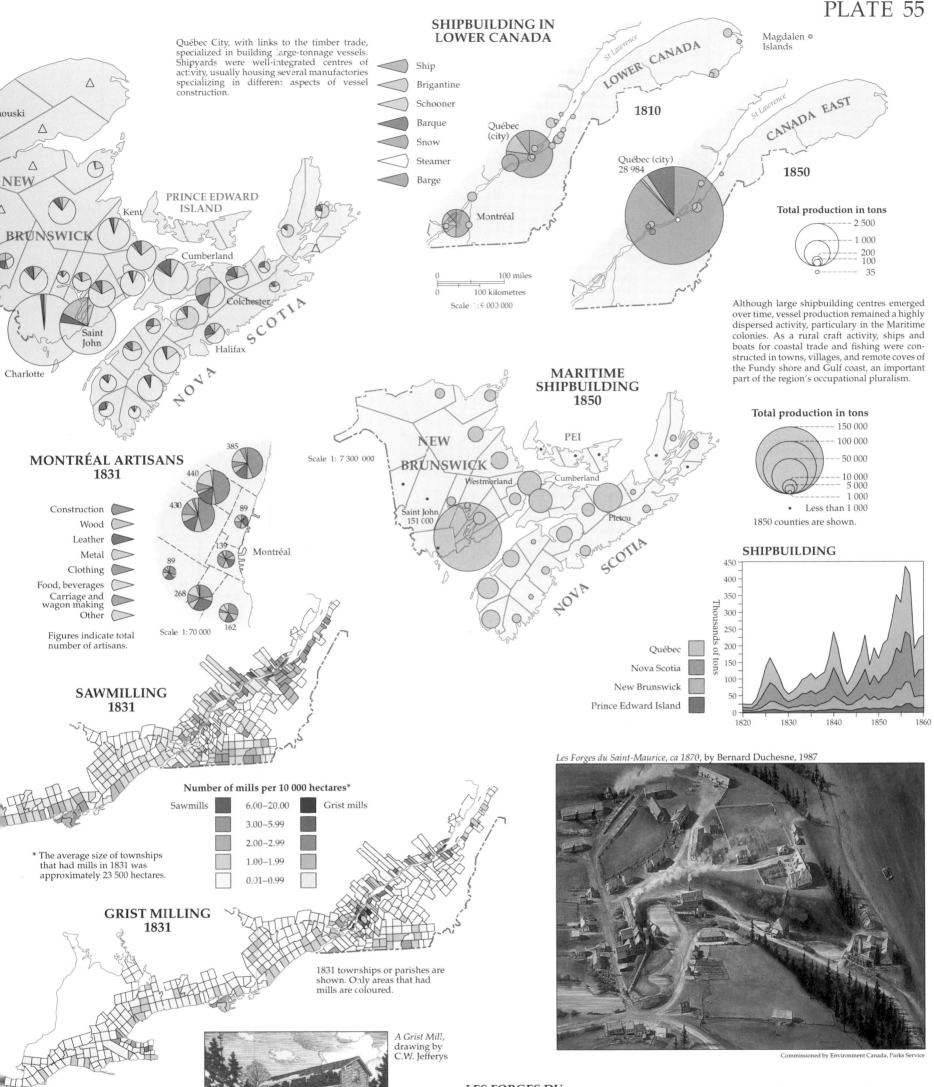

SHIPBUILDING IN LOWER CANADA

Québec City, with links to the timber trade, specialized in building large-tonnage vessels. Shipyards were well-integrated centres of activity, usually housing several manufactories specializing in different aspects of vessel construction.

Ship
Brigantine
Schooner
Barque
Snow
Steamer
Barge

1810

1850

Québec (city) 28 984

Total production in tons
2 500
1 000
200
100
35

Although large shipbuilding centres emerged over time, vessel production remained a highly dispersed activity, particularly in the Maritime colonies. As a rural craft activity, ships and boats for coastal trade and fishing were constructed in towns, villages, and remote coves of the Fundy shore and Gulf coast, an important part of the region's occupational pluralism.

Total production in tons
150 000
100 000
50 000
10 000
5 000
1 000
• Less than 1 000
1850 counties are shown.

MARITIME SHIPBUILDING 1850

Scale 1: 7 300 000

NEW BRUNSWICK

PEI

Westmorland

Cumberland

Saint John 151 000

Pictou

MONTRÉAL ARTISANS 1831

Construction
Wood
Leather
Metal
Clothing
Food, beverages
Carriage and wagon making
Other

Figures indicate total number of artisans.

385
440
430
89
139
89
268
162

Montréal

Scale 1: 70 000

SHIPBUILDING

Québec
Nova Scotia
New Brunswick
Prince Edward Island

Thousands of tons

1820 1830 1840 1850 1860

SAWMILLING 1831

Number of mills per 10 000 hectares*
Sawmills		Grist mills
	6.00–20.00	
	3.00–5.99	
	2.00–2.99	
	1.00–1.99	
	0.01–0.99	

* The average size of townships that had mills in 1831 was approximately 23 500 hectares.

GRIST MILLING 1831

1831 townships or parishes are shown. Only areas that had mills are coloured.

Scale 1: 8 400 000

rist milling

rly grist mills or later ones in remote areas
ere often rudimentary wooden structures
mploying exposed overshot water wheels for
wer. Operation was frequently disrupted by
e and snow even though, for farmers, the
nsportation of grain was easiest on winter
ads.

Les Forges du Saint-Maurice, ca 1870, by Bernard Duchesne, 1987

Commissioned by Environment Canada, Parks Service

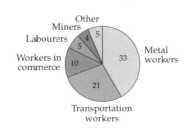

A Grist Mill, drawing by C.W. Jefferys

Courtesy of National Archives of Canada, Ottawa, C 69700

LES FORGES DU SAINT-MAURICE WORKFORCE, 1831

Other
Miners
Labourers
Workers in commerce
Transportation workers
Metal workers

5
5
5
4
10
21
33

Strategically located near the St Lawrence River with abundant bog-iron and hardwood-forest resources close by, Les Forges operated from 1729 to 1883, producing a wide variety of goods for markets throughout British North America. An integrated industrial community, Les Forges could be considered Canada's first company town, providing workers with housing, food, and other necessities of daily life. At the heart of the community, straddling the Ruisseau du Lavoir, were the three iron-processing complexes which used the extensively modified water course to power refining equipment. The blast furnace, to the west, processed the bog iron into pig iron. At the upper forge at the centre and the lower forge adjacent to the Saint-Maurice River the pig iron was refined into various products.

CONCISE EDITION

THE DEVELOPING INDUSTRIAL HEARTLAND, 1871–1891

Authors: Ronald H. Walder, Daniel Hiebert (Toronto clothing)

With Confederation came the expectation of a prosperous industrial economy, to be achieved through tariff protection and the economic opportunities promised by the development of the Canadian West. Despite depressions during the mid-1870s and early 1890s, the Canadian economy produced moderate but steady growth in the decades following Confederation. Although the industrial economy was still dominated by primary production of resource staples, considerable expansion and diversification also occurred in the secondary manufacturing sector.

By 1891 there was a clearly developing industrial heartland centred in southern Ontario and in and around Montréal. These regions possessed a large population base, capable industrial entrepreneurs, a powerful service sector, location at the centre of a well-developed transportation system, and proximity to a burgeoning economic power to the south. Secondary manufacturing in the heartland developed on several fronts. Meat packing, butter and cheese production, agricultural implements, and railway equipment indicate expansion fostered by a continuing emphasis on resource staples. Sugar refining, cotton textiles, and musical instruments were new developments in consumer goods dependent on tariff protection.

With an existing core of metal-products industries and a skilled labour force southern Ontario specialized in producer goods such as agricultural implements and factory machinery. Capitalizing on a large, cheap labour pool, Montréal's development was oriented towards labour-intensive manufacturing of consumer goods such as textiles, clothing, and shoes. From a regional economy rooted in mercantilism the Maritimes developed a highly dispersed community-based system of manufacturing and entrepreneurship. Despite early success in sugar refining, cotton textiles, and iron and steel, its manufacturing base declined in the face of competition from the developing industrial heartland in central Canada.

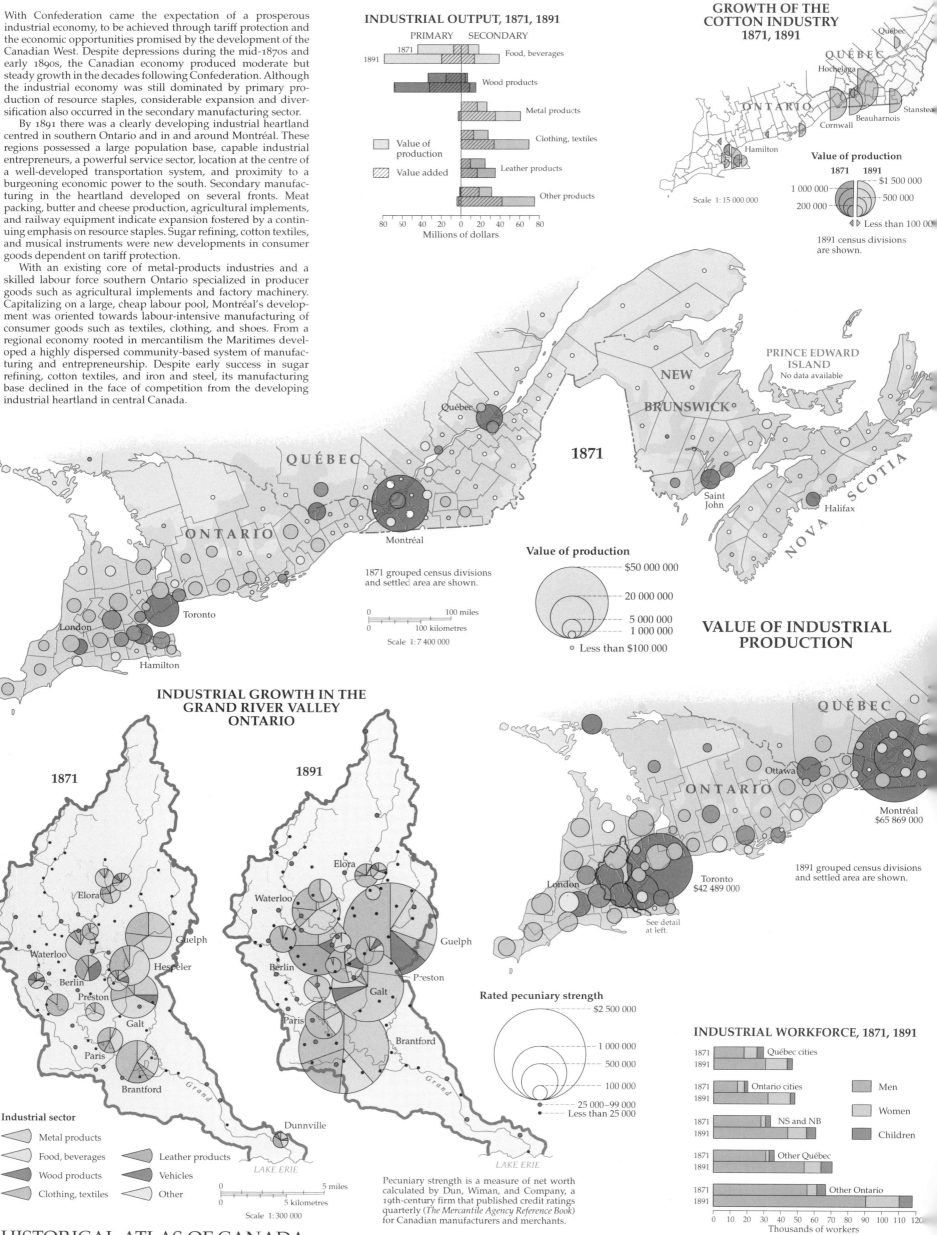

INDUSTRIAL OUTPUT, 1871, 1891

PRIMARY   SECONDARY

Food, beverages
Wood products
Metal products
Clothing, textiles
Leather products
Other products

Value of production
Value added

80 50 20 0 20 40 60 80
Millions of dollars

GROWTH OF THE COTTON INDUSTRY 1871, 1891

Québec
Hochelaga
Stanstead
Cornwall
Beauharnois
Hamilton

Value of production
1871   1891
$1 500 000
1 000 000
500 000
200 000
Less than 100 000

1891 census divisions are shown.

Scale 1: 15 000 000

1871

QUÉBEC
ONTARIO
Québec
Montréal
Toronto
London
Hamilton
NEW BRUNSWICK
PRINCE EDWARD ISLAND
No data available
Saint John
Halifax
NOVA SCOTIA

1871 grouped census divisions and settled area are shown.

0 — 100 miles
0 — 100 kilometres
Scale 1:7 400 000

VALUE OF INDUSTRIAL PRODUCTION

Value of production
$50 000 000
20 000 000
5 000 000
1 000 000
Less than $100 000

INDUSTRIAL GROWTH IN THE GRAND RIVER VALLEY ONTARIO

1871

Elora
Waterloo
Guelph
Berlin
Hespeler
Preston
Galt
Paris
Brantford

1891

Elora
Waterloo
Berlin
Guelph
Preston
Galt
Paris
Brantford

Dunnville

LAKE ERIE

Industrial sector
- Metal products
- Food, beverages
- Wood products
- Clothing, textiles
- Leather products
- Vehicles
- Other

0 — 5 miles
0 — 5 kilometres
Scale 1:300 000

QUÉBEC / ONTARIO (1891 detail)

Ottawa
Montréal
$65 869 000
London
Toronto
$42 489 000
See detail at left.

1891 grouped census divisions and settled area are shown.

Rated pecuniary strength

$2 500 000
1 000 000
500 000
100 000
25 000–99 000
Less than 25 000

LAKE ERIE

Pecuniary strength is a measure of net worth calculated by Dun, Wiman, and Company, a 19th-century firm that published credit ratings quarterly (*The Mercantile Agency Reference Book*) for Canadian manufacturers and merchants.

INDUSTRIAL WORKFORCE, 1871, 1891

	Men	Women	Children
1871 / 1891 Québec cities			
1871 / 1891 Ontario cities			
1871 / 1891 NS and NB			
1871 / 1891 Other Québec			
1871 / 1891 Other Ontario			

0 10 20 30 40 50 60 70 80 90 100 110 120
Thousands of workers

HISTORICAL ATLAS OF CANADA

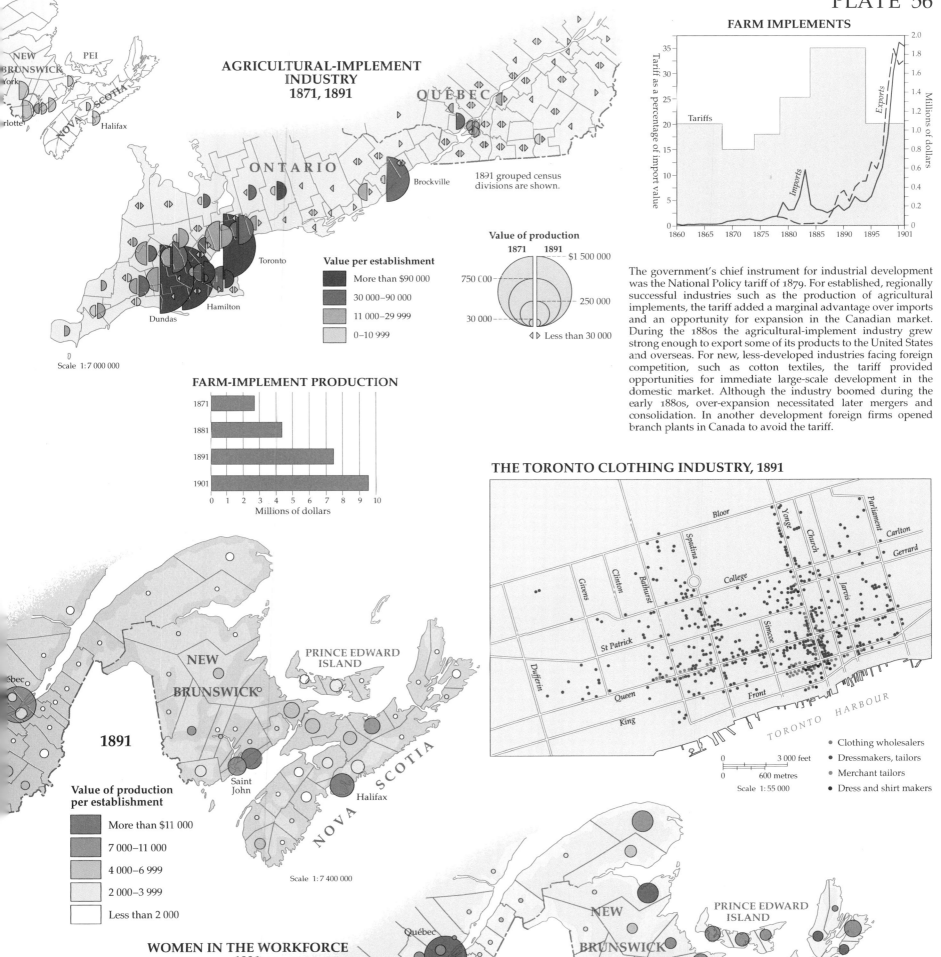

FARM IMPLEMENTS

AGRICULTURAL-IMPLEMENT INDUSTRY 1871, 1891

1891 grouped census divisions are shown.

Value per establishment
- More than $90 000
- 30 000–90 000
- 11 000–29 999
- 0–10 999

Value of production

1871 1891

$1 500 000
750 000
250 000
30 000
Less than 30 000

Scale 1:7 000 000

FARM-IMPLEMENT PRODUCTION

1871
1881
1891
1901

0 1 2 3 4 5 6 7 8 9 10
Millions of dollars

The government's chief instrument for industrial development was the National Policy tariff of 1879. For established, regionally successful industries such as the production of agricultural implements, the tariff added a marginal advantage over imports and an opportunity for expansion in the Canadian market. During the 1880s the agricultural-implement industry grew strong enough to export some of its products to the United States and overseas. For new, less-developed industries facing foreign competition, such as cotton textiles, the tariff provided opportunities for immediate large-scale development in the domestic market. Although the industry boomed during the early 1880s, over-expansion necessitated later mergers and consolidation. In another development foreign firms opened branch plants in Canada to avoid the tariff.

THE TORONTO CLOTHING INDUSTRY, 1891

- ● Clothing wholesalers
- ◆ Dressmakers, tailors
- ● Merchant tailors
- ● Dress and shirt makers

0   3 000 feet
0   600 metres
Scale 1:55 000

1891

Value of production per establishment
- More than $11 000
- 7 000–11 000
- 4 000–6 999
- 2 000–3 999
- Less than 2 000

Scale 1:7 400 000

WOMEN IN THE WORKFORCE 1891

1891 grouped census divisions and settled area are shown.

Number of women

9 500
5 000
2 000
500
100
Less than 100

Percentage of women in the workforce
- More than 25%
- 16–25
- 11–15
- 0–10

0   150 miles
0   150 kilometres
Scale 1:8 000 000

The factory system of production had profound effects on the composition of the workforce. From 1871 to 1891 the number of women workers tripled. By 1891 they comprised 20% of the workforce not including the large numbers employed as domestic servants. In manufacturing women occupied the lowest-paying jobs in the production of textiles, tobacco, shoes, clothing, and matches, and in printing shops. They often worked long hours under poor conditions executing simple, repetitive tasks. Taking jobs in order to help support their working-class families, most female workers were between 12 and 24 years of age, and many worked only until they married.

CONCISE EDITION

SOCIAL CHANGE IN MONTRÉAL, 1842–1901

Authors: Sherry Olson, David Hanna

In the early 19th century Montréal looked ahead to its role as the pre-eminent middleman and shipper for British North America. Population growth was moderate but steady, from 18 800 inhabitants in 1821 to 40 400 in 1842. The old order passed in the 1850s. Montréal was at the heart of a new railway system linking the Atlantic coast with Ontario and the American midwest. The growth of financial services and large-scale industrialization followed. Population soared. French Canadians from the rural areas and Irish immigrants from abroad poured into what soon became Canada's leading industrial city. Overnight the formation of industrial districts established the framework of class segregation, forming residential patterns that would persist into the next century. On these maps common occupations identify five levels of social class, each with a distinct pattern of rent-paying capacity, as shown for 1881. Labourers outnumbered any other occupation, but merchants and professionals, who paid higher rents, outweighed blue-collar workers in the housing market. After 1842 the city unfolded like a flower out of Old Montréal. In each surge of growth all classes occupied new territory. By the end of the century we see an orderly gradient between the mountain and the river. Culturally the balance between populations of French and British origins shifted to a French majority, but the balance between Catholics and Protestants remained rather stable.

MONTRÉAL 1847

Like other North American cities, Montré[al] grew in boom-and-bust fashion, as is eviden[t] from the numbers of building permits issued each year. Population is shown by the number of households. In the first interval (1847–61) numbers doubled; in the second (1861–81) they almost trebled; by 1901 they had almos[t] doubled again.

Selected occupations

- Merchants
- Doctors, lawyers
- Clerks
- Joiners
- Labourers

MONTRÉAL 1861

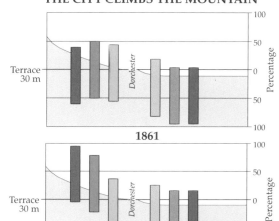

SELECTED OCCUPATIONS AND RENT CLASSES, 1881

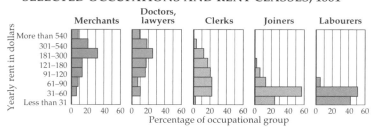

Yearly rent in dollars: More than 540 / 301–540 / 181–300 / 121–180 / 91–120 / 61–90 / 31–60 / Less than 31
Percentage of occupational group

Merchants · Doctors, lawyers · Clerks · Joiners · Labourers

HEADS OF HOUSEHOLDS   RENT

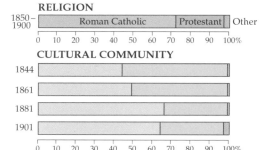

Total number and total rent paid by occupational group

Of a total of approximately 33 400 households in Montréal in 1881, an estimated 9 400 heads of households fell into these occupational groups. The rent paid totalled almost three million dollars.

RELIGION

| 1850–1900 | Roman Catholic | Protestant | Other |

0 10 20 30 40 50 60 70 80 90 100%

CULTURAL COMMUNITY

1844
1861
1881
1901

0 10 20 30 40 50 60 70 80 90 100%

- French
- British
- Other

THE CITY CLIMBS THE MOUNTAIN

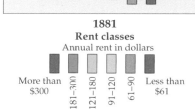

Terrace 30 m — Dorchester — 1861

Terrace 30 m — Dorchester — 1881

Percentage: 100 50 0 50 100

Rent classes
Annual rent in dollars

- More than $300
- 181–300
- 121–180
- 91–120
- 61–90
- Less than $61

In the years 1861–1901 the city crept up the slope of the mountain. The wealthy led the climb. The bar of colour for each rent level shows what percentage of the households lived above and below an elevation of 30 metres, the Dorchester Street terrace. A street of houses was an exacting sieve for social class. The professionals — doctors, dentists, lawyers, and notaries — were moving out of Old Montréal, occupying handsome streets like Dorchester and Sherbrooke (west), Saint-Denis, Saint-Hubert, and Berri. They clustered in Place Viger (1861), then in Saint-Louis Square (1901). New dwellings, built in the boom of the 1870s, commanded annual rents ranging from less than $40 to more than $1 200. Most streets had only two or three types of dwellings, stacked as shown, most of them duplex units. The cubes shown below are proportional to the space in the dwelling unit.

A SCALE OF LIVING SPACE
A typology of new housing

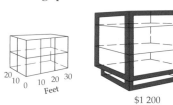

Carmen Jensen

Dwelling space and annual rents

20 10 0 10 20 30 Feet

$1 200 $700 $450 $250 $180 $140 $140 $120 $75 $60

Dwelling units
Dimensions are shown in f[eet]. Annual rents are shown in dollars and colour-coded according to rent class.

$40 $40
$40 $40

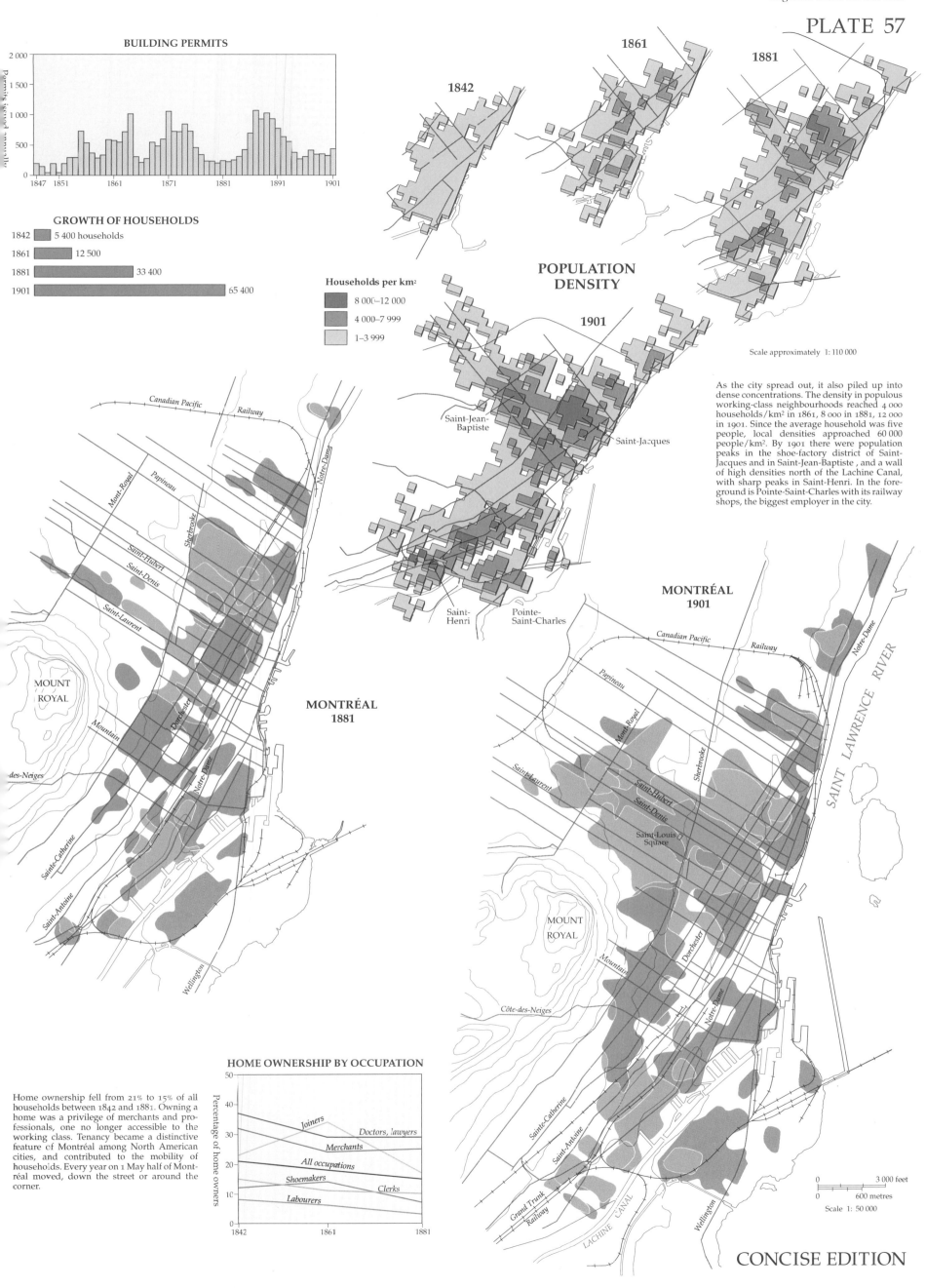

BUILDING PERMITS

Permits issued annually

2 000
1 500
1 000
500
100

1847   1851   1861   1871   1881   1891   1901

GROWTH OF HOUSEHOLDS

1842   5 400 households
1861   12 500
1881   33 400
1901   65 400

POPULATION DENSITY

1842

1861

1881

1901

Households per km²

8 000–12 000
4 000–7 999
1–3 999

Scale approximately 1: 110 000

Saint-Jean-Baptiste

Saint-Jacques

Saint-Henri

Pointe-Saint-Charles

As the city spread out, it also piled up into dense concentrations. The density in populous working-class neighbourhoods reached 4 000 households/km² in 1861, 8 000 in 1881, 12 000 in 1901. Since the average household was five people, local densities approached 60 000 people/km². By 1901 there were population peaks in the shoe-factory district of Saint-Jacques and in Saint-Jean-Baptiste , and a wall of high densities north of the Lachine Canal, with sharp peaks in Saint-Henri. In the foreground is Pointe-Saint-Charles with its railway shops, the biggest employer in the city.

MONTRÉAL 1881

Canadian Pacific   Railway
Mont-Royal
Papineau
Sherbrooke
Saint-Hubert
Saint-Denis
Saint-Laurent
Notre-Dame
MOUNT ROYAL
Mountain
Dorchester
des-Neiges
Sainte-Catherine
Saint-Antoine
Wellington

MONTRÉAL 1901

Canadian Pacific   Railway
Papineau
Mont-Royal
Sherbrooke
Saint-Laurent
Saint-Hubert
Saint-Denis
Saint-Louis Square
MOUNT ROYAL
Mountain
Dorchester
Notre-Dame
Côte-des-Neiges
Sainte-Catherine
Saint-Antoine
Grand Trunk Railway
LACHINE CANAL
Wellington
Notre-Dame
SAINT LAWRENCE RIVER

0   3 000 feet
0   600 metres
Scale 1: 50 000

HOME OWNERSHIP BY OCCUPATION

Percentage of home owners

50
40
30
20
10

Joiners
Doctors, lawyers
Merchants
All occupations
Shoemakers
Clerks
Labourers

1842   1861   1881

Home ownership fell from 21% to 15% of all households between 1842 and 1881. Owning a home was a privilege of merchants and professionals, one no longer accessible to the working class. Tenancy became a distinctive feature of Montréal among North American cities, and contributed to the mobility of households. Every year on 1 May half of Montréal moved, down the street or around the corner.

CONCISE EDITION

THE EMERGENCE OF CORPORATE TORONTO, 1890–1930

Authors: Gunter Gad, Deryck W. Holdsworth

By 1914 Toronto had consolidated its position as the leading industrial centre for Ontario. Industrial growth occurred close to the city centre, along the railway corridors, and at the outer edge of the city. The printing and later the garment industry moved west from the King/Bay area to Spadina Avenue, engineering and transportation-equipment firms expanded along the railroad belts, and meat-packing and other food-processing industries dominated the city's northwest corner. Significant expansion occurred at the edges of the central business district. Substantial blocks of land in public use for most of the 19th century became sites for railway freight yards, factories, and warehouses. As King Street was transformed from the city's specialty retail street into a canyon of Edwardian office towers, Yonge and Queen, where the rapidly expanding Eaton's and Simpson's department stores were located, became the new focus for retailing. Increasingly serving national markets and relying to some extent on their own manufacturing, Eaton's and Simpson's developed large mail-order operations and factories which, in the case of Eaton's, were adjacent to the retail store.

EXPANSION OF BUILT-UP AND INDUSTRIAL AREAS

Built-up area

Over 50% by 1890

Over 50% 1890–1923

City limits

1890

1923

Industrial area

Existing in 1890

Additions by 1923

Mixed commercial and industrial use

Scale 1:145 000

0 — 2 miles
0 — 2 kilometres

Harbour development

1890

1923

INVESTMENT IN INDUSTRIAL BUILDINGS, 1912

Type of industry

Metals, machinery

Food products

Clothing, textiles

Printing, bookbinding

Other

Investment in thousands of dollars

100.0 or more

50.0–99.9

5.0–49.9

Less than 5.0

Scale 1:145 000

EXPANSION OF EATON'S AND SIMPSON'S

Date of first occupancy

1890

1891–1900

1901–1910

1911–1920

1921–1930

Major use by 1930

S Retail store

M Mail-order department

F Factory

W Warehouse

G Support functions (garage, workshop)

P Parking lot

EATON'S

SIMPSON'S

City Hall and Courthouse

500 feet
100 metres

Scale 1:4 800

DOMINION BANK, 1911
National employment

Rest of Western Canada

Winnipeg

Montréal

Rest of Ontario

Other branches

Main branch

Head office

Total 506 persons

Outline of the Canadian Bank of Commerce Building, erected 1929–31 on the site of the old head office and two adjacent properties

CENTRAL-AREA LAND USE

1890

1 St Lawrence Market
2 City Hall
3 Court House
4 Toronto Stock Exchange
5 Union Station
6 Parliament Buildings
7 Government House
8 Upper Canada College

Office

Retail

Wholesale

Manufacturing

Mixed commercial

Hotel, restaurant, place of entertainment

Public building/grounds, church

Transportation, utility, storage

Residential

Vacant lot or land

Park

2 000 feet
500 metres

Scale 1:21 000

1914

1 St Lawrence Market
2 City Hall and Court House
3 Eaton's store
4 Toronto Stock Exchange
5 Union Station
6 Grand Trunk Railway freight yard
7 Canadian Pacific Railway freight yards
8 Site of new Union Station

EAST

CPR Building 1911–1913

Yonge Street

Dominion Bank Building 1913–1914

Before 1860

Michie and Co 1894–1895

Standard Bank Building 1910–19

Detail not available

Yonge Street

Dominion Bank Chambers 1878–1879

HISTORICAL ATLAS OF CANADA

PRESIDENCIES AND DIRECTORSHIPS OF TORONTO'S PLUTOCRATS

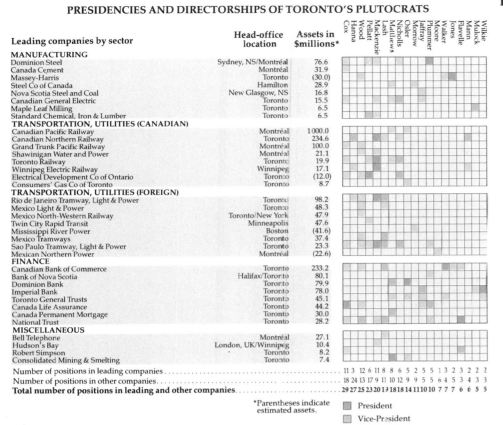

Leading companies by sector	Head-office location	Assets in $millions*	Cox	Wood	Hanna	Pellatt	Mackenzie	Lash	Matthews	Nicholls	Osler	Jaffray	Morrow	Moore	Walker	Flavelle	Jones	Plummer	Mulock	Mann	Mann	Wilkie
MANUFACTURING																					
Dominion Steel	Sydney, NS/Montréal	76.6																				
Canada Cement	Montréal	31.9																				
Massey-Harris	Toronto	(30.0)																				
Steel Co of Canada	Hamilton	28.9																				
Nova Scotia Steel and Coal	New Glasgow, NS	16.8																				
Canadian General Electric	Toronto	15.5																				
Maple Leaf Milling	Toronto	6.5																				
Standard Chemical, Iron & Lumber	Toronto	6.5																				
TRANSPORTATION, UTILITIES (CANADIAN)																						
Canadian Pacific Railway	Montréal	1000.0																				
Canadian Northern Railway	Toronto	234.6																				
Grand Trunk Pacific Railway	Montréal	100.0																				
Shawinigan Water and Power	Montréal	21.1																				
Toronto Railway	Toronto	19.9																				
Winnipeg Electric Railway	Winnipeg	17.1																				
Electrical Development Co of Ontario	Toronto	(12.0)																				
Consumers' Gas Co of Toronto	Toronto	8.7																				
TRANSPORTATION, UTILITIES (FOREIGN)																						
Rio de Janeiro Tramway, Light & Power	Toronto	98.2																				
Mexico Light & Power	Toronto	48.3																				
Mexico North-Western Railway	Toronto/New York	47.9																				
Twin City Rapid Transit	Minneapolis	47.6																				
Mississippi River Power	Boston	(41.6)																				
Mexico Tramways	Toronto	37.4																				
Sao Paulo Tramway, Light & Power	Toronto	23.3																				
Mexican Northern Power	Montréal	(22.6)																				
FINANCE																						
Canadian Bank of Commerce	Toronto	233.2																				
Bank of Nova Scotia	Halifax/Toronto	80.1																				
Dominion Bank	Toronto	79.9																				
Imperial Bank	Toronto	78.0																				
Toronto General Trusts	Toronto	45.1																				
Canada Life Assurance	Toronto	44.2																				
Canada Permanent Mortgage	Toronto	30.0																				
National Trust	Toronto	28.2																				
MISCELLANEOUS																						
Bell Telephone	Montréal	27.1																				
Hudson's Bay	London, UK/Winnipeg	10.4																				
Robert Simpson	Toronto	8.2																				
Consolidated Mining & Smelting	Toronto	7.4																				

Number of positions in leading companies 11 3 12 6 11 8 8 6 5 2 5 5 1 3 2 3 2 2 2

Number of positions in other companies 18 24 13 17 9 11 10 12 9 9 5 5 6 4 5 3 4 3 3

Total number of positions in leading and other companies. 29 27 25 23 20 19 18 18 14 11 10 10 7 7 7 6 6 5 5

Parentheses indicate estimated assets.

- ▓ President
- ▒ Vice-President
- □ Director

TORONTO 'PLUTOCRATS'

Identified by the *Grain Growers' Guide*, 1913 (see end notes)

INTERLOCKING DIRECTORSHIPS
Companies with Toronto plutocrats as president

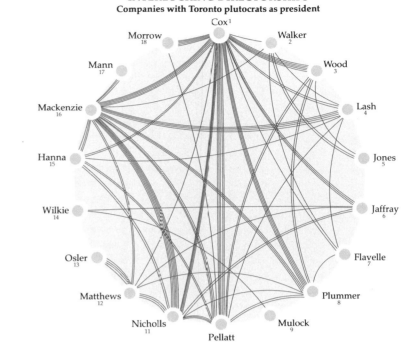

Red connecting lines indicate number of interlocking directorships. Red numbers refer to locations of offices of plutocrats on the map below left. Messrs Jones, Flavelle, and Nichols were located outside this core area. Moore (whose office was located at #19) is not shown in the diagram; see end notes.

Toronto-based enterprises became increasingly important nationally during the first decades of the 20th century. Toronto banks and insurance companies grew in stature, sometimes through acquisitions and mergers, sometimes by relocation from other cities to Toronto, to profit from new economic activity in Central Canada, the West, and the United States. A small group of Toronto entrepreneurs created new companies to develop utilities, streetcar systems, railway lines, real estate, and mines across the nation and beyond. Many of these 'plutocrats' sat as directors on one another's boards.

New forms of enterprises and the concentration of business in Toronto created the need for stockbrokers, lawyers, accountants, and other services ancillary to corporate capitalism. Demand for office space led to new, taller buildings. The first structures over six storeys were built in the 1890s, and by 1928 there were more than 40 buildings over six storeys high. The core of the office district moved westward along King Street to Yonge Street and its western limit reached Bay Street. A new city hall and court house at Bay and Queen added to the westward shift of the office district. The new office towers housed more than their names suggest: the Canadian Pacific Railway (CPR) and Dominion Bank buildings contained many legal, financial, and manufacturing firms as well as their primary occupants. The Canadian Bank of Commerce outgrew its 1890 head-office building by the 1920s and its new 32-storey tower, the tallest in the British Empire, anticipated further expansion of the company; most of the tower was rented out, and the bank's main branch and head office occupied only the first seven floors.

OFFICES OF COMPANY PRESIDENTS, 1913

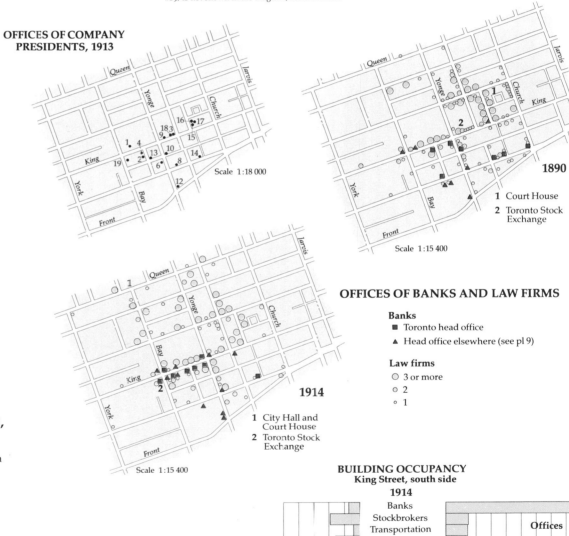

Scale 1:18 000

1 Court House
2 Toronto Stock Exchange

Scale 1:15 400

1890

1914

1 City Hall and Court House
2 Toronto Stock Exchange

Scale 1:15 400

OFFICES OF BANKS AND LAW FIRMS

Banks
- ■ Toronto head office
- ▲ Head office elsewhere (see pl 9)

Law firms
- ◎ 3 or more
- ◦ 2
- ∘ 1

KING STREET, SOUTH SIDE, 1890 AND 1914

Building name and date of construction indicated where possible

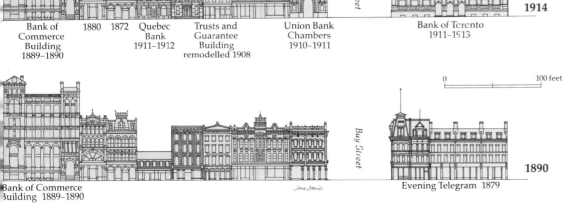

Bank of Nova Scotia 1902–1904

Colonial Building 1880

Bay Street

WEST

1914

Bank of Commerce Building 1889–1890 | 1880 | 1872 | Quebec Bank 1911–1912 | Trusts and Guarantee Building remodelled 1908 | Union Bank Chambers 1910–1911 | Bank of Toronto 1911–1913

Bay Street

1890

Bank of Commerce Building 1889–1890

Evening Telegram 1879

0   100 feet

BUILDING OCCUPANCY
King Street, south side

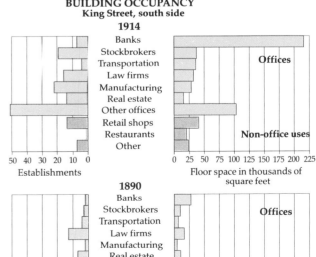

1914

Banks
Stockbrokers
Transportation
Law firms
Manufacturing
Real estate
Other offices
Retail shops
Restaurants
Other

Offices

Non-office uses

50 40 30 20 10 0
Establishments

0 25 50 75 100 125 150 175 200 225
Floor space in thousands of square feet

1890

Banks
Stockbrokers
Transportation
Law firms
Manufacturing
Real estate
Other offices
Retail shops
Restaurants
Other

Offices

Non-office uses

50 40 30 20 10 0

0 25 50 75 100 125 150 175 200 225

CONCISE EDITION

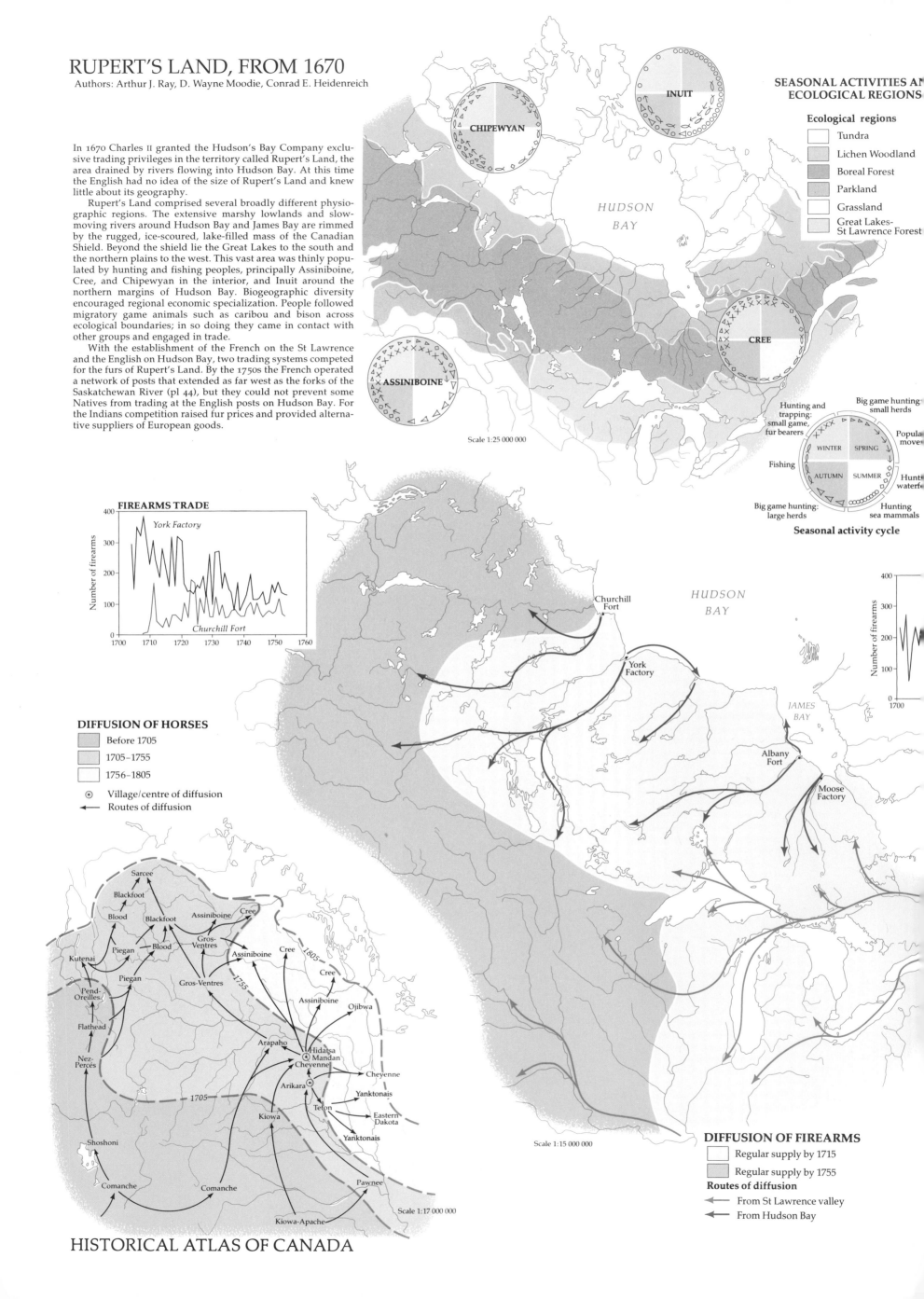

RUPERT'S LAND, FROM 1670

Authors: Arthur J. Ray, D. Wayne Moodie, Conrad E. Heidenreich

In 1670 Charles II granted the Hudson's Bay Company exclusive trading privileges in the territory called Rupert's Land, the area drained by rivers flowing into Hudson Bay. At this time the English had no idea of the size of Rupert's Land and knew little about its geography.

Rupert's Land comprised several broadly different physiographic regions. The extensive marshy lowlands and slow-moving rivers around Hudson Bay and James Bay are rimmed by the rugged, ice-scoured, lake-filled mass of the Canadian Shield. Beyond the shield lie the Great Lakes to the south and the northern plains to the west. This vast area was thinly populated by hunting and fishing peoples, principally Assiniboine, Cree, and Chipewyan in the interior, and Inuit around the northern margins of Hudson Bay. Biogeographic diversity encouraged regional economic specialization. People followed migratory game animals such as caribou and bison across ecological boundaries; in so doing they came in contact with other groups and engaged in trade.

With the establishment of the French on the St Lawrence and the English on Hudson Bay, two trading systems competed for the furs of Rupert's Land. By the 1750s the French operated a network of posts that extended as far west as the forks of the Saskatchewan River (pl 44), but they could not prevent some Natives from trading at the English posts on Hudson Bay. For the Indians competition raised fur prices and provided alternative suppliers of European goods.

SEASONAL ACTIVITIES AND ECOLOGICAL REGIONS

Ecological regions

- Tundra
- Lichen Woodland
- Boreal Forest
- Parkland
- Grassland
- Great Lakes-St Lawrence Forest

CHIPEWYAN

INUIT

CREE

ASSINIBOINE

Scale 1:25 000 000

Seasonal activity cycle

Hunting and trapping: small game, fur bearers

Big game hunting: small herds

Population movements

Fishing

WINTER | SPRING
AUTUMN | SUMMER

Hunting waterfowl

Big game hunting: large herds

Hunting sea mammals

FIREARMS TRADE

York Factory

Churchill Fort

Number of firearms

400 — 300 — 200 — 100 — 0

1700 1710 1720 1730 1740 1750 1760

DIFFUSION OF HORSES

- Before 1705
- 1705–1755
- 1756–1805
- ⊙ Village/centre of diffusion
- ← Routes of diffusion

Sarcee
Blackfoot
Blood
Blackfoot
Assiniboine
Cree
Piegan
Blood
Gros-Ventres
Kutenai
Piegan
Assiniboine
Cree
Pend-Oreilles
Gros-Ventres
Cree
Flathead
Assiniboine
Ojibwa
Nez-Percés
Arapaho
Hidatsa
Mandan
Cheyenne
Cheyenne
Arikara
Yanktonais
Kiowa
Teton
Eastern Dakota
Yanktonais
Shoshoni
Comanche
Comanche
Pawnee
Kiowa-Apache

1805
1755
1705

Scale 1:17 000 000

HUDSON BAY

Churchill Fort

York Factory

JAMES BAY

Albany Fort

Moose Factory

Number of firearms

400 — 300 — 200 — 100 — 0

1700

Scale 1:15 000 000

DIFFUSION OF FIREARMS

- Regular supply by 1715
- Regular supply by 1755

Routes of diffusion
- ← From St Lawrence valley
- ← From Hudson Bay

HISTORICAL ATLAS OF CANADA

ECONOMIC REGIONS, ca 1670

- Barren-ground caribou
- Fish, woodland caribou, waterfowl
- Moose, woodland caribou, fish
- Fish, moose, waterfowl
- Fish, moose, wild rice, waterfowl
- Bison, moose, red deer
- Bison

HUDSON BAY

Scale 1:25 000 000

NATIVE GROUPS, ca 1670

- Assiniboine
- Chipewyan
- Cree
- Inuit

General direction of population movement

- ⇠ Spring or summer
- ← Fall

FIREARMS TRADE

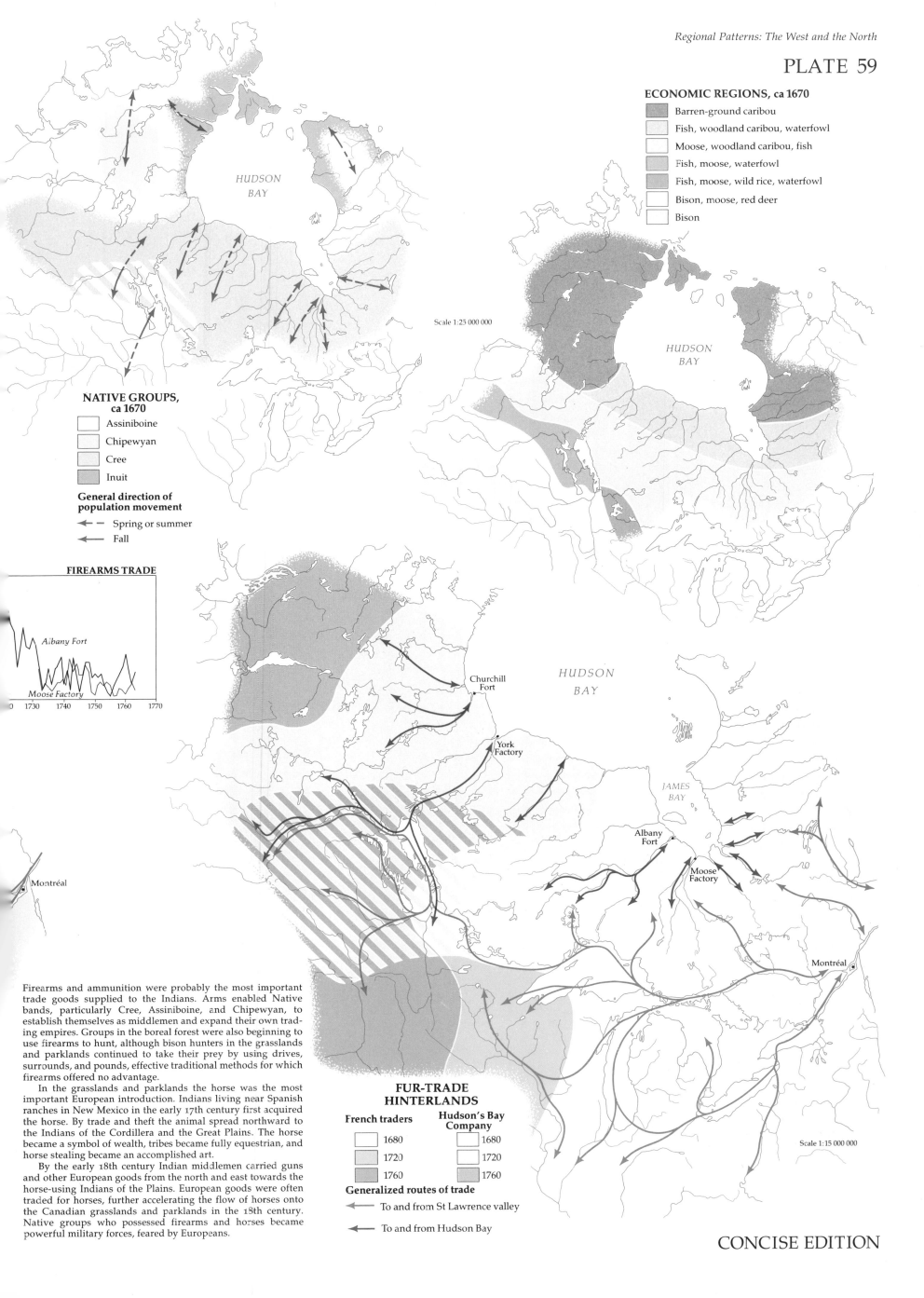

Albany Fort

Moose Factory

1730   1740   1750   1760   1770

HUDSON BAY

JAMES BAY

Churchill Fort

York Factory

Albany Fort

Moose Factory

Montréal

Montréal

Firearms and ammunition were probably the most important trade goods supplied to the Indians. Arms enabled Native bands, particularly Cree, Assiniboine, and Chipewyan, to establish themselves as middlemen and expand their own trading empires. Groups in the boreal forest were also beginning to use firearms to hunt, although bison hunters in the grasslands and parklands continued to take their prey by using drives, surrounds, and pounds, effective traditional methods for which firearms offered no advantage.

In the grasslands and parklands the horse was the most important European introduction. Indians living near Spanish ranches in New Mexico in the early 17th century first acquired the horse. By trade and theft the animal spread northward to the Indians of the Cordillera and the Great Plains. The horse became a symbol of wealth, tribes became fully equestrian, and horse stealing became an accomplished art.

By the early 18th century Indian middlemen carried guns and other European goods from the north and east towards the horse-using Indians of the Plains. European goods were often traded for horses, further accelerating the flow of horses onto the Canadian grasslands and parklands in the 18th century. Native groups who possessed firearms and horses became powerful military forces, feared by Europeans.

FUR-TRADE HINTERLANDS

French traders		Hudson's Bay Company	
	1680		1680
	1720		1720
	1760		1760

Generalized routes of trade

- → To and from St Lawrence valley
- → To and from Hudson Bay

Scale 1:15 000 000

CONCISE EDITION

FUR TRADE IN THE INTERIOR, 1760–1825

Authors: D. Wayne Moodie, Victor P. Lytwyn, Barry Kaye, Arthur J. Ray

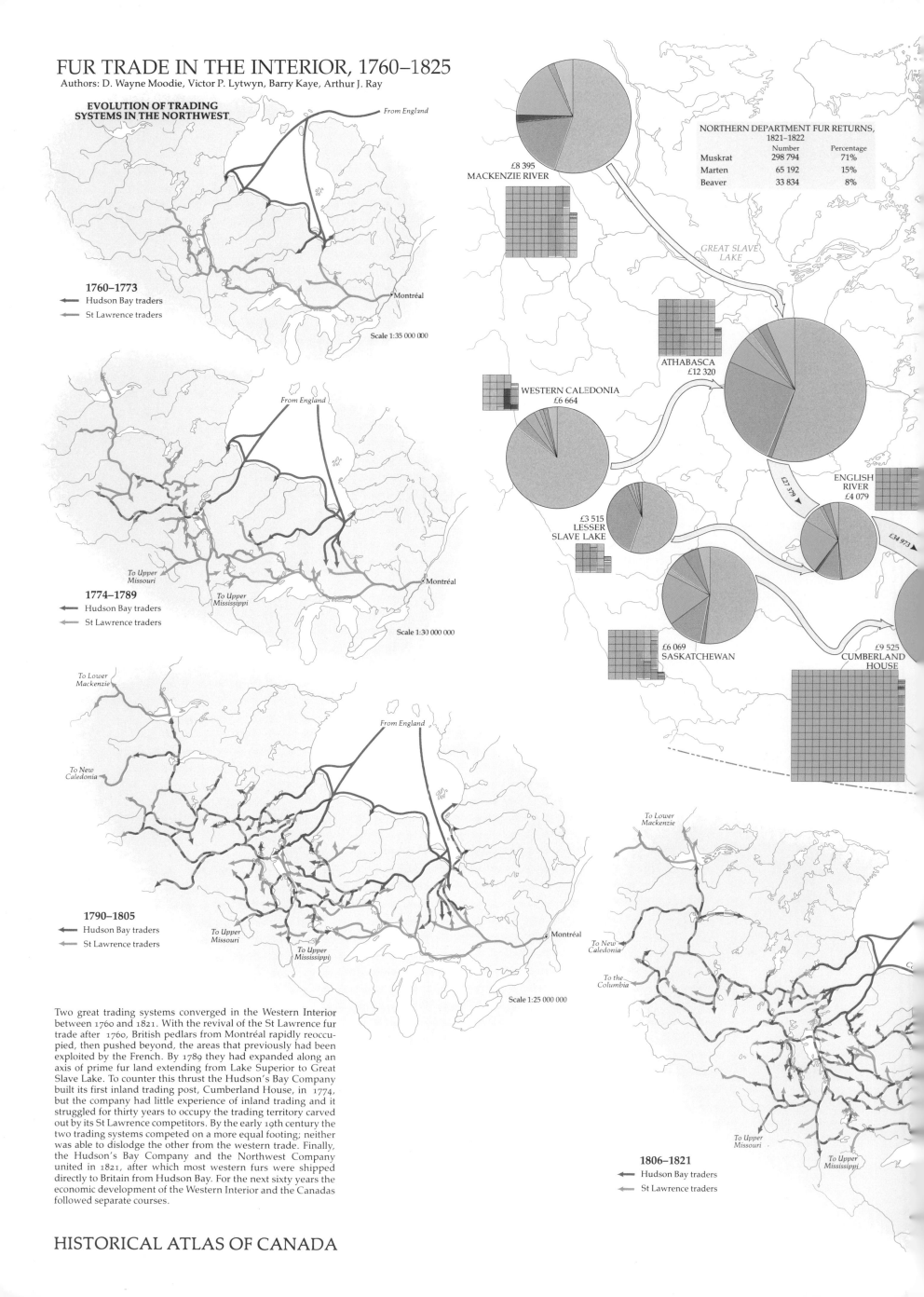

EVOLUTION OF TRADING SYSTEMS IN THE NORTHWEST

1760–1773
→ Hudson Bay traders
→ St Lawrence traders

From England

Montréal

Scale 1:35 000 000

1774–1789
→ Hudson Bay traders
→ St Lawrence traders

From England

To Upper Missouri
To Upper Mississippi
Montréal

Scale 1:30 000 000

1790–1805
→ Hudson Bay traders
→ St Lawrence traders

To Lower Mackenzie
To New Caledonia
From England
To Upper Missouri
To Upper Mississippi
Montréal

Scale 1:25 000 000

1806–1821
→ Hudson Bay traders
→ St Lawrence traders

To Lower Mackenzie
To New Caledonia
To the Columbia
To Upper Missouri
To Upper Mississippi

NORTHERN DEPARTMENT FUR RETURNS, 1821–1822		
	Number	Percentage
Muskrat	298 794	71%
Marten	65 192	15%
Beaver	33 834	8%

£8 395
MACKENZIE RIVER

GREAT SLAVE LAKE

ATHABASCA
£12 320

WESTERN CALEDONIA
£6 664

£3 515
LESSER SLAVE LAKE

£6 069
SASKATCHEWAN

ENGLISH RIVER
£4 079

£34 973

£9 525
CUMBERLAND HOUSE

Two great trading systems converged in the Western Interior between 1760 and 1821. With the revival of the St Lawrence fur trade after 1760, British pedlars from Montréal rapidly reoccupied, then pushed beyond, the areas that previously had been exploited by the French. By 1789 they had expanded along an axis of prime fur land extending from Lake Superior to Great Slave Lake. To counter this thrust the Hudson's Bay Company built its first inland trading post, Cumberland House, in 1774, but the company had little experience of inland trading and it struggled for thirty years to occupy the trading territory carved out by its St Lawrence competitors. By the early 19th century the two trading systems competed on a more equal footing; neither was able to dislodge the other from the western trade. Finally, the Hudson's Bay Company and the Northwest Company united in 1821, after which most western furs were shipped directly to Britain from Hudson Bay. For the next sixty years the economic development of the Western Interior and the Canadas followed separate courses.

HISTORICAL ATLAS OF CANADA

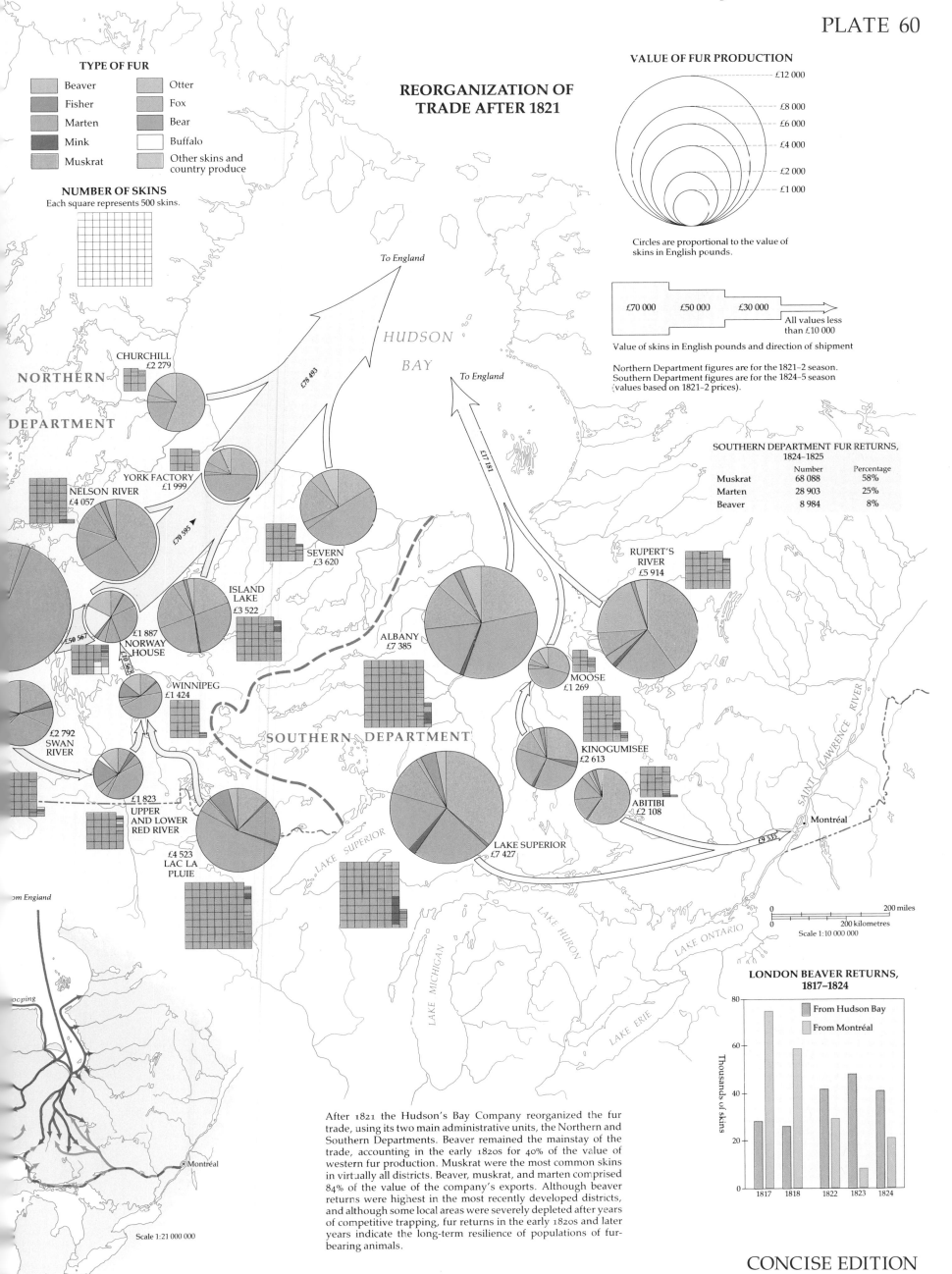

REORGANIZATION OF TRADE AFTER 1821

TYPE OF FUR

Beaver
Fisher
Marten
Mink
Muskrat

Otter
Fox
Bear
Buffalo
Other skins and country produce

NUMBER OF SKINS
Each square represents 500 skins.

VALUE OF FUR PRODUCTION

£12 000
£8 000
£6 000
£4 000
£2 000
£1 000

Circles are proportional to the value of skins in English pounds.

£70 000   £50 000   £30 000
All values less than £10 000

Value of skins in English pounds and direction of shipment

Northern Department figures are for the 1821–2 season.
Southern Department figures are for the 1824–5 season
(values based on 1821–2 prices).

To England

HUDSON BAY

To England

NORTHERN
DEPARTMENT

CHURCHILL
£2 279

£78 493

YORK FACTORY
£1 999

NELSON RIVER
£4 057

£70 595

SEVERN
£3 620

ISLAND LAKE
£3 522

£1 887
NORWAY HOUSE

£50 567

£10 562

WINNIPEG
£1 424

ALBANY
£7 385

£2 792
SWAN RIVER

SOUTHERN DEPARTMENT

£1 823
UPPER AND LOWER RED RIVER

£4 523
LAC LA PLUIE

£17 181

RUPERT'S RIVER
£5 914

MOOSE
£1 269

KINOGUMISEE
£2 613

ABITIBI
£2 108

LAKE SUPERIOR
£7 427

Montréal

£9 535

SAINT LAWRENCE RIVER

SOUTHERN DEPARTMENT FUR RETURNS, 1824–1825

	Number	Percentage
Muskrat	68 088	58%
Marten	28 903	25%
Beaver	8 984	8%

LAKE SUPERIOR
LAKE MICHIGAN
LAKE HURON
LAKE ONTARIO
LAKE ERIE

0   200 miles
0   200 kilometres
Scale 1:10 000 000

om England
ooping
Montréal
Scale 1:21 000 000

After 1821 the Hudson's Bay Company reorganized the fur trade, using its two main administrative units, the Northern and Southern Departments. Beaver remained the mainstay of the trade, accounting in the early 1820s for 40% of the value of western fur production. Muskrat were the most common skins in virtually all districts. Beaver, muskrat, and marten comprised 84% of the value of the company's exports. Although beaver returns were highest in the most recently developed districts, and although some local areas were severely depleted after years of competitive trapping, fur returns in the early 1820s and later years indicate the long-term resilience of populations of fur-bearing animals.

LONDON BEAVER RETURNS, 1817–1824

From Hudson Bay
From Montréal

Thousands of skins

80
60
40
20
0

1817   1818   1822   1823   1824

CONCISE EDITION

HOMESTEADING AND AGRICULTURE IN THE WEST, 1872–1891

Authors: James M. Richtik, Don Measner

By the 1870s a new kind of settlement had appeared in the West, replacing the old order based on fur-trading posts and river-lot farms. The new emphasis was on the use of land for commercial agriculture. By the early 1870s most of Manitoba had been surveyed into townships six miles square (9.6 km²) and sections one mile square (1.6 km²). Hand in hand with the survey went the granting of homesteads by the Canadian government. The homesteader was required to pay a fee of $10 for entry and to maintain a three-year period of occupancy and cultivation to qualify for a patent.

In the early 1870s almost all homesteaders took land as near Winnipeg as availability permitted, with the largest concentration on silty soils south of Lake Manitoba. By 1880 the homesteading frontier was just reaching the present western boundary of Manitoba, with the main westward thrust along proposed railway routes near the American border and north of the Assiniboine River. The greatest expansion occurred in the early 1880s when settlement followed the proposed railway routes into Saskatchewan, particularly extending onto the prairie along the transcontinental route, as finally approved, through Regina.

The settlement nodes of 1884 served as foci for further settlement. In spite of the large number of homestead entries, the only new areas opened up were along the transcontinental railway north of Cypress Hills, along the new railway line north of Calgary, and in the Lethbridge coal-mining area.

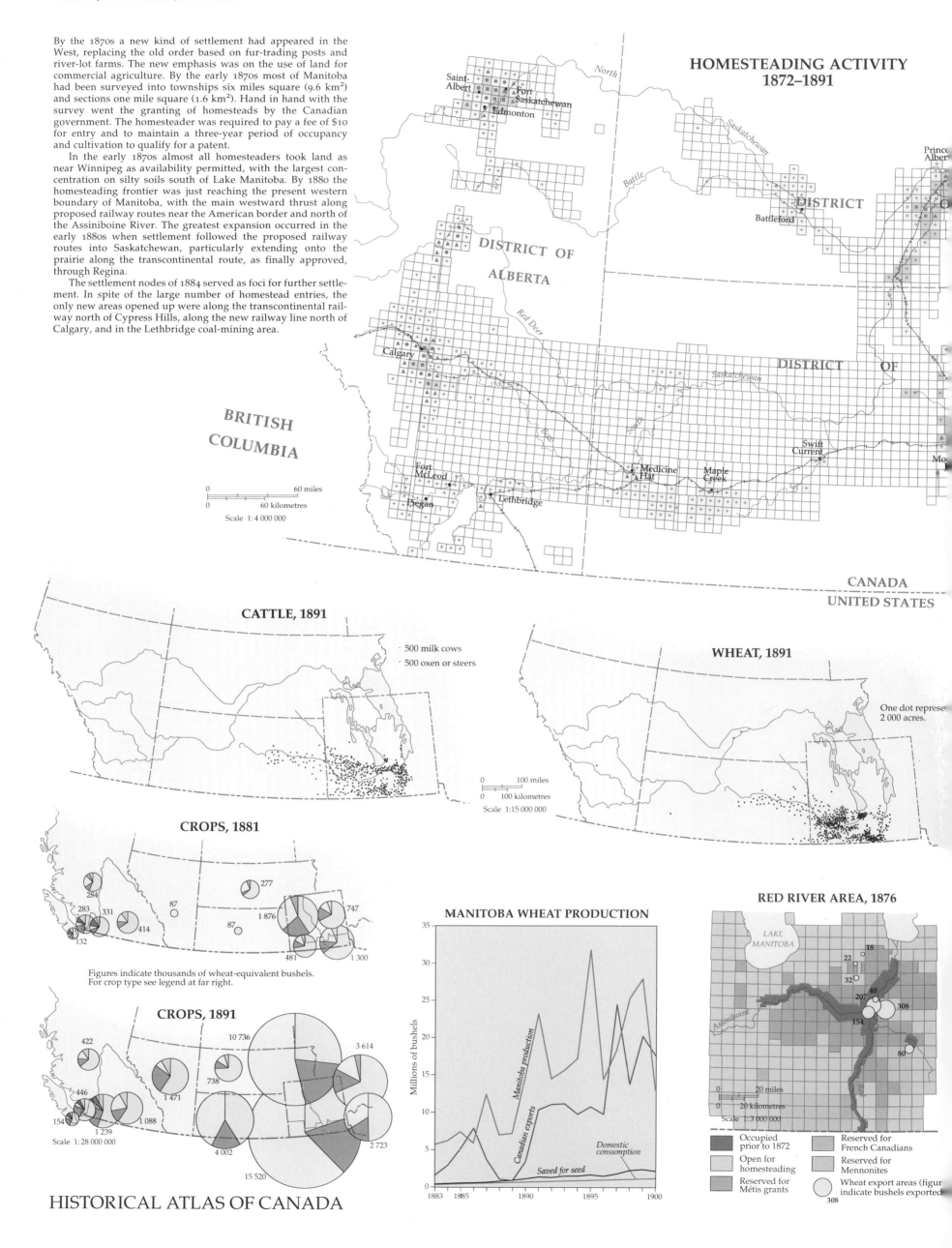

HOMESTEADING ACTIVITY 1872–1891

Scale 1:4 000 000

CATTLE, 1891

· 500 milk cows
· 500 oxen or steers

Scale 1:15 000 000

WHEAT, 1891

One dot represents 2 000 acres.

CROPS, 1881

Figures indicate thousands of wheat-equivalent bushels.
For crop type see legend at far right.

CROPS, 1891

Scale 1:28 000 000

MANITOBA WHEAT PRODUCTION

Manitoba production
Canadian exports
Domestic consumption
Saved for seed

Millions of bushels

RED RIVER AREA, 1876

Scale 1:3 000 000

Occupied prior to 1872
Open for homesteading
Reserved for Métis grants
Reserved for French Canadians
Reserved for Mennonites
Wheat export areas (figures indicate bushels exported)

HISTORICAL ATLAS OF CANADA

Date of initial township settlement

- 1872–1876
- 1877–1880
- 1881–1884
- 1885–1891
- Unoccupied in 1891

Percentage of township homesteaded,* 1891

- ■ More than 74%
- ● 50–74
- ▲ 25–49
- + 0–24

Period of railway construction

- +++ 1877–1880
- ++ 1881–1884
- +↓ 1885–1891

1891 surveyed township lines are shown.

* In each township 50% of the land was available for homesteading. The amounts shown above are the percentages of the land available for homesteading which had been opened for settlement.

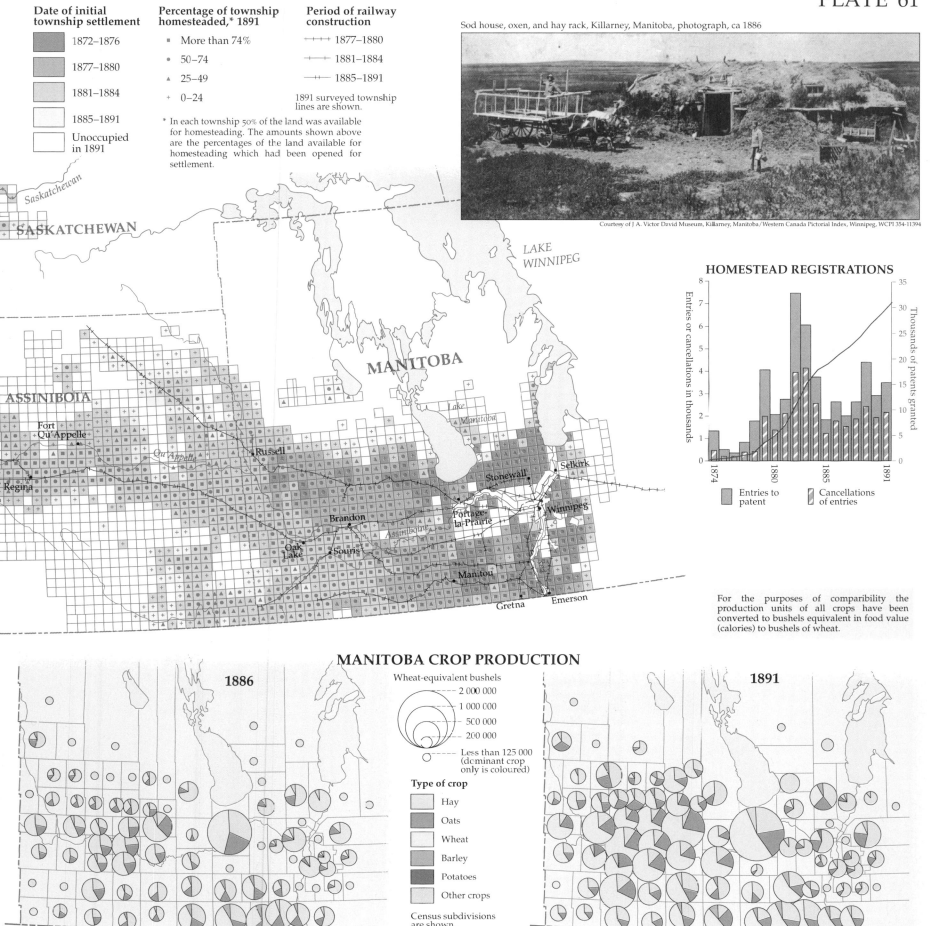

Sod house, oxen, and hay rack, Killarney, Manitoba, photograph, ca 1886

Courtesy of J A. Victor David Museum, Killarney, Manitoba / Western Canada Pictorial Index, Winnipeg, WCPI 354-11394

HOMESTEAD REGISTRATIONS

- Entries to patent
- Cancellations of entries

For the purposes of comparibility the production units of all crops have been converted to bushels equivalent in food value (calories) to bushels of wheat.

MANITOBA CROP PRODUCTION

1886   **1891**

Wheat-equivalent bushels

- 2 000 000
- 1 000 000
- 500 000
- 200 000
- ○ Less than 125 000 (dominant crop only is coloured)

Type of crop

- Hay
- Oats
- Wheat
- Barley
- Potatoes
- Other crops

Census subdivisions are shown.

Scale 1: 4 000 000   Scale 1: 4 000 000

ELEVATOR STORAGE AND WHEAT SHIPMENTS, 1891

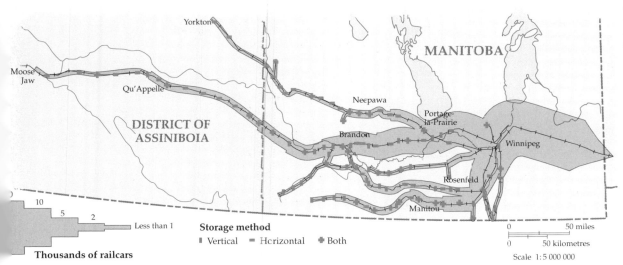

Thousands of railcars

Storage method

- ▮ Vertical
- ▬ Horizontal
- ✦ Both

0   50 miles

0   50 kilometres

Scale 1: 5 000 000

The expansion of the occupied area during the 1880s coincided with increases in crop and animal production, setting the stage for the massive increases to follow. Before 1891 crop production was concentrated in Manitoba, the area first settled. The emphasis was on wheat as the export crop, with smaller acreages devoted to animal feeds such as hay and oats for horses and cattle for the potential export of beef and dairy products. Cattle distributions in 1891 also point to a rising beef-cattle industry on the ranching frontier in southern Alberta.

Wheat acreage continued to increase in the late 1880s, particularly in the heavily settled districts of Manitoba and along railway lines. Grain-elevator capacity to handle the increased production was another factor favouring wheat growing, and by 1891 an economy based on vertical elevators had spread throughout Manitoba and to the larger centres west along the transcontinental railway. The export of wheat in 1876 from the area around Winnipeg established the reputation of Manitoba wheat and began the process of making the prairies the bread basket of the empire. By 1891 significantly larger shipments of wheat were transported almost entirely through Winnipeg and eastward along the Canadian transcontinental railway to Lake Superior.

CONCISE EDITION

PEOPLING THE PRAIRIES, 1891–1931

Authors: William J. Carlyle, John C. Lehr, G.E. Mills (homesteaders' shelter)

The Canadian Prairies were seen as the Last Best West: their settlement marked the end of an era of agricultural settlement that had brought millions of homesteaders to the North American plains since the 1860s. At the margins of agriculture, in terms of both climate and soils, the Prairies could be settled only after effective seed types and transportation systems had been developed. Settlement followed the parkland belt northwest from Winnipeg towards Edmonton, and between Edmonton and Calgary, filling in the margins to the south and north in the 1920s. Land was surveyed into 160-acre parcels by the Dominion Lands Survey. The government and other agencies, including railroad companies, the Hudson's Bay Company, and land colonization companies, disposed of the land to settlers. Not all the land was appropriate for farming, and in many townships outmigration began during the 1920s.

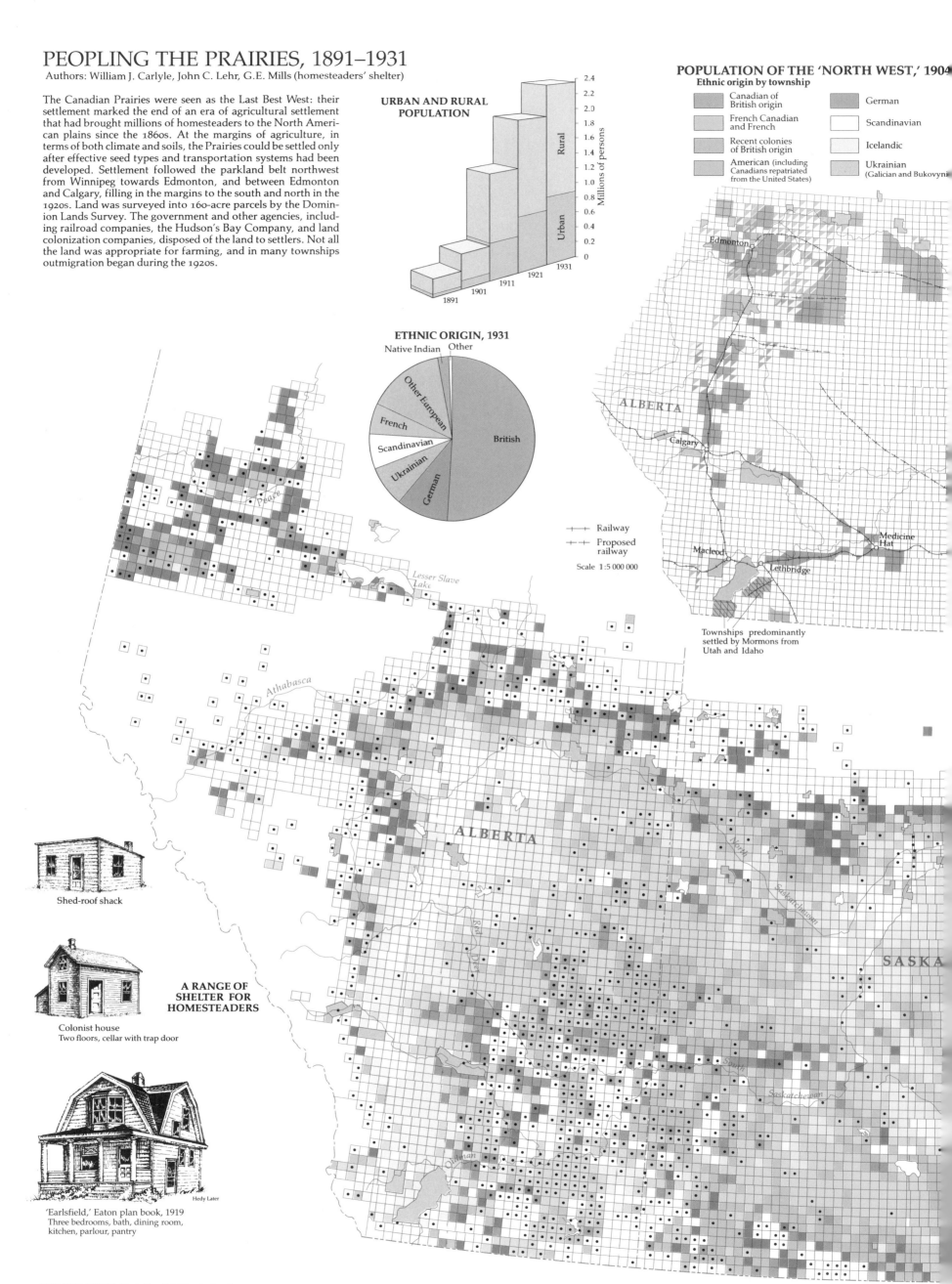

URBAN AND RURAL POPULATION

Millions of persons

2.4 2.2 2.0 1.8 1.6 1.4 1.2 1.0 0.8 0.6 0.4 0.2 0

Rural

Urban

1891 1901 1911 1921 1931

POPULATION OF THE 'NORTH WEST,' 1904
Ethnic origin by township

- Canadian of British origin
- French Canadian and French
- Recent colonies of British origin
- American (including Canadians repatriated from the United States)
- German
- Scandinavian
- Icelandic
- Ukrainian (Galician and Bukovynian)

Edmonton

ALBERTA

Calgary

Macleod

Medicine Hat

Lethbridge

Townships predominantly settled by Mormons from Utah and Idaho

ETHNIC ORIGIN, 1931

Native Indian   Other

Other European

French

Scandinavian

Ukrainian

German

British

Railway

Proposed railway

Scale 1:5 000 000

Peace

Lesser Slave Lake

Athabasca

ALBERTA

North Saskatchewan

Red Deer

Bow

SASKA...

Saskatchewan

South Saskatchewan

Oldman

Shed-roof shack

A RANGE OF SHELTER FOR HOMESTEADERS

Colonist house
Two floors, cellar with trap door

'Earlsfield,' Eaton plan book, 1919
Three bedrooms, bath, dining room, kitchen, parlour, pantry

Hedy Later

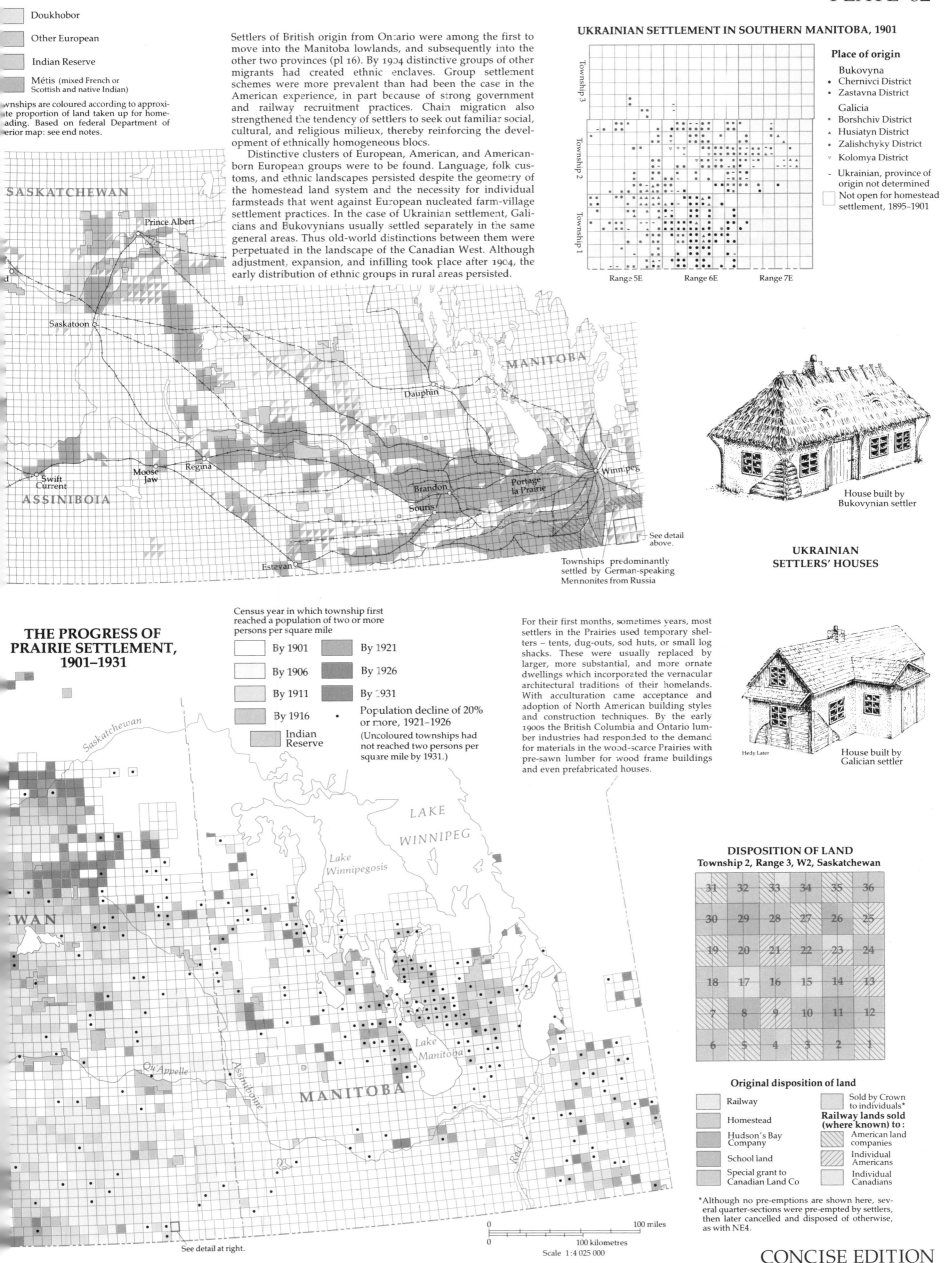

Legend (top left)

- Doukhobor
- Other European
- Indian Reserve
- Métis (mixed French or Scottish and native Indian)

ownships are coloured according to approxi-te proportion of land taken up for home-ading. Based on federal Department of erior map: see end notes.

Settlers of British origin from Ontario were among the first to move into the Manitoba lowlands, and subsequently into the other two provinces (pl 16). By 1904 distinctive groups of other migrants had created ethnic enclaves. Group settlement schemes were more prevalent than had been the case in the American experience, in part because of strong government and railway recruitment practices. Chain migration also strengthened the tendency of settlers to seek out familiar social, cultural, and religious milieux, thereby reinforcing the development of ethnically homogeneous blocs.

Distinctive clusters of European, American, and American-born European groups were to be found. Language, folk customs, and ethnic landscapes persisted despite the geometry of the homestead land system and the necessity for individual farmsteads that went against European nucleated farm-village settlement practices. In the case of Ukrainian settlement, Galicians and Bukovynians usually settled separately in the same general areas. Thus old-world distinctions between them were perpetuated in the landscape of the Canadian West. Although adjustment, expansion, and infilling took place after 1904, the early distribution of ethnic groups in rural areas persisted.

UKRAINIAN SETTLEMENT IN SOUTHERN MANITOBA, 1901

Place of origin

Bukovyna
- Chernivci District
- Zastavna District

Galicia
- Borshchiv District
- Husiatyn District
- Zalishchyky District
- Kolomya District

- Ukrainian, province of origin not determined

☐ Not open for homestead settlement, 1895–1901

Township 3 · Township 2 · Township 1

Range 5E · Range 6E · Range 7E

Townships predominantly settled by German-speaking Mennonites from Russia

See detail above.

House built by Bukovynian settler

UKRAINIAN SETTLERS' HOUSES

For their first months, sometimes years, most settlers in the Prairies used temporary shelters – tents, dug-outs, sod huts, or small log shacks. These were usually replaced by larger, more substantial, and more ornate dwellings which incorporated the vernacular architectural traditions of their homelands. With acculturation came acceptance and adoption of North American building styles and construction techniques. By the early 1900s the British Columbia and Ontario lumber industries had responded to the demand for materials in the wood-scarce Prairies with pre-sawn lumber for wood frame buildings and even prefabricated houses.

Hedy Later

House built by Galician settler

THE PROGRESS OF PRAIRIE SETTLEMENT, 1901–1931

Census year in which township first reached a population of two or more persons per square mile

- By 1901
- By 1906
- By 1911
- By 1916
- By 1921
- By 1926
- By 1931
- Indian Reserve
- • Population decline of 20% or more, 1921–1926

(Uncoloured townships had not reached two persons per square mile by 1931.)

LAKE WINNIPEG · Lake Winnipegosis · Lake Manitoba · MANITOBA · Qu'Appelle · Assiniboine · Red

0 — 100 miles
0 — 100 kilometres
Scale 1:4 025 000

See detail at right.

DISPOSITION OF LAND
Township 2, Range 3, W2, Saskatchewan

31	32	33	34	35	36
30	29	28	27	26	25
19	20	21	22	23	24
18	17	16	15	14	13
7	8	9	10	11	12
6	5	4	3	2	1

Original disposition of land

- Railway
- Homestead
- Hudson's Bay Company
- School land
- Special grant to Canadian Land Co
- Sold by Crown to individuals*

Railway lands sold (where known) to:
- American land companies
- Individual Americans
- Individual Canadians

*Although no pre-emptions are shown here, several quarter-sections were pre-empted by settlers, then later cancelled and disposed of otherwise, as with NE4.

Map labels (main settlement map)

SASKATCHEWAN · Prince Albert · Saskatoon · Swift Current · ASSINIBOIA · Moose Jaw · Regina · Estevan · Brandon · Souris · Portage la Prairie · Dauphin · MANITOBA · Winnipeg

DROUGHT AND DEPRESSION ON THE PRAIRIES, 1930s

Author : Murdo MacPherson

WHEAT RETURNS BY AREA, 1921–1929 AND 1930–1938

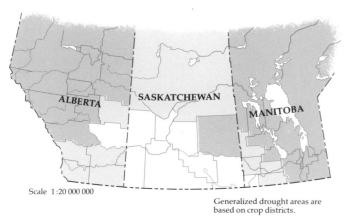

Scale 1:20 000 000

Generalized drought areas are based on crop districts.

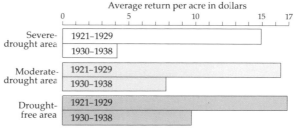

Average return per acre in dollars

	0	5	10	15	17
Severe-drought area	1921–1929				
	1930–1938				
Moderate-drought area	1921–1929				
	1930–1938				
Drought-free area	1921–1929				
	1930–1938				

The effect of economic depression alone is seen in the reduced returns for the drought-free area. The addition of severe drought rendered economic wheat production impossible. Little more than subsistence was possible in the moderate-drought area.

MARKET VALUE OF WHEAT

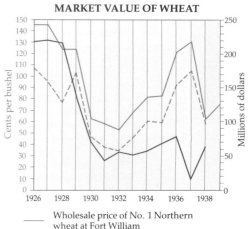

— Wholesale price of No. 1 Northern wheat at Fort William

--- Wheat price at local elevator in Saskatchewan

— Estimated value of wheat sold from Saskatchewan farms

INDEX OF NET FARM INCOME

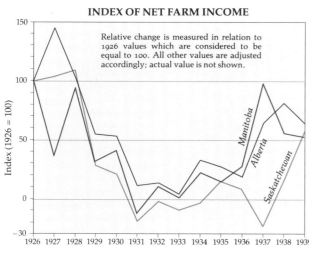

Relative change is measured in relation to 1926 values which are considered to be equal to 100. All other values are adjusted accordingly; actual value is not shown.

Index (1926 = 100)

Manitoba
Alberta
Saskatchewan

The combined effects of economic collapse and prolonged drought meant that the Depression was felt more severely in the Prairies than in any other part of Canada. Restriction of the world export grain market, as a result of newly erected tariff barriers and increased foreign production, reduced the value of Prairie wheat by almost one-third between 1929 and 1932. At the same time a series of droughts between 1930 and 1937 brought about complete or partial crop failures over extensive areas.

Although there was yearly variation in the effects of the drought across the Prairies, there was little respite for south-central Saskatchewan and the wheat crop there was severely and consistently devastated. Low wheat prices and low yields resulted in a steep drop in net farm income. In Saskatchewan per capita income plunged by 72% between 1928 and 1933 and returns from farming could not cover costs from 1931 to 1934 and again during the severe drought of 1937, when farmers in Manitoba and Alberta were well on the way to recovery. It was impossible for most Prairie farmers, and especially those in Saskatchewan, to survive without some form of government relief. Saskatchewan's relief payments reflected the severity of the drought in that province, and in the worst-hit areas entire municipalities were at times supported by relief.

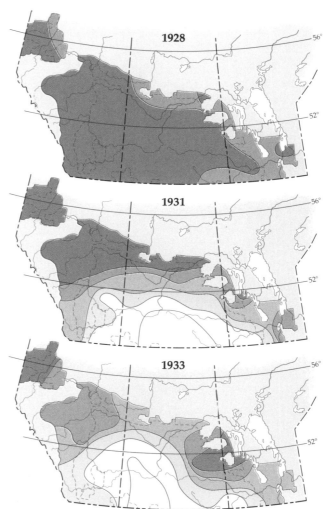

1928

1931

1933

Scale 1:22 000 000

WHEAT YIELDS

Bushels per acre

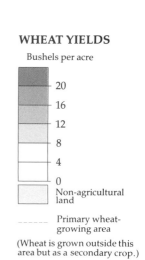

	20
	16
	12
	8
	4
	0
	Non-agricultural land

--- Primary wheat-growing area

(Wheat is grown outside this area but as a secondary crop.)

Wheat yields reflect the cumulative effect of various natural forces. Although deficiency of rainfall was undoubtedly the single most important factor, other problems such as a grasshopper plague in 1933 and rust disease in 1935 contributed to crop devastation. Destruction of crop and vegetation cover also left the land susceptible to soil erosion under the high prairie winds, and dust bowls further reduced productive capacity.

GOVERNMENT-ASSISTED SETTLE

FARM RELIEF, SASKATCHEWAN, 1929–1938

Saskatoon

Regina

Relief per occupied farm

	4 000 dollars or more
	3 000–3 999
	2 000–2 999
	1 000–1 999
	Less than 1 000

Based on rural municipalities

In Saskatchewan relief also involved the provision of working capital to enable farmers to regain their livelihood and self-sufficiency. This additional burden of agricultural aid accounted for the province's massive relief expenditure.

0		100 miles
0		100 kilometres

Scale 1:7 500 000

ORIGINS

· One settler family

○ Concentrations of settler families

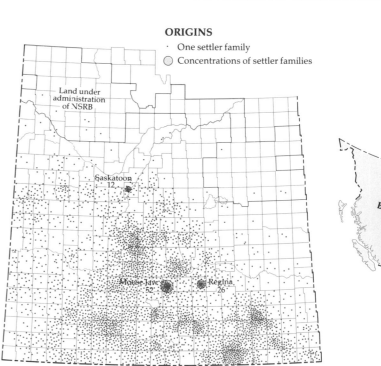

Land under administration of NSRB

Saskatoon
12

Mouse Jaw
52

Regina
26

BC

12

HISTORICAL ATLAS OF CANADA

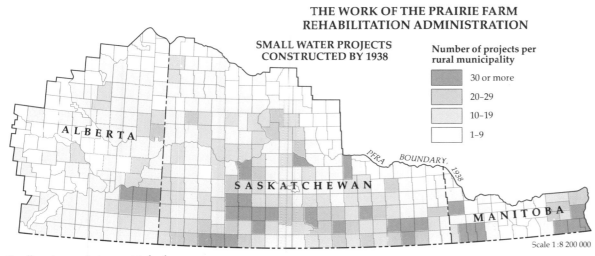

THE WORK OF THE PRAIRIE FARM REHABILITATION ADMINISTRATION

SMALL WATER PROJECTS CONSTRUCTED BY 1938

Number of projects per
rural municipality

30 or more
20–29
10–19
1–9

Scale 1:8 200 000

By the mid-1930s it appeared that large areas of the prairie would be lost to agriculture. In April 1935 the dominion government responded with the Prairie Farm Rehabilitation Act (PFRA) which established remedial programs. New agricultural practices, such as strip farming, cover cropping, and shelter belts were introduced. Submarginal crop land was fenced, re-grassed, and permanently converted into community pastures which counteracted the worst of the soil drifting. The limited water resources of the Prairies were more effectively utilized through development of water-holding and irrigation projects. The smaller of these water projects were most immediately beneficial to farmers while the larger and more expensive ones attempted to provide long-term solutions. In combination, water and pasture development enabled a diversification in Prairie agriculture through expanded livestock production.

Small water projects consisted of dugouts, ponds for watering stock, and small irrigation works constructed relatively cheaply on individual farms. Dugouts, on average 60 ft by 160 ft and 10 ft deep (18 m by 49 m and 3 m deep), were the most numerous and effective of these projects.

Large water projects were mainly concerned with irrigation and aided the resettlement of farmers. The management of community pastures was under federal jurisdiction but such an arrangement was resisted by Alberta until 1962.

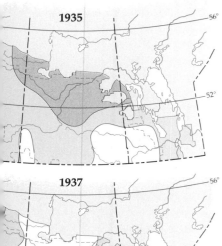

1935

1937

1939

SKATCHEWAN, 1930–1938

LARGE WATER PROJECTS AND COMMUNITY PASTURES COMPLETED BY 1940

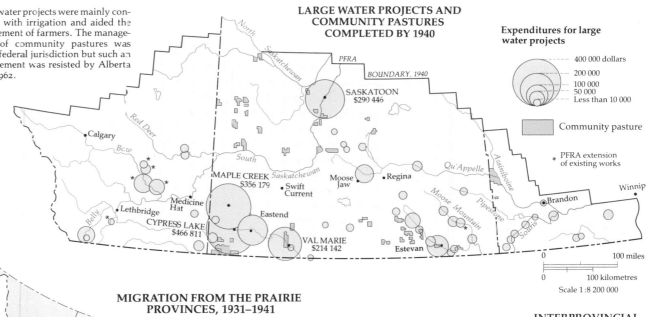

Expenditures for large
water projects

400 000 dollars
200 000
100 000
50 000
Less than 10 000

Community pasture

* PFRA extension
of existing works

Scale 1:8 200 000

MIGRATION FROM THE PRAIRIE PROVINCES, 1931–1941

Scale 1:40 000 000

For many farmers packing up and abandoning their farms was the only way they could respond to the catastrophe surrounding them. The Saskatchewan government established a program to assist farmers who wished to move out of the drought area to northern Crown lands and even outside the province. The northern forest fringes posed a new hardship to many settlers who had no experience of bush clearing or practising mixed agriculture on damp, heavy soils. As the decade progressed, more assisted settlers chose destinations outside Saskatchewan. Between 1931 and 1941 almost 200 000 people left the Prairie Provinces entirely, resulting in a net loss of population.

INTERPROVINCIAL MIGRATION, CANADA, 1931–1941

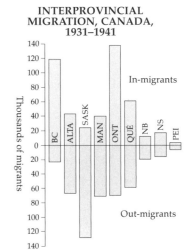

In-migrants

Out-migrants

Percentage change

50.0 or more
25.0–49.9
5.0–24.9
-4.9 – 4.9
-5.0 – -24.9
-25.0 or more

DESTINATIONS

• One settler family

Forest land not
open for settlement

SASKATCHEWAN

Scale 1:7 500 000

CHANGE IN DESTINATIONS

1930–1932
1933–1935 Within Saskatchewan
1936–1938 Outside Saskatchewan

0   500   1 000

Number of settler families

These settlers, assisted by the Saskatchewan Relief Commission and the Northern Settlers Re-Establishment Branch (NSRB), represented over one-third of the estimated 9 000 families who moved into the northern Crown lands during the Depression.

Scale 1:45 000 000

RURAL POPULATION CHANGE, SASKATCHEWAN, 1931–1941

Numbers show population
increase from 0.

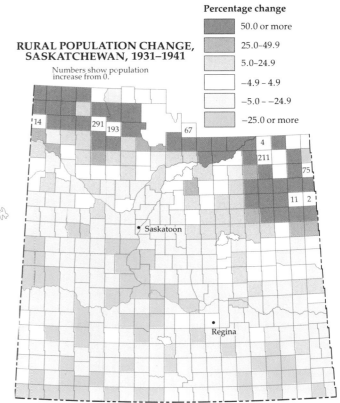

Saskatoon

Regina

GOLD AND POPULATION IN BRITISH COLUMBIA, 1858–1881

Authors: Robert Galois, R. Cole Harris

The extension of placer mining into the northern Cordillera transformed its social, economic, and political life. Over 30 000 people participated in the Fraser River gold rush of 1858, disrupting and displacing indigenous and fur-trade societies. The colony of British Columbia was established to impose administrative order on this sudden influx. After 1858 mining expanded further inland. Important discoveries were made in the Cariboo region late in 1860 and another major rush followed. With Williams Creek as the principal focus, population and gold production peaked in 1863. Despite other discoveries, including those at Kootenay in 1864, Big Bend in 1865, Omineca in 1870, and Cassiar in 1873, the Cariboo remained the heart of the mining economy.

Mining in the interior required construction of new transportation links with the coast. The Cariboo Wagon Road, from Yale to Barkerville, became the system's central artery, supplemented by trails to other areas. Placer mining also stimulated the growth of commercial and supply centres, primarily on the coast. Their relatively stable population contrasted with the highly mobile and overwhelmingly male societies of the mining areas.

REGIONAL POPULATIONS, 1861–1870

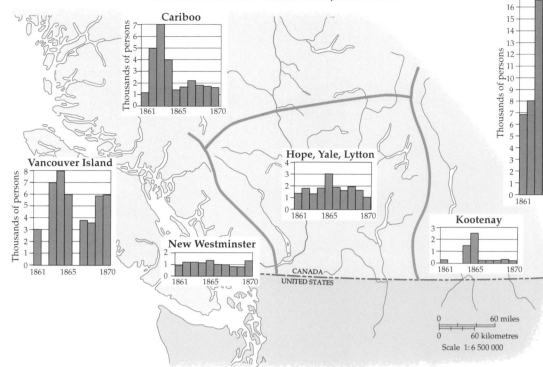

PLACER-GOLD PRODUCTION

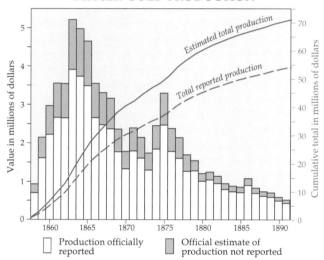

Production officially reported

Official estimate of production not reported

BRITISH COLUMBIA EXPORTS

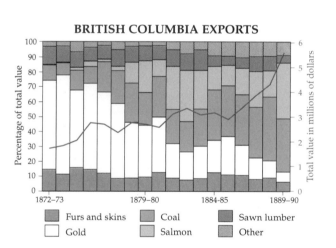

Furs and skins Coal Sawn lumber
Gold Salmon Other

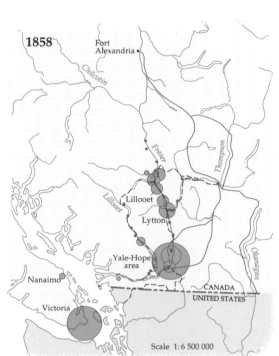

1858

1863

Scale 1:6 500 000

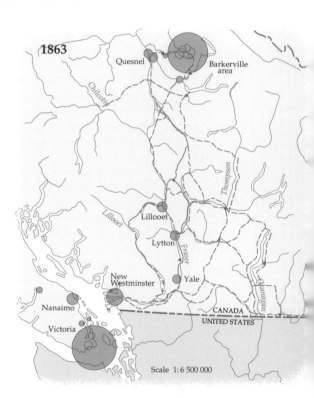

Cameronville, Williams Creek, BC, watercolour by E.M. Richardson, 1863–1865

Collection of Glenbow Museum, Calgary, Alberta, 98?

BARKERVILLE AREA, 1860–1876

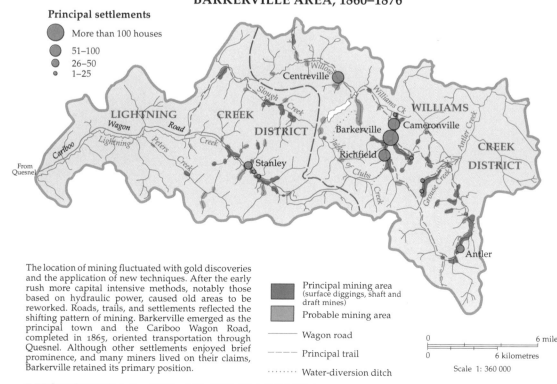

Principal settlements

More than 100 houses
51–100
26–50
1–25

The location of mining fluctuated with gold discoveries and the application of new techniques. After the early rush more capital intensive methods, notably those based on hydraulic power, caused old areas to be reworked. Roads, trails, and settlements reflected the shifting pattern of mining. Barkerville emerged as the principal town and the Cariboo Wagon Road, completed in 1865, oriented transportation through Quesnel. Although other settlements enjoyed brief prominence, and many miners lived on their claims, Barkerville retained its primary position.

Principal mining area
(surface diggings, shaft and draft mines)
Probable mining area

Wagon road
Principal trail
Water-diversion ditch

Scale 1:360 000

HISTORICAL ATLAS OF CANADA

PLACER MINING IN BRITISH COLUMBIA, 1876

	Cassiar	Lightning Creek	Williams Creek	Other Cariboo	Other BC
Production value (dollars)	464 000	224 000	137 000	83 000	73 000
Claims worked (number)	165	44	58	41	34
Hydraulic sites (number)	2	2	22	2	14
Value/worker (dollars)	370	355	245	315	260
Value/claim (dollars)	2 810	5 090	2 370	2 010	2 150
Workers/mine (non-native)	8	14	10	6	8

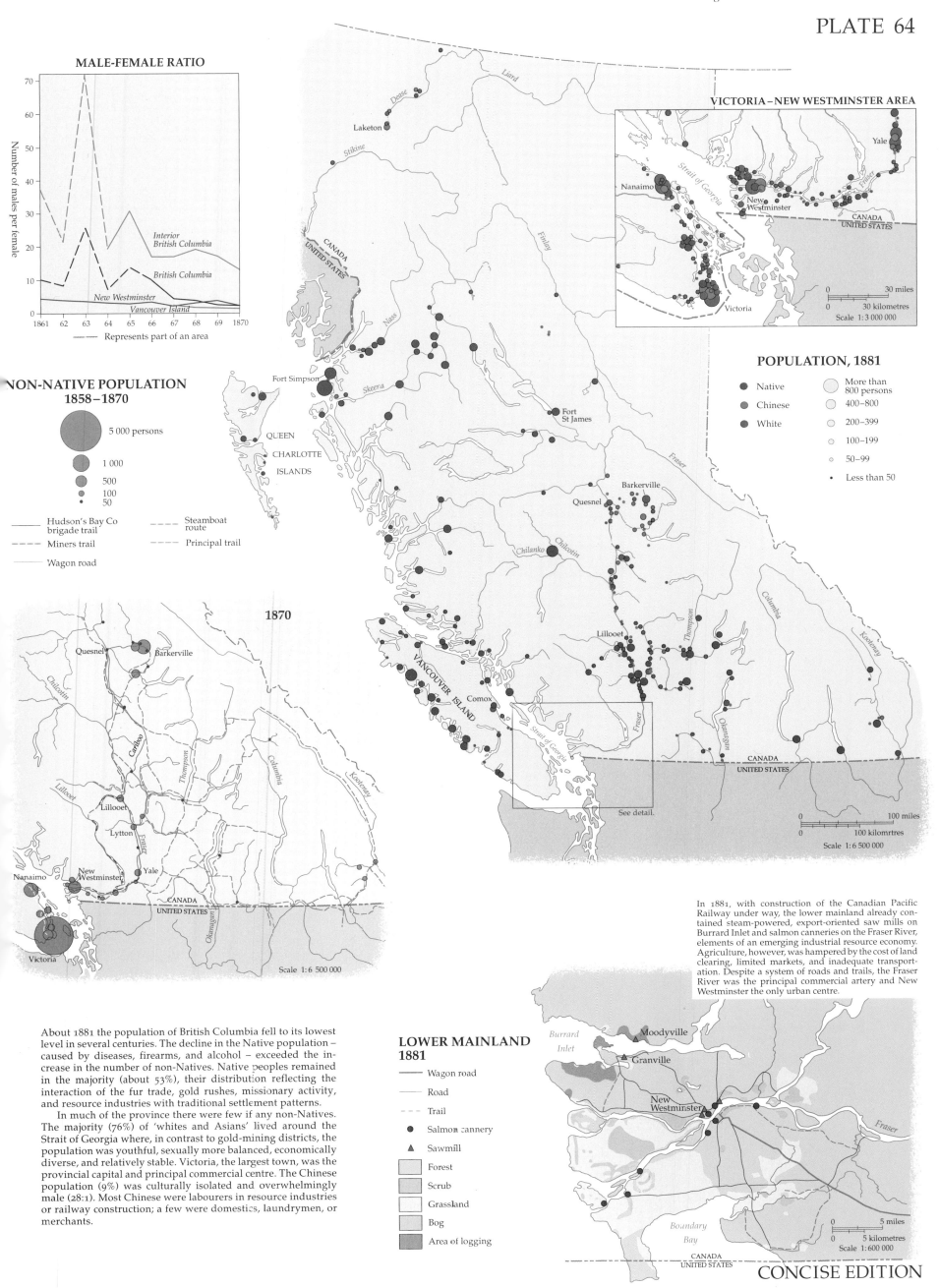

MALE-FEMALE RATIO

Number of males per female

Interior British Columbia

British Columbia

New Westminster

Vancouver Island

1861 62 63 64 65 66 67 68 69 1870

----- Represents part of an area

NON-NATIVE POPULATION 1858–1870

5 000 persons

1 000

500

100

50

—— Hudson's Bay Co brigade trail

- - - Miners trail

—— Wagon road

— — Steamboat route

— — Principal trail

1870

Quesnel Barkerville

Chilcotin *Cariboo* *Thompson* *Columbia*

Lillooet

Lillooet

Lytton

Fraser

Nanaimo

New Westminster Yale

Okanagan

Victoria

CANADA
UNITED STATES

Scale 1: 6 500 000

VICTORIA – NEW WESTMINSTER AREA

Yale

Strait of Georgia

Nanaimo

New Westminster

Fraser

CANADA
UNITED STATES

Victoria

0   30 miles

0   30 kilometres

Scale 1: 3 000 000

POPULATION, 1881

● Native

● Chinese

● White

○ More than 800 persons

○ 400–800

○ 200–399

○ 100–199

○ 50–99

• Less than 50

Liard

Dease

Laketon

Stikine

Finlay

CANADA
UNITED STATES

Ness

Fort Simpson

Skeena

Fort St James

QUEEN

CHARLOTTE

ISLANDS

Barkerville

Quesnel

Chilanko *Chilcotin*

Fraser

Lillooet

Thompson

Columbia

Kootenay

VANCOUVER ISLAND

Comox

Strait of Georgia

Fraser

Okanagan

See detail.

CANADA
UNITED STATES

0   100 miles

0   100 kilomrtres

Scale 1: 6 500 000

In 1881, with construction of the Canadian Pacific Railway under way, the lower mainland already contained steam-powered, export-oriented saw mills on Burrard Inlet and salmon canneries on the Fraser River, elements of an emerging industrial resource economy. Agriculture, however, was hampered by the cost of land clearing, limited markets, and inadequate transportation. Despite a system of roads and trails, the Fraser River was the principal commercial artery and New Westminster the only urban centre.

About 1881 the population of British Columbia fell to its lowest level in several centuries. The decline in the Native population – caused by diseases, firearms, and alcohol – exceeded the increase in the number of non-Natives. Native peoples remained in the majority (about 53%), their distribution reflecting the interaction of the fur trade, gold rushes, missionary activity, and resource industries with traditional settlement patterns.

In much of the province there were few if any non-Natives. The majority (76%) of 'whites and Asians' lived around the Strait of Georgia where, in contrast to gold-mining districts, the population was youthful, sexually more balanced, economically diverse, and relatively stable. Victoria, the largest town, was the provincial capital and principal commercial centre. The Chinese population (9%) was culturally isolated and overwhelmingly male (28:1). Most Chinese were labourers in resource industries or railway construction; a few were domestics, laundrymen, or merchants.

LOWER MAINLAND 1881

—— Wagon road

— Road

- - - Trail

● Salmon cannery

▲ Sawmill

Forest

Scrub

Grassland

Bog

Area of logging

Burrard Inlet

▲ Moodyville

▲ Granville

New Westminster

Fraser

Boundary Bay

CANADA
UNITED STATES

0   5 miles

0   5 kilometres

Scale 1: 600 000

CONCISE EDITION

BRITISH COLUMBIA RESOURCES, 1891–1928

Author: Robert Galois

Prior to the opening of the Canadian Pacific Railway (CPR) to Vancouver in 1887, the economy of British Columbia was dependent on maritime linkages, via the south coast, for the export of staple commodities (coal, gold, fish, fur, and lumber). On the mainland the Cariboo Wagon Road served as the axis of economic activity for placer mining and ranching.

In 1891 the geographic pattern of staples extraction had changed relatively little, but coal, lumber, and fish had assumed greater importance. Overseas markets still predominated. The railway constituted a new axis of development on the mainland but, as yet, the effective transportation corridor remained narrow; the lack of branch lines left much of the southern interior poorly integrated, hampering resource development, especially lode mining. Victoria, the provincial capital, remained the largest city but the emergence of Vancouver at the intersection of the rail and ocean transport systems signalled a new importance for the Lower Mainland as a processing and transportation centre.

VALUE OF RESOURCES

Contribution to provincial revenues

- Forestry
- Wild lands*
- Mining

*Tax on land including mining and forest lands

Percentage of BC revenue

Production in millions of dollars

Forestry · Mining · Fishery

1891 · 1901 · 1911 · 1921 · 1928

BRITISH COLUMBIA RESOURCES

Salmon canneries
Annual production in cases

- 30 000 or more
- 20 000–29 999
- 10 000–19 999
- 1–9 999

Sawmills and shingle mills
Capacity in thousands of board feet per day

- 200 or more
- 100–199
- 50–99
- 1–49
- No data available

Pulp and paper mills
Capacity in tons per day

- 400 or more
- 200–399
- 100–199
- 1–99

Metal (lode) mines
Annual production in tons of ore

- 100 000 or more
- 10 000–99 999
- 1 000–9 999
- 100–999

Coal mines
Annual production in tons

- 300 000 or more
- 150 000–299 999
- 50 000–149 999
- 100–49 999

Transportation

- Railway
- Railway under construction
- Steamboat service

1891 MAP ONLY

Placer mining
Annual value in dollars

- 50 000 or more
- Less than 50 000
- Lode-mining development

Transportation

- All-weather wagon road
- Coastal passenger service

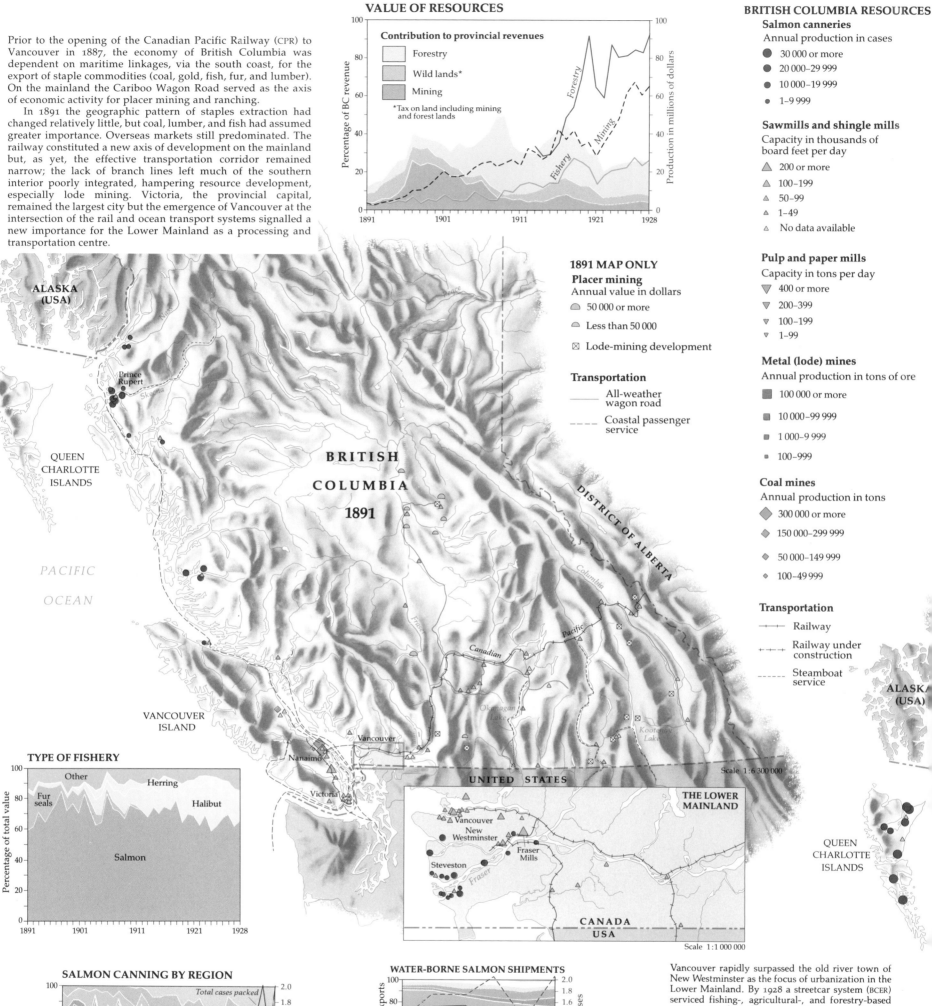

ALASKA (USA)

Prince Rupert · Skeena

QUEEN CHARLOTTE ISLANDS

PACIFIC OCEAN

BRITISH COLUMBIA 1891

DISTRICT OF ALBERTA

Columbia · Canadian · Pacific · Okanagan Lake · Kootenay Lake

VANCOUVER ISLAND

Vancouver

Nanaimo

Victoria

UNITED STATES

Scale 1:6 300 000

ALASKA (USA)

QUEEN CHARLOTTE ISLANDS

THE LOWER MAINLAND

Vancouver · New Westminster · Fraser Mills · Steveston · Fraser

CANADA / USA

Scale 1:1 000 000

TYPE OF FISHERY

Percentage of total value

Fur seals · Other · Herring · Halibut · Salmon

1891 · 1901 · 1911 · 1921 · 1928

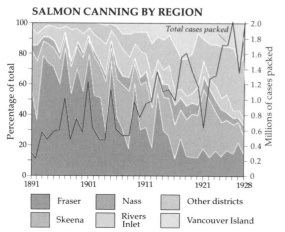

SALMON CANNING BY REGION

Percentage of total · Millions of cases packed

Total cases packed

1891 · 1901 · 1911 · 1921 · 1928

- Fraser
- Skeena
- Nass
- Rivers Inlet
- Other districts
- Vancouver Island

WATER-BORNE SALMON SHIPMENTS

Percentage of total exports · Millions of cases

1923 · 1924 · 1925 · 1926 · 1927 · 1928

Destinations

- United Kingdom, Europe
- Australia, Pacific Islands
- South and Central America
- Atlantic Coast
- South and East Asia
- Africa
- Other
- Total cases packed
- Total cases shipped

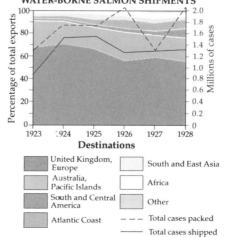

Vancouver rapidly surpassed the old river town of New Westminster as the focus of urbanization in the Lower Mainland. By 1928 a streetcar system (BCER) serviced fishing-, agricultural-, and forestry-based communities from Steveston to Chilliwack; 48.8% of the provincial population lived in the area, 35.5% (246 593) in Vancouver.

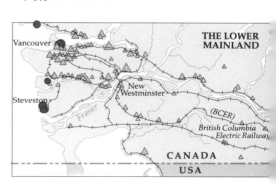

THE LOWER MAINLAND

Vancouver · New Westminster · Steveston · Fraser · (BCER) British Columbia Electric Railway

CANADA / USA

HISTORICAL ATLAS OF CANADA

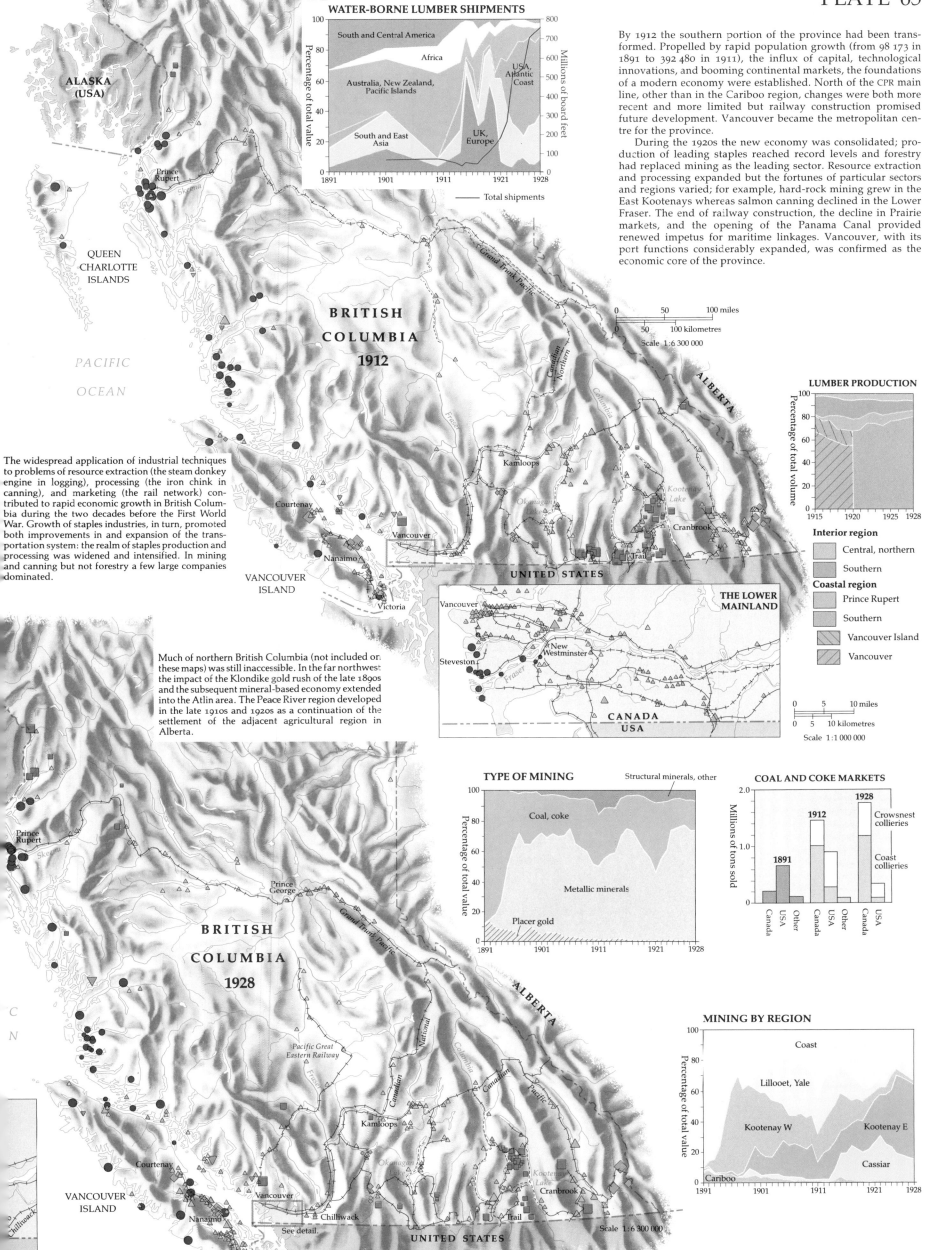

WATER-BORNE LUMBER SHIPMENTS

By 1912 the southern portion of the province had been transformed. Propelled by rapid population growth (from 98 173 in 1891 to 392 480 in 1911), the influx of capital, technological innovations, and booming continental markets, the foundations of a modern economy were established. North of the CPR main line, other than in the Cariboo region, changes were both more recent and more limited but railway construction promised future development. Vancouver became the metropolitan centre for the province.

During the 1920s the new economy was consolidated; production of leading staples reached record levels and forestry had replaced mining as the leading sector. Resource extraction and processing expanded but the fortunes of particular sectors and regions varied; for example, hard-rock mining grew in the East Kootenays whereas salmon canning declined in the Lower Fraser. The end of railway construction, the decline in Prairie markets, and the opening of the Panama Canal provided renewed impetus for maritime linkages. Vancouver, with its port functions considerably expanded, was confirmed as the economic core of the province.

The widespread application of industrial techniques to problems of resource extraction (the steam donkey engine in logging), processing (the iron chink in canning), and marketing (the rail network) contributed to rapid economic growth in British Columbia during the two decades before the First World War. Growth of staples industries, in turn, promoted both improvements in and expansion of the transportation system: the realm of staples production and processing was widened and intensified. In mining and canning but not forestry a few large companies dominated.

Much of northern British Columbia (not included on these maps) was still inaccessible. In the far northwest the impact of the Klondike gold rush of the late 1890s and the subsequent mineral-based economy extended into the Atlin area. The Peace River region developed in the late 1910s and 1920s as a continuation of the settlement of the adjacent agricultural region in Alberta.

LUMBER PRODUCTION

Interior region
Central, northern
Southern

Coastal region
Prince Rupert
Southern
Vancouver Island
Vancouver

THE LOWER MAINLAND

Scale 1:1 000 000

TYPE OF MINING

COAL AND COKE MARKETS

MINING BY REGION

CONCISE EDITION

RESOURCE DEVELOPMENT ON THE SHIELD, 1891–1928

Author: Susan L. Laskin

At the end of the 19th and the beginning of the 20th century the Precambrian Shield was transformed from a largely undeveloped territory into a resource hinterland for Central Canada (and to some extent the United States). The changing technology in the production of pulp from wood, the new techniques of producing hydroelectric power from running water, American demand for newsprint, provincial legislation prohibiting the export of pulpwood (1900 in Ontario, 1910 in Québec), and American legislation allowing the import of duty-free newsprint (1913) gave rise to large-scale pulp and paper mills based on the Shield's spruce forests and power from its fast-flowing rivers.

New processes to refine complex ores (both to separate copper and nickel and to separate out gold), new techniques of producing hydroelectric power, demand for minerals in the growing industrial economies of Central Canada and the United States, and the discovery of silver- and gold-bearing veins of rock produced a mining boom in northern Ontario.

By the late 1920s the heavy investment in the pulp and paper industry of the late 1910s and early 1920s was beginning to create overcapacity. The enormous power potential of the Shield was confirmed in the establishment of an American-controlled aluminum smelter at Arvida based on imported bauxite and a planned hydroelectric capacity of 800 000 hp. The number of head offices of mining companies located in Toronto confirmed Toronto's pre-eminent position in developing the Shield's mining frontier.

SILVER SHIPMENTS

Value in millions of dollars / Total number of producing mines

Other
Cobalt area

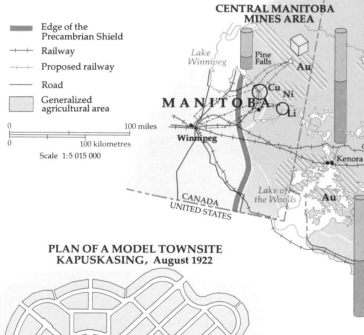

A Northern Silver Mine, Franklin Carmichael, 1930

Courtesy of McMichael Canadian Art Collection, gift of Mrs. A. J. Latner, 1971.9.

RESOURCE DEVELOPMENT, 1928

Edge of the Precambrian Shield
Railway
Proposed railway
Road
Generalized agricultural area

Scale 1:5 015 000

CENTRAL MANITOBA MINES AREA

Lake Winnipeg
Pine Falls
MANITOBA
Winnipeg
Kenora
Dryden
Fort Frances
Atikokan
Fort William
Port Arthur
Nipigon
Lake Nipigon
ONTARIO
Red Lake
Lac Seul
Michipicoten
Algoma Central Railway
Sault Ste Marie
SUDBURY AREA

Cu Ni Li
Au, Fe, Cu, Ag, Zn, Pb, Pt

CANADA / UNITED STATES
Lake of the Woods
CNR
CPR

PLAN OF A MODEL TOWNSITE
KAPUSKASING, August 1922

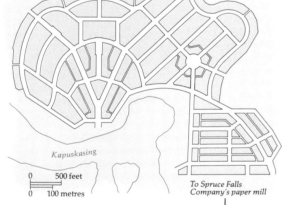

Kapuskasing

To Spruce Falls Company's paper mill

In the late 19th century settlement around small-scale mining operations was unplanned and growth was haphazard. When later resource developments required large-scale capital investment, companies increasingly built their own towns. The layout of these townsites created spatial segregation based on job status at the workplace. In Kapuskasing, the first community on the Shield where a provincial government became involved in planning, curvilinear streets, attention to topography, and other aspects of contemporary British garden-city planning were adopted.

Resource communities on the Shield, like Copper Cliff, depended on a single industry and attracted immigrant labour. Sudbury initially developed as a service centre for the surrounding mining communities and its work-force and ethnic composition were more diversified.

THE SUDBURY AREA

Levack
Zn
Pb
SUDBURY
Creighton
Pt
Frood
Copper Cliff
Garson
Coniston
Fe
Ni
Cu

Scale 1:1 200 000

ETHNIC ORIGIN OF POPULATION, 1931

Other
Scandinavian
Eastern European
German, Dutch
Italian
French
British

Copper Cliff 3 173   **Sudbury 18 518**

COMPOSITION OF THE WORKFORCE, 1931

Unspecified, other
Trapping
Mining
Service
Manufacturing
Finance
Trade
Construction
Transportation, communication
Mining, smelting, refining

Copper Cliff 1 018   **Sudbury 7 652**

SMELTING IN THE SUDBURY AREA

Thousands of tons / Value in millions of dollars

Copper
Nickel

No data available

Mineral production

△ Major mine
◇ Smelter
⬧ Smelter and refinery

Cobalt
Copper
Gold
Lead
Nickel
Platinum
Silver
Zinc

One block represents $1 000 000.

Gold and silver production for Québec not shown; see end notes.

HISTORICAL ATLAS OF CANADA

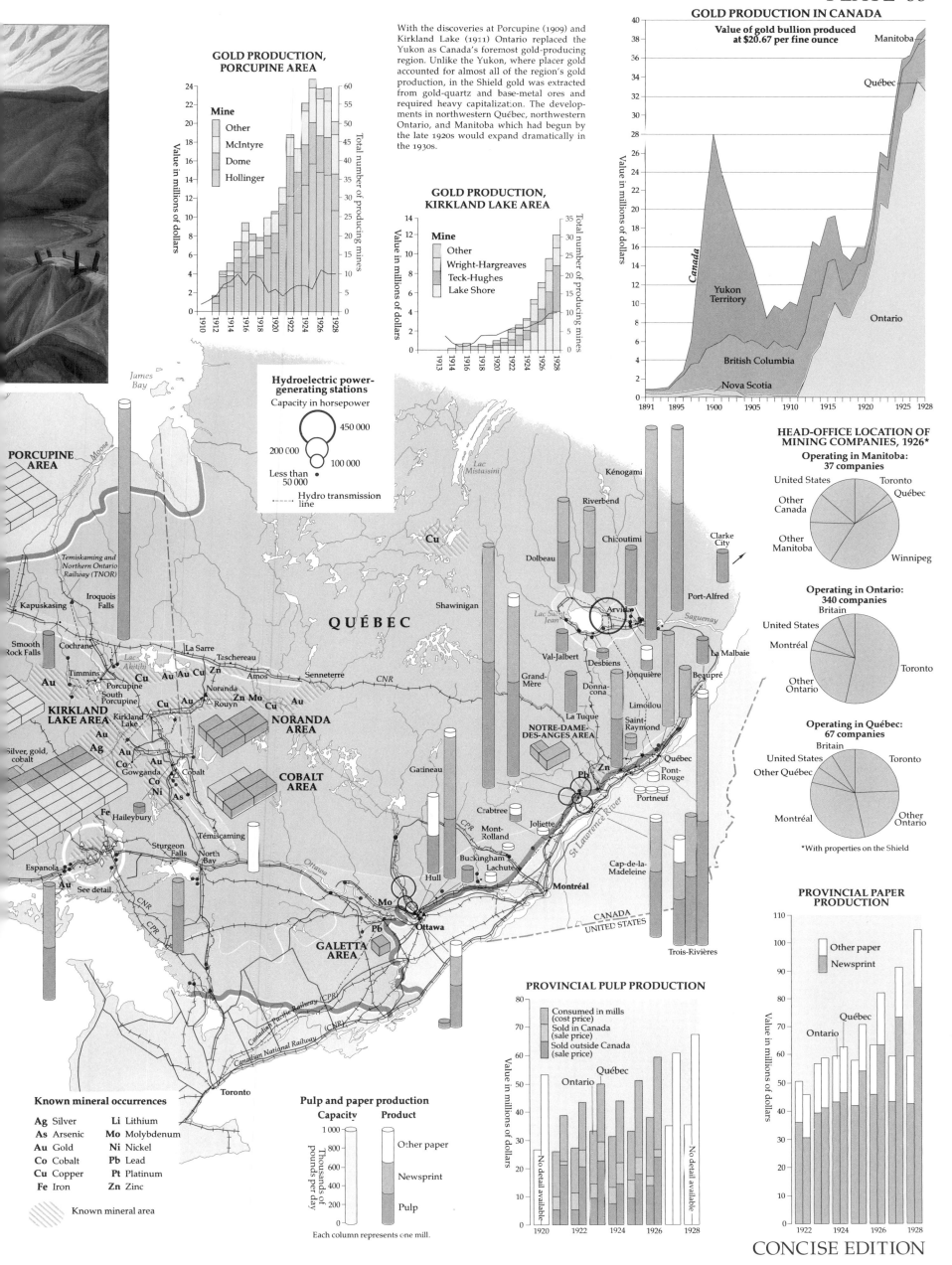

GOLD PRODUCTION, PORCUPINE AREA

Mine
- Other
- McIntyre
- Dome
- Hollinger

Value in millions of dollars
Total number of producing mines

GOLD PRODUCTION, KIRKLAND LAKE AREA

Mine
- Other
- Wright-Hargreaves
- Teck-Hughes
- Lake Shore

Value in millions of dollars
Total number of producing mines

With the discoveries at Porcupine (1909) and Kirkland Lake (1911) Ontario replaced the Yukon as Canada's foremost gold-producing region. Unlike the Yukon, where placer gold accounted for almost all of the region's gold production, in the Shield gold was extracted from gold-quartz and base-metal ores and required heavy capitalization. The developments in northwestern Québec, northwestern Ontario, and Manitoba which had begun by the late 1920s would expand dramatically in the 1930s.

GOLD PRODUCTION IN CANADA

Value of gold bullion produced at $20.67 per fine ounce

Value in millions of dollars

Canada
Yukon Territory
British Columbia
Nova Scotia
Ontario
Manitoba
Québec

HEAD-OFFICE LOCATION OF MINING COMPANIES, 1926*

Operating in Manitoba: 37 companies
- United States
- Other Canada
- Other Manitoba
- Toronto
- Québec
- Winnipeg

Operating in Ontario: 340 companies
- Britain
- United States
- Montréal
- Other Ontario
- Toronto

Operating in Québec: 67 companies
- Britain
- United States
- Other Québec
- Montréal
- Toronto
- Other Ontario

*With properties on the Shield

Hydroelectric power-generating stations
Capacity in horsepower
- 450 000
- 200 000
- 100 000
- Less than 50 000
- - - Hydro transmission line

PROVINCIAL PAPER PRODUCTION

- Other paper
- Newsprint

Value in millions of dollars
Ontario
Québec

PROVINCIAL PULP PRODUCTION

- Consumed in mills (cost price)
- Sold in Canada (sale price)
- Sold outside Canada (sale price)

Value in millions of dollars
Ontario
Québec
No detail available

Known mineral occurrences

Ag	Silver	Li	Lithium
As	Arsenic	Mo	Molybdenum
Au	Gold	Ni	Nickel
Co	Cobalt	Pb	Lead
Cu	Copper	Pt	Platinum
Fe	Iron	Zn	Zinc

Known mineral area

Pulp and paper production
Capacity
Thousands of pounds per day
- 1 000
- 800
- 600
- 400
- 200
- 0

Product
- Other paper
- Newsprint
- Pulp

Each column represents one mill.

CONCISE EDITION

SOCIETIES AND ECONOMIES IN THE NORTH, 1891–1961

Author: Peter J. Usher

POPULATION COMPOSITION

YUKON TERRITORY

NORTHWEST TERRITORIES*

Thousands of persons

Non-native

Inuit

Indian

1901 1911 1921 1931 1941 1951 1961

1921 1931 1941 1951 1961

* No pre-1921 data

BIRTHPLACE OF IMMIGRANTS

YUKON TERRITORY

NORTHWEST TERRITORIES

Percentage

Other
Rest of Europe
Northwest Europe
Scandinavia
United States
Great Britain
Atlantic Provinces
Québec
Ontario — Canada
Prairies
British Columbia

1911 1921 1931 1941 1951 1961

1911 1921 1931 1941 1951 1961

NON-NATIVE INSTITUTIONS
1891–1910 See central legend.

Existing in 1891 or established 1891–1895

Existing in 1910

Abandoned by 1910

Established 1896–1910

Existing in 1910

Abandoned by 1910

Two distinct systems of economic activity coexisted in the North: the locally based hunting, fishing, and trapping economy of the indigenous peoples, and the metropolitan-based staples and defence economies, involving non-Native residents. The chief link between the two was the fur trade.

In 1891 the Native population (Dene and Métis in the Sub-Arctic, Inuit in the Arctic) was widely dispersed in small seasonal encampments. Non-Native activity was limited to fur trade posts (where there were also religious missions) along the Mackenzie River and the whale fishery, which had a few shore stations on the Beaufort Sea, northern Hudson Bay, and east Baffin Island. The gold rush of 1898 brought a large transient population to the Yukon River. After 1900 both gold mining and whaling declined. The Canadian state established its presence in the North with police posts between 1895 and 1903.

While Natives were the main labour force of the fur trade, the whale fishery was operated by non-residents. In the Northwest Territories the foreign-born were largely British and northwestern European, reflecting the employment policies of the Hudson's Bay Company and the religious missions. In contrast, the early years of the gold rush brought numerous Americans, as well as some southern and eastern Europeans, to the Yukon.

NON-NATIVE INSTITUTIONS
1911–1939 See central legend.

Existing in 1911 or established 1911–1920

Existing in 1939

Abandoned by 1939

Established 1921–1939

Existing in 1939

Abandoned by 1939

TRAPPING AND HUNTING

Approximate area used by non-Native trappers, ca 1920–1940

Game preserves (Native use only) established 1918–1942

NON-NATIVE ACTIVITY

Economic

● Fur - trade post

▼ Mine

⬬ Whaling station

Social

⬛ Mission

⬛ School or hospital

■ Post office

Institutional

▲ RCMP post

✳ Defence installation

⬟ Weather station

Hollow symbols indicate abandonment; see individual legends for time periods.

Scale 1:16 000 000

0 — 300 miles

0 — 300 kilometres

BEAUFORT SEA

BANKS ISLAND

M'Clure Strait

Amundsen Gulf

VICTORIA ISLAND

Herschel Island

Fort McPherson

Dawson

Fort Good Hope

YUKON TERRITORY

NORTHWEST

Fort Norman

Mackenzie

Great Bear Lake

Whitehorse

Fort Simpson

Fort Rae

Great Slave Lake

Fort Providence

Fort Liard

Hay River

Fort Resolution

Fort Smith

POLAR ICE CAP

Extension to the North Pole, 1925

BEAUFORT SEA

Tuktoyaktuk

Aklavik

YUKON TERRITORY

Mayo

NORTHWEST

Viscount Melville Sound

BAFFIN BAY

Pond Inlet

Coppermine

Port Radium

Cambridge Bay

TERRITORIES

Pangnirtung

FOXE BASIN

Yellowknife

Baker Lake

Lake Harbour

Chesterfield Inlet

HUDSON BAY

Hudson Strait

Eskimo Point

QUÉBEC

Scale 1:16 000 000

HISTORICAL ATLAS OF CANADA

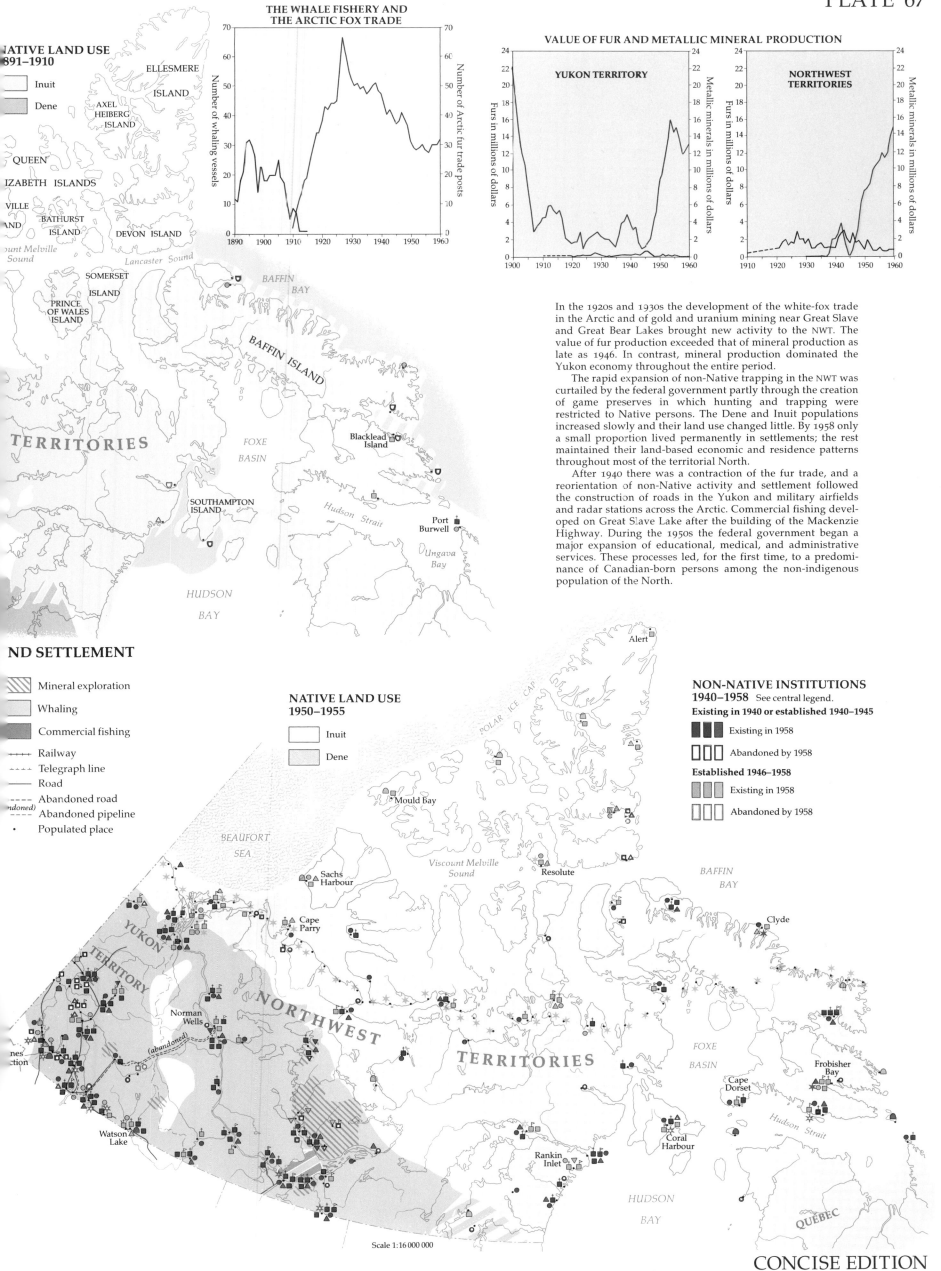

NATIVE LAND USE 1891–1910

- Inuit
- Dene

THE WHALE FISHERY AND THE ARCTIC FOX TRADE

Number of whaling vessels

Number of Arctic fur trade posts

VALUE OF FUR AND METALLIC MINERAL PRODUCTION

YUKON TERRITORY

Furs in millions of dollars / Metallic minerals in millions of dollars

NORTHWEST TERRITORIES

Furs in millions of dollars / Metallic minerals in millions of dollars

In the 1920s and 1930s the development of the white-fox trade in the Arctic and of gold and uranium mining near Great Slave and Great Bear Lakes brought new activity to the NWT. The value of fur production exceeded that of mineral production as late as 1946. In contrast, mineral production dominated the Yukon economy throughout the entire period.

The rapid expansion of non-Native trapping in the NWT was curtailed by the federal government partly through the creation of game preserves in which hunting and trapping were restricted to Native persons. The Dene and Inuit populations increased slowly and their land use changed little. By 1958 only a small proportion lived permanently in settlements; the rest maintained their land-based economic and residence patterns throughout most of the territorial North.

After 1940 there was a contraction of the fur trade, and a reorientation of non-Native activity and settlement followed the construction of roads in the Yukon and military airfields and radar stations across the Arctic. Commercial fishing developed on Great Slave Lake after the building of the Mackenzie Highway. During the 1950s the federal government began a major expansion of educational, medical, and administrative services. These processes led, for the first time, to a predominance of Canadian-born persons among the non-indigenous population of the North.

...ND SETTLEMENT

- Mineral exploration
- Whaling
- Commercial fishing
- Railway
- Telegraph line
- Road
- Abandoned road
- Abandoned pipeline
- Populated place

NATIVE LAND USE 1950–1955

- Inuit
- Dene

NON-NATIVE INSTITUTIONS 1940–1958 See central legend.

Existing in 1940 or established 1940–1945
- Existing in 1958
- Abandoned by 1958

Established 1946–1958
- Existing in 1958
- Abandoned by 1958

Scale 1:16 000 000

CONCISE EDITION

Notes and Sources

Abbreviations and Shortened References

ANQ	Archives nationales du Québec
CE	*The Canadian Encyclopedia*. 2nd ed. 4 vols. Edmonton: Hurtig, 1988
CHR	*Canadian Historical Review*
CMC	Canadian Museum of Civilization (formerly National Museum of Man)
CO	Colonial Office (London)
CPR	Canadian Pacific Railway
DBS	Canada. Dominion Bureau of Statistics
DCB	*Dictionary of Canadian Biography*. 14 vols published. Toronto: University of Toronto Press, 1966–
DU	Dalhousie University
ECHP	Environment Canada, National Historic Parks (formerly Parks Canada)
GSC	Geological Survey of Canada
HAC	*Historical Atlas of Canada*. 3 vols. Toronto: University of Toronto Press, 1987–93
HBC	Hudson's Bay Company
Hist Soc	*Histoire sociale / Social History*
MAU	Mount Allison University
McGU	McGill University
MUN	Memorial University of Newfoundland
NAC	National Archives of Canada
NMC	National Map Collection, Public Archives of Canada

NMM	National Museum of Man (see also CMC)
PAC	Public Archives of Canada
PAM	Provincial Archives of Manitoba
PANL	Provincial Archives of Newfoundland and Labrador
PANS	Public Archives of Nova Scotia
PRO	Public Record Office (London)
QU	Queen's University
ROM	Royal Ontario Museum
SFU	Simon Fraser University
SP	Canada. *Sessional Papers*
UA	University of Alberta
UBC	University of British Columbia
UC	University of Calgary
UL	Université Laval
UMan	University of Manitoba
UMonc	Université de Moncton
UMont	Université de Montréal
UO	University of Ottawa
UT	University of Toronto
WLU	Wilfrid Laurier University
YU	York University

Canada Year Book

Canada. Department of Agriculture. *The Statistical Year-Book of Canada*. 1891–1904
Canada. Department of Agriculture. Census and Statistics Office. *The Canada Year Book*. 2nd series. 1905–10
Canada. Department of Trade and Commerce. Census and Statistics Office. *The Canada Year Book*. 2nd series. 1911–17
Canada. Department of Trade and Commerce. Dominion Bureau of Statistics. *Canada Year Book*. 1918–61

Census

Canada. Dominion Bureau of Statistics. *Census of Canada*

Documents published by the federal government were printed in Ottawa by the King's Printer or the Queen's Printer unless otherwise indicated.

Titles of annual reports of government documents and the names of the departments themselves may have changed over time.

Leacy. *Historical Statistics*

Leacy, F.H., ed. *Historical Statistics of Canada*. 2nd ed. Ottawa: Statistics Canada with the Social Science Federation of Canada, 1983. This is a revision of the original compilation prepared by Urquhart and Buckley in 1965.

Urquhart and Buckley. *Historical Statistics*

Urquhart, M.C., and K.A.H. Buckley, eds. *Historical Statistics of Canada*. Toronto: Macmillan, 1965

Census Data

Data enumerated for a given census year normally apply to that year. Where production figures are given, however, they are normally derived from the previous year. For further discussion of the censuses see the following:

Drummond, Ian M. *Progress without Planning: The Economic History of Ontario from Confederation to the Second World War*. Toronto: University of Toronto Press, 1987. App B
Pomfret, Richard. *The Economic Development of Canada*. Toronto: Methuen, 1981. Especially pp 47–9

Currency and Rates of Exchange

The first Canadian coins were not issued until late in 1858, and the government of Canada did not begin to issue monetary notes until 1866. Up to this time, and for some years after, the principal currency and means of exchange were at first French and Spanish coins and later British and American coins. Notes issued by local chartered banks had become an important part of the money system after 1820.

The British North American monetary system was based on an officially designated currency called the *Halifax currency*, which rated the Spanish dollar at 5 shillings. The Halifax currency became for the most part the standard in which accounts were kept. Some confusion arose, however, when some preferred the New York standard, which rated the Spanish dollar at 8 shillings. In addition, accounts in Lower Canada has used *livres françaises ancien cours*, which related to the Paris currency of *livres tournois*, of which 9 were the equivalent of 10 ancien cours. In Halifax currency 24 livres ancien cours equalled £1. Post-revolutionary French coins also became legal tender in Lower Canada in 1819, but the union of Lower and Upper Canada in 1840 resulted in the retention of the Halifax system with adjustments in the ratings assigned to coins. The fixed relationships may be tabulated as follows (McCalla, p 246; McCullough, p 292, table 43):

£1 (all currencies) = 20 shillings = 240 pence
1 livre = 20 sols (sous) = 240 deniers (d)
$1 = 100 cents

£1 Halifax currency = $4.00
£1 New York (or York) currency = $2.50
£1 Halifax currency = 24 livres françaises ancien cours (or livres courantes françaises)
The fluctuating relationships were:
£1 sterling = ca £1.111 Halifax currency (to 1820)
£1 sterling = ca £1.217 Halifax currency (from 1820)
£1 sterling = ca $4.8667 (from 1858)
Because there are so many unknowns, clear uncomplicated conversions are not always possible.

Legislation in 1853 incorporated the pound, dollar, shilling, penny, and cent as units of Canadian currency. This was a first step towards a common currency based on the decimal system. In 1871, despite the objections of the banks, an act was passed which provided uniform currency for Canada and established legal currency in Manitoba. The denominations were to be the dollar, cent, and mill. Pounds, shillings, and pence were no longer accepted as an alternative method of accounting. In 1875 the Uniform Currency Act was extended to the Northwest Territories and in 1881 to Prince Edward Island and British Columbia.

McCalla, Douglas. *Planting the Province: The Economic History of Upper Canada*. Toronto: University of Toronto Press, 1993. App A
McCullough, A.B. *Money and Exchange in Canada to 1900*. Toronto: Dundurn Press / Charlottetown: Parks Canada and the Canadian Government Publishing Centre, 1984
Shortt, Adam, and Arthur G. Doughty. *Canada and Its Provinces*. Toronto: Glasgow, Brook, and Co, 1914. Vol 5, pp 273–6

Notes to the Reader

- The affiliations of the authors listed at the head of each of the plate notes are as of the date when the plate was published (1987–93), and may have changed. Similarly, with a few exceptions, the references have not been updated.
- Any unpublished reports submitted to the HAC project and cited below are available at the National Archives of Canada, the repository for HAC working materials.

PLATE 1

Environmental Change after 9000 BCE

J.H. McANDREWS   Botany, Royal Ontario Museum and University of Toronto
K.-B. LIU   Geography and Anthropology, Louisiana State University
G.C. MANVILLE   Botany, Academy of Natural Sciences, Philadelphia
V.K. PREST   Glacial Geology, Geological Survey of Canada
J.-S. VINCENT   Glacial Geology, Geological Survey of Canada

Sources

Bernabo, J.C., and T. Webb. 'Changing Patterns in the Holocene Pollen Record of Northeastern North America: A Mapped Summary.' *Quaternary Research* 8 (1977): 64–97
Delcourt, P.A., and H.A. Delcourt. 'Vegetation Maps for Eastern North America: 40,000 yr BP to the Present.' In R.C. Romans, ed. *Geobotany II*. New York: Plenum, 1981
Denton, G.H., and T.J. Hughes, eds. *The Last Great Ice Sheets*. New York: Wiley, 1981
Hopkins, D.M., J.V. Matthews, Jr, C.E. Schweger, and S.B. Young, eds. *Paleoecology of Beringia*. New York: Academic Press, 1982
Liu, K.-B. 'Pollen Evidence of Late-Quaternary Climatic Changes in Canada: A Review. Part I: Western Canada.' *Ontario Geography* 15 (1980): 83–101
– 'Pollen Evidence of Late-Quaternary Climatic Changes in Canada: A Review. Part II: Eastern Arctic and Sub-Arctic Canada.' *Ontario Geography* 17 (1981): 61–82
Matthews, J.V., Jr. 'Tertiary and Quaternary Environments: Historical Background for an Analysis of the Canadian Insect Fauna'. In *Canada and Its Insects*. Ed. H.V. Danks. *Memoirs of the Entomological Society of Canada* 108 (1979): 31–86
Prest, V.K. 'Quaternary Geology of Canada.' In R.J.W. Douglas, ed. *The Geology and Economic Minerals of Canada*. GSC, Economic Report No. 1. Ottawa, 1970. Pp 677–763
Ritchie, J.C. *Past and Present Vegetation of the Far Northwest of Canada*. Toronto: University of Toronto Press, 1984
Wright, H.E., Jr, ed. *Late-Quaternary Environments of the United States*. 2 vols. Minneapolis: University of Minnesota Press, 1983

PLATE 2

Native Cultural Sequences, 6th Century to European Contact

J.V. WRIGHT   Archaeological Survey of Canada, Canadian Museum of Civilization

This plate includes one of the first comprehensive maps of the prehistory of Canada. It is based on technical published reports, unpublished manuscripts, consultation with colleagues in the Archaeological Survey of Canada, CMC, the responses of 20 archaeologists across the country to initial drafts, and information provided on request by colleagues throughout Canada. A substantial amount of the information used here is either unpublished or in publications that are not easily obtained. Other maps in this series may be found in HAC vol I, pll 6, 7, 8, 12, 14, and 15.

The extent of glacial ice has been determined by the systematic mapping of ice-marginal features. The time contol of the margins is based on radiocarbon dating of organic deposits (shells, wood, peat, lake deposits, etc.).

Sources

'Development in Canadian Prehistory since 1970 – A Symposium held at the Annual CAA Convention, Hamilton, 1982.' *Canadian Journal of Archaeology* 6 (1982): 47–218
Epp, Henry T., and Ian Dyck, eds. *Tracking Ancient Hunters: Prehistoric Archaeology in Saskatchewan*. Regina: Saskatchewan Archaeological Society, 1983
Fladmark, K.R. *Prehistory of British Columbia*. Ottawa: NMM, 1986
McGhee, Robert. *Canadian Arctic Prehistory*. Toronto: Van Nostrand Reinhold, 1978
Prest, V.K. *Retreat of Wisconsin and Recent Ice in North America*. GSC, Map 1257A. 1969
Prest, V.K., D.R. Grant, and V.N. Rampton. *Glacial Map of Canada*. GSC, Map 1253A. 1968
Tuck, James A. *Newfoundland and Labrador Prehistory*. Ottawa: NMM, 1976
– *Maritime Provinces Prehistory*. Ottawa: NMM, 1984
Wright, J.V. *Ontario Prehistory: An Eleven-Thousand-Year Archaeological Outline*. Ottawa: NMM, 1972
– *Quebec Prehistory*. Toronto: Van Nostrand Reinhold, 1979
– 'The Development of Prehistory in Canada, 1935–1985.' *American Antiquity* 50, no. 4 (1985): 421–33

PLATE 3

Native Population and Subsistence, 17th Century

CONRAD E. HEIDENREICH   Geography, York University
J.V. WRIGHT   Archaeological Survey of Canada, Canadian Museum of Civilization

Population, early 17th century

Early population data are meagre. The populations given here are estimates based on a few references to pre-epidemic populations. These references were transferred to other groups in similar environments with similar socioeconomic conditions.

Linguistic families, 17th century

This list is based on secondary sources with some adjustments in distribution indicated by primary sources.

Subsistence, ethnohistoric data, 17th century

This map is based on secondary sources with extensive adjustments according to earliest European observations.

Sources

Banfield, A.W.F. *The Mammals of Canada*. Toronto: University of Toronto Press, 1981
Biggar, Henry P., ed. *The Works of Samuel de Champlain*. 6 vols. Toronto: Champlain Society, 1922–36
Handbook of North American Indians. Vol 6: *Subarctic*. Ed J. Helm. Washington: Smithsonian Institution, 1981
Handbook of North American Indians. Vol 15: *Northeast*. Ed B.G. Trigger. Washington: Smithsonian Institution, 1978
Jenness, D. *The Indians of Canada*. 7th ed. Toronto: University of Toronto Press, 1977
NAC, NMC. Maps from the period 1600–60
Sagard, Gabriel (Théodat). *Histoire du Canada et voyages que les Frères mineurs Recollets y ont faicts pour la conversion des infidelles ...* 4 vols. Paris: Tross, 1866
– *The Long Journey to the Country of the Hurons*. Ed. G.M. Wrong; trans H.H. Langton. Toronto: Champlain Society, 1939
Thwaites, R.G., ed. *The Jesuit Relations and Allied Documents*. 73 vols. Cleveland: Burrows Bros., 1896–1901

See also references to pll 6 and 43.

PLATE 4

Native Canada, ca 1820

CONRAD E. HEIDENREICH   Geography, York University
ROBERT GALOIS   Geography, University of British Columbia

We gratefully acknowledge permission to consult the HBC Archives, PAM, as well as the help of the archivists, especially Shirlee A. Smith; and also the staff in Special Collections, the Library, UBC.

Much of the HBC census material is complete for men, women, and children. In cases where only men were counted, a total population was extrapolated using population ratios derived from nearby groups living in a similar environment with a similar economy. Where later censuses had to be used for Native groups who were affected by epidemic diseases after 1821 (eg, Tlingit), the population totals were adjusted upward by one-third. Data for some of the Plains groups (eg, Blackfoot, Assiniboine) were originally given in numbers of tents. These were converted to population numbers on the basis of eight people per tent, as suggested by contemporary observers. It is impossible to determine how accurate the early censuses and estimates were.

Early 19th-century populations in the Cordillera are particularly difficult to establish. There were 11 HBC censuses of various areas, some overlapping, none surviving in original form. The copies that do survive, made in 1878 by one of H.H. Bancroft's researchers, usually do not indicate the date of the enumeration. Given these limitations it is no easy matter to resolve the contradictions arising between different, overlapping estimates. For example, there are five separate censuses of some or all of the Southern Kwakiutl but only one includes a date (summer 1838), and none indicates who was responsible for the compilation. Wilson Duff used this material and his own large knowledge of Native British Columbia to prepare the population map in *The Indian History of British Columbia*. We have been over the same ground, correcting some mistakes on Duff's map while following its general patterns. A comprehensive analysis of these censuses and other estimates of early-contact Native populations in the northern Cordillera remains to be done.

Sources

Great Britain, House of Commons. British North American Provinces. 'Copies of Extracts of Correspondence ... Respecting the Indians, 17 June, 1839.' In *British Parliamentary Papers*. Colonies, Canada, 12. Irish University Press, 1969
– House of Commons. Indian Department, Canada. 'Copies or Extracts of Recent Correspondence Respecting ... Indian Departments in Canada, 2 June, 1856.' In *British Parliamentary Papers*. Colonies, Canada, 21. Irish University Press, 1970
– Parliament. 'Aboriginal Tribes.' In *Imperial Blue Books on Affairs Relating to Canada* 5 (1834–6), paper 617: 1–229
Hind, N.Y. *Explorations of the Interior of the Labrador Peninsula, the Country of the Montagnais and Nasquapee Indians*. 2 vols. London: Longman, James, 1863
Keating, W.H. *Narrative of an Expedition to the Sources of St. Peter's River ... Performed in the Year 1823*. Philadelphia: H.C. Carey and I. Lea, 1824
Mason, P.P., ed. *Schoolcraft's Expedition to Lake Itasca*. East Lansing: Michigan State University, 1958
New Brunswick, *Journal of the House of Assembly*. 6th Session, 12th General Assembly, pp xcii–cxvii. Fredericton, 1842
NAC, RG10, vol 708, Census Records, 1810–36; vol 747, Census Records, 1840–52
– NMC. All maps by A. Arrowsmith and D. Thompson
PAM, HBC Archives. B/e: District Reports (Abitibi, B1/e/2, 1822–3 to York Factory, B239/e/3, 182) approximately covering the years 1818–25. B/2: various censuses compiled between 1815 and 1839. Maps: all maps drawn between 1815 and 1827
PANS. RG1, vol 431, Papers relating to Indians, 1832–6; vol. 432, Papers relating to Indians, 1842–3
Provincial Archives of British Columbia. Douglas papers, Second series, Microfilm 737A, pp 7–33; Transcript B/20/1853, pp 5–31. The originals are in the Bancroft Library, San Francisco.

Further readings

Boas, F. *The Central Eskimo*. Smithsonian Institution, Bureau of American Ethnology, 6th Annual Report. Washington, 1888
Brice-Bennett, C., ed. *Our Footprints Are Everywhere: Inuit Land Use and Occupancy in Labrador*. Nain: Labrador Inuit Association, 1977
Duff, W. *The Indian History of British Columbia*. Vol 1: *The Impact of the White Man*. Provincial Museum of Natural History and Anthropology, Memoir 5, 1964. Victoria, 1965
Freeman, M.M.R., ed. *Inuit Land Use and Occupancy Project*. 3 vols. Ottawa: Minister of Supply and Services, 1976
Handbook of North American Indians. Vol 6: *Subarctic*. Ed J. Helm. Washington: Smithsonian Institution, 1981
Handbook of North American Indians. Vol 15: *Northeast*. Ed B.G. Trigger. Washington: Smithsonian Institution, 1978

Hodge, F.W., ed. *Handbook of Indians North of Mexico*. 2 vols. Smithsonian Institution, Bureau of American Ethnology, Bulletin 30. Washington, 1907, 1910

Horr, D.A., ed. *Coast Salish and Western Washington Indians*. 5 vols. New York: Garland, 1974

– *Interior Salish and Eastern Washington Indians*. 5 vols. New York: Garland, 1974

Howley, J.P. *The Beothucks or Red Indians: The Aboriginal Inhabitants of Newfoundland*. Cambridge: Cambridge University Press, 1915

Krause, A. *The Tlingit Indians*. Trans E. Gunther. 1st ed. 1885. Seattle: University of Washington, 1956

Tanner, V. 'Outlines of the Geography, Life and Customs of Newfoundland-Labrador.' *Acta Geographica* 8, no. 1 (1944): 1–907

PLATE 5

Exploring the Atlantic Coast, 16th and 17th Centuries

RICHARD I. RUGGLES Geography, Queen's University

Baffin, William (1584–1622) DCB 1: 74–5
Bellenger, Étienne (fl 1580–4) DCB 1: 87–9
Button, Sir Thomas (ca 1577–1634) DCB 1: 144–5
Bylot, Robert (fl 1610–16) DCB 1: 145
Cabot, John (fl 1497–8) DCB 1: 146–52
Cartier, Jacques (1491–1557) DCB 1: 165–72
Corte-Real, Gaspar (ca 1450–1501) DCB 1: 234–6
Corte-Real, Miguel (ca 1450–1502) DCB1: 236
Davis, John (ca 1550–1605) DCB 1: 251–2
Fagundes, João Alvares (fl 1521) DCB 1: 303–4
Foxe (Fox), Luke (1586–1635) DCB 1: 311–12
Frobisher, Sir Martin (ca 1535–94) DCB 1: 316–19
Gómez, Esteban (in Portuguese Estevão Gomes) (1484–1538) DCB 1: 342–3
Hudson, Henry (fl 1607–11) DCB 1: 374–9
James, Thomas (ca 1593–1635) DCB 1: 384–5
La Rocque de Roberval, Jean-François de (1500–60) DCB 1: 422–5
Munk, Jens (1579–1628) DCB 1: 514–15
Ribeiro, Diogo (d 1533) Portuguese royal cartographer in Spanish service
Verrazzano, Giovanni da (ca 1485–1528) DCB 1: 657–60

Further readings

Brebner, J.B. *The Explorers of North America, 1492–1806*. London: A. & C. Black, 1933
Cooke, Alan, and Clive Holland. *The Exploration of Northern Canada, 500–1920: A Chronology*. Toronto: Arctic History Press, 1978
Crone, Gerald. *The Discovery of America*. London: Hamilton, 1969
Cumming, W.P., R.A. Skelton, and D.B. Quinn. *The Discovery of North America*. London: Elek, 1971
Klemp, Egon. *America in Maps, Dating from 1500 to 1856*. London: Holmes & Meier, 1976
Morison, Samuel E. *The European Discovery of America*. New York: Oxford University Press, 1971–4
The National Atlas of Canada. 4th ed, rev. Ottawa: Department of Energy, Mines and Resources and Information Canada / Toronto: Macmillan, 1974
Quinn, D.B. *England and the Discovery of America 1481–1620*. New York: Knopf, 1974
Tooley, R.V., and Charles Bricker. *Landmarks of Mapmaking; An Illustrated Survey of Maps and Mapmakers*. New York: Crowell, 1968

PLATE 6

Exploration, 17th, 18th Centuries

RICHARD I. RUGGLES Geography, Queen's University
CONRAD E. HEIDENREICH Geography, York University

Allouez, Claude (1622–89) DCB 1: 57–8
Bellin, Jacques-Nicolas (1703–72) Cartographer attached to French Marine Office
Bonnécamps, Joseph-Pierre de (1707–90) DCB 4: 76–7
Brûlé, Étienne (1592–1633) DCB 1: 130–3
Buache, Philippe (1700–73) French geographer
Cavelier de La Salle, René-Robert (1643–87) DCB 1: 172–84
Champlain, Samuel de (1570–1635) DCB 1: 186–99
Chaussegros de Léry, Gaspard-Joseph (1682–1756) DCB 3: 116–19
Coronelli, Vincenzo Maria (1650–1718) Venetian cartographer
Delisle, Joseph-Nicolas (1688–1768) French astronomer and cartographer working in St Petersburg, Russia
Denys de La Ronde, Pierre (1631–1708) DCB 2: 178–9
Franquelin, Jean-Baptiste-Louis (b 1651, d after 1712) DCB 2: 228–30
Gaultier de Varennes et de La Vérendrye, Pierre (1685–1749) DCB 3: 246–54
Hennepin, Louis (1626–1705) DCB 2: 277–82
Jolliet, Louis (1645–1700) DCB 1: 392–8
Laure, Pierre-Michel (1688–1738) DCB 2: 357–8
Nicollet de Belleborne, Jean (1598–1642) DCB 1: 516–18
Sanson, Nicolas (1600–67) Founder of 17th-century French school of cartography

Sources

NAC. NMC. 17th- and 18th-century maps. As far as possible all surviving primary records of exploration were consulted.

Further readings

DCB, vols 1–4
Heidenreich, C.E. 'Mapping the Great Lakes: The Period of Exploration, 1603–1700.' *Cartographica* 17 (1980): 32–64
– 'Mapping the Great Lakes: The Period of Imperial Rivalries.' *Cartographica* 18 (1981): 74–109

PLATE 7

Exploration from Hudson Bay, 18th Century

RICHARD I. RUGGLES Geography, Queen's University

Bayly, Charles (fl ca 1630–80) DCB 1: 81–4
Chouart Des Groseilliers, Médard (1618–96?) DCB 1: 223–8
Coats, William (d 1752) DCB 3: 127–8
Cocking, Matthew (1743–99) DCB 4: 156–8
Gillam, Zachariah (1636–82) DCB 1: 336–8
Gorst, Thomas (fl ca 1668–87) DCB 1: 343
Grimington, Michael (d 1710) DCB 2: 264–7
Hearne, Samuel (1745–92) DCB 4: 339–42
Henday, Anthony (fl 1750–62) DCB 3: 285–7
Kelsey, Henry (1667–1724) DCB 2: 307–15
Middleton, Christopher (d 1770) DCB 3: 446–50
Mitchell, Thomas (fl 1743–51) DCB 3: 453–4
Nixon, John (1623–92) DCB 1: 518–20
Norton, Moses (1735–73) DCB 4: 583–5
Norton, Richard (1701–41) DCB 3: 489–90
Radisson, Pierre–Esprit (1640–1710) DCB 2: 535–40
Scroggs, John (fl 1718–24) DCB 2: 604
Smith, Joseph (d 1765) DCB 3: 594–5
Walker, Nehemiah (fl ca 1670–90) DCB 1: 666

The following were also Hudson's Bay Company traders: George Atkinson, Jr, Alex Brand, Thomas Buchan, John Clarke, James Clouston, John Isbister, Thomas Isbister, George Jackman, Christopher Norton, William Pink, James Robertson, William Robinson, William Stewart, William Tomison, Joseph Waggoner. Joseph Frobisher and Thomas Frobisher were Montréal traders.

Sources

The originals of the maps by Thornton, Coats, Norton, and Graham are in the HBC Archives, PAM. The map attributed to Dobbs, actually the work of Joseph La France, appeared in Arthur Dobbs, *An Account of the Countries Adjoining to Hudson's Bay in the North-West Part of America...* (London, 1744). The depictions of explorers' routes and of territory explored are largely based on extensive research in the HBC Archives, particularly in the correspondence (A5, A6, A10, A11), in the post journals and letters between posts (B3/a and B3/b), and in the map collection. Much use has also been made of the map collection at the NAC.

Further readings

Cooke, Alan, and Clive Holland. *The Exploration of Northern Canada, 500–1920: A Chronology*. Toronto, Arctic History Press, 1978
Cummings, W.P., S.E. Hillier, D.B. Quinn, and G. Williams. *The Exploration of North America, 1630–1776*. Toronto: McClelland and Stewart, 1974
Rich, Edwin Ernest. *The History of the Hudson's Bay Company, 1670–1870*. 2 vols. London: HBC Record Society, 1958–9
Thomson, Don W. *Men and Meridians: The History of Surveying and Mapping in Canada*. Vol 1. Ottawa: Queen's Printer, 1966
Warkentin, John, and Richard I. Ruggles. *Historical Atlas of Manitoba, 1612–1969*. Winnipeg: Manitoba Historical Society, 1970

PLATE 8

Exploration in the Far Northwest, 18th and 19th Centuries

RICHARD I. RUGGLES Geography, Queen's University

RUSSIAN EXPLORERS
Vitus Joanassen Bering; Alexei Chirikov; Grigor Ivanovich Shelikov; Gerasim Grigorievich Ismailov; Master Bocharov; Joseph Billings, DCB 5: 79–81; Gavriil Andreevich Sarychev

SPANISH EXPLORERS
Juan Josef Pérez Hernández, DCB 4: 622–3; Juan Francisco de la Bodega y Quadra, DCB 4: 72–4; Francisco de Eliza y Reventa; Salvador Fidalgo; Cayetano Valdés y Flores Bazán; Dionisio Alcalá-Galiano, DCB 5: 11–12; Jacinto Caamano

BRITISH EXPLORERS
James Cook, DCB 4: 162–7; George Vancouver, DCB 4: 743–8

EXPLORERS OF THE INTERIOR
Peter Pond, DCB 5: 681–6; Alexander Mackenzie, DCB 5: 537–43; Philip Turnor, DCB 4: 740–2; Peter Fidler, DCB 6: 249–52; Malcolm (Malcolm) Ross, DCB 4: 684–5; David Thompson, DCB 8: 878–84; Edward Jarvis, DCB 4: 389–90; John Kipling; George Sutherland, DCB 4: 726–7; James Sutherland, DCB 4: 727–8; James Hudson

EXPLORERS OF THE ARCTIC
John Ross, DCB 8: 770–4; William Edward Parry, DCB 8: 683–6; John Franklin; John Richardson, DCB 9: 658–61; George Back, DCB 10: 26–9

Sources

The Pond, Arrowsmith, and Taylor maps are from the collection at the NAC. The Hodgson map is from the collection in the HBC Archives, PAM. The original of the Thompson map is in the Ontario Archives; the version on this plate is based on a simplified drawing of the Thompson map published by the Champlain Society. For HBC sources see notes for pl 7.

Further readings

Cooke, Alan, and Clive Holland. *The Exploration of Northern Canada, 500–1920: A Chronology*. Toronto: Arctic History Press, 1978
Morton, A.S. *A History of the Canadian West to 1870–71*. Toronto: Nelson, 1939
Moulton. Gary E., ed. *Atlas of the Lewis and Clark Expedition*. Lincoln: University of Nebraska Press, 1983
Rich, Edwin Ernest. *The History of the Hudson's Bay Company, 1670–1870*. 2 vols. London: HBC Record Society, 1958–9

Ruggles, Richard I. 'The West of Canada in 1763: Imagination and Reality.' *The Canadian Geographer* 15, no. 4 (1971)
Schwartz, Seymour I., and Ralph E. Ehrenberg. *The Mapping of America*. New York: Abrams, 1980
Stuart-Stubbs, Basil, and Coolie Verner. *The Northpart of America*. Don Mills, Ont: Academic Press, 1979
Thomson, Don W. *Men and Meridians: The History of Surveying and Mapping in Canada*. Vol 1. Ottawa: Queen's Printer, 1966
Warkentin, John. *The Western Interior of Canada*. The Carleton Library, no. 15. Toronto: McClelland and Stewart, 1964
Warkentin, John, and Richard I. Ruggles. *Historical Atlas of Manitoba, 1612–1969*. Winnipeg: Manitoba Historical Society, 1970

PLATE 9

Exploration and Assessment to 1891

RICHARD I. RUGGLES   Geography, Queen's University

General exploration

BRITISH EXPLORERS

Adams, William (d 1890), captain of the whaler *Arctic*   Alan Cooke and Clive Holland, *The Exploration of Northern Canada, 500–1920: A Chronology* (Toronto: Arctic History Press, 1978), p 234
Belcher, Edward (1799–1877)   CE 1: 199; DCB 10: 42–3
Bellot, Joseph-René (1826–53)   DCB 8: 79–81
Collinson, Richard (1811–83)   DCB 11: 198–201
Griffin, Jane (Lady Franklin) (1792–1875)   DCB 10: 319–20
Inglefield, Edward Augustus (1820–94)   *Dictionary of National Biography* (DNB) (London: Smith, Elder, 1885–1901) Suppl 22: 904–5; *The Encyclopedia Americana* (EA) (Danbury, Conn: Grolier, 1991), 15: 174
Jago, C.T.   Cooke and Holland, pp 196, 206
Kellett, Henry (1806–75)   CE 2: 1130; DCB 10: 396–7
Kennedy, William (1814–90)   DCB 11: 470–1
McClintock, Francis Leopold (1819–1907)   CE 2: 1256
Nares, George Strong (1831–1915)   CE 3: 1426; EA 6: 247
Osborn, Sherard (1822–75)   DCB 10: 561–3
Richards, George Henry (baptized 1819–96)   DCB 12: 892–3
Young, Allen William (1827–1915)   DCB 10: 320; 12: 955

HUDSON'S BAY COMPANY EXPLORERS

The depiction of HBC explorers' routes is based on extensive research in the Hudson's Bay Company Archives of the Provincial Archives of Manitoba, especially on manuscript maps, post journals, and correspondence with company headquarters in London, and between posts.

Anderson, James (1812–67)   DCB 9: 5–6
MacFarlane, Roderick (1833–1920)   DCB 9: 6; 10: 276; Cooke and Holland, pp 213, 220
Mackinlay, James   Cooke and Holland, pp 262, 297, 318
Pike, Warburton (ca 1861–1915)   *Encyclopedia Canadiana* (EC) (Ottawa: Canadian Co, 1957–8) 8: 205
Rae, John (1813–93)   DCB 12: 876–9; DNB 16: 594–6
Stewart, James Green (1825–81)   DCB 11: 854–5

AMERICAN EXPLORERS

Fisher, Elnathan B., captain of a whaler   Cooke and Holland, p 230
Greely, Adolphus Washington (1844–1935)   *Dictionary of American Biography* (DAB) (New York: Scribner's, 1957) Suppl 1: 352–5
Hall, Charles Francis (1821–71)   CE 2: 954; DCB 10: 327–9
Hayes, Isaac Israel (1832–81)   DCB 11: 393–4
Kane, Elisha Kent (1820–57)   CE 2: 1126–7; DCB 8: 448–50
Schwatka, Frederick (1849–92)   DCB 12: 954–5; DAB 8: 481–2
Spicer, John O., captain of a whaler   Cooke and Holland, p 244

Scientific expeditions

Bell, Robert (1841–1917)   CE 1: 201
Boas, Franz (1858–1942)   EA 4: 118
Drexler, Charles   Cooke and Holland, p 218
Gordon, Andrew Robertson (1851–93)   Cooke and Holland, p 252; DCB 12: 382–3
Hector, James (1834–1907)   CE 2: 976
Hind, Henry Youle (1823–1907)   CE 2: 988; EC 5: 128
Hind, William G.R. (1833–89)   CE 2: 988; EC 5: 128
Kennicott, Robert (1835–66)   DAB 5: 338–9
Palliser, John (1817–87)   CE 3: 1610; DCB 11: 661–4

Geological Survey of Canada

LAND-AREA RECONNAISSANCE

Dawson, George Mercer (1849–1901)   CE 1: 573–4
Dowling, Donaldson B. (1858–1925)   Cooke and Holland, p 264
McConnell, Richard George (1857–1942)   EC 6: 240
Ord, L.R.   Morris Zaslow, *Reading the Rocks: The Story of the Geological Survey of Canada 1842–1872* (Ottawa: Department of Energy, Mines and Resources and Information Canada / Toronto: Macmillan, 1975), p 120
Richardson, James (1810–83)   EC 9: 21
Tyrrell, Joseph Burr (1858–1957)   CE 4: 2205
Vennor, Henry G. (1840–84)   DCB 11: 898–900

WESTERN CANADA EXPEDITIONS

Macoun, John (1831–1920)   CE 2: 1280–1
Ogilvie, William (1849–1912)   CE 3: 1561
Selwyn, Alfred Richard Cecil (1824–1902)   CE 3: 1977
Spencer, J.W. (1851–1921)   Zaslow, pp 116, 133

EASTERN CANADA EXPEDITIONS

Cochrane, A.S. (d 1894)   Zaslow, p 136
Low, Albert Peter (1861–1942)   CE 2: 1247
McOuat, Walter (1842–75)   Zaslow, p 124

Missionary journeys, Eastern Canada

Babel, Father Louis-François (1826–1912)   Cooke and Holland, p 227
Petitot, Father Émile (1838–1917)   Cooke and Holland, p 224

Geology of British North America

Hall, Stanley. *A New General Atlas*. London: Longman, Rees, Orme, Brown and Green, 1830. Pl 45
Richardson, John. *Arctic Searching Expedition: A Journal of a Boat Voyage through Rupert's Land and the Arctic Sea in Search of the Discovery Ships under Command of Sir John Franklin, with an Appendix on the Physical Geography of North America*. 2 vols. London: Longman, Brown, Green and Longman, 1851

Climate of British North America

Lorin Blodget's climatology maps were originally compiled and published in 1857. The map on this plate is based on the 1875 publication by Walling, who used Blodget's 1857 maps.

Blodget, Lorin. *Climatology of the United States, and of the Temperate Latitudes of the North American Continent*. Philadelphia: Lippincott, 1857. Isotherm map facing p 210; isohyets (precipitation) map facing p 220
Walling, H.F. *Tackabury's Atlas of the Dominion of Canada*. Montréal, Toronto, London: George N. Tackabury, 1875. Pp 98–101

Prairie levels

Palliser, John. *The Journals, Detailed Reports, and Observations Relative to the Explorations by Captain Palliser ... during the years 1857, 1858, 1859 and 1860*. London: Parliamentary Papers, 1863. Pp 6–13
– *Papers Relative to the Exploration by Captain Palliser of That Portion of British North America Which Lies Between the Northern Branch of River Saskatchewan and Rocky Mountains*. Presented to both Houses of Parliament by Command of Her Majesty, June 1859. London: Eyre and Spottiswoode, 1859, 1860. Repr New York: Greenwood Press, 1969

Natural regions of the Prairies, 1857–1859

Hector, James. 'Physical Features of the Central Part of British North America, with Special Reference to Its Botanical Physiognomy.' *Edinburgh New Philosophical Journal*, new series, 14, no. 11 (1861): 216–22, 230–4
Palliser, *Papers Relative to the Exploration by Captain Palliser*. 1859, 1860

Further readings

Baird, Patrick D. *Expeditions to the Canadian Arctic*. Repr from *The Beaver* (Winnipeg: HBC) no. 279 (Mar 1949): 44–7; no. 280 (June 1949): 41–7; (Sep 1949): 44–8
Belcher, Sir Edward. *The Last of the Arctic Voyages: Being a Narrative of the Expedition in H.M.S. 'Assistance,' under the Command of the Captain Sir Edward Belcher, C.B., in Search of Sir John Franklin, During the Years 1852–53–54*. 2 vols. London: Lovell Reeve, 1855
Berton, Pierre. *The Arctic Grail: The Quest for the Northwest Passage and the North Pole, 1818–1904*. Toronto: McClelland and Stewart, 1988
Carrière, Gaston. *Explorateur pour le Christ: Louis Babel, o.m.i., 1826–1912*. Montréal: Rayonnement, 1963
Chapman, J.D., A.L. Farley, R.I. Ruggles, and D.B. Turner, eds. *British Columbia Atlas of Resources*. Vancouver: British Columbia Natural Resources Conference, 1956
Hind, Henry Youle. *Narrative of the Canadian Red River Exploring Expedition of 1857 and of the Assiniboine and Saskatchewan Exploring Expedition of 1858*. 2 vols. London: Longman, Green, Longman and Roberts, 1860
Houston, C. Stuart, ed. *Arctic Ordeal: The Journal of John Richardson, Surgeon-Naturalist with Franklin 1820–1822*. Montréal and Kingston: McGill-Queen's University Press, 1984
Kupsch, W.O., and W.A.S. Sarjeant, eds. *History of Concepts in Precambrian Geology*. Geological Association of Canada, Special Paper 19. Ottawa, 1979
Markham, Albert H. *A Whaling Cruise to Baffin's Bay and the Gulf of Boothia ...* London: S. Low, Marston, Low and Searle, 1875
Morton, Arthur S. *A History of the Canadian West to 1870–1*. Toronto: University of Toronto Press, 1939; repr 1973
The National Atlas of Canada. 4th ed, rev. Ottawa: Department of Energy, Mines and Resources and Information Canada / Toronto: Macmillan, 1974
Petitot, Émile. 'Géographie de l'Athabaskaw-Mackenzie et des grands lacs du bassin arctique.' *Société de Géographie (Paris) Bulletin*. Ser. 6, no. 10 (1875): 5–42, 126–83, 242–90
Rich, Edwin Ernest. *The History of the Hudson's Bay Company 1670–1870*. 2 vols. London: Hudson's Bay Record Society, 1958–9
Ruggles, Richard I. *A Country So Interesting: The Hudson's Bay Company and Two Centuries of Mapping, 1670–1870*. Montréal and Kingston: McGill-Queen's University Press, 1991
Spry, Irene M. *The Palliser Expedition: An Account of John Palliser's British North American Expedition 1857–1860*. Toronto: Macmillan, 1963
Taylor, Andrew. *Geographical Discovery and Exploration in the Queen Elizabeth Islands*. Geographical Branch, Department of Mines and Technical Surveys, Memoir 3. Ottawa, 1955
Thomson, Don W. *Men and Meridians: The History of Surveying and Mapping in Canada*. Vols 1, 2. Ottawa: Queen's Printer, 1966, 1967
Wallace, Hugh N. 'Geographical Explorations to 1880.' In Morris Zaslow, ed. *A Century of Canada's Arctic Islands: 1880–1980*. Ottawa: Royal Society of Canada, 1981. Pp 15–32
– *The Navy, the Company and Richard King: British Exploration in the Canadian Arctic, 1829–1860*. Montréal and Kingston: McGill-Queen's University Press, 1980
Warkentin, John. *The Western Interior of Canada: A Record of Geographic Discovery 1612–1917*. Carleton Library no. 15. Toronto: McClelland and Stewart, 1964
Warkentin, John, and Richard I. Ruggles. *Manitoba Historical Atlas: A Selection of Facsimile Maps, Plans and Sketches from 1612*. Winnipeg: Historical and Scientific Society of Manitoba, 1970
Wonders, William C. 'Unrolling the Map of Canada's Arctic.' In Zaslow, ed. *A Century of Canada's Arctic Islands*. 1981. Pp 1–14

PLATE 10

From Sea to Sea: Territorial Growth to 1900

NORMAN L. NICHOLSON   Deceased
CHARLES F.J. WHEBELL   Geography, University of Western Ontario

Before he died in Nov 1984 Norman L. Nicholson had provided us with maps and other research materials along with written advice on how to use them for this plate. During his varied career Professor Nicholson had been successively director of the Geographic Branch in Ottawa and chairman of the Geography Department, assistant dean of the Graduate School, then principal of University College, University of Western Ontario. From 1951 to 1960 he was the first editor of the *Canadian Geographer*, which he helped to found. An able administrator, he was also a dedicated scholar whose PhD thesis on the boundaries of Canada, its provinces, and territories, later published as *Boundaries of the Canadian Confederation* (Toronto: Macmillan, 1979), remains one of the definitive statements on that subject.

Canada in 1900
The National Atlas of Canada. 4th ed, rev. Ottawa: Department of Energy, Mines and
   Resources and Information Canada / Toronto: Macmillan, 1974. Pp 85–6
The National Atlas of Canada, 5th ed. Ottawa: Department of Energy, Mines and
   Resources, Geographical Services Directorate, 1982. 'Canada – Territorial Evolu-
   tion 1867 – 1981'
Nicholson, Normal L. *The Boundaries of Canada, Its Provinces and Territories*. Geograph-
   ical Branch Memoir 2. Ottawa: Queen's Printer, 1964

Canada: 1791; 1825; 1849; 1873
The National Atlas of Canada. 1974. Pp 83–4

Alaska Panhandle boundary dispute, 1873–1903
Nicholson. *The Boundaries of Canada*. 1964. Pp 38–54
Paullin, Charles O. *Atlas of the Historical Geography of the United States*, ed J. K. Wright.
   Baltimore: Hoen, 1932. Pl 96, map A
White, James. 'Boundary Disputes and Treaties.' In Adam Shortt and Arthur G.
   Doughty, eds. *Canada and Its Provinces: A History of the Canadian People and Their
   Institutions*. Toronto: Glasgow, Brook and Co, 1914–17. Vol 8, part 3, map facing
   p 918

San Juan boundary dispute, 1846–1874
Paullin. *Atlas of the Historical Geography of the United States*. 1932. Pl 96, map C
White. 'Boundary Disputes and Treaties.' 1914–17. Vol 8, map facing p 870

Oregon Territory boundary dispute, 1820–1848
Paullin. *Atlas of the Historical Geography of the United States*. 1932. Pl 93, map C
White. 'Boundary Disputes and Treaties.' 1914–17. Vol 8, pp 839–71

Lake Superior boundary dispute, 1826–1842
Ontario. *Northwestern Ontario: Its Boundaries, Resources and Communications*. Toronto:
   Hunter, Rose, 1879
Paullin. *Atlas of the Historical Geography of the United States*. 1932. Pl 91, map B
White. 'Boundary Disputes and Treaties.' 1914–17. Vol 8, map facing p 894

Maine boundary dispute, 1798–1842
Paullin. *Atlas of the Historical Geography of the United States*. 1932. Pl 91, maps A, C; pl
   93, map D
White. 'Boundary Disputes and Treaties.' 1914–17. Vol 8, map facing p 782

Québec–New Brunswick boundary dispute, 1798–1851
Ganong, W.G. 'A Monograph of the Evolution of the Boundaries of New Brunswick.'
   Proceedings and Transactions of the Royal Society of Canada. 2nd series, vol 7, section 2
   (1901): 139–449

PLATE 11

Territorial Evolution, 1891–1961

NORMAN L. NICHOLSON   Deceased
ROBERT GALOIS   Geography, University of British Columbia
MICHAEL STAVELEY   Geography, Memorial University of Newfoundland

Two views of land in British Columbia
The map of the Gitskan and Wet'suwet'en territories was compiled under the authority of the hereditary chiefs. Many thanks are due to the Tribal Council for providing
the map and refining the text, and to Richard Overstall for providing liaison during
this process.

British Columbia. Department of Lands. Pre-Emptor's Map. 'Bulkley Sheet,' 192.

Regional share of territory: 1891; 1949
Land area indicated as 1949 uses 1951 data; 1951 was the first time Newfoundland
was included.

Canada Year Book. 1892: p 115. 1952: p 129

Canada, 1891–1961
The National Atlas of Canada. 5th ed. rev. Ottawa: Energy, Mines and Resources
   Canada, 1985. Pl 13.5

Proposals for the Prairie Provinces, 1905
Nicholson, Norman L. *The Boundaries of Canada, Its Provinces and Territories*. Ottawa:
   Queen's Printer, 1954. Pp 129–38

Arctic exploration
There were other explorers who ventured into the Arctic region between 1891 and
1961. Those shown on the map were the first to travel to particular areas.

Taylor, Andrew. *Geographical Discovery and Exploration in the Queen Elizabeth Islands*.
   Geographical Branch Memoir No. 3. Department of Mines and Technical Surveys.
   Ottawa, 1955

Newfoundland joins Confederation
The Newfoundland Gazette. Aug 1948

PLATE 12

Eastern Canada, ca 1800

R. COLE HARRIS   Geography, University of British Columbia
DAVID WOOD   Geography, York University

The content of this plate has depended upon the expertise and advice of Conrad E.
Heidenreich, Mario Lalancette, Victor P. Lytwyn, John Mannion, D. Wayne Moodie,
and Graeme Wynn.

The data on settlement and the fisheries in Newfoundland are drawn from pl 46;
HAC, vol I, pll 26–7; and from the Newfoundland census of 1797 (PRO, CO 194/40). The
data of settlement and trade in the Maritimes are derived from pl 48. The data on settlement and fisheries in the northern and western Gulf of St Lawrence are drawn
from HAC, vol I, pl 54.
   The population of Lower Canada is based on the estimate in pl 49. The distribution
of settlement and the extent of cleared land in Lower Canada are derived from
Joseph Bouchette, *A Topographical Description of the Province of Lower Canada ...* (London: Faden, 1815). The distribution of English-speaking settlers in Québec is a considered estimate – as much as can be done until this matter is the subject of a specialized
study. Fur routes are generalized and simplified, and are not intended to show exact
locations. Nor does the plate attempt to show all trading posts (for a more comprehensive distribution of posts in much of this territory see HAC, vol I, pl 62). The distribution of native people is derived from HAC, vol I, pl 69, from sources mentioned in
the notes for that plate. The small native populations in the Canadian Shield cannot
be usefully shown at the scale used on this plate and have been omitted.
   Estimates of the size and distribution of population in Upper Canada are based on
Lieutenant Governor Simcoe's correspondence (E.A. Cruikshank, ed, *The Correspondence of Lt Governor Simcoe*, 5 vols [Toronto: Ontario Historical Society, 1924]), the
militia returns, and the civil secretary's papers (NAC, RG 5 B26). The following have
been helpful: county histories; Robert Gourlay's *Statistical Account of Upper Canada ...*
(London: Simpkin and Marshall, 1822), abridged and with an introduction by S.R.
Mealing (Toronto: McClelland and Stewart, 1974); and the dates of township survey
given in W.G. Dean and G.J. Matthews, *Economic Atlas of Ontario* (Toronto: University
of Toronto Press, 1969), pl 99. Data on trade in Upper Canada have been derived in
part from Douglas McCalla, 'The "Loyalist" Economy of Upper Canada, 1784–1806,'
Histoire sociale / Social History 16 (1983): 279–304. William G. Dean prepared the information on roads and settled areas in the United States from Charles O. Paullin, *Atlas
of the Historical Geography of the United States* (Baltimore: Hoen, 1932), pll 60E,
76C, 138J.

PLATE 13

Population in the Canadas and the Atlantic Region to 1857

BRIAN S. OSBORNE   Geography, Queen's University
JEAN-CLAUDE ROBERT   Histoire, Université du Québec à Montréal
DAVID A. SUTHERLAND   History, Dalhousie University

Population distribution: ca 1825; ca 1851
Dots are plotted in a random rather than a uniform manner, with greater concentration along lakes and rivers, based on historical evidence. Because aggregate values
are used, the exact location of the settlers is unknown. It is not known whether or not
there was a clustering around parish churches in Lower Canada, and even the location of most parish churches is unknown. Accordingly, the exact location of parish
boundaries in Lower Canada has been assumed. A random location is more plausible
than a clustering around assumed parish centroids.
   The ca 1825 map reflects 1821 data for Upper Canada, 1824 data for New Brunswick, 1825 data for Lower Canada, and 1827 data for Nova Scotia and Prince
Edward Island.

Canada. *Census*. 1851. Vol 1, Census by Ages, pp 112–505
Lower Canada. *Census*. 1825
NAC. RG 5 B26. Population of Upper Canada. 1821, 1831, 1851
New Brunswick. *Census*. 1824, 1851
Newfoundland. *Census*. 1857
Nova Scotia. *Census*. 1827, table 1; 1851
Prince Edward Island. *Census*. 1848

Growth of cities, 1825–1891
Canada. *Census*. Various census years
Censuses of individual provinces. Various census years. Summarized in Canada.
   Census. 1871. Vol 4
Simmons, J., and Geoff Dobilas. 'The Population of Urban Nodes.' HAC research
   report. 1980

Growth of provinces, 1851–1891
Urquhart and Buckley, *Historical Statistics of Canada*. Series A 2–14, 'Population of
Canada, by Province. Census dates, 1851 to 1976'

Male–female ratio in Upper Canada, 1824–1851
The graph reflects the data in the censuses although there is a large upward shift in
the single year between 1841 and 1842. The census of 1842 is considered faulty.

Canada. *Census*. 1871. Vol 4. Census of Upper Canada, Annual 1824–42, table 4; 1848,
table 4; 1851

Population pyramids
The population pyramids for Eastern Canada are shown for the individual provinces
and are broken down into major urban areas and other parts of each province. No
consolidation of provincial data was feasible because the age groups for the data
were generally different.

Sources for the data used in constructing the population pyramids are the same as those used for the maps of population distribution, above.

Further readings

Bouchette, Joseph. *The British Dominions in North America* ... London: Longman, Rees, Orme, Brown, Green and Longman, 1832. Vol 2, ch 11

Campbell, Duncan. *History of Prince Edward Island*. Charlottetown: Bremner Brothers, 1875

Clark, Andrew Hill. *Three Centuries and the Island: A Historical Geography of Settlement and Agriculture in Prince Edward Island, Canada*. Toronto: University of Toronto Press, 1959

McGregor, John. *British America*. Edinburgh: Blackwood / London: Cadell, 1832. Book 4

– *Historical and Descriptive Sketches of the Maritime Colonies of British America*. London: Longman, Rees, Orme, Brown and Green, 1828. Chs 1–8

Martin, R. Montgomery. *The British Colonies: Their History, Extent, Condition, and Resources*. London and New York: London Printing and Publishing Co, 1851– . Vol 1, book 4

– *History of the Colonies of the British Empire ... From the Official Records of the Colonial Office*. London: Wm. H. Allen and George Routledge, 1843. Book 3

– *History of Nova Scotia, Cape Breton, the Sable Islands, New Brunswick, Prince Edward Island, the Bermudas, Newfoundland, &c. &c.* London: Whitaker, 1837. Ch 3

Meacham, J.H., and Co. *Illustrated Historical Atlas of the Province of Prince Edward Island*. Philadelphia: Meacham, 1880. Repr Oshawa: Maracle Press, 1973

Stewart, John. *An Account of Prince Edward Island, in the Gulph of St. Lawrence, North America ...* London: Winchester and Son, 1806

PLATE 14

The Canadian Population, 1871, 1891

DON MEASNER Historical Atlas of Canada, Toronto
CHRISTINE HAMPSON Geography, Brock University

Population distribution: 1871; 1891

The rural population was based on census-subdivision areas. Reference was made to other dot-distribution maps, to county atlases, and to present-day medium-scale topographic maps to help ensure that the placement of dots within census subdivisions was as accurate as possible.

For Québec the 1951 census-subdivision map boundaries were carried backward to 1871 in order to determine the census-subdivision boundaries for 1871 and 1891. Because the 1871 census year was arranged geographically by both census division and subdivision, it was used as the base year. Subdivision-population remainders of less than 300 were added to an adjacent subdivision so no numbers were dropped in any one province. For incorporated areas urban-centre populations were drawn from the census, and for unincorporated areas from a research report on the population of urban nodes prepared for the HAC project. Incorporated areas with a population of fewer than 1 000 were considered rural and added to the rural population for the surrounding census subdivision. The populations of unincorporated urban nodes of more than 1 000 were subtracted from the population of the surrounding census subdivisions.

Native people were underenumerated in both the 1871 and the 1891 censuses, especially in the West. The distribution of Native people may be seen HAC, vol II, pll 32, 33, 34, and 35, and pl 64 of this volume.

Canada. *Census*. 1871. Vol 1, table 1
– *Census*. 1891. Vol 1, table 2
Newfoundland. *Census*. 1884

Urban populations, 1851, 1871, 1891
Urban centres, 1851, 1871, 1891
Canada. Various censuses. Urban populations
Simmons, J., and G. Dobilas. 'The Population of Urban Nodes, 1871–1951.' Unpublished HAC research report. 1980

Population pyramids

The population pyramids were constructed from census data that give the population by sex and grouped ages. For comparability with population data at mid-century (pl 13) some age groups were consolidated. The male-female ratio is indicated for each age group on each pyramid. In each age group the larger population (male or female) was divided by the smaller population, multiplied by 100, and then rounded to the nearest whole number.

Canada. *Census*. 1871. Vol 2, table 7
– *Census*. 1891. Vol 2, table 1
Newfoundland. *Census*. 1884

Further reading
Walling, H.F. *Tackabury's Atlas of the Dominion of Canada*. Montréal, Toronto, London: Tackabury, 1875

PLATE 15

The Exodus: Migrations, 1860–1900

PATRICIA A. THORNTON Geography, Concordia University
RONALD H. WALDER Historical Atlas of Canada, Toronto
ELIZABETH BUCHANAN University of Toronto Schools

Migration types, 1871–1891
Thornton, Patricia. 'The Problem of Out-Migration from Atlantic Canada, 1871–1921: A New Look.' *Acadiensis* 15, no. 1 (1985): 3–34
Widdis, Randy W. 'Scale and Context: Approaches to the Study of Canadian Migration Patterns in the Nineteenth Century.' *Social Science History* 12, no. 3 (1988): 269–303

Migration rates: 1871–1881; 1881–1891
Estimates of net migration between censuses always grossly understate the extent of movement, identifying only the net balance of migrations. Moreover county-level data often disguise opposing economic and demographic processes occurring within the county. This is a particular problem in counties that include both old and newly settled regions, rural and urban parts, and agricultural and industrial areas. The method we used to calculate intercensal net migration is termed *cohort analysis*. By this method net migration was calculated as the difference in the total number of people in each age group from one census to the next, less those who died in the interim. Given the age and sex structure of the population in a census year and a comparable age structure for the same population 10 years later, survival factors were used to project forward from the first census the number expected to have survived until the next census. The difference between the expected and the actual populations provided an estimate of net migration for each age and sex group. These estimates were then added together to give the total net migration and converted into rates by dividing the estimates by the average of the base populations for the two censuses.

For reasons of reliability only those born before the initial census and younger than 60 were used to calculate net migration, although the total population was used in the denominator to calculate rates. This assumed that migration among the very young and very old was negligible.

In the absence of registration of vital statistics in Canada at the time, life-table estimates of 10-year survival factors were used, based on Bourbeau and Légaré (1982). In light of the acknowledged significantly higher mortality in Québec than in the rest of Canada at this time, especially among infants, the Bourbeau and Légaré estimates for Québec for 1871 and 1881, respectively, were used for that province and their estimates for Canada were used for Ontario and the Maritimes.

Newfoundland was ignored because the data were not comparable.

The unit of measurement was the census division in 1871, 1881, and 1891. In a few cases in Ontario and Québec, boundaries were modified or adjacent divisions aggregated to ensure geographic continuity throughout the 20-year period.

Bourbeau, Robert, and Jacques Légaré. *Évolution de la mortalité au Canada et au Québec, 1831–1931*. Montréal: Les Presses de l'Université de Montréal, 1982
Canada. *Census*. 1871. Vol 2, table 7
– *Census*. 1881. Vol 2, table 8
– *Census*. 1891. Vol 1, table 6; vol 2, table 1
Thornton. 'The Problem of Out-Migration from Atlantic Canada.' 1985

Biological kinship linkages, northern Ontario, 1889
The data from which the kinship linkages were derived were collected as part of a much larger project designed to explore the importance of 19th-century kinship relations in Ontario to individual permanence within townships and to geographical mobility (Buchanan, 1989). Included in the study were all persons arriving in the townships of Day, Bright, and Bright Additional in Algoma East between 1879, when the area was opened for settlement, and 1939, after which most social-welfare programs began to be universally available in Canada.

Of greatest importance for this map were the manuscript censuses of 1881 and 1891 for the study area, and the manuscript censuses of 1861 and 1871 for the places of origin of those who migrated from southern Ontario to the study area. Cases of members of families originating elsewhere had to be treated individually. The manuscript censuses are a reliable source of basic data about individuals and their relationships within their families. Other sources are land records; newspaper announcements of births, deaths, marriages, and obituaries; along with cemetery inscriptions. Less complete, reliable, or accessible records for the area were civil registrations, directories, county atlases, and church records. The local *Tweedsmuir Village History* (compiled by the Women's Institute) and local residents who were direct descendants of many of the original settlers helped in the resolution of ambiguities or with anomalous data in the records.

Data from such sources were consolidated into family-group record sheets. These genealogical sheets provided an individual's life history within the context of the family of orientation (parents, siblings, grandparents) and the family of procreation (spouse and children). The year of arrival in the study area and the year of death within the study area or of departure to another destination were also used. Thus it became possible to identify all individuals present in the study area for any given year in the context of their local kinship network.

Buchanan, Elizabeth. 'In Search of Security: Kinship and the Farm Family on the North Shore of Lake Huron, 1879–1930.' PhD thesis, McMaster University, 1989

Canadians in New England, 1900
Faucher, Albert. 'L'émigration des Canadiens français au XIXᵉ siècle: position du problème et perspectives.' *Recherches sociographiques* 5, no. 3 (1961): 277–317
Paquet, Gilles, and Wayne R. Smith. 'L'émigration des Canadiens français vers les États-Unis, 1790–1940: problématique et coups de sonde.' *L'actualité économique* 59, no. 3 (1983): 423–53
United States. *Census*. 1900. Vol 1, part 1, table 34

Selected occupations of Canadian-born in the northeastern United States, 1880
United States. *Census*. 1880. Vol 1 (Population), table 31

Canadian-born in the United States, 1880
United States. *Census*. 1880. Vol 1 (Population), table 27

Migration estimates, 1850s–1900s
Canada. *Census*. 1871. Vol 4, tables for 1851, 1861, 1871
See also 'Migration rates: 1871–1881; 1881–1891' above.

Place of birth, 1861, 1891
Canada. *Census*. 1861. Vol 1, table 3
– *Census*. 1891. Vol 1, table 5

Further readings
Bouchard, Gérard. 'Family Structures and Geographic Mobility at Laterrière, 1851–1935.' *Journal of Family History* 2, no. 4 (1977): 350–69
Elliot, Bruce S. *Irish Migrants in the Canadas: A New Approach*. Montréal and Kingston: McGill-Queen's University Press, 1988
Houston, Cecil J., and William J. Smyth. *Irish Emigration and Canadian Settlement: Patterns, Links and Letters*. Toronto: University of Toronto Press, 1990
Hudson, John C. 'Migration to an American Frontier.' *Annals of the Association of American Geographers* 66, no. 2 (1976): 242–65

Keyfitz, Nathan. 'The Growth of the Canadian Population.' *Population Studies* 4, no. 1 (1950): 47–63

Lavoie, Yolande. 'Les mouvements migratoires des Canadiens entre leur pays et les États-Unis au XIXe et XXe siècles: étude quantitative.' In Hubert Charbonneau, ed. *La population du Québec: études retrospectives*. Montréal: Boréal, 1973. Pp 73–88

McDougall, Duncan M. 'Immigration into Canada, 1851–1920.' *Canadian Journal of Economics and Political Science* 27, no. 2 (1961): 162–75

Paquet, Gilles. 'L'émigration des Canadiens français vers la Nouvelle Angleterre, 1870–1910: prises de vue quantitative.' *Recherches sociographiques* 5, no. 3 (1964): 319–70

Studness, Charles M. 'Economic Opportunity and the Westward Migration of Canadians during the Late Nineteenth Century.' *Canadian Journal of Economics and Political Science* 30, no. 4 (1961): 570–84

Vicero, R.D. 'Immigration of French Canadians to New England, 1840–1900: A Geographical Analysis.' PhD thesis, University of Wisconsin, 1968

PLATE 16

Migration, 1891–1930

MARVIN McINNIS   Economics, Queen's University

Special acknowledgment should be made to the important contribution of Michael Percy (Economics, University of Alberta) in the study of the Ontario origin of Prairie settlers.

The move to the West, 1891–1914
This map is based on two separate bodies of evidence. The interprovincial movement of Canadian-born people was estimated directly from census data on province of birth, cross-tabulated with province of residence. For the Prairie Provinces the 1916 total of those born out of the province was derived from the census of that year. For other provinces the 1914 numbers were interpolated from the 1911 and 1921 censuses. The number of persons in each province of destination from each province of origin was compared with the 1891 number adjusted for survival over the 25-year period; the survival rates used were those from Bourbeau and Légaré (1982). Variations in the concentrations of Ontario-born settlers in the Prairie Provinces can be drawn directly from the 1916 census. Data on districts of origin within Ontario were based on a sample of Prairie newspaper obituaries (McInnis and Percy, 1989). For the calculations some Ontario counties/districts were grouped: Muskoka and Parry Sound, Peterborough and Haliburton, Frontenac and Addington, Leeds and Grenville, Brant and Wentworth.

Bourbeau, Robert, and Jacques Légaré. *Évolution de la mortalité au Canada et au Québec, 1831–1931*. Montréal: Les Presses de l'Université de Montréal, 1982

Canada. *Census*. 1891: Vol 2, Table V. 1921: Vol 2, Table LIII
– *Census of the Prairie Provinces*. 1916. Table XXII

McInnis, Marvin, and Michael Percy. 'Dead Men Can Tell Tales: The Ontario Origins of Canadian Settlers on the Canadian Plains.' Unpublished report submitted to the Historical Atlas of Canada project, Vol III, 1989

Immigration, 1896–1914
Immigration to the Prairies, 1896–1914
The migration flows are based on changes in the numbers of foreign-born in Canada over the period between 1891 and 1914. The immigrant population in the 1921 census is tabulated by period of arrival so that post-1914 immigrants can be netted out. By covering the whole period in a net fashion a lower figure for immigration to Canada is derived, well below the cumulated annual inflow (graph of 'Immigration to Canada'). Survival rates from the model life tables given in Bourbeau and Légaré (1982) for the twenty-five-year interval are applied to the number of foreign-born in 1891. For some areas the numbers shown on the flow lines do not correspond to the totals on the pie graphs because no specific flow lines are shown for the Asian population moving beyond British Columbia.

Bourbeau and Légaré. *Évolution de la mortalité*. 1982
Canada. *Census*. 1891: Vol 1, Table V. 1921: Vol 2, Table XLII
– *Census of the Prairie Provinces*. 1916. Table XLII

Immigration to Canada, 1891–1961
Urquhart and Buckley. *Historical Statistics*. Series A254

Asian immigration, 1891–1931
Urquhart and Buckley. *Historical Statistics*. Series A333, A334, A335

Distribution of immigrant population, 1921
Canada. *Census*. 1921. Vol 2, Table XLI

Canadians moving to the United States, 1890–1914
Canadians living in the United States, 1930
Truesdell, Leon E. *The Canadian Born in the United States*. New Haven: Yale University Press, 1943. Table 40, Fig 8

Origins of American homesteaders on the Prairies, 1890–1914
Canada. Department of the Interior. *Annual Report of the Deputy Minister*. 1890–1914. Data for the plate compiled by Michael Percy

Percy, Michael B., and Tamara Woroby. 'American Homesteaders and the Canadian Prairies, 1899 and 1909.' *Explorations in Economic History* 24, no. 1 (Jan 1987): 77–100

PLATE 17

Population Changes, 1941–1961

MARVIN McINNIS   Economics, Queen's University
WARREN KALBACH   Sociology, University of Toronto
DONALD KERR   Geography, University of Toronto

Interprovincial migration, 1956–1961
Canada. *Census*. 1961. Vol 4, Pt 1 (Bull 4.1–9), Table 14

George, M.V. *Internal Migration in Canada: Demographic Analyses*. DBS. 1961 Census Monograph. Ottawa, 1970. Ch 6, Appendix (various tables)

Stone, Leroy O. *Migration in Canada: Some Regional Aspects*. DBS. 1961 Census Monograph. Ottawa, 1969. Section 2.2, Appendix (various tables)

Demographic change, 1951–1961
For non-metropolitan urban areas and for rural sectors of counties and census divisions containing metropolitan urbanized areas, estimates have been made by McInnis based on the census.
Canada. *Census*. 1961. Vol 7, Pt 1 (Bull 7.1–2), Table x

Immigrant population, 1946–1961
'Canada. *Census*. 1961. Vol 1, Pt 1 (Bull 1.3–11), Tables 125–6

Net migration, 1951–1961
Canada. *Census*. 1961. Vol 7, Pt 1, Table 2

Gross reproduction rate, 1941–1961
The Gross Reproduction Rate (GRR) is a widely used measure of fertility that is free from the influence of age composition. For that reason it is better suited than crude birth rates for comparison across geographic areas. The GRR is usually interpreted in a cohort sense, that is, if age-specific fertility rates continued at their given level, the GRR would measure the number of female children women would bear, on average, over their span of reproductive years. A GRR value of 1.00 would indicate a population that is just reproducing itself. No adjustment is made for survival (hence the *gross* rate). Another way of describing the GRR is as the sum of age-specific fertility rates, multiplied by the fraction of births that is female children. The age weights are taken to be equal (a rectangular distribution).

The choice of GRR is, in part, dictated by the availability of those rates for counties, cities, and towns of more than 5 000 population for 1940–2. Those are found in the 1941 census monograph on fertility by Charles (1948). They are the only properly constructed measures of fertility available for subprovincial areas in Canada for that date. In most parts of the nation fertility in 1941 was still very close to the all-time low reached in the mid-1930s. Nationally the GRR reached its Baby Boom peak in 1959, but it fell slowly at first and by 1961 was down only 2½% from the peak. The period shown thus spans the full extent of the Baby Boom. A tabulation of births by place of residence of mother is readily available for the 1960–2 births period. The problem is that there are no age-specific fertility rates for counties and towns. The GRR for 1960–2 is approximated by factoring the GRR into two component indices that can be separately calculated and recombined. The procedure ignores a small, indeterminate interaction term. An index of births to women 15–49 years of age as a whole could be directly calculated. It was then modified by an index of the deviation of local from national age composition of women (where women in each age group are weighted by the national average age-specific fertility rates). A comparison of this estimated GRR with values directly calculated for provinces and large cities (for which the requisite data are available) shows a close match. See McInnis (1988).

Canada. DBS. *Vital Statistics*. 1900, 1961, 1962. Tables S6, S7

Charles, Enid. *The Changing Size of the Family in Canada*. 1941 Census Monograph No 1. Ottawa, 1948

McInnis, Marvin. 'Geographic Dimensions of the Baby Boom in Canada.' Unpublished report submitted to the Historical Atlas of Canada project, Vol III, 1988

Total fertility rate, 1926–1961
Canada. Statistics Canada. *Vital Statistics*. Cats. 84–204, 84–206. 1971

Natural increase, 1881–1961
Net migration, 1881–1961
Canada. Statistics Canada. *Vital Statistics*. Cats. 84–204, 84–206. 1971
Urquhart and Buckley. *Historical Statistics*. Series A233–43, A244–53

Further readings
Beaujot, Rodric, and Kevin McQuillan. *Canadian Dualism: The Demographic Development of Canadian Society*. Toronto: Gage, 1982

Butz, William, and Michael P. Ward. 'Will U.S. Fertility Remain Low? A New Economic Interpretation.' *Population and Development Review* 5 (1979): 663–88

Easterlin, Richard. *Birth and Fortune*. New York: Basic Books, 1980

Kalbach, W.E. *The Impact of Immigration on Canada's Population*. DBS. 1961 Census Monograph. Ottawa, 1970

Kalbach, W.E., and W.E. McVey. *Demographic Bases of Canadian Society*. 2nd ed. Toronto: McGraw-Hill Ryerson, Toronto, 1979

PLATE 18

Population Composition, 1891–1961

DONALD CARTWRIGHT   Geography, University of Western Ontario
MURDO MacPHERSON   Historical Atlas of Canada, Toronto

Ethnic origin: 1901; 1931; 1961
Since the 1901 and 1935 censuses of Newfoundland and Labrador gave only place of birth and not ethnic origin, Newfoundland is not included in 1891 and 1931. Graphs of cities specify ethnic groups of 0.4% or larger; graphs of provinces specify groups of 1.0% or more except 'other' which may be less than 1.0%.

Canada. Census. 1901: Vol 1, Table XI. 1931: Vol 2, Tables 32, 34. 1961: Vol 1, Pt 2, Tables 37, 38

Major ethnic groups: 1901; 1931; 1961
Canada. *Census*. 1901: Vol 1, Table XI. 1931: Vol 2, Table 31. 1961: Vol 1, Pt 2, Table 35

Population profile: 1901; 1931; 1961
Canada. *Census*. 1961. Vol 1, Pt 2, Table 20

Urban and rural population: 1901; 1931; 1961
Estimates of Newfoundland population were provided by Michael Staveley (Geography, Memorial University of Newfoundland).

Canada. *Census.* 1901–61. Various tables
Newfoundland. *Census of Newfoundland and Labrador.* Various years

Population growth, 1891–1961
Leacy. *Historical Statistics.* Series A67–9

The bilingual belt, 1961
With the exception of Montréal, urban areas have been incorporated with the census subdivisions in which they are located. On the map adjacent census subdivisions with similar values and thus of the same category are amalgamated into a single unit. Individual subdivisions are shown only when they are of a different category from surrounding divisions.
Canada. *Census.* 1961. Vol 1, Pt 1, Table 7; Series SP, Bulletin SP–5

Further readings
Canada. Royal Commission on Bilingualism and Biculturalism. *The Official Languages.* Book I. 1967
Coons, W.H., D.M. Taylor, and M.-A. Tremblay, eds. *The Individual, Language and Society in Canada.* Ottawa: The Canada Council, 1977
Joy, Richard J. *Languages in Conflict: The Canadian Experience.* Toronto: McClelland and Stewart, 1972
Lachapelle, Réjean, and Jacques Henripin. *La situation démolinguistique au Canada: évolution passée et pros.* Montréal: Institut de recherches politiques, 1980. Also issued in English as *The Demolinguistic Situation in Canada: Past Trends and Future Prospects* in 1982
Lieberson, Stanley. *Language and Ethnic Relations in Canada.* New York: Wiley. 1970
Maheu, Robert. *Les francophones du Canada: 1941–1991.* Montréal: Éditions Parti pris, 1970

PLATE 19

The Emergence of a Transportation System, 1837–1852

ANDREW F. BURGHARDT   Geography, McMaster University

Gratitude is expressed to Darrell Norris (State University of New York, Geneseo) for his careful research and collection of data on the canal systems.

Transportation service, Summer 1837
The map was compiled from data in local newspapers of the time and from published sources.
Aiton, Grace. 'Communications – Trail, Portage and Rivers in the Early Days of New Brunswick.' *Collections of the New Brunswick Historical Society* no. 19 (1966): 47–51
Evans, Reginald D. 'Transportation and Communications in Nova Scotia, 1815 to 1850.' MA thesis, Dalhousie University, 1936
Guillet, Edwin C. *Pioneer Travel in Upper Canada.* Toronto: University of Toronto Press, 1933
Haliburton, Thomas C. *History of Nova Scotia.* 2 vols. Halifax: Joseph Howe, 1829. Repr Belleville, Ont: Mika, 1973
O'Neill, Paul. *A Seaport Legacy: The Story of St. John's, Newfoundland.* Erin, Ont: Press Porcépic, 1976
Parker, William Henry. 'The Geography of the Province of Lower Canada, in 1837.' PhD thesis, Oxford University, 1958
Taylor, Mary L. 'Traffic on the St. John River.' *Collections of the New Brunswick Historical Society* no. 16 (1961): 24–36

Scheduled passenger service, Summer 1852
This map was constructed from a large number of local and county histories, notices and advertisements in newspapers, the sources listed above, and the following:
MacKay, Robert W.S. *The Canada Directory.* Montréal: Lovell, 1851
Martell, J.S. 'Intercolonial Communications, 1840–1867.' In George A. Rawlyk, ed. *Historical Essays on the Atlantic Provinces.* Toronto: McClelland and Stewart, 1967. Pp 179–206
Munro, Alexander. *New Brunswick: With a Brief Outline of Nova Scotia and Prince Edward Island.* Halifax: Nugent, 1855. Repr Belleville, Ont: Mika, 1972
Perley, Moses H. *Handbook of Information for Emigrants to New Brunswick.* Saint John: Chubb, 1854
Smith, William Henry. *Canada, Past, Present and Future: Being a Historical, Geographical, Geological, and Statistical Account of Canada West.* Toronto: Maclear, 1851

Travel times from Liverpool, England: 1837; 1852
Travel times were extracted from the sources listed for the maps above. The isochrones are based on a few key points such as Montréal and the Atlantic ports. Known travel times were used to extend the lines along rivers and coasts. Times for various distances inland were estimated from the overland travel rates of the time.

Welland Canal system, 1851
Guillet. *Pioneer Travel in Upper Canada.* 1933

Traffic volume on London-area toll roads, 1844
Molson, John (1787–1860) DCB 8: 630–4
Simcoe, John Graves (1752–1806) DCB 5: 754–9
Weller, William (1799–1863) DCB 9: 825–6
Canada, Province of. *Journals of the Legislative Assembly.* 1845. App, letter A, nos 2, 3, 4, 5, 7

Cargo origins and destinations, 1851–1852
Canada, Province of. *Journals of the Legislative Assembly.* 1852. Tables of Trade and Navigation. No. 8, p 27; no. 9, p 28

Welland Canal cargo, 1834–1844
Canada. Province of. *Journals of the Legislative Assembly.* 1835–45. Tables of Trade and Navigation

Average travel costs per mile, 1850
Travel costs were calculated by averaging fares advertised in 13 newspapers from across Canada West in 1850.

PLATE 20

Linking Canada, 1867–1891

THOMAS F. McILWRAITH   Geography, University of Toronto

The research assistance and advice of Christopher Andreae, Historical Research, London, and Susan Knox, Mississauga, are gratefully acknowledged.

Building the transcontinental railway
Corporate histories of the Canadian Pacific, Grand Trunk, and other lines provided much of the evidence for this map, with precise alignments taken from topographic maps. Information on surveys, alternative routes, and dates of completion came from legislation and published sources. Transborder details have been compiled from the sources cited below and various corporate histories.
Andreae, Christopher. 'Historical Atlas of the Railways of Canada.' Unpublished ms maps. 1976. Published as *Lines of Country.* Toronto: Stoddart, 1997.
Berton, Pierre. *The National Dream: The Great Railway, 1871–1881.* Toronto: McClelland and Stewart, 1970
Lavallée, Omer S.A. *Van Horne's Road: An Illustrated Account of the Construction and First Years of Operation of the Canadian Pacific Transcontinental Railway.* Montréal: Railfare Enterprises, 1974
McIlwraith, Thomas F. 'Transport in the Borderland,' In Robert Lecker, ed. *A Borderland Anthology.* Toronto: ECW Press, 1991. Pp 54–79
Wilgus, William John. *The Railway Interrelations of the United States and Canada.* New Haven: Yale University Press, 1937

Travel time from Ottawa: 1867; 1891
Published schedules for railways and ships were used to establish the travelling time where public common-carrier transportation was available. For regions beyond the reach of these services the journals and accounts of more than 200 travellers were analysed. Some of these trips had occurred as much as a century earlier, while others took place during the 20th century. If the methods used (canoe and foot, mainly) were the only ones available in 1867 or 1890, the experience was not considered to be out of date.
For each date the data were consolidated on a large base map, permitting days of travel to be accumulated from route to route. A system of reference points resulted, each identified by the number of days of travel from Ottawa. The isochrones (lines of equal time-distance from Ottawa) were interpolated through these points. Trip times tend to be optimistic, as travel and exploration commonly took place in seasons of favourable weather. There was, however, a great deal of variability, reflected in the broadening generalization of the isochrones towards the extremities of the country.
The following published timetables and newspapers were consulted:
British Columbian (New Westminster). 3 July 1867
Halifax Citizen. 20 Oct 1866
The Manitoban (Winnipeg). 11 Apr, 13 June 1874
New Brunswick Reporter (Fredericton). 28 June, 5 July 1867
Quebec Mercury. 21 July 1867
Saint John Morning News. 24 June 1867
Travelers' Official Railway Guide, for the United States and Canada. New York: Pratt, June 1868
Winnipeg Free Press. 30 Sep 1890
The more important traveller accounts are as follows:
The Beaver. Publ by the HBC. 1935–80. About 35 articles consulted
Cooke, Alan, and Clive Holland. *The Exploration of Northern Canada, 500 to 1920: A Chronology.* Toronto: Arctic History Press, 1978
Hanbury, David T. *Sport and Travel in the Northland of Canada.* London: Edward Arnold, 1904
Morse, Eric W. *Fur Trade Canoe Routes of Canada, Then and Now.* Toronto: University of Toronto Press, 1968
Papers of the Historical and Scientific Society of Manitoba. Winnipeg
Pike, Warburton. *The Barren Ground of Northern Canada.* London: Macmillan, 1892
Sheldon, Charles. *The Wilderness of the Upper Yukon.* Toronto: Copp Clark, 1911
Simpson, Alexander. *The Life and Travels of Thomas Simpson, the Arctic Discoverer.* London: Bentley, 1845. Repr Toronto: Canadian Heritage Series Library Edition, 1963
Spry, Irene M. *The Palliser Expedition: An Account of John Palliser's British North American Expedition, 1857–1860.* Toronto: Macmillan, 1963
Thomas, Lewis G., ed. *The Prairie West to 1905.* Toronto: Oxford University Press, 1975
Tyrrell, Joseph B. *Across the Sub-Arctics of Canada.* London, 1898. Repr Toronto: Coles Facsimile Edition, 1973
Wallace, W. Stewart. *John McLean's Notes of Twenty-Five Years' Service in the Hudson's Bay Territory.* Toronto: Champlain Society, 1932
Wallace, W. Stewart, ed. 'Sir Henry Lefroy's Journey to the North-West in 1843–4.' In Royal Society of Canada, *Proceedings and Transactions.* Series 3, 32, section 2 (1938): 67–96
Zaslow, Morris. *The Opening of the Canadian North, 1870–1914.* Toronto: McClelland and Stewart, 1971

Major trips of the governor-general, 1873–1877
Dufferin, Frederick Temple Blackwood, Marquis of (1826–1902) CE 1: 632
Dufferin, Marchioness of. *My Canadian Journal 1872–78.* London, 1891. Repr Toronto: Coles Facsimile Edition, 1971
Leggo, William. *The History of the Administration of Dufferin.* Montréal: Lovell, 1878
Stewart, George. *Canada under the Administration of the Earl of Dufferin.* Toronto: Rose-Belford, 1878

Profile of the transcontinental route
White, James. *Altitudes in Canada.* Ottawa: Commission of Conservation, 1915

'Around the World with Canadian Pacific'
CPR. 'Annotated Time Table.' Corrected to 19 July 1892

Sleeping car 'Honolulu'
Drawings by J.A. Shields, Montréal. Reprinted with permission from Lavallée, *Van Horne's Road* (1974), p 255

PLATE 21

The Emergence of the Urban System, 1888–1932

JAMES W. SIMMONS   Geography, University of Toronto
MICHAEL CONZEN   Committee on Geographical Studies, University of Chicago
DONALD KERR   Geography, University of Toronto

The urban network: 1891; 1921
Population change, 1891–1921
In the measurement and mapping of urbanization there are problems of definition: what is the threshold size below which places are not considered to be urban; and what is the areal demarcation used to separate an urban place from its rural surroundings? In Canada there is no alternative to using population data as compiled in decennial censuses. Prior to 1951, the DBS defined the urban population as those persons residing within *incorporated* cities, towns, and villages of whatever population. Between 1941 and 1951 the rapid expansion of suburban populations within rural municipalities led to a redefinition. In 1951 the definition of urban population was modified to include all persons living in cities, towns, and villages with populations of 1 000 and over, *incorporated or not*, as well as the residents of *metropolitan areas*. This latter concept included municipalities and parts of townships adjacent to major centres with populations of over 100 000.

A decision was made to adopt the 1951 definition to identify urban centres in 1891 and 1921 on these maps. Unincorporated places were considered, closely linked urban centres were aggregated together, and the urbanized parts of rural municipalities were assigned to the appropriate urban place.

Allen, E.S., compiler. *The Official Guide of the Railways and Steam Navigation Lines of the United States, Puerto Rico, Canada, Mexico, and Cuba.* New York: National Railway Publication Company, 1921
Allen, W.F., compiler. *Travellers' Official Railway Guide for the United States and Canada.* New York: National Railway Publication Company, 1891
Canada. *Census.* 1891. 1921. Various tables, data modified by author
Simmons, J.W., and G. Dobilas. 'Population Nodes, 1871–1951.' Unpublished report submitted to the Historical Atlas of Canada project, Vol III, 1984

The long-distance telephone network, 1888–1932
Telephone connections from Montréal, 1888–1932
From the early 20th century on, Canadian telephone facilities were greatly decentralized, being controlled by eight major companies and several smaller ones. Each province in western Canada and Nova Scotia, New Brunswick, and Newfoundland had its own telephone company; the Bell Telephone Company controlled facilities in Ontario and Québec. The variable quality and general lack of comparability of the historical records make research difficult. Without question the archives and historical section of Bell Canada in Montréal are the largest and most valuable source of information. Very few records are available in provincial or federal archives.

Using maps as sources of information had limitations. The existence of a line between two points on a map did not necessarily mean that there was a reliable long-distance service between the two points. Further research is needed to establish more precisely the spread of the service in terms of reliability and frequency of calls.

A special acknowledgment is made to the staff of the Bell Canada Archives in Montréal and especially Stephanie Sykes, Director of the Historical and Information Resource Centre, and Catherine Lowe, Manager of the Historical Research Division, for providing maps and other source material as well as answering countless questions. Without their help it would have been impossible to prepare the maps.

Dick Priest and later Robert Lewis of the American Telephone and Telegraph Company in New York were extremely helpful. Research commissioned under their supervision to answer our questions is gratefully acknowledged. Additional invaluable assistance was received from across Canada: Tony Cashman of Edmonton, retired historian of the Alberta Telephone Company; R. Cole Harris, Geography, University of British Columbia; Ted Chown of Saskatchewan Telephone; and L.D. McCann, Geography, Mount Allison University.

American Telephone and Telegraph Company Archives. New York. 'Growth of the Long Lines Plant 1881–1941.' 21 June 1946. Map
Archives Bell Canada, Montréal. Reference No. 1544, 'Bell Telephone Company of Canada: Long Distance Lines and Connections, October 1891' and 'United States Connections.' Reference No. 14258, 'Bell Telephone Company of Canada: Wire Map Long Distance Lines, 1909.' Maps
'British Columbia Telephone Company Ltd.: Toll Circuit and Route Map.' *Telephone Talk* (Dec 1919): 13
Kee, C.A. *History of Telephone Service in New Brunswick.* 1920 (unpublished). Maps 1 and 2, 'New Brunswick Toll Lines, August 1906', pp 71A, 71B. A copy of the manuscript has been deposited in the NAC.
NAC. National Map Collection. 'Route of Trans-Canada Telephone System.' 1932
Saskatchewan Telephone and Telegraph Company, Regina. Historical Records. 'Saskatchewan Government: Long Distance Telephone System and Connections.' 1913, 1920, 1924. Maps
United States. Federal Communications Commission Special Investigation. Docket No.1, 'Telephone and Telegraph Trunk Routes of the American Telephone and Telegraph Company Long Lines Department, 1935.' Exhibit 134, Report on American Telephone and Telegraph Company, Washington, Apr 15, 1936. Map

Further readings
Abler, Ronald. 'The Telephone and the Evolution of the American Metropolitan System.' In Itheil de Sola Pool, ed. *The Social Impact of the Telephone.* Cambridge, Mass: Massachusetts Institute of Technology Press, 1977. Pp 318–41
Armstrong, Christopher, and H.V. Nelles. *Monopoly's Moment: The Organization and Regulation of Canadian Utilities.* Philadelphia: Temple University Press, 1986 / Toronto: University of Toronto Press, 1987
Cashman, Anthony W. *Singing Wires – The Telephone in Alberta.* Edmonton: Alberta Government Telephones Commission, 1972
George, M.V. 'Population Growth In Canada.' Profile Study. 1971 Census Monograph. Bulletin 5.1–1. Cat. 99–701. Ottawa: Statistics Canada, 1976
Langdale, John V. 'The Growth of Long Distance Telephony in the Bell System: 1875–1907.' *Journal of Historical Geography* 4, no. 2 (1978): 145–59
Ogle, Edmond B. *Long Distance Please: The Story of the TransCanada Telephone System.* Don Mills: Collins, 1979
Patten, William. 'Pioneering the Telephone in Canada.' Montréal, 1926 (privately printed)
Simmons, James W. 'The Growth of the Canadian Urban System.' Centre for Urban and Community Studies, University of Toronto, Research Paper No. 65. 1974
Simmons, J.W., and Bourne, L.S. 'Defining Urban Places: Differing Concepts of the Urban System.' In L.S. Bourne and J.W. Simmons, eds. *System of Cities: Readings on Structure, Growth and Policy.* New York: Oxford University Press, 1978. Pp 28–41
Stone, Leroy O. *Urban Development in Canada.* 1961 Census Monograph. Ottawa: DBS, 1967
Trotier, Louis. 'La genèse du réseau urbain du Québec.' *Recherches sociographiques* 9, no. 1 (Jan 1968): 23–32
Wasserman, Neil H. *From Invention to Innovation: Long Distance Telephone Transmission at the Turn of the Century.* Baltimore: The Johns Hopkins University Press, 1985

PLATE 22

The Integration of the Urban System, 1921–1961

JAMES W. SIMMONS   Geography, University of Toronto
MICHAEL CONZEN   Committee on Geographical Studies, University of Chicago

We would like to acknowledge the assistance of Charles Baker and Michael Bloor in preparing material for this plate. For a discussion of the definition of 'urban' see pl 21.

Population change, 1921–1951
The urban network, 1951
Material was drawn from various tables in the census and carefully synthesized by the authors.

Canada. *Census.* 1921–51
Burns, A.J., compiler. *The Official Guide of the Railways and Steam Navigation Lines of the United States, Puerto Rico, Canada, Mexico and Cuba.* New York: National Railway Publication Company, 1951

Economic specialization, 1961
This map was constructed by: (1) grouping the countries and census divisions of Canada around urban places with populations of approximately 10 000, except in BC where the census divisions were used as given; (2) examining the labour force by industry as given in the 1961 census; (3) modifying the breakdown into sectors by reallocating the resource processing part of manufacturing, such as pulp making, into the appropriate primary activity; and (4) examining more closely those sectors contributing more than 10% of the labour force. Four individual primary specializations were indicated with provision for a multiple primary role (fish/forest, mine/forest, etc). Manufacturing could occur alone or in combination with a primary activity, always agriculture except for the Sydney (mining) and Sault Ste Marie (forest) regions, or a tertiary activity, often transportation. Tertiary specializations were limited to transportation or public administration, because each of the cities contains a high proportion of retail, finance, and service jobs.

Canada. *Census.* 1961
– DBS. *Geographical Distribution of Manufacturing Industries of Canada.* Cat. 31–209. 1961

Intercity air-passenger flows, 1961
The help of Flemming Leicht, Statistical Officer, Air Transport Bureau, International Civil Aviation Organization, Montréal, in providing data on trans-border flights is gratefully acknowledged. It was not until 1966 that the Canadian Air Transport Board published data on trans-border flights for carriers other than Canadian. The International Civil Aviation Organization (ICAO) published data on a quarterly basis for all carriers. The Canadian data are not precisely comparable with ICAO data because they derive from a continuous statistical sample for the whole year whereas the ICAO data derive from four specific months.

Canada. Department of Transportation. Statistics Section. *Origin and Destination Statistics, Mainline Revenue Passengers Domestic Survey, 1960–61.* Ottawa, 1962
International Civil Aviation Organization. *Digest of Statistics of the Traffic by Flight Stage.* Montréal, 1961 (Mar, June, Sep, Dec issues)

Further readings
See pl 21.

PLATE 23

The Growth of Road and Air Transport, 20th Century

GERALD BLOOMFIELD   Geography, University of Guelph
MURDO MacPHERSON   Historical Atlas of Canada, Toronto
DAVID NEUFELD   Canadian Parks Service, Winnipeg

Canadian airlines: 1937; 1963
NAC. RG 12. Department of Transport files. Vol 2154, f. 5562–18, pt 2
Winnipeg Evening Tribune. 8 Dec 1937. P 63, map, 'Canadian Air Lines,' amended by author

CARGO VOLUME BY REGION
Canada. Department of Transport. 'Quarterly Civil Air Liaison Letter.' no. 38, 39, 40, 41

AIR FREIGHT
Canada. Department of Trade and Commerce. Transportation and Public Utilities Branch. *Civil Aviation in Canada 1937.* 1938
– *Aviation in Canada 1971: A Statistical Handbook of Canadian Civil Aviation.* Aviation Statistics Centre, 1972
Canadian Aviation. Various issues, Oct 1936–Mar 1938
Cunningham, H. *Development of Commercial Air Services in Canada 1919–1944.* Directorate of Air Development, Department of Reconstruction and Supply, 1946
NAC. G 12. Department of Transport files
Provincial Archives of Manitoba. MG 11A 34. Canadian Airways Collection
University of Saskatchewan Archives. Tweddell Papers. 'The Bullentin,' Canadian Airways Newsletter

Origins of the major airlines, 1921–1964
Canada. Department of Industry, Trade, and Commerce. *Aviation in Canada, 1971.* Fig 1.2
Fuller, G.A., J.A. Griffin, and K.M. Molson. *125 Years of Canadian Aeronautics: A Chronology 1840–1965.* Willowdale, Ont: Canadian Aviation Historical Society, 1983

Canadian airlines, 1963
Canada Year Book. 1962. P 823
A Comparative Economic Analysis of EPA and Its Role in the Development of the Atlantic Provinces. Aug 1965. P 48, map, amended by author
Davies, R.E.G. *A History of the World's Airlines.* London: Oxford University Press, 1964. P 373 Pacific Western Airlines. 17th Annual Report. 1963
Quebecair. *Financial Report.* 1963
– *Wings in Space.* Oct 1964
Transair. *Annual Report.* 1962
Trans-Canada Airlines. *Annual Report.* 1963
Wagner, U. Stan, Senior Operations Manager for Transair from the 1950s to 1974. Interview, Jan 1988

Passenger miles and commercial pilots, 1921–1961
Canada. DBS. Cat. 51–202. 1936–69
– Department of Industry, Trade, and Commerce. *Aviation in Canada,* 1971
– Department of Marine. Civil Aviation Branch. *Annual Report.* 1923–36

Evolution of the road network
Canada. Department of Mines and Technical Surveys. Geographical Branch. 'Major Roads.' Ottawa, 1962. Map
– Department of Resources and Development. Canadian Government Travel Bureau. 'Highway Map of Canada and Northern United States.' Ottawa, 1961
– Department of Resources and Development. Canadian Government Travel Bureau. 'Main Automobile Roads Between United States and Canada.' Ottawa, 1950. Map
Imperial Oil Ltd. 'Imperial Oil Map of Eastern Canada.' 1937. Maps 1–3
– 'Imperial Oil Map of Western Canada.' 1937. Maps 4, 5
Newfoundland. Department of Natural Resources. Crown Land and Surveys Branch. 'Ten Mile Map of Newfoundland.' St John's, 1941

Trans-Canada Highway
Canada, DBS. Cat. 53–201. 1963

Main highways, 1930
Fragmentary evidence points to some errors on the Firestone map (1930). More research is needed to confirm its accuracy.
Canada. Department of the Interior. 'Map Indicating Main Automobile Roads Between Canada and the United States.' Ottawa, 1930
Firestone's Road Maps of Canada and Northern United States. Preston, Ont: Peerless Vulcanizing Co, 1930

Motor-vehicle registrations, 1901–1961
Canada. DBS. Cat. 53–201. 1938, 1951, 1961
Urquhart and Buckley. *Historical Statistics.* Series S222–35

Surfaced roads, 1921–1961
Canada Year Book. 1962. P 771
Urquhart and Buckley. *Historical Statistics.* Series S215–21

Paved roads, 1921–1961
Canada. DBS. Cat. 53–201. 1945–57, 1959–75
Canada Year Book. 1956: p 834. 1958: p 793. 1960: pp 798–9. 1962: p 771

Movement of passengers, 1891–1961
For motor vehicles, estimate was based on total number of registrations multiplied by ten.
Leacy. *Historical Statistics.* Series T39–46, T147–94, T195–8
Urquhart and Buckley. *Historical Statistics.* Series S39–52, S112–19, S236–9

Further readings
Bloomfield, G.T. 'Canadian Highways and the Automobile.' Unpublished report submitted to the Historical Atlas of Canada project, Vol III, 1983
Guillet, E.C. *The Story of Canadian Roads.* Toronto: University of Toronto Press, 1966
Main, J.R.K. *Voyageurs of the Air: Canadian Civil Aviation, 1858–1967.* Ottawa: Queen's Printer, 1967
Molson, K.M. *Pioneering in Canadian Air Transport.* Winnipeg: James Richardson & Sons, 1974
Neufeld, D. 'Canada: Air Transport in 1939.' Manuscript map and supporting documents prepared for *The National Atlas of Canada,* 1989

PLATE 24

Canadian North Atlantic Trade, 17th and 18th Centuries

THOMAS WIEN   History, McGill University
JAMES PRITCHARD   History, Queen's University

We gratefully acknowledge the assistance of L. Dechêne (History, McGill University), J. Gwyn (University of Ottawa), and J. Mathieu (Université Laval); of V. Chabot, NAC, and P. McCann and M. Treen Sears. The sketches of the ships were made from drawings provided by Musée de la Marine, Palais de Chaillot, Paris, and from Eric Rieth, 'Célébration des Goélettes,' *Cols bleus,* no. 1811 (28 July–4 August 1984).

The Québec cargo of *La Revanche* was evaluated using 1733 prices. Calculations of the value of exports in 1771 do not include shipments of dressed deerskins and a few of the less important fancy furs. The values of North American fur exports and London fur imports were calculated on the basis of the lowest price paid in London for prime Canadian furs. In calculating exports of beaver we have assumed that one skin weighs 1.5 lbs. (1.39 livres or 0.681 kg).
Hides: Here defined as the skins, dressed or not, of deer, elk or wapiti, and moose

Sources

BEAVER EXPORTS
Archives nationales, Paris, France. Fonds des Colonies, C[11A]; F[2B], vol II
– Section Outre-mer. G[1], vol 466
British Library, London, Eng. Add Mss 21861
NAC. MG23 G1, vol 10, p 66
PRO. Shelburne Mss, vol 64, pp 161–4
Thwaites, R.G., ed. *The Jesuit Relations and Allied Documents.* 73 vols. Cleveland: Burrows Bros, 1896–1901

EUROPEAN SHIPPING
Archives départementales, France. Port records
British Library. Add Mss 21861 (NAC *Report,* 1882)
PRO. Customs 16/1
Quebec Gazette

FUR IMPORTS
Archives de l'Université de Montréal, Montréal. P58, Collection Baby, fiches 1625ff
Archives municipales. Archives de la Chambre de Commerce, La Rochelle, nos 9385–9424
PRO. Customs 3 and 17

NORTH AMERICAN FUR EXPORTS
Archives de l'Université de Montréal. P58, Collection Baby, fiches 1625ff
PRO, Customs 17

PRICES, VALUES
ANQ, Québec. Collection J. Spears and Collection Séminaire de Québec, C34, C36
Archives nationales. Fonds des Colonies, C[11A], vol 121, fol 126
NAC. MG23 G III 28, Pierre Guy, livre no. 10; MG19 A2 series 3, vol 86, Lawrence Ermatinger
Quebec Gazette, account books

TRADE PATTERNS, SHIPPING
Archives nationales. Fonds des Colonies, F2B
PRO. customs 16/1

VOYAGES
Archives nationales. Fonds des Colonies, F[2B], vol 11; C[11C], vol 9, fol 81[V]; C[8B], cart. 17
Archives départementales. Charente-Maritime, La Rochelle, B4202–4203

Further readings

Lunn, A.J.E. 'Economic Development in New France, 1713–1760.' PhD thesis, McGU, 1942. Trans as *Développement économique de la Nouvelle-France 1713–1760.* Montréal: Les Presses de l'Université de Montréal, 1986
McCann, Paul. 'Québec's Balance of Payments, 1768, 1772.' MA thesis, UO, 1982
Mathieu, Jacques. *Le commerce entre la Nouvelle-France et les Antilles au XVIIIe siècle.* Montreal: Fides, 1981
Miquelon, Dale. *Dugard of Rouen.* Montréal: McGill-Queen's University Press, 1978
Moore, Christopher. 'The Other Louisbourg: Trade and Merchant Enterprise in Ile Royale 1713–58.' *Hist Soc* 12 (1979): 79–96
Ouellet, Fernand. *Histoire économique et sociale du Québec, 1760–1850.* Montréal: Fides, 1966
Pritchard, James. 'The Voyage of the *Fier.*' *Hist Soc* 6 (1973): 75–97
– 'The Pattern of French Colonial Shipping to Canada before 1760.' *Revue française d'histoire d'outre-mer* 63 (1976): 189–210

PLATE 25

Canada in 1891

MARVIN McINNIS   Economics, Queen's University
PETER J. USHER   P.J. Usher Consulting Services, Ottawa

Non-native land use: agriculture, fishing, mining, forestry, manufacturing

Net agricultural output by county was estimated from census data, supplemented by data on market prices, using a complex procedure involving a FORTRAN algorithm of more than 300 lines. Full details of the method will be reported in a forthcoming study by McInnis. The general form of the procedure and the motivation for its particular steps are discussed by Lewis and McInnis (1984) in the context of estimates made for Québec counties in 1851.

Manufacturing and forestry output were drawn directly from the census although it must be noted that the reported number of pine logs cut in Essex County, Ontario, is far too large when compared with related data and has been adjusted. Mineral production was based on quantities of output reported in DBS Reference Paper No. 68 (1957), converted to values in some instances and prices reported in annual reports of the provincial departments of mines.

Canada. *Census*. 1891. Vols 3, 4
– DBS. *Canadian Mineral Statistics, 70 Years, 1886–1956*. Reference Paper No. 68. 1957
– *SP*. 1892. No. 11A, App A
Lewis, Frank D., and Marvin McInnis. 'Agricultural Output and Efficiency in Lower Canada, 1851.' *Research in Economic History* 9 (1984): 45–87

Non-native land use: missions
As far as possible, the missions shown represent permanent posts.

Beech, H.P. *A Geography and Atlas of Protestant Missions*. Vol 2. New York: Student Volunteer Movement for Foreign Missions, 1903
Carrière, Gaston. *Histoire documentaire de la Congrégation des missionaires oblats de Marie-Immaculée dans l'Est du Canada*. Pt 2. Vol 9. Ottawa: Éditions de l'Université d'Ottawa, 1970
Champagne, Claude. *Les débuts de la mission dans de Nord-Ouest canadien: mission et église chez Mgr Vital Grandin, o.m.i., 1829–1902*. Ottawa: Éditions de l'Université Saint-Paul, 1983
Levasseur, Donat. *Histoire des Missionaires oblats de Marie Immaculée: essai de synthèse*. Vol 1: (1815–1898). Montréal: Maison provinciale, 1983
Musée du Québec. *Le grand héritage: l'église catholique et la société du Québec*. Vol 2. Québec, 1984

Non-native land use: fur trading posts
Many thanks to Arthur J. Ray (History, University of British Columbia) for providing the information on fur-trade posts south of 60°.

Hudson's Bay Company Archives. A 74/1. 'Annual Reports, Outfit 1891 Contents'
– A 12/L 58/2 fo. 21. 'Map showing the Position of the Trading Establishments of the Hudson's Bay Company'
The National Atlas of Canada. 4th ed, rev. Ottawa: Department of Energy, Mines and Resources and Information Canada / Toronto: Macmillan, 1974. Information from original research files of P.J. Usher
Ray, A.J. 'The Hudson's Bay Company and Native People.' In W.E. Washburn, ed. *History of Indian-White Relations*. Vol 4 of *Handbook of North American Indians*, ed W.C. Sturtevant. Washington: Smithsonian Institution, 1988. Pp 335–50
– *The Canadian Fur Trade in the Industrial Age*. Toronto: University of Toronto Press, 1990. Information from original research files of Arthur J. Ray

Non-native land use: whaling stations
Native land use
The National Atlas of Canada. 4th ed, rev. Information from original research files of P.J. Usher

The land
Adjustments to the extent of land unexplored by Europeans were made on the advice of Wm G. Dean, University of Toronto, Richard I. Ruggles, Queen's University, Alan Cooke, Montréal, and J. Garth Taylor, Museum of Civilization, Hull.

HAC, vol I
The National Atlas of Canada. 4th ed, rev.

PLATE 26

Primary Production, 1891–1926

MARVIN McINNIS   Economics, Queen's University

Agricultural production, 1891 and 1921
Procedures used to estimate net agricultural output in dollars by county and by province are exceedingly complex, the estimating algorithms alone taking at least 300 lines of FORTRAN. Production data have been drawn from the agricultural census and price data from a wide variety of sources. The main complexity of the estimation procedure lies in the conversion of census data on stocks of animals, sales and production of animal products, and production of field crops into measures of net output, to give the net amount of crops used for animal feed. The method is an adaptation of one first developed by Lewis and McInnis (1984) in a study of mid-19th-century Québec and later modified by McInnis (full details to be discussed by McInnis in a forthcoming monograph).

Three categories of agricultural commodities are shown: livestock and animal products such as milk, butter, and wool; the net production (not counting crops used for animal feed) of the conventional field crops such as wheat, barley, and hay sold to the non-agricultural sectors of the economy; and an assortment of other products such as tobacco, apples, beans, and clover seed that were typically grown in only a few specific areas. Dots representing given amounts of each of the first two categories of agricultural production have been distributed randomly by a computer program within the settled area of each township. Dots for the specialty products were located manually in locations known to have large concentrations of those products. On the map of the whole nation in 1921 agricultural production is aggregated into a single product. This is a counterpart to the 1891 map shown on pl 25. The agricultural detail has been mapped separately for Central Canada in 1891 and 1921 and for the Prairie Provinces in 1921.

The provincial and national totals of agricultural production are aggregations of the county totals. National aggregates for 1891 and 1921 obtained in this way agree quite closely with national estimates for GDP originating in agriculture made by a quite different method and reported by McInnis (1986) in a study of trends in agricultural productivity.

Canada. *Census*. 1891: Vol 3. 1921: Vol 5
Lewis, Frank D., and Marvin McInnis. 'Agricultural Output and Efficiency in Lower Canada, 1851.' *Research in Economic History* 9 (1984): 45–87, esp App, 'The estimation of net agricultural productivity'
McInnis, Marvin. 'Output and Productivity in Canadian Agriculture, 1870–71 to 1926–27.' In Stanley L. Engerman and Robert E. Gallman, eds. *Long-Term Factors in American Economic Growth*. National Bureau of Economic Research. Studies in Income and Wealth, Vol 51. Chicago: University of Chicago Press, 1986. Pp 737–78

Mining production, 1891–1926
Value of mineral production has unavoidably been upwardly biased because minerals are valued at market prices. No data are available for pithead prices and consequently transport and other costs are built into the price used for conversion to value of production.

Canada. DBS. *Canadian Mineral Statistics, 70 Years, 1886–1956*. Reference Paper No. 68. 1957
Various annual reports of provincial departments of mines were also used.

Forestry production, 1891–1926
Value of forestry production is based on national figures for GDP originating in forestry, as estimated by Urquhart (1986), allocated to provinces on the basis of the value of woods operations reported by DBS (1926). The value of forest production includes transport to the sawmills and pulp mills. The symbols on the map representing value of forestry production do not take into account farm cut which was widely dispersed; this omission is especially noteworthy in Québec.

Canada. *Census*. 1891. Vol 6
– DBS. *Forest Industries of Canada, 1926*. 'Operations in the woods'
Urquhart, M.C. 'New Estimates of Gross National Product, Canada 1870–1926: Some Implications for Canadian Development.' In Engerman and Gallman, eds. *Long-Term Factors*. 1986. Pp 9–94

Fishing production, 1891–1926
Canada. DBS. *Fishery Statistics of Canada*. Cat. 24–201. 1921
Urquhart. 'New Estimates of Gross National Product.' 1986. Esp Table 2:1

PLATE 27

Farming and Fishing, 1941–1961

GERALD BLOOMFIELD   Geography, University of Guelph
PHILIP D. KEDDIE   Geography, University of Guelph
ERIC W. SAGER   History, University of Victoria

The research assistance of Garry Penner in assembling the information on fishing is gratefully acknowledged. For data on fishing the value of the fish caught is the value at the boat's landing, based on sale to first buyer. Inland provinces include Ontario, Manitoba, Saskatchewan, and Alberta.

Value of catch by species, 1961
Canada. DBS. *Fisheries Statistics of Canada*. 1961. Table 2

Value of fish caught, 1926–1961
Prior to 1952 annual figures for value of all fish landed are not available for Newfoundland. The nearest equivalent is total export value of salt cod and this was used for 1926 to 1952. The British Columbia figure in 1961 includes halibut landed in US ports and fish caught in the Yukon Territory.

Government of Newfoundland and Labrador. *Historical Statistics of Newfoundland*. St John's, 1970. Table K-7
Leacy. *Historical Statistics*. Series N1–11
Newfoundland. *Journals of the House of Assembly*. 'Customs Returns'

Fishing labour force, 1891–1961
Statistics for Newfoundland are for number of fishermen in the cod fishery only; for other regions the number of persons engaged in primary fishing operations was used.

Canada. DBS. *Fisheries Statistics of Canada*. 1917–62
– Department of Marine and Fisheries. *Annual Report*. 1891–1917
Canadian Fisheries Annual. 1952–61
Leacy. *Historical Statistics*. Series N38–48, N139–42

Fish caught, ICNAF areas, 1958: total and by region
International Commission for the Northwest Atlantic Fisheries (ICNAF). *Statistical Bulletin*. 1958. Vol 8, Pt 1, p 7; Pt 2, pp 12–13

Fish caught, 1951–61
Alexander, David. *Decay of Trade: An Economic History of the Newfoundland Saltfish Trade, 1935–1965*. St John's: Institute of Social and Economic Research, 1977. P 151
ICNAF. *Statistical Bulletin*. 1958. Vols 1–11
Leacy. *Historical Statistics*. N125–7

North Pacific salmon catch by nation, 1955–1959
International North Pacific Fisheries Commission. *Bulletin*. Vol 39. 1978

Net farming income, 1926–1961
Net returns from farming operations were used as net farm income.

Leacy. *Historical Statistics*. Series M119–28

Change in improved acreage, 1941–1961
Canada. *Census*. 1941: Vol 8, Table 52. 1961: Vol 5, Table 28

Crop combinations in the Prairies: 1941; 1961
When wheat is designated as the only crop, at least 75% and more commonly over 80% of the cropland is devoted to wheat. When wheat is combined with one other crop, it is generally the more important of the two dominant crops. In the combination of wheat, hay, and one other the third crop is generally either oats or barley, but flax is popular in Manitoba. The combination of four or more crops, including wheat, generally includes oats, barley, and hay; other crops appearing in these combinations are rye, flax, and canola (rapeseed) (in 1961). The most prominent crops grown singly or in combination not including wheat are hay and oats; barley is generally added to these in a three-crop combination.

Canada. *Census*. 1941: Vol 8, Table 54. 1961: Vol 5, Table 30

Varieties of Prairie bread wheat, 1941–1961

Data on varietal composition are based on information from Line Elevator Farm Service (see below) provided by J.R. Rogalsky, Chief, Crops Section, Agriculture Manitoba at the Agriculture Canada Research Station, Winnipeg.

'Other rust-resistant' varieties include Apex (first licensed in 1937), Renown (1937), Regent (1939), Redman (1946), and Lee (1950). Marquis was first distributed to farmers in 1909. Red Bobs was first licensed in 1926, Thatcher in 1935, Rescue in 1946, Chinook in 1952, Selkirk in 1953.

Bushuk, W. 'Development, Licensing and Distribution of New Varieties of Grain in Canada.' *Grains and Oilseeds, Handling, Marketing, Processing.* 3rd rev ed. Winnipeg: Canadian International Grains Institute, 1982. Pp 443–62

Greaney, F.J., and J. Barnes. *Distribution of Wheat Varieties in the Prairie Provinces, 1941 to 1950.* Circular No. 15. Winnipeg: Line Elevator Farm Service, 1953

Line Elevator Farm Service. Winnipeg. Distribution of wheat varieties for the crop districts of Manitoba, Saskatchewan, and Alberta, 1955–61. Untitled and unpublished annual tables

Line Elevator Farm Service. Winnipeg. 'Distribution of Wheat Varieties in the Prairie Provinces (1951 to 1955).' Unpublished table

Farms with tractors, 1921–1961

Canada. *Census.* 1921: Vol 5, Table 38. 1931: Vol 8, Table XXIX. 1941: Vol 8, Tables 28, 48. 1951: Vol 6, Table 24. 1961: Vol 5, Table 29

Further readings

Bennett, John W. *Northern Plainsmen: Adaptive Strategy and Agrarian Life.* Chicago: Aldine, 1969

Canada. *Navigating Troubled Waters: A New Policy for the Atlantic Fisheries.* Ottawa: Supply and Services Canada, 1983

MacEwan, G. *Harvest of Bread.* Saskatoon: Western Producer, 1969

Marchak, Patricia, N. Guppy, and J. McMullan, eds. *Uncommon Property: The Fishing and Fish Processing Industries in British Columbia.* Toronto: Methuen, 1987

Sinclair, Peter R. *From Traps to Draggers: Domestic Commodity Production in Northwest Newfoundland, 1850–1982.* St John's: Institute of Social and Economic Research, 1985

– ed. *A Question of Survival: The Fisheries and Newfoundland Society.* St John's: Institute of Social and Economic Research, 1988

PLATE 28

The Changing Structure of Manufacturing, 1879–1930

GERALD BLOOMFIELD   Geography, University of Guelph
MICHAEL HINTON   Montréal
TED REGEHR   History, University of Saskatchewan, Saskatoon
GLEN WILLIAMS   Political Science, Carleton University

We wish to acknowledge the help of Stephen Bellinger in the preparation of this plate.

Manufacturing production and employment

All the primary sources of manufacturing statistics suffer from three major problems – classification, coverage, and comparability. Classifications of manufacturing in the earlier censuses include many activities which are no longer regarded as manufacturing (eg, electric-power generation, dyeing and cleaning, blacksmithing). Until the 1920s when classification systems based primarily on materials were adopted, there was little attempt to group manufacturing activities. All the census reports merely present an alphabetical listing of industries (the 1911 census has 228 separate categories from 'abrasive goods' to 'wool pulling'). The coverage of industrial activity is variable over time. Prior to 1901 all industrial establishments regardless of size were included in the census. From 1901 to 1911 establishments with fewer than five employees were excluded although some activities such as cheese making were included even if they had fewer than five employees. The 1916 *Postal Census of Manufactures* covered only establishments with an annual output of $2 500 or more.

Comparability is, then, a major problem in using the primary published materials. It has been difficult to revise the data to make them comparable because in earlier periods an activity may have been insufficiently defined and, to avoid disclosure of an individual establishment, the data were sometimes included under 'all other industries.' The problems of disclosure are greatest at the subprovincial level and it is virtually impossible to construct data for small areas by industrial group.

For the most part the various sectors or subdivisions of Canadian manufacturing are well covered in the primary sources. Indeed it would seem that the greatest original interest in and use of the statistics was by sector of manufacturing. Until the 1920s there was little attempt to develop higher-order aggregations of statistics. The 1907 and 1913 *Canada Year Books* had a 15-group classification for contemporary statistics and retrospective summaries. The schemes developed in the 1920s were based on similarity of materials and therefore included some curious groups of industries.

The introduction of a Standard Industrial Classification by the DBS in 1948 reorganized the classification of manufacturing activities. This 1948 classification was used by Bertram (1964) and Urquhart and Buckley (1965) to develop a comparable series of statistics from 1870 to the 1950s. Bertram's (1964) compilations of sectors by provinces have made it possible to prepare data to show production by industry by province for 1890, 1910, and 1929.

Bertram, G.W. 'Historical Statistics on Growth and Structure of Manufacturing in Canada 1870–1957.' In J. Henripin and A. Asimakopulos, eds. *Conferences on Statistics 1962 and 1963, Papers.* Canadian Political Studies Association. Toronto: University of Toronto Press, 1964. Pp 93–151

Bloomfield, G.T. 'General Statistics on Canadian Manufacturing to 1929.' Unpublished report submitted to the Historical Atlas of Canada project, Vol III, 1982

Canada. *Census.* 1891: Vol 3. 1911: Vol 3

– DBS. *Annual Survey of Manufactures.* 1929. Series 31–D–20–7

Canada Year Book. 1932. Pp 305–35

Drummond, Ian M. *Progress without Planning: The Economic History of Ontario from*

Confederation to the Second World War. Ontario Historical Studies Series. Toronto: University of Toronto Press, 1987. App B, pp 353–9

Urquhart and Buckley. *Historical Statistics.* Section Q, pp 455–92

American branch plants, 1913

Field (1914) provides the only early listing of American firms operating in Canada. Although Field's estimates of the dollar value of foreign capital investments in Canada have been criticized, his compilation of American firms is generally accepted. However, Hooper (1983) revealed a few flaws in Field's list of American firms operating in Hamilton in 1913.

Bellinger, S.L. 'American Firms in Canada: Data Sources and Review.' Unpublished report submitted to the Historical Atlas of Canada project, Vol III, 1984

Field, Frederick William. *Capital Investments in Canada.* Montréal: Monetary Times, 1914

Hooper, Diana. 'Foreign Ownership and the Evolution of Canada's Industrial Structure: A Case Study of Hamilton, Ontario.' MA thesis, University of Toronto, 1983

The motor-vehicle industry

Data on companies are drawn from company files.

Bloomfield, G.T. 'Elements of the Canadian Motor Vehicle Industry to 1929.' Unpublished report submitted to the Historical Atlas of Canada project, Vol III, 1982

Canada. DBS. *Automobile Statistics for Canada.* Cat. 42–209. 1930

The emergence of corporate ownership in the newsprint industry: 1925; 1930

Comprehensive statistical data are available on capacity of mills but data on production are fragmentary and in some cases unreliable.

Financial Post. 4 Sep 1925. 26 Sep 1931. Supplemented by other statistical data published in various issues of the *Financial Post, Financial Times, Pulp and Paper Directory of Canada, Pulp and Paper Business Directory of Canada, Pulp and Paper Canada, National Directory of the Canadian Pulp and Paper Industries*

Urquhart and Buckley. *Historical Statistics.* Series K156–68

Corporate concentration in the cotton industry

Manuscript material from Michael Hinton (Montréal)

Origin of capital investment in growth industries, 1920

Williams, Glen. *Not for Export.* Toronto: McClelland and Stewart, 1983. Ch 2, Table 2, p 29

Further readings

Acheson, T.W. 'The National Policy and the Industrialization of the Maritimes, 1880–1910.' *Acadiensis* 1, no. 1 (Spring 1972): 3–28

Bertram, Gordon W. 'Economic Growth in Canadian Industry, 1870–1915: The Staple Model and the Take-off Hypothesis.' *Canadian Journal of Economics and Political Science* 29, no. 2 (May 1963): 162–84. Repr in W.T. Easterbrook and Mel Watkins, eds. *Approaches to Canadian Economic History.* Toronto: McClelland and Stewart, 1967. Pp 74–98

Bloomfield, Gerald. *The World Automotive Industry.* Newton Abbot: David and Charles, 1987

Gilmour, James M., and Kenneth Murricane. 'Structural Divergence in Canada's Manufacturing Belt.' *Canadian Geographer* 17, no. 1 (Spring 1973): 1–18

Guthrie, John Alexander. *The Newsprint Paper Industry.* Cambridge, Mass: Harvard University Press, 1941

Kerr, Donald. 'The Emergence of the Industrial Heartland c. 1750–1950.' In L.D. McCann, ed. *Heartland and Hinterland: A Geography of Canada.* Scarborough: Prentice-Hall, 1982. Pp 64–99

Linteau, Paul-André, René Durocher, and Jean-Claude Robert. *Quebec: A History 1867–1929*, trans Robert Chodos. Toronto: Lorimer, 1983

Marshall, Herbert, Frank Southard, and Kenneth Wiffen Taylor. *Canadian-American Industry: A Study of International Investment.* New York: Russel & Russel, 1970. Repr Toronto: McClelland and Stewart, 1976

Piedalue, Gilles. 'Les Groupes Financiers et la Guerre du Papier au Canada 1920–1930.' *Revue d'histoire de l'Amérique française* 30, no. 2 (Sep 1976): 223–58

Rae, John B. *The American Automotive Industry.* Boston: Twayne, 1984

Rouillard, Jacques. *Les travailleurs du coton au Québec 1900–1915.* Montréal: Les Presses de l'Université du Québec, 1974

Weldon, J.C. 'Consolidations in Canadian Industry 1900–1948.' In Lawrence Alexander Skeoch, ed. *Restrictive Trade Practices in Canada.* Toronto: McClelland and Stewart, 1966. Pp 228–79

PLATE 29

19th-Century Images of Canada

JOHN H. WADLAND   Canadian Studies Program, Trent University
MARGARET HOBBS   Women's Studies Program, Trent University

The authors are deeply indebted to the following for their assistance in the preparation of this plate: Andrew Birrell, François-Marc Gagnon, Fernand Harvey, Joy Houston, Joan Murray, Hellen Ostler, Mary Jane Penfold, Dennis Reid, Alan Toff, Helle Viirlaid, John Warkentin. Special thanks are accorded Joan Schwartz for permission to use her unpublished research to identify the locations of Frederick Dally photographs.

On this plate we trace the movements of some representative 19th-century landscape painters and photographers, using as our points of reference published evidence of their work. The topographical artists who preceded the railway and the photograph were primarily watercolourists with military training. The easy portability of their medium reflected their role and the often harsh conditions they endured. Their job was to document the terrain over which they travelled, to give it definition comprehensible to analytical viewers at home. The engineers, surveyors, generals, politicians, and settlement agents depending upon such pictorial data would interpret it for their own practical purposes – but so would many others, since images made by such artists were published and in print well before mid-century.

Later survey and expeditionary artists like W.G.R. Hind reached artistic maturity simultaneously with the birth of commercial photography and the railway. Hind had studied art in England and Europe before coming to Canada and he brought to the oils and watercolours which chronicle his extensive travels across Canada an eye for microscopic detail. He shared Paul Kane's fascination for indigenous peoples, whom both men clearly regarded as integral parts of the wilderness landscapes they most loved, but Hind was equally at ease painting the pastoral and maritime scenes pictured on this plate. Chromolithographs by Hind were published as early as 1863, to illustrate his brother's book of their joint *Explorations in the Interior of the Labrador Peninsula*.

Professional artists – those who made a living by painting – often required institutional patronage. Both Peter Rindisbacher and Paul Kane were sustained at intervals by the HBC and its officials. Lucius R. O'Brien and J.A. Fraser were commissioned by William Van Horne to make views for the CPR.

Like the topographic artists, Paul Kane made sketches, often in watercolour, in the field. These he brought back to his studio as the raw material for larger oil paintings. As these paintings were often revised to accommodate the aesthetic tastes of their buyers, it is the sketches which we often turn to for more dependable representations of the land and the native people.

After the arrival of the collodion wet-plate the portrait photograph became a commonplace, ensuring the success of commercial houses like William Notman's studio in Montréal. Notman hired aspiring young painters like Fraser to colour his photographs – indeed, the Notman Studio was to late 19th-century landscape artists what Grip would become for the Group of Seven. Fraser organized sketching expeditions for the other Notman artists during the 1860s and in 1867 he was involved in founding the Society of Canadian Artists. After moving to Toronto in 1868 to establish the Notman and Fraser Studio, he joined with O'Brien, T. Mower Martin and others to form the Ontario Society of Artists in 1872. Many of these 'railway artists,' as they later became known, were charter members of the Royal Canadian Academy at its founding in 1880. The first president of the Academy was O'Brien, an Ontario-born civil engineer who did not take up painting seriously until he was 40. He travelled from one end of Canada to the other, by train, by wagon, by canoe, and on foot, frequently camping under the night sky, usually sketching from nature.

Nevertheless he included in *Picturesque Canada* (1882), of which he was art editor, some images that he himself had made by copying photographs originally taken many years earlier by Benjamin Baltzly, Frederick Dally, Charles Horetzky, and others. Fraser occasionally did the same thing, duplicating and embellishing photographs for publicity pictures commissioned by the CPR. Thus images have turned up in publications or on posters as 'true' representations of places an artist may never have been. By the end of his career O'Brien was taking his own photographs in the field during the summer and working up oil paintings based upon them in the warmth of his studio during the winter.

On this plate we have identified places painted by O'Brien and later reproduced and published, in order not only to document O'Brien's attempts to grasp the whole of Canada and give it definition, but also to demonstrate the growing capacity of the printing press to bring individual landscape works by this extraordinary painter to a wider public. Martin attempted several years later to duplicate the success of *Picturesque Canada*, preparing 77 landscapes which were printed in colour in Wilfred Campbell's book *Canada* (1907). However, they never captured the imagination of the public, whose tastes, by the turn of the century, were being revolutionized by the very advances in photography which had made reproduction of the paintings possible. By then a new generation of artists, particularly painters like Homer Watson who were touched by the Barbizon school and Impressionism, felt compelled to leave the realistic depiction of the land to the photographers.

Developments in photography have proved extremely difficult to map. The route of the contingent of Royal Engineers responsible for photography for the North American Boundary Commission demonstrates that one can find documentary images which, in sequence, hold large expanses of Canada fixed in time and in the eye of the cameraman. Humphrey Lloyd Hime, who travelled with Henry Youle Hind on the Assiniboine and Saskatchewan expedition of 1858, and Alexander Henderson, whose camera captured the newly constructed Intercolonial and Canadian Pacific railways, have left us invaluable photographic images of the vast territories they traversed before the imposition of the land surveys which would redefine landscape and culture forever.

This plate emphasizes photographic activity in British Columbia. As the new western terminus of the CPR after 1885 it provided an exotic destination for the eastern tourist armed, by 1888, with George Eastman's Kodak box camera. The rugged topography of the province also provided incentives to modernize conventional survey methods. One must imagine Benjamin Baltzly, working for the Geological Survey of Canada in the summer of 1871, hauling the 500 pounds of paraphernalia associated with collodion wet-plate technology through the valley of the Thompson River. He not only had to expose and develop his glass plates on site but also to concoct from toxic chemicals his own emulsions.

Charles Horetzky, who worked on the CPR survey throughout the 1870s, pioneered the use of the collodion dry-plate process in similar terrain, simplifying travel by reducing his apparatus to camera, plates, and tripod. In the 1890s the Rocky Mountains challenged Édouard Deville, Surveyor General of Canada, to adapt an existing European technique, photogrammetry, to carry the Dominion Land Survey from the western edge of Alberta to the Pacific Coast. Deville's method of photogrammetry was also employed by the Alaska Boundary Commission Survey (1893–5) to define the British Columbia border adjacent to the Alaska Panhandle. In addition to tourists and surveyors, anthropologists were drawn to the far west by the wide diversity of indigenous linguistic groups to be found along the coast and in the interior. Photographers like Edward Dossetter and Frederick Dally have left a rich and evocative record of their encounters with native people, documenting in exquisite detail the complexities of their cultures and their relationships to land and sea before the arrival of the railway. Locations for which we have images photographed by Dally between 1866 and 1870 are identified on the plate.

It is common for contemporary critics to be critical of 19th-century realist landscape painting, partly because many modern practitioners of the genre have made it a sentimental cliché. But what should be clear from this plate is that, while the majority of artists and photographers attempting to capture the diversity of Canadian terrain were foreign born and frequently foreign trained in formal conventions like the sublime and the picturesque, in going *into* the new land they attempted not only to absorb the wilderness of which they had had no previous experience, but to reshape their perceptions, to begin the arduous process of finding a new visual language truly capable of expressing this place they would call home.

Victorian class distinctions were attached to paintings and photographs. Original paintings appealed to the wealthy because they were unique: no print could be made that would reproduce the touch, the manual applicaiton of colour by the artist. The aesthetic sensibility of potential purchasers remained a major obstacle to innovation by artists throughout this period. The original photograph, however, was valuable to the photographer only if the prints made from it were sold over and over again. Photography was distinguished by its novelty, by its speed, and by its realism. It fostered the advertising industry and promoted tourism. It brought immortality through the family album. By way of the stereograph it lured unsolicited geography lessons about Africa and Asia into the front parlour on Saturday nights. Shortly after Confederation the half-tone plate could reproduce paintings, political events, and landscape views in books, magazines, and newspapers. These in turn could be shipped by rail to progressively more remote destinations, revolutionizing the visual understanding of Canada by a people whose huge country had largely been imagined from words and engravings.

The following table briefly chronicles the development of new technologies in the 19th century. Readers are encouraged to juxtapose this information with that on the plate, to establish relationships between painting and photography, on the one hand, and, on the other, the revolution in the visual perception of landscape which new printing technologies brought to the reading public of 19th-century Canada.

A checklist of developments in the visual arts and in photographic, printing, and transportation technologies

Steel, copper, and wood engravings were printed in Canada throughout the 19th century, but photomechanical processes gradually displaced them. Photography, printing, and railway travel combined to explode the conventions of visualization.

1826 First evidence of commercial lithography in Canada
1839 Invention of the daguerreotype and calotype
1851 Invention of the collodion wet-plate photographic process (used by Frederick Dally, Alexander Henderson, and the Royal Engineers on the North American Boundary Commission)
1853 Completion of the St Lawrence and Atlantic Railroad
1856 The first commercial coloured lithograph printed in Canada by Fuller and Benecke of Toronto (a reproduction of Paul Kane's *The Death of Big Snake*)
1860 Completion of the Grand Trunk Railway, Sarnia–Rivière-du-Loup
Founding of the Art Association of Montreal
1865 *Canada Classified Directory* (Toronto: Mitchell and Co, 1865–6) lists more than 360 photographers
1867 First appearance of the collodion dry-plate photographic process in Canada (used by Charles Horetzky)
Founding of the Society of Canadian Artists in Montréal
1869 First commercial appearance of half-tone screen photo engravings. Processes patented in Canada by William Augustus Leggo included granulated photography, leggotyping, and photolithography, examples of which appeared in *The Canadian Illustrated News* (1869–83), Sandford Fleming's *The Intercolonial* (1876), and George Monro Grant's *Ocean to Ocean* (1872)
1870 First issue of *Opinion publique*
1871 Establishment of the Dominion Lands Survey
1872 Founding of the Ontario Society of Artists
1873 Completion of the Toronto, Grey and Bruce Railway, Toronto–Owen Sound
1876 Completion of the Intercolonial Railway, Rivière-du-Loup–Halifax
1878 Development of the gelatino-bromide dry-plate photographic process
1880 Founding of the Royal Canadian Academy, Lucius R. O'Brien, president
1882 Publication of *Picturesque Canada* with 500 wood engravings, Lucius R. O'Brien, art editor
1886 Beginning of CPR transcontinental passenger service
1887 First photogrammetric surveys in Canada conducted by W.S. Drewry and J.J. McArthur using techniques pioneered in Canada by Édouard Deville
1888 George Eastman introduces the Kodak No. 1 camera incorporating roll film. This was followed in 1889 by the Kodak No. 2 camera incorporating celluloid roll film. Both used a dry gelatin emulsion. This camera was used by Joseph Burr Tyrrell in his work on the Geological Survey. It was also available to tourists who now had a simple method of recording their personal travels.
First issue of *The Dominion Illustrated* (1888–93)
1891 Photogravure illustrations appear for the first time in a Canadian daily newspaper (*The Globe*)

Illustrations

1 Frederick Dally. Ox team at Clinton, Cariboo Road, BC. 1868. Photograph. Glenbow Archives, Calgary. NA-674-38
2 William G.R. Hind. *Strait of San Juan*. Ca 1862. Watercolour on paper. McCord Museum of Canadian History, Montréal. M473
3 Lucius R. O'Brien. 1832–1899. *Through the Rocky Mountains, A Pass on the Canadian Highway*. 1887. Watercolour on paper. Private collection, Toronto. Photograph courtesy of Art Gallery of Ontario
4 J.B. Tyrrell. Eskimo camp on the barren land, NWT, 18 Aug 1894. Photograph. National Archives of Canada, Geological Survey of Canada Collection. PA-050939
5 Charles Horetzky. Peace River at Fort Dunvegan, October 4, 1872. 1872. Photograph. National Archives of Canada, W.J. Topley Collection. PA-9244
6 Paul Kane (1810–1871). *Camping on the Prairie*. 1845. Oil. Stark Museum of Art, Orange, Texas. 31.78/156, POP18
7 Royal Engineers, George Dawson / North American Boundary Commission. Ox train at Dead Horse Creek, on their way West. Ca 1873. Photograph. National Archives of Canada, Dr Thomas Millman Collection. PA-74645
8 Peter Rindisbacher. *Winter Fishing on the Ice of the Assynoibain and Red River*. 1821. Watercolour with pen and black ink on paper. National Archives of Canada. C-001932
9 Paul Kane (1810–1871). *French River Rapids*. 1845. Oil. Stark Museum of Art, Orange, Texas. 31.78/159, POP22

10 Peter Rindisbacher. *Occupation of the Unfortunate Colonists within sight of a mass of ice of 5700 cubic [metres?], June 30, 1821*. 1821. Watercolour and ink. National Archives of Canada. C-1905

11 Frederick C. Lowe, after Lucius R. O'Brien. *View of Cobourg*. Ca 1852. Wood engraving on paper. From *Anglo American Magazine* (Toronto), 2 (Feb 1853). Metropolitan Toronto Reference Library, J. Ross Robertson Collection. T 18073

12 Lucius Richard O'Brien. Canadian 1832–1899. *Among the Islands of Georgian Bay*. 1886. Watercolour on paper. 26.7 x 39.4 cm. Art Gallery of Ontario, Toronto. Bequest of Mrs Florence L. Cody, 1951. T 260 1

13 L.R. O'Brien. *Sunrise on the Saguenay*. Ca 1882. Oil on canvas. National Gallery of Canada, Ottawa. 113

14 J.A. Fraser. *September Afternoon, Eastern Townships*. 1873. Oil on canvas. National Gallery of Canada, Ottawa. 18159

15 Alexander Henderson. Intercolonial Railway. On the Matapedia River. Ca 1872. Albumen print. National Archives of Canada, Sir Sandford Fleming Collection. PA-022071

16 W.G.R. Hind. *Harvesting Hay*, Sussex, New Brunswick. Ca 1880. Oil on commercial board. National Archives of Canada, Ottawa. C-103003

Selected bibliography

PAINTING

Bell, Michael. *Painters in a New Land*. Toronto: McClelland and Stewart, 1973

Bovay, E.H. *Le Canada et les Suisses, 1604–1974*. Fribourg, Switzerland: Éditions universitaires, 1976. This study contains a catalogue of the work of Peter Rindisbacher.

Gagnon, François-Marc. 'Painting and Sculpture.' In Paul-André Linteau et al. *Quebec: A History, 1867–1929*. Toronto: Lorimer, 1983. Pp 292–302, 552–63

Harper, J. Russell. *William G.R. Hind, 1833–1889*. Ottawa: National Gallery of Canada, 1976

Harper, J. Russell, ed. *Paul Kane's Frontier, including Wanderings of an Artist among the Indians of North America*. Toronto: University of Toronto Press, 1971

Hind, Henry Youle. *Explorations in the Interior of the Labrador Peninsula, the Country of the Montagnais and Nasquapee Indians*. 2 vols. London: Longman, Green, Longman, Roberts and Green, 1863

– *Narrative of the Canadian Red River Exploring Expedition of 1857 and of the Assiniboine and Saskatchewan Exploring Expedition of 1858*. 2 vols. London: Longman, Green, Longman and Roberts, 1860

Josephy, Alvin M. *The Artist Was a Young Man: The Life Story of Peter Rindisbacher*. Fort Worth, Texas: Amon Carter Museum, 1970

Lavallée, Omer. *Van Horne's Road: An Illustrated Account of the Construction and First Years of Operation of the Canadian Pacific Transcontinental Railway*. Montréal: Railfare Enterprises, 1974

McMann, Evelyn de R. *Royal Canadian Academy of Arts: Exhibitions and Members, 1880–1979*. Toronto: University of Toronto Press, 1981

Murray, Joan. *Ontario Society of Artists: 100 Years*. Toronto: Art Gallery of Ontario, 1972

Rees, Ronald. *Land of Earth and Sky: Landscape Painting in Western Canada*. Saskatoon: Western Producer Prairie Books, 1985

Reid, Dennis. *Lucius R. O'Brien: Visions of Victorian Canada*. Toronto: Art Gallery of Ontario, 1990

– *'Our Own Country Canada': Being an Account of the Principal Landscape Artists in Montreal & Toronto, 1860–1890*. Ottawa: National Gallery of Canada, 1979

Thibault, Claude. *L'art du paysage au Québec, 1800–1940*. Québec: Musée du Québec, 1978

Walker, Doreen E. 'Some Early British Columbia Views and Their Photographic Sources.' *The Beaver* (Summer 1983): 44–51

Willistead Art Gallery of Windsor. *William G.R. Hind: A Confederation Painter in Canada*, text by J. Russell Harper. Windsor: The Gallery, 1967

PHOTOGRAPHY AND THE PICTORIAL PRESS

Birrell, Andrew J. *Benjamin Baltzly: Photographs and Journal of an Expedition through British Columbia*. Toronto: Coach House Press, 1973

– 'Fortunes of a Misfit: Charles Horetzky.' *Alberta Historical Review* 19 (Winter 1971): 9–25

Cavell, Edward. *Journeys to the Far West: Accounts of the Adventurers in Western Canada, 1858–1885*. Toronto: Lorimer, 1979. This study contains many fine examples of images captured by Dally, Dossetter, and others.

Deville, Édouard. *Photographic Surveying: Including the Elements of Descriptive Geometry and Perspective*. Ottawa: Survey Office, 1889

Fleming, Sandford. *The Intercolonial: A Historical Sketch of the Inception, Location, Construction and Completion of the Line of Railway Uniting the Inland and Atlantic Provinces of the Dominion, with Maps and Numerous Illustrations*. Montréal: Dawson Brothers, 1876

Grant, George Monro. *Ocean to Ocean: Sandford Fleming's Expedition through Canada in 1872*. Toronto: J. Campbell, 1873

Grant, George Monro, ed. *Picturesque Canada: The Country As It Was and Is*. Illustrated under the supervision of L.R. O'Brien, with over 500 engravings on wood. 2 vols. Toronto: Belden Brothers, 1882. *Picturesque Canada* was released in 36 parts between Jan 1882 and Sep 1884; gathered, bound copies were not available until 1884.

Green, Lewis. *The Boundary Hunters*. Vancouver: University of British Columbia Press, 1982

Greenhill, Ralph, and Andrew J. Birrell. *Canadian Photography, 1839–1920*. Toronto: Coach House Press, 1979

Hart, E.J. *The Selling of Canada: The CPR and the Beginnings of Canadian Tourism*. Banff: Altitude Publishing, 1983

Horetzky, Charles. *Canada on the Pacific: An Account of a Journey from Edmonton to the Pacific by the Peace River Falls and a Winter Voyage along the Western Coast of the Dominion that Remarks on the Physical Features of the Pacific Railway Route and Notations of the Indian Tribes of British Columbia*. Montréal: Dawson Brothers, 1874

– 'Report on Explorations from Douglass, Gardner and Dean Inlets, Eastward in the Cascade Mountains.' In Sandford Fleming, *Report on Surveys and Preliminary Operations on the Canadian Pacific Railway up to January, 1877*. Ottawa: MacLean, Roger and Co, 1877. Pp 137–44

Huyda, Richard J. *Camera in the Interior, 1858: H.L. Hime, Photographer. The Assiniboine and Saskatchewan Exploring Expedition*. Toronto: Coach House Press, 1975

Inglis, Alex. *Northern Vagabond: The Life and Career of J.B. Tyrrell*. Toronto: McClelland and Stewart, 1978

Koltun, Lilly, ed. *Private Realms of Light: Amateur Photography in Canada, 1839–1940*. Toronto: Fitzhenry and Whiteside, 1984

McKenzie, Karen, and Mary F. Williamson. *The Art and Pictorial Press in Canada: Two Centuries of Art Magazines*. Toronto: Art Gallery of Ontario, 1979

Martin, William T. Mower, and Wilfred Campbell. *Canada*. London: A. and C. Black, 1907

Moritz, Albert. *Canada Illustrated: The Art of Nineteenth Century Engraving*. Toronto: Dreadnaught, 1982

Parker, George L. *The Beginnings of the Book Trade in Canada*. Toronto: University of Toronto Press, 1985

Pringle, Allan. 'William Cornelius Van Horne, Art Director, Canadian Pacific Railway.' *Journal of Canadian Art History* 8, no. 1 (1984): 50–79

Schwartz, Joan M. 'The Past in Focus: Photography and British Columbia, 1858–1914.' *BC Studies* 52 (Winter 1981–2): 5–15

– 'The Photographic Record of Pre-Confederation British Columbia.' *Archivaria* 5 (Winter 1977–8): 17–44

Schwartz, Joan M., and Lilly Koltun. 'A Visual Cliché: Five Views of Yale.' *BC Studies* 52 (Winter 1981–2): 113–28

Triggs, Stanley G. 'Alexander Henderson: Nineteenth-Century Landscape Photographer.' *Archivaria* 5 (Winter 1977–8): 45–59

– *William Notman: The Stamp of a Studio*. Toronto: Art Gallery of Ontario and Coach House Press, 1985

PLATE 30

The Look of Domestic Building, 1891

PETER ENNALS   Geography, Mount Allison University
DERYCK W. HOLDSWORTH   Geography, Pennsylvania State University

In spite of efforts to create a major machine-readable data base (the Canadian Inventory of Historical Buildings) it has not been possible so far to carry out a comprehensive detailed mapping of the thousands of buildings surviving from the 19th century. While some efforts have been made to formulate an appropriate classification system for house types which might be used in this process, there remains a good deal of disagreement on the principles of such a typology. Moreover, such an exercise risks overlooking the existence and the extent of a wide assortment of very ordinary 19th-century buildings that have not survived or that were not documented by contemporaries. The research for this plate arose from a careful reading of the existing literature on Canada's architectural history, coupled with extensive field observation. However, in the absence of a more scientific basis for analysis, the treatment is necessarily impressionistic.

Hall and parlour: The term *hall* refers to the 'great room' found at many scales in English housing during the medieval periods and thereafter. This room was a multi-purpose space in which cooking, dining, domestic manufacture, and sleeping took place. It should not be confused with the entry spaces or passageways that are often called *halls* in the modern dwelling.

Further readings

Butterfield, David K., and Edward M. Ledohowski. *Architectural Heritage and the Brandon and Area Planning District*. Winnipeg: Department of Culture, Heritage and Recreation, 1984

Ennals, Peter, and Deryck W. Holdsworth. 'Vernacular Architecture and the Cultural Landscape of the Maritime Provinces: A Reconnaissance.' *Acadiensis* 10 (Spring 1981): 86–105

Gowans, Alan. *Building Canada: An Architectural History of Canadian Life*. Toronto: Oxford University Press, 1966

Lessard, Michel, and Huguette Marquis. *Encyclopédie de la maison québécoise*. Montréal: Les Éditions de l'homme, 1974

MacRae, Marion, and Anthony Adamson. *The Ancestral Roof: Domestic Architecture of Upper Canada*. Toronto: Clarke, Irwin, 1963

Mannion, John J. *Irish Settlement in Eastern Canada*. Toronto: University of Toronto Press, 1974

Mills, David. 'The Development of Folk Housing in Trinity Bay, Newfoundland.' In John J. Mannion, ed. *The Peopling of Newfoundland: Essays in Historical Geography*. St John's: Institute of Social and Economic Research, 1977

Rempel, John I. *Building with Wood and Other Aspects of Nineteenth-Century Building in Ontario*. Toronto: University of Toronto Press, 1967

Segger, Martin, and Douglas Franklin. *Victoria: A Primer for Regional History in Architecture*. Watkins Glen, NY: American Life Foundation, 1979

Wonders, William C., and Mark A. Rasmussen. 'Log Buildings of West Central Alberta.' *Prairie Forum* 5 (1980): 197–217

PLATE 31

The Printed Word, 18th and 19th Centuries

JOHN H. WADLAND   Canadian Studies Program, Trent University
MARGARET HOBBS   Women's Studies Program, Trent University

The authors are deeply indebted to John Wiseman, Fernand Harvey, and George Parker for their assistance in the preparation of this plate.

Newspapers, 1891

This map identifies communities in which newspapers survived until 1891. Almost invariably the most independent newspapers were those based in major urban centres, not because their occupants were more intelligent but because they constituted the densest consumer market. As time passed, the symbiotic relationship between advertising and circulation strengthened. Advertisements consumed between one-third and two-thirds of the space in any given newspaper; by 1900 big-city dailies

At the outbreak of war the vessels were largely converted merchant vessels, but later they were specially built near the sites where they would be used. Towards the end of the war a massive race in naval construction was under way at Kingston and at Sackets Harbor on Lake Ontario. The warships completed or under construction by the end of the war were larger and more heavily armed than Admiral Nelson's flagship *Victory*.

Everest. *The War of 1812 in the Champlain Valley*. 1981. Ch 11
Roosevelt, Theodore. *The Naval War of 1812*. Vols 1, 2. New York: Putnam. 1883
Thatcher, Joseph M. 'A Fleet in the Wilderness: Shipbuilding at Sackets Harbor.' In R. Arthur Bowler, ed. *War along the Niagara: Essays on the War of 1812 and Its Legacy*. Youngstown, NY: Old Fort Niagara Association, 1991. Pp 53–9
Zaslow and Turner, eds. *The Defended Border*. 1964

Illustration
Charles W. Jefferys (1869–1951) *The Battle of Lundy's Lane*. 1909. Watercolour on paper. 47.7 × 70.2 cm. Courtesy of the City of Toronto Archives. A75-61

Further readings
Burt, Alfred L. *The United States, Great Britain and British North America from the Revolution to the Establishment of Peace after the War of 1812*. New Haven: Yale University Press, 1940
Coffin, W.F. *1812, The War and Its Moral: A Canadian Chronicle*. Montréal: J. Lovell, 1864
Dunlop, William. *Tiger Dunlop's Upper Canada ...* Toronto: McClelland and Stewart, 1967

PLATE 39

Transatlantic Migrations, 1815–1865

JOHN C. WEAVER   History, McMaster University
JAMES DE JONGE   Canadian Parks Service, Ottawa
DARRELL NORRIS   Geography, State University of New York, Geneseo

Immigration to British North America: 1831–1836; 1846–1851
The data for these maps are based on assorted reports and despatches sent by the colonial administrators to the CO and often published in *British Parliamentary Papers*. Some minor fragments of information were unpublished and scattered throughout the original correspondence of the CO in the appropriate series: for Canada, CO 42; for New Brunswick, CO 188; for Newfoundland, CO 194; for Nova Scotia and Cape Breton Island, CO 217. Regardless of the final destination on form, data and estimates were assembled by the executive officers of the colonial governments from newspapers' accounts of ships and passengers arriving or from the reports of the emigration agents located in major ports. The British Parliament began to publish more or less routine reports on emigration in the mid-1830s; some reports contained data for prior years. Because the titles of these reports changed over time and some reports were not part of a series, a complete listing of sources used would be excessively long. Abbreviated titles for published reports can be found under the heading 'emigration,' in *British Parliamentary Papers*.

Great Britain. *British Parliamentary Papers: General Index to Accounts and Papers Printed by Order of the House of Commons and the Papers Presented by Command, 1801–1853*. Shannon: Irish University Press, 1968

Final residences: Wellington County
Historical Atlas of the County of Wellington, Ontario. Toronto: Historical Atlas Publishing Co, 1906. Pp 10–71. The data are derived from biographies of original settlers whose final residences were in Wellington County.

Travels of immigrant J. Thomson, 1844–1864
Preston, Richard A., ed. *For Friends at Home: A Scottish Emigrant's Letters from Canada, California and the Cariboo*. Montréal and Kingston: McGill-Queen's University Press, 1974

Emigration from the British Isles, 1815–1865
This graph is based on the work of Helen Cowan.

Cowan, Helen I. *British Immigration to British North America: The First Hundred Years*. Toronto: University of Toronto Press, 1961
– *British Immigration before Confederation*. Ottawa: Canadian Historical Association, 1968

Occupations of male immigrants, 1846–1851
This graph was prepared from the reports compiled by A.C Buchanan, the chief emigration agent at Québec. They appeared in *British Parliamentary Papers* among the returns from Canada for 1846–51. Because the British government was interested in the numbers who left the United Kingdom, Buchanan's count included those adult males who died at sea or in quarantine.

Further readings
Adams, William Forbes. *Ireland and Irish Emigration to the New World from 1815 to the Famine*. New Haven: Yale University Press, 1932
Akenson, Donald Harman. *The Irish in Ontario: A Study in Rural History*. Montréal and Kingston: McGill-Queen's University Press, 1984
Elliot, Bruce S. *Irish Migrants in the Canadas: A New Approach*. Montréal and Kingston: McGill-Queen's University Press, 1988
Erickson, Charlotte. *Invisible Immigrants: The Adaptation of English and Scottish Migrants in Nineteenth Century America*. London: Weidenfeld and Nicolson, 1972
Mannion, John. *Irish Settlements in Eastern Canada: A Study of Cultural Transfer and Adaptation*. Toronto: University of Toronto Press, 1974
Martell, J.S. *Immigration to and Emigration from Nova Scotia, 1815–1838*. Halifax: Public Archives of Nova Scotia, 1942

PLATE 40

The Great War, 1914–1918

CHRISTOPHER A. SHARPE   Geography, Memorial University of Newfoundland

Enlistment and military installations
The data for Canadian Expeditionary Force (CEF) training camps and winter camps are combined; when they occur at the same place, only one camp is indicated. CEF includes 124 588 male recruits raised by the Military Service Act; it does not include 2 854 women who volunteered as nursing sisters. Eligible population is that of 1911.
    Enlistment is shown by place of enlistment and does not include those who enlisted in the CEF in the United States (6 986) or the United Kingdom (3 079). Newfoundland enlistment was in the Royal Newfoundland Regiment, not the CEF.
    There were 8 579 'aliens' interned in the camps, 5 417 of whom were civilians: 5 954 were Austro-Hungarian, 2 009 German, and 616 of other nationalities.

Canada. *Census*. 1911. Unpublished folio CXXXVI, Table 4
– *SP*. 1919. No. 246, Department of Justice, 'Report of the Military Service Branch of the Ministry of Justice on the Operation of the Military Service Act, 1917'
Carter, David J. *Behind Canadian Barbed Wire: Alien, Refugee and Prisoner of War Camps in Canada*. Calgary: Tumbleweed Press, 1980. P 308
Duguid, Col. A.F. *Official History of the Canadian Forces in the Great War, 1914–1919*. Vol 1. Ottawa: King's Printer, 1938
NAC. Militia Defence Records. RG 24. Vol 1842, Files GAQ 10–42, GAQ 10–44, GAQ 10–47, Vol 1. Vol 1843, File GAQ 10–47E. Vol 1892, No. 109

Victory loan campaigns, 1917, 1918
Data for per capita contributions for 1917 and 1918, combined, were graphed because these were the only years for which a provincial breakdown is available. Prior to the campaigns to enlist small investors (with subscriptions as low as $50), there were loans in 1915, 1916, and 1917 to attract large-scale investment. These loans were supplemented by additional funds from New York but when the United States entered the war in Apr 1917, it became increasingly difficult for foreign nations to enter the New York market. Canada therefore had to rely on its own internal resources.

Canada. *SP*. 1919. No. 181. Not published
Canada Year Book. 1920
Hunt, M.S. *Nova Scotia's Part in the Great War*. Halifax, 1920
Hopkins, J. Castell. *The Province of Ontario in the War: A Record of Government and People*. Toronto: Warwick and Rutter, 1919
NAC. Department of Finance Records. RG 19. Vol 588, File 155–1D. Vol 607, File 155–87–6. Vol 608, File 155–88–6

Canadian patriotic fund, 1914–1919
Graph includes money paid into the Canadian Fund between Aug 1914 and 31 Mar 1919. Manitoba had a separate provincial fund which raised $6 315 209, of which $2 405 126 came from voluntary subscriptions. It disbursed $6 282 331. Newfoundland had its own patriotic fund which took in $122 706. There were also local funds in Ontario – Toronto and York, Lincoln County, Fort William, Preston, Kenora, Orillia – and one in Cumberland County, BC. There is some ambiguity about the patriotic fund in Vancouver and Victoria; these organizations refused to affiliate with the provincial organizations and it is unclear whether these two cities are included in the BC total.

Bray, R.M. 'Canadian Patriotic Response to the Great War.' PhD thesis, York University, 1977
Canada Year Book. 1920
Hopkins. *The Province of Ontario in the War*. 1919
Morris, Philip, ed. 'Canadian Patriotic Fund. A Record of Its Activities from 1914–1919.' nd
Newfoundland. *Journals of the House of Assembly*. 1920. 'Report of the Patriotic Fund'

Imperial Munitions Boards contracts, 1915–1919
Not included are investments made in munitions contracts in the United States ($130 123 000), the United Kingdom ($7 726 000), and Newfoundland ($261 000).

Carnegie, David. *History of Munitions Supply in Canada 1914–1918*. Toronto: Longmans, 1925
NAC. G 30. B4, Vol 36, 'Imperial Munitions Board Report'

Provincial share of manufacturing and war trade, 1915
The data are taken from the 1916 *Postal Census of Manufactures* which for 1915 'asked each manufacturer to report on such products of his establishment as he had reason to believe were destined for war purposes, whether supplied directly or indirectly.'

Canada. Department of Trade and Commerce. Census and Statistics Office. *Postal Census of Manufactures*. 1916

Casualty rates of selected battalions
Fetherstonhaugh, R.C. *The 24th Battalion, C.E.F., Victoria Rifles of Canada, 1914–1919*. Montréal: Gazette Printing Company, 1930
An Historical Sketch of the Seventy-Seventh Battalion Canadian Expeditionary Force. Ottawa: War Publications Ltd, 1926
McEvoy, Bernard, and Capt. A.H. Finley. *A History of the 62nd Canadian Infantry Battalion: Seaforth Highlanders of Canada*. Vancouver: Cowan and Brookhouse, 1920
McWilliams, James L., and R. James Steel. *The Suicide Battalion*. Edmonton: Hurtig, 1978
Murray, Col. W.W. *The History of the 2nd Canadian Battalion (East. Ontario Regiment), Canadian Expeditionary Force in the Great War, 1914–1918*. Ottawa: The Historical Committee, 2nd Battalion, CEF, 1947
NAC. *Reports of the Militia Department*. 1919–20
Stevens, George Roy. *A City Goes to War: 49th Infantry Battalion (Loyal Edmonton Regiment)*. Brampton: Charters, 1964

The Royal Newfoundland Regiment
Newfoundland. Department of Militia. *Report*. 1919, 1920
Provincial Archives of Newfoundland. *Regimental Rolls*. 'Royal Newfoundland Regiment'

'St John's, Nfld Plan.' 1914. Repr Oct 1925. Toronto and Montréal: Underwriters Survey Bureau

Military Service Act, 1917

The graph includes registration, call-up, and exemption from military service of all male British subjects, unmarried or widowed without children, aged 20–32 years. For Manitoba and Ontario the sum of the agricultural, medical, and occupational exemptions did not equal the total number of exemptions granted. Kenora District of Ontario had been included in the three Manitoba exemption categories but in the Ontario totals. The discrepancy was 1 997 and it was divided equally among the three categories; for the graph the data were subtracted from those of Manitoba and added to those of Ontario.

Canada. *SP.* 1919. No. 246. 'Report of the Director on the Operation of the Military Service Act, 1919'
NAC. RG 24. Vol 1824. File GAQ 10–44, GAQ 10–47, Vol 1
– Department of Militia and Defence. European War Memorandum No. 6. 1919

Revenue and public debt, 1900–1939
Taxes, 1915–1939
Canada Year Book. 1940

Canadian military hospitals and cemeteries in Europe
Casualties and medical-care facilities

The Canadian General Hospital (CGH) category includes eight stationary hospitals, smaller than general hospitals and originally set up as resting places on the line for casualties on their way back to base. Given the short lines of communications, they became small general hospitals. Some hospitals operated at various locations; in these cases the maximum capacity at the location where that maximum occurred was mapped. There are three exceptions where the maximum capacity was at Salonica, but the hospitals appear on the map in locations in England (Basingstoke, Hastings, and Liverpool) to which they were transferred in 1917 and 1918. Hospitals in Europe outside the map area: in Britain, Buxton (2 special), Kirkdale (1 CGH), Liverpool (1 CGH), Matlock Bath (1 convalescent); in France, Joinville (1 CGH), Champagnoles (1 Forestry Corps Hospital, FCH), La Joux/Jura (1 FCH), Gérardmer/Vosges (1 FCH).

Canada. *Report of the Ministry: Overseas Military Forces of Canada.* London, 1918
– *SP.* 1917. No. 158. Not published
NAC. G 24. Vol 1843, File GAQ 10–47E. Vol 1844, File GAQ 11–10
Nicholson, G.W.L. *Seventy Years of Service: A History of the Royal Canadian Army Medical Corps.* Ottawa: Borealis Press, 1977
Statistics of the Military Effort of the British Empire during the Great War. London: HMSO, 1922
Wood, Herbert Farlie, and John Swettenham. *Silent Witnesses.* Toronto: Hakkert, 1974

PLATE 41
The Impact of the Great Depression, 1930s

MURDO MacPHERSON   Historical Atlas of Canada, Toronto
DERYCK W. HOLDSWORTH   Geography, Pennsylvania State University

The unemployed and relief, 1926–1940

Reliable data on unemployment during the Depression are available only at the national level. The provincial situation can only be displayed indirectly through the distribution of relief (see 'Relief recipients by province').

Canada. *Census.* 1931. Vol 13, monograph on unemployment, pp 274–6
– DBS. *Statistics Relating to Labour Supply Under War Conditions.* Cat. 71–D–52. 194 P 14
– Department of Labour. *Annual Report of the Dominion Commissioner of Unemployment Relief.* 1932–41
Marsh, Leonard C. *Canadians In and Out of Work: A Survey of Economic Classes and Their Relation to the Labour Market.* Toronto: Oxford University Press, 1940. P 364

Relief recipients by province, 1930–1940

The yearly average number on relief shown on all provincial graphs was calculated from the monthly totals given in the Department of Labour's annual reports.
Cape Breton cities include Sydney, Glace Bay, Sydney Mines, and North Sydney.
Canada. Department of Labour. *Annual Reports of the Dominion Commissioner of Unemployment Relief.* 1930–41
Goldenberg, H. Carl. *Municipal Finance in Canada.* A Study Prepared for the Royal Commission on Dominion-Provincial Relations. Ottawa, 1939. P 70
Provincial Archives of Newfoundland. Records of the Department of Public Health and Welfare, Newfoundland Commission of Government
Newfoundland. *Census of Newfoundland and Labrador.* 1935

Occupational classification of workers on relief, 1935

'Other manual' includes longshoremen, miners, fishermen, and seamen. Number of persons included in the regional totals: Western Provinces 27 904; Ontario 53 251; Québec 60 897; Maritime Provinces 5 575.
Marsh. *Canadians In and Out of Work.* 1940. P 472

'Riding the rails'
Glenbow Archives, Calgary. NC6–12955(b)

The trek in search of work
Johnstone, Bill. *'Coal Dust in My Blood': The Autobiography of a Coal Miner.* British Columbia Provincial Museum, Heritage Record No. 9. Victoria, 1980
Knight, Rolf. *A Very Ordinary Life.* Vancouver: New Star Books, 1974
Thibault, Nelson. Interview conducted by Deryck W. Holdsworth. Winnipeg, 10 Apr 1985

Monthly relief budgets, 1936
Marsh, Leonard, A. Grant Fleming, and C.F. Blackler. *Health and Unemployment: Some Studies of Their Relationships.* Toronto: Oxford University Press, 1938. P 163

Monthly food allowances, 1936
The 'low cost restricted emergency diet' was a minimum-level food budget drawn up by the United States Department of Agriculture, Bureau of Home Economics. Marsh, Fleming, and Blackler (1938) adapted this budget for Canadian prices (pp 160–72). This diet was not recommended for prolonged use.

Marsh, Fleming, and Blackler. *Health and Unemployment.* 1938. P 169

Relief budget, 1932
Horn, Michael Steven Daniel, ed. *The Dirty Thirties: Canadians in the Great Depression.* Toronto: Copp Clark, 1972. P 284

Deportations, 1903–1960
Urquhart and Buckley. *Historical Statistics.* Series A342–7

Price and wage indices, 1926–1940
Wage rate and purchasing power, 1926–1940
For the retail indices, 1940 figures from the 1940 *Canadian Year Book*, which were represented on a 1935–9 base, had to be converted to a 1926 base. 'Purchasing power,' or 'real' wages, was calculated by dividing the wage-rate index by the cost-of-living index.

Bank of Canada. *Statistical Summary.* Ottawa, 1941. P 34
Canada Year Book. 1939: p 860–1. 1941: p 717

Further readings
Cassidy, Harry Morris. *Unemployment and Relief in Ontario, 1929–1932.* Toronto: Dent, 1932
Drystek, Henry F. 'The Simplest and Cheapest Mode of Dealing with Them: Deportation from Canada before World War II.' *Histoire sociale / Sociale History* 15, no. 30 (Nov 1982): 407–41
Richter, Lothar, ed. *Canada's Unemployment Problem.* Toronto: Macmillan, 1939
Sautter, Udo. 'Measuring Unemployment in Canada: Federal Efforts before World War II.' *Histoire sociale / Social History* 15, no. 30 (Nov 1982): 475–87
Struthers, James. *No Fault of Their Own: Unemployment and the Canadian Welfare State, 1914–1941.* Toronto: University of Toronto Press, 1983

PLATE 42
The Second World War, 1939–1945

CHRISTOPHER A. SHARPE   Geography, Memorial University of Newfoundland

This plate benefited enormously from the expertise of Norman Hillmer, Ben Greenhaus, and Roger Sarty of the Directorate of History, National Defence Headquarters, Ottawa. Thanks also are due to Michael Hadley for his advice.

Military mobilization
Enlistment of women
Canada. *Census.* 1941. Vol 1, Tables 18, 35, 37
– National Personnel Records Centre. 'Canadian Army Statistics, War 1939–45,' 'Royal Canadian Air Force Statistics, War 1939–45,' 'Canadian Navy Statistics, War 1939–45'
Douglas, W.A.B. *The Creation of a National Air Force.* Vol 2 of *The Official History of the Royal Canadian Air Force*, ed Norman Hillmer. Toronto: University of Toronto Press, 1986. 'British Commonwealth Air Training Plan' (foldout maps)
NAC. RG 24. G3 Files 133.008 (D103), 133.009 (D131)
'Report on the operations of military mobilization in Canada during World War Two.' Prepared by the Associate Director of National Selection Service (Mobilization Division) in collaboration with the Research and Statistics Branch, Department of Labour. 10 Feb 1947. Typescript held at National Defence Headquarters, Historical Division
Stacey, C.P. *Six Years of War: The Army in Canada, Britain and the Pacific.* Ottawa: Queen's Printer, 1955. App D
Tucker, G.N. *Naval Service of Canada.* Ottawa: King's Printer, 1952

Ill-Fated Trio
Rikki Cameron of the Canadian War Museum assisted in the search for an appropriate war painting and Douglas Champion generously displayed his works for the editors.

Douglas Champion, a resident of Toronto known for his marine art under the name of Alfred Leete, enlisted in the Royal Navy in the spring of 1940 and saw service in the Arctic, the North Atlantic, and the Mediterranean. His painting *Ill-Fated Trio* (North Atlantic Convoys ONS18 and ON202 combined, Sep 1943) shows HMCS *St Croix* and HMS *Itchen* of support group EC9 and HMS *Polyanthus* of C2 escort group. All three were lost to acoustic torpedo attack by U-boats in a fierce battle to protect the big combined convoy. *St Croix* and *Polyanthus* were sunk on 20 Sep. Survivors from both ships were picked up by *Itchen*. On 22 Sep *Itchen* was hit and sank, taking all but three survivors from the combined ships' companies with her.

Canadian War Museum. Ottawa. Cat. 87061

Canadian fatalities in two world wars
Military fatalities in the Second World War
Canada. Department of Veteran's Affairs, Newfoundland District Office. 'Service Ledger, Royal Navy Enlistments (Newfoundland)'
– National Personnel Records Centre. *Canadian Medical Service 1939–45*
Canada Year Book. 1947. Pp 1120–30
Dupuy, R. Ernest, and Trevor N. Dupuy. *The Encyclopedia of Military History.* 2nd rev ed. New York: Harper and Row, 1986
Singer, J. David, and M. Small. *The Wages of War.* New York: Wiley, 1972
Stacey, C.P. *Arms, Men and Government: The War Policies of Canada 1939–1945.* Ottawa: Queen's Printer, 1970

Canadian war graves
Wood, Herbert Farlie, and John Swettenham. *Silent Witnesses.* Toronto: Hakkert, 1974

Canadian forces in Europe and the North Atlantic; Pacific Coast

Roger Sarty, Directorate of History, National Defence Headquarters, made available recently released material from the British Navy Historical Branch which made it possible to refine information concerning military ship losses. The data from the secondary sources listed below were updated using these sources, as well as books by Douglas (1986) and Rohwer (1983).

Barraclough, Geoffrey, ed. *The Times Atlas of World History*. London: Times Books, 1978. P 273

Britain. Historical Section Admiralty. Naval Staff History Second World War. 'Defeat of the Enemy Attack on Shipping 1939–1945: A Study of Policy and Operations.' Vols 1A, 1B. 1957

Coppock, R.M. 'Reassessments concerning the destruction of *FAA Di Bruno*, U-163, U-756, U-311.' Written for Britain. Ministry of Defence Dec 1982–Sep 1987. Not published. Copies held at Directorate of History, National Defence Headquarters, Ottawa

Douglas. *The Creation of a National Air Force*. 1986

Douglas, W.A.B., and B. Greenhaus. *Out of the Shadows: Canada in the Second World War*. Toronto: Oxford University Press, 1977

Goodspeed, D.J. *The Armed Forces of Canada, 1867–1967, A Century of Achievement*. Ottawa: Directorate of History, Canadian Forces Headquarters, 1967

Hadley, M. *U-Boats Against Canada: German Submarines on Canadian Waters*. Montréal: McGill-Queen's University Press, 1977

Kostenuk, Samuel, and John Griffen. *R.C.A.F. Squadron Histories and Aircraft, 1924–1968*. Toronto/Sarasota: Hakkert/Samuel Stevens, 1977

Rohwer, Jurgen. *Axis Submarine Successes, 1939–1945*. Annapolis, Md: Naval Institute Press, 1983

Schull, Joseph. *The Far Distant Ships, An Official Account of Canadian Naval Operation*. Ottawa: King's Printer, 1950

Stacey. *Six Years of War*. 1955

Tucker. *Naval Service of Canada*. 1952

Further readings

Granatstein, J.L. *Canada's War: Policies of the MacKenzie King Government 1939–1945*. Toronto: Oxford University Press, 1975

Morton, Desmond. *Canada and War: A Political and Military History*. Toronto: Butterworths, 1981

PLATE 43

Trade in Interior America, 1654–1666

CONRAD E. HEIDENREICH   Geography, York University

Congé: A licence issued by the governor or intendant permitting a trader to send one canoe load of trade goods and three men into the interior

Coureurs de bois: Men trading in the interior without a licence or any other form of permission

Entrepôt: A major interior post with storage facilities and merchant residences where goods and furs were trans-shipped to other posts or Montréal

Livre (pesant): Unit of weight, about 1 pound (489.5 gms)

Pack of furs: Furs bundled for canoe transportation, usually weighing 80–100 pounds (36–45 kg)

Société: A small company, usually of short duration, composed of a number of partners

Native groups were mapped according to references in the documents and maps. Spelling of names and linguistic affiliations are, as far as possible, according to entries in the *Handbook of North American Indians* (1978; 1981). In mapping Native groups the assumption has been made that, if a group was in a certain location at an early date and was in the same location at a later date, it was also there in the intervening years, providing there is no evidence to the contrary. The same assumption was made in mapping posts, forts, and missions.

Sources

Adams, A.T., ed. *The Explorations of Pierre Esprit Radisson*. Minneapolis: Ross and Haines, 1961

Alvord, C.W., and C.E. Carter, eds. *The Critical Period, 1763–1765*. Illinois State Historical Library Collections, 10, British series I. Springfield: The Library, 1915

– *The New Régime, 1765–1767*. Illinois State Historical Library Collections, 11, British series II. Springfield: The Library, 1916

ANQ. *Rapport de l'archiviste de la province de Québec*. 'Les Journaux de M. de Léry' (1926–7): 334–71. 'Correspondance entre M. de Vaudreuil et la Cour' (1938–9): 10–179; (1939–40): 355–463; (1942–3): 399–443; (1946–7): 371–460; (1947–8): 137–339. 'Journal de Louis Jolliet allant à la descouverte de Labrador, 1694' (1943–4): 149–206

Blair, E.H., ed and transl. *The Indian Tribes of the Upper Mississippi Valley and Region of the Great Lakes, as Described by Nicolas Perrot ...; Bacqueville de la Potherie ...* 2 vols. Cleveland: Arthur H. Clark, 1911–12

Burpee, L.J., ed. 'York Factory to the Blackfeet Country – The Journal of Anthony Henday, 1754–55.' In *Transactions of the Royal Society of Canada*. 3rd series. 1, section II (1907): 307–64

– *Journals and Letters of Pierre Gaultier de Varennes de La Vérendrye and His Sons ...* Toronto: Champlain Society, 1927

Carver, J. *Travels through the Interior Parts of North America in the Years 1766, 1767 and 1768*. London: G. Robinson, 1778

Charlevoix, P.F.X. de. *Histoire et description générale de la Nouvelle France, avec le journal historique d'un voyage fait par ordre du roi dans l'Amérique septentrionale*. 6 vols. Paris: Rolin Fils, 1744

[Dollier de Casson, François.] *A History of Montreal, 1640–1672, from the French of Dollier de Casson*. Ed and trans R. Flenley. Toronto, 1928

Doughty, A.G., and C. Martin, eds. *The Kelsey Papers*. Ottawa: PAC, 1929

Houck, L., ed. *The Spanish Régime in Missouri; A Collection of Papers and Documents Relating to Upper Louisiana Principally Within the Present Limits of Missouri During the*

Dominion of Spain, from the Archives of the Indies at Seville. Chicago: R.R. Donnelly, 1909

Jameson, J.F., ed. *Narratives of New Netherlands, 1609–1664*. New York: Barnes and Noble, 1909

[Jérémie, Nicolas.] *Twenty Years of York Factory 1694–1714: Jérémie's Account of Hudson Strait and Bay*. Trans R. Douglas and J.N. Wallace. Toronto: Thorburn and Abbott, 1926

Lamontagne, L., ed, R.A. Preston, trans. *Royal Fort Frontenac*. Toronto: Champlain Society, 1958

McIlwain, C.H. *An Abridgement of the Indian Affairs Contained in Four Folio Volumes, Transacted in the Colony of New York, from the Year 1678 to the Year 1751*. Ed P. Wraxhall. Harvard Historical Studies, XXI. Cambridge, Mass., 1915

'Memoir or Summary Journal of the Expedition of Jacques Repentigny Legardeur de Saint Pierre ... Charged with the Discovery of the Western Sea ... 1752.' PAC, *Report, 1886*, note C: clviii-clxix. Ottawa, 1887

Michigan Pioneer Collections. 40 vols. See esp vols 33–4: 'The Cadillac Papers,' 1903, 1904. Lansing, 1874–1929

NAC. MG18, B12, 'Détail des noms et de la distance de chaque Nation, tant du Nord du lac Supérieur, que des terres découvertes et établis dans l'Ouest, présenté à Monsieur Le Marquis de Beauharnois ... Par le Sr. de la Vérendrye ...' [ca 1740]. 6 pp

– NMC. An effort was made to consult all holdings dating from 1600 to 1763. For a summary of useful maps see Heidenreich, 1980, 1981, below.

O'Callaghan, E.B., and B. Fernow, eds. *Documents Relative to the Colonial History of the State of New York; Procured in Holland, England and France by John Romeyn Brodhead*. 15 vols. Albany: Weed, Parsons, 1853–87

Pease, T.C., and R.C. Werner, eds. *The French Foundations, 1680–1693*. Illinois State Historical Library Collections, 23, French Series, 1. Springfield: The Library, 1934

Preston, R.A., ed. *Kingston before the War of 1812: A Collection of Documents*. Toronto: Champlain Society, 1959

Prouville de Tracy, Alexandre de (1596–1670)   DCB 1: 554–7

Rich, E.E., and A.M. Johnson, eds. *James Isham's Observations on Hudsons Bay, 1743 and Notes and Observations on a Book Entitled 'A Voyage to Hudsons Bay in the Dobbs Galley,' 1749*. London: The Hudson's Bay Record Society, 1949

Rochemonteix, C. de, ed. *Relation par lettres de l'Amérique septentrionale années 1709 et 1710*. Paris, 1904

Rowland, D., and A.G. Sanders, eds. *Mississippi Provincial Archives, 1701–1740, French Dominion*. 2 vols. Jackson, 1927–9

Thwaites, R.G., ed. *The Jesuit Relations and Allied Documents*. 73 vols. Cleveland: Burrows Bros, 1896–1901

– *Wisconsin State Historical Society Collections*. Vol 16: *The French Régime in Wisconsin, I: 1634–1727*. Vol 17: *The French Régime in Wisconsin, II: 1727–1748*. Vol 18: 'The French Régime in Wisconsin, 1743–1760.' Madison: The Society, 1902–8

– *A New Discovery of a Vast Country in America, by Father Louis Hennepin*. Repr from the second London issue of 1698. Chicago: A.C. McClung, 1903

– *Early Western Travels, 1748–1846*. 38 vols. Cleveland: Arthur H. Clark, 1904–7

– *New Voyages to North-America, by the Baron de Lahontan*. Repr from the English edition of 1703. 2 vols. Chicago: A.C. McClung, 1905

Tyrrell, J.B., ed. *Documents Relating to the Early History of Hudson Bay*. Toronto: Champlain Society, 1931

Further readings

Alvord, C.W. *The Illinois Country, 1673–1818*. Springfield: Illinois Centennial Commission, 1920

Bond, B.W. *The History of the State of Ohio*. Ed C. Witke. 2 vols. Columbus: Ohio State Archaeological and Historical Society, 1941–4

Caldwell, N.W. *The French in the Mississippi Valley, 1740–1750*. Philadelphia: Porcupine Press, 1974

Cooke, A., and C. Holland. *The Exploration of Northern Canada, 500 to 1920: A Chronology*. Toronto: Arctic History Press, 1978

Eccles, W.J. *Canada Under Louis XIV, 1663–1701*. Toronto: McClelland and Stewart, 1964

– *The Canadian Frontier, 1534–1760*. New York: Holt, Rinehart and Winston, 1969

Handbook of North American Indians. Vol 6: *Subarctic*. Ed J. Helm. Washington: Smithsonian Institution, 1981

Handbook of North American Indians. Vol 15: *Northeast*. Ed B.G. Trigger. Washington: Smithsonian Institution, 1978

Heidenreich, C.E. 'Mapping the Great Lakes: The Period of Exploration, 1603–1700.' *Cartographica* 17 (1980): 32–64

– 'Mapping the Great Lakes: the Period of Imperial Rivalries, 1700–1760.' *Cartographica* 18 (1981): 74–109

– 'Mapping the Location of Native Groups, 1600–1760.' *Mapping History* 2 (1981): 6–13

Hodge, F.W., ed. *Handbook of Indians North of Mexico*. 2 vols. Smithsonian Institution, Bureau of American Ethnology, Bulletin 30. Washington, 1907, 1910

Innis, H.A. *The Fur Trade in Canada*. Rev ed. Toronto: University of Toronto Press, 1956

Jennings, F. *The Ambiguous Iroquois Empire*. New York: Norton, 1984

Kellogg, Louise P. *The French Régime in Wisconsin and the Northwest*. Madison: State Historical Society of Wisconsin, 1925

Lanctot, G. *A History of Canada*. 3 vols. Toronto: Clarke Irwin, 1963

Morton, A.S. *A History of the Canadian West to 1870–71*. Toronto: University of Toronto Press, 1939

Norton, Thomas E. *The Fur Trade in Colonial New York, 1686–1776*. Madison: University of Wisconsin Press, 1974

Ray, A.J. *Indians in the Fur Trade, 1660–1870*. Toronto: University of Toronto Press, 1974

Severance, F.H. *An Old Frontier of New France: The Niagara Region and Adjacent Lakes under French Control*. 2 vols. New York: Dodd, Mead 1917

Stanley, G.F.G. *New France: The Last Phase, 1744–1760*. Toronto: McClelland and Stewart, 1968

Trudel, M. *The Beginnings of New France, 1524–1663*. Toronto: McClelland and Stewart, 1973

PLATE 44

France Secures the Interior, 1740–1755

CONRAD E. HEIDENREICH   Geography, York University
FRANÇOISE NOËL   History, Memorial University of Newfoundland

See pl 43.

Céloron de Blainville, Pierre-Joseph, 1693–1759   DCB 3: 99–101

PLATE 45

The Migratory Fisheries, 18th Century

JOHN MANNION   Geography, Memorial University of Newfoundland
C. GRANT HEAD   Geography, Wilfrid Laurier University

Thanks are due to Sandy Balcomb, ECHP, Halifax; and to Edward Tompkins, PANL, St John's.

The labour costs given on the graph are calculated on the assumption of one boat's master at £23 per season and four other men at £12 each; see CO 194/15, folios 22–3.

Sources
Archives nationales, Paris, France. Fonds des Colonies, C¹²ᴬ, vol 10. Also in NAC, NMC 19196
Duhamel Du Monceau, Henri-Louis. *Traité général des pêches*. Paris: Saillant et Nyon, 1769–82
PRO. CO 194/15, folios 22–3; CO 194/21, folio 39

Further readings
Bosher, J.F. 'A Fishing Company of Louisbourg, Les Sables d'Olonne and Paris: La Société du Baron d'Huart, 1750–1775.' *French Historical Studies* 9, no. 2 (1975). 263–77
Brière, Jean-François. 'Le Trafic terre-neuvier malouin dans la première moitié du XVIIIᵉ siècle, 1713–1755.' *Hist Soc* 11, no. 2 (1978): 356–74
Cell, Gillian T. *English Enterprise in Newfoundland, 1577–1660*. Toronto: University of Toronto Press, 1969
Head, C. Grant. *Eighteenth Century Newfoundland: A Geographer's Perspective*. Toronto: McClelland and Stewart, 1976
Innis, Harold A. *The Cod Fisheries: The History of an International Economy*. Rev ed. Toronto: University of Toronto Press, 1954
La Morandière, Charles de. *Histoire de la pêche française de la morue dans l'Amérique septentrionale … 3 vols*. Paris: Maisonneuve et Larose, 1962–6
Quinn, D.B. *New American World: A Documentary History of North America to 1612*. New York: Arno Press, 1979

PLATE 46

The Newfoundland Fishery, 18th Century

JOHN MANNION   Geography, Memorial University of Newfoundland
GORDON HANDCOCK   Geography, Memorial University of Newfoundland
ALAN MACPHERSON   Geography, Memorial University of Newfoundland

Thanks are due to R.H. Mackinnon (UBC), Maura Mannion, and Edward Tompkins (PANL).

Sources
FRANCE
Ships and men departing France, 1765–72, and distribution of French fisheries in Newfoundland: Archives nationales, Paris. Fonds des Colonies, C11F, vols 3, 4: État des pêches françaises sur les bancs et à Saint-Pierre, 1770–4. Archives nationales. Fonds des Colonies, C12, vol 19
French fishing vessels, totals: Archives nationales, Paris. Fonds de la Marine. CC 598, C5, vol 52 (1787). Bibliothèque nationale, Nouvelles acquisitions françaises 2550 (1725)
GREAT BRITAIN
Ships departing England, 1765–74: PANL. GB/5, Second Report, State of Trade to Newfoundland, 24 April 1793. Appendix 6B, 425–6
Maritime History Archives, MUN. Lloyd's List and Registers of Shipping, London, 1765–74
British cod fishery: PRO. CO/194, Governors' returns on the inhabitants and fisheries at Newfoundland, 1700–1820

Further readings
Brière, Jean-François. 'Le trafic terre-neuvier malouin dans la première moitié du XVIIIᵉ siècle, 1713–1755.' *Hist Soc* 11, no. 2 (1978): 356–74
– 'Le reflux des Terre-Neuviers malouins sur les côtes du Canada dans la première moitié du XVIIIᵉ siècle: réponse à un changement de climat?' *Hist Soc*, 12, no. 23 (1979): 166–9
Handcock, W. Gordon. 'English Migration to Newfoundland.' In John J. Mannion, ed. *The Peopling of Newfoundland: Essays in Historical Geography*, 15–48. St John's: Institute of Social and Economic Research, Memorial University of Newfoundland, 1977
– 'The West Country Migrations to Newfoundland.' *Bulletin of Canadian Studies* 5, no. 1 (1981): 5–24
Head, C. Grant. *Eighteenth-Century Newfoundland: A Geographer's Perspective*. Toronto: McClelland and Stewart, 1976

Innis, Harold A. *The Cod Fisheries: The History of an International Economy*. Rev ed. Toronto: University of Toronto Press, 1954
Lounsbury, R.G. *British Fishery at Newfoundland, 1634–1763*. New Haven: Yale University Press, 1934
La Morandière, Charles de. *Histoire de la pêche française de la morue dans l'Amérique septentrionale … 3 vols*. Paris: Maisonneuve et Larose, 1962–6
Macpherson, Alan G. 'A Modal Sequence in the Peopling of Central Bonavista Bay, 1676–1857.' In John J. Mannion, ed. *The Peopling of Newfoundland: Essays in Historical Geography*. St John's: Institute of Social and Economic Research, Memorial University of Newfoundland, 1977
Mannion, John J. 'The Waterford Merchants and the Irish-Newfoundland Provisions Trade, 1770–1820.' In D.H. Akenson, ed. *Canadian Papers in Rural History III*. 178–203. Gananoque: Langdale Press, 1982
Ommer, Rosemary E. '"A Peculiar and Immediate Dependence of the Crown": The Basis of the Jersey Merchant Triangle.' *Business History* 25, no. 2 (1983): 107–24
Turgeon, Laurier. 'La crise de l'armement morutier basco-bayonnais dans la première moitié du XVIIIᵉ siècle. *Société des Sciences, Lettres et Arts de Bayonne* 139 (1983): 75–91
Whiteley, W.H. 'Governor Hugh Palliser and the Newfoundland and Labrador Fishery, 1764–1768.' *CHR* 50, no. 2 (1969): 141–63
– 'James Cook, Hugh Palliser and the Newfoundland Fishery.' *The Newfoundland Historical Society* 5, no. 1 (1972): 17–22
– 'Newfoundland, Quebec and the Administration of the Coast of Labrador, 1774–1783.' *Acadiensis* 6, no. 1 (1976): 92–111

PLATE 47

Acadian Marshland Settlement, 1671–1714

JEAN DAIGLE   Histoire, Université de Moncton

Sources
Acadian censuses: Archives nationales, Paris, France. Section Outre-mer, G1, vol 466
Dièreville. 'Voyage à l'Acadie, 1699–1700.' La Société historique acadienne, *Les cahiers* 16, nos. 3–4 (1985): 9–173
Maps of explorers, travellers, and cartographers of the seventeenth and eighteenth centuries: Bibliothèque nationale, Paris, France. Service hydrographique de la Marine, Cartes et plans

Further readings
Arseneault, Samuel, et al. *Atlas de l'Acadie. Petit atlas des francophones des Maritimes*. Moncton: Éditions d'Acadie, 1976
Christianson, David J. *Belleisle 1983: Excavations at a Pre-Expulsion Acadian Site*. Nova Scotia Museum, Curatorial Report no. 48. Halifax, 1984
Clark, Andrew H. *Acadia: The Geography of Early Nova Scotia to 1760*. Madison: University of Wisconsin Press, 1968
Daigle, Jean, ed. *Les Acadiens des Maritimes: études thématiques*. Moncton: Centre d'études acadiennes, 1980
– ed. *The Acadians of the Maritimes: Thematic Studies*. Moncton: Centre d'études acadiennes, 1982
De Grâce, Eloi. *Noms géographiques de l'Acadie*. Moncton: Société historique acadienne, 1974
Lapierre, J.-W., and M. Roy. *Les Acadiens*. Paris: Presses universitaires de France, 1983

PLATE 48

Maritime Canada, Late 18th Century

GRAEME WYNN   Geography, University of British Columbia
L.D. McCANN   Geography, Mount Allison University

Thanks are due to Peter M. Ennals (Geography, Mount Allison University) for comment on building types and Stephen Hornsby for alerting us to the map of Sydney.

Sources
Campbell, Patrick. *Travels in the Interior Inhabited Parts of North America in the Years 1791 and 1792*. New ed. Ed H.H. Langton and W. Francis. Toronto: Champlain Society, 1937
NAC. MG23 D1 (1), vol 24, General Returns of Loyalists
PANS. RG1, vol 443, 444, 444½, Poll Tax Returns
[Perkins, Simeon]. *The Diary of Simeon Perkins*. Ed H.A. Innis, D.C. Harvey, and C.B. Fergusson. 5 vols. Toronto: Champlain Society, 1948–78
'Report on Nova Scotia by Col. Robert Morse, R.E., 1784.' *PAC, Report, 1884*, note C, xxvii–lix. Ottawa, 1885
Raymond, W.O., ed. *Winslow Papers, A.D. 1776–1826*. Saint John: Sun Printing Co., 1901

Further readings
Condon, A.G. *The Envy of the American States: The Loyalist Dream for New Brunswick*. Fredericton: New Ireland Press, 1984
Ells, M. 'Clearing the Decks for the Loyalists.' Canadian Historical Association. *Report* (1933): 56–8
– 'Settling the Loyalists in Nova Scotia.' Canadian Historical Association. *Report* (1935): 105–9
Temperley, H. 'Frontierism, Capital and the American Loyalists in Canada.' *Journal of American Studies* 13 (1979): 5–27
Walker, James W. St G. *The Black Loyalists. The Search for a Promised Land in Nova Scotia and Sierra Leone, 1783–1870*. New York: Africana Publishing Co., 1976
Wright, E.C. *The Loyalists of New Brunswick*. Moncton: Moncton Publishing Co., [1972]